W9-BLE-924

THE LONGMAN READER

ELEVENTH EDITION

Judith Nadell

John Langan

New!
2016
MLA
Updates

with contributions from

Deborah Coxwell-Teague
Florida State University

PEARSON

Boston   Columbus   Hoboken   Indianapolis   New York   San Francisco   Amsterdam
Cape Town   Dubai   London   Madrid   Milan   Munich   Paris   Montréal   Toronto
Delhi   Mexico City   São Paulo   Sydney   Hong Kong   Seoul   Singapore   Taipei   Tokyo

Senior Acquisitions Editor:
Brad Potthoff
Program Manager: Eric Jorgensen
Development Editor: Linda Stern
Product Marketing Manager: Ali Arnold
Field Marketing Manager:
Mark Robinson
Executive Digital Producer:
Stefanie Snajder
Content Specialist: Erin E. Jenkins
Project Manager: Donna Campion

**Project Coordination, Text Design,
and Electronic Page Makeup:**
Integra Software Services Pvt. Ltd
Design Lead: Beth Paquin
Cover Designer: Studio Montage
Cover Illustration/Photo:
Shutterstock/Alexander Chaikin
Senior Manufacturing Buyer:
Roy L. Pickering, Jr.
Printer/Binder: RR Donnelley/Crawfordsville
Cover Printer: Courier/Westford

Acknowledgments of third-party content appear on pages 630–633, which constitute an extension of this copyright page.

PEARSON, ALWAYS LEARNING, and MYWRITINGLAB are exclusive trademarks owned by Pearson Education, Inc. or its affiliates in the United States and/or other countries.

Unless otherwise indicated herein, any third-party trademarks that may appear in this work are the property of their respective owners and any references to third-party trademarks, logos, or other trade dress are for demonstrative or descriptive purposes only. Such references are not intended to imply any sponsorship, endorsement, authorization, or promotion of Pearson's products by the owners of such marks, or any relationship between the owner and Pearson Education, Inc., or its affiliates, authors, licensees, or distributors.

Library of Congress Cataloging-in-Publication Data

Nadell, Judith, author.
　The Longman Reader / Judith Nadell, John Langan, Deborah Coxwell-Teague.—Eleventh Edition.
　　pages cm
　ISBN 13: 978-0-13-386295-9
　ISBN 10: 0-13-386295-X
　1. College readers.　2. English language—Rhetoric—Problems, exercises, etc.　3. Report writing—Problems, exercises, etc.　I. Langan, John, 1942- author.　II. Coxwell-Teague, Deborah, author.　III. Title.
　PE1417.N33 2015
　808'.0427—dc23
　　　　　　　　　　　　　　　　　　　　　　　　　　2014038784

Copyright © 2016, 2012, 2010 by Pearson Education, Inc.

All Rights Reserved. Printed in the United States of America. This publication is protected by copyright, and permission should be obtained from the publisher prior to any prohibited reproduction, storage in a retrieval system, or transmission in any form or by any means, electronic, mechanical, photocopying, recording, or otherwise. For information regarding permissions, request forms and the appropriate contacts within the Pearson Education Global Rights & Permissions Department, please visit www.pearsoned.com/permissions/.

1　16

www.pearsonhighered.com

Student Edition ISBN-10:　　0-13-458643-3
ISBN-13: 978-0-13-458643-4
A la Carte ISBN-10:　　0-13-458262-4
ISBN-13: 978-0-13-458262-7

CONTENTS

Parents are told to switch the dial if they don't want their kids watching
something on TV. But what should parents do when the entire culture
warrants being switched off?

3 DESCRIPTION   78

The truth of the old adage "beauty lies in the eye of the beholder" is illustrated in this description of the place the author calls home. While his *barrio* may be considered unattractive by outsiders, it is beautiful to Mario Suárez because of the people who live there and the culture they embrace.

Three weeks after Hurricane Katrina, an environmentalist tours New Orleans and the Gulf Coast to assess damage and the prospects for recovery.

4 NARRATION   121

9 CAUSE-EFFECT   352

APPENDIX B: AVOIDING TEN COMMON WRITING ERRORS

605

THEMATIC CONTENTS

ETHICS AND MORALITY

FAMILY AND CHILDREN

GOVERNMENT AND LAW

HEALTH AND PSYCHOLOGY

HUMAN GROUPS AND SOCIETY

HUMOR AND SATIRE

MEANING IN LIFE

MEDIA AND TECHNOLOGY

MEMORIES AND AUTOBIOGRAPHY

MEN AND WOMEN

NATURE AND SCIENCE

PREFACE

Much about our world has changed since the first edition of *The Longman Reader* (previously titled *The Macmillan Reader*) was published in 1987. In those days, students did not sit in coffee shops with their laptops or tablets before them as they worked on drafts of their essays; they didn't have Internet access or smartphones; and the word *texting* did not yet exist. However, although the ways writers compose, conduct research, and communicate with others has changed drastically over the past several decades, one factor that has remained constant is the need for students to be able to communicate their ideas clearly through writing. Something else that has not changed since this text's authors and production team worked on that first edition is the commitment to publishing a book that helps students develop sound writing skills.

As in the first ten editions, in this eleventh edition we have aimed for a different kind of text—one that would offer fresh examples of professional prose, one that would take a more active role in helping students become stronger readers, thinkers, and writers. *The Longman Reader* continues to include widely read and classic essays, as well as fresh new pieces, such as Alex Horton's "On Getting By" and Lynda Barry's "The Sanctuary of School." We've been careful to choose selections that range widely in subject matter and approach, from the humorous to the informative, from personal meditation to polemic. We've also made sure that each selection captures students' interest and clearly illustrates a specific pattern of development or a combination of such patterns.

As before, we have also tried to help students bridge the gap between the product and process approaches to reading and writing. Throughout, we describe possible sequences and structures but emphasize that such steps and formats are not meant to be viewed as rigid prescriptions; rather, they are strategies for helping students discover what works best in a particular situation.

WHAT'S NEW IN THE ELEVENTH EDITION OF *THE LONGMAN READER*

In preparing this edition, we looked closely at the reviews completed by instructors using the book. Their comments helped us identify new directions the book might take. Here are some of the new features of this edition of *The Longman Reader*.

- **Increased emphasis on academic writing,** with seven professional selections now including MLA and APA in-text references and works cited or reference lists. Additional coverage of academic writing is integrated into writing process steps. Also, the number of professional readings using third-person point of view is increased to twenty-eight, from nineteen in the last edition.
- **A new discussion on how to read graphs as visuals** has been added to Chapter 1's coverage of reading visuals to help students think critically about why and how statistical information is used in documents to better prepare them for the sorts of documents they will encounter in other course areas. In addition, seven professional selections use images as an integral feature, a threefold increase from the last edition. Finally, a new set of assignments on employing visuals in essays on specific topics appears at the end of each pattern of development chapter.
- **Sixteen of the fifty-eight selections are new.** Whether written by a journalist such as Bianca Bosker ("How Teens Are Really Using Facebook: It's a 'Social Burden,' Pew Study Finds"), a prominent figure such as Hillary Rodham Clinton ("Remarks to the United Nations Fourth Conference on Women Plenary Session"), or a literary figure such as Mario Suárez ("El Hoyo"), the new selections are bound to stimulate strong writing on a variety of topics—education, technology, body image, and identity, to name a few.
- **All new student essays—eleven in all**—with many written using third-person point of view, MLA documentation, and integrated illustrations. New student essays cover a range of subjects, from academic (review of a piece of art) to personal (relationships) to political (gender equality).
- **A completely revised Chapter 2 that follows a new student essay** through the steps of the writing process—from assignment to final draft, complete with works cited list. The chapter puts a new emphasis on academic writing while retaining the time-tested writing process steps established in previous editions.
- **A new pair of pro-con essays** in the argumentation-persuasion chapter further expands coverage of refutation strategies: Michael Marlow and Sherzod Abdukadirov's "Government Intervention Will Not Solve Our Obesity Problem" and Mark Bittman's "What Causes Weight Gain"—two readings that explore the issue of government regulation of citizen's food choices (Chapter 11).
- **Chapter objectives** have been added to help students prepare for and assess their work.
- **A revised treatment of plagiarism,** including discussions of intentional and unintentional plagiarism and "patchwork writing," appears in Appendix A.

ORGANIZATION OF *THE LONGMAN READER*

Buoyed by compliments about the previous editions' teachability, we haven't tinkered with the book's underlying format. Such a structure, we've been told, does indeed help students read more critically, think more logically, and write more skillfully. Here is the book's basic format.

Chapter 1, "Reading Critically"

Designed to reflect current theories about the interaction of reading, thinking, and writing, this chapter provides guided practice in a three-part process for reading with close attention and a high level of interpretive skill. This step-by-step process sharpens students' understanding of the book's selections and promotes the rigorous thinking needed to write effective essays.

An activity at the end of the chapter gives students a chance to use the three-step process. First, they read an essay by the journalist Ellen Goodman. The essay has been annotated both to show students the reading process in action and to illustrate how close critical reading can pave the way to promising writing topics. Then students respond to sample questions and writing assignments, all similar to those accompanying each of the book's selections. The chapter thus does more than just tell students how to sharpen their reading abilities; it guides them through a clearly sequenced plan for developing critical reading skills, including the skills needed to read and evaluate images.

Chapter 2, "The Writing Process"

In this revised chapter, as an introduction to essay writing and to make the composing process easier for students to grasp, we continue to provide a separate section for each of the following stages: prewriting, identifying a thesis, supporting the thesis with evidence, organizing the evidence, writing the first draft, revising, and editing and proofreading. The stages are also illustrated in a diagram, "Stages of the Writing Process."

From the start, we point out that the stages are fluid. Indeed, the case history of an evolving student paper—a new sample essay for this edition—illustrates just how recursive and individualized the writing process can be. Guided activities at the end of each section give students practice taking their essays through successive stages in the composing process.

To illustrate the link between reading and writing, the writing chapter presents the progressive stages of a student paper written in response to Ellen Goodman's "Family Counterculture," the selection presented in Chapter 1. An easy-to-spot symbol in the margin 〰 makes it possible to locate—at a glance—this evolving student essay. Commentary following the student paper highlights the essay's strengths and points out spots that could use additional work. In short, by the end of the second chapter, the entire reading–writing process has been illustrated, from reading a selection to writing about it.

Chapters 3 to 11: Patterns of Development

The chapters contain selections grouped according to nine patterns of development: description, narration, exemplification, division-classification, process analysis, comparison-contrast, cause-effect, definition, and argumentation-persuasion. The sequence progresses from the more personal and expressive patterns to the more public and analytic. However, because each chapter is self-contained, the patterns may be covered in any order. Instructors preferring a thematic approach will find the Thematic Contents helpful.

The Longman Reader treats the patterns separately because such an approach helps students grasp the distinctive characteristics of each pattern. At the same time, the book continually shows the way writers usually combine patterns in their work. We also encourage students to view the patterns as strategies for generating and organizing ideas. Writers, we explain, rarely set out to compose an essay in a specific pattern. Rather, they choose a pattern or combination of patterns because it suits their purpose, audience, and subject.

Each of the nine pattern-of-development chapters follows the format detailed here.

1. A **striking visual** opens every pattern-of-development chapter. Instructors may use the image as a prompt for a pattern-related writing activity that encourages students to consider issues of purpose and audience in a piece of real-world writing.
2. **Chapter objectives**, new in this edition, introduce the chapter's aims. Students can use the objectives to monitor their progress and formulate their personal goals.
3. **A detailed explanation of the pattern** begins the chapter. The explanation includes (a) a definition of the pattern, (b) a description of the way the pattern helps a writer accommodate his or her purpose and audience, and (c) step-by-step strategies for using the pattern.
4. **A development diagram** in each chapter illustrates how the pattern is expressed in each stage of the writing process.
5. **A section of revision strategies**, with a revision/peer review checklist, then follows.
6. **An annotated student essay** using the pattern of development appears next. Written in response to one of the professional selections in the chapter, each essay illustrates the characteristic features of the pattern discussed in the chapter. These student essays, all new

in this edition, model a range of features from third-person point of view, to integrated images, to MLA works cited lists.

7. **Commentary** after each student essay points out the blend of patterns in the piece, identifies the paper's strengths, and locates areas needing improvement. "First draft" and "revised" versions of one section of the essay reveal how the student writer went about revising, which illustrates the relationship between the final draft and the steps taken to produce it.

8. **Prewriting and revising activities** in shaded boxes after the sample student essay help students understand the unique demands posed by the pattern being studied.

9. **Professional selections** in the pattern-of-development chapters are accompanied by these items:

    • **An essay structure diagram** for the first essay in each section shows how the essay makes use of patterns of development.

    • **A biographical note** and **Pre-Reading Journal Entry assignment** give students a perspective on the author and create interest in the piece. The journal assignment encourages students to explore—in a loose, unpressured way—their thoughts about an issue that will be raised in the selection. The journal entry thus motivates students to read the piece with extra care, attention, and personal investment.

    • **Questions for Close Reading**, four in all, help students dig into and interpret the selection's content. The first question asks them to identify the selection's thesis.

    • **Questions About the Writer's Craft**, four in all, deal with such matters as purpose, audience, tone, organization, sentence structure, diction, figures of speech, visual illustrations, and use of documentation. The first question in the series (labeled "The Pattern") focuses on the distinctive features of the pattern used in the selection. And usually there's another question (labeled "Other Patterns") that asks students to analyze the writer's use of additional patterns in the piece.

    • **Writing Assignments**, three in all, follow each selection. Packed with suggestions on how to proceed, the assignments use the selection as a springboard. The first two assignments ask students to write an essay using the same pattern as the one used in the selection; the last assignment encourages students to experiment with a combination of patterns in their own essay.

    In some cases, assignments are accompanied by the symbol , indicating that students might benefit from conducting library or Internet research.

10. **Three sets of Additional Writing Topics** close each pattern of development chapter: "General Assignments," "Assignments Using Visuals," and "Assignments with a Specific Purpose, Audience, and Point of View." The first set provides open-ended topics that prompt students to discover the best way to use a specific pattern; the second set suggests visuals for use with specific essay topics; the third set develops students' sensitivity to rhetorical context by asking them to apply the pattern in a real-world situation ("Academic Life," "Civic Activity," or "Workplace Action").

Chapter 12, "Combining the Patterns"

The final chapter offers a sample student essay as well as four essays by different prose stylists. Annotations on the student essay and on one of the professional selections show how writers often blend patterns of development in their work. The chapter also provides guidelines to help students analyze this fusing of patterns.

Appendixes and Glossary

Appendix A, "A Guide to Using Sources," provides guidelines for evaluating, analyzing, and synthesizing sources; using quotations, summaries, and paraphrases to integrate sources into a paper; and documenting sources following the latest MLA style guidelines. **Appendix B, "Avoiding Ten Common Writing Errors,"** targets common problem areas in student writing and offers quick, accessible solutions for each. The **Glossary** lists and defines all the key terms presented in the text.

RESOURCES FOR STUDENTS AND INSTRUCTORS

MyWritingLab
`MyWritingLab`

MyWritingLab is an online homework, tutorial, and assessment program that provides engaging experiences to today's instructors and students. By incorporating rubrics into the writing assignments, faculty can create meaningful assignments, grade them based on their desired criteria, and analyze class performance through advanced reporting. For students who enter the course underprepared, MyWritingLab offers a diagnostic test and personalized remediation so that students see improved results and instructors spend less time in class reviewing the basics. Rich multimedia resources, including a text-specific ebook in many courses, are built in to engage students and support faculty throughout the course. Visit www.mywritinglab.com for more information.

Instructor's Manual

A comprehensive Instructor's Manual contains the following: in-depth answers to the "Questions for Close Reading" and "Questions About the Writer's Craft"; suggested activities; pointers about using the book; a detailed syllabus; and an analysis of the blend of patterns in the selections in the "Combining the Patterns" chapter.

ACKNOWLEDGMENTS

We are most indebted to Deborah Coxwell-Teague of Florida State University for her significant, conscientious, and expert contributions to the eleventh edition, including the selection of new and contemporary readings; new questions and activities; a new emphasis on incorporating visuals and sources; a thorough revision of writing process steps in Chapter 2; commentary on new student papers; and even new chapter opening images.

At Pearson, our thanks go to Brad Potthoff for his perceptive editorial guidance and enthusiasm for *The Longman Reader*. We're also indebted to Linda Stern, our Development Editor, and to Stephanie Raga of Integra-Chicago and Eric Jorgensen and Donna Campion of Pearson for their skillful handling of the never-ending complexities of the production process.

Over the years, many writing instructors have reviewed *The Longman Reader* and responded to detailed questionnaires about its selections and pedagogy. Their comments have guided our work every step of the way. We are particularly indebted to the following reviewers for the valuable assistance they have provided during the preparation of the eleventh edition of *The Longman Reader*: Denise Cady Arbeau, North Shore Community College; Jesse Doiron, Lamar University; Amy Fox, Central Texas College–Fort Knox Campus; Mary Sue Fox, Central New Mexico Community College; Dr. Harry A. Maxson, Wesley College; Stephen Raynie, Gordon State College; Lisa G. Rosa, Polk State College; Mary Stahoviak, Victoria College; Alex Tavares, Hillsborough Community College; and Matthew F. Wegener, Olympic College. Their reactions to various drafts of material sharpened our thinking and helped focus our work. And we are especially indebted to the students whose essays are included in the book. Their thoughtful, carefully revised papers dramatize the potential of student writing and the power of the composing process.

JUDITH NADELL
JOHN LANGAN

READING CRITICALLY

More than two hundred years ago, essayist Joseph Addison commented, "Of all the diversions of life, there is none so proper to fill up its empty spaces as the reading of useful and entertaining authors." Addison might have added that reading also challenges our beliefs, deepens our awareness, and stimulates our imagination. And the more challenging the material, the more actively involved the reader must be.

The essays in this book, which range from the classic to the contemporary, call for active reading. They contain language that will move you, images that will enlarge your understanding of other people, and ideas that will transform your views on complex issues. They will also help you develop a repertoire of reading skills that will benefit you throughout life.

The novelist Saul Bellow observed, "A writer is a reader moved to emulation." As you become a better reader, your own writing will become more insightful and polished. Increasingly, you'll be able to employ the techniques that professional writers use to express ideas.

The three-stage approach outlined here will help you learn to read more critically and get the most out of the readings in this book, as well as any other readings, including those with visuals. Ultimately, becoming a stronger reader will also help you grow as a writer.

STAGE 1: GET AN OVERVIEW OF THE SELECTION

Ideally, you should get settled in a quiet place that encourages concentration. Once you're settled, it's time to read the selection. To ensure a good first reading, try the following hints.

☑ FIRST READING: A CHECKLIST

❏ Get an overview of the essay and its author. Start by checking out the author's credentials. If a biographical note precedes the selection, as in this book, you'll want to read it for background that will help you evaluate the writer's credibility, as well as his or her slant on the subject. For other materials, do a computer search for information on the author and the publication or website where the reading appears.

❏ Consider the selection's title. A good title often expresses the essay's main idea, giving you insight into the selection even before you read it.

❏ Read the selection straight through purely for pleasure. Allow yourself to be drawn into the world the author has created. Because you bring your own experiences and viewpoints to the piece, your reading will be unique.

❏ If a reading has visuals, ask yourself these questions: Who created the visual? Is the source reliable? What does the caption say? If the visual is an image, what general mood, feeling, or other impression does it convey? If it is a graphic, is information clearly labeled and presented?

❏ After this initial reading of the selection, briefly describe the piece and your reaction to it.

STAGE 2: DEEPEN YOUR SENSE OF THE SELECTION

At this point, you're ready to move more deeply into the selection. A second reading will help you identify the specific features that triggered your initial reaction.

There are a number of techniques you can use during this second, more focused reading. Mortimer Adler, a well-known writer and editor, argued passionately for marking up the material we read. The physical act of annotating, he believed, etches the writer's ideas more sharply in the mind, helping readers grasp and remember those ideas more easily. Adler also described various annotation techniques he used when reading. Several of these techniques, adapted somewhat, are presented in the following checklist.

☑ SECOND READING: A CHECKLIST

Using a pen (or pencil) and highlighter for print texts—or digital commenting and highlighting features if you're reading online—you might...

❑ Underline or highlight the selection's main idea, or thesis, often found near the beginning or end. If the thesis isn't stated explicitly, write down your own version of the selection's main idea. If you're reading the selection online, you might add a digital sticky note or comment with your version of the thesis.

❑ Locate the main supporting evidence used to develop the thesis. Number the key supporting points by writing in the margin or adding digital sticky notes.

❑ Circle or put an asterisk next to key ideas that are stated more than once.

❑ Take a minute to write "Yes" or "No" or to insert these comments digitally beside points with which you strongly agree or disagree. Your reaction to these points often explains your feelings about the aptness of the selection's ideas.

❑ Return to any unclear passages you encountered during the first reading. The feeling you now have for the piece as a whole will *probably* help you make sense of initially confusing spots. You may possibly discover that the writer's thinking isn't as clear as it could be.

❑ Use a print or online dictionary to check the meanings of any unfamiliar words.

❑ Take some quick notes about any visuals. If you're reading online, you might choose to make digital comments. What is the author's purpose? Do images such as photos tell a story? Do they make assumptions about viewers' beliefs or knowledge? What elements stand out? How do the colors and composition (arrangement of elements) work to convey an impression? Are any graphs and similar visuals adequately discussed in the text? Is the information current and presented without distortion? Is it relevant to the text discussion?

❑ If your initial impression of the selection has changed in any way, try to determine why you reacted differently during this reading.

STAGE 3: EVALUATE THE SELECTION

Now that you have a good grasp of the selection, you may want to read it a third time, especially if the piece is long or complex. This time, your goal is to make judgments about the essay's effectiveness. Keep in mind, though, that you shouldn't evaluate the selection until after you have a strong hold on it. Whether positive or negative, any reaction is valid only if it's based on an accurate reading.

To evaluate the essay, ask yourself the following questions.

☑ EVALUATING A SELECTION: A CHECKLIST

❑ *Where does support for the selection's thesis seem logical and sufficient? Where does support seem weak?* Which of the author's supporting facts, arguments, and examples seem pertinent and convincing? Which don't?

❑ *Is the selection unified? If not, why not?* Where does something in the selection not seem relevant? Where are there any unnecessary digressions or detours?

❑ *How does the writer make the selection move smoothly from beginning to end?* Are any parts of the essay abrupt and jarring? Which ones?

❑ *Which stylistic devices are used to good effect in the selection?* How do paragraph development, sentence structure, word choice (diction), and tone contribute to the piece's overall effect? Where does the writer use *figures of speech* effectively? (Consult the index to see where these devices are explained.)

❑ *How do any visuals improve the reading and support the writer's main points?* Are the visuals adequately discussed in the text? Are images such as photos thought-provoking without being sensationalistic? Do graphs and similar visuals give relevant, persuasive details?

❑ *How does the selection encourage further thought?* What new perspective on an issue does the writer provide? What ideas has the selection prompted you to explore in an essay of your own?

ASSESSING VISUALS IN A READING

Writers may use visuals—images and graphics—to help convey their message. You can incorporate your "reading" of these visuals into the three-stage process you use for reading print texts: In stage 1, *preview* the visuals at the same time that you get an overview of the print text. In stage 2, *analyze and interpret* the visuals as a means of deepening your sense of the reading. Finally, in stage 3, *evaluate* the visuals as part of your evaluation of the entire selection.

Some kinds of visuals you are likely to find are listed here. Following this list are two examples of assessing visuals using the three-stage process.

Illustrations

- Photographs, paintings, drawings, and prints
    Illustrate a particular scene, time period, activity, event, idea, person, and so on.

- Cartoons and comics
    May make a joke, comment on a situation, or tell a story.

Graphics

- Tables
    Use columns and rows to present information, especially specific numbers, concisely.

- Bar graphs
    Use rectangular bars of different sizes to compare information about two or more items.

- Line graphs
    Use horizontal lines moving from point to point to show changes over time.

- Pie charts
    Use a circle divided into wedges to show proportions.

- Charts and diagrams
    Use different shapes and lines to show flow of information, organization of a group, layouts such as room plans, or assembly instructions.

- Maps
    Present information by geographical location.

Photos, paintings, and similar illustrations may appear in web pages, periodicals, books, and advertisements. Graphics regularly appear in academic, technical, and business writing. You can evaluate all these visuals just as you would print texts.

Assessing an Image: An Example

Suppose a reading aims to persuade readers that the international community must set up an organization that stands ready to implement an immediate and coordinated response to natural diasters, no matter where they occur. The reading includes a photo (see the next page) taken in the aftermath of the magnitude 7 earthquake that hit Haiti on January 12, 2010. How can we evaluate this image and its effectiveness for the reader?

Previewing the Photo. We see that the photo was found at *Time* magazine online and was taken by a photographer for the Associated Press (AP)—both reliable sources that we can trust. The author of the essay has written

Using whatever implements are at their disposal, Haitians searched for survivors—and victims—of the catastrophic earthquake that devastated Port-au-Prince and many surrounding areas on January 12, 2010.

Source: Arduengo, Ricardo. "Search and Rescue." *Devastation from the Haiti Earthquake*. Photo essay. *Time.com*, Jan. 2010, content.time.com/time/photogallery/0,29307,1953257_2024130,00.html.

a caption that clearly explains the image, and the phrase "Using whatever implements are at their disposal" supports the author's point that an immediate response is needed. We also notice, however, that the caption uses strong language, for example, "catastrophic" and "devastated." Information in the reading will have to support the use of these terms. Still, our first response to the photo would be one of sympathy and perhaps compassion for the people of Haiti.

Analyzing and Interpreting the Photo.   The photo tells a story of people coming together to help one another in the aftermath of the earthquake. The elements in the photo are arranged so that we first see people silhouetted against clouds, working with hand tools. Then we realize the people are standing atop a collapsed building, and we see the startling image of cars crushed beneath that structure. Now we understand the scope of the wreckage. The startling image of the ruined cars and the hopeful brightness of the sky are punctuated by the dark, massive bulk of the collapsed structure. Though we cannot see people's faces, we can imagine their determination. But we can also tell that their tools are unlikely to be adequate for the urgent task of finding those buried in the rubble.

Evaluating the Photo.   The photo powerfully illustrates the scale of the work facing Haiti and the probable inadequacy of the country's resources. The contrast between the crushed cars and building below and the determined workers above conveys a sense of the hopefulness of the human spirit even in dire situations. Many readers will feel an emotional response to these people, will see that they need help, and will want to help them. The photo and caption together, therefore, successfully support the idea that some countries may not have the means to cope effectively with huge natural disasters. The text of the reading will have to convince the reader that setting up an international organization to coordinate responses to these crises is the right solution.

Assessing a Graph: An Example

Imagine that a reading's purpose is to show that people need to do more to eradicate disease in the poorest countries and that the article includes the pie chart in Figure 1.1. How can we approach this graphic element and assess its usefulness to the reader?

Previewing the Graph.   We see right away that the author has created a pie chart comparing cases of malaria in regions of the world. The chart is clearly labeled, and a full caption tells us the information is from a reliable source— the World Health Organization, which is part of the United Nations.

FIGURE 1.1

Distribution of the 219 Million Cases of Malaria Reported Worldwide in 2010

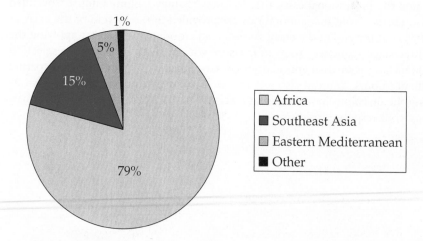

Source: From data reported in the *World Malaria Report 2012* (World Health Organization, www.who.int/malaria/publications/world_malaria_report_2012/report/en/)

Analyzing and Interpreting the Graph.   The source's date tells us that the information is not only reliable, but also current. The chart clearly shows that the greatest percentage of malaria cases reported in 2010 occurred in Africa. However, percentages can be misleading. If there were only 1,000 malaria cases altogether, 85 percent would not represent a very big number of cases. But because the figure title gives us the number of cases—and that number is very large (219 million)—we can conclude that malaria is a serious health problem in Africa.

Evaluating the Graph.   Without being sensationalistic, the chart is striking. It effectively dramatizes the point that the poorest regions of the world suffer substantially more from certain diseases than the developed regions do. The chart appeals to our sense of fairness. After all, if we can do more to prevent malaria in poor regions, shouldn't we? The author must still persuade us that it's really possible to do more, but the graph strongly supports at least part of the author's main idea.

A MODEL ANNOTATED READING

It takes some work to follow the three-step approach just described, but the selections in *The Longman Reader* are worth the effort. Bear in mind that none of the selections sprang full-blown from the pen of its author. Rather, each essay is the result of hours of work—hours of thinking, writing, rethinking, and revising. As a reader, you should show the same willingness to work with the selections, to read them carefully and thoughtfully.

To illustrate the multi-stage reading process just described, we've annotated the professional essay that follows: "Family Counterculture" by Ellen Goodman. Note that annotations are provided in the margin of the essay as well as at the end of the essay. As you read Goodman's essay, try applying the three-stage sequence. You can measure your ability to dig into the selection by making your own annotations on Goodman's essay and then comparing them to ours. You can also see how well you evaluated the piece by answering the questions in "Evaluating a Selection: A Checklist" and then comparing your responses to ours on pages 12–13.

A recipient of a Pulitzer Prize for Distinguished Commentary, Ellen Goodman (1941–) graduated *cum laude* from Radcliffe College in 1963. She worked for *Newsweek* and the *Detroit Free Press* before joining the staff of *The Boston Globe* in 1967. She began writing a column focused on social change in 1974, and the column has been nationally syndicated by the Washington Post Writers Group since 1976. Her books include *Turning Points* (1979) and, with coauthor Patricia O'Brien, *I Know Just What You Mean: The Power of Friendship in Women's Lives* (2000). She has also published six collections of her columns, including *Value Judgments* (1993), in which the following selection appears.

Pre-Reading Journal Entry

MyWritingLab

Television and other media are often blamed for having a harmful effect on children. Do you think this criticism is merited? In what ways do elements of today's culture exert a negative influence on children? In what ways do they exert a positive influence? Take a few minutes to respond to these questions in your journal.

Marginal Annotations

Family Counterculture

Interesting take on the term "counterculture"

Time frame established

    Sooner or later, most Americans become card-carrying 1 members of the counterculture. This is not an underground holdout of hippies. No beads are required. All you need to join is a child.

Light humor; easy, casual tone

Time frame picked up

Thesis, developed overall by cause-effect pattern

First research-based example to support thesis

    At some point between Lamaze and the PTA, it 2 becomes clear that one of your main jobs as a parent is to counter the culture. What the media delivers to children by the masses, you are expected to rebut one at a time.

    The latest evidence of this frustrating piece of the 3 parenting job description came from pediatricians. This summer, the American Academy of Pediatrics called for a ban on television food ads. Their plea was hard on the heels of a study showing that one Saturday morning of TV cartoons contained 202 junk-food ads.

    The kids see, want, and nag. That is, after all, the 4 theory behind advertising to children, since few six-year-olds have their own trust funds. The end result, said the pediatricians, is obesity and high cholesterol.

    Their call for a ban was predictably attacked by the 5 grocers' association. But it was also attacked by people assembled under the umbrella marked "parental responsibility." We don't need bans, said these "PR" people; we need parents who know how to say "no."

Relevant paragraph? Identifies Goodman as a parent, but interrupts flow

Well, I bow to no one in my capacity for naysaying. I agree that it's a well-honed skill of child raising. By the time my daughter was seven, she qualified as a media critic.

6

Transition doesn't work but would if ¶6 were cut

But it occurs to me now that the call for "parental responsibility" is increasing in direct proportion to the irresponsibility of the marketplace. Parents are expected to protect their children from an increasingly hostile environment.

7

Series of questions and brief answers consistent with overall casual tone

Are the kids being sold junk food? Just say no. Is TV bad? Turn it off. Are there messages about sex, drugs, violence all around? Counter the culture.

8

Brief real-life examples support thesis

Fragments

Mothers and fathers are expected to screen virtually every aspect of their children's lives. To check the ratings on the movies, to read the labels on the CDs, to find out if there's MTV in the house next door. All the while keeping in touch with school and, in their free time, earning a living.

9

More examples

In real life, most parents do a great deal of this monitoring and just-say-no-ing. Any trip to the supermarket produces at least one scene of a child grabbing for something only to have it returned to the shelf by a frazzled parent. An extraordinary number of the family arguments are over the goodies—sneakers, clothes, games—that the young know only because of ads.

10

Another weak transition—no contrast

But at times it seems that the media have become the mainstream culture in children's lives. Parents have become the alternative.

11

Restatement of thesis

Second research-based example to support thesis

Barbara Dafoe Whitehead, a research associate at the Institute for American Values, found this out in interviews with middle-class parents. "A common complaint I heard from parents was their sense of being overwhelmed by the culture. They felt their voice was a lot weaker. And they felt relatively more helpless than their parents.

12

Citing an expert reinforces thesis

Restatement of thesis

"Parents," she notes, "see themselves in a struggle for the hearts and minds of their own children." It isn't that they can't say no. It's that there's so much more to say no to.

13

Without wallowing in false nostalgia, there has been a fundamental shift. Americans once expected parents to raise their children in accordance with the dominant

14

Comparison-
contrast pattern—
signaled by "once,"
"Today," "Once,"
and "Now"

cultural messages. Today they are expected to raise their children in opposition.

Once the chorus of cultural values was full of ministers, teachers, neighbors, leaders. They demanded more conformity, but offered more support. Now the messengers are Ninja Turtles, Madonna, rap groups, and celebrities pushing sneakers. Parents are considered "responsible" only if they are successful in their resistance. 15

Restatement
of thesis

It's what makes child raising harder. It's why parents feel more isolated. It's not just that American families have less time with their kids. It's that we have to spend more of this time doing battle with our own culture. 16

Conveys the
challenges that
parents face

It's rather like trying to get your kids to eat their green beans after they've been told all day about the wonders of Milky Way. Come to think of it, it's exactly like that. 17

Annotations at End of Selection

Thesis: First stated in paragraph 2 ("...it becomes clear that one of your main jobs as a parent is to counter the culture. What the media delivers to children by the masses, you are expected to rebut one at a time.") and then restated in paragraphs 11 ("the media have become the mainstream culture in children's lives. Parents have become the alternative."); 13 (Parents are frustrated, not because "...they can't say no. It's that there's so much more to say no to."); and 16 ("It's not just that American families have less time with their kids. It's that we have to spend more of this time doing battle with our own culture.").

First reading: A quick take on a serious subject. Informal tone and to-the-point style gets to the heart of the media vs. parenting problem. Easy to relate to.

Second and third readings:
1. Uses the findings of the American Academy of Pediatrics, a statement made by Barbara Dafoe Whitehead, and a number of brief examples to illustrate the relentless work parents must do to counter the culture.
2. Uses cause-effect overall to support thesis and comparison-contrast to show how parenting nowadays is more difficult than it used to be.
3. Not everything works (reference to her daughter as a media critic, repetitive and often inappropriate use of "but" as a transition), but overall the essay succeeds.
4. At first, the ending seems weak. But it feels just right after an additional reading. Shows how parents' attempts to counter the culture are as commonplace as their attempts to get kids to eat vegetables. It's an ongoing and constant battle that makes parenting more difficult than it has to be and less enjoyable than it should be.
5. Possible essay topics: A humorous paper about the strategies kids use to get around their parents' saying "no" or a serious paper on the negative effects on kids of another aspect of television culture (cable television, tabloid-style talk shows, and so on).

The following answers to the questions in "Evaluating a Selection: A Checklist" on page 4 will help crystallize your reaction to Goodman's essay.

1. *Where does support for the selection's thesis seem logical and sufficient? Where does support seem weak?*

Goodman begins to provide evidence for her thesis when she cites the American Academy of Pediatrics' call for a "ban on television food ads" (paragraphs 3–5). The ban followed a study showing that kids are exposed to 202 junk-food ads during a single Saturday morning of television cartoons. Goodman further buoys her thesis with a list of brief "countering the culture" examples (8–10) and a slightly more detailed example (10) describing the parent-child conflicts that occur on a typical trip to the supermarket. By citing Barbara Dafoe Whitehead's findings later on (12–13), Goodman further reinforces her point that the need for constant rebuttal makes parenting especially frustrating: Because parents have to say "no" to virtually everything, more and more family time ends up being spent "doing battle" with the culture (16).

2. *Is the selection unified? If not, why not?*

In the first two paragraphs, Goodman identifies the problem and then provides solid evidence of its existence (3–4, 8–10). But Goodman's comments in paragraph 6 about her daughter's skill as a media critic seem distracting. Even so, paragraph 6 serves a purpose because it establishes Goodman's credibility by showing that she, too, is a parent and has been compelled to be a constant naysayer with her child. From paragraph 7 on, the piece stays on course by focusing on the way parents have to compete with the media for control of their children. The concluding paragraphs (16–17) reinforce Goodman's thesis by suggesting that parents' struggle to counteract the media is as common—and as exasperating—as trying to get children to eat their vegetables when all the kids want is to gorge on candy.

3. *How does the writer make the selection move smoothly from beginning to end?*

The first two paragraphs of Goodman's essay are clearly connected: The phrase "sooner or later" at the beginning of the first paragraph establishes a time frame that is then picked up at the beginning of the second paragraph with the phrase "at some point between Lamaze and the PTA." And Goodman's use in paragraph 3 of the word *this* ("The latest evidence of *this* frustrating piece of the parenting job description...") provides a link to the preceding paragraph. Other connecting strategies can be found in the piece. For example, the words *once, Today, Once,* and *Now* in paragraphs 14–15 provide an easy-to-follow contrast between parenting in earlier times and parenting in this era. However, because paragraph 6 contains a distracting aside, the contrast implied by the word *But* at the beginning of paragraph 7 doesn't work. Nor does Goodman's use of the word *But* at the beginning of paragraph 11 work; the point there emphasizes rather than contrasts with the one made in paragraph 10. From this point on, though, the essay is tightly written and moves smoothly along to its conclusion.

4. *Which stylistic devices are used to good effect in the selection?*

Goodman uses several patterns of development in her essay. The selection as a whole shows the *effect* of the mass media on kids and their parents. In paragraphs 3 and 12, Goodman provides *examples in the form of research data* to support her thesis, whereas paragraphs 8–10 provide a series of *brief real-life examples.* Paragraphs 12–15 use *contrast,* and paragraph 17 makes a *comparison* to punctuate Goodman's concluding point. Throughout, Goodman's *informal, conversational tone* draws readers in, and her *no-holds-barred style* drives her point home forcefully. In paragraph 8, she uses a *question-and-answer format* ("Are the kids being sold junk food? Just say no.") and *short sentences* ("Turn it off" and "Counter the culture") to illustrate how pervasive the situation is. And in paragraph 9, she uses *fragments* ("To check the ratings…" and "All the while keeping in touch with school…") to focus attention on the problem. These varied stylistic devices help make the essay a quick, enjoyable read. Finally, although Goodman is concerned about the corrosive effects of the media, she leavens her essay with dashes of *humor.* For example, the image of parents as counterculturists (1) and the comments about green beans and Milky Ways (17) probably elicit smiles or gentle laughter from most readers.

5. *How does the selection encourage further thought?*

Goodman's essay touches on a problem most parents face at some time or another—having to counter the culture to protect their children. Her main concern is how difficult it is for parents to say "no" to virtually every aspect of the culture. Although Goodman offers no immediate solutions, her presentation of the issue urges us to decide for ourselves which aspects of the culture should be countered and which should not.

If, for each essay you read in this book, you consider the checklist questions, you'll be able to respond thoughtfully to the *Questions for Close Reading* and *Questions About the Writer's Craft* presented after each selection. Your responses will, in turn, prepare you for the writing assignments that follow the questions. Interesting and varied, the assignments invite you to examine issues raised by the selections and encourage you to experiment with various writing styles and organizational patterns.

Following are some sample questions and writing assignments based on the Goodman essay; all are similar to the sort that appear later in this book. Note that the final writing assignment paves the way for a student essay, the stages of which are illustrated in Chapter 2.

Questions for Close Reading

MyWritingLab

1. According to Goodman, what does it mean to "counter the culture"? Why is this harder now than ever before?

2. Which two groups, according to Goodman, protested the American Academy of Pediatrics's ban on television food ads? Which of these two groups does she take more seriously? Why?

Questions About the Writer's Craft

1. What audience do you think Goodman had in mind when she wrote this piece? How do you know? Where does she address this audience directly?
2. What word appears four times in paragraph 16? Why do you think Goodman repeats this word so often? What is the effect of this repetition?

Writing Assignments

1. Goodman believes that parents are forced to say "no" to almost everything the media offer. Write an essay illustrating the idea that not everything the media present is bad for children.
2. Singling out television as a medium that conveys negative messages about food, Goodman calls today's culture "an increasingly hostile environment" for kids. Do you agree? Why or why not? Drawing on but not limiting yourself to the material in your pre-reading journal, write an essay in which you support or reject this viewpoint. Consider focusing on one particular form of media. Although you are not required to include information from outside sources in your essay, feel free to do so if you think additional information from reputable sources would make your essay more effective.

The benefits of active reading are many. Books in general and the selections in *The Longman Reader* in particular will bring you face to face with issues that concern all of us. If you study the selections and the questions that follow them, you'll be on the way to discovering ideas for your own compositions. Chapter 2, "The Writing Process," offers practical suggestions for turning those ideas into well-organized, thoughtful essays.

MyWritingLab Visit Chapter 1, "Reading Critically," in MyWritingLab to complete the Pre-Reading Journal Entry activity and Questions for Close Reading, and to test your understanding of the chapter objectives.

THE WRITING PROCESS

How do you typically react when your college professor assigns an essay? Are you so excited that you can hardly wait to get started? Perhaps—if you are lucky enough to immediately think of what you want to say and how you want to say it. But for many, if not most, putting pen or pencil to paper—or fingers to keyboard—is a little scary, and for good reason.

When you write, you put what's going on in your brain—your innermost thoughts—down for others to see. If they read what you've written and react positively, with a comment such as "Wow! You are an amazing writer!" you feel wonderful. Their reaction has made you feel validated as a student, as a thinker, and as an intelligent person. But if the writing in your early drafts needs lots of improvement, don't despair. That doesn't mean that you are not smart or that you're not a "good" writer. What it does mean is that, more often than not, writing is hard work, and the words don't simply pour perfectly and effortlessly out of your brain and on to the page or screen—and that's true for almost everyone. Although your final draft may, indeed, be engaging, interesting, and polished, chances are that your writing did not start out that way. Writing truly is a process, and you need to think carefully about the steps you take that will lead to a final draft you can be proud to share with your audience.

Because writing is a process, shaky starts and changes in direction aren't uncommon. Although there's no way to eliminate the work needed to write effectively, certain approaches can make the process more manageable and rewarding. This chapter describes a sequence of steps for writing essays.

Familiarity with a specific sequence develops your awareness of strategies and choices, making you feel more confident when it comes time to write. You're less likely to look at a blank piece of paper and think, "Help! Now what do I do?" During the sequence, you do the following:

1. Prewrite.
2. Identify the thesis.
3. Support the thesis with evidence.
4. Organize the evidence.
5. Write the first draft.
6. Revise the essay.
7. Edit and proofread.

We present the sequence as a series of stages, but we urge you not to view it as a formula to be followed rigidly. Most people develop personalized approaches to the writing process. Some writers mull over a topic in their heads and then move quickly into a promising first draft; others outline their essays in detail before beginning to write. Between these two extremes are any number of effective approaches. The sequence here—illustrated in Figure 2.1—can be streamlined or otherwise altered to fit individual writing styles as well as the needs of specific assignments.

STAGE 1: PREWRITE

Prewriting refers to strategies you can use to generate ideas *before* starting the first draft of a paper. Prewriting techniques are like the warm-ups you do before going out to jog—they loosen you up, get you moving, and help you develop a sense of well-being and confidence. Because prewriting techniques encourage imaginative exploration, they also help you discover what interests you most about your subject.

During prewriting, you deliberately ignore your internal critic. Your purpose is simply to get ideas down on paper *without evaluating* their effectiveness. Writing without immediately judging what you produce can be liberating. Once you feel less pressure, you'll probably find that you can generate a good deal of material. And that can make your confidence soar.

Keep a Journal

Of all the prewriting techniques, keeping a journal (daily or almost daily) is most likely to make writing a part of your life. Some entries focus on a single theme; others wander from topic to topic. Your starting point may be a dream, a snippet of overheard conversation, a song, a political cartoon, an issue raised in class or in your reading—anything that surprises, interests, angers, depresses, confuses, or amuses you. You may also use a journal to

FIGURE 2.1
Stages of the Writing Process

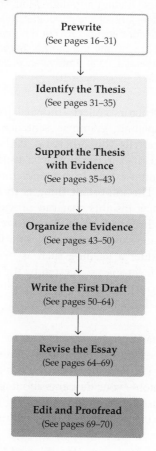

experiment with your writing style—say, to vary your sentence structure if you tend to use predictable patterns.

Here is a fairly focused excerpt from a student's journal:

Today I had to show Paul around school. He and Mom got here by 9. I didn't let on that this was the earliest I've gotten up all semester! He got out of the car looking kind of nervous. Maybe he thought his big brother would be different after a couple of months of college. I walked him around part of the campus and then he went with me to Am. Civ. and then to lunch. He met Greg and some other guys. Everyone seemed to like him. He's got a nice, quiet sense of humor.

When I went to Bio., I told him that he could walk around on his own since he wasn't crazy about sitting in on a science class. But he said "I'd rather stick with you." Was he flattering me or was he just scared? Anyway it made me feel good. Later when he was leaving, he told me he's definitely going to apply. I guess that'd be kind of nice, having him here. Mom thinks it's great and she's pushing it. I don't know. I feel kind of like it would invade my privacy. I found this school and have made a life for myself here. Let him find his own school!

But it could be great having my kid brother here. I guess this is a classic case of what my psych teacher calls ambivalence. Part of me wants him to come, and part of me doesn't! (November 10)

Although some instructors collect students' journals, you needn't be overly concerned with spelling, grammar, sentence structure, or organization, unless your teacher tells you otherwise. Although journal writing is typically more structured than freewriting, you usually don't have to strive for entries that read like mini-essays. In fact, sometimes you may find it helpful to use a simple list. The important thing is to let your journal writing prompt reflection and new insights that can provide you with material to draw on in your writing. It is, then, a good idea to reread each week's entries to identify recurring themes and concerns. Keep a list of these issues at the back of your journal, under a heading such as "Possible Essay Subjects." Here, for instance, are a few topics suggested by the preceding journal entry: deciding which college to attend, leaving home, sibling rivalry. Each of these topics could be developed in a full-length essay.

The Pre-Reading Journal Entry.   To reinforce the value of journal writing, we've included a journal assignment before every reading selection in the book. This assignment, called Pre-Reading Journal Entry, encourages you to explore—in a tentative fashion—your thoughts about an issue that will be raised in the selection. Here, once again, is the Pre-Reading Journal Entry assignment that precedes Ellen Goodman's "Family Counterculture" in Chapter 1:

> Television and other media are often blamed for having a harmful effect on children. Do you think this criticism is merited? In what ways do elements of today's culture exert a negative influence on children? In what ways do they exert a positive influence? Take a few minutes to respond to these questions in your journal.

The following journal entry shows how one student, Caylah Francis, responded to the journal assignment. An eighteen-year-old college student with two younger brothers who spend hours each week playing video games, Caylah was intrigued by the assignment; she decided to focus her journal entry on the negative and positive effects of playing video games. As you'll see, Caylah used a listing strategy to prepare her journal entry. She found that lists are perfect for dealing with the essentially "for or against" nature of the journal assignment.

Video Games' Negative Influence on Kids	Video Games' Positive Influence on Kids
Teaches negative behaviors (violence, sex, swearing, drugs, alcohol, etc.)	Teaches important problem-solving skills
Cuts down on time spent using imagination to come up with fun things to do that don't involve sitting in front of a screen	Exposes kids to new images and worlds (*Skylanders, Disney Infinity*)
Cuts down on time spent with parents (talking, reading, playing board games together)	Can inspire important discussions (about morals, sexuality, drugs, etc.) between kids and parents
Encourages parents' lack of involvement with kids	Gives parents a needed break from kids
Frightens kids excessively by showing images of real-life violence (terrorist attacks, war, murders, etc.)	Educates kids about the painful realities in the world
Encourages isolation (interacting with a screen rather than interacting with other kids)	Creates common ground among kids, basis of conversations and games
De-emphasizes reading and creates need for constant stimulation	Sharpens eye-hand coordination skills and promotes faster reaction times
Cuts down on time spent playing outside and getting much needed exercise	Keeps kids occupied inside in the safety of their homes instead of outside in a potentially dangerous environment

As you've just seen, journal writing can stimulate thinking in a loose, unstructured way; it can also prompt the focused thinking required by a specific writing assignment. When you have a specific piece to write, you should approach prewriting in a purposeful, focused manner. You need to:

- Understand the boundaries of the assignment.
- Determine your purpose, audience, and tone.
- Discover your essay's limited subject.
- Generate raw material about your limited subject.
- Organize the raw material.

Understand the Boundaries of the Assignment

Before you start writing a paper, learn what's expected. First, clarify the *kind of paper* the instructor has in mind. Suppose the instructor asks you to discuss the key ideas in an assigned reading. What does the instructor want you to do? Should you include a brief summary of the selection? Should you compare the author's ideas with your own view of the subject? Should you determine if the author's view is supported by valid evidence? If you're not sure about an assignment, ask your instructor to make the requirements clear.

In particular, clarify whether your instructor expects you to consult researched sources for your essay. If that is the expectation, then be sure to find out the following:

- The number and kinds of sources you need to include in your essay.
- Whether you need to use both primary and secondary sources or only one or the other.
- Whether you are expected to use a combination of print and online sources, and of books, magazines, journals, and so on.
- The note-taking procedure your teacher expects you to use (for example, note cards, a research journal, or a research log).
- The required documentation style—for example, the style favored by the Modern Language Association (MLA) or the American Psychological Association (APA).
- Whether you are expected to include visuals to clarify or illustrate points you make in your essay, and if so, what kinds of visuals (for example, graphs, charts, or photos).

You will also need to find out anything else you need to know to effectively complete the assignment, including *how long* the essay is expected to be. Many instructors will indicate the approximate length of the writings they assign. If no length requirements are provided, discuss with the instructor what you plan to cover and indicate how long you think your essay will be. The instructor will either give you the go-ahead or help you refine the direction and scope of your work.

Determine Your Purpose, Audience, and Tone

Once you understand the requirements for a writing assignment, you're ready to begin thinking about the essay. What is its *purpose*? For what *audience* will it be written? What *tone* will you use? Later on, you may modify your decisions about these issues. That's fine. But you need to understand the way these considerations influence your work in the early phases of the writing process.

Purpose.   The essays you write in college are usually meant to *inform* or *explain*, to *convince* or *persuade*, to *analyze* or *evaluate*, and sometimes to *entertain*. In practice, writing often combines purposes. For example, you might write an essay trying to *convince* people to support a new trash recycling program in your community. But before you win readers over, you most likely would have to *explain* something about current waste disposal technology.

When purposes blend this way, the predominant one determines the essay's content, organization, emphasis, and choice of words. Assume you're writing about a political campaign. If your primary goal is to inform your readers of the views of the various candidates, you might want to focus your essay on explaining where each one stands on important issues. But if your primary purpose is to *persuade* readers that one candidate is clearly the best qualified for the position and that the views of that particular candidate are in the best interest of the community, you might focus on pointing out the strengths of that candidate over the others.

Audience. To write effectively, you need to identify who your readers are and to take their expectations and needs into account. An essay about the artificial preservatives in the food served by the campus cafeteria would take one form if submitted to your chemistry professor and a different form if written for the college newspaper. The chemistry report would probably be formal and technical, complete with chemical formulations and scientific data: "Distillation revealed sodium benzoate particles suspended in a gelatinous medium." But such technical material would be inappropriate in a newspaper column intended for general readers. In this case, you might provide specific examples of cafeteria foods containing additives—"Those deliciously smoky cold cuts are loaded with nitrates and nitrites, both known to cause cancer in laboratory animals"—and suggest ways to eat healthier: "Pass by the deli counter and fill up instead on vegetarian pizza and fruit juices."

When analyzing your audience, ask yourself the following questions.

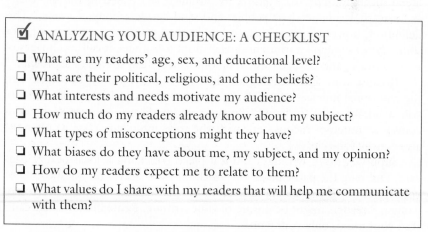

✔ ANALYZING YOUR AUDIENCE: A CHECKLIST

- ❏ What are my readers' age, sex, and educational level?
- ❏ What are their political, religious, and other beliefs?
- ❏ What interests and needs motivate my audience?
- ❏ How much do my readers already know about my subject?
- ❏ What types of misconceptions might they have?
- ❏ What biases do they have about me, my subject, and my opinion?
- ❏ How do my readers expect me to relate to them?
- ❏ What values do I share with my readers that will help me communicate with them?

Tone. Just as a voice projects a range of feelings, writing can convey one or more *tones,* or emotional states: enthusiasm, anger, resignation, and so on. Tone is integral to meaning; it permeates writing and reflects your attitude toward yourself, your purpose, your subject, and your readers. How do you project tone?

1. Use appropriate sentence structure.   *Sentence structure* refers to the way sentences are shaped. Although the two paragraphs that follow deal with exactly the same subject, note how differences in sentence structure create sharply dissimilar tones:

> During the 1960s, many inner-city minorities considered the police an occupying force and an oppressive agent of control. As a result, violence against police grew in poorer neighborhoods, as did the number of residents killed by police.

> An occupying force. An agent of control. An oppressor. That's how many inner-city minorities in the '60s viewed the police. Violence against police soared. Police killings of residents mounted.

Informative in its approach, the first paragraph projects a neutral, almost dispassionate tone. The sentences are fairly long, and clear transitions ("During the 1960s"; "As a result") mark the progression of thought. But the second paragraph, with its dramatic, almost alarmist tone, seems intended to elicit a strong emotional response; its short sentences, fragments, and abrupt transitions reflect the turbulence of those earlier times.

2. Choose effective words.   *Word choice* also plays a role in establishing the tone of an essay. Words have *denotations,* neutral dictionary meanings, as well as *connotations,* which are emotional associations that go beyond the literal meaning. The word *beach,* for instance, is defined in the dictionary as "a nearly level stretch of pebbles and sand beside a body of water." This definition, however, doesn't capture individual responses to the word. For some, *beach* suggests warmth and relaxation; for others, it calls up images of hospital waste and sewage washed up on a once-clean stretch of shoreline.

Because tone and meaning are tightly bound, you must be sensitive to the emotional nuances of words. In a respectful essay about police officers, you wouldn't refer to "cops," "narcs," or "flatfoots" because such terms convey a contempt inconsistent with the tone intended. Your words must also convey tone clearly.

Suppose you're writing a satirical piece criticizing a local beauty pageant. Dubbing the participants "livestock on view" leaves no question about your tone. But if you simply referred to the participants as "attractive young women," readers might be unsure of your attitude. Remember, readers can't read your mind, only your words.

3. Use a formal tone for most academic writing.   In most academic writing, the author is expected to use a formal tone. The kind of casual language you are likely to use in conversation with a friend or in texts you send them is almost never appropriate in academic writing. Your instructor might ask you to adhere to these guidelines:

- Writing from third-person point of view (using the pronouns *he*, *she*, *it*, *one*, and *they*), instead of using first person (*I* or *we*) or second person (*you*).
- Using few or no contractions and abbreviations.
- Omitting slang expressions.

For example, a sentence such as "You don't eat junk like donuts and puff pastries, just the healthy stuff, if you want a great bod" is not appropriate in an academic essay. The sentence might be revised as follows: "Avoiding sugary treats and eating healthy foods such as whole grains, fruits, and vegetables is an important part of staying in shape." A good rule to follow is to save informal language for informal situations.

Discover Your Essay's Limited Subject

Because too broad a subject can result in a diffuse, rambling essay, be sure to restrict your general subject before starting to write. The following examples show the difference between general subjects that are too broad for an essay and limited subjects that are appropriate and workable. The examples, of course, represent only a few among many possibilities.

General Subject	Less General	Limited
Education	Computers in education	Computers in elementary school arithmetic classes
	High school education	High school electives
Transportation	Low-cost travel	Hitchhiking
	Getting around a metropolitan area	The transit system in a nearby city
Work	Planning for a career	College internships
	Women in the work force	Women's success as managers

How do you move from a general to a narrow subject? Imagine that you're asked to prepare a straightforward, informative essay for your writing class. Reprinted here is writing assignment 2 from Chapter 1. The assignment, prompted by Ellen Goodman's essay "Family Counterculture," is an extension of the journal-writing assignment given earlier in that chapter.

Singling out television as a medium that conveys negative messages about food, Goodman calls today's culture "an increasingly hostile environment" for kids. Do you agree? Why or why not? Drawing on but not limiting yourself to the material in your pre-reading journal, write an essay in which you support or reject this viewpoint. Consider focusing on one particular form of media. Although you are not required to include information from outside sources in your essay, feel free to do so if you think additional information from reputable sources would make your essay more effective.

Two techniques—*questioning* and *brainstorming*—can help you limit such a general assignment. Although these techniques encourage you to roam freely over a subject, they also help restrict the discussion by revealing which aspects of the subject interest you most.

1. Question the general subject.   One way to narrow a subject is to ask a series of *who, how, why, where, when,* and *what* questions. The following example shows how Caylah used this technique to limit the Goodman assignment.

You may recall that, before reading Goodman's essay, Caylah had used her journal to explore—using a listing strategy—video games' effects on children. After reading "Family Counterculture," Caylah concluded that she essentially agreed with Goodman; like Goodman, she felt that parents nowadays are indeed forced to raise their kids in an "increasingly hostile environment." She was pleased that the writing assignment gave her an opportunity to expand preliminary ideas she had jotted down in her journal.

Caylah soon realized that she had to narrow the Goodman assignment. She started by asking a number of pointed questions about the general topic. As she proceeded, she was aware that the same questions could have led to different limited subjects—just as other questions would have.

General Subject: Do children live in an "increasingly hostile environment"?

Question	Limited Subject
Who is to blame for the difficult conditions in which children grow up?	Parents' casual attitude toward child-rearing
How have schools contributed to the problems children face?	Not enough counseling programs for kids in distress
Why do children feel frightened?	Too much time spent alone while parents are at work
Where do kids go to escape?	Video games, which can make the world seem even more dangerous
When are children most vulnerable?	The special problems of adolescents
What dangers or fears should parents discuss with their children?	Drugs, alcohol, crime, sexually transmitted diseases

2. Brainstorm the general subject. Another way to focus on a limited subject is to list quickly everything about the general topic that pops into your mind. Just jot down brief words, phrases, and abbreviations to capture your free-floating thoughts. Writing in complete sentences will slow you down. Don't try to organize or censor your ideas. Even the most fleeting, random, or seemingly outrageous thoughts can be productive. An example of brainstorming appears later in this chapter.

Questioning and brainstorming can suggest many possible limited subjects. To identify especially promising ones, reread your material. What arouses your interest, anger, or curiosity? What themes seem to dominate and cut to the heart of the matter? Star or circle ideas with potential.

After marking the material, write several phrases or sentences summariz- ing the most promising limited subjects. Here are just a few that emerged from Caylah's prewriting for the Goodman assignment:

- Various popular media partly to blame for kids having such a hard time
- Schools also at fault
- Kids need to get outside more and play the way we used to
- Violent video games especially harmful to kids today

Looking back at the work she did for her pre-reading journal assignment, Caylah decided to write on the last of these limited subjects—the harmful effects of playing violent video games.

Generate Raw Material about Your Limited Subject

When a limited subject strikes you as having possibilities, use these techniques to see if you have enough interesting things to say about the subject to write an effective essay.

1. Freewrite on your limited subject. *Freewriting* means jotting down in rough sentences or phrases everything that comes to mind. To capture this continuous stream of thought, write nonstop for ten minutes or more. Don't censor anything; put down whatever pops into your head. Don't reread, edit, or pay attention to organization, spelling, or grammar. If your mind goes blank, repeat words until another thought emerges.

Here is part of the freewriting that Caylah generated about her limited subject, "The harmful effects of playing violent video games":

Kids today have tough problems to face. Lots of dangers. The Internet first and foremost. Also crimes of violence against kids. Parents have to keep up with cost of living, everything costs more, kids want and expect more. My brothers sure expect and get more than I did when I was their age. Today, both parents almost always have full-time jobs. Parents have to work more hours than ever before to give their kids everything they need and want. Sometimes parents give in and buy them things that are not good for them. Like some of the games my brothers play. What were my parents thinking? Why would they buy those games for Brandon and Josh? Kids are left alone at home more than they ever were before. Kids grow up too fast, too fast. Kids grow up too fast, too fast. Drugs and alcohol. Witness real-life violence on TV, like terrorist attacks and school shootings. Kids can't handle knowing too much at an early age. Both parents at work much of the day. Kids spend too much time at home alone. Can do pretty much anything they want when parents aren't around. Another problem is getting kids to do homework, lots of other things to do. Especially like texting friends or checking out the latest Facebook posts. When I was young, we did homework after dinner, no excuses accepted by my parents. My parents are sure a lot easier on my brothers than they were on me. That's not a good thing.

2. Brainstorm your limited subject.   Let your mind wander freely, as you did when using brainstorming to narrow your subject. This time, list every idea, fact, and example that occurs to you about your limited subject. Use brief words and phrases. For now, don't worry if ideas fit together or if the points listed make sense.

To gather additional material on her limited subject for the Goodman assignment ("The harmful effects of playing violent video games"), Caylah brainstormed the following list:

Kids today spend way too much time playing violent video games they have no business playing.

Parents work long hours and don't know what their kids are doing while they're home alone.

Kids expecting more and more things like video games and cell phones.

Clothes so important, even to boys like my brothers who think they can only wear Ralph Lauren polo shirts and khakis.

- I remember seeing something on TV about violent video games making some kids become more aggressive—maybe I can look this up.
- Sitting in front of a screen for so many hours not good for kids.
- Violent games become addictive to some kids, like my younger brother.
- Sex everywhere—TV, movies, magazines, Internet.
- Kids grow up too fast—see too much.
- Sexual abuse of kids.
- Violence against kids when parents abuse drugs.
- Meth, Ecstasy, alcohol, heroin, cocaine, STDs.
- Schools have to teach kids about these things.
- Schools emphasize testing too much—not as good as they used to be.
- Not enough homework assigned—kids unprepared.
- Kids not doing homework when it is assigned.
- Parents letting kids have too much freedom and do things they shouldn't let them do.
- Distractions from homework—video games, Internet—especially social networking sites, TV, cell phones.

3. Use group brainstorming.   Brainstorming can also be conducted as a group activity. Thrashing out ideas with other people stretches the imagination and reveals possibilities you may not have considered on your own. Group brainstorming doesn't have to be conducted in a formal classroom situation. You can bounce ideas around with friends and family anywhere— over lunch, at the student center, and so on.

4. Map out the limited subject.   If you're the kind of person who doodles while thinking, you may want to try *mapping,* sometimes called *diagramming* or *clustering.* Like other prewriting techniques, mapping proceeds rapidly and encourages the free flow of ideas. Begin by expressing your limited subject in a crisp phrase and placing it in the center of a blank sheet of paper. As ideas come to you, put them along lines or in boxes or circles around the limited subject. Draw arrows and lines to show the relationships among ideas. Don't stop there, however. Focus on each idea; as subpoints and details come to you, connect them to their source idea, again using boxes, lines, circles, or arrows to clarify how everything relates.

5. Use the patterns of development.   Throughout this book, we show how writers use various patterns of development (narration, process analysis, definition, and so on), singly or in combination, to develop and organize their ideas. Because each pattern has its own distinctive logic, the patterns encourage you—when you prewrite—to think about a subject in different ways, causing insights to surface that might otherwise remain submerged. The patterns of development are discussed in detail in Chapters 3–11.

The following chart shows the way each pattern can generate raw material for a limited subject.

Limited Subject: The harmful effects of playing violent video games.

Pattern	Purpose	Raw Material
Description	To detail what a person, place, or object is like	Detail what the games are like—the sexy images, the language used, the thrill of the chase, the danger and excitement of battle
Narration	To relate an event	Recount what happened when neighbors tried to forbid their kids from playing violent games that their friends were playing
Exemplification	To provide specific instances or examples	Offer examples of particular games and the violence in them

(Continued)

Pattern	Purpose	Raw Material
Division-classification	To divide something into parts or to group related things in categories	Identify different kinds of violent games—those about war, those about high-speed chases from law enforcement, those about abduction, etc.
Process analysis	To explain how something happens or how something is done	Explain step by step how family life can disintegrate when parents have to work long hours and children are left home unsupervised
Comparison-contrast	To point out similarities and/or dissimilarities	Contrast families today with those of a generation ago
Cause-effect	To analyze reasons and consequences	Explain why parents are not around to be with their kids: Everything costs so much and we expect more luxuries today than our parents and grandparents expected—such as large houses and cars for everyone in the family who is old enough to drive
		Explain the consequences of absentee parents: Kids left alone too much with time to do whatever they want; they spend hours on the Internet; they spend far too many hours each week playing violent video games
Definition	To explain the meaning of a term or concept	What is meant by "tough love"?
Argumentation-persuasion	To win people over to a point of view	Convince parents that they must learn how to say "no" to their kids and not let them do something just because their friends are doing it

Conduct research. Depending on your topic, you may find it helpful to visit the library or to go online to identify books and articles about your limited subject. At this point, you don't need to read closely the material you find. Just skim and perhaps take a few brief notes on ideas and points that could be useful.

 Early in the drafting process, Caylah realized that she needed to conduct research to find out more about her subject: the harmful effects of violent video games. She had lots of ideas about possible harmful effects, but she needed to find out what reputable sources had to say about her subject. She knew her essay would not be effective unless she included documented sources to support her claims.

In researching for her assignment Caylah looked under the following headings and subheadings:

The most popular violent video games on the market today
Effects of playing violent video games
    Isolation and video game play
    Obesity and video game play
    Aggression and video game play
Family
Parent-child relationships
Children of working parents
School and home

Caylah eventually identified several sources that offered important material on her subject. She read these sources critically and made sure they were reputable. She also made sure the sources were relevant to her topic and provided trustworthy information. Many of the sources she found came from Internet sites, and Caylah took a close look at who hosted the sites, who authored the articles, the links the sites provided, and whether the information on the sites was supported with documentation. As she took notes, she was careful to place quotation marks around words and phrases she copied directly from the sources and to record all of the information she would need when she was ready to begin compiling her list of works cited. In addition, she made copies of her source materials so that she could easily return to them as needed.

Organize the Raw Material

Later on in this chapter, we talk about the more formal outline you may eventually need in the writing process. However, a *scratch outline* or *scratch list* can be an effective strategy for imposing order on the tentative ideas generated during prewriting.

Reread your exploratory thoughts about the limited subject. Cross out anything not appropriate for your purpose, audience, and tone; add points that didn't originally occur to you. Star or circle compelling items that warrant further development. Then draw arrows between related items; your goal is to group such material under a common heading. Finally, determine what seems to be the best order for those headings.

By giving you a sense of the way your free-form material might fit together, a scratch outline makes the writing process more manageable. You're less likely to feel overwhelmed once you actually start writing because you'll already have some idea about how to shape your material into a meaningful statement. Remember, though, the scratch outline can, and most likely will, be modified along the way.

The following scratch outline shows how Caylah began to shape her brainstorming into a more organized format. Note the way she eliminated some items (for example, the points about drugs, wearing particular brands of clothes, and sexual abuse), added others (for example, the psychological effects of playing violent video games), and grouped the brainstormed items under four main headings, with the appropriate details listed underneath. (Caylah's more formal outline and her first draft, appear later on in this chapter.)

Limited Subject: The harmful effects of playing violent video games.

1. Home life today
   • Parents at work long hours
   • Kids left alone
   • Kids have too much freedom
   • Parents too permissive
2. Kids more aggressive
   • They start acting like the characters in the games they play
   • Playing games more likely to lead to aggression than watching violence on TV
3. Become addicted to games
   • The more they play, the more likely they'll become addicted
   • Spend more and more time alone
4. Can damage their health
   • Obesity
   • Procrastination

The prewriting strategies just described provide a solid foundation for the next stages of your work. But invention and imaginative exploration don't end when prewriting is completed. As you'll see, remaining open to new ideas is crucial during all phases of the writing process.

Activities: Prewrite   MyWritingLab

1. Number the items in each set from 1 (*broadest subject*) to 5 (*most limited subject*):

   Set A
   Abortion
   Controversial social issue
   Cutting state abortion funds
   Federal funding of abortions
   Social issues

   Set B
   Business majors
   Students' majors
   College students
   Kinds of students on campus
   Why many students major in business

2. Which of the following topics are too broad for an essay of two to five typewritten pages: reality TV's appeal to college students; day care; trying to "kick" the junk food habit; romantic relationships; international terrorism?

3. Use the techniques indicated in parentheses to limit each general topic listed. Then, identify a specific purpose, audience, and tone for the one limited subject you consider most interesting. Next, with the help of the patterns of development,

generate raw material about that limited subject. (You may find it helpful to work with others when developing this material.) Finally, shape your raw material into a scratch outline—crossing out, combining, and adding ideas as needed. (Save your scratch outline so you can work with it further after reading about the next stage in the writing process.)

Friendship *(journal writing)*

Malls *(mapping)*

Leisure *(freewriting)*

Social media sites *(brainstorming)*

Required courses *(group brainstorming)*

Manners *(questioning)*

STAGE 2: IDENTIFY THE THESIS

The process of prewriting—discovering a limited subject and generating ideas about it—prepares you for the next stage in writing an essay: identifying the paper's *thesis,* or controlling idea. The thesis, which presents your opinion on a subject, should focus on an interesting and significant issue, one that engages your energies and merits your consideration. You may think of the thesis as the essay's hub—the central point around which all the other material revolves. Your thesis determines what does and does not belong in the essay. The thesis, especially when it occurs early in an essay, also helps focus the reader on the piece's central point.

Sometimes the thesis emerges early in the prewriting stage. Often, though, you'll need to do some work to determine your thesis. For some topics, you may need to do some library research. For others, the best way to identify a promising thesis is to look through your prewriting and ask yourself questions such as these: What statement does all this prewriting support? What aspect of the limited subject is covered in most detail? What is the focus of the most provocative material?

From the scratch outline that Caylah prepared for the limited subject "The harmful effects of playing violent video games" (see page 30), Caylah devised the following thesis: "Playing violent video games can have many negative effects on kids. It can lead to increased levels of aggression, video game addiction, and serious health issues."

Writing an Effective Thesis

Generally expressed in one or two sentences, a thesis statement often has two parts. One part presents the *limited subject;* the other gives your *point of view,* or *attitude,* about that subject. Here are some examples of moving from general subject to limited subject to thesis statement. In each thesis statement, the limited subject is underlined once and the attitude twice.

General Subject	Limited Subject	Thesis
Education	Computers in elementary school arithmetic classes	<u>Computer programs in arithmetic can individualize instruction more effectively than the average elementary school teacher can.</u>
Transportation	A metropolitan transit system	Although the <u>city's transit system</u> still has problems, <u>it has become safer and more efficient in the last two years.</u>
Work	College internships	<u>College internships provide valuable opportunities to students uncertain about what to do after graduation.</u>
Our anti-child world	The harmful effects of playing violent video games	<u>Playing violent video games can have many negative effects on kids. It can lead to increased levels of aggression, video game addiction, and serious health issues.</u>

(*Reminder:* The last thesis statement is Caylah's, devised for the essay she planned to write for the Goodman assignment in Chapter 1. Caylah's first draft appears later on in this chapter.)

Avoiding Thesis Pitfalls

Because identifying your thesis statement is an important step in writing a sharply focused essay, you need to avoid three common problems that lead to an ineffective thesis.

Don't make an announcement. Some writers use the thesis statement merely to announce the limited subject of their paper and forget to indicate their attitude toward the subject. Such statements are announcements of intent, not thesis statements.

Compare the following three announcements with the thesis statements beside them.

Announcements	Thesis Statements
My essay will discuss whether a student pub should exist on campus.	This college should not allow a student pub on campus.
Assault weapons legislation is the subject of this paper.	Regulating the purchase of assault weapons is a crucial step in controlling crime in the United States.
I want to discuss cable television.	Cable television has not delivered on its promise to provide an alternative to network programming.

Don't make a factual statement. Your thesis, and thus, your essay should focus on an issue capable of being developed. If a fact is used as a thesis, you have no place to go; a fact generally doesn't invite much discussion. Notice the difference between these factual statements and thesis statements.

Factual Statements	Thesis Statements
Many businesses pollute the environment.	A carbon tax should be levied against businesses that pollute the environment.
Nowadays, many movies are violent.	Movie violence provides a healthy outlet for aggression.
The population of the United States is growing older.	The aging of the U.S. population will eventually create a crisis in the delivery of health-care services.

Don't make a broad statement. Avoid stating your thesis in vague, general, or sweeping terms. Broad statements make it difficult for readers to grasp your essay's point. Moreover, if you start with a broad thesis, you're saddled with the impossible task of trying to develop a book-length idea in an essay that runs only several pages.

The following examples contrast statements that are too broad with thesis statements that are focused effectively.

Broad Statements	Thesis Statements
Nowadays, high school education is often meaningless.	High school diplomas have been devalued by grade inflation.
Popular magazines cater to the taste of the American public.	The success of *People* magazine indicates that many people are intrigued by celebrity culture and want to learn more about the day-to-day lives of pop culture icons.
The computer revolution is not all that we have been led to believe it is.	Having easy access to computers is one reason children are growing up too fast today.

The thesis is often stated near the beginning, but it may be delayed, especially if you need to provide background information before it can be understood. Sometimes the thesis is reiterated—with fresh words—in the essay's conclusion or elsewhere. You may even leave the thesis unstated, relying on strong evidence to convey the essay's central idea.

One final point: Once you start writing your first draft, some feelings, thoughts, and examples may emerge that qualify, or even contradict, your initial thesis. Don't resist these new ideas; they frequently move you toward a clearer statement of your main point. Remember, though, your essay must have a thesis. Without this central concept, you have no reason for writing.

Activities: Identify the Thesis   MyWritingLab

1. For each of the following limited subjects, four possible thesis statements are given. Indicate whether each is an announcement (*A*), a factual statement (*FS*), too broad a statement (*TB*), or an effective thesis (*OK*). Then, for each effective thesis, identify a possible purpose, audience, and tone.

    Limited Subject: The ethics of treating severely handicapped infants

    Some babies born with severe handicaps have been allowed to die.

    There are many serious issues involved in the treatment of handicapped newborns.

    The government should pass legislation requiring medical treatment for handicapped newborns.

    This essay will analyze the controversy surrounding the treatment of severely handicapped babies who would die without medical care.

    Limited Subject: Privacy and computerized records

    Computers raise some significant and crucial questions for all of us.

    Computerized records keep track of consumer spending habits, credit records, travel patterns, and other personal information.

    Computerized records have turned our private lives into public property. In this paper, the relationship between computerized records and the right to privacy will be discussed.

2. Each of the following sets lists the key points in an essay. Using the information provided, prepare a possible thesis for each essay.

    ### Set A
    - One evidence of this growing conservatism is the reemerging popularity of fraternities and sororities.
    - Beauty contests, ROTC training, and corporate recruiting—once rejected by students on many campuses—are again popular.
    - Most important, many students no longer choose risky careers that enable them to contribute to society but select, instead, safe fields with moneymaking potential.

    ### Set B
    - We do not know how engineering new forms of life might affect the Earth's delicate ecological balance.
    - Another danger of genetic research is its potential for unleashing new forms of disease.
    - Even beneficial attempts to eliminate genetic defects could contribute to the dangerous idea that only perfect individuals are entitled to live.

3. Following are four pairs of general and limited subjects. Generate an appropriate thesis statement for each pair. Select one thesis, and determine which pattern of development would support it most effectively. Use that pattern to draft a paragraph developing the thesis. (Save the paragraph so you can work with it further after reading about the next stage in the writing process.)

General Subject	Limited Subject
Psychology	The power struggles in a classroom
Health	Doctors' attitudes toward patients
U.S. politics	Television's coverage of presidential campaigns
Work	Minimum-wage jobs for young people

4. Return to the scratch outline you prepared for Activity 3 on page 30. After examining the outline, identify a thesis that conveys the central idea behind most of the raw material. Then, ask others to evaluate your thesis in light of the material in the outline. Finally, keeping the thesis—as well as your purpose, audience, and tone—in mind, refine the scratch outline by deleting inappropriate items, adding relevant ones, and indicating where more material is needed. (Save your refined scratch outline and thesis so you can work with them further after reading about the next stage in the writing process.)

STAGE 3: SUPPORT THE THESIS WITH EVIDENCE

Supporting material grounds your essay, showing readers you have good reason for feeling as you do about your subject. Your evidence also adds interest and color to your writing. In college essays of 500 to 1500 words, you usually need at least three major points of evidence to develop your thesis. These major points—each focusing on related but separate aspects of the thesis—eventually become the supporting paragraphs in the body of the essay.

What Is Evidence?

By *evidence*, we mean a number of different kinds of support. *Examples* are just one option. To develop your thesis, you might also include *reasons, facts, details, statistics, anecdotes,* and *quotations from experts.* Imagine you're writing an essay with the thesis "People normally unconcerned about the environment can be galvanized to constructive action if they feel personally affected by an environmental problem." You could support this thesis with any combination of the following types of evidence:

- *Examples* of successful recycling efforts in several neighborhoods.
- *Reasons* people got involved in a neighborhood recycling effort.

- *Facts* about other residents' efforts to preserve the quality of their well water.
- *Details* about the steps that people can take to get involved in environmental issues.
- *Statistics* showing the number of Americans concerned about the environment.
- An *anecdote* about your involvement in environmental efforts.
- A *quotation* from a well-known scientist about the impact that citizens can have on environmental legislation.

Where Do You Find Evidence?

Where do you find the examples, anecdotes, details, and other types of evidence needed to support your thesis? As you saw when you followed Caylah's strategies for gathering material for an essay, a good deal of evidence is generated during the prewriting stage. In this phase of the writing process, you tap into your personal experiences, draw on other people's observations, or perhaps interview a person with special knowledge about your subject. The library and the Internet, with their abundant material, are also rich sources of supporting evidence, and Caylah made extensive use of both of these as she prepared to write her essay on the harmful effects of playing violent video games. In addition, the various patterns of development are a valuable source of evidence.

How the Patterns of Development Help Generate Evidence

Just as patterns of development can help generate material about a limited subject they can also help develop support for a thesis. The following chart shows how three patterns can generate evidence for this thesis: "To those who haven't done it, babysitting looks easy. In practice, though, babysitting can be difficult, frightening, even dangerous."

Pattern	Evidence Generated
Division-classification	A typical babysitting evening divided into stages: playing with the kids; putting them to bed; dealing with their nighttime fears once they're in bed
	Kids' nighttime fears classified by type: monsters under their beds; bad dreams; being abandoned by their parents
Process analysis	Step-by-step account of what a babysitter should do if a child becomes ill or injured
Comparison-contrast	Contrast between two babysitters: one well prepared and the other unprepared

Characteristics of Evidence

No matter how it is generated, all types of supporting evidence share the characteristics described in the following sections. You should keep these characteristics in mind as you review your thesis and scratch outline. That way, you can make the changes needed to strengthen the evidence gathered previously. As you'll see shortly, Caylah focused on many of these issues as she worked with the evidence she collected during the prewriting phase.

The evidence is relevant and unified.   All the evidence in an essay must clearly support the thesis. It makes no difference how riveting material might be; if it doesn't *relate directly* to the essay's central point, the material should be eliminated. Irrelevant material can weaken your position by implying that no relevant support exists. It also distracts readers from your controlling idea, which disrupts the paper's overall unity.

The following paragraph, from an essay on changes in Americans' movie-viewing habits, focuses on people's reasons for watching movies at home instead of in movie theatres. As you'll see, the paragraph lacks unity because it contains points (underlined) unrelated to its main idea. Specifically, the comments about parents who are more annoying that crying babies should be deleted. Although this observation brings up interesting points, it shifts the paragraph's focus from reasons for watching movies at home to problems with parents, and this is not the intended focus of the paragraph.

Nonunified Support

Many people prefer to watch movies in the comfort of their own living rooms instead of in movie theaters. They enjoy wearing their comfortable pajamas, sitting in their favorite recliner, and drinking a beverage of their choice while they watch a movie that just came out on Netflix, On-Demand, or Redbox. They appreciate the option of pausing the movie when they need to answer the phone or get clothes out of the dryer, and they are happy not having to put up with the couple behind them who talk throughout the movie or the baby who won't stop crying and whose parents aren't polite enough to step outside the theater until the baby quiets down. Those parents can actually be more annoying than the crying baby. Babies cry—that's a natural thing—but parents should realize that they are being inconsiderate and downright rude when they remain in the theater with a baby who is disturbing others. Watching movies at home can also be more convenient. Viewers who have only an hour of free time can watch a movie for 60 minutes and save the rest for another time. It's hardly surprising that movie theater ticket sales are down whereas Netflix, On-Demand, and Redbox are doing booming business.

Early in the writing process, Caylah was aware of the importance of relevant evidence. Take a moment to compare Caylah's brainstorming (page 26) and her scratch outline (page 30). Even though Caylah hadn't identified her thesis when she prepared the scratch outline, she realized she should delete a number of items from her brainstorming—for example, the items about clothes, drugs, sexual abuse, and school. Caylah eliminated these points because they weren't consistent with the focus of her limited subject.

The evidence is specific.   When evidence is vague and general, readers lose interest in what you're saying, become skeptical of your ideas' validity, and feel puzzled about your meaning. In contrast, *specific, concrete evidence* provides sharp *word pictures* that engage your readers, persuade them that your thinking is sound, and clarify meaning.

Consider, for example, the differences between the following two sentences: "The young man had trouble lifting the box out of an old car" and "Joe, only twenty years old but severely weakened by a recent bout with the flu, struggled to lift the heavy wooden crate out of the rusty, dented Chevrolet." The first sentence, filled with generalities, is fuzzy and imprecise, whereas the second sentence, filled with specifics, is crisp and clear.

As the preceding sentences illustrate, three strategies can be used, singly or in combination, to make writing specific. First, you can provide answers to *who, which, what,* and similar *questions.* (The question "How does the car look?" prompts a change in which "an old car" becomes "a rusty, dented Chevrolet.") Second, you can use *vigorous verbs* ("had trouble lifting" becomes "struggled to lift"). Finally, you can replace *vague, abstract* nouns with *vivid, concrete* nouns or phrases ("the young man" becomes "Joe, only twenty years old but severely weakened by a recent bout with the flu").

Following are two versions of a paragraph from an essay about trends in the business community. Although both paragraphs focus on one such trend—working from home—note how the first version's bland language fails to engage the reader and how its vague generalities leave the meaning unclear. Why, for example, are employees "happier" when they work from home, and how does working from home help them "lead more balanced lives and also save money"? The second paragraph answers these questions (as well as several others) with clear specifics; it also uses strong, energetic language. As a result, the second paragraph is more informative and more interesting than the first.

Nonspecific Support

More and more businesses are beginning to allow employees to work from home, and this is working out very well for both employees and businesses. The employees are happier. They lead more balanced lives and also save money. The companies are saving money as well and have better employees than they did before allowing employees to work from home. The trend to allow employees to work from home is likely to become more and more widespread.

Specific Support

Gone are the days when all employees were expected to follow a rigid schedule, arriving at their offices and clocking in at 8 A.M., going to lunch from noon to 1 P.M., and clocking out at 5 P.M. More and more businesses are beginning to allow employees to work from home, and this trend is working out very well for both employees and businesses. For one thing, the employees are happier. Their stress levels have dramatically decreased because they do not have to deal with commuter traffic or long bus or train rides. They lead more balanced lives because they can schedule their work hours around their daily lives, which allows them to spend more time with friends and family. They can even work in more time for exercise—time they once had to spend going to and from their offices. Working from home also helps employees save money. They no longer have to purchase expensive clothes to wear to the office or pay for after-school care. Instead of spending a chunk of their income each day on costly lunches, they can walk into their kitchen and make a sandwich. The companies who hire them are saving money as well. They no longer have to provide high-priced office space. In addition, they have better employees than they did before allowing employees to work from home. Their pool of possible job candidates grows considerably when they can hire individuals from anywhere in the world—not just from within a 30-mile radius of their business location. With so many benefits for both employees and businesses, the trend to allow employees to work from home is likely to become more and more widespread.

At this point, it will be helpful to compare once again Caylah's brainstorming (page 26) and her scratch outline (page 30). Note the way she added new details in the outline to make her evidence more specific. For example, after conducting research relating to her brainstorming statement "I remember seeing something on TV about violent video games making some kids more aggressive," she created the heading "Kids more aggressive" and she added new examples: "They start acting like the characters in the games they play" and "Playing games more likely to lead to aggression than watching violence on TV." And, as you'll see when you read Caylah's first and final drafts later in this chapter, she added even more vigorous specifics during later stages of the writing process.

The evidence is adequate.   Readers won't automatically accept your thesis; you need to provide *enough specific evidence* to support your viewpoint. On occasion, a single extended example will suffice. Generally, though, you'll need various kinds of evidence: facts, examples, reasons, personal observations, expert opinion, and so on.

Following are two versions of a paragraph from a paper showing how difficult it is to get personal, attentive service nowadays at gas stations, supermarkets, and department stores. Both paragraphs focus on the problem at gas stations, but one paragraph is much more effective. As you'll see, the first paragraph starts with good, specific support, yet fails to provide enough of it. The second paragraph offers additional examples, descriptive details, and dialogue—all of which make the writing stronger and more convincing.

Inadequate Support

For a good example of this lack of personal service, consider gas stations. Gone are the attendants of yesteryear who pumped your gas for you. Today, motorists pull up to a combination convenience store and gas island where they pay for their gas by inserting a credit card into a card reader that is part of the gas pump, or if they are paying with cash, go inside the store and wait in line to pay the clerk sitting behind the cash register. Then drivers must pump their own gas. That's a real inconvenience, especially in comparison with the way service stations used to be run.

Adequate Support

For a good example of this lack of personal service, consider gas stations. Gone are the attendants of yesteryear who pumped your gas for you. Today, motorists pull up to a combination convenience store and gas island where they pay for their gas by inserting a credit card into a card reader that is part of the gas pump, or if they are paying with cash, go inside the store and wait in line to pay the clerk sitting behind the cash register. Then drivers must pump their own gas. Gone are the days when "pump jockeys" walked up to your window as soon as you pulled up next to the gas pump and asked, "Check your oil? Wash your windshield?" Today, if you're lucky, you may discover a bucket of water and a squeegee you can use to clean your own windshield.

And customers with a fretful engine or a nonfunctioning heater are out of luck. Why? Gas stations have eliminated on-duty mechanics. The skillful mechanic who could replace a belt or fix a tire in a few minutes has been replaced by a card reader for you to stick your credit card into.

Now take a final look at Caylah's scratch outline from previously in this chapter (page 30). Caylah realized she needed more than one block of supporting material to develop her limited subject; that's why she identified four separate blocks of evidence ("Home life today," "Kids more aggressive," "Become addicted to games," and "Can damage their health"). When Caylah prepared her first and final drafts, she decided to include information about home life today in her introduction and conclusion instead of using it as the topic of one of her supporting paragraphs. She realized that the three body paragraphs needed to provide information that supported her thesis on the harmful effects of video games and that a paragraph on home life today would not serve that purpose.

The evidence is accurate.   When you have a strong belief and want readers to see things your way, you may be tempted to overstate or downplay facts, disregard information, misquote, or make up details. Suppose you plan to write an essay making the point that dormitory security is lax. You begin supporting your thesis by narrating the time you were nearly mugged in your dorm hallway. Realizing the essay would be more persuasive if you also mentioned other episodes, you decide to invent some material. Perhaps you describe several supposed burglaries on your dorm floor or exaggerate the amount of time it took campus security to respond to an emergency call from a residence hall. Yes, you've supported your point—but at the expense of truth. Keep in mind that hypothetical examples are okay to use, as long as readers know they did not actually happen.

The evidence is representative.   Using representative evidence means that you rely on the typical and usual to show that your point is valid. Contrary to the maxim, exceptions don't prove the rule. Perhaps you plan to write an essay contending that the value of seat belts has been exaggerated. To support your position, you mention a friend who survived a head-on collision without wearing a seat belt. Such an example isn't representative because the facts and figures on accidents suggest your friend's survival was a fluke.

Borrowed evidence is documented.   If you include evidence from outside sources (for example, books, articles, interviews, or websites) as Caylah did in her essay, you need to acknowledge where that information comes from. If you don't, readers may consider your evidence nothing more than your point of view, or they may regard as dishonest your failure to cite your indebtedness to others for ideas that are not your own. As Caylah composed her essay, she was careful to use quotation marks around language that came directly from her sources and to use parenthetical documentation so that her readers would know where she obtained the outside information she included. She also carefully prepared her Works Cited page so that her readers could easily locate her sources. (For information on acknowledging sources in longer, more formal papers, refer to Appendix A.)

Strong supporting evidence is at the heart of effective writing. Without it, essays lack energy and fail to convey the writer's perspective. Such lifeless writing is more apt to put readers to sleep than to engage their interest and convince them that the points being made are valid. Taking the time to accumulate solid supporting material is, then, a critical step in the writing process.

Activities: Support the Thesis with Evidence   MyWritingLab

1. Each of the following sets includes a thesis statement and four points of support. In each set, identify the one point that is off target.

Set A

Thesis: Colleges should put less emphasis on sports.

Encourages grade fixing
Creates a strong following among former graduates
Distracts from real goals of education
Causes extensive and expensive injuries

Set B

Thesis: The United States is becoming a homogenized country.

Regional accents vanishing
Chain stores blanket country
Americans proud of their ethnic identities
Metropolitan areas almost indistinguishable from one another

2. For each of the following thesis statements, develop three points of relevant support. Then use the patterns of development to generate evidence for each point of support.

Thesis: The trend toward disposable, throwaway products has gone too far.
Thesis: The local (or college) library fails to meet the needs of those it is supposed to serve.
Thesis: Television portrays men as incompetent creatures.

3. Choose one of the following thesis statements. Then identify an appropriate purpose, audience, and tone for an essay with this thesis. Using freewriting, mapping, or the questioning technique, generate at least three supporting points for the thesis. Last, write a paragraph about one of the points, making sure your evidence reflects the characteristics discussed in these pages. Alternatively, you may go ahead and prepare the first draft of an essay having the selected thesis. (If you choose the second option, you may want to turn to Figure 2.2, "Structure of an Essay," in this chapter for a diagram showing how to organize a first draft.) Save whatever you prepare so you can work with it further after reading about the next stage in the writing process.

   - Winning the lottery may not always be a blessing.
   - All of us can take steps to reduce the country's trash crisis.
   - Drug education programs in public schools are (or are not) effective.

4. Select one of the following thesis statements. Then determine your purpose, audience, and tone for an essay with this thesis. Next, use the patterns of development to generate at least three supporting points for the thesis. Finally, write a paragraph about one of the points, making sure that your evidence demonstrates

the characteristics discussed in these pages. Alternatively, you may go ahead and prepare a first draft of an essay having the thesis selected. (If you choose the latter option, you may want to turn to Figure 2.2, "Structure of an Essay," in this chapter for a diagram showing how to organize a first draft.) Save whatever you prepare so you can work with it further after reading about the next stage in the writing process.

- Teenagers should (or should not) be able to obtain birth control devices without their parents' permission.
- The college's system for awarding student loans needs to be overhauled.
- Texting has changed for the worse (or the better) the way Americans communicate with each other.

5. Retrieve the paragraph you wrote in response to Activity 3 on page 35. Keeping in mind the characteristics of effective evidence, make whatever changes are needed to strengthen the paragraph. (Save the paragraph so you can work with it further after reading about the next stage in the writing process.)

6. Look at the thesis and refined scratch outline you prepared in response to Activity 4 on page 35. Where do you see gaps in the support for your thesis? By brainstorming with others, generate material to fill these gaps. If some of the new points generated suggest that you should modify your thesis, make the appropriate changes now. (Save this material so you can work with it further after reading about the next stage in the writing process.)

STAGE 4: ORGANIZE THE EVIDENCE

After you've generated supporting evidence, you're ready to *organize* that material. Even highly compelling evidence won't illustrate the validity of your thesis or achieve your purpose if readers have to plow through a maze of chaotic evidence. Some writers can move quickly from generating support to writing a clearly structured first draft. (They usually say they have sequenced their ideas in their heads.) Most, however, need to spend some time sorting out their thoughts on paper before starting the first draft; otherwise, they tend to lose their way in a tangle of ideas.

When moving to the organizing stage, you should have in front of you your scratch outline and thesis plus any supporting material—for example, notes from research—that you've accumulated. To find a logical framework for all this material, you'll need to

- Determine the main pattern of development implied in your evidence.
- Select one of four basic approaches for organizing your evidence.
- Outline your evidence.

Use the Patterns of Development

Each pattern of development (description, narration, exemplification, division-classification, process analysis, comparison-contrast, cause-effect, definition, and argumentation-persuasion) has its own internal logic that makes it appropriate for some writing purposes but not for others. Once you see which pattern (or combination of patterns) is implied by your purpose, you can block out your paper's general structure. Imagine that you're writing an essay *explaining why* some students drop out of college during the first semester. You might organize the essay around a three-part discussion of the key *causes* contributing to the difficulty that students have adjusting to college: (1) they miss friends and family, (2) they take inappropriate courses, and (3) they experience conflicts with roommates.

Some essays follow a single pattern, but most blend them, with a predominant pattern providing the piece's organizational framework. In our example essay, you might include a brief *description* of an overwhelmed first-year college student; you might *define* the psychological term "separation anxiety"; you might end the paper by briefly explaining a *process* for making students' adjustment to college easier. Still, the essay's overall organizational pattern would be *cause-effect* because the paper's primary purpose is to explain why students drop out of college. (For more information on the way patterns often blend in writing, see Chapter 12 "Combining the Patterns.")

Although writers often combine the patterns of development, writing an essay organized according to a single pattern can help you understand a particular pattern's unique demands. Keep in mind, though, that most writing begins not with a specific pattern but with a specific *purpose*. The pattern or combination of patterns evolves out of that purpose.

Select an Organizational Approach

No matter which pattern(s) of development you select, you need to know four general approaches for organizing supporting evidence—chronological, spatial, emphatic, and simple-to-complex.

Chronological approach. When an essay is organized *chronologically*, supporting material is arranged in a clear time sequence, usually starting with what happened first and ending with what happened last. Occasionally, chronological sequences can be rearranged to create flashback or flash-forward effects, which are two techniques discussed in Chapter 4 on narration. Essays using narration (for example, an experience with prejudice) or process analysis (for instance, how to deliver an effective speech) are most likely to be organized chronologically. The paper on public speaking might use a time sequence to present its points: how to prepare a few days before the presentation is due; what to do right before the speech; what to concentrate on during the speech itself.

Spatial approach.   When you arrange supporting evidence *spatially*, you discuss details as they occur in space, or from certain locations. This strategy is particularly appropriate for description. Imagine that you plan to write an essay describing the happy times you spent as a child playing by a towering old oak tree in the neighborhood park. Using spatial organization, you start by describing the rich animal life (the plump earthworms, swarming anthills, and numerous animal tracks) you observed while hunkered down *at the base* of the tree. Next, you recreate the contented feeling you experienced sitting on a branch *in the middle* of the tree. Finally, you end by describing the glorious view of the world you had *from the top* of the tree.

Although spatial arrangement is flexible (you could, for instance, start with a description from the top of the tree), you should always proceed systematically. And once you select a particular spatial order, you should usually maintain that sequence throughout the essay; otherwise, readers may get lost along the way.

Emphatic approach.   In *emphatic* order, the most compelling evidence is usually saved for last. This arrangement is based on the principle that people remember best what they experience last. Sometimes, though, an essay captures the audience's attention by giving the most important point first. Emphatic order is especially effective in argumentation-persuasion essays, in papers developed through examples, and in pieces involving comparison-contrast, division-classification, or causal analysis.

Consider an essay analyzing the negative effect that workaholic parents can have on their children. The paper might start with a brief discussion of relatively minor effects such as the family's eating mostly frozen or takeout foods. Paragraphs on more serious effects might follow: children get no parental help with homework; they try to resolve personal problems without parental advice. Finally, the essay might close with a detailed discussion of the most significant effect—children's lack of self-esteem because they feel unimportant in their parents' lives.

Simple-to-complex approach.   A final way to organize an essay is to proceed from relatively *simple* concepts to more *complex* ones. By starting with easy-to-grasp, generally accepted evidence, you establish rapport with your readers and assure them that the essay is firmly grounded in shared experience. In contrast, if you open with difficult or highly technical material, you risk confusing and alienating your audience.

Assume you plan to write a paper arguing that your college has endangered students' health by not making an all-out effort to remove asbestos from dormitories and classroom buildings. It probably wouldn't be a good idea to begin with a medically sophisticated explanation of precisely how asbestos damages lung tissue. Instead, you might start with an observation that is likely to be familiar to your readers—one that is part of their everyday experience. You could, for example, open with a description of asbestos—as readers might see it—wrapped around air ducts and furnaces or used as electrical insulation and fireproofing material. Having provided a basic, easy-to-visualize description, you could then go on to explain the complicated process by which asbestos can cause chronic lung inflammation.

Depending on your purpose, any one of these four organizational approaches might be appropriate. For example, assume that you planned to write an essay developing Caylah's thesis: "Playing violent video games can have many negative effects on young children. It can lead to increased levels of aggression, video game addiction, and serious health issues." To emphasize that the harmful effects are directly related to the types of games children play at particular ages, you might select a *chronological* sequence. To show that harmful effects vary depending on whether children are playing at home alone, with friends at their homes, or in other settings, you might choose a *spatial* sequence. To stress the range of harmful effects (from less to more serious), you might use an *emphatic* sequence. To illustrate why video games today require more commitment of player's time and energy than they used to, you might take a *simple-to-complex* approach in describing the simpler games of decades ago and then the increasingly sophisticated and complicated games of today.

Prepare an Outline

Having an outline—a skeletal version of your paper—*before* you begin the first draft can make the writing process much more manageable. The outline helps you organize your thoughts beforehand, and it guides your writing as you work on the draft. Even though ideas continue to evolve during the draft, an outline clarifies how ideas fit together, which points are major, which should come first, and so on. An outline may also reveal places where evidence is weak, underscoring the need, perhaps, for more prewriting.

Some people prepare highly structured outlines; others make only a few informal jottings. Sometimes outlining will go quickly, with points falling easily into place; at other times you'll have to work hard to figure out how points are related. If that happens, be glad you caught the problem while outlining rather than while writing the first draft.

To prepare an effective outline, you should reread and evaluate your scratch outline and thesis as well as any other evidence you've generated since the prewriting stage. Then decide which pattern of development (description, cause-effect, and so on) seems to be suggested by your evidence. Also determine whether your evidence lends itself to a chronological, a spatial, an emphatic, or a simple-to-complex order. Having done all that, you're ready to identify and sequence your main and supporting points.

The amount of detail in an outline will vary according to the paper's length and the instructor's requirements. A scratch outline (like the one shown under the heading "Organize the Raw Material" previously in this chapter) is often sufficient, but for longer papers, you'll probably need a more detailed and formal outline. In such cases, the suggestions in the accompanying checklist will help you develop a sound plan. Feel free to modify these guidelines to suit your needs.

✔ OUTLINING: A CHECKLIST

- ❏ Write your purpose, audience, tone, and thesis at the top.
- ❏ Below the thesis, enter the pattern of development you've chosen.
- ❏ Record the organizational approach you've selected.
- ❏ Delete from your supporting material anything that doesn't develop the thesis or that isn't appropriate for your purpose, audience, and tone.
- ❏ Add any new points or material. Group related items together. Give each group a heading that represents a main topic in support of your thesis.
- ❏ Label these main topics with Roman numerals (I, II, III, and so on). Let the order of the numerals indicate the best sequence.
- ❏ Identify subtopics and group them under the appropriate main topics. Indent and label these subtopics with capital letters (A, B, C, and so on). Let the order of the letters indicate the best sequence.
- ❏ Identify supporting points (often, reasons and examples) and group them under the appropriate subtopics. Indent and label these supporting points with Arabic numbers (1, 2, 3, and so on). Let the numbers indicate the best sequence.
- ❏ Identify specific details (secondary examples, facts, statistics, expert opinions, and quotations from outside sources you plan to use in your essay) and group them under the appropriate supporting points. Indent and label these specific details with lowercase letters (a, b, c, and so on). Let the letters indicate the best sequence.
- ❏ Examine your outline, looking for places where evidence is weak. Where appropriate, add new evidence.
- ❏ Double-check that all main topics, subtopics, supporting points, and specific details develop some aspect of the thesis. Also confirm that all items are arranged in the most logical order.

The sample outline that follows develops the thesis "Playing violent video games can have many negative effects on kids. It can lead to increased levels of aggression, video game addiction, and serious health issues." The thesis is the one that Caylah devised for the essay she planned to write in response to the Goodman assignment in Chapter 1. Caylah's scratch list appears previously in this chapter (page 30). When you compare Caylah's scratch list and outline, you'll find some differences. On the whole, the outline contains more specifics, but it doesn't include all the material in the scratch list. For example, after reconsidering her purpose, audience, tone, and thesis, Caylah decided to omit from her outline the section on the connection between parents and kids playing video games. After further thought, she realized this information would not support her thesis and that she could use some of these ideas in the introduction.

The plan shown here is called a *topic outline* because it uses phrases, or topics, for each entry. For a lengthier or more complex paper, a *sentence outline* would be more appropriate.

Purpose: To persuade

Audience: Instructor as well as class members, most of whom are 18–20 years old

Tone: Serious and straightforward; formal, academic language

Thesis: Playing video games can have many negative effects on kids. It can lead to increased levels of aggression, video game addiction, and serious health issues.

Pattern of development: Argumentation-persuasion

Organizational approach: Emphatic order
 I. Increased levels of aggression and violence
    A. Imitation of aggression in violent video games (Include first Willoughby quote)
    B. Effects of playing versus watching violent video games (Include second Willoughby quote)
    C. Effects of playing violent video games versus watching television violence (Include first and second Polman quotes)
 II. Addiction
    A. Relationship between time spent playing and probability of addiction (Include first Porter quote)
    B. Effects of addiction (Include Young quote)
       1. Preoccupation with gaming
       2. Lying about gaming
       3. Loss of interest in other activities
       4. Withdrawal from family and friends
    C. Factors that lead to addiction
       1. Positive reinforcement
       2. Positive sanctions
    D. Extreme effects of addiction (Include paraphrase of Porter)
       1. Mental illness.
       2. Physical exhaustion
       3. Death
 III. Health dangers
    A. Obesity
    B. Procrastination

Before starting to write your first draft, show your outline to several people (your instructor, friends, classmates) for their reactions, especially about areas needing additional work. After making whatever changes are needed, you're in a good position to go ahead and write the first draft of your essay.

Activities: Organize the Evidence

MyWritingLab

1. The thesis statement here is followed by a scrambled list of supporting points. Prepare an outline for a potential essay, making sure to distinguish between major and secondary points.

    Thesis: Our schools, now in crisis, could be improved in several ways.

    Certification requirements for teachers
    Schedules
    Teachers
    Longer school year
    Merit pay for outstanding teachers
    Curriculum
    Better textbooks for classroom use
    Longer school days
    More challenging content in courses

2. Assume you plan to write an essay based on the following brief outline, which consists of a thesis and several points of support. Determine which pattern of development you would probably use for the essay's overall framework. Also identify which organizational approach you would most likely adopt to sequence the points of support listed. Then, use one or more patterns of development to generate material to support those points. Having done that, review the material generated, deleting, adding, combining, and arranging ideas in logical order. Finally, make an outline for the body of the essay. (Save your outline so you can work with it further after reading about the next stage in the writing process.)

    Thesis: Friends of the opposite sex fall into one of several categories: the pal, the confidant, or the pest.

    • Frequently, an opposite-sex friend is simply a "pal."
    • Sometimes, though, a pal turns, step by step, into a confidant.
    • If a confidant begins to have romantic thoughts, he or she may become a pest, thus disrupting the friendship.

3. Retrieve the writing you prepared in response to Activity 3, 4, or 5 on pages 42–43. As needed, reshape that material, applying the organizational principles discussed in these pages. Be sure, for example, that you select the approach (chronological, spatial, emphatic, or simple-to-complex) that would be most appropriate, given your main idea, purpose, audience, and tone. (Save whatever you prepare so you can work with it further after reading about the next stage in the writing process.)

(continued)

Activities: Organize the Evidence (*continued*)

4. Look again at the thesis and scratch outline you refined and elaborated in response to Activity 6 on page 43. Reevaluate this material by deleting, adding, combining, and rearranging ideas as needed. Also, keeping your purpose, audience, and tone in mind, consider whether a chronological, a spatial, an emphatic, or a simple-to-complex approach will be most appropriate. Now prepare an outline of your ideas. Finally, ask at least one person to evaluate your organizational plan. (Save your outline. After reading about the next stage in the writing process, you can use it to write the essay's first draft.)

STAGE 5: WRITE THE FIRST DRAFT

Your *first draft* —a rough, provisional version of your essay—may flow quite smoothly. But don't be discouraged if it doesn't. You may find that your thesis has to be reshaped, that a point no longer fits, that you need to return to a prewriting activity to generate additional material. Such stopping and starting is to be expected. Writing the first draft is a process of discovery, involving the continual clarification and refining of ideas.

How to Proceed

There's no single right way to prepare a first draft. For example, some writers rely heavily on their scratch lists or outlines, whereas others glance at them only occasionally. However you choose to proceed, consider the suggestions in the following checklist when moving from an outline or scratch list to a first draft.

✔ TURNING OUTLINE INTO FIRST DRAFT: A CHECKLIST

❑ Make the outline's *main topics* (I, II, III) the *topic sentences* of the essay's supporting paragraphs. (Topic sentences are discussed later in this chapter.)

❑ Make the outline's *subtopics* (A, B, C) the *subpoints* in each paragraph.

❑ Make the outline's *supporting points* (1, 2, 3) the key *examples* and *reasons* in each paragraph.

❑ Make the outline's *specific details* (a, b, c) the *secondary examples, facts, statistics, expert opinions,* and *quotations* in each paragraph.

Although outlines and lists are valuable for guiding your work, don't be so dependent on them that you shy away from new ideas that surface during your writing of the first draft. If promising new thoughts pop up, jot them down in the margin. Then, at the appropriate point, go back and evaluate them: Do they support your thesis? Are they appropriate for your essay's purpose, audience, and tone? If so, go ahead and include the material in your draft.

It's easy to get bogged down while preparing the first draft if you try to edit as you write. Remember: A draft isn't intended to be perfect. For the time being, adopt a relaxed, noncritical attitude. Work as quickly as you can, don't stop to check spelling, correct grammar, or refine sentence structure. Save these tasks for later.

You may find that using a computer considerably facilitates the drafting process because saving and revising text, as well as cutting and pasting material, can be done easily and quickly. Remember to give your drafts clear filenames—for example, "Video games draft 1"—so that you can locate the most recent version of an essay. If you are using direct quotations from notes that you have in a computer file, carefully cut and paste the quotations from the notes file to your draft, making sure to use quotation marks and to indicate the source at the end of the quote.

What should you do if you get stuck while writing your first draft? Stay calm and try to write something—no matter how awkward or imprecise it may seem. Just jot a reminder to yourself in the margin ("Fix this," "Redo," or "Ugh!") to fine-tune the section later. Or leave a blank space to hold a spot for the right words when they finally break loose. It may also help to reread—out loud is best—what you've already written. Regaining a sense of the larger context is often enough to get you moving again. You might also try talking your way through a troublesome section. By speaking aloud, you tap your natural oral fluency and put it to work in your writing.

If a section of the essay is particularly difficult, don't spend time struggling with it. Move on to an easier section, write that, and then return to the challenging part. If you're still getting nowhere, take a break. Listen to music, talk with friends, or take a walk. While you're giving your mind a break, your thoughts may loosen up and untangle the knotty section.

Because you read essays from beginning to end, you may assume that writers work the same way, starting with the introduction and going straight through to the conclusion. Often, however, this isn't the case. In fact, because an introduction depends so heavily on everything that follows, it's usually best to write the introduction *after* the essay's body.

When preparing your first draft, you may find it helpful to follow this sequence:

1. Write the supporting paragraphs.
2. Connect ideas in the supporting paragraphs.
3. Write the introduction.
4. Write the conclusion.
5. Write the title.

Write the Supporting Paragraphs

Drawn from the main sections in your outline or scratch list (I, II, III, etc.), each *supporting paragraph* should develop an aspect of your essay's thesis. A strong supporting paragraph is (1) often focused by a topic sentence and (2) organized around one or more patterns of development. As you write, keep in mind that you shouldn't expect your draft paragraphs to be perfect; you'll have a chance to revise them later on.

Use topic sentences.   Frequently, a *topic sentence* functions as a kind of mini-thesis for a supporting paragraph. Generally one or two sentences in length, the topic sentence usually appears at or near the beginning of the paragraph. However, it may also appear at the end, in the middle, or—with varied wording—several times within the paragraph.

The topic sentence states the paragraph's main idea, whereas the other sentences in the paragraph provide support for this central point in the form of examples, facts, expert opinion, and so on. Like a thesis statement, the topic sentence *signals the paragraph's subject* and frequently *indicates the writer's attitude* toward that subject. In the topic sentences that follow, the subject of the paragraph is underlined once and the attitude toward that subject is underlined twice:

> Some students select a particular field of study for the wrong reasons.
> The ocean dumping of radioactive waste is a ticking time bomb.
> Several contemporary rock groups show unexpected sensitivity to social issues.
> Political candidates are sold like slickly packaged products.

As you work on the first draft, you may find yourself writing paragraphs without paying too much attention to topic sentences. That's fine, as long as you evaluate the paragraphs later on. When revising, you can provide a topic sentence for a paragraph that needs a sharper focus, recast a topic sentence for a paragraph that ended up taking an unexpected turn, or even eliminate a topic sentence altogether if a paragraph's content is sufficiently unified to imply its point.

Use the patterns of development.   As you saw previously, an entire essay can be organized around one or more patterns of development (narration, process analysis, definition, and so forth). These patterns can also provide the organizational framework for an essay's supporting paragraphs. Assume you're writing an article for your town newspaper with the thesis "Year-round residents of an ocean community must take an active role in safeguarding the seashore environment." Your supporting paragraphs could develop this thesis through a variety of patterns, with each paragraph's topic sentence suggesting a specific pattern or combination of patterns.

For example, one paragraph might start with the topic sentence "In a nearby ocean community, signs of environmental danger are everywhere" and go on to *describe* a seaside town with polluted waters, blighted trees, and diseased marine life. The next paragraph might have the topic sentence "Fortunately, not all seaside towns are plagued by such environmental problems" and continue by *contrasting* the troubled community with another, more ecologically sound shore town. A later paragraph, focused by the topic sentence "Residents can get involved in a variety of pro-environment activities," might use *division-classification* to elaborate on activities at the neighborhood, town, and municipal levels.

Connect Ideas in the Supporting Paragraphs

While writing the supporting paragraphs, you can try to smooth out the progression of ideas within and between paragraphs. In a *coherent* essay, the relationship between points is clear; readers can easily follow the development of your thoughts. (Sometimes, working on coherence causes a first draft to get bogged down; if this happens, move on, and wait until the revision stage to focus on such matters.)

The following paragraph lacks coherence for two main reasons. First, it sequences ideas improperly. (Thinking about the deadline for registration should come first in the order of things to consider, not last; and thinking about which instructors to avoid and which have been recommended should come after considering such pragmatic concerns as hours of credit needed and personal schedule.) Second, it doesn't include much needed signal words such as "The first thing you're likely to want to consider..." or "After you have considered these issues, think about..." that help the reader understand the relationship among the ideas.)

Incoherent Support

Registering for classes is an important task students must complete. Think about instructors you would like to avoid and others who have been recommended to you. Figure out which courses you need to take. Do you have prerequisite courses that must be completed? How many hours of credit do you need to earn? If you are on financial aid, it is likely that you are required to register for a minimum number of credit hours each term to maintain your eligibility. Consider your personal schedule. If you work while attending school, what days and times does your employer expect you to be available for work? If you don't have a job, what schedule would work best for you? Are you more productive when taking classes daily, or do you accomplish more when you take classes two or three days a week and save other days for homework? Consider the deadline for registration. Do you have two days or two months to work out your schedule? Considering these issues will help you plan the perfect course schedule.

Coherent Support

Registering for classes is an important task students must complete prior to the beginning of each school term. <u>The first thing you're likely to want to consider</u> is the deadline for registration. Do you have two days or two months to work out the schedule that will work best for you? <u>Another issue</u> to consider early in the process is figuring out which courses you need to take. Do you have prerequisite courses that must be completed by the end of the following term? If so, making sure you include those in your schedule should be a priority. <u>After you have considered these issues</u>, think about the number of hours of credit you need to earn. If you are on financial aid, it is likely that you are required to register for a minimum number of credit hours each term to maintain your eligibility. <u>Next</u>, consider your personal schedule. If you work while attending school, what days and times does your employer expect you to be available for work? If you don't have a job, what schedule would work best for you? Are you more productive when taking classes daily, or do you accomplish more when you take classes two or three days a week and save other days for homework? <u>And finally</u>, are there particular instructors you would like to avoid and others who have been recommended to you? Considering these issues will help you plan the perfect course schedule.

To avoid the kinds of problems found in the incoherent paragraph, use—as the revised version does—two key strategies: (1) a clearly *chronological, spatial, emphatic* ("*Worst of all,* attendants say . . ."), or *simple-to-complex* approach and (2) *signal devices* (underlined in the revised paragraph) to show how ideas are connected. The following paragraphs describe signal devices. Once you determine a logical approach for presenting your points, you need to make sure readers can follow the progression of those points. Signal devices provide readers with cues, reminding them where they have been and indicating where they are going.

Aim to include some signals—however awkward or temporary—in your first draft. If you find you *can't,* that's probably a warning that your ideas may not be arranged logically. A light touch should be your goal with such signals. Too many call attention to themselves, making the essay mechanical and plodding. In any case, here are some signaling devices to consider.

1. Transitions. Words and phrases that ease readers from one idea to another are called transitions. The following lists give a variety of such signals.

TRANSITIONS

Time

after, afterward, at the same time, before, earlier, previously, finally, eventually, first, next, immediately, in the meantime, meanwhile, simultaneously, subsequently, later, then, now

Space

above, below, next to, behind

Addition or Sequence

and, also, too, besides, finally, last, first,...second,...third, furthermore, moreover, in addition, next, one...another

Examples

for instance, for example, namely, specifically, to illustrate

Contrast

although, though, but, however, conversely, despite, even though, in contrast, nevertheless, nonetheless, on the contrary, whereas, on the one (other) hand, otherwise, yet, still

Comparison

also, too, likewise, in comparison, in the same way, similarly

Cause or Effect

as a result, because, since, consequently, in turn, so, therefore, then

Summary or Conclusion

in conclusion, in short, therefore, thus

Here's a previous paragraph from this chapter. Note how the transitions (underlined) show readers how ideas fit together.

> <u>After</u> you've generated supporting evidence, you're ready to *organ-ize* that material. Even highly compelling evidence won't illustrate the validity of your thesis or achieve your purpose if readers have to plow through a maze of chaotic evidence. Some writers can move quickly from generating support to writing a clearly structured first draft. (They usually say they have sequenced their ideas in their heads.) Most, <u>however</u>, need to spend some time sorting out their thoughts on paper before starting the first draft; <u>otherwise</u>, they tend to lose their way in a tangle of ideas.

2. Bridging sentences.   Although bridging sentences may be used within a paragraph, they are more often used to move readers from one paragraph to the next. Look again at the first sentence in the preceding paragraph. Note that the sentence consists of two parts: The first part reminds readers that the previous discussion focused on techniques for generating evidence; the second part tells readers that the focus will now be the organization of such evidence.

3. Repeated words, synonyms, and pronouns.   The repetition of impor-tant words maintains continuity, reassures readers that they are on the right track, and highlights key ideas. *Synonyms*—words similar in meaning—also provide coherence, but without unimaginative and tedious repetitions.

Finally, pronouns (*he, she, it, they, this, that*) enhance coherence by causing readers to think back to the original word the pronoun replaces (antecedent). When using pronouns, however, be sure there is no ambiguity about antecedents.

Reprinted here is another paragraph from this chapter annotated to illustrate how these techniques were used to integrate the paragraph's ideas. Repeated words are underlined once and their synonyms are underlined twice; pronouns and their antecedents are printed in bold type.

The process of prewriting—discovering **a limited subject** and generating ideas about **it**—prepares you for the next stage in writing an essay: identifying the paper's *thesis,* or controlling idea. The thesis, which presents your opinion on a subject, should focus on an interesting and significant **issue, one** that engages your energies and merits your consideration. You may think of the thesis as the essay's hub—the central point around which all the other material revolves. Your thesis determines what does and does not belong in the essay. The **thesis,** especially when **it** occurs early in an essay, also helps focus the reader on the piece's central point.

Write the Introduction

Many writers don't prepare an introduction until they have started to revise; others feel more comfortable if their first draft includes in basic form all parts of the final essay. If that's how you feel, you'll probably write the introduction as you complete your first draft. No matter when you prepare it, keep in mind how crucial the introduction is to your essay's success. Specifically, the introduction serves three distinct functions: It arouses readers' interest, introduces your subject, and presents your thesis.

The length of your introduction will vary according to your paper's scope and purpose. Most essays you write, however, will be served best by a one- or two-paragraph beginning. To write an effective introduction, use any of the following methods, singly or in combination. The thesis statement in each sample introduction is underlined.

Broad Statement Narrowing to a Limited Subject

For generations, morality has been molded primarily by parents, religion, and schools. Children traditionally acquired their ideas about what is right and wrong, which goals are important in life, and how other people should be treated from these three sources collectively. But in the past few decades, a single force—television—has undermined the beneficial influence that parents, religion, and school have on children's moral development. Indeed, television often implants in children negative values about sex, work, and family life.

Brief Anecdote

At a local high school recently, students in a psychology course were given a hint of what it is like to be the parents of a newborn. Each "parent" had to carry a raw egg around at all times to symbolize the responsibilities of parenthood. The egg could not be left alone; it limited the "parents'" activities; it placed a full-time emotional burden on "Mom" and "Dad." This class exercise illustrates a common problem facing the majority of new mothers and fathers. Most people receive little preparation for the job of being parents.

Idea That Is the Opposite of the One Developed

We hear a great deal about divorce's disastrous impact on children. We are deluged with advice on ways to make divorce as painless as possible for youngsters; we listen to heartbreaking stories about the confused, grieving children of divorced parents. Little attention has been paid, however, to a different kind of effect that divorce may have on children. Children from divorced families may become skilled manipulators, playing off one parent against the other, worsening an already painful situation.

Series of Short Questions

What happens if a child is caught vandalizing school property? What happens if a child goes for a joyride in a stolen car and accidentally hits a pedestrian? Should parents be liable for their children's mistakes? Should parents have to pay what might be hundreds of thousands of dollars in damages? Adults have begun to think seriously about such questions because the laws concerning the limits of parental responsibility are changing rapidly. With unfortunate frequency, courts have begun to hold parents legally and financially accountable for their children's misdeeds.

Quotation

Educator Neil Postman believes that television has blurred the line between childhood and adulthood. According to Postman, "All the secrets that a print culture kept from children...are revealed all at once by media that do not, and cannot, exclude any audience." This media barrage of information, once intended only for adults, has changed childhood for the worse.

Refutation of a Common Belief

Adolescents care only about material things; their lives revolve around brand-name sneakers, designer jeans, the latest fad in electronics. They resist education, don't read, barely know who is president, mainline rock 'n' roll, experiment with drugs, and exist on a steady diet of Ring-Dings, nachos, and beer. This is what many adults, including parents, seem to believe about the young. The reality is, however, that young people today show more maturity and common sense than most adults give them credit for.

Dramatic Fact or Statistic

Seventy percent of the respondents in a poll conducted by columnist Ann Landers stated that if they could live their lives over, they would choose not to have children. This startling statistic makes one wonder what these people believed parenthood would be like. <u>Most parents, it seems, have unrealistic expectations about their children.</u> Parents want their children to accept their values, follow their paths, and succeed where they failed.

Introductory paragraphs sometimes end with a *plan of development:* a quick preview of the essay's major points in the order in which those points will be discussed. The plan of development is usually considered part of the thesis, even if it is stated in a separate sentence. Because the plan of development outlines the essay's organizational structure, it helps prepare the reader for the essay's progression of ideas. In a brief essay, readers can often keep track of the ideas without this extra help. In a longer paper, though, a plan of development can be an effective unifying device because it highlights the main ideas the essay will develop.

Write the Conclusion

You may have come across essays that ended with jarring abruptness because they had no conclusions at all. Other papers may have had conclusions, but they sputtered to a weak close, a sure sign that the writers had run out of steam and wanted to finish as quickly as possible. Just as satisfying closes are an important part of everyday life (we feel cheated if dinner doesn't end with dessert or if a friend leaves without saying goodbye), a strong conclusion is an important part of an effective essay.

Generally one or two paragraphs, the conclusion should give the reader a feeling of completeness and finality. One way to achieve this sense of "rounding off" is to return to an image, idea, or anecdote from the introduction. Because people tend to remember most clearly the points they read last, the conclusion is also a good place to remind readers of your thesis. You may also use the conclusion to make a final point about your subject. Be careful, though, not to open an entirely new line of thought at the essay's close.

Illustrated briefly here are several strategies for writing sound conclusions. These techniques may be used singly or in combination. The first strategy, the summary conclusion, can be especially helpful in long, complex essays because readers may appreciate a review of your points. Tacked onto a short essay, though, a summary conclusion often seems boring and mechanical.

Summary

Contrary to what many adults think, most adolescents are not only aware of the important issues of the times but also deeply concerned about them. They are sensitive to the plight of the homeless, the destruction of the environment, and the pitfalls of rampant materialism. Indeed, today's young people are not less mature and sensible than their parents were. If anything, they are more so.

Prediction

The growing tendency on the part of the judicial system to hold parents responsible for the actions of their wayward children can have a disturbing impact on all of us. Parents will feel bitter toward their own children and cynical about a system that holds them accountable for the actions of minors. Children, continuing to escape the consequences of their actions, will become even more lawless and destructive. Society cannot afford two such possibilities.

Quotation

The comic W. C. Fields is reputed to have said, "Anyone who hates children and dogs can't be all bad." Most people do not share Fields's cynicism. Viewing childhood as a time of purity, they are alarmed at the way television exposes children to the seamy side of life, stripping youngsters of their innocence and giving them a glib sophistication that is a poor substitute for wisdom.

Statistic

Granted, divorce may, in some cases, be the best thing for families torn apart by parents who battle one another. However, in longitudinal studies of children from divorced families, psychologist Judith Wallerstein found that only 10 percent of the youngsters felt relief at their parents' divorce; the remaining 90 percent felt devastated. Such statistics surely call into question parents' claims that they are divorcing for their children's sake.

Recommendation or Call for Action

It is a mistake to leave parenting to instinct. Instead, we should make parenting skills a required course in schools. In addition, a nationwide hotline should be established to help parents deal with crises. Such training and continuing support would help adults deal more effectively with many of the problems they face as parents.

Write the Title

Some writers say that they began a certain piece with only a title in mind. But for most people, writing a title is a finishing touch. Although creating a title for your paper is usually one of the last steps in writing an essay, it shouldn't be done haphazardly. It may take time to write an effective title—one that hints at the essay's thesis and snares the reader's interest.

Good titles may make use of the following techniques: repetition of sounds (*The Great Gatsby*); questions (*What Color Is Your Parachute?*); and humor (*Since You're Leaving Anyway, Take Out the Trash*). More often, though, titles are straightforward phrases derived from the essay's subject or thesis: "How I Survived My First Year of College" and "My Path to Happiness," for example.

Pull It All Together

Now that you know how to prepare a first draft, you might find it helpful to examine Figure 2.2 to see how the different parts of a draft can fit together. Keep in mind that not every essay you write will take this shape. As your purpose, audience, and tone change, so will your essay's structure. An introduction or conclusion, for instance, may be developed in more than one paragraph; the thesis statement may be implied or delayed until the essay's middle or end; not all paragraphs may have topic sentences; and several supporting paragraphs may be needed to develop a single topic sentence. Even so, the basic format presented here offers a strategy for organizing a variety of writing assignments—from term papers to lab reports. Once you feel comfortable with the structure, you have a foundation on which to base your variations. (This book's student and professional essays illustrate some possibilities.) Even when using a specific format, you always have room to give your spirit and imagination free play. The language you use, the details you select, the perspective you offer are uniquely yours. They are what make your essay different from everyone else's.

FIGURE 2.2
Structure of an Essay

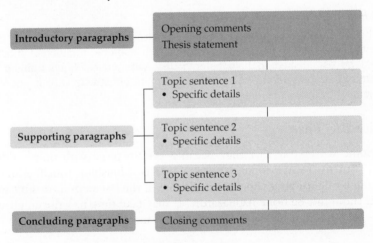

Sample First Draft

Here is the first draft of Caylah's essay, which she wrote in response to the following assignment:

> Singling out television as a medium that conveys negative messages about food, Goodman calls today's culture "an increasingly hostile environment" for kids. Do you agree? Why or why not? Drawing on but not limiting yourself to the material in your prereading journal, write an essay in which you support or reject this viewpoint. Consider focusing on one particular form of media. Although you are not required to include information from outside sources in your essay, feel free to do so if think additional information from reputable sources would make your essay more effective.

Caylah wrote the draft in one sitting. Working at a computer, she started by typing her thesis at the top of the first page. Then, following the guidelines in the checklist on turning an outline into a first draft, she moved the material in her outline to her draft. Caylah worked rapidly; she started with the first body paragraph and wrote straight through to the last supporting paragraph.

By moving quickly, Caylah got down her essay's basic text rather easily. She had already conducted her research and made notes in her outline regarding where she would include supporting material from her outside sources. Once she felt she had captured in rough form what she wanted to say in her three body paragraphs, she reread her draft to get a sense of how she might open and close the essay. She already knew that she wanted to include information about changing family life and the role of parents in monitoring video game play in her introduction, but she didn't have a plan for her conclusion. Both her introduction and conclusion appear here, together with the body of the essay. The commentary following the draft will give you a clearer sense of how Caylah proceeded. (Note that the marginal annotations reflect Caylah's comments to herself about areas she needs to address when revising her first draft.)

Kids and Video Games

The incredible advancement of technology has created a world where many American houses not only have one television, one computer, and one video game console, but many have several of these media devices. Parents try everything to please their kids such as buying them a variety of video games from violent first person shooter games to fantasy games. Parents that work many hours a week and

Name specific games

Reword?

Weak trans.

have kids try their best to preoccupy their children to aid in the parenting process. With that said, the use of video games has become a popular activity among many kids. In result, there have been many negative and positive effects on young people who play video games. More specifically this has created concerns for kids who play video games an excessive amount of time. Playing violent video games can have many negative effects on kids. It can lead to increased levels of aggression, video game addiction, and serious health issues.

Integrate quotes better

One concern that many people have for violent video games is their children learning to be more aggressive and violent. "From a social learning perspective, adolescents who play violent video games may imitate the aggression that they observe in the games" (Willoughby 1044). According to Willoughby in "A Longitudinal Study of the Association Between Violent Video Game Play and Aggression among Adolecents," "greater violent video game play predicted higher levels of aggression over time," while nonviolent video game play did not predict higher levels of aggressive behavior" (Willoughby 1044). Another study revealed that "playing a violent video game caused boys to become more aggressive than merely watching the same violent video game" (Polman 256). This study goes on to state that "specifically for boys, playing a violent video game could lead to more aggression than watching television violence" (Polman 256). There is no doubt that children can learn to be more aggressive and violent by playing a simple video game.

Integrate quote better

Violent video games and the creation of aggressive children is only one of many negative effects. Another negative effect is video game addiction. In a 2010 study, 1,945 people were surveyed about video game use. The study found that "almost one-half (48.7%) of the participants spent 1-3 hours per day playing video games, and approximately one-third (32.9%) spent 4-8 hours per day doing so" (Porter 123). As young children play video games, the probability that the child will grow up addicted to video games is very high. "They become preoccupied with gaming, lie about their gaming use, lose interest in other activities just to game, withdrawal from family and friends to game, and use gaming as a means to psychologically escape" (Young 356). Games usually offer positive reinforcement and positive sanctions. For example, games that are first person shooter games often offer their positive reinforcement in terms of new weapons, perks, vehicles, and ranks. As many play these video games online they can communicate to others through a simple microphone. This allows many positive sanctions from other people. Gaming addiction has also had associated with mental illness, physical exhaustion, and death (Porter 2010).

Same trans. as prev. para. Revise?

Video game addiction and aggressive learning are two of many negative effects. Another effect is the danger to the child's health. The United States of America is known for obesity. Video games offer the lack of movement; this can cause an increase in risk for obesity. Not only is the child's physical health at risk, but, the risk of poor psychological health is also at risk. If one were to play video games for many hours, procrastination can become a factor. If one were to not go to work to play video games enough, they would eventually be fired

Word choice?

from their position. If a young child were to put off his/her daily chores, this could put extra pressure on parents. In result, it can affect parent's job performance and could cause the termination of their position.

Weak trans. Redo concl.

Above all, video games have many negative effects on young children. Video games are a very popular activity for young children. Research shows that children can become more aggressive and violent after playing violent video games. Extensive research also shows that many become addicted to video games. Gaming addiction can cause procrastination and unhealthy habits such as the withdrawal from family to play video games. Also video games can cause physical and psychological health issues.

Commentary

As you can see, Caylah's draft is rough. Because she knew she would revise later on, she focused on getting all of her ideas down and incorporating outside source material. She did not take time at this point in the drafting process to polish her prose or create smooth transitions.

Writing a first draft may seem like quite a challenge, but the tips offered in these pages should help you proceed with confidence. Indeed, as you work on the draft, you may be surprised how much you enjoy writing. After all, this is your chance to get down on paper something you want to say.

Activities: Write the First Draft   MyWritingLab

1. Retrieve the writing you prepared in response to Activity 3 on page 49. Applying the principles just presented, rework that material. If you wrote a single paragraph previously, expand the material into a full essay draft. If you prepared an essay, strengthen what you wrote. In both cases, remember to consider your purpose, audience, and tone as you write the body of the essay as well as its intro-

(continued)

Activities: Write the First Draft (*continued*)

> duction and conclusion. (Save your draft so you can rework it even further after reading about the next stage in the writing process.)
>
> 2. Referring to the outline you prepared in response to Activity 2 on page 49 or Activity 4 on page 50, draft the body of your essay, making your evidence as strong as possible. As you work, keep your purpose, audience, and tone in mind. After reading what you've prepared, go ahead and draft a rough introduction, conclusion, and title. Finally, ask at least one other person to react to your draft by listing its strengths and weaknesses. (Save the draft so you can work with it further after reading about the next stage in the writing process.)

STAGE 6: REVISE THE ESSAY

By now, you've probably abandoned any preconceptions you might have had about good writers sitting down and creating a finished product in one easy step. Alexander Pope's comment that "true ease in writing comes from art, not chance" is as true today as it was more than two hundred years ago. Writing that seems effortlessly clear is often the result of sustained work, not of good luck or even inborn talent. And much of this work takes place during the final stage of the writing process when ideas, paragraphs, sentences, and words are refined and reshaped.

Professional writers—novelists, journalists, textbook authors—seldom submit a piece of writing that hasn't been revised. They recognize that rough, unpolished work doesn't do them justice. What's more, they often look forward to revising. Columnist Ellen Goodman put it this way: "What makes me happy is rewriting. . . . It's like cleaning house, getting rid of all the junk, getting things in the right order, tightening up."

In a sense, revision occurs throughout the writing process: At some previous stage, you may have dropped an idea, overhauled your thesis, or shifted paragraph order. What, then, is different about the rewriting that occurs in the revision stage? The answer has to do with the literal meaning of the word *revision*—to re-see, or to see again. Genuine revision involves casting clear eyes on your work, viewing it as though you're a reader rather than the writer. Revision means that you go through your paper looking for trouble, ready to pick a fight with your own writing. And then you must be willing to sit down and make the changes needed for your writing to be as effective as possible.

Revision is not, as some believe, simply touch-up work—changing a sentence here or a word there, eliminating spelling errors, preparing a neat final copy. Revision means cutting dead wood, rearranging paragraphs, substituting new words for old ones, recasting sentences, improving coherence, and even generating new material when appropriate. With experience, you'll learn how to streamline the process so you can focus on the most critical issues for a particular piece of writing. (For advice on correcting some common writing errors, see Appendix B.)

Five Revision Strategies

Because revision is challenging, you may find yourself unsure about how to proceed. Keep in mind that there are no hard-and-fast rules about the revision process. Even so, the following pointers should help get you going if you balk at or feel overwhelmed by revising.

- *Set your draft aside for a while* before revising. When you pick up your paper again, you'll have a fresh, more objective point of view.
- *Work from printed-out material* whenever possible. Reading your essay on paper instead of on a computer screen helps you see the essay in a new way. Each time you make major changes, try to print out a copy of that section so that you can see it anew.
- *Read your draft aloud* as often as you can. Hearing how your writing sounds helps you pick up problems that you passed by before: places where sentences are awkward, meaning is ambiguous, words are imprecise. Even better, have another person read aloud to you what you have written. If the reader slows to a crawl over a murky paragraph or trips over a convoluted sentence, you know where you have to do some rewriting.
- *View revision as a series of steps.* Don't try to tackle all of a draft's problems at once; instead, proceed step by step, starting with the most pressing issues. Although there are bound to be occasions when you have time for only one quick pass over a draft, whenever possible, read your draft several times; each time focus on different matters and ask yourself different questions. Move from a broad view of the draft to an up-close look at its mechanics.
- *Evaluate and respond to instructor feedback.* Often, instructors collect and respond to students' first drafts. Like many students, you may be tempted to look only briefly at your instructor's comments. Perhaps you've "had it" with the essay and don't want to think about revising the paper to reflect the instructor's remarks. But taking your instructor's comments into account when revising is often what's needed to turn a shaky first draft into a strong final draft.

When an instructor returns a final draft graded, you may think that the grade is all that counts. Remember, though: Grades are important, but comments are even more so. They can help you *improve* your writing—if not in this paper, then in the next one. If you don't understand or agree with the instructor's observations, don't hesitate to request a conference. Getting together gives both you and the instructor a chance to clarify your respective points of view.

Peer Review: An Additional Revision Strategy

Many instructors include in-class or at-home peer review as a regular part of a composition course. Peer review—the critical reading of another person's writing with the intention of suggesting changes—accomplishes several important goals. First, peer review helps you gain a more objective perspective on your work. When you write something, you're often too close to what you've prepared to evaluate it fairly; you may have trouble seeing where the writing is strong and where it needs to be strengthened. Peer review supplies the fresh, neutral perspective you need. Second, reviewing your classmates' work broadens your own composing options. You may be inspired to experiment with a technique you admired in a classmate's writing but wouldn't have thought of on your own. Finally, peer review trains you to be a better reader and critic of your *own* writing. When you get into the habit of critically reading other students' writing, you become more adept at critiquing your own.

The Peer Review/Revision Checklist on the inside front cover of this book will help focus your revision—whether you're reworking your own paper or responding to a peer's. Your instructor may have you respond to all questions on the checklist or to several selected items. What follows is a peer review worksheet that Caylah's instructor prepared to help students respond to first drafts for the Goodman assignment (see pages 23–24). Wanting students to focus on four areas (thesis statement, support for thesis statement, overall organization, and signal devices), the instructor drew on relevant sections from the Peer Review/Revision Checklist. With this customized worksheet in hand, Caylah's classmate Taylor Young was able to give Caylah constructive feedback on her first draft. (*Note:* Because Caylah didn't want to influence Taylor's reaction, the draft she gave Taylor didn't include her marginal notations to herself.)

Peer Review Worksheet

Essay Author's Name: <u>Caylah Francis</u>   Reviewer's Name: <u>Taylor Young</u>

1. What is the essay's thesis? Is it explicit or implied? Does the thesis focus on a limited subject and express the writer's attitude toward that subject?

   Thesis: "Playing violent video games can have many negative effects on kids. It can lead to increased levels of aggression, video game addiction, and serious health issues."

The thesis is limited, but it's pretty long; it's made up of two sentences, with the plan of development in the second one. You could omit the second sentence and add something about the research you did. You do a great job of including lots of sources to back up your claims, but there's no mention of that made in the introduction.

2. **What are the main points supporting the thesis? List the points. Is each supporting point developed sufficiently? If not, where is more support needed?**

(1) Playing violent video games can make children become more aggressive and violent.
(2) Playing violent video games can lead to video game addiction.
(3) Playing violent video games can affect a child's health.

The supporting points are good and are explained pretty well, except for a few places.

In the last sentence in para. 2 you refer to "a simple video game." I'm not sure that's what you really meant. The violent video games I have seen are not simple, and even if some are, I'm not sure that's the point you're trying to make.

About half way through para. 3, you use the word "withdrawal" in the quote from Young, pg. 356. You might want to check the source. I don't think that's the right word. It doesn't make sense there.

In para. 4 on how playing violent video games can endanger a child's health, you don't incorporate any outside sources the way you do in the other body paragraphs. Your essay might be stronger if you did. Also in that paragraph, you bring in the idea that playing video games can lead to procrastination, which can result in getting fired and putting off chores. I'm not sure how that relates to a child's health. I know conclusions are not easy to write—they sure aren't for me. But in your conclusion you pretty much just restate what you have already said. I can see why you might want to do that in a long essay, but since this is not a long one, I wonder if there's another approach you could take—maybe go back to the ideas in your introduction about parents and their role in helping their kids not get hooked on playing violent games and then just briefly remind readers of the essay's main points. And if you do remove the part about procrastination from para. 4, you'll want to remove it from the conclusion too.

3. **What overall format (chronological, spatial, emphatic, simple-to-complex) is used to sequence the essay's main points? Does this format work? Why or why not? What organizational format is used in each supporting paragraph? Does the format work? Why or why not?**

The paper's overall emphatic organization seems good. I like the way you use exemplification in your three supporting paragraphs to back up your topic

(continued)

Peer Review Worksheet (*continued*)

> sentences for each paragraph. That works well—except in para. 4. I mentioned this before, but you could use at least one source to back up your claims, and you might take out the references to procrastination.
>
> 4. What signal devices are used to connect ideas within and between paragraphs? Are there too few signal devices or too many? Where?
>
> You do a nice job, overall, with transitions from one sentence to another and from one paragraph to another. But I did notice some areas you might want to work on.
>
> About halfway through para. 1, you use the signal device "with that said," and in the next sentence you use the phrase "in result." You might want to play with your wording in those two places. The two phrases sound kind of strange to me, as if you couldn't quite find the words you were looking for.
>
> Something else you might consider is your signal device at the beginning of your conclusion: "Above all." You might be able to come up with a more effective bridge there.

As you can see, Taylor flagged several areas that Caylah herself also noted needed work. But Taylor also commented on entirely new areas (for example, the lack of outside support and the reference to procrastination in paragraph 4), offering Caylah a fresh perspective on what she needed to do to polish her draft. To see which of Taylor's suggestions Caylah followed, take a look at her final draft later in the chapter and at the "Commentary" following the essay.

Becoming a skilled peer reviewer.   Even with the help of a checklist, preparing a helpful peer review is a skill that takes time to develop. At first, you, like many students, may be too easy or too critical. Effective peer review calls for rigor and care; you should give classmates the conscientious feedback that you hope for in return. Peer review also requires tact and kindness; feedback should always be constructive and include observations about what works well in a piece of writing. People have difficulty mustering the energy to revise if they feel there's nothing worth revising.

If your instructor doesn't include peer review, you can set up peer review sessions outside of class, with classmates getting together to respond to each other's drafts. Or you may select non-classmates who are objective (not a lovestruck admirer or a doting grandparent) and skilled enough to provide useful commentary.

To focus your readers' comments, you may adapt the Peer Review/Revision Checklist on the inside front cover of this book, or you may develop your own questions. If you prepare the questions yourself, be sure to solicit *specific* observations about what does and doesn't work in your writing. If you simply ask, "How's this?" you may receive a vague comment like "It's not very effective." What you want are concrete observations and suggestions: "I'm confused because what you say in the fifth sentence contradicts what you say in the second." To promote such specific responses, ask your readers targeted (preferably written) questions like "I'm having trouble moving from my second to my third point. How can I make the transition smoother?" Such questions require more than "yes" or "no" responses; they encourage readers to dig into your writing where you sense it needs work. (If it's feasible, encourage readers to *write* their responses to your questions.)

If you and your peer reviewers can't meet in person, e-mail can provide a crucial means of contact. With a couple of clicks, you can simply send each other computer files of your work. You and your reviewers also need to decide exactly how to exchange comments about your drafts. You might conclude, for example, that you'll type your responses, perhaps in bold capitals, into the file itself. Or you might decide to print out the drafts and reply to the comments in writing, later exchanging the annotated drafts in person. No matter what you and your peers decide, you'll probably find e-mail an invaluable tool in the writing process.

Evaluating and responding to peer review.   Accepting criticism isn't easy (even if you asked for it), and not all peer reviewers will be diplomatic. Even so, try to listen with an open mind to those giving you feedback. Take notes on their oral observations or have them fill out relevant sections from the Peer Review/Revision Checklist. Later, when you're ready to revise your paper, reread your notes. Which reviewer remarks seem valid? Which don't? Rank the problems and solutions that your reviewers identified, designating the most critical as number 1. Using the peer feedback, enter your own notes for revising in the margins of a clean copy of your draft. This way, you'll know exactly what changes need to be made in your draft as you proceed. Then, keeping the problems and remedies in mind, start revising. Type in your changes, or handwrite changes directly on the draft above the appropriate line. (Rework extensive sections on a separate piece of paper.) When revising, always keep in mind that you may not agree with every reviewer suggestion. That's fine. It's *your* paper, and it's *your* decision to implement or reject the suggestions made by your peers.

STAGE 7: EDIT AND PROOFREAD

Your essay is not finished until you have dealt with errors in grammar, punctuation, and spelling. As Caylah carefully reviewed her final draft to make sure she had corrected all of her errors, she realized that she had not corrected two typos from her rough draft. She had failed to change *Adolecents* to *Adolescents* in the title of one of her sources in the second paragraph, and she had not changed *withdrawal* to *withdraw* in a quote in her third paragraph. She had checked the quote and found the typo previously, but after reading Taylor's suggestion, she realized that she forgotten to go back to her draft and make the correction. Almost missing these obvious mistakes reminded Caylah of the importance of proofreading and editing carefully before submitting the final draft of an essay.

As you proofread and edit your final draft, use your computer's spelling check program to identify and correct misspelled words. Read the screen slowly, looking for wrong words (such as *there* when you mean *their*), errors in proper names, and errors in grammar. Double-check to make sure you have formatted the essay using your instructor's guidelines, and then print a copy. Proofread the printed text slowly to catch typos and other mistakes. Often, you will catch mistakes when reading from a printed text that you don't see when reading your text on a screen.

STUDENT ESSAY

In this chapter, we've taken you through the various stages in the writing process. You've seen how Caylah used prewriting and outlining to arrive at her first draft. You've also seen how Caylah's peer reviewer, Taylor, critiqued her first draft. In the following pages, you'll look at Caylah's final draft—the paper she submitted to her instructor.

Caylah, an eighteen-year-old first-year college student with two younger brothers who spent hours each week playing video games, wanted to write an informative paper with a straightforward, serious tone. While preparing her essay, she kept in mind that her audience would include her course instructor as well as her classmates. This is the assignment that prompted Caylah's essay:

> Singling out television as a medium that conveys negative messages about food, Goodman calls today's culture "an increasingly hostile environment" for kids. Do you agree? Why or why not? Drawing on but not limiting yourself to the material in your pre-reading journal, write an essay in which you support or reject this viewpoint. Consider focusing on one particular form of media. Although you are not required to include information from outside sources in your essay, feel free to do so if you think additional information from reputable sources would make your essay more effective.

Caylah's essay is annotated so that you can see how it illustrates the essay format shown in Figure 2.2. As you read her essay, try to determine how well it reflects the principles of effective writing. The commentary following the paper will help you look at the essay more closely and give you some sense of the way Caylah went about revising her first draft.

Page number

Heading

Caylah Francis

Professor Hernandez

English 1102

18 March 2014

Title

Aggression, Addiction, Isolation, and More:

The Dark Side of Video Game Play

Introduction

Advancements in technology have resulted in a world in which   1

many American homes have not just one television, one computer,

and one video game console, but more than one of each of these media

devices. To please their children and help keep them occupied, many

parents buy them a variety of video games, ranging from seemingly

innocent, fun games such as *Dance Dance Revolution* to survival

horror games like *Outlast* and violent first-person-shooter games such

as *Call of Duty*. Many parents are working more hours than ever before

trying to provide for their families. They are not always home as much

as they would like to be to spend time with their children, and when

these parents are home, there is much that demands their attention.

As a result, many children are keeping themselves occupied by

Thesis

spending hours each day playing video games. While some argue that

playing video games does not have harmful effects, research proves

otherwise.

First
supporting
paragraph

One concern many people, including experts, have is that   2

playing some of these video games makes children become

more aggressive and violent. A 2011 article on the relationship

between playing violent video games and increased aggression

Topic
sentence

revealed that playing these games can cause players to "imitate

the aggression that they observe in the games" (Willoughby et al.

1044). Researchers who conducted this study found that "greater

violent video game play predicted higher levels of aggression

over time" while "nonviolent video game play did not predict

Francis 2

higher levels of aggressive behavior" (1044). Another study that focused on the difference in the effects of playing versus watching violent video games reports that "playing a violent video game caused boys to become more aggressive than merely watching the same violent video game" (Polman et al. 256). This study goes on to state that "specifically for boys, playing a violent video game could lead to more aggression than watching television violence" (256). There is no doubt that children generally and boys in particular can learn to be more aggressive and violent by playing video games.

Second supporting paragraph

Topic sentence

A tendency toward increased aggression and violence is only one of many negative effects of spending time playing these games; another negative effect is video game addiction. In a 2010 study, 1,945 participants were surveyed about video game use. Findings of the study showed that "almost one-half (48.7%) of the participants spent 1-3 hours per day playing video games, and approximately one-third (32.9%) spent 4-8 hours per day doing so" (Porter et al. 123). As children spend more and more time playing video games, the chance that they will grow up addicted to playing them increases. Another study reports that video gamers can "become preoccupied with gaming, lie about their gaming use, lose interest in other activities just to game, withdraw from family and friends to game, and use gaming as a means to psychologically escape" (Young 356). Violent video games usually offer positive reinforcement and positive sanctions for violent acts. For example, first-person-shooter games often offer positive reinforcement in terms of new weapons, perks, vehicles, and ranks. Many who play these video games online communicate with others through a simple microphone as they

3

Francis 3

play the games. This allows them to receive even more positive sanctions for their violent behavior. Gaming addiction has also been associated with mental illness, physical exhaustion, and death (Porter et al. 120).

Third supporting paragraph

Topic sentence

Increased aggression and video game addiction are two of many negative effects; another effect is the danger to the child's health. The United States has become known as a nation filled with obese individuals. Children who spend hours each day playing video games are most likely not getting enough exercise; this can cause an increase in risk for obesity. Not only is the child's physical health at risk; there is also a risk of poor psychological health. A 2013 study conducted in Great Britain reveals that children who spend time playing video games experience higher levels of emotional distress, anxiety, and depression than other children and that the greater the amount of screen time, the higher the likelihood of these negative effects (United Kingdom).

4

Conclusion

Playing video games can have many negative effects on children. While playing these games is a very popular activity among children, research shows that playing violent video games can result in increased levels of aggression and that children can become addicted. Gaming addiction can lead to hours of screen time each day, which, in turn, can lead to obesity and greater chances of psychological issues such as emotional distress, anxiety, and depression. Parents need to think carefully before caving in to their children's pleas for the latest video game. The dangers associated with video gaming cannot be denied and should not be ignored.

5

Francis 4

Works Cited

How Healthy Behaviour Supports Children's Wellbeing. Public
    Health England, 28 Aug. 2013.

Polman, Hanneke, et al. "Experimental Study of the Differential
    Effects of Playing versus Watching Violent Video Games
    on Children's Aggressive Behavior." *Aggressive Behavior,*
    vol. 34, no. 3, May/June 2008, pp. 256-64. *Wiley Online
    Library,* doi:10.1002/ab.20245.

Porter, Guy, et al. "Recognizing Problem Video Game Use."
    Australian & New Zealand Journal of Psychiatry, vol. 44,
    no. 2, 2010, pp. 120-28. *Taylor & Francis Online,*
    doi:10.3109/00048670903279812.

Willoughby, Teena, et al. "A Longitudinal Study of the
    Association between Violent Video Game Play and
    Aggression among Adolescents." *Developmental
    Psychology,* vol. 48, no. 4, July 2012, pp. 1044-57.

Young, Kimberly. "Understanding Online Gaming Addiction
    and Treatment Issues for Adolescents." *American Journal
    of Family Therapy,* vol. 37, no. 5, 2009, pp. 355-72.

> Works Cited list on a separate page

COMMENTARY

 Introduction and thesis.   The opening paragraph attracts readers' interest by pointing out how recent advancements in technology have drastically changed the number and kinds of media devices that many people now have in their homes. Instead of immediately focusing on the negative effects of one form of media, video games, Caylah acknowledges that there are many different types of games and that parents often purchase them to help keep children occupied while the parents are working long hours to provide for their families. Then she transitions smoothly to her *thesis,* which she revised according to peer review feedback from Taylor: "While some argue that playing video games does not have harmful effects, research proves otherwise." Her statement acknowledges that this is a controversial issue, reveals her stance on the issue, and lets her readers know that she will be supporting her assertion with evidence from research.

Plan of development.   Instead of following her thesis with a *plan of development* that anticipates the three major points to be covered in the essay's supporting paragraphs, Caylah ends the introduction with her thesis. She had included the three major points (that playing violent video games can lead to increased levels of aggression, video game addiction, and serious health issues) in her first draft that she shared with peer reviewer Taylor, but she chose to follow Taylor's recommendation to cut the two awkward sentences and end the introduction with a stronger, clearer statement. Caylah decided that it was unnecessarily repetitive to state the three major points in the introduction and also in the topic sentences of the three supporting paragraphs.

Patterns of development.   Caylah's primary pattern of development is *argumentation-persuasion*. She develops her thesis by making assertions about the harmful effects of playing violent video games and supporting those assertions with evidence from documented sources. However, she incorporates other *patterns of development* throughout her essay. For example, she employs *comparison-contrast* when she compares the number and types of media devices in many American homes today with those present before recent advancements in technology. She employs *division-classification* when she refers to various types of video games: "seemingly innocent fun games such as *Dance Dance Revolution*, survival horror games like *Outlast*, and violent first-person shooter games such as *Call of Duty.*" She also uses *exemplification* through her use of researched *examples* substantiating her claim that playing violent video games can have harmful effects on children.

Purpose, audience, and tone.   Given the essay's *purpose* and *audience*, Caylah adopts a serious tone, providing no-nonsense evidence to support her thesis. Suppose, however, that she had been asked to write a column for her school newspaper on video games that can help college students stay in shape. Aiming for a different tone, purpose, and audience, Caylah would have taken another approach. Drawing on her personal experience, she might have shared how she and her friends love spending hours playing *Dance Dance Revolution* and about how such video games, as well as games like *Wii Fit*, *Kinect Sports*, and *Zumba Fitness,* can have positive, rather than harmful effects. Such a column would have been written in a lighter, less formal tone.

Organization.   Structuring the essay around three major points (increased levels of aggression, video game addiction, and serious health issues), Caylah uses *emphatic order* to sequence those claims. Although each claim is important, Caylah decided to try to keep her readers interested by starting with a major concern for society and parents (aggression), then moving on to a more personal concern for parents (addiction), and finally discussing the most tangential concern (health). She decided that it would make sense to start with the issue most readers would be anxious about (because it's the result most likely to affect them) and then to give the substantially less alarming potential consequences (at least for society) as additional support.

The essay also displays Caylah's familiarity with other kinds of organizational strategies. Each supporting paragraph opens with a *topic sentence.* Further, *signal devices* are used throughout the essay to show how ideas are related to one another: *transitions* ("As a result, many children are keeping themselves occupied by spending hours each day playing video games"; *pronouns* ("many parents...they"); and *bridging sentences* ("A tendency toward increased aggression and violence is only one of many negative effects of spending time playing these games; another negative effect is video game addiction").

Two minor problems.   Caylah's efforts to write a well-organized essay result in a somewhat predictable structure. She might have increased the essay's appeal if she had rewritten one of the paragraphs, perhaps embedding the topic sentence in the middle of the paragraph or saving it for the end. Similarly, Caylah's signal devices are a little heavy-handed. Even so, an essay with a sharp focus and clear signals is preferable to one with a confusing or inaccessible structure. As she gains more experience, Caylah can work on making the structure of her essays more subtle.

Conclusion.   Following Taylor's suggestion, Caylah dropped from the final paragraph the problematic reference to procrastination. Having done that, she was able to bring the essay to a satisfying *close* by reminding readers of the essay's central idea and three main points. The final paragraph also extends the essay's scope by introducing a new but related issue: that "parents need to think carefully before caving in to their children's pleas for the latest video game."

Realizing that writing is a process, Caylah left herself enough time to revise—and to carefully consider Taylor's peer review comments. Early in her composition course, Caylah learned that attention to the various stages in the writing process yields satisfying results, for writer and reader alike.

Activity: Revise the Essay   MyWritingLab

Return to the draft you wrote in response to either Activity 1 on page 63 or Activity 2 on page 64. Also look at any written feedback you received on the draft. To identify any further problems in the draft, get together with several people (classmates, friends, or family members) and request that one of them read the draft aloud to you. Then ask your audience focused questions about the areas you sense need work, or use the checklist on the inside front cover to focus the feedback. In either case, summarize and rank the comments on a feedback chart or in marginal annotations. Then, using the comments as a guide, go ahead and revise the draft. Either type a new version or do your revising by hand, perhaps on a photocopy of the draft. Don't forget to proofread closely before submitting the paper to your instructor.

MyWritingLab Visit Chapter 2, "The Writing Process," in MyWritingLab to complete the chapter activities, and to test your understanding of the chapter objectives.

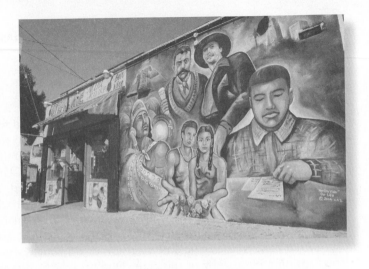

3

DESCRIPTION

In this chapter, you will learn:

3.1 To use the pattern of description to develop your essays.

3.2 To consider how description can fit your purpose and audience.

3.3 To develop strategies for using description in an essay.

3.4 To develop strategies for revising a description essay.

3.5 To analyze how description is used effectively in student-written and professionally authored selections.

3.6 To write your own essays using description as a strategy.

WHAT IS DESCRIPTION?

All of us respond in a strong way to sensory stimulation. The sweet perfume of a candy shop takes us back to childhood; the blank white walls of the campus infirmary remind us of long vigils at a hospital where a grandmother lay dying; the screech of a subway car sets our nerves on edge.

Without any sensory stimulation, we sink into a less-than-human state. Neglected babies, left alone with no human touch, no colors, and no lullabies, become withdrawn and unresponsive. And prisoners dread solitary confinement, knowing that the sensory deprivation can be unbearable, even to the point of madness.

Because sensory impressions are so potent, descriptive writing has a unique power and appeal. *Description* can be defined as the expression, in vivid language, of what the five senses experience. A richly rendered description freezes a subject in time, evoking sights, smells, sounds, textures, and tastes in such a way that readers become one with the writer's world.

HOW DESCRIPTION FITS YOUR
PURPOSE AND AUDIENCE

Description can be a supportive technique that develops part of an essay, or it can be the dominant technique used throughout an essay. Here are some examples of the way description can help you meet the objective of an essay developed chiefly through another pattern of development:

- In a *causal analysis* showing the *consequences* of pet overpopulation, you might describe the desperate appearance of a pack of starving stray dogs.
- In an *argumentation-persuasion* essay urging more rigorous handgun control, you might start with a description of a violent family confrontation that ended in murder.
- In a *process analysis* explaining the pleasure of making ice cream at home, you might describe the beauty of an old-fashioned, hand-cranked ice-cream maker.
- In a *narrative essay* recounting a day in the life of a street musician, you might describe the musician's energy and the joyous appreciation of passersby.

In each case, the essay's overall purpose would affect the amount of description needed.

Your readers also influence how much description to include. As you write, ask yourself, "What do my particular readers need to know to understand and experience keenly what I'm describing? What descriptive details will they enjoy most?" Your answers to these and similar questions will help you tailor your description to specific readers. Consider an article intended for professional horticulturists; its purpose is to explain a new technique for controlling spider mites. Because of readers' expertise, there would be little need for a lengthy description of the insects. Written for a college newspaper, however, the article would probably provide a detailed description of the mites so student gardeners could distinguish between the pesky parasites and flecks of dust.

Although your purpose and audience define *how much* to describe, you have great freedom deciding *what* to describe. Description is especially suited to objects (your car or desk, for example), but you can also describe a person, an animal, a place, a time, and a phenomenon or concept. You might write an effective description of a friend who runs marathons (person), a pair of ducks that return each year to a neighbor's pond (animals), the kitchen of a fast-food restaurant (place), a period when you were unemployed (time), the "fight-or-flight" response to danger (phenomenon or concept).

Description can be divided into two types: *objective* and *subjective*. In an objective description, you describe the subject in a straightforward and literal way, without revealing your attitude or feelings. Reporters, as well as technical and scientific writers, specialize in objective description; their jobs depend on their ability to detail experiences without emotional bias. For example, a reporter may write an unemotional account of a township meeting that ended in a fistfight. Or a marine biologist may write a factual report describing the way sea mammals are killed by the plastic refuse (sandwich wrappings, straws, fishing lines) that humans throw into the ocean.

In contrast, when writing a subjective description, you convey a highly personal view of your subject and seek to elicit a strong emotional response from your readers. Such subjective descriptions often take the form of reflective pieces or character studies. For example, in an essay describing the rich plant life in an inner-city garden, you might reflect on people's longing to connect with the soil and express admiration for the gardeners' hard work, which is an admiration you'd like readers to share. Or, in a character study of your grandfather, you might describe his stern appearance and gentle behavior, hoping that the contradiction will move readers as much as it moves you.

The *tone* of a subjective description is determined by your purpose, your attitude toward the subject, and the reader response you wish to evoke. Consider an essay about a dynamic woman who runs a center for disturbed children. If you want readers to admire the woman, your tone will be serious and appreciative. But if you want to criticize her high-pressure tactics and management style, your tone will be disapproving and severe.

The language of a descriptive piece also depends, to a great extent, on whether your purpose is primarily objective or subjective. If the description is objective, the language is straightforward, precise, and factual. Such *denotative* language consists of neutral dictionary meanings. To describe as dispassionately as possible fans' violent behavior at a football game, you might write about the "large crowd" and its "mass movement onto the field." But for a subjective piece that inspires outrage in readers, you might write about the "swelling mob" and its "rowdy stampede onto the field." In the latter case, the language you used would be *connotative* and emotionally charged so that readers would share your feelings.

Subjective and objective descriptions often overlap. Sometimes a single sentence contains both objective and subjective elements: "Although his hands were large and misshapen by arthritis, they were gentle to the touch, inspiring confidence and trust." Other times, part of an essay may provide a factual description (the physical appearance of a summer cabin your family rented), whereas another part of the essay may be highly subjective (how you felt in the cabin, sitting in front of a fire on a rainy day).

STRATEGIES FOR USING DESCRIPTION IN AN ESSAY

The suggestions here and in Figure 3.1 below will be helpful whether you use description as a dominant or a supportive pattern of development.

1. Focus a descriptive essay around a dominant impression.   Like other kinds of writing, a descriptive essay must have a thesis, or main point. In a descriptive essay with a subjective slant, the thesis usually centers on the *dominant impression* you have about your subject. Suppose you decide to write an essay on your ninth-grade history teacher, Ms. Hazzard. You want the paper to convey how unconventional and flamboyant she was. The essay could, of course, focus on a different dominant impression—how insensitive she could be to students, for example. What's important is that you establish

FIGURE 3.1
Development Diagram: Writing a Description Essay

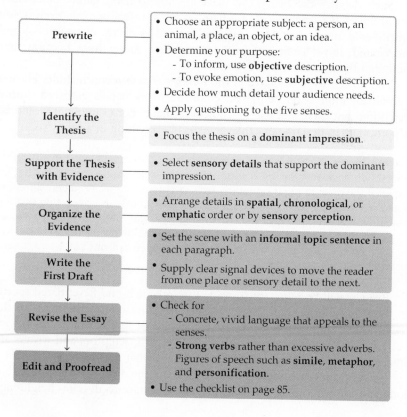

early in the paper the dominant impression you intend to convey. Although descriptive essays often imply, rather than explicitly state, the dominant impression, that impression should be unmistakable.

2. Select the details to include.   The power of description hinges on your ability to select from all possible details only those that support the dominant impression. All others, no matter how vivid or interesting, must be left out. If you're describing how flamboyant Ms. Hazzard could be, the details in the following paragraph would be appropriate.

> A large-boned woman, Ms. Hazzard wore her bright red hair piled on top of her head, where it perched precariously. By the end of class, wayward strands of hair tumbled down and fell into eyes fringed by spiky false eyelashes. Ms. Hazzard's nails, filed into crisp points, were painted either bloody burgundy or neon pink. Plastic bangle bracelets, also either burgundy or pink, clattered up and down her ample arms as she scrawled on the board the historical dates that had, she claimed, "changed the world."

Such details—the heavy eye makeup, stiletto nails, gaudy bracelets—contribute to the impression of a flamboyant, unusual person. Even if you remembered times that Ms. Hazzard seemed perfectly conventional and understated, most likely you wouldn't describe those times because they contradict the dominant impression.

You must also be selective in the *number of details* you include. Having a dominant impression helps you eliminate many details gathered during prewriting, but there still will be choices to make. For example, it would be inappropriate to describe in exhaustive detail everything in a messy room:

> The brown desk, made of a grained plastic laminate, is directly under a small window covered by a torn yellow-and-gold plaid curtain. In the left corner of the desk are four crumbled balls of blue-lined yellow paper, three red markers, two fine-point blue pens, an ink eraser, and four letters, two bearing special wildlife stamps. A green down-filled vest and a red cable-knit sweater are thrown over the back of the bright blue metal bridge chair pushed under the desk. Under the chair is an oval braided rug, its once brilliant blues and greens spotted by old coffee stains.

Readers will be reluctant to wade through such undifferentiated specifics. Even more important, such excessive detailing dilutes the focus of the essay. You end up with a seemingly endless list of specifics rather than with a carefully crafted picture in words. In this regard, sculptors and writers are similar—what they take away is as important as what they leave in.

Perhaps you're wondering how to generate the details that support your dominant impression. As you can imagine, you have to develop heightened powers of observation and recall. To sharpen these key faculties, it can be helpful to make up a chart with separate columns for each of the five senses. If you can observe your subject directly, enter in the appropriate columns what you see, hear, taste, and so on. If you're attempting to remember something from the past, try to recollect details under each of these sense headings. Ask yourself questions ("How did it smell? What did I hear?") and list each memory recaptured. You'll be surprised how this simple technique can tune you in to your experiences and help uncover the specific details needed to develop your dominant impression.

3. Organize the descriptive details.   Select the organizational pattern (or combination of patterns) that best supports your dominant impression. The paragraphs in a descriptive essay are usually sequenced *spatially* (from top to bottom, interior to exterior, near to far) or *chronologically* (as the subject is experienced in time). But the paragraphs can also be ordered *emphatically* (ending with your subject's most striking elements) or by *sensory impression* (first smell, then taste, then touch, and so on).

You might, for instance, use a *spatial* pattern to organize a description of a large city as you viewed it from the air, a taxi, and a subway car. A description of your first day on a new job might move *chronologically*, starting with how you felt the first hour on the job and proceeding through the rest of the day. In a paper describing a bout with the flu, you might arrange details *emphatically*, beginning with a description of your low-level aches and pains and concluding with an account of your raging fever. An essay about a neighborhood garbage dump, euphemistically called an "ecology landfill" by its owners, could be organized by *sensory impressions:* the sights of the dump, its smells, its sounds. Regardless of the organizational pattern you use, provide enough *signal devices* (for example, *about, next, worst of all*) so that readers can follow the description easily.

Finally, although descriptive essays don't always have conventional topic sentences, each descriptive paragraph should have a clear focus. Often this focus is indicated by a sentence early in the paragraph that names the scene, object, or individual to be described. Such a sentence functions as a kind of *informal topic sentence;* the paragraph's descriptive details then develop that topic sentence.

4. Use vivid sensory language and varied sentence structure.   The connotative language typical of subjective description should be richly evocative. The words you select must etch in readers' minds the same picture that you have in yours. For this reason, rather than relying on vague generalities, you must use language that involves readers' senses. Consider the difference between the following paired descriptions.

Vague	Vivid
The food was unappetizing.	The stew congealed into an oval pool of milky-brown fat.
The toothpaste was refreshing.	The toothpaste, tasting minty sweet, felt good against slippery teeth, free finally from braces.
Filled with passengers and baggage, the car moved slowly down the road.	Burdened with its load of clamoring children and well-worn suitcases, the car labored down the interstate on bald tires and worn shocks, emitting puffs of blue exhaust and an occasional backfire.

Unlike the *concrete, sensory-packed* sentences on the right, the sentences on the left fail to create vivid word pictures that engage readers. Although all good writing blends abstract and concrete language, descriptive writing demands an abundance of specific sensory language.

Keep in mind, too, that *verbs pack more of a wallop* than adverbs. The following sentence has to rely on adverbs (italicized) because its verbs are so weak: "She walked *casually* into the room and *deliberately* tried not to pay much attention to their stares." Rewritten, so that verbs (italicized), not adverbs, do the bulk of the work, the sentence becomes more powerful: "She *strolled* into the room and *ignored* their stares."

Figures of speech—nonliteral, imaginative comparisons between two basically dissimilar things—are another way to enliven descriptive writing. *Similes* use the words *like* or *as* when comparing; *metaphors* state or imply that two things being compared are alike; and *personification* attributes human characteristics to inanimate things.

The examples that follow show how effective figurative language can be in descriptive writing.

> Moving as jerkily as a marionette on strings, the old man picked himself up off the sidewalk and staggered down the street. (*simile*)
>
> Stalking their prey, the hall monitors remained hidden in the corridors, motionless and ready to spring on any unsuspecting student who dared to sneak into class late. (*metaphor*)
>
> The scoop of vanilla ice cream, plain and unadorned, cried out for hot-fudge sauce and a sprinkling of sliced pecans. (*personification*)

Finally, when writing descriptive passages, you need to *vary sentence structure*. Don't use the same subject-verb pattern in all sentences. The second example, for instance, could have been written as follows: "The hall monitors stalked their prey. They hid in the corridors. They remained motionless and ready to spring on any unsuspecting student who tried to sneak into class late." But the sentence is richer and more interesting when the descriptive elements are embedded, eliminating what would otherwise have been a clipped and predictable subject-verb pattern.

REVISION STRATEGIES

Once you have a draft of the essay, you're ready to revise. The following checklist will help you and those giving you feedback apply to description some of the revision techniques discussed in Chapter 2.

☑ DESCRIPTION: A REVISION/PEER REVIEW CHECKLIST

Revise Overall Meaning and Structure

❑ What dominant impression does the essay convey? Is the dominant impression stated or implied? Where? Should it be made more obvious or more subtle?

❑ Is the essay primarily objective or subjective? Should the essay be more emotionally charged or less so?

❑ Which descriptive details don't support the dominant impression? Should they be deleted, or should the dominant impression be adjusted to encompass the details?

Revise Paragraph Development

❑ How are the essay's descriptive paragraphs organized—spatially, chronologically, emphatically, or by sensory impression? Would another organizational pattern be more effective? Which one(s)?

❑ Which paragraphs lack a distinctive focus?

❑ Which descriptive paragraphs are mere lists of sensory impressions?

❑ Which descriptive paragraphs fail to engage the reader's senses? How could they be made more concrete?

Revise Sentences and Words

❑ What signal devices guide readers through the description? Are there enough signals? Too many?

❑ Where should sentence structure be varied to make it less predictable?

❑ Which sentences should include more sensory images?

❑ Which flat verbs should be replaced with vigorous verbs?

❑ Where should there be more or fewer adjectives?

❑ Do any figures of speech seem contrived or trite? Which ones?

STUDENT ESSAY

The following student essay was written by Leanna Stoufer in response to this assignment:

> The essay "El Hoyo" is a poignant piece about a place that holds special significance to the author. Write an essay about a place, a person, or an object that holds rich significance for you, centering the description on a dominant impression.

While reading Leanna's essay, try to determine how well it applies the principles of description. The annotations on Leanna's essay and the commentary following it will help you look at the essay more closely.

Enduring with Dignity: *Akua's Surviving Children*
by Leanna Stoufer

Introduction

Spatial sequence at beginning of essay

It is often the first piece that catches the eye of a visitor   1
walking through the doorway of El Anatsui's exhibit, "When
I Last Wrote to You about Africa," featured at the Denver
Art Museum. (See Fig. 1.) The structure, created in 1996,
is titled *Akua's Surviving Children* and sits on an 8-inch
platform, approximately 12 feet wide and 8 feet deep. The
platform itself is a flat grey color and appears to have been

FIG. 1
El Anatsui. *Akua's Surviving Children*. 1996, collection of
the artist and October Gallery, London. Photo: Andy Keate.
Courtesy of the artist and Jack Shainman Gallery, New York.
© El Anatsui. (El Anatsui)

provided by the Denver Art Museum, rather than being an integral part of the artwork. There are twenty-seven figures standing on the platform. Each one is unique, with heights varying between approximately 2 feet and 5 feet. Each figure has a "body" that is described by the artist as a piece of driftwood; however, these bodies appear to have been shaped by man at one time—perhaps they are the broken remnants of piers, or docks, or maybe shards left from a shoreline house or a boat. What is clear is that each piece has had a difficult life. Each of the twenty-seven bodies has its own mélange of scars, splits, gouges, and worm-eaten holes, and each is attached to the platform with a simple pair of metal brackets. Several have charred areas, and one has a section of threaded rod protruding through the bottom, with a rusty washer and nut still attached.

Dominant impression (thesis)

Personification

Each figure also has a "head" attached at the top; these heads are smaller chunks of worn and battered wood. In fact, some are made up of several small chunks of wood wired together. One appears to have been attached to the body with wire wrappings, but most have a gigantic spike driven through the head, with a small space between head and body where the spike forms a neck of sorts. Nearly every one of the heads is charred, which gives it a much darker appearance than the body beneath. It is not possible to say with assuredness which way these figures are facing, but they appear to all be facing in one direction (to the viewer's left), with the exception of one figure near the front of the platform and on the right-hand side, which seems to be looking back—perhaps toward its homeland.

Topic sentence: First of three paragraphs in an emphatic sequence

Personification

El Anatsui's statement regarding his creation shares not only that each of the "bodies" is composed of a piece of driftwood, but also that the piece was created while he was in Denmark. He adds that this piece is "representative of individual Africans who crossed tumultuous oceans" during the days of the Danish slave trade. Regarding his work, El Anatsui states, "Rather than recounting history, my art is telling about what history has provoked" (qtd. in Binder 83).

Topic sentence: Second of three paragraphs in an emphatic sequence

El Anatsui and his crew used a wide variety of materials and processes as they created the multiple pieces included in the exhibit. His most famous works are the moveable blankets or sheets, made up of thousands of pieces of plastic from bottle necks and lids. The tiny pieces are stitched together with copper wire, creating massive blankets, with many colors and textures. These have been shaped and draped on walls and on the exteriors of buildings, and also hung from cables. Each of his pieces is evocative of the transformation of materials, and perhaps of the transformation of peoples as well.

Topic sentence: Third paragraph in the emphatic sequence

Akua's Surviving Children captures the onlooker's attention partly because of the poignancy of seeing such battered pieces

Conclusion

2

3

4

5

of wood used to create works of art, and partly because of the title, which brings to mind images of survivors—those who have survived violence, cancer, AIDS, and other diseases—along with images of those who do not survive. These figures, battered and scarred though they are, stand straight, with heads upright, and they seem to wear the mantle of survivorship with great dignity. These are not figures that go quietly into a dusty, ignoble history, but rather they seem to still be speaking to future generations of their toils, their travels, and their strength in bearing the unbearable. The story they tell is deeply moving.

Personification — [marginal note pointing to "scarred though they are, stand straight, with heads upright"]

Echo of idea in introduction — [marginal note pointing to "tions of their toils, their travels, and their strength in bearing the"]

Work Cited

Binder, Lisa M., editor. *El Anatsui: When I Last Wrote to You about Africa*. New York, Museum for African Art, 2012.

COMMENTARY

The dominant impression.   Leanna responded to the assignment by writing a moving tribute to a sculpture having special meaning for her—El Anatsui's *Akua's Surviving Children*. Like most descriptive pieces, Leanna's essay is organized around a dominant impression: the poignant story told by twenty-seven charred and scarred wooden figures who are "representative of individual Africans who crossed tumultuous oceans" during the days of the Danish slave trade. The essay's introduction provides a context for the dominant impression with two images of the work of art—one through the writer's words and another through a photo of the sculpture.

Combining patterns of development.   In addition to vivid *description* throughout her essay, Leanna uses *process analysis* when explaining how El Anatsui creates his sculptures. In the second paragraph she says that some of the "heads" "are made up of several small chunks of wood wired together." She goes on explain: "One appears to have been attached to the body with wire wrappings, but most have a gigantic spike driven through the head, with a small space between head and body where the spike forms a neck of sorts." And in the fourth paragraph she explains that El Anatsui's "most famous works are the moveable blankets or sheets." She tells how the works are made from bottle necks and lids: "The tiny pieces are stitched together with copper wire, creating massive blankets, with many colors and textures."

The essay also contains a strong element of *narration* in that Leanna shares the story the wooden figures tell. In paragraph 1 she states, "What is clear is that each piece has had a difficult life. Each of the twenty-seven bodies has its own mélange of scars, splits, gouges and worm-eaten holes,…" and in paragraph 2 she tells us that all of the figures except one are facing in the same direction, and that the one who is looking in the opposite direction "seems to be looking back—perhaps toward its homeland." Then in the following paragraph she adds to the story she is weaving into her description when she quotes El Anatsui as saying that *Akua's Surviving Children* is "'representative of individual Africans who crossed tumultuous oceans' during the days of the Danish slave trade," and that "rather than recounting history, [his] art is telling about what history has provoked." Leanna completes her story in the final sentences of the closing paragraph: "These are not figures that go quietly into a dusty, ignoble history, but rather they seem to still be speaking to future generations of their toils, their travels, and their strength in bearing the unbearable. The story they tell is deeply moving."

Sensory language.   Leanna's essay is rich with concrete, sensory-packed sentences and connotative language such as "mélange of scars, splits, gouges and worm-eaten holes" and "attached...with a simple pair of metal brackets" (paragraph 1); and "Most have a gigantic spike driven through the head, with a small space between head and body where the spike forms a neck of sorts" (paragraph 2).

Figurative language, vigorous verbs, and varied sentence structure. You might have noted that *figurative language, vigorous verbs,* and *varied sentence patterns* contribute to the essay's descriptive power. Leanna uses personification throughout the essay as she attributes human characteristics to wooden figures; she refers to the "difficult life" of each figure in paragraph 1, the heads of the figures and the lone figure as looking back toward its homeland in paragraph 2, and the figures' "deeply moving story" in paragraph 5. Moreover, throughout the essay she uses lively verbs ("wired," "driven," "stitched," "shaped and draped") to capture the work of the artist. She even ascribes "dignity" to the figures: "These figures, battered and scarred though they are, stand straight, with heads upright, and they seem to wear the mantle of survivorship with great dignity" (paragraph 5).

Similarly, Leanna enhances descriptive passages by varying the length of her sentences. Long, fairly elaborate sentences are interspersed with shorter, dramatic statements. In the opening paragraph, for example, a long sentence ("Each figure has a 'body' that is described by the artist as a piece of driftwood; however, they appear to have been shaped by man at one time—perhaps they are the broken remnants of piers, or docks, or maybe shards left from a shoreline house or a boat") is followed by a brief statement, "What is clear is that each piece has had a difficult life." And in the concluding paragraph, the long sentence "These are not figures that go quietly into a dusty, ignoble history, but rather they seem to still be speaking to future generations of their toils, their travels, and their strength in bearing the unbearable" is followed by the simple and poignant closing statement "The story they tell is deeply moving."

Organization.   Leanna uses an easy-to-follow combination of *spatial* and *emphatic* patterns in her essay. Although the essay begins with a spatial pattern, it relies primarily on emphatic arrangement because the three body paragraphs focus on the different elements of the sculpture that combine to create the story it tells. Leanna begins by using spatial order as she describes what it is like to walk through the doorway of the room that houses the exhibit by El Anatsui and to have one's attention immediately drawn to the piece that is the focus of her essay: *Akua's Surviving Children*. However, from that point on, she uses emphatic order as she tells the story of people who were taken from their homeland and sold into slavery. In the first body paragraph she focuses on describing the heads of the wooden figures and their human characteristics; in the second body paragraph she incorporates quotes from El Anatsui, the creator of the piece, sharing his statement that the "piece is representative of individual Africans who crossed tumultuous oceans"; and in the final supporting paragraph she describes how the artist creates pieces that are "evocative of the transformation of materials, and perhaps of the transformation of peoples as well." Using an emphatic pattern allows her to effectively tell the story of people who were treated horribly yet managed to survive.

Conclusion.   The concluding paragraph brings the essay to a powerful close. It begins by connecting with the first sentence of the essay and the reference to "the first piece that catches the visitor's eye" but goes beyond that image to reflect on why the image is so captivating, noting not only "the poignancy of seeing such battered pieces of wood used to create works of art" but also the significance "of the title, which brings to mind images of survivors—those who have survived violence, cancer, AIDS, and other diseases—along with images of those who do not survive." She goes on to describe images that "wear the mantle of survivorship with great dignity" and refuse to "go quietly into a dusty, ignoble history, but rather...seem to still be speaking to future generations of their toils, their travels, and their strength in bearing the unbearable."

Revising the first draft.   When Leanna met with a small group of her classmates during a peer review session, the students agreed that Leanna's first draft was strong and moving. However, one group member pointed out that as he read her concluding paragraph, he thought that perhaps her essay would be more effective if written from third-person point of view. He went on to explain that he thought the move to third-person might be appropriate because the essay wasn't really about Leanna and her trip to the museum, but rather about the sculpture. Consequently, it was less about her personal experience at the museum than it was a critical commentary. Following is the first-draft version of Leanna's concluding paragraph.

Original Version of the Conclusion

Akua's Surviving Children captured my attention partly because of poignancy of seeing such battered pieces of wood used to create works of art, and partly because of the title. I was immediately struck by the idea of survivors, and thought of the survivors of violence, survivors of cancer and other diseases, and the many that do not survive. The many images that coursed through my mind on reading the title compelled me to spend some time appreciating this piece. These figures, battered and scarred though they are, stand straight, with heads upright, and they seem to wear the mantle of survivorship with great dignity. These are not figures that go quietly into a dusty, ignoble history, but rather they seem to still be speaking to future generations of their toils, their travels, and their strength in bearing the unbearable. Speaking only for myself, I was deeply moved by their story.

When Leanna looked more carefully at the paragraph, she agreed that her use of first-person point of view detracted from the main focus of the essay: the piece of art itself. As she revised the concluding paragraph and switched from first person to third person, she combined the ideas in the first three sentences of the first draft and wrote one tighter, more effective sentence: "*Akua's Surviving Children* captures the onlooker's attention partly because of the poignancy of seeing such battered pieces of wood used to create works of art, and partly because of the title, which brings to mind images of survivors—those who have survived violence, cancer, AIDS and other diseases—along with images of those who do not survive." As she continued her move from first person to third person in that paragraph, she also revised her closing sentence, making it more emphatic and pointed: "The story they tell is deeply moving."

As she continued revising her essay, Leanna switched from first-person to third-person point of view throughout and intensified the sensory images in her opening paragraph. She changed "perhaps they are broken pieces of piers or docks" to "perhaps they are the broken remnants of piers, or docks, or maybe shards left from a shoreline house or a boat." And in the fourth paragraph "The small pieces are joined with wire, making huge, colorful blankets" became "The tiny pieces are stitched together with copper wire, creating massive blankets, with many colors and textures."

These are just some of the changes Leanna made while rewriting her essay. Her skillful revisions provided the polish needed to make an already strong essay even more evocative.

Activities: Description   MyWritingLab
Prewriting Activities

1. Imagine you're writing two essays: One explains the *process* by which students get "burned out"; the other *argues* that being a spendthrift is better (or worse) than being frugal. Jot down ways you might use description in each essay.

2. Go to a place on campus where students congregate. In preparation for an *objective* description of this place, make notes of various sights, sounds, smells, and textures, as well as the overall "feel" of the place. Then, in preparation

(continued)

Activities: Description (*continued*)

for a *subjective* description, observe and take notes on another sheet of paper. Compare the two sets of material. What differences do you see in word choice and selection of details?

Revising Activities

3. Revise each of the following sentence sets twice. The first time, create an unmistakable mood; the second time, create a sharply contrasting mood. To convey atmosphere, vary sentence structure, use vigorous verbs, provide rich sensory details, and pay special attention to words' connotations.

   a. The card players sat around the table. The table was old. The players were, too.
   b. A long line formed outside the movie theater. People didn't want to miss the show. The movie had received a lot of attention recently.
   c. A girl walked down the street in her first pair of high heels. This was a new experience for her.

4. The following descriptive paragraph is from the first draft of an essay showing that personal growth may result when romanticized notions and reality collide. How effective is the paragraph in illustrating the essay's thesis? Which details are powerful? Which could be more concrete? Which should be deleted? Where should sentence structure be more varied? How could the description be made more coherent? Revise the paragraph, correcting any problems you discover and adding whatever sensory details are needed to enliven the description. Feel free to break the paragraph into two or more separate ones.

   As a child, I was intrigued by stories about the farm in Harrison County, Maine, where my father spent his teens. Being raised on a farm seemed more interesting than growing up in the suburbs. So about a year ago, I decided to see for myself what the farm was like. I got there by driving on Route 334, a surprisingly easy-to-drive, four-lane highway that had recently been built with matching state and federal funds. I turned into the dirt road leading to the farm and got out of my car. It had been washed and waxed for the occasion. Then I headed for a dirt-colored barn. Its roof was full of huge, rotted holes. As I rounded the bushes, I saw the house. It too was dirt-colored. Its paint must have worn off decades ago. A couple of dead-looking old cars were sprawled in front of the barn. They were dented and windowless. Also by the barn was an ancient refrigerator, crushed like a discarded accordion. The porch steps to the house were slanted and wobbly. Through the open windows came a stale smell and the sound of television. Looking in the front door screen, I could see two chickens jumping around inside. Everything looked dirty both inside and out. Secretly grateful that no one answered my knock, I bolted down the stairs, got into my clean, shiny car, and drove away.

Mario Suárez

Mario Suárez (1923–1998), author of *Chicano Sketches,* which is a collection of short stories (2004), is considered by many to be the first contemporary Chicano writer. Suárez was one of five children born to Mexican immigrants who moved to Arizona. After serving in the U.S. Navy during World War II, he attended the University of Arizona, and while still an undergraduate, he wrote for the *Arizona Quarterly.* A journalist and college teacher, Suárez wrote primarily about the lives of immigrants and life in El Hoyo, the barrio where he grew up.

For ideas on how this description essay is organized, see Figure 3.2 on page 95.

Pre-Reading Journal Entry

MyWritingLab

Think of a place that is important to you from your childhood or adolescence—perhaps the place (or one of the places) where you grew up. Why was the place important to you? How would you describe it to someone who had never been there?

El Hoyo

From the center of downtown Tucson, the ground slopes gently away   1
to Main Street, drops a few feet, and then rolls to the banks of the Santa Cruz River. Here lies the section of the city known as El Hoyo. Why it is called El Hoyo is not very clear. In no sense is it a hole as its name would imply; it is simply the river's immediate valley. Its inhabitants are chicanos who raise hell on Saturday night and listen to Padre Estanislao on Sunday morning. While the term *chicano* is the short way of saying Mexicano, it is not restricted to the paisanos who came from old Mexico with the territory or the last famine to work for the railroad, labor, sing, and go on relief. Chicano is the easy way of referring to everybody. Pablo Gut'errez married the Chinese grocer's daughter and now runs a meat department; his sons are chicanos. So are the sons of Killer Jones who threw a fight in Harlem and fled to El Hoyo to marry Cristina Mendez. And so are all of them. However, it is doubtful that all these spiritual sons of Mexico live in El Hoyo because they love each other—many fight and bicker constantly. It is doubtful they live in El Hoyo because of its scenic beauty—it is everything but beautiful. Its houses are simple affairs of unplastered adobe, wood, and abandoned car parts. Its narrow streets are mostly clearings which have, in time, acquired names. Except for some tall trees which nobody has ever cared to identify, nurse, or destroy, the main things known to grow in the general area are weeds, garbage piles, dark-eyed chavalos, and dogs. And it is doubtful that the chicanos live in El Hoyo because it is safe—many times the Santa Cruz has risen and inundated the area.

In other respects, living in El Hoyo has its advantages. If one is born   2
with a weakness for acquiring bills, El Hoyo is where the collectors are
less likely to find you. If one has acquired the habit of listening to Octavio
Perea's Mexican Hour in the wee hours of the morning with the radio
on at full blast, El Hoyo is where you are less likely to be reported to the
authorities. Besides, Perea is very popular and sooner or later to everyone
"Smoke in the Eyes" is dedicated between the pinto beans and white
flour commercials. If one, for any reason whatever, comes on an extended
period of hard times, where, if not in El Hoyo, are the neighbors more
willing to offer solace? When Teofila Malacara's house burned to the
ground with all her belongings and two children, a benevolent gentleman
carried through the gesture that made tolerable her burden. He made a
list of five hundred names and solicited from each a dollar. At the end of a
month, he turned over to the tearful but grateful señora one hundred dollars in cold cash and then accompanied her on a short vacation. When the
new manager of a local store decided that no more chicanas were to work
behind the counters, it was the chicanos of El Hoyo who, on taking their
individually small but collectively great buying power elsewhere, drove
the manager out and the girls returned to their jobs. When the Mexican
Army was en route to Baja, California, and the chicanos found out that
the enlisted men ate only at infrequent intervals, it was El Hoyo's chicanos
who crusaded across town with pots of beans and trays of tortillas to meet
the train. When someone gets married, celebrating is not restricted to the
immediate friends of the couple. Everybody is invited. Anything calls for a
celebration, and a celebration calls for anything. On Memorial Day there
are no less than half a dozen good fights at the Riverside Dance Hall. On
Mexican Independence Day, more than one flag is sworn allegiance to
amid cheers for the queen.

And El Hoyo is something more. It is this something more which   3
brought Felipe Sanchez back from the wars after having killed a score of
Vietnamese with his body resembling a patchwork quilt to marry Julia
Armijo. It brought Joe Zepeda, a gunner,... back to compose boleros. He
has a metal plate for a skull. Perhaps El Hoyo is proof that those people
exist, and perhaps exist best, who have as yet failed to observe the more popular modes of human conduct. Perhaps the humble appearance of El Hoyo
justifies the indifferent shrug of those made aware of its existence. Perhaps
El Hoyo's simplicity motivates an occasional chicano to move away from
its narrow streets, babbling comadres, and shrieking children to deny the
bloodwell from which he springs and to claim the blood of a conquistador
while his hair is straight and his face beardless. Yet El Hoyo is not an outpost
of a few families against the world. It fights for no causes except those which
soothe its immediate angers. It laughs and cries with the same amount of
passion in times of plenty and of want.

Perhaps El Hoyo, its inhabitants, and its essence can best be explained   4
by telling a bit about a dish called capirotada. Its origin is uncertain. But,
according to the time and the circumstance, it is made of old, new, or hard
bread. It is softened with water and then cooked with peanuts, raisins,
onions, cheese, and panocha. It is fired with sherry wine. Then it is served
hot, cold, or just "on the weather" as they say in El Hoyo. The Sermeños
like it one way, the Garcias another, and the Ortegas still another. While
it might differ greatly from one home to another; nevertheless, it is still
capirotada. And so it is with El Hoyo's chicanos. While being divided from
within and from without, like the capirotada, they remain chicanos.

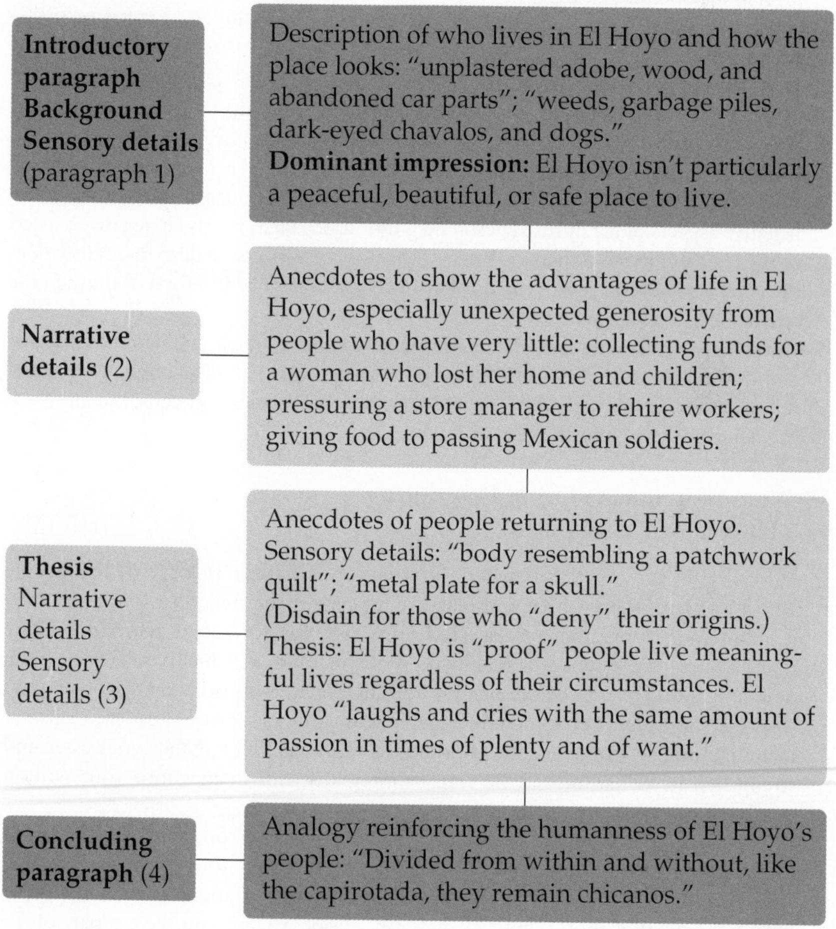

FIGURE 3.2
Essay Structure Diagram: "El Hoyo" by Mario Suárez

Introductory paragraph **Background** **Sensory details** (paragraph 1)	Description of who lives in El Hoyo and how the place looks: "unplastered adobe, wood, and abandoned car parts"; "weeds, garbage piles, dark-eyed chavalos, and dogs." **Dominant impression:** El Hoyo isn't particularly a peaceful, beautiful, or safe place to live.
Narrative details (2)	Anecdotes to show the advantages of life in El Hoyo, especially unexpected generosity from people who have very little: collecting funds for a woman who lost her home and children; pressuring a store manager to rehire workers; giving food to passing Mexican soldiers.
Thesis **Narrative details** **Sensory details** (3)	Anecdotes of people returning to El Hoyo. Sensory details: "body resembling a patchwork quilt"; "metal plate for a skull." (Disdain for those who "deny" their origins.) Thesis: El Hoyo is "proof" people live meaningful lives regardless of their circumstances. El Hoyo "laughs and cries with the same amount of passion in times of plenty and of want."
Concluding paragraph (4)	Analogy reinforcing the humanness of El Hoyo's people: "Divided from within and without, like the capirotada, they remain chicanos."

Questions for Close Reading

MyWritingLab

1. What is the selection's thesis (or dominant impression)? Locate the sentence(s) in which Suárez states his main idea. If he doesn't state the thesis explicitly, express it in your own words.
2. According to the author, what do the words *el hoyo* and *chicano* mean?
3. Why do people choose to live in El Hoyo?
4. Suárez tries to create an essay that describes for his readers the place where he grew up and why it is important in his life. Do you think his essay succeeds in communicating his ideas? Why or why not?

Questions about the Writer's Craft

1. **The pattern.** Focus on the first paragraph of "El Hoyo." Carefully re-read the paragraph and make notes regarding its organization. What does Suárez accomplish in his opening paragraph? What negative aspects of El Hoyo does he include, and why do you think he includes these in the opening paragraph? What might be his purpose?
2. How would you characterize the author's tone? Serious? Humorous? Down to earth? Give some examples to support your idea. Why do you think the author adopts the tone that he uses?
3. **Other patterns.** Although the primary focus of "El Hoyo" is on describing the barrio where Suárez grew up, the essay also *compares* and *contrasts* both positive and negative aspects of life in this Tucson neighborhood. First, list three negative aspects of the community, and then list three of the positive aspects he describes. How does the inclusion of both positive and negative characteristics of El Hoyo strengthen the overall impact of the essay?
4. In the closing paragraph of the essay Suárez creates an analogy between El Hoyo and *capirotada*, a Mexican dish made of leftovers. In what ways might *capirotada* represent life in the barrio? Make a list of three similarities you can draw between the neighborhood and the dish.

Writing Assignments Using Description as a Pattern of Development

1. Suárez describes the barrio where he grew up: where it is located, the people who live there, the positive and negative aspects of the neighborhood, and how it is different from other places. He brings his essay to closure with an analogy that captures the essence of El Hoyo. Write an essay in which you describe the neighborhood (or one of the neighborhoods) where you grew up. Do your best to present a multifaceted view of your neighborhood for your reader. Consider including images of the neighborhood or its residents that enhance your essay and strengthen its visual impact. Be sure to integrate your images into your written text by referencing them in your essay.
2. In his essay Suárez mentions specific individuals who stood out for him from the community—among them Pablo Gut'errez, Killer Jones, Felipe Sanchez, Julia Amijo, and Joe Zepeda. Write a descriptive essay about particular people from your neighborhood, your elementary school, a team you were a part of, or

another group that played a role in your life. Go beyond describing these individuals and reflect on why they stand out in your mind. Why did they create a lasting impression on you? Consider integrating images that enhance your essay and strengthen its visual impact. Be sure to integrate your images into your written text by referencing them in your essay.

Writing Assignment Combining Patterns of Development

3. Although El Hoyo is the barrio where Suárez grew up—a neighborhood he cherishes—it is clearly not the upscale, upper-class part of town. Write an essay in which you *compare* and *contrast* two neighborhoods—or two cities or countries—you are familiar with. Describe both areas, but also compare the ways they are alike and the ways they differ. Bring in outside sources as needed to strengthen your essay, and consider using images such as a pie chart showing income or education levels, or perhaps a map of the areas discussed in your essay.

David Helvarg

David Helvarg is a journalist and environmental activist. Born in 1951, he started his career as a freelance journalist and then became a war correspondent. Today he writes primarily about politics, AIDS, and marine life. Helvarg is also the founder and president of Blue Frontier Campaign, a marine conservation lobbying group that was inspired by his book about the world's oceans, *Blue Frontier.* Helvarg's lobbying on environmental issues grows out of his experiences covering war, political conflict, and marine biology. This article, about the aftermath of Hurricane Katrina, which devastated New Orleans and the Gulf Coast in 2005, is excerpted from the September/October 2005 issue of *Multinational Monitor,* a magazine that examines multinational corporations and also covers issues relating to the environment and development.

Pre-Reading Journal Entry   MyWritingLab

Although humans have shaped the environment in many ways, we are still at the mercy of nature at times. Recall a hurricane, tornado, thunderstorm, windstorm, mudslide, earthquake, volcanic eruption, tsunami, drought, flood, or other natural event that affected you and your community. What was the event? What was the experience like? Use your journal to answer these questions.

The Storm This Time

Urban Floodplain

I arrive in Baton Rouge with a planeload of relief workers, FEMA   1
functionaries and crew cut contractors, all working their cell phones and BlackBerrys. After renting a car and making my way through the daily traffic jam (Baton Rouge's population has exploded since the storm) I head

south on Interstate 10, tuning into the United Radio Broadcasters of New Orleans, a consortium of local stations playing 24/7 information and call-in reports on Katrina's aftermath.

A police spokesperson assures listeners there are still 20 to 30 roadblocks   2 around New Orleans and 11,000 guardsmen in the city. The mayor wants to open the city back up to residents but the approach of Hurricane Rita has forced him to postpone his plan.

Around the New Orleans airport in Jefferson Parish, I begin to see   3 box stores, warehouses and motels with their roofs ripped off or caved in, downed trees and broken street signs, house roofs covered in blue tarps and high-rises with glass windows popped out like broken eyes. I hit a traffic jam and follow an SUV across the median strip to an exit where I stop to take a picture of a small office complex with its second story front and roof gone. Rain-soaked cardboard boxes fill the exposed floor above a CPA's office. I talk to a carpet-store owner removing samples. He helps me locate where we are on a map. I get a call from a contact at the New Orleans Aquarium. They lost most of their fish when the pumps failed but managed to evacuate the penguins and sea otters to Monterey. I get on a wide boulevard that leads to a roadblock where a police officer checks my press identification. "This is only for emergency vehicles, but go ahead," she says.

I drive into Lakeview, one of the large sections of the city that sat under-   4 water for two weeks and will likely have to be bulldozed. It reminds me of war zones I've been in after heavy street fighting. There are trees and power poles down, electric lines hanging, metal sheets and street signs on mud-caked pavement, smashed cars, boats on sidewalks and torn-open houses, all colored in sepia tones of gray and brown. Unable to drive far in the debris chocked streets, I get out of my car, half expecting the sweet, rotting smell of death. Instead, I'm confronted with an equally noxious odor. It's what I'll come to think of as the smell of a dead city, like dried cow pies and mold with a stinging chemical aftertaste. Fine yellow dust starts rising up from under my boots and infiltrating the car. I retreat. The I-10 exit is barricaded, forcing me north again. I do a U-turn at a major roadblock and get chased down by some angry cops. I explain that I'm just following another cop's helpful directions and soon find myself speeding along a near-empty freeway bridge approaching downtown.

The rusted ruined roof of the Superdome inspires me to choose an exit   5 and, after getting turned around at a friendly National Guard checkpoint, I'm soon in the deserted streets of the central business district, checking out the rubble piles and empty highrises. A big wind-damaged 'Doubletree' hotel sign reads D UL EE. The French Quarter is still intact with even a few bars open for soldiers, FBI agents and fire fighters. On Canal Street, it looks like a Woodstock for first responders with Red Cross and media satellite trucks, tents and RVs pulled up on the central streetcar median by the Sheraton. Red-bereted troops from the 82nd Airborne cruise by in

New Orleans house showing flood line and searcher's graffiti. The zero indicates that no bodies were found in the house. (©*David Helvarg*)

open-sided trucks, M-4s at the ready in case the undead should appear at sunset. Uptown, some boats lie in the middle of the street, along with cars crushed by a falling wall and a pharmacy trashed by looters. Further on are the smashed homes and muddied boulevards and still-flooded underpasses and cemeteries, abandoned cars and broken levees of an eerily hollow city.

In the coming days. I'll travel across this new urban landscape, tracing the brown floodwater line that marks tens of thousands of homes, schools, offices, banks, churches, grocery stores and other ruined structures, including the main sewage plant. I'll cross paths with animal rescue crews, military patrols, utility crews from New York and Pennsylvania, and body recovery search teams with K-9 dogs using orange spray paint to mark the doors of still unexamined buildings, writing the date and adding a zero for no bodies or numbers where bodies have been found.... 6

Life After Katrina

I put up with an AP colleague in the less damaged Algiers Point section of the city just across the Mississippi from where the helicopter assault ship Iwo Jima and Carnival Cruise Line ship Ecstasy are being used to house city employees and relief workers. Blackhawk helicopters fly overhead at sunset while a Red Cross truck down the street offers hot food to the handful of residents still here. 7

Bob Chick examines his flood-ruined house in the Lakeview section of New Orleans. (©*David Helvarg*)

Back in Lakeview, I encounter Bob Chick. Bob snuck past the check-   8
points to see if he can salvage anything from his green Cajun Cottage near
where the 17th Street floodwall breached.

He hasn't had much luck, "just some tools that might be OK," he says.   9
"I left all my photos on top of a chest of drawers thinking the water wouldn't
get that high. They say if you have more than five inches of water in your house
for five days it's a loss. We had eight feet for two weeks." He's found one of his
cats dead but thinks the other two might have escaped. He invites me to look
inside. From the door it's a jumble of furniture, including a sofa, table, twisted
carpet, lamps and wooden pieces all covered in black and gray gunk, reeking
of mold and rotted cat food. I try not to breathe too deeply. "I had a collection of Jazz Fest T shirts going back to '79 but they're gone." He's wearing a
mask, rubber boots and gloves, but still manages to give an expressive shrug of
resignation when I take his picture. "I lived in this house 16 years. We'd have
been fine if the levee hadn't broke. We'd be moving back right now...."

A Disappeared Town

I catch a ride along the west bank of the Mississippi in Plaquemines   10
Parish south of New Orleans with deputy Sheriff Ken Harvey. This is where
towns of several thousand, like Empire and Buras, got washed away and
some oil tank farms ruptured. Where the road's cut by water, we drive up on
the eroded levee and keep going. There are boats on the land, and houses in

the water or washed onto the road or turned into woodpiles. At one point where the levee broke and the water poured through, there's nothing but a field where Diamond, an unincorporated town of about 300 including many trailer-park residents, stood. Those folks never seem to catch a break.

I take a picture of an antebellum white mansion in the water along with a 11 floating pickup, a larger truck hanging off a tree, a semi-trailer cab under the bottom of an uplifted house, a speedboat through a picture window, the Buras water tower collapsed next to a wrecked store, shrimp boats on the levee, on the road and in the bushes with military patrols passing by. We stop and stare in awe at a 200-foot barge tossed atop the levee like a bath toy on a tub rim.

Approaching the Empire Bridge, I note the white church facing north 12 towards us is still intact and suggest that's a hopeful sign. "It used to face the road," Ken points out....

Unfortunately, as I drive east through Mississippi and Alabama I find 13 most of [the] coastal trees and wetlands festooned with plastic like Tibetan prayer flags (as if monks were praying over dead turtles and seabirds). In Biloxi, along with smashed casinos, historic homes and neighborhoods, I find miles of beachfront covered in plastic buckets and insulation, mattresses, furniture, chunks of drywall and Styrofoam pellets that the seabirds are eyeing as potential snack food. I wave down a truck marked "Department of Natural Resources," but the guys inside are from Indiana.

I feel like an eco-geek being more concerned about the gulls and wet- 14 lands than the lost revenue from the casinos that everyone else seems to be obsessing on. The waterside wing of the new Hard Rock Casino is now a smashed tangle of twisted girders and concrete. I pull over by an 8,000 ton, 600-foot-long casino barge that was pushed half a mile by the storm, landing on Beach Drive. Somewhere underneath its barnacle-encrusted black hull is a historic mansion. Nearby, the Grand Casino barge has taken out much of the stately facade of the six story yellow brick Biloxi Yacht Club before grounding next to it. Another barge landed on the Holiday Inn, where more than 25 people may have been trying to ride out the hurricane. No one's been able to do a body-recovery there yet.

Because Southern Baptist and other religious conservatives objected to 15 "land-based" gambling in Mississippi, much of Biloxi's wetlands were torn up to make way for these floating casinos.

I talk with Phil Sturgeon, a Harrah's security agent hanging out with 16 some cops from Winter Park, Florida. He's in jeans and a gray shirt with a toothbrush and pen sticking out the pocket. He tells me the storm surge crested at about 35 feet, at least five feet higher than Camille in '69.

In Waveland, I drive over twisted railroad tracks where the eye of Katrina 17 passed into neighborhoods of jagged wooden debris. A middle-aged couple is trying to clear the drive to the lot where their home once stood. A surfboard leans up against one of the live oaks that seem to have fared better then the houses in between them.

"Are you an adjuster," the woman asks.   18
"No, a reporter."   19
"Good, because we don't like adjusters. Nationwide was not on our side."   20
Apparently they've been offered $1,700 on their $422,000 home.   21
    "At least you've got your surfboard," I tell John, her husband, "Oh,   22
that's not my surfboard," he grins, pointing around. "And that's not my boat,
and that's not my Corvette (buried to its hood in the rubble), and that's not
our roof. We think it might belong to the house at the end of the street...."

Starting Again

I'm back in New Orleans on Canal Street, where the Salvation Army   23
offers me cold water, a baloney sandwich (I decline) and a fruit cocktail. It's
been a long day with the Army Corps of Engineers, who've leased helicopters that are dropping 3,000 and 7,000 pound sandbags on the latest breach
in the Industrial Canal which has reflooded the Lower Ninth Ward. I enter
the Sheraton after getting cleared by muscular Blackwater Security guys in
tan and khaki tee shirts and shorts with Glocks on their hips. Another one
sits by the elevators checking room IDs. I wonder if being a professional
mercenary is good training for concierge duty. I sit by the Pelican bar in the
lobby looking out the big three-story glass window at the media RVs and
SUVs on the street—feeling as if I've been in this hotel before in various war
zones and Third World capitals like Managua, Tegucigalpa, and Suva.

The Gulf region is now very much like a war zone, only with fewer   24
deaths (about 1,200 bodies recovered at the time of my visit) and far more
extensive damage. It also offers many of the same ironies and bizarre moments. Unity Radio announces that if you're going to tonight's Louisiana
State University football game in Baton Rouge you can return after curfew
provided you show your game stubs to the deputies at the roadblocks.

Three years ago I made a decision. I'd lost a key person in my life and   25
was trying to decide what to do next. I was considering either going back to
war reporting, as George Bush was clearly planning a pre-emptive invasion
of Iraq, or turning from journalism to ocean advocacy....Finally, I decided
that while we'll probably always have wars, we may not always have living
reefs, wild fish or protective coastal wetlands.

What we know we are going to have are more environmental disasters   26
like the Hurricane Season of '05 linked to fossil-fuel-fired climate change
and bad coastal policies driven by saltwater special interests.

Still, destruction on a biblical scale also offers Noah-like opportunities   27
for restoration after the flood. There are practical solutions to the dangers
we confront, along with models of how to live safely by the sea. Things can
be done right in terms of building wisely along the coasts, and advancing social and environmental equity. But it will take a new wave of citizen activism
to avoid repetition of old mistakes, with even more dire consequences.

Questions for Close Reading

1. What is the selection's thesis? Locate the sentence(s) in which Helvarg states his main idea. If he doesn't state his thesis explicitly, express it in your own words.
2. Helvarg uses headings to divide his essay into sections. What is the subject of the section titled "Urban Floodplain"? How does this section frame the remainder of the essay?
3. Most of the details in Helvarg's essay focus on the destruction caused by the hurricane and the recovery effort. However, he does give a description of an activity that shows life going on as normal. What is it? Why does Helvarg include this description?
4. Some words are so new they are not yet in dictionaries. Helvarg uses such a word when he describes himself as an "eco-geek" in paragraph 14. Given the context, and the meanings of the root *eco* and the word *geek,* how would you define this word?

Questions About the Writer's Craft

1. **The pattern.** How does Helvarg organize his points in this essay? What transitional words and phrases does he use to keep the reader oriented as his essay progresses?
2. Most of the description in this essay focuses on visual details, but Helvarg also describes some other sensations. Find the passages in which Helvarg describes something other than the sights of the post-Katrina landscape, and evaluate their vividness. What do these passages contribute to the essay?
3. In paragraphs 4 and 24, to what does Helvarg compare the post-Katrina Gulf Coast? How does this analogy help the reader envision the destruction? How does it help express the dominant impression of the essay?
4. Helvarg took the photographs that accompany this essay. Compare the photograph of the marked door on page 99 with the author's description of it in paragraph 6. Does this photograph add to the description in the essay, or is the author's description so vivid that the photograph is unnecessary? Now compare the photograph of Bob Chick on page 100 with the author's description of him in paragraph 9. Does this photograph add to the description of Bob in the essay, or is the author's description so vivid that the photograph is unnecessary? If you were writing this essay, would you include the photographs? If so, how would they affect the way you wrote the essay?

Writing Assignments Using Description as a Pattern of Development

1. One reason Helvarg's essay has such an impact is that destruction of the normal Gulf Coast environment was sudden as well as devastating. Not all environmental destruction is so dramatic, however. Find something in your own environment— your home, neighborhood, city, or region—that has been damaged or destroyed by gradual overuse or neglect. For example, your home may have a shabby room, or part of your yard may be overgrown. Or your neighborhood may have a run-down playground or park, or roads full of potholes, or an abandoned building. Select a location that has been neglected or overused, and write an essay in which you describe this damaged environment.

2. Although severe weather, like Hurricane Katrina, provides good subject matter for description, so does more common, less destructive weather. Think of a day on which the weather was important to you but turned out badly. For example, you might have planned an outdoor event and it rained, or you might have scheduled a trip and it snowed, or you might have worn great new clothes and been too hot or too cold. Write an essay in which you describe this uncooperative weather. Use sensory details and figures of speech to convey your feelings about this day.

Writing Assignment Combining Patterns of Development

3. In "The Storm This Time," the environmental devastation was caused by a natural event. However, much destruction of the environment is caused by people rather than by weather or other natural disasters. Select a place you know that has changed for the worse through human use. For example, you might choose an industrial site, a polluted river or lake, or a park. *Compare* and *contrast* the place as it once was and as it is now. Provide vivid *descriptions* of how the place has changed.

Riverbend

The author known by the pseudonym, or fictitious name, Riverbend is an Iraqi woman in her twenties. In 2003, she began writing a blog, *Baghdad Burning,* in which she described her personal experiences of the U.S. invasion and occupation of Iraq. The blog entries have been collected in two books—*Baghdad Burning: Girl Blog from Iraq* (2005) and *Baghdad Burning II: More Girl Blog from Iraq* (2006)— published by The Feminist Press. "Bloggers Without Borders..." is Riverbend's last blog entry, posted on October 22, 2007.

Pre-Reading Journal Entry   MyWritingLab

Can you remember a time you endured a frustrating situation? Maybe you were appealing a ticket in traffic court or waiting to board an airplane. In your journal, jot down what you recall about the scene. What was the setting like? Who else was present? Why was the situation frustrating? How else did you feel in the situation?

Bloggers Without Borders...

Syria is a beautiful country—at least I think it is. I say "I think" because   1
while I perceive it to be beautiful, I sometimes wonder if I mistake safety, security and normalcy for 'beauty.' In so many ways, Damascus is like Baghdad before the war—bustling streets, occasional traffic jams, markets seemingly always full of shoppers[.]...And in so many ways it's different. The buildings are higher, the streets are generally narrower and there's a mountain, Qasiyoun, that looms in the distance.

The mountain distracts me, as it does many Iraqis—especially those   2
from Baghdad. Northern Iraq is full of mountains, but the rest of Iraq is
quite flat. At night, Qasiyoun blends into the black sky and the only indication of its presence is a multitude of little, glimmering spots of light—houses
and restaurants built right up there on the mountain. Every time I take a
picture, I try to work Qasiyoun into it—I try to position the person so that
Qasiyoun is in the background.

The first weeks here were something of a cultural shock. It has taken   3
me these last three months to work away certain habits I'd acquired in Iraq
after the war. It's funny how you learn to act a certain way and don't even
know you're doing strange things—like avoiding people's eyes in the street
or crazily murmuring prayers to yourself when stuck in traffic. It took me at
least three weeks to teach myself to walk properly again—with head lifted,
not constantly looking behind me.

It is estimated that there are at least 1.5 million Iraqis in Syria today.   4
I believe it. Walking down the streets of Damascus, you can hear the Iraqi
accent everywhere. There are areas like Geramana and Qudsiya that are
packed full of Iraqi refugees. Syrians are few and far between in these areas.
Even the public schools in the areas are full of Iraqi children. A cousin of
mine is now attending a school in Qudsiya and his class is composed of 26
Iraqi children, and 5 Syrian children. It's beyond belief sometimes. Most of
the families have nothing to live on beyond their savings which are quickly
being depleted with rent and the costs of living.

Within a month of our being here, we began hearing talk about Syria re-   5
quiring visas from Iraqis, like most other countries. Apparently, our esteemed
puppets in power met with Syrian and Jordanian authorities and decided they
wanted to take away the last two safe havens remaining for Iraqis—Damascus
and Amman. The talk began in late August and was only talk until recently—
early October. Iraqis entering Syria now need a visa from the Syrian consulate
or embassy in the country they are currently in. In the case of Iraqis still in
Iraq, it is said that an approval from the Ministry of Interior is also required
(which kind of makes it difficult for people running away from militias OF
the Ministry of Interior...). Today, there's talk of a possible fifty dollar visa
at the border.

Iraqis who entered Syria before the visa was implemented were getting a   6
one month visitation visa at the border. As soon as that month was over, you
could take your passport and visit the local immigration bureau. If you were
lucky, they would give you an additional month or two. When talk about
visas from the Syrian embassy began, they stopped giving an extension on
the initial border visa. We, as a family, had a brilliant idea. Before the com-
motion of visas began, and before we started needing a renewal, we decided
to go to one of the border crossings, cross into Iraq, and come back into
Syria—everyone was doing it. It would buy us some time—at least 2 months.

We chose a hot day in early September and drove the six hours to   7
Kameshli, a border town in northern Syria. My aunt and her son came with
us—they also needed an extension on their visa. There is a border crossing
in Kameshli called Yaarubiya. It's one of the simpler crossings because the
Iraqi and Syrian borders are only a matter of several meters. You walk out of
Syrian territory and then walk into Iraqi territory—simple and safe.

When we got to the Yaarubiya border patrol, it hit us that thousands   8
of Iraqis had had our brilliant idea simultaneously—the lines to the border
patrol office were endless. Hundreds of Iraqis stood in a long line waiting to
have their passports stamped with an exit visa. We joined the line of people
and waited. And waited. And waited...

It took four hours to leave the Syrian border after which came the lines   9
of the Iraqi border post. Those were even longer. We joined one of the
lines of weary, impatient Iraqis. "It's looking like a gasoline line[.]..." My
younger cousin joked. That was the beginning of another four hours of
waiting under the sun, taking baby steps, moving forward ever so slowly.
The line kept getting longer. At one point, we could see neither the beginning of the line, where passports were being stamped to enter Iraq, nor the
end. Running up and down the line were little boys selling glasses of water,
chewing gum and cigarettes. My aunt caught one of them by the arm as he
zipped past us, "How many people are in front of us?" He whistled and took
a few steps back to assess the situation, "A hundred! A thousand!" He was
almost gleeful as he ran off to make business.

I had such mixed feelings standing in that line. I was caught between a   10
feeling of yearning, a certain homesickness that sometimes catches me at the
oddest moments, and a heavy feeling of dread. What if they didn't agree to
let us out again? It wasn't really possible, but what if it happened? What if
this was the last time I'd see the Iraqi border? What if we were no longer allowed to enter Iraq for some reason? What if we were never allowed to leave?

We spent the four hours standing, crouching, sitting and leaning in the   11
line. The sun beat down on everyone equally—Sunnis, Shia and Kurds alike.
E. tried to convince the aunt to faint so it would speed the process up for
the family, but she just gave us a withering look and stood straighter. People
just stood there, chatting, cursing or silent. It was yet another gathering of
Iraqis—the perfect opportunity to swap sad stories and ask about distant relations or acquaintances.

We met two families we knew while waiting for our turn. We greeted   12
each other like long lost friends and exchanged phone numbers and addresses in Damascus, promising to visit. I noticed the 23-year-old son, K.,
from one of the families was missing. I beat down my curiosity and refused
to ask where he was. The mother was looking older than I remembered
and the father looked constantly lost in thought, or maybe it was grief.
I didn't want to know if K. was dead or alive. I'd just have to believe he

was alive and thriving somewhere, not worrying about borders or visas. Ignorance really is bliss sometimes...

Back at the Syrian border, we waited in a large group, tired and hungry, 13 having handed over our passports for a stamp. The Syrian immigration man sifting through dozens of passports called out names and looked at faces as he handed over the passports patiently, "Stand back please—stand back." There was a general cry towards the back of the crowded hall where we were standing as someone collapsed—as they lifted him I recognized an old man who was there with his family being chaperoned by his sons, leaning on a walking stick.

By the time we had reentered the Syrian border and were headed back to 14 the cab ready to take us into Kameshli, I had resigned myself to the fact that we were refugees. I read about refugees on the Internet daily...in the newspapers...hear about them on TV. I hear about the estimated 1.5 million plus Iraqi refugees in Syria and shake my head, never really considering myself or my family as one of them. After all, refugees are people who sleep in tents and have no potable water or plumbing, right? Refugees carry their belongings in bags instead of suitcases and they don't have cell phones or Internet access, right? Grasping my passport in my hand like my life depended on it, with two extra months in Syria stamped inside, it hit me how wrong I was. We were all refugees. I was suddenly a number. No matter how wealthy or educated or comfortable, a refugee is a refugee. A refugee is someone who isn't really welcome in any country—including their own...especially their own.

We live in an apartment building where two other Iraqis are renting. The 15 people in the floor above us are a Christian family from northern Iraq who got chased out of their village by Peshmerga and the family on our floor is a Kurdish family who lost their home in Baghdad to militias and were waiting for immigration to Sweden or Switzerland or some such European refugee haven.

The first evening we arrived, exhausted, dragging suitcases behind us, 16 morale a little bit bruised, the Kurdish family sent over their representative— a 9 year old boy missing two front teeth, holding a lopsided cake, "We're Abu Mohammed's house—across from you—mama says if you need anything, just ask—this is our number. Abu Dalia's family live upstairs, this is their number. We're all Iraqi too...Welcome to the building."

I cried that night because for the first time in a long time, so far away 17 from home, I felt the unity that had been stolen from us in 2003.

Questions for Close Reading

MyWritingLab

1. What is the selection's thesis (or dominant impression)? Locate the sentence(s) in which Riverbend states her main idea. If she doesn't state her thesis explicitly, express it in your own words.
2. At the start of the reading, the author compares Damascus, the capital of Syria, with her native Baghdad. How do the cities seem the same? How do they seem different? Why do you think the author is "distracted" by the mountain Qasiyoun?

3. The author uses two numerical examples. What are they? What are the sources for these examples? How do the examples contribute to the dominant impression of the reading?
4. For much of the selection, the author describes the scene as she and her family cross the border into Iraq and then immediately cross back into Syria. Why have they decided to take these actions? What realization does the author have as a result?

Questions About the Writer's Craft

1. **The pattern.** How does the author use description in the selection? What phrases convey the physical discomfort of the border-crossing experience? Why does the author spend so much of the selection describing the experience?
2. At times, the selection expresses an ironic or humorously sardonic tone. Which specific sentences does the author use to achieve this tone? What is the effect of the selection's tone for the reader?
3. **Other patterns.** The author *compares* Damascus to Baghdad at the start of the reading and then *narrates* the story of the border crossing. In addition, the author gives at least four personal *anecdotes* from the border crossing and afterward. What are these anecdotes, and what do they illustrate for the reader?
4. What is the significance of the selection's title, "Blogging Without Borders…"? Is the title effective?

Writing Assignments Using Description as a Pattern of Development

1. The author uses the phrase "Ignorance is bliss" to underscore that she would rather continue imagining a young family friend as "alive and thriving somewhere" than risk finding out for sure that he was dead or missing. Like the author, we may suddenly find ourselves reminded of the possibility of death. For example, we may hear about a friend's serious accident or illness. Write an essay in which you describe your thoughts and feelings in response to such a reminder. Did you feel sad, afraid, angry, vulnerable, or lucky? How were you affected by the experience?
2. Riverbend describes the "culture shock" she experiences in Damascus. Have you ever spent time in a place that is very different from your home? For example, if you live in the city, have you ever spent a summer on a farm? Or if you live in a warm region, have you spent a winter holiday in a cold climate? In an essay, describe your experience in that strange place. Use colorful details to tell readers about the environment, food, customs, and other aspects of the place and its inhabitants.

Writing Assignment Combining Patterns of Development

3. The author implies that Syria imposed new visa requirements in an attempt to control the number of Iraqi refugees. With Syria now in civil turmoil, the refugee problem across the Middle East has become acute. Do some research into conditions for Middle Eastern refugees and their host countries—primarily Jordan, Egypt, Turkey, and the United States. In an essay, *argue* for or against the policies of one host country, using your researched evidence to support your view.

Judith Ortiz Cofer

Born in Puerto Rico, raised both on her native island and in the United States, and educated in sites that included Oxford University in England, Judith Ortiz Cofer (1952–) knows what it is to move between cultures, absorbing from each while keeping mindful of her own heritage. Cofer earned a master's degree in English from the University of Florida before spending a year in graduate study at Oxford. Following a stint as a bilingual teacher, Cofer taught English at several colleges and universities and currently teaches Creative Writing at the University of Georgia. She has published collections of poetry, including *Peregrine* (1986), *Terms of Survival* (1995), *Reaching for the Mainland and Selected New Poems* (1995), and *A Love Story Beginning in Spanish* (2005); novels, *The Line of the Sun* (1989), *The Meaning of Consuelo* (2003), and *Call Me Maria* (2004); and four books of essays, *Silent Dancing: A Partial Remembrance of a Puerto Rican Childhood* (1990), *The Latin Deli: Telling the Lives of Barrio Women* (1993), *An Island Like You: Stories of the Barrio* (1995), and *Woman in Front of the Sun* (2000). The following essay is taken from *Silent Dancing*.

Pre-Reading Journal Entry

MyWritingLab

Everyone loves a good story. But stories do more than merely entertain us. Use your journal to reflect on two or more stories that adults told you in your childhood as a way to teach an important lesson about life. In addition to sketching out the stories themselves, outline the circumstances of hearing the stories: who told them, where you were when you heard the stories, why the stories were recounted.

A Partial Remembrance of a Puerto Rican Childhood

At three or four o'clock in the afternoon, the hour of *café con leche*,[1] the   1
women of my family gathered in Mamá's living room to speak of important things and retell familiar stories meant to be overheard by us young girls, their daughters. In Mamá's house (everyone called my grandmother Mamá) was a large parlor built by my grandfather to his wife's exact specifications so that it was always cool, facing away from the sun. The doorway was on the side of the house so no one could walk directly into her living room. First they had to take a little stroll through and around her beautiful garden where prize-winning orchids grew in the trunk of an ancient tree she had hollowed out for that purpose. This room was furnished with several mahogany rocking chairs, acquired at the births of her children, and one intricately carved rocker that had passed down to Mamá at the death of her own mother.

[1]Spanish for "coffee with milk" (editors' note).

It was on these rockers that my mother, her sisters, and my grandmother   2
sat on these afternoons of my childhood to tell their stories, teaching each
other, and my cousin and me, what it was like to be a woman, more specifically, a Puerto Rican woman. They talked about life on the island, and life in
Los Nueva Yores, their way of referring to the United States from New York
City to California: the other place, not home, all the same. They told real-life
stories though, as I later learned, always embellishing them with a little or a
lot of dramatic detail. And they told *cuentos,* the morality and cautionary tales
told by the women in our family for generations: stories that became a part of
my subconscious as I grew up in two worlds, the tropical island and the cold
city, and that would later surface in my dreams and in my poetry.

One of these tales was about the woman who was left at the altar. Mamá   3
liked to tell that one with histrionic intensity. I remember the rise and fall
of her voice, the sighs, and her constantly gesturing hands, like two birds
swooping through her words. This particular story usually would come up
in a conversation as a result of someone mentioning a forthcoming engagement or wedding. The first time I remember hearing it, I was sitting on the
floor at Mamá's feet, pretending to read a comic book. I may have been
eleven or twelve years old, at that difficult age when a girl was no longer a
child who could be ordered to leave the room if the women wanted freedom
to take their talk into forbidden zones, nor really old enough to be considered a part of their conclave. I could only sit quietly, pretending to be in
another world, while absorbing it all in a sort of unspoken agreement of my
status as silent auditor. On this day, Mamá had taken my long, tangled mane
of hair into her ever-busy hands. Without looking down at me and with no
interruption of her flow of words, she began braiding my hair, working at it
with the quickness and determination that characterized all her actions. My
mother was watching us impassively from her rocker across the room. On
her lips played a little ironic smile. I would never sit still for *her* ministrations,
but even then, I instinctively knew that she did not possess Mamá's matriar-
chal power to command and keep everyone's attention. This was never more
evident than in the spell she cast when telling a story.

"It is not like it used to be when I was a girl," Mamá announced. "Then,   4
a man could leave a girl standing at the church altar with a bouquet of fresh
flowers in her hands and disappear off the face of the earth. No way to track
him down if he was from another town. He could be a married man, with
maybe even two or three families all over the island. There was no way to
know. And there were men who did this. *Hombres*[2] with the devil in their flesh
who would come to a *pueblo,*[3] like this one, take a job at one of the *haciendas,*[4]
never meaning to stay, only to have a good time and to seduce the women."

[2]Spanish for "men" (editors' note).
[3]Spanish for "community" (editors' note).
[4]Spanish for "large estate" or "ranch" (editors' note).

The whole time she was speaking, Mamá would be weaving my hair into   5
a flat plait that required pulling apart the two sections of hair with little jerks
that made my eyes water; but knowing how grandmother detested whining
and *boba* (sissy) tears, as she called them, I just sat up as straight and stiff as
I did at La Escuela San Jose, where the nuns enforced good posture with a
flexible plastic ruler they bounced off of slumped shoulders and heads. As
Mamá's story progressed, I noticed how my young Aunt Laura lowered her
eyes, refusing to meet Mamá's meaningful gaze. Laura was seventeen, in her
last year of high school, and already engaged to a boy from another town
who had staked his claim with a tiny diamond ring, then left for Los Nueva
Yores to make his fortune. They were planning to get married in a year.
Mamá had expressed serious doubts that the wedding would ever take place.
In Mamá's eyes, a man set free without a legal contract was a man lost. She
believed that marriage was not something men desired, but simply the price
they had to pay for the privilege of children and, of course, for what no decent (synonymous with "smart") woman would give away for free.

"María La Loca was only seventeen when *it* happened to her." I lis-   6
tened closely at the mention of this name. María was a town character, a
fat middle-aged woman who lived with her old mother on the outskirts of
town. She was to be seen around the pueblo delivering the meat pies the two
women made for a living. The most peculiar thing about María, in my eyes,
was that she walked and moved like a little girl though she had the thick
body and wrinkled face of an old woman. She would swing her hips in an exaggerated, clownish way, and sometimes even hop and skip up to someone's
house. She spoke to no one. Even if you asked her a question, she would just
look at you and smile, showing her yellow teeth. But I had heard that if you
got close enough, you could hear her humming a tune without words. The
kids yelled out nasty things at her, calling her *La Loca*,[5] and the men who
hung out at the *bodega*[6] playing dominoes sometimes whistled mockingly as
she passed by with her funny, outlandish walk. But María seemed impervious
to it all, carrying her basket of *pasteles*[7] like a grotesque Little Red Riding
Hood through the forest.

María La Loca interested me, as did all the eccentrics and crazies of our   7
pueblo. Their weirdness was a measuring stick I used in my serious quest
for a definition of normal. As a Navy brat shuttling between New Jersey and
the pueblo, I was constantly made to feel like an oddball by my peers, who
made fun of my two-way accent: a Spanish accent when I spoke English, and
when I spoke Spanish I was told that I sounded like a *Gringa*.[8] Being the
outsider had already turned my brother and me into cultural chameleons.

[5]Spanish for "crazy one" (editors' note).
[6]Spanish for a neighborhood grocery store (editors' note).
[7]Spanish for "pastries" (editors' note).
[8]A negatively charged Latin American slang expression for a female foreigner (editors' note).

We developed early on the ability to blend into a crowd, to sit and read quietly in a fifth story apartment building for days and days when it was too bitterly cold to play outside, or, set free, to run wild in Mamá's realm, where she took charge of our lives, releasing Mother for a while from the intense fear for our safety that our father's absences instilled in her. In order to keep us from harm when Father was away, Mother kept us under strict surveillance. She even walked us to and from Public School No. 11, which we attended during the months we lived in Paterson, New Jersey, our home base in the States. Mamá freed all three of us like pigeons from a cage. I saw her as my liberator and my model. Her stories were parables from which to glean the *Truth*.

"María La Loca was once a beautiful girl. Everyone thought she would   8 marry the Méndez boy." As everyone knew, Rogelio Méndez was the richest man in town. "But," Mamá continued, knitting my hair with the same intensity she was putting into her story, "this *macho* made a fool out of her and ruined her life." She paused for the effect of her use of the word "macho," which at that time had not yet become a popular epithet for an unliberated man. This word had for us the crude and comical connotation of "male of the species," stud; a *macho* was what you put in a pen to increase your stock.

I peeked over my comic book at my mother. She too was under Mamá's   9 spell, smiling conspiratorially at this little swipe at men. She was safe from Mamá's contempt in this area. Married at an early age, an unspotted lamb, she had been accepted by a good family of strict Spaniards whose name was old and respected, though their fortune had been lost long before my birth. In a rocker Papá had painted sky blue sat Mamá's oldest child, Aunt Nena. Mother of three children, stepmother of two more, she was a quiet woman who liked books but had married an ignorant and abusive widower whose main interest in life was accumulating wealth. He too was in the mainland working on his dream of returning home rich and triumphant to buy the *finca*[9] of his dreams. She was waiting for him to send for her. She would leave her children with Mamá for several years while the two of them slaved away in factories. He would one day be a rich man, and she a sadder woman. Even now her life-light was dimming. She spoke little, an aberration in Mamá's house, and she read avidly, as if storing up spiritual food for the long winters that awaited her in Los Nueva Yores without her family. But even Aunt Nena came alive to Mamá's words, rocking gently, her hands over a thick book in her lap.

Her daughter, my cousin Sara, played jacks by herself on the tile porch   10 outside the room where we sat. She was a year older than I. We shared a bed and all our family's secrets. Collaborators in search of answers, Sara

[9]Spanish for "farm" or "ranch" (editors' note).

and I discussed everything we heard the women say, trying to fit it all together like a puzzle that, once assembled, would reveal life's mysteries to us. Though she and I still enjoyed taking part in boys' games—chase, volleyball, and even *vaqueros,* the island version of cowboys and Indians involving cap-gun battles and violent shoot-outs under the mango tree in Mamá's backyard—we loved best the quiet hours in the afternoon when the men were still at work, and the boys had gone to play serious baseball at the park. Then Mamá's house belonged only to us women. The aroma of coffee perking in the kitchen, the mesmerizing creaks and groans of the rockers, and the women telling their lives in *cuentos* are forever woven into the fabric of my imagination, braided like my hair that day I felt my grandmother's hands teaching me about strength, her voice convincing me of the power of storytelling.

That day Mamá told how the beautiful María had fallen prey to a man   11
whose name was never the same in subsequent versions of the story; it was Juan one time, José, Rafael, Diego, another. We understood that neither the name or any of the *facts* were important, only that a woman had allowed love to defeat her. Mamá put each of us in María's place by describing her wedding dress in loving detail: how she looked like a princess in her lace as she waited at the altar. Then, as Mamá approached the tragic denouement of her story, I was distracted by the sound of my Aunt Laura's violent rocking. She seemed on the verge of tears. She knew the fable was intended for her. That week she was going to have her wedding gown fitted, though no firm date had been set for the marriage. Mamá ignored Laura's obvious discomfort, digging out a ribbon from the sewing basket she kept by her rocker while describing María's long illness, "a fever that would not break for days." She spoke of a mother's despair: "that woman climbed the church steps on her knees every morning, wore only black as a *promesa* to the Holy Virgin in exchange for her daughter's health." By the time María returned from her honeymoon with death, she was ravished, no longer young or sane. "As you can see, she is almost as old as her mother already," Mamá lamented while tying the ribbon to the ends of my hair, pulling it back with such force that I just knew I would never be able to close my eyes completely again.

"That María's getting crazier every day." Mamá's voice would take a   12
lighter tone now, expressing satisfaction, either for the perfection of my braid, or for a story well told—it was hard to tell. "You know that tune María is always humming?" Carried away by her enthusiasm, I tried to nod, but Mamá still had me pinned between her knees.

"Well, that's the wedding march." Surprising us all, Mamá sang out,   13
"Da, da, dara...da, da, dara." Then lifting me off the floor by my skinny shoulders, she would lead me around the room in an impromptu waltz—another session ending with the laughter of women, all of us caught up in the infectious joke of our lives.

Questions for Close Reading

MyWritingLab

1. What is the selection's thesis (or dominant impression)? Locate the sentence(s) in which Cofer states her main idea. If she doesn't state the thesis explicitly, express it in your own words.
2. Who are the women who participate in the storytelling sessions? Why is Cofer allowed to join them? Why aren't men or boys part of the group?
3. What lessons about men and women does Mamá intend the story of María La Loca to teach?
4. What information does Cofer provide about her aunts and her mother? What similarities and/or differences are there between each of their lives and the story of María La Loca?

Questions About the Writer's Craft

1. **The pattern.** Of all the women mentioned in the essay, only María La Loca is described in detail. What descriptive details does Cofer offer about her? Why do you suppose Cofer provides so much description about this particular woman?
2. In paragraph 7, Cofer provides some specifics about her childhood as a "Navy brat." What would have been lost if Cofer hadn't included this material?
3. **Other patterns.** Reread paragraphs 4, 6, 8, and 11–13, where Cofer *recounts* her grandmother's story. Why do you think Cofer doesn't tell the story straight through, without interruptions? What purpose do the interruptions serve? How does Cofer signal when she is moving away from the story or back to it?
4. Why might Cofer have mentioned in several spots the braiding of her hair, which goes on the whole time Mamá tells María's story? What similarities are there between the braiding and the storytelling session? What similarities are there between the braiding and Cofer's descriptive style (consider especially the last sentence of paragraph 10)?

Writing Assignments Using Description as a Pattern of Development

1. Cofer paints a vivid picture of a childhood ritual: the telling of stories among the women in her family. Think of a specific scene, event, or ritual from your own childhood or youth that has special meaning for you. Then write a descriptive essay conveying the distinctive flavor of that occasion. Draw on vivid sensory language to capture your dominant impression of that time. Consider using dialogue, as Cofer does, to add texture to your description and reveal character.
2. To Cofer, Mamá was a "liberator" and a "model." Think of a person in your life who served as a role model or opened doors for you, and write an essay describing that person. Like Cofer, place the person in a characteristic setting and supply vigorous details about the person's actions, speech, looks, and so forth. Make sure that all the descriptive details reinforce your dominant impression of the individual.

Writing Assignment Combining Patterns of Development

3. The stories Cofer heard taught her "what it was like to be a woman." What information and experiences shaped your understanding of your gender? Write an essay showing how your perception of your gender identity was *influenced* by what you heard, witnessed, and experienced as a child. Along the way, you might briefly *narrate* one or more of these gender-shaping interactions.

Cherokee Paul McDonald

Cherokee Paul McDonald (1949–) is a fiction writer and journalist, a military veteran, and a former ten-year member of the Fort Lauderdale (Florida) Police Force. His publications include *Into the Green* (2001), in which he draws on his experiences as an Army lieutenant, and *Blue Truth* (1992), a graphic memoir of his day-to-day life as a police officer. He is also a fisherman and the father of three children. "A View from the Bridge" was first published February 12, 1989, in the Florida *Sun Sentinel*.

Pre-Reading Journal Entry   MyWritingLab

Think of a time when you did something to help someone—perhaps a friend, a family member, a classmate, or a stranger—and later realized that your actions had benefitted you just as much as, or perhaps even more than, they had helped the other person.

A View from the Bridge

I was coming up on the little bridge in the Rio Vista neighborhood of 1 Fort Lauderdale, deepening my stride and my breathing to negotiate the slight incline without altering my pace. And then, as I neared the crest, I saw the kid.

He was a lumpy little guy with baggy shorts, a faded T-shirt, and heavy 2 sweat socks falling down over old sneakers.

Partially covering his shaggy blond hair was one of those blue baseball 3 caps with gold braid on the bill and a sailfish patch sewn onto the peak. Covering his eyes and part of his face was a pair of those stupid-looking '50s-style wrap-around sunglasses.

He was fumbling with a beat-up rod and reel, and he had a little bait 4 bucket by his feet. I puffed on by, glancing down into the empty bucket as I passed.

"Hey, mister! Would you help me, please?" 5

The shrill voice penetrated my jogger's concentration, and I was deter- 6 mined to ignore it. But for some reason, I stopped.

With my hands on my hips and the sweat dripping from my nose I 7 asked, "What do you want, kid?"

"Would you please help me find my shrimp? It's my last one and I've 8 been getting bites and I know I can catch a fish if I can just find that shrimp. He jumped outta my hand as I was getting him from the bucket."

Exasperated, I walked slowly back to the kid, and pointed. 9

"There's the damn shrimp by your left foot. You stopped me for *that*?" 10

As I said it, the kid reached down and trapped the shrimp. 11

"Thanks a lot, mister," he said.   12

I watched as the kid dropped the baited hook down into the canal. Then   13
I turned to start back down the bridge.

That's when the kid let out a "Hey! Hey!" and the prettiest tarpon I'd   14
ever seen came almost six feet out of the water, twisting and turning as he
fell through the air.

"I got one!" the kid yelled as the fish hit the water with a loud splash   15
and took off down the canal.

I watched the line being burned off the reel at an alarming rate. The   16
kid's left hand held the crank while the extended fingers felt for the drag
setting.

"No, kid!" I shouted. "Leave the drag alone...just keep that damn rod   17
tip up!"

Then I glanced at the reel and saw there were just a few loops of line left   18
on the spool.

"Why don't you get yourself some decent equipment?" I said, but be-   19
fore the kid could answer I saw the line go slack.

"Ohhh, I lost him," the kid said. I saw the flash of silver as the fish   20
turned.

"Crank, kid, crank! You didn't lose him. He's coming back toward you.   21
Bring in the slack!"

The kid cranked like mad, and a beautiful grin spread across his face.   22

"He's heading in for the pilings," I said. "Keep him out of those   23
pilings!"

The kid played it perfectly. When the fish made its play for the pilings,   24
he kept just enough pressure on to force the fish out. When the water exploded and the silver missile hurled into the air, the kid kept the rod tip up
and the line tight.

As the fish came to the surface and began a slow circle in the middle of   25
the canal, I said, "Whooee, is that a nice fish or what?"

The kid didn't say anything, so I said, "Okay, move to the edge of the   26
bridge and I'll climb down to the seawall and pull him out."

When I reached the seawall I pulled in the leader, leaving the fish lying   27
on its side in the water.

"How's that?" I said.   28

"Hey, mister, tell me what it looks like."   29

"Look down here and check him out," I said, "He's beautiful."   30

But then I looked up into those stupid-looking sunglasses and it hit me.   31
The kid was blind.

"Could you tell me what he looks like, mister?" he said again.   32

"Well, he's just under three, uh, he's about as long as one of your arms,"   33
I said. "I'd guess he goes about 15, 20 pounds. He's mostly silver, but the

silver is somehow made up of *all* the colors, if you know what I mean."
I stopped. "Do you know what I mean by colors?"

The kid nodded.   34

"Okay. He has all these big scales, like armor all over his body. They're   35
silver too, and when he moves they sparkle. He has a strong body and a large
powerful tail. He has big round eyes, bigger than a quarter, and a lower jaw
that sticks out past the upper one and is very tough. His belly is almost white
and his back is a gunmetal gray. When he jumped he came out of the water
about six feet, and his scales caught the sun and flashed it all over the place."

By now the fish had righted itself, and I could see the bright-red gills as   36
the gill plates opened and closed. I explained this to the kid, and then said,
more to myself, "He's a beauty."

"Can you get him off the hook?" the kid asked. "I don't want to kill   37
him."

I watched as the tarpon began to slowly swim away, tired but still alive.   38

By the time I got back up to the top of the bridge the kid had his line   39
secured and his bait bucket in one hand.

He grinned and said, "Just in time. My mom drops me off here, and   40
she'll be back to pick me up any minute."

He used the back of one hand to wipe his nose.   41

"Thanks for helping me catch that tarpon," he said, "and for helping me   42
to see it."

I looked at him, shook my head, and said, "No, my friend, thank you   43
for letting *me* see that fish."

I took off, but before I got far the kid yelled again.   44

"Hey, mister!"   45

I stopped.   46

"Someday I'm gonna catch a sailfish and a blue marlin and a giant tuna   47
and all those big sportfish!"

As I looked into those sunglasses I knew he probably would. I wished I   48
could be there when it happened.

Questions for Close Reading [MyWritingLab]

1. What is the selection's thesis (or dominant impression)? Locate the sentence(s) in which McDonald states his main idea. If he doesn't state the thesis explicitly, express it in your own words.
2. Why is McDonald initially determined to ignore the boy's request for help? Why does he hesitate to stop for the boy?
3. What details are provided to let the reader know that the boy is blind, and at what point does McDonald finally come to this realization?
4. Why do you think McDonald titled this "A View from the Bridge," and how does the view change—both literally and figuratively— as the essay progresses?

Questions About the Writer's Craft

1. **The pattern.** Choose a passage that you consider to be especially rich in detail and description, and make a list of the descriptors McDonald uses in the passage to draw a picture in words of the image. Then using those descriptors, take a few minutes to sketch out the image as you see it in your mind.
2. How does McDonald organize his essay? What transitional words and phrases does he use to keep the reader oriented as his essay progresses?
3. **Other patterns.** Because McDonald's descriptive essay has a strong *narrative* component, there is extensive dialogue in the selection. How does the use of dialogue enrich the essay? In what ways might the essay be less effective if the reader could not "hear" what McDonald and the boy said to each other?
4. Most of the description in this essay focuses on visual details, but McDonald also describes some other sensations. Find the passages in which McDonald presents other details that help the reader have a clearer understanding of the changing dynamic between the two characters as the essay moves along.

Writing Assignments Using Description as a Pattern of Development

1. In his essay, McDonald uses description to allow his readers to "see" the jogger-narrator (McDonald), the boy, the fish they caught, the view from the bridge, and more. Think of a scene that you came upon suddenly—a vista you encountered hiking, a street musician playing for spare change, a solitary animal at the zoo. Use vivid language to describe the scene and its impact on you.
2. Although stories of incidents in our lives provide rich contexts for description, so do a host of other subjects. Write an essay in which you describe a place that is meaningful to you—perhaps the house where you grew up, the home of a friend or relative, the elementary school you attended, or a place where you and your friends spend time together. Be sure to convey a dominant impression: Did you feel safe in this place? comfortable? on edge? invisible? Select descriptive terms that enhance your feelings.

Writing Assignment Combining Patterns of Development

3. McDonald's essay describes the process of catching a fish. Write an essay in which you guide the reader through a familiar *process*, for example, baking cookies, planting flowers, or uploading a video to a social media site such as *YouTube*. *Describe* how each stage of the process would look, sound, smell, feel, or taste. You might want to research images online to *illustrate* your essay. If so, write a descriptive caption for each image.

Additional Writing Topics

DESCRIPTION

MyWritingLab

General Assignments

Using description, develop one of these topics into an essay.

1. A favorite item of clothing
2. A school as a young child might see it
3. A coffee shop, bus shelter, newsstand, or some other small place
4. A parade or victory celebration
5. One drawer in a desk or bureau
6. A TV, film, or music celebrity
7. The inside of something, such as a cave, boat, car, shed, or machine
8. A friend, roommate, or other person you know well
9. An essential or a useless gadget
10. A once-in-a-lifetime event

Assignments Using Visuals

Use the suggested visuals to help develop a descriptive essay on one of these topics:

1. Your best friend and the role that person has played in your life (photos)
2. Effective Super Bowl advertisements (links to ads on *YouTube*)
3. The best (or worst) gift you have received (photo or web link)
4. Your vision of an ideal house (sketches or photos)
5. A place you love to visit and why (photos and/or web links)

Assignments with a Specific Purpose, Audience, and Point of View

1. **Academic life.** For an audience of incoming first-year students, prepare a speech describing registration day at your college. Use specific details to help prepare students for the actual event. Choose an adjective that represents your dominant impression of the experience, and keep that word in mind as you write.
2. **Academic life.** Your college has decided to replace an old campus structure (for example, a dorm or dining hall) with a new version. Write a letter of protest to the administration, describing the place so vividly and appealingly that its value and need for preservation are unquestionable.
3. **Academic life.** As a staff member of the campus newspaper, you have been asked to write a weekly column of social news and gossip. For your first column, you plan to describe a recent campus event—a dance, party, concert, or other social activity. With a straightforward or tongue-in-cheek tone, describe where the event was held, the appearance of the people who attended, and so on.

4. **Civic activity.** As a subscriber to a community-wide dating service, you've been asked to submit a description of the kind of person you'd like to meet. Describe your ideal date. Focus on specifics about physical appearance, personal habits, character traits, and interests.

5. **Civic activity.** As a resident of a particular town, you're angered by the appearance of a certain spot and by the activities that take place there. Write a letter to the town council, describing in detail the undesirable nature of this place (an adult bookstore, a bar, a bus station, a neglected park or beach). End with some suggestions about ways to improve the situation.

6. **Workplace action.** You've noticed a recurring problem in your workplace and want to bring it to the attention of your boss, who typically is inattentive. Write a letter to your boss describing the problem. Your goal is not to provide solutions, but rather, to provide a vivid description—complete with sensory details—so that your boss can no longer deny the problem.

MyWritingLab Visit Chapter 3, "Description," in MyWritingLab to complete the chapter activities, Pre-Reading Journal Entry activities, Questions for Close Reading, and Additional Writing Topics assignments and to test your understanding of the chapter objectives.

NARRATION

In this chapter, you will learn:

4.1 To use the pattern of narration to develop your essays.

4.2 To consider how narration can fit your purpose and audience.

4.3 To develop strategies for using narration in an essay.

4.4 To develop strategies for revising a narration essay.

4.5 To analyze how narration is used effectively in student-written and professionally authored selections.

4.6 To write your own essays using narration as a strategy.

WHAT IS NARRATION?

Human beings are instinctively storytellers. In prehistoric times, our ancestors huddled around campfires to hear tales of hunting and magic. In ancient times, warriors gathered in halls to listen to bards praise in song the exploits of epic heroes. Things are no different today. Boisterous children invariably settle down to listen when their parents read to them; millions of people tune in day after day to the ongoing drama of their favorite soap operas; vacationers sit motionless on the beach, caught up in the latest best-sellers; and all of us enjoy saying, "Just listen to what happened to me today." Our hunger for storytelling is a basic part of us.

Narration means telling a single story or several related stories. The story can be a way to support a main idea or thesis. For instance, to demonstrate that many individuals are becoming too dependent on technology, you might narrate a story about a friend who loved to stay connected to her friends via social networking sites and thought she would go crazy when she spent several days in a remote area where there was no Internet service.

Narration is powerful. Every public speaker—from politician to classroom teacher—knows that stories capture the attention of listeners as nothing else can. Narration speaks to us strongly because it is about us; we want to know what happened to others, not simply because we're curious, but because their experiences shed light on the nature of our own lives. Narration lends force to opinions, triggers the flow of memory, and evokes places and times in ways that are compelling and affecting.

HOW NARRATION FITS YOUR PURPOSE AND AUDIENCE

Narration can appear in essays as a supplemental pattern of development. For example, if your purpose in a paper is to *persuade* apathetic readers that airport security regulations must be followed strictly, you might lead off with a brief account of a friend who inadvertently tried to board a plane with a pocket knife in his backpack. In a paper *defining* good teaching, you might keep readers engaged by including satirical anecdotes about one hapless instructor, the antithesis of an effective teacher. An essay on the *effects* of an overburdened judicial system might provide a dramatic account of the way one clearly guilty murderer plea-bargained his way to freedom.

Narration can also serve as an essay's dominant pattern of development. You might choose to narrate the events of a day spent with your three-year-old nephew as a way of revealing how you rediscovered the importance of family life. Or you might relate the story of your roommate's mugging, evoking the powerlessness and terror of being a victim. Any story can form the basis for a narrative essay as long as you convey the essence of the experience and evoke its meaning.

STRATEGIES FOR USING NARRATION IN AN ESSAY

The suggestions here and in Figure 4.1 on page 123 will be helpful whether you use narration as a dominant or a supportive pattern of development.

1. Identify the conflict in the event.

The power of many narratives is rooted in a special kind of tension that "hooks" readers and makes them want to follow the story to its end. This narrative tension is often a by-product of some form of *conflict* within the story. Many narratives revolve around an internal conflict experienced by a key person in the story. Or the conflict may be between people in the story or between a pivotal character and some social institution or natural phenomenon.

FIGURE 4.1
Development Diagram: Writing a Narration Essay

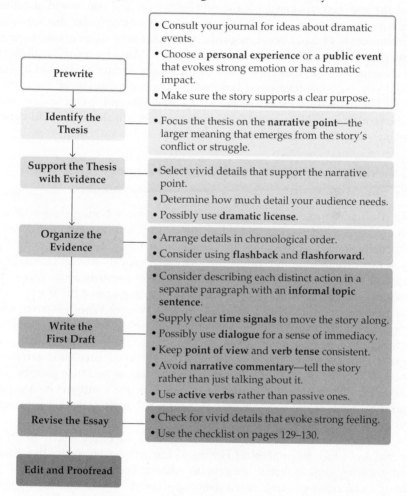

Prewrite	• Consult your journal for ideas about dramatic events. • Choose a **personal experience** or a **public event** that evokes strong emotion or has dramatic impact. • Make sure the story supports a clear purpose.
Identify the Thesis	• Focus the thesis on the **narrative point**—the larger meaning that emerges from the story's conflict or struggle.
Support the Thesis with Evidence	• Select vivid details that support the narrative point. • Determine how much detail your audience needs. • Possibly use **dramatic license**.
Organize the Evidence	• Arrange details in chronological order. • Consider using **flashback** and **flashforward**.
Write the First Draft	• Consider describing each distinct action in a separate paragraph with an **informal topic sentence**. • Supply clear **time signals** to move the story along. • Possibly use **dialogue** for a sense of immediacy. • Keep **point of view** and **verb tense** consistent. • Avoid **narrative commentary**—tell the story rather than just talking about it. • Use **active verbs** rather than passive ones.
Revise the Essay	• Check for vivid details that evoke strong feeling. • Use the checklist on pages 129–130.
Edit and Proofread	

2. Identify the point of the narrative.

In *The Adventures of Huckleberry Finn,* Mark Twain warned: "Persons attempting to find a motive in this narrative will be prosecuted; persons attempting to find a moral in it will be banished; persons attempting to find a plot in it will be shot." Twain was, of course, being ironic; his novel's richness lies in its "motives" and "morals." Similarly, when you recount a narrative, it's your responsibility to convey the event's *significance* or *meaning.* In other words, be sure readers are clear about your *narrative point,* or thesis.

Suppose you decide to write about the time you got locked in a mall late at night. Your narrative might focus on the way the mall looked after hours and the way you struggled with mounting terror. But you would also use the narrative to make a point. Perhaps you want to emphasize that fear can be instructive. Or your point might be that malls have a disturbing, surreal underside. You could state this thesis explicitly. ("After hours, the mall shed its cheerful daytime demeanor and took on a more sinister quality.") Or you could rely on your details and language to convey the point of the narrative: "The mannequins stared at me with glazed eyes and frozen smiles" and "The steel grates pulled over each store's entrance glinted in the cold light, making each shop look like a prison cell."

3. Develop only those details that advance the narrative point.

You know from experience that nothing is more boring than a storyteller who gets sidetracked and drags out a story with nonessential details. If a friend started to tell about the time his car broke down in the middle of an expressway—but interrupted his story to complain at length about the slipshod work done by his auto repair shop—you might become annoyed, wishing your friend would get back to the interesting part of the story.

Brainstorming ("What happened? When? Where? Who was involved? Why did it happen?") can be valuable for helping you amass narrative details. Then, after generating the specifics, you cull the nonessential and devote your energies to the key specifics needed to advance your narrative point. When telling a story, you maintain an effective narrative pace by focusing on that point and eliminating details that don't support it. A good narrative depends not only on what is included, but also on what has been left out.

But how do you determine which specifics to omit, which to treat briefly, and which to emphasize? Having a clear sense of your narrative point and knowing your audience are crucial. Assume you're writing a narrative about a disastrous get-acquainted dance sponsored by your college the first week of the academic year. In addition to telling what happened, you want to make a point; perhaps you want to emphasize that, despite the college's good intentions, such official events actually make it difficult to meet people. So you might write about how stiff and unnatural students seemed, eager to make a positive impression but nervous because they knew no one else there; you might narrate snatches of strained conversation; you might describe the way the room emptied long before midnight, when the dance was scheduled to end. All these details would support your narrative point.

Because you don't want to get away from that point, you would leave out details about the top-notch band and the appetizing refreshments. The music and food may have been surprisingly good, but because these details don't advance the point you want to make, they should be omitted.

You also need to keep your audience in mind when selecting narrative details. If the audience consists of your instructor and other students—all of them familiar with the new student center where the dance was held—specific details about the center probably wouldn't have to be provided. But imagine that the essay is going to appear in the quarterly magazine published by the college's community relations office. Many of the magazine's readers are former graduates who haven't been on campus for several years. They may need some additional specifics about the student center: its location, how many people it holds, how it is furnished.

As you write, keep asking yourself, "Is this detail or character or snippet of conversation essential? Does my audience need this detail to understand the conflict in the situation? Does this detail advance or intensify the narrative action?" Summarize details that have some importance but do not deserve lengthy treatment ("Two hours went by..."). And try to limit *narrative commentary*—statements that tell rather than show what happened—because such remarks interrupt the narrative flow. Focus instead on the specifics that propel action forward in a vigorous way.

Sometimes, especially if the narrative recreates an event from the past, you won't be able to remember what happened detail for detail. In such a case, you should take advantage of what is called *dramatic license*. Using as a guide your powers of recall as well as the perspective you now have of that particular time, feel free to reshape events to suit your narrative point.

4. Organize the narrative sequence.

Every narrative begins somewhere, presents a span of time, and ends at a certain point. Frequently, you'll want to use a straightforward time order, following the event *chronologically* from beginning to end: first this happened, next this happened, finally this happened.

But sometimes a strict chronological recounting may not be effective—especially if the high point of the narrative gets lost somewhere in the middle of the time sequence. To avoid that possibility, you may want to disrupt chronology, plunge the reader into the middle of the story, and then return in a *flashback* to the beginning of the tale. You're probably familiar with the way flashback is used on television and in film. You see someone appealing to the main character for financial help, then return to an earlier time when both were students in the same class, before learning how the rest of the story unfolds. Narratives can also use *flash-forward*. You give readers a glimpse of the future (the main character being jailed) before the story continues in the present (the events leading to the arrest). These techniques shift the story onto several planes and keep it from becoming a step-by-step, predictable account. Reserve flash-forwards and flashbacks, however, for crucial incidents only, because breaking out of chronological order acts as emphasis. Here are examples of how flashback and flash-forward can be used:

Flashback

Standing behind the wooden counter, Greg wielded his knife expertly as he shucked clams—one every ten seconds—with practiced ease. The scene contrasted sharply with his first day on the job, when his hands broke out in blisters and when splitting each shell was like prying open a safe.

Flash-forward

Rushing to move my car from the no-parking zone, I waved a quick goodbye to Karen as she climbed the steps to the bus. I didn't know then that by the time I picked her up at the bus station later that day, she would have made a decision that would affect both our lives.

Whether or not you choose to include flashbacks or flash-forwards in an essay, remember to limit the time span covered by the narrative. Otherwise, you will have trouble generating the details needed to give the story depth and meaning. Also, regardless of the time sequence you select, organize the tale so that it drives toward a strong finish. Be careful that your story doesn't trail off into minor, anticlimactic details.

5. Make the narrative easy to follow.

Describing each distinct action in a separate paragraph helps readers grasp the flow of events. Although narrative essays don't always have conventional topic sentences, each narrative paragraph should have a clear focus. Often this focus is indicated by a sentence early in the paragraph that directs attention to the action taking place. Such a sentence functions as a kind of *informal topic sentence;* the rest of the paragraph then develops that topic sentence. You should also be sure to use time signals when narrating a story. Words like *now, then, next, after,* and *later* ensure that your reader won't get lost as the story progresses.

6. Make the narrative vigorous and immediate.

A compelling narrative provides an abundance of specific details, making readers feel as if they're experiencing the story being told. Readers must be able to see, hear, touch, smell, and taste the event you're narrating. *Vivid sensory description* is, therefore, an essential part of an effective narrative. Not only do specific sensory details make writing a pleasure to read—we all enjoy learning the particulars about people, places, and things—but they also give the narrative the stamp of reality. The specifics convince the reader that the event actually did, or could, occur.

Compare the following excerpts from a narrative essay. The first version is lifeless and dull; the revised version, packed with sensory images, grabs readers with its sense of foreboding:

> That eventful day started out like every other summer day. My sister Madison and I made several elaborate mud pies, which we decorated with care. A little later on, as we were spraying each other with the garden hose, we heard my father walk up the path.

> That sad summer day started out uneventfully enough. My sister Madison and I spent a few hours mixing and decorating mud pies. Our hands caked with dry mud, we sprinkled each lopsided pie with alternating rows of dandelion and clover petals. Later when the sun got hotter, we tossed our white T-shirts over the red picket fence–forgetting my grandmother's frequent warnings to be more ladylike. Our sweaty backs bared to the sun, we doused each other with icy sprays from the garden hose. Caught up in the primitive pleasure of it all, we barely heard my father as he walked up the garden path, the gravel crunching under his heavy work boots.

A caution: Sensory language enlivens narration, but it also slows the pace. Be sure that the slower pace suits your purpose. For example, a lengthy description fits an account of a leisurely summer vacation but is inappropriate in a tale about a frantic search for a misplaced wallet.

Another way to create an aura of narrative immediacy is to use *dialogue.* Our sense of other people comes, in part, from what they say and how they sound. Dialogue allows the reader to experience characters directly. Compare the following fragments of a narrative, one with dialogue and one without, noting how much more energetic the second version is.

> When I finally found my way back to the campsite, the trail guide commented on my disheveled appearance.

> When I finally found my way back to the campsite, the trail guide took one look at me and drawled, "What on earth happened to you, Daniel Boone? You look as though you've been dragged through a haystack backwards."
>
> "I'd look a lot worse if I hadn't run back here. When a bullet whizzes by me, I don't stick around to see who's doing the shooting."

When using dialogue, begin a new paragraph to indicate a shift from one person's speech to another's (as in the second example above).

Using *varied sentence structure* is another strategy for making narratives lively and vigorous. Sentences that plod along predictably (subject-verb, subject-verb) put readers to sleep. Experiment with your sentences by juggling length and sentence type; mix long and short sentences, simple and complex. Compare the following original and revised versions to get an idea of how effective varied sentence rhythm can be in narrative writing.

Original

The store manager went to the walk-in refrigerator every day. The heavy metal door clanged shut behind her. I had visions of her freezing to death among the hanging carcasses. The shiny door finally swung open. She waddled out.

Revised

Each time the store manager went to the walk-in refrigerator, the heavy metal door clanged shut behind her. Visions of her freezing to death among the hanging carcasses crept into my mind until the shiny door finally swung open and she waddled out.

Original

The yellow-and-blue-striped fish struggled on the line. Its scales shimmered in the sunlight. Its tail waved frantically. I saw its desire to live. I decided to let it go.

Revised

Scales shimmering in the sunlight, tail waving frantically, the yellow-and-blue-striped fish struggled on the line. Seeing its desire to live, I let it go.

Finally, *vigorous verbs* lend energy to narratives. Use active verb forms ("The boss *yelled at* him") rather than passive ones ("He *was yelled at* by the boss"), and try to replace anemic *to be* verbs ("She *was* a good basketball player") with more dynamic constructions ("She *played* basketball well").

7. Keep your point of view and verb tense consistent.

All stories have a *narrator,* the person who tells the story. If you, as narrator, tell a story as you experienced it, the story is written in the *first-person point of view* ("*I* saw the dog pull loose"). But if you observed the event (or heard about it from others) and want to tell how someone else experienced the incident, you would use the *third-person point of view* ("*Haley* saw the dog pull loose"). Each point of view has advantages and limitations. First person allows you to express ordinarily private thoughts and to recreate an event as you actually experienced it. This point of view is limited, though, in its ability to depict the inner thoughts of other people involved in the event. By way of contrast, third person makes it easier to provide insight into the thoughts of all the participants. However, its objective, broad perspective may undercut some of the subjective immediacy of the "I was there" point of view. No matter which you select, stay with that vantage point throughout the narrative.

Knowing whether to use the *past* or *present tense* ("I *strolled* into the room" as opposed to "I *stroll* into the room") is important. In most narrations, the past tense predominates, enabling the writer to span a considerable period of time. Although more rarely used, the present tense can be powerful for events of short duration—a wrestling match or a medical emergency, for instance. A narrative in the present tense prolongs each moment, intensifying the reader's sense of participation. Be careful, though; unless the event is intense and fast-paced, the present tense can seem contrived. Whichever tense you choose, avoid shifting midstream—starting, let's say, in the past tense ("she skated") and switching to the present ("she runs").

REVISION STRATEGIES

Once you have a draft of the essay, you're ready to revise. The following checklist will help you and those giving you feedback apply to narration some of the revision techniques discussed in Chapter 2.

☑ NARRATION: A REVISION/PEER REVIEW CHECKLIST

Revise Overall Meaning and Structure

❑ What is the essay's main point? Is it stated explicitly or is it implied? Where? Could the point be conveyed more clearly? How?

❑ What is the narrative's conflict? Is it stated explicitly or is it implied? Where? Could the conflict be made more dramatic? How?

❑ From what point of view is the narrative told? Is it the most effective point of view for this essay? Why or why not?

Revise Paragraph Development

❑ Which paragraphs fail to advance the action, reveal character, or contribute to the story's mood? Should these sections be condensed or eliminated?

❑ Where should the narrative pace be slowed down or quickened?

❑ Where is it difficult to follow the chronology of events? Should the order of paragraphs be changed? How? Where would additional time signals help?

❑ How could flashback or flash-forward paragraphs be used to highlight key events?

❑ Would dramatic dialogue or mood-setting description help make the essay's opening paragraph more compelling?

❑ What could be done to make the essay's closing paragraph more effective? Should the essay end earlier? Should it close by echoing an idea or image from the opening?

(continued)

Narration: A Revision/Peer Review Checklist (*continued*)

Revise Sentences and Words

❏ Where is sentence structure monotonous? Where would combining sentences, mixing sentence types, and alternating sentence length help?

❏ Where could dialogue replace commentary to convey character and propel the story forward?

❏ Which sentences and words are inconsistent with the essay's tone?

❏ Where do vigorous verbs convey action? Where could active verbs replace passive ones? Where could dull *to be* verbs be converted to more dynamic forms?

❏ Where are there inappropriate shifts in point of view or verb tense?

STUDENT ESSAY

The following student essay was written by Laura Rose Dunn in response to this assignment:

> In her essay, "The Fourth of July," Audre Lorde shares a disturbing experience that brought her childhood to an end and changed the way she thought about "her" country. Write a narrative about an experience from your childhood that had a profound effect on you. Your essay does not necessarily have to be about a disturbing experience, but it should focus on something from your childhood that played a role in shaping you into the person you are today.

While reading Laura Rose's essay, try to determine how well it applies the principles of narration. The annotations on Laura Rose's essay and the commentary following it will help you look at the essay more closely.

Letters from Dad
by Laura Rose Dunn

Introduction · Time signal
        When I was in kindergarten, my teacher asked each of us   1
to write a paper about our parents. The first "open house" of
the school year was a few days away, and she wanted to post
our early essay attempts on the classroom walls. I began my
essay by telling the world about my mom and how beautiful
and kind she was. I wrote about how she was my hero and
how I was so proud to be her daughter. I went on and on like
that for the whole page, not once mentioning good old dad.
I soon realized this, and at the very end of my paper, after I
had practically serenaded my mom, I added six short words:
"My dad, his name is Bill." That was it. That was all I had to
say about my dad. Naturally, my dad was crushed when he

Narrative tension established — read my paper at open house, and I am sure he will never forget my insinuation in that kindergarten essay that he did not play an important role in my life. In fact, he still teases me about the way I slighted him in that paper. So in the spirit of making up for past neglect, I want to now make clear that my dad has always been an important figure in my life, even when he was thousands of miles away. He has not only helped

Narrative point (thesis) — me develop my reading and writing skills, but has also played a major role in expanding my view of the world.

Informal topic sentence —   My dad and I have always been close, despite his fre-   2
quent absences. You see, my dad has been and always will be a United States Marine, and with that title come certain obligations. He has been overseas more times than I can count and has seen more of the world than I could ever imag-

Time signal — ine. From the time I was three, my dad has written me letters every week of every deployment. Although at first I could not read them on my own, I never grew weary of trying. Those letters were my only link to him while he was away, and I held on to every single one. Each night that he was gone, I would pull them out of my drawer and read my letters from him as if it were for the first time, and I anxiously awaited the arrival of the next one.

Informal topic sentence starting with a time signal —   At the time, I loved those letters almost as much as the   3
man behind them. When I was very young and hadn't yet learned how to read, he would illustrate key words below each sentence to help me grasp his meaning. To this day, my favor-

Time signal — ite letter from Dad features drawings of a fish, a cat, a dog, and Jabba the Hutt. Needless to say, it was a very interesting let-

Sensory details — ter. Although his illustrations were juvenile at best (no offense, Dad), they gave me a way to connect with the words he wrote. With the pictures there to guide me, I felt more encouraged to take a real stab at reading. I even started writing my own letters to him.

Informal topic sentence —   My first letters to my dad were very interesting speci-   4
mens. Some consisted of more glitter-glue than actual vo-cabulary, but day-by-day, my letters became more readable.

Time signal — By the time I hit age six, I was very good at thinking about what I wanted to say and putting those thoughts on a piece of paper. Upon receiving my letters, my dad would read and en-joy them, and then critique and criticize. Along with my dad's usual letters, I would also receive my letters with corrections on them. Part of me wants to think that he did this to help pass the time, but I know in my heart that what it really comes down to is that my dad runs the "grammar police." Even when he was home, he would drill me on my vocabulary, spelling, and sentence structure. Despite my protests at the time, I will admit that now, I am grateful for the instruction he gave me.

Time signal — By the time I was in fifth grade, I was a writing pro. The only thing I failed to comprehend was sarcasm. So when my dad signed at the end of his letter, "Laura Rose, I love you as if you were my own daughter, but you have got to work on your handwriting," I naturally assumed that I had been adopted. And as you might imagine, sarcasm was the next concept he helped me tackle.

Informal topic sentence ⎯⎯⎯→ My dad's letters not only gave me the tools I needed to   5 grow as a writer; they also helped me see a new side of the world. Dad wrote to me of the beautiful Alps in Switzerland, the vast deserts of the Middle East, the complex beauty of The Med, and the heart-breaking reality of war. I got a firsthand look at the world just by reading his letters, and I know I am lucky to have had that. I was able to make connections between what he shared with me in his letters and what I was reading about in school. When it came time for my geography and history classes, I had an advantage over most of my classmates.

Informal topic sentence ⎯⎯⎯→ Although I enjoyed our relationship as pen pals, it is al-   6 ways so much better to have my dad at home. Life for me is still hard when he is gone. As I have gotten older, I have not **Time signal** ⏋ "gotten used to it." In fact, knowing that he is on the other side of the world is almost harder now. The only thing that gets me through my dad being away is the promise of a letter, once a week. Those letters *are* my dad, and he has taught me more through his letters than any book could have taught me. My dad has missed more birthdays, soccer games, and award ceremonies than I even care to count. He has missed chunks of my life that are impossible to make up, but in his absence **Sensory details** ⏋ my dad gave me so much more than a cheer from the crowd or a swing on the merry-go-round. He shared his world with me and taught me not only how to read and write, but how vast the world is and how I can use its history to enrich my life.

Echoing of narrative point in the introduction ⏋ I thank my dad for all that he has taught me that has   7 helped me grow as a reader, a writer, and a person. I thank him for playing a huge role in making me who I am today. I am so proud to be the daughter of a United States Marine.

Concluding statement Oh, and my mom, her name is Mimi.   8

COMMENTARY

Point of view, tense, and narrative tension. Laura Rose chose to write "Letters from Dad" from the *first-person point of view*, a logical choice because she appears as a main character in her own story. Using a combination of *past* and *present tense*, Laura Rose recounts a story from her past but also moves to the present as she shares with her readers how her dad has played a major role in shaping her into the reader, writer, and individual she has become. In pointing out that her dad was "crushed" because she did not mention him in her first school paper, Laura Rose introduces some mild *narrative tension* that contributes to the point of her essay.

Narrative point.   It isn't always necessary to state the *narrative point* of an essay; the point can be implied. But Laura Rose decided to express the controlling idea of her narrative in two places. First, in the introduction, she includes two sentences that work together to make her narrative point: "So in the spirit of making up for past neglect, I want to make clear that my dad has always been an important figure in my life, even when he was thousands of miles away. He has not only helped me develop my reading and writing skills, but has also played a major role in expanding my view of the world." She makes her narrative point again in the next-to-last paragraph, where she thanks her dad for his positive influence on her life. All of the essay's narrative details contribute to the point of the piece; Laura Rose does not include any extraneous information that would detract from the central idea she wants to convey.

Organization.   The narrative is *organized chronologically*, as Laura Rose reflects on the important role her dad has played in her life. Although the story she tells spans fifteen years, from when she was three years old to the present, Laura Rose chooses specific examples from across the years as she shares with her readers the role her dad has played in shaping her into the person she has become. To help the reader follow the course of the narrative, Laura Rose uses *time signals*: "When I was in kindergarten..." (1); "From the time I was three..." (2); "At the time...," "When I was very young...," "To this day..." (3); "By the time I hit age six,..." "By the time I was in fifth grade,..." (4); "As I have gotten older,..." (6).

The paragraphs also contain *informal topic sentences* that direct attention to the specific parts of the story being narrated. Indeed, each paragraph focuses on a particular aspect of her story: how a kindergarten assignment led to an essay for a college class, why her dad has been away from home for much of her life, why she loved receiving letters from him, what those early letters to him and his responses to her were like, how her dad's letters enriched her life, how his absence over the years has affected her, and why he means so much to her today.

Combining patterns of development.   The chronological structure of Laura Rose's reflection, from her childhood years to the present, use *cause* and *effect* to explain how the letters from her dad have shaped the person she has become, and the *description* she uses throughout her essay brings her story to life with rich *sensory details* to engage the reader. For example, the two following sentences allow her readers to "see" what his letters to her looked like and understand how they helped her learn to read: "When I was very young and hadn't yet learned how to read, he would illustrate key words below each sentence to help me grasp his meaning. To this day, my favorite letter from Dad features drawings of a fish, a cat, a dog and Jabba the Hutt" (3).

Conclusion. The primary purpose of an essay's conclusion is to bring the composition to closure, and Laura Rose does this in a creative way. Although her next-to-last paragraph adheres to a more typical essay structure by restating the main idea she has communicated to her readers—that she appreciates all that her dad has done over the years to help her grow as a reader, a writer, and a person—she doesn't stop there. Laura Rose goes on to include one short, terse, concluding sentence that brings her readers back to her reason for writing this essay: that she slighted her dad in an essay she wrote in kindergarten in which she focused on her mom. She evens the score—resolving the narrative tension expressed in paragraph 1—by ending her college essay with a humorously ironic nod to her mom: "Oh, and my mom, her name is Mimi."

Revising the first draft. Comparing the final version of the essay's first paragraph with the following preliminary version reveals some of the changes Laura Rose made while revising the essay.

Original Version of the Introductory Paragraph

When I was in Kindergarten, my teacher had our class sit down and write a paper about our parents. I began my paper by telling the world about my mom and how beautiful and kind she was. I wrote about how she was my hero and how I was so proud to be her daughter. I went on and on like that for the whole page, not once mentioning good old dad. I soon realized this and at the very end of my paper, after I had practically serenaded my mom, I added six short words: "My dad, his name is Bill." That was it. That was all I had to say about my dad. Naturally, my dad was crushed when he read my paper at open house, and I am sure that he will never let me live it down as he still teases me about it to this day. So, in the spirit of making up for past neglect, I must now say that my dad has really helped me come into my own and has given me the practice I needed to become a successful reader and writer.

After putting the original draft aside for a while, Laura Rose reread what she had written and realized that she needed to make some major changes in her opening paragraph. She began her revisions by tackling the easy issues: correcting a capitalization or punctuation error (changing *Kindergarten* to *kindergarten*, adding a needed comma in her fifth sentence); omitting unnecessary words (such as "sit down" in the first sentence and "that" in other sentences); and playing with her wording to make sentences more accurately reflect her intentions (such as changing "I must now say..." to "I want to now make clear...").

Next, Laura Rose decided to add a sentence that would allow her readers to understand early in the essay that the papers she and her classmates were writing in kindergarten were going to be posted around the room at her school's upcoming open house. In her first draft, she had waited until more than half way through the paragraph to mention this event. As she revised, Laura Rose was clearly thinking more about her readers and making changes that would help them more easily follow her story line.

She also realized that her pronoun reference was both repetitive and unclear in the last part of one of her sentences in the original draft: "... and I am sure that he will never let me live *it* down as he still teases me about *it* to this day." In her revision, she gets rid of the unclear pronoun reference by including concrete language and using two sentences instead of one to make her point: "... and I am sure he will never forget my insinuation in that kindergarten essay that he did not play an important role in my life. In fact, he still teases me about the way I slighted him in that paper."

Finally, she realized that her last sentence in the paragraph needed to be revised. When she started drafting her essay, she intended to focus on how her dad had helped her develop as a reader and writer, but as she was drafting her essay, she went on to include additional information on how her dad helped expand her view of the world. As is the case for many writers, Laura Rose's thesis changed as she worked on her essay, and she needed to revise the thesis statement to reflect that change.

The revisions she made in her opening paragraph made for a stronger, more polished piece of narrative writing. Consideration of her audience as she revised helped Laura Rose see how she could improve her opening paragraph, as well as the rest of her essay.

Activities: Narration

MyWritingLab

Prewriting Activities

1. Imagine you're writing two essays: One analyzes the *effect* of insensitive teachers on young children; the other *argues* the importance of family traditions. With the help of your journal or freewriting, identify different narratives you could use to open each essay.

2. For each of the situations, identify two different conflicts that would make a story worth relating. Then prepare six to ten lines of natural-sounding dialogue for each potential conflict in *one* of the situations.
   a. Going to the supermarket with a friend
   b. Telling your parents which college you've decided to attend
   c. Participating in a demonstration
   d. Preparing for an exam in a difficult course

(continued)

Activities: Narration (*continued*)

Revising Activities

1. Revise each of the following narrative sentence groups twice: once with words that carry negative connotations, and again with words that carry positive connotations. Use varied sentence structure, sensory details, and vigorous verbs to convey mood.

   a. The bell rang. It rang loudly. Students knew the last day of class was over.

   b. Last weekend, our neighbors burned leaves in their yard. We went over to speak with them.

   c. The sun shone in through my bedroom window. It made me sit up in bed. Daylight was finally here, I told myself.

2. The following paragraph is the introduction from the first draft of an essay proposing harsher penalties for drunk drivers. Revise this narrative paragraph to make it more effective. How can you make sentence structure less predictable? Which details should you delete? As you revise, provide language that conveys the event's sights, smells, and sounds. Also, clarify the chronological sequence.

   As I drove down the street in my bright blue sports car, I saw a car coming rapidly around the curve. The car didn't slow down as it headed toward the traffic light. The light turned yellow and then red. A young couple, dressed like models, started crossing the street. When the woman saw the car, she called out to her husband. He jumped onto the shoulder. The man wasn't hurt but, seconds later, it was clear the woman was. I ran to a nearby emergency phone and called the police. The ambulance arrived, but the woman was already dead. The driver, who looked terrible, failed the sobriety test, and the police found out that he had two previous offenses. It's apparent that better ways have to be found for getting drunk drivers off the road.

Named poet laureate of the state of New York in 1991, Audre Lorde (1934–1992) was a New Yorker born of African-Caribbean parents. After earning degrees at Hunter College and Columbia University, Lorde held numerous teaching positions throughout the New York City area. She later toured the world as a lecturer, forming women's rights coalitions in the Caribbean, Africa, and Europe. Best known as a feminist theorist, Lorde combined social criticism and personal revelation in her writing on such topics as race, gender relations, and sexuality. Her numerous poems and nonfiction pieces were published in a variety of magazines and literary journals. Her books include *The Black Unicorn: Poems* (1978), *Sister Outsider: Essays and Speeches* (1984), and *A Burst of Light* (1988). The following selection is an excerpt from her autobiography, *Zami: A New Spelling of My Name* (1982).

For ideas about how this narration essay is organized, see Figure 4.2 on page 141.

Pre-Reading Journal Entry

MyWritingLab

When you were a child, what beliefs about the United States did you have? List these beliefs. For each, indicate whether subsequent experience maintained or shattered your childhood understanding of these beliefs. Take time to explore these issues in your journal.

The Fourth of July

The first time I went to Washington, D.C., was on the edge of the summer when I was supposed to stop being a child. At least that's what they said to us all at graduation from the eighth grade. My sister Phyllis graduated at the same time from high school. I don't know what she was supposed to stop being. But as graduation presents for us both, the whole family took a Fourth of July trip to Washington, D.C., the fabled and famous capital of our country.

It was the first time I'd ever been on a railroad train during the day. When I was little, and we used to go to the Connecticut shore, we always went at night on the milk train, because it was cheaper.

Preparations were in the air around our house before school was even over. We packed for a week. There were two very large suitcases that my father carried, and a box filled with food. In fact, my first trip to Washington was a mobile feast; I started eating as soon as we were comfortably ensconced in our seats, and did not stop until somewhere after Philadelphia. I remember it was Philadelphia because I was disappointed not to have passed by the Liberty Bell.

1

2

3

My mother had roasted two chickens and cut them up into dainty bite-   4
size pieces. She packed slices of brown bread and butter and green pepper
and carrot sticks. There were little violently yellow iced cakes with scalloped
edges called "marigolds," that came from Cushman's Bakery. There was
a spice bun and rock-cakes from Newton's, the West Indian bakery across
Lenox Avenue from St. Mark's School, and iced tea in a wrapped mayon-
naise jar. There were sweet pickles for us and dill pickles for my father, and
peaches with the fuzz still on them, individually wrapped to keep them
from bruising. And, for neatness, there were piles of napkins and a little tin
box with a washcloth dampened with rosewater and glycerine for wiping
sticky mouths.

I wanted to eat in the dining car because I had read all about them,   5
but my mother reminded me for the umpteenth time that dining car food
always costs too much money and besides, you never could tell whose hands
had been playing all over that food, nor where those same hands had been
just before. My mother never mentioned that Black people were not allowed into railroad dining cars headed south in 1947. As usual, whatever my
mother did not like and could not change, she ignored. Perhaps it would go
away, deprived of her attention.

I learned later that Phyllis's high school senior class trip had been to   6
Washington, but the nuns had given her back her deposit in private, explaining to her that the class, all of whom were white, except Phyllis, would be
staying in a hotel where Phyllis "would not be happy," meaning, Daddy explained to her, also in private, that they did not rent rooms to Negroes. "We
will take you to Washington, ourselves," my father had avowed, "and not
just for an overnight in some measly fleabag hotel."

American racism was a new and crushing reality that my parents had   7
to deal with every day of their lives once they came to this country. They
handled it as a private woe. My mother and father believed that they could
best protect their children from the realities of race in america and the fact
of american racism by never giving them name, much less discussing their
nature. We were told we must never trust white people, but *why* was never
explained, nor the nature of their ill will. Like so many other vital pieces of
information in my childhood, I was supposed to know without being told. It
always seemed like a very strange injunction coming from my mother, who
looked so much like one of those people we were never supposed to trust.
But something always warned me not to ask my mother why she wasn't
white, and why Auntie Lillah and Auntie Etta weren't, even though they
were all that same problematic color so different from my father and me,
even from my sisters, who were somewhere in-between.

In Washington, D.C., we had one large room with two double beds and   8
an extra cot for me. It was a back-street hotel that belonged to a friend of
my father's who was in real estate, and I spent the whole next day after Mass

squinting up at the Lincoln Memorial where Marian Anderson[1] had sung after the D.A.R.[2] refused to allow her to sing in their auditorium because she was Black. Or because she was "Colored," my father said as he told us the story. Except that what he probably said was "Negro," because for his time, my father was quite progressive.

I was squinting because I was in that silent agony that characterized all   9
of my childhood summers, from the time school let out in June to the end of July, brought about by my dilated and vulnerable eyes exposed to the summer brightness.

I viewed Julys through an agonizing corolla of dazzling whiteness and   10
I always hated the Fourth of July, even before I came to realize the travesty such a celebration was for Black people in this country.

My parents did not approve of sunglasses, nor of their expense.   11

I spent the afternoon squinting up at monuments to freedom and past   12
presidencies and democracy, and wondering why the light and heat were both so much stronger in Washington, D.C., than back home in New York City. Even the pavement on the streets was a shade lighter in color than back home.

Late that Washington afternoon my family and I walked back down   13
Pennsylvania Avenue. We were a proper caravan, mother bright and father brown, the three of us girls step-standards in-between. Moved by our historical surroundings and the heat of the early evening, my father decreed yet another treat. He had a great sense of history, a flair for the quietly dramatic and the sense of specialness of an occasion and a trip.

"Shall we stop and have a little something to cool off, Lin?"   14

Two blocks away from our hotel, the family stopped for a dish of vanilla   15
ice cream at a Breyer's ice cream and soda fountain. Indoors, the soda fountain was dim and fan-cooled, deliciously relieving to my scorched eyes.

Corded and crisp and pinafored, the five of us seated ourselves one by   16
one at the counter. There was I between my mother and father, and my two sisters on the other side of my mother. We settled ourselves along the white mottled marble counter, and when the waitress spoke at first no one understood what she was saying, and so the five of us just sat there.

The waitress moved along the line of us closer to my father and spoke   17
again. "I said I kin give you to take out, but you can't eat here. Sorry." Then she dropped her eyes looking very embarrassed, and suddenly we heard what it was she was saying all at the same time, loud and clear.

---

[1]Acclaimed African-American opera singer (1902–93), famed for her renderings of Black spirituals (editors' note).

[2]Daughters of the American Revolution. A society, founded in 1890, for women who can prove direct lineage to soldiers or others who aided in winning American independence from Great Britain during the Revolutionary War (1775–83) (editors' note).

Straight-backed and indignant, one by one, my family and I got down   18
from the counter stools and turned around and marched out of the store,
quiet and outraged, as if we had never been Black before. No one would answer my emphatic questions with anything other than a guilty silence. "But
we hadn't done anything!" This wasn't right or fair! Hadn't I written poems
about Bataan and freedom and democracy for all?

My parents wouldn't speak of this injustice, not because they had contrib-   19
uted to it, but because they felt they should have anticipated it and avoided
it. This made me even angrier. My fury was not going to be acknowledged
by a like fury. Even my two sisters copied my parents' pretense that nothing
unusual and anti-american had occurred. I was left to write my angry letter to
the president of the united states all by myself, although my father did promise I could type it out on the office typewriter next week, after I showed it to
him in my copybook diary.

The waitress was white, and the counter was white, and the ice cream I   20
never ate in Washington, D.C., that summer I left childhood was white, and
the white heat and the white pavement and the white stone monuments of
my first Washington summer made me sick to my stomach for the whole rest
of that trip and it wasn't much of a graduation present after all.

Questions for Close Reading   MyWritingLab

1. What is the selection's thesis (or narrative point)? Locate the sentence(s) in which
   Lorde states her main idea. If she doesn't state the thesis explicitly, express it in
   your own words.
2. In paragraph 4, Lorde describes the elaborate picnic her mother prepared for the
   trip to Washington, D.C. Why did Lorde's mother make such elaborate preparations? What do these preparations tell us about Lorde's mother?
3. Why does Lorde have trouble understanding her parents' dictate that she "never
   trust white people" (paragraph 7)?
4. In general, how do Lorde's parents handle racism? How does the family as a
   whole deal with the racism they encounter in the ice-cream parlor? How does the
   family's reaction to the ice-cream parlor incident make Lorde feel?

Questions About the Writer's Craft

1. **The pattern.** What techniques does Lorde use to help readers follow the unfold-
   ing of the story as it occurs in both time and space?
2. When telling a story, skilled writers limit narrative commentary—statements that
   tell rather than show what happened—because it tends to interrupt the narrative
   flow. Lorde, however, provides narrative commentary in several spots. Find these
   instances. How is the information she provides essential to her narrative?
3. In paragraphs 7 and 19, Lorde uses all lowercase letters for *America, American,*
   and *President of the United States.* Why do you suppose she doesn't follow the
   rules of capitalization? In what ways does her rejection of these rules reinforce
   what she is trying to convey through the essay's title?

FIGURE 4.2
Essay Structure Diagram: "The Fourth of July" by Audre Lorde

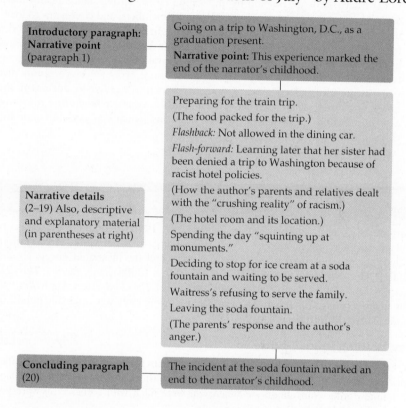

Introductory paragraph: **Narrative point** (paragraph 1)	Going on a trip to Washington, D.C., as a graduation present. **Narrative point:** This experience marked the end of the narrator's childhood.
Narrative details (2–19) Also, descriptive and explanatory material (in parentheses at right)	Preparing for the train trip. (The food packed for the trip.) *Flashback:* Not allowed in the dining car. *Flash-forward:* Learning later that her sister had been denied a trip to Washington because of racist hotel policies. (How the author's parents and relatives dealt with the "crushing reality" of racism.) (The hotel room and its location.) Spending the day "squinting up at monuments." Deciding to stop for ice cream at a soda fountain and waiting to be served. Waitress's refusing to serve the family. Leaving the soda fountain. (The parents' response and the author's anger.)
Concluding paragraph (20)	The incident at the soda fountain marked an end to the narrator's childhood.

4. What key word does Lorde repeat in paragraph 20? What effect do you think she hopes the repetition will have on readers?

Writing Assignments Using Narration as a Pattern of Development

1. Lorde recounts an incident during which she was treated unfairly. Write a narrative about a time when either you were treated unjustly or you treated someone else in an unfair manner. Like Lorde, use vivid details to make the incident come alive and to convey how it affected you.

2. Write a narrative about an experience that dramatically changed your view of the world. The experience might have been jarring and painful, or it may have been positive and uplifting. In either case, recount the incident with compelling narrative details. To illustrate the shift in your perspective, begin with a brief statement of the way you viewed the world before the experience.

Writing Assignment Combining Patterns of Development

3. In her essay, Lorde decries and by implication takes a strong stance against racial discrimination. Brainstorm with friends, family members, and classmates to identify other injustices in American society. You might begin by considering attitudes toward the elderly, the overweight, the physically disabled; the funding of schools in poor and affluent neighborhoods; the portrayal of a specific ethnic group on television; and so on. Focusing on *one* such injustice, write an essay *arguing* that such an injustice indeed exists. Conduct research as needed to document the nature and extent of the injustice. You should also consider *recounting* your own and other people's experiences. Acknowledge and, when you can, dismantle the views of those who think there isn't a problem.

Lynda Barry

Cartoonist, novelist, and playwright, Lynda Barry (1956–) combines the genres of collage, memoir, novel, graphic novel, and workbook in her work. Her creations include the syndicated strip *Ernie Pook's Comeek* and the illustrated novels *Cruddy* (2001), *One Hundred Demons* (2002), *What It Is* (2008), and *Picture This: The Near-Sighted Monkey Book* (2010). Her 2002 novel *The Good Times Are Killing Me* was adapted into an off-Broadway play. The following essay was originally published in the *Baltimore Sun* on January 24, 1992.

Pre-Reading Journal Entry

MyWritingLab

In her essay, Lynda Barry writes about a time in her childhood when she was "filled with a panic...like the panic that strikes kids when they realize they are lost." Think of a time during your childhood when you were filled with panic. Why were you afraid? How did you feel? What did you do?

The Sanctuary of School

I was 7 years old the first time I snuck out of the house in the dark. It was winter and my parents had been fighting all night. They were short on money and long on relatives who kept "temporarily" moving into our house because they had nowhere else to go.

My brother and I were used to giving up our bedroom. We slept on the couch, something we actually liked because it put us that much closer to the light of our lives, our television.

At night when everyone was asleep, we lay on our pillows watching it with the sound off. We watched Steve Allen's mouth moving. We watched Johnny Carson's mouth moving. We watched movies filled with gangsters shooting machine guns into packed rooms, dying soldiers hurling a last grenade and beautiful women crying at windows. Then the sign-off finally came and we tried to sleep.

The morning I snuck out, I woke up filled with a panic about needing   4
to get to school. The sun wasn't quite up yet but my anxiety was so fierce that I just got dressed, walked quietly across the kitchen and let myself out the back door.

It was quiet outside. Stars were still out. Nothing moved and no one was   5
in the street. It was as if someone had turned the sound off on the world.

I walked the alley, breaking thin ice over the puddles with my shoes. I   6
didn't know why I was walking to school in the dark. I didn't think about it. All I knew was a feeling of panic, like the panic that strikes kids when they realize they are lost.

That feeling eased the moment I turned the corner and saw the dark outline   7
of my school at the top of the hill. My school was made up of about 15 nondescript portable classrooms set down on a fenced concrete lot in a rundown Seattle neighborhood, but it had the most beautiful view of the Cascade Mountains. You could see them from anywhere on the playfield and you could see them from the windows of my classroom—Room 2.

I walked over to the monkey bars and hooked my arms around the cold   8
metal. I stood for a long time just looking across Rainier Valley. The sky was beginning to whiten and I could hear a few birds.

In a perfect world my absence at home would not have gone unnoticed. I   9
would have had two parents in a panic to locate me, instead of two parents in a panic to locate an answer to the hard question of survival during a deep financial and emotional crisis.

But in an overcrowded and unhappy home, it's incredibly easy for any child   10
to slip away. The high levels of frustration, depression and anger in my house made my brother and me invisible. We were children with the sound turned off. And for us, as for the steadily increasing number of neglected children in this country, the only place where we could count on being noticed was at school.

"Hey there, young lady. Did you forget to go home last night?" It was   11
Mr. Gunderson, our janitor, whom we all loved. He was nice and he was funny and he was old with white hair, thick glasses and an unbelievable number of keys. I could hear them jingling as he walked across the playfield. I felt incredibly happy to see him.

He let me push his wheeled garbage can between the different portables   12
as he unlocked each room. He let me turn on the lights and raise the window shades and I saw my school slowly come to life. I saw Mrs. Holman, our school secretary, walk into the office without her orange lipstick on yet. She waved.

I saw the fifth-grade teacher, Mr. Cunningham, walking under the   13
breezeway eating a hard roll. He waved.

And I saw my teacher, Mrs. Claire LeSane, walking toward us in a red   14
coat and calling my name in a very happy and surprised way, and suddenly
my throat got tight and my eyes stung and I ran toward her crying. It was
something that surprised us both.

It's only thinking about it now, 28 years later, that I realize I was crying   15
from relief. I was with my teacher, and in a while I was going to sit at my
desk, with my crayons and pencils and books and classmates all around me,
and for the next six hours I was going to enjoy a thoroughly secure, warm
and stable world. It was a world I absolutely relied on. Without it, I don't
know where I would have gone that morning.

Mrs. LeSane asked me what was wrong and when I said "Nothing," she   16
seemingly left it at that. But she asked me if I would carry her purse for her,
an honor above all honors, and she asked if I wanted to come into Room 2
early and paint.

She believed in the natural healing power of painting and drawing for trou-   17
bled children. In the back of her room there was always a drawing table and
an easel with plenty of supplies, and sometimes during the day she would
come up to you for what seemed like no good reason and quietly ask if you
wanted to go to the back table and "make some pictures for Mrs. LeSane."
We all had a chance at it—to sit apart from the class for a while to paint, draw
and silently work out impossible problems on 11 × 17 sheets of newsprint.

Drawing came to mean everything to me. At the back table in Room 2,   18
I learned to build myself a life preserver that I could carry into my home.

We all know that a good education system saves lives, but the people of   19
this country are still told that cutting the budget for public schools is necessary, that poor salaries for teachers are all we can manage and that art, music
and all creative activities must be the first to go when times are lean.

Before- and after-school programs are cut and we are told that public schools   20
are not made for baby-sitting children. If parents are neglectful temporarily
or permanently, for whatever reason, it's certainly sad, but their unlucky
children must fend for themselves. Or slip through the cracks. Or wander in
a dark night alone.

We are told in a thousand ways that not only are public schools not im-   21
portant, but that the children who attend them, the children who need them
most, are not important either. We leave them to learn from the blind eye of
a television, or to the mercy of "a thousand points of light"[1] that can be as
far away as stars.

---

[1]In his inaugural address, President George H. W. Bush used this phrase to encourage nongovernmental community action (editors' note).

I was lucky. I had Mrs. LeSane. I had Mr. Gunderson. I had an abun-   22
dance of art supplies. And I had a particular brand of neglect in my home
that allowed me to slip away and get to them. But what about the rest of the
kids who weren't as lucky? What happened to them?

By the time the bell rang that morning I had finished my drawing and   23
Mrs. LeSane pinned it up on the special bulletin board she reserved for
drawings from the back table. It was the same picture I always drew—a sun
in the corner of a blue sky over a nice house with flowers all around it.

Mrs. LeSane asked us to please stand, face the flag, place our right hands   24
over our hearts and say the Pledge of Allegiance. Children across the country
do it faithfully. I wonder now when the country will face its children and say
a pledge right back.

Questions for Close Reading

MyWritingLab

1. What is the selection's thesis? Locate the sentence(s) in which Barry states her
main idea. If she doesn't state the thesis explicitly, express it in your own words.
2. Various details from Barry's narrative essay let the reader know that her childhood
home life was far from perfect. Skim back over the essay and make a list of the
details she includes to describe what she refers to as "a particular brand of neglect
in [her] home" (paragraph 22).
3. Barry says that the first time she sneaked out of her house early that morning
when she was seven, she did not know why she was leaving and she "did not
think about it" (paragraph 6). She only knew that she was seized by panic and
had to escape. From what was she escaping, and what was there about her school
that made it a "sanctuary" for her? Why do you think she "did not want to think
about" why she was sneaking away from home?
4. What details both for and against budget cuts in education are included in Barry's
essay?

Questions About the Writer's Craft

1. **The pattern.** What kind of organizational pattern does Barry use in her narrative
essay, and in what ways is this an appropriate choice for organizing the selection?
2. In her essay Barry uses repeated references to the absence of sound. Locate those
references and reflect on how she uses them. In what ways do you think they add
to or take away from the essay's effectiveness?
3. **Other patterns.** Although the primary focus of Barry's essay is on narrating a
story from her childhood and the important role school played as a safe refuge,
her essay is also *persuasive*. She takes a stand and makes a strong *argument*. In
what ways does the personal anecdote she tells in the first sixteen paragraphs of
the essay make her political argument stronger than it would be had she not included her own story?
4. In the essay, Barry reflects on her childhood experience and comes to realizations
about herself that she did not make when she was a small child. Read through the
essay, listing the discoveries she makes about herself as she reflects. In what ways
do Barry's reflections add to the effectiveness of her essay?

Writing Assignments Using Narration as a Pattern of Development

1. Barry's essay tells about a time when she was seized by panic and felt that she had to escape. Write an essay about a time in your life when you felt that you had to get away from a particular situation—a time when you had to make a change in your life. Go beyond telling your story and reflect on *why* you needed to get away and *why* you took the steps needed to make the change.
2. Barry writes about individuals in her life who were there when she desperately needed them. Write a narrative essay about a time when someone reached out to you and helped you when you especially needed help. Use vivid details and believable dialogue to enrich your essay.

Writing Assignment Combining Patterns of Development

3. In her essay Barry combines *narration* and *argumentation-persuasion*. Write an essay in which you *argue* for an educational or child-rearing issue that matters to you. Include a story that helps the reader understand why the issue is important to you. Take time to conduct any research needed to substantiate your claims, and include those findings in your essay. Consider using images—perhaps charts or graphs—that illustrate your findings for your readers.

Joan Murray

Joan Murray—a poet, writer, editor, and playwright—was born in New York City in 1945. She attended Hunter College and New York University, and published her first volume of poetry, which she also illustrated, in 1975. Three of her poetry books—*Queen of the Mist, Looking for the Parade,* and *The Same Water*—have won prizes. Her most recent volume of poetry is *Dancing on the Edge,* published in 2002. This essay appeared in the "Lives" section of the weekly *New York Times Magazine* on May 13, 2007.

Pre-Reading Journal Entry

MyWritingLab

We are used to having our mothers care for us, but sometimes we have to care for our mothers. Reflect on an occasion when you had to do something important for your mother or other caregiver. What was the situation? How did you help? How did you feel about helping someone who normally helped you? Use your journal to respond to these questions.

Someone's Mother

Hitchhiking is generally illegal where I live in upstate New York, but   1
it's not unusual to see someone along Route 20 with an outstretched thumb or a handmade sign saying "Boston." This hitchhiker, though, was

waving both arms in the air and grinning like a president boarding Air Force One.

I was doing 60—eager to get home after a dental appointment in Albany—and I was a mile past the hitchhiker before something made me turn back. I couldn't say if the hitchhiker was a man or a woman. All I knew was that the hitchhiker was old. 2

As I drove back up the hill, I eyed the hitchhiker in the distance: dark blue raincoat, jaunty black beret. Thin arms waving, spine a little bent. Wisps of white hair lilting as the trucks whizzed by. I made a U-turn and pulled up on the gravel, face to face with an eager old woman who kept waving till I stopped. I saw no broken-down vehicle. There was no vehicle at all. She wore the same broad grin I noticed when I passed her. 3

I rolled my window down. "Can I call someone for you?" 4

"No, I'm fine—I just need a ride." 5

"Where are you going?" 6

"Nassau." 7

That was three miles away. "Are you going there to shop?" 8

"No. I live there." 9

"What are you doing here?" I asked with a tone I hadn't used since my son was a teenager. 10

"I was out for a walk." 11

I glanced down the road: Jet's Autobody. Copeland Coating. Thoma Tire Company. And the half-mile hill outside Nassau—so steep that there's a second lane for trucks. She must have climbed the shoulder of that hill. And the next one. And the next. Until something made her stop and throw her hands in the air. 12

"Did you get lost?" I asked, trying to conceal my alarm. 13

"It was a nice day," she said with a little cry. "Can't an old lady go for a walk on a nice day and get lost?" 14

It wasn't a question meant to be answered. She came around to the passenger side, opened the door and sat down. On our way to Nassau, she admitted to being 92. Though she ducked my questions about her name, her address and her family. "Just leave me at the drugstore," she said. 15

"I'll take you home," I said. "Then you can call someone." 16

"Please," she said, "just leave me at the drugstore." 17

"I can't leave you there," I replied just as firmly. "I'm going to take you to your house. Or else to the police station." 18

"No, no," she begged. She was agitated now. "If my son finds out, he'll put me in a home." 19

Already I was seeing my own mother, who's 90. A few years ago, she was living in her house on Long Island, surrounded by her neighbors, her bird feeders, her azaleas. Then one morning she phoned my brother to say she didn't remember how to get dressed anymore. A few weeks later, with sorrow and worry, we arranged her move to a nursing home. 20

I noticed that the hitchhiker had a white dove pinned to her collar. "Do   21
you belong to a church?" I tried. "Yes," she said. She was grinning. "I'd like
to take you there," I said. "No, please," she said again. "My son will find out."

Things were getting clearer. "You've gotten lost before?"   22

"A few times," she shrugged. "But I always find my way home. Just take   23
me to the drugstore."

As we drove, I kept thinking about my mother, watched over and cared   24
for in a bright, clean place. I also thought about her empty bird feeders, her
azaleas blooming for no one, the way she whispers on the phone, "I don't
know anyone here."

When I pulled into the parking strip beside the drugstore, the hitchhiker   25
let herself out. "I just need to sit on the step for a while," she said before
closing the door. I stepped out after her. "Can't I take you home?" I asked
as gently as I could.

She looked into my eyes for a moment. "I don't know where I live,"   26
she said in the tiniest voice. "But someone will come along who knows me.
They always do."

I watched as she sat herself down on the step. Already she had dismissed   27
me from her service. She was staring ahead with her grin intact, waiting for
the next person who would aid her.

I should call the police, I thought. But then surely her son would be   28
told. I should speak with the pharmacists. Surely they might know her—
though they might know her son as well. Yet who was I to keep this incident
from him? And yet how could I help him put the hitchhiker in a home?

"Promise me you'll tell the druggist if no one comes soon," I said to her   29
with great seriousness.

"I promise," she said with a cheerful little wave.   30

Questions for Close Reading

MyWritingLab

1. What is the selection's thesis? Locate the sentence(s) in which Murray states her main idea. If she doesn't state her thesis explicitly, express it in your own words.
2. What is the external conflict Murray experiences in this essay? What is the internal conflict?
3. In paragraph 22, the author says "Things were getting clearer." What does she mean by this?
4. Why does Murray finally go along with the hitchhiker's wishes?

Questions About the Writer's Craft

1. **The pattern.** How does Murray organize the events in this essay? How does she keep the reader oriented as her story progresses?
2. **Other patterns.** In some passages, Murray *describes* the hitchhiker's appearance. What do these descriptions contribute to the narrative?
3. In paragraphs 12, 20, 24, and 28, Murray tells us her thoughts. What effect do these sections have on the pace of the narrative? How do they affect our understanding of what is happening?
4. Murray uses a lot of dialogue in this essay. Explain why the use of dialogue is (or is not) effective. What function does the dialogue have?

Writing Assignments Using Narration as a Pattern of Development

1. Murray's encounter with the hitchhiker happens as she is driving home. Recall a time when you were traveling in a car, bus, or other vehicle and something surprising occurred. Were you frightened, puzzled, amused? Did you learn something about people or about yourself? Tell the story using first-person narration, being sure to include your thoughts as well as your actions and the actions of others.
2. Write a narrative about an incident in your life in which a stranger helped you, and explain how this made you feel. The experience might have made you grateful, resentful, or anxious like the hitchhiker. Use either flashback or flashforward to emphasize an event in your narrative.

Writing Assignment Combining Patterns of Development

3. Did Murray do the right thing when she left the elderly woman sitting in front of the drugstore? Write an essay in which you *argue* that Murray did or did not act properly. You can support your argument using *examples* from the essay showing the hitchhiker's state of mental and physical health. You can also support your argument by presenting the possible positive or negative effects of Murray's action, depending on your point of view.

Langston Hughes

One of the foremost members of the 1920s literary movement known as the Harlem Renaissance, Langston Hughes (1902–1967) committed himself to portraying the richness of Black life in the United States. A poet and a writer of short stories, Hughes was greatly influenced by the rhythms of blues and jazz. In his later years, he published two autobiographical works, *The Big Sea* (1940) and *I Wonder as I Wander* (1956), and he wrote a history of the National Association for the Advancement of Colored People (NAACP). The following selection is from *The Big Sea*.

Pre-Reading Journal Entry

MyWritingLab

Young people often feel pressured by family and community to adopt certain values, beliefs, or traditions. In your journal, reflect on some of the pressures that you've experienced. What was your response to these pressures? What have been the consequences of your response? Do you think your experience with these family or community pressures was unique or fairly common?

Salvation

I was saved from sin when I was going on thirteen. But not really saved. It happened like this. There was a big revival at my Auntie Reed's church. Every night for weeks there had been much preaching, singing, praying, and shouting, and some very hardened sinners had been brought to Christ, and the membership of the church had grown by leaps and bounds. Then just before the revival ended, they held a special meeting for children, "to bring the young lambs to the fold." My aunt spoke of it for days ahead. That night I was escorted to the front row and placed on the mourners' bench with all the other young sinners, who had not yet been brought to Jesus.

My aunt told me that when you were saved you saw a light, and something happened to you inside! And Jesus came into your life! And God was with you from then on! She said you could see and hear and feel Jesus in your soul. I believed her. I had heard a great many old people say the same thing and it seemed to me they ought to know. So I sat there calmly in the hot, crowded church, waiting for Jesus to come to me.

The preacher preached a wonderful rhythmical sermon, all moans and shouts and lonely cries and dire pictures of hell, and then he sang a song about the ninety and nine safe in the fold, but one little lamb was left out in the cold. Then he said: "Won't you come? Won't you come to Jesus? Young lambs, won't you come?" And he held out his arms to all us young sinners there on the mourners' bench. And the little girls cried. And some of them jumped up and went to Jesus right away. But most of us just sat there.

1

2

3

A great many older people came and knelt around us and prayed, old 4
women with jet-black faces and braided hair, old men with work-gnarled
hands. And the church sang a song about the lower lights are burning, some
poor sinners to be saved. And the whole building rocked with prayer and song.

Still I kept waiting to *see* Jesus. 5

Finally all the young people had gone to the altar and were saved, but 6
one boy and me. He was a rounder's son named Westley. Westley and I were
surrounded by sisters and deacons praying. It was very hot in the church, and
getting late now. Finally Westley said to me in a whisper: "God damn! I'm
tired o' sitting here. Let's get up and be saved." So he got up and was saved.

Then I was left all alone on the mourners' bench. My aunt came and 7
knelt at my knees and cried, while prayers and songs swirled all around me in
the little church. The whole congregation prayed for me alone, in a mighty
wail of moans and voices. And I kept waiting serenely for Jesus, waiting,
waiting—but he didn't come. I wanted to see him, but nothing happened to
me. Nothing! I wanted something to happen to me, but nothing happened.

I heard the songs and the minister saying: "Why don't you come? My 8
dear child, why don't you come to Jesus? Jesus is waiting for you. He wants
you. Why don't you come? Sister Reed, what is this child's name?"

"Langston," my aunt sobbed. 9

"Langston, why don't you come? Why don't you come and be saved? 10
Oh, Lamb of God! Why don't you come?"

Now it was really getting late. I began to be ashamed of myself, holding 11
everything up so long. I began to wonder what God thought about Westley,
who certainly hadn't seen Jesus either, but who was now sitting proudly on
the platform, swinging his knickerbockered legs and grinning down at me,
surrounded by deacons and old women on their knees praying. God had not
struck Westley dead for taking his name in vain or for lying in the temple. So
I decided that maybe to save further trouble, I'd better lie, too, and say that
Jesus had come, and get up and be saved.

So I got up. 12

Suddenly the whole room broke into a sea of shouting, as they saw me 13
rise. Waves of rejoicing swept the place. Women leaped in the air. My aunt
threw her arms around me. The minister took me by the hand and led me to
the platform.

When things quieted down, in a hushed silence, punctuated by a few 14
ecstatic "Amens," all the new young lambs were blessed in the name of God.
Then joyous singing filled the room.

That night, for the last time in my life but one—for I was a big boy 15
twelve years old—I cried. I cried, in bed alone, and couldn't stop. I buried
my head under the quilts, but my aunt heard me. She woke up and told my
uncle I was crying because the Holy Ghost had come into my life, and because I had seen Jesus. But I was really crying because I couldn't bear to tell

her that I had lied, that I had deceived everybody in the church, and I hadn't seen Jesus, and that now I didn't believe there was a Jesus any more, since he didn't come to help me.

Questions for Close Reading

MyWritingLab

1. What is the selection's thesis (or narrative point)? Locate the sentence(s) in which Hughes states his main idea. If Hughes doesn't state the thesis explicitly, express it in your own words.
2. During the revival meeting, what pressures are put on the young Langston to get up and be saved?
3. How does Westley's attitude differ from Hughes's?
4. Does the narrator's Auntie Reed really understand him? Why can't he tell her the truth about his experience in the church?

Questions About the Writer's Craft

1. **The pattern.** A narrative's power can often be traced to a conflict within the event being recounted. What conflict does the narrator of "Salvation" experience? How does Hughes create tension about this conflict?
2. What key role does Westley serve in the resolution of the narrator's dilemma? How does Hughes's inclusion of Westley in the story help us to understand the narrator better?
3. **Other patterns.** The thirteenth paragraph presents a *metaphor* of the church as an ocean. What images develop this metaphor? What does the metaphor tell us about Hughes's feelings and those of the church people?
4. The singing of hymns is a major part of this religious service. Why do you think Hughes has the narrator reveal the subjects and even the lyrics of some of the hymns?

Writing Assignments Using Narration as a Pattern of Development

1. Like Hughes, we sometimes believe that deception is our best alternative. Write a narrative about a time you felt deception was the best way either to protect those you care about or to maintain the respect of those important to you.
2. Write a narrative essay about a chain of events that caused you to become disillusioned about a person or institution you had previously regarded highly. Begin as Hughes does by presenting your initial beliefs. Relate the sequence of events that changed your evaluation of the person or organization. In the conclusion, explain the short- and long-term effects of the incident.

Writing Assignment Combining Patterns of Development

3. Write a *persuasive* essay *arguing* either that lying is sometimes right or that lying is always wrong. Apply your thesis to particular situations and show how lying is or is not the right course of action. Be sure to keep your *narration* of these situations brief and focused on your point. Remember to acknowledge the opposing viewpoint.

Barbara Ehrenreich

Barbara Ehrenreich was born in Montana in 1941. Early on, she studied science, earning a Ph.D. in cell biology from Rockefeller University. But her interest soon turned to social issues, and she became an activist for peace, women's rights, health care, and economic justice. Ehrenreich has published articles in *Time, Mother Jones, The Nation,* and the *New York Times.* Her books include *For Her Own Good: Two Centuries of the Experts' Advice to Women* (2005), *Bait and Switch: The (Futile) Pursuit of the American Dream* (2006), *Bright-Sided: How the Relentless Promotion of Positive Thinking Has Undermined America* (2009), and most recently *Living with a Wild God* (2014). The following excerpt is from her book *Nickel and Dimed: On (Not) Getting By in America* (2001), in which she chronicles her experiences as a worker in low-wage, blue collar jobs.

Pre-Reading Journal Entry

MyWritingLab

Ehrenreich says that her experience as a server changed her, but not necessarily in a good way. Think of experiences that you feel have changed you for the better—perhaps made you more thoughtful, serious, optimistic, helpful, or caring. Was the change gradual or sudden? Write some notes in your journal.

Serving in Florida

Picture a fat person's hell, and I don't mean a place with no food. 1 Instead there is everything you might eat if eating had no bodily consequences—the cheese fries, the chicken-fried steaks, the fudge-laden desserts—only here every bite must be paid for, one way or another, in human discomfort. The kitchen is a cavern, a stomach leading to the lower intestine that is the garbage and dishwashing area, from which issue bizarre smells combining the edible and the offal: creamy carrion, pizza barf, and that unique and enigmatic Jerry's[1] scent, citrus fart. The floor is slick with spills, forcing us to walk through the kitchen with tiny steps, like Susan McDougal[2] in leg irons. Sinks everywhere are clogged with scraps of lettuce, decomposing lemon wedges, water-logged toast crusts. Put your hand down on any counter and you risk being stuck to it by the film of ancient syrup spills, and this is unfortunate because hands are utensils here, used for scooping up lettuce onto the salad plates, lifting out pie slices, and even moving hash browns from one plate to another. The regulation poster in the single unisex rest room admonishes us to wash our hands thoroughly, and

[1]"Jerry's" is the fictitious name for the "national chain" where the author worked (editors' note).
[2]Susan McDougal was imprisoned for refusing to testify against President Bill Clinton and Hillary Clinton before the 1996 Whitewater grand jury (editors' note).

even offers instructions for doing so, but there is always some vital substance missing—soap, paper towels, toilet paper—and I never found all three at once. You learn to stuff your pockets with napkins before going in there, and too bad about the customers, who must eat, although they don't realize it, almost literally out of our hands.

The break room summarizes the whole situation: there is none, because   2 there are no breaks at Jerry's. For six to eight hours in a row, you never sit except to pee. Actually, there are three folding chairs at a table immediately adjacent to the bathroom, but hardly anyone ever sits in this, the very rectum of the gastroarchitectural system. Rather, the function of the peri-toilet area is to house the ashtrays in which servers and dishwashers leave their cigarettes burning at all times, like votive candles, so they don't have to waste time lighting up again when they dash back here for a puff. Almost everyone smokes as if their pulmonary well-being depended on it—the multinational mélange of cooks; the dishwashers, who are all Czechs here; the servers, who are American natives—creating an atmosphere in which oxygen is only an occasional pollutant. My first morning at Jerry's, when the hypoglycemic shakes set in, I complain to one of my fellow servers that I don't understand how she can go so long without food. "Well, I don't understand how *you* can go so long without a cigarette," she responds in a tone of reproach. Because work is what you do for others; smoking is what you do for yourself. I don't know why the antismoking crusaders have never grasped the element of defiant self-nurturance that makes the habit so endearing to its victims—as if, in the American workplace, the only thing people have to call their own is the tumors they are nourishing and the spare moments they devote to feeding them.

Now, the Industrial Revolution[3] is not an easy transition, especially, in   3 my experience, when you have to zip through it in just a couple of days. I have gone from craft work straight into the factory, from the air-conditioned morgue of the Hearthside[4] directly into the flames. Customers arrive in human waves, sometimes disgorged fifty at a time from their tour buses, puckish and whiny. Instead of two "girls" on the floor at once, there can be as many as six of us running around in our brilliant pink-and-orange Hawaiian shirts. Conversations, either with customers or with fellow employees, seldom last more than twenty seconds at a time. On my first day, in fact, I am hurt by my sister servers' coldness. My mentor for the day is a supremely competent, emotionally uninflected twenty-three-year-old, and the others, who gossip a little among themselves about the real reason someone is out sick today and

[3]"Industrial Revolution" refers to the rapid social and economic change occurring when machine-made production is introduced into a society, as in England in the late eighteenth century (editors' note).
[4]"Hearthside" is the fictitious name for the other restaurant where the author worked (editors' note).

the size of the bail bond someone else has had to pay, ignore me completely. On my second day, I find out why. "Well, it's good to see *you* again," one of them says in greeting. "Hardly anyone comes back after the first day." I feel powerfully vindicated—a survivor—but it would take a long time, probably months, before I could hope to be accepted into this sorority.

I start out with the beautiful, heroic idea of handling the two jobs at   4 once, and for two days I almost do it: working the breakfast/lunch shift at Jerry's from 8:00 till 2:00, arriving at the Hearthside a few minutes late, at 2:10, and attempting to hold out until 10:00. In the few minutes I have between jobs, I pick up a spicy chicken sandwich at the Wendy's drive-through window, gobble it down in the car, and change from khaki slacks to black, from Hawaiian to rust-colored polo. There is a problem, though. When, during the 3:00-4:00 o'clock dead time, I finally sit down to wrap silver, my flesh seems to bond to the seat. I try to refuel with a purloined cup of clam chowder, as I've seen Gail[5] and Joan do dozens of times, but Stu catches me and hisses "No *eating!*" although there's not a customer around to be offended by the sight of food making contact with a server's lips. So I tell Gail I'm going to quit, and she hugs me and says she might just follow me to Jerry's herself.

But the chances of this are minuscule. She has left the flophouse and her   5 annoying roommate and is back to living in her truck. But, guess what, she reports to me excitedly later that evening, Phillip has given her permission to park overnight in the hotel parking lot, as long as she keeps out of sight, and the parking lot should be totally safe since it's patrolled by a hotel security guard! With the Hearthside offering benefits like that, how could anyone think of leaving? This must be Phillip's theory, anyway. He accepts my resignation with a shrug, his main concern being that I return my two polo shirts and aprons.

Gail would have triumphed at Jerry's, I'm sure, but for me it's a crash   6 course in exhaustion management. Years ago, the kindly fry cook who trained me to waitress at a Los Angeles truck stop used to say: Never make an unnecessary trip; if you don't have to walk fast, walk slow; if you don't have to walk, stand. But at Jerry's the effort of distinguishing necessary from unnecessary and urgent from whenever would itself be too much of an energy drain. The only thing to do is to treat each shift as a one-time-only emergency: you've got fifty starving people out there, lying scattered on the battlefield, so get out there and feed them! Forget that you will have to do this again tomorrow, forget that you will have to be alert enough to dodge the drunks on the drive home tonight—just burn, burn, burn! Ideally, at some point you enter what servers call a "rhythm" and psychologists term a "flow state," where signals pass from the sense organs directly to the

[5]Gail, Joan, Stu, and Phillip (in the next paragraph) work at the Hearthside (editors' note).

muscles, bypassing the cerebral cortex, and a Zen-like emptiness sets in. I'm on a 2:00-10:00 P.M. shift now, and a male server from the morning shift tells me about the time he "pulled a triple"—three shifts in a row, all the way around the clock—and then got off and had a drink and met this girl, and maybe he shouldn't tell me this, but they had sex right then and there and it was like *beautiful.*

But there's another capacity of the neuromuscular system, which is pain. 7
I start tossing back drugstore-brand ibuprofens as if they were vitamin C, four before each shift, because an old mouse-related repetitive-stress injury in my upper back has come back to full-spasm strength, thanks to the tray carrying. In my ordinary life, this level of disability might justify a day of ice packs and stretching. Here I comfort myself with the Aleve commercial where the cute blue-collar guy asks: If you quit after working four hours, what would your boss say? And the not-so-cute blue-collar guy, who's lugging a metal beam on his back, answers: He'd fire me, that's what. But fortunately, the commercial tells us, we workers can exert the same kind of authority over our painkillers that our bosses exert over us. If Tylenol doesn't want to work for more than four hours, you just fire its ass and switch to Aleve.

True, I take occasional breaks from this life, going home now and then 8
to catch up on e-mail and for conjugal visits (though I am careful to "pay" for everything I eat here, at $5 for a dinner, which I put in a jar), seeing *The Truman Show*[6] with friends and letting them buy my ticket. And I still have those what-am-I-doing-here moments at work, when I get so homesick for the printed word that I obsessively reread the six-page menu. But as the days go by, my old life is beginning to look exceedingly strange. The e-mails and phone messages addressed to my former self come from a distant race of people with exotic concerns and far too much time on their hands. The neighborly market I used to cruise for produce now looks forbiddingly like a Manhattan yuppie emporium. And when I sit down one morning in my real home to pay bills from my past life, I am dazzled by the two- and three-figure sums owed to outfits like Club Body Tech and Amazon.com.

Management at Jerry's is generally calmer and more "professional" 9
than at the Hearthside, with two exceptions. One is Joy, a plump, blowsy woman in her early thirties who once kindly devoted several minutes of her time to instructing me in the correct one-handed method of tray carrying but whose moods change disconcertingly from shift to shift and even within one. The other is B.J., aka B.J. the Bitch, whose contribution is to stand by the kitchen counter and yell, "Nita, your order's up, move it!" or "Barbara, didn't you see you've got another table out there? Come *on*, girl!" Among other things, she is hated for having replaced the whipped cream squirt cans

[6]In *The Truman Show*, a 1998 movie, a man discovers he has lived his whole life as a kind of reality television show (editors' note).

with big plastic whipped-cream-filled baggies that have to be squeezed with both hands—because, reportedly, she saw or thought she saw employees trying to inhale the propellant gas from the squirt cans, in the hope that it might be nitrous oxide. On my third night, she pulls me aside abruptly and brings her face so close that it looks like she's planning to butt me with her forehead. But instead of saying "You're fired," she says, "You're doing fine." The only trouble is I'm spending time chatting with customers: "That's how they're getting you." Furthermore I am letting them "run me," which means harassment by sequential demands: you bring the catsup and they decide they want extra Thousand Island; you bring that and they announce they now need a side of fries, and so on into distraction. Finally she tells me not to take her wrong. She tries to say things in a nice way, but "you get into a mode, you know, because everything has to move so fast."[7]

I mumble thanks for the advice, feeling like I've just been stripped naked   10 by the crazed enforcer of some ancient sumptuary law:[8] No chatting for *you*, girl. No fancy service ethic allowed for the serfs: Chatting with customers is for the good-looking young college-educated servers in the downtown carpaccio and ceviche joints, the kids who can make $70–$100 a night. What had I been thinking? My job is to move orders from tables to kitchen and then trays from kitchen to tables. Customers are in fact the major obstacle to the smooth transformation of information into food and food into money— they are, in short, the enemy. And the painful thing is that I'm beginning to see it this way myself. There are the traditional asshole types—frat boys who down multiple Buds and then make a fuss because the steaks are so emaciated and the fries so sparse—as well as the variously impaired—due to age, diabetes, or literacy issues—who require patient nutritional counseling. The worst, for some reason, are the Visible Christians—like the ten-person table, all jolly and sanctified after Sunday night service, who run me mercilessly and then leave me $1 on a $92 bill. Or the guy with the crucifixion T-shirt (SOMEONE TO LOOK UP TO) who complains that his baked potato is too hard and his iced tea too icy (I cheerfully fix both) and leaves no tip at all. As a general rule, people wearing crosses or WWJD? ("What Would Jesus Do?") buttons look at us disapprovingly no matter what we do, as if they were confusing waitressing with Mary Magdalene's original profession.

I make friends, over time, with the other "girls" who work my shift: 11 Nita, the tattooed twenty-something who taunts us by going around

---

[7] In *Workers in a Lean World: Unions in the International Economy* (Verso, 1997), Kim Moody cites studies finding an increase in stress-related workplace injuries and illness between the mid-1980s and the early 1990s. He argues that rising stress levels reflect a new system of "management by stress" in which workers in a variety of industries are being squeezed to extract maximum productivity, to the detriment of their health (author's note).

[8] A sumptuary law regulates personal habits, especially regarding food and dress, on the basis of a community's moral or religious beliefs (editors' note).

saying brightly, "Have we started making money yet?" Ellen, whose teen-age son cooks on the graveyard shift and who once managed a restaurant in Massachusetts but won't try out for management here because she prefers being a "common worker" and not "ordering people around." Easygoing fiftyish Lucy, with the raucous laugh, who limps toward the end of the shift because of something that has gone wrong with her leg, the exact nature of which cannot be determined without health insurance. We talk about the usual girl things—men, children, and the sinister allure of Jerry's chocolate peanut-butter cream pie—though no one, I notice, ever brings up anything potentially expensive, like shopping or movies. As at the Hearthside, the only recreation ever referred to is partying, which requires little more than some beer, a joint, and a few close friends. Still, no one is homeless, or cops to it anyway, thanks usually to a working husband or boyfriend. All in all, we form a reliable mutual-support group: if one of us is feeling sick or over-whelmed, another one will "bev" a table or even carry trays for her. If one of us is off sneaking a cigarette or a pee, the others will do their best to conceal her absence from the enforcers of corporate rationality.[9]

But my saving human connection—my oxytocin receptor, as it were—   12
is George, the nineteen-year-old Czech dishwasher who has been in this country exactly one week. We get talking when he asks me, tortuously, how much cigarettes cost at Jerry's. I do my best to explain that they cost over a dollar more here than at a regular store and suggest that he just take one from the half-filled packs that are always lying around on the break table. But that would be unthinkable. Except for the one tiny earring signaling his allegiance to some vaguely alternative point of view, George is a perfect straight arrow—crew-cut, hardworking, and hungry for eye contact. "Czech Republic," I ask, "or Slovakia?" and he seems delighted that I know the dif-ference. "Vaclav Havel."[10] I try, "Velvet Revolution, Frank Zappa?" "Yes, yes, 1989," he says, and 1 realize that for him this is already history.

---

[9]Until April 1998, there was no federally mandated right to bathroom breaks. According to Marc Linder and Ingrid Nygaard, authors of *Void Where Prohibited: Rest Breaks and the Right to Urinate on Company Time* (Cornell University Press, 1997), "The right to rest and void at work is not high on the list of social or political causes supported by professional or executive employees, who enjoy personal workplace liberties that millions of factory workers can only dream about....While we were dismayed to discover that workers lacked an acknowledged right to void at work, [the workers] were amazed by outsiders' naïve belief that their employers would permit them to perform this basic bodily function when necessary....A factory worker, not allowed a break for six-hour stretches, voided into pads worn inside her uniform; and a kindergarten teacher in a school without aides had to take all twenty children with her to the bathroom and line them up outside the stall door while she voided" (author's note).

[10]Vaclav Havel, a writer and dissident, became the first president of the Czech Republic, which was established after the 1989 Velvet Revolution, a nonviolent revolution that ended commu-nism in Czechoslovakia (editors' note).

My project is to teach George English. "How are you today, George?" I   13
say at the start of each shift. "I am good, and how are you today, Barbara?"
I learn that he is not paid by Jerry's but by the "agent" who shipped him
over—$5 an hour, with the agent getting the dollar or so difference between
that and what Jerry's pays dishwashers. I learn also that he shares an apartment with a crowd of other Czech "dishers," as he calls them, and that he
cannot sleep until one of them goes off for his shift, leaving a vacant bed.
We are having one of our ESL sessions late one afternoon when B.J. catches
us at it and orders "Joseph" to take up the rubber mats on the floor near
the dishwashing sinks and mop underneath. "I thought your name was
George," I say loud enough for B.J. to hear as she strides off back to the
counter. Is she embarrassed? Maybe a little, because she greets me back at
the counter with "George, Joseph—there are so many of them!" I say nothing, neither nodding nor smiling, and for this I am punished later, when I
think I am ready to go and she announces that I need to roll fifty more sets
of silverware, and isn't it time I mixed up a fresh four-gallon batch of blue-
cheese dressing? May you grow old in this place, B.J., is the curse I beam out
at her when I am finally permitted to leave. May the syrup spills glue your
feet to the floor....

In line with my reduced living conditions, a new form of ugliness arises   14
at Jerry's. First we are confronted—via an announcement on the computers
through which we input orders—with the new rule that the hotel bar, the
Driftwood, is henceforth off-limits to restaurant employees. The culprit, I
learn through the grapevine, is the ultraefficient twenty-three-year-old who
trained me—another trailer home dweller and a mother of three. Something
had set her off one morning, so she slipped out for a nip and returned to
the floor impaired. The restriction mostly hurts Ellen, whose habit it is to
free her hair from its rubber band and drop by the Driftwood for a couple
of Zins before heading home at the end of her shift, but all of us feel the
chill. Then the next day, when I go for straws, I find the dry-storage room
locked. It's never been locked before; we go in and out of it all day—for
napkins, jelly containers, Styrofoam cups for takeout. Vic, the portly assistant
manager who opens it for me, explains that he caught one of the dishwashers
attempting to steal something and, unfortunately, the miscreant will be with
us until a replacement can be found—hence the locked door. I neglect to ask
what he had been trying to steal but Vic tells me who he is—the kid with the
buzz cut and the earning, you know, he's back there right now.

I wish I could say I rushed back and confronted George to get his side   15
of the story. I wish I could say I stood up to Vic and insisted that George
be given a translator and allowed to defend himself or announced that I'd
find a lawyer who'd handle the case pro bono. At the very least I should
have testified as to the kid's honesty. The mystery to me is that there's not
much worth stealing in the dry-storage room, at least not in any fenceable

quantity: "Is Gyorgi here, and am having 200—maybe 250—catsup packets. What do you say?" My guess is that he had taken—if he had taken anything at all—some Saltines or a can of cherry pie mix and that the motive for taking it was hunger.

So why didn't I intervene? Certainly not because I was held back by the kind of moral paralysis that can mask as journalistic objectivity. On the contrary, something new—something loathsome and servile—had infected me, along with the kitchen odors that I could still sniff on my bra when I finally undressed at night. In real life I am moderately brave, but plenty of brave people shed their courage in POW camps, and maybe something similar goes on in the infinitely more congenial milieu of the low-wage American workplace. Maybe, in a month or two more at Jerry's, I might have regained my crusading spirit. Then again, in a month or two I might have turned into a different person altogether—say, the kind of person who would have turned George in.... [16]

I can do this two-job thing, is my theory, if I can drink enough caffeine and avoid getting distracted by George's ever more obvious suffering.[11] The first few days after the alleged theft, he seemed not to understand the trouble he was in, and our chirpy little conversations had continued. But the last couple of shifts he's been listless and unshaven, and tonight he looks like the ghost we all know him to be, with dark half-moons hanging from his eyes. At one point, when I am briefly immobilized by the task of filling little paper cups with sour cream for baked potatoes, he comes over and looks as if he'd like to explore the limits of our shared vocabulary, but I am called to the floor for a table. I resolve to give him all my tips that night, and to hell with the experiment in low-wage money management. At eight, Ellen and I grab a snack together standing at the mephitic end of the kitchen counter, but I can only manage two or three mozzarella sticks, and lunch had been a mere handful of McNuggets. I am not tired at all, I assure myself, though it may be that there is simply no more "I" left to do the tiredness monitoring. What I would see if I were more alert to the situation is that the forces of destruction are already massing against me. There is only one cook on duty, a young man named Jesus ("Hay-Sue," that is), and he is new to the job. And there is Joy, who shows up to take over in the middle of the shift dressed in high heels and a long, clingy white dress and fuming as if she'd just been stood up in some cocktail bar. [17]

[11]In 1996 the number of persons holding two or more jobs averaged 7.8 million, or 6.2 percent of the workforce. It was about the same rate for men and women (6.1 versus 6.2). About two-thirds of multiple jobholders work one job full-time and the other part-time. Only a heroic minority—4 percent of men and 2 percent of women—work two full-time jobs simultaneously (John F. Stinson Jr., "New Data on Multiple Jobholding Available from the CPS," *Monthly Labor Review*, March 1997) (author's note).

Then it comes, the perfect storm. Four of my tables fill up at once. Four   18
tables is nothing for me now, but only so long as they are obligingly stag-
gered. As I bev table 27, tables 25, 28, and 24 are watching enviously. As I
bev 25, 24 glowers because their bevs haven't even been ordered. Twenty-
eight is four yuppyish types, meaning everything on the side and agonizing
instructions as to the chicken Caesars. Twenty-five is a middle-aged black
couple who complain, with some justice, that the iced tea isn't fresh and the
tabletop is sticky. But table 24 is the meteorological event of the century: ten
British tourists who seem to have made the decision to absorb the American
experience entirely by mouth. Here everyone has at least two drinks—iced
tea *and* milk shake, Michelob *and* water (with lemon slice in the water,
please)—and a huge, promiscuous orgy of breakfast specials, mozz sticks,
chicken strips, quesadillas, burgers with cheese and without, sides of hash
browns with cheddar, with onions, with gravy, seasoned fries, plain fries, ba-
nana splits. Poor Jesus! Poor me! Because when I arrive with their first tray
of food—after three prior trips just to refill bevs—Princess Di refuses to eat
her chicken strips with her pancake and sausage special since, as she now reveals, the strips were meant to be an appetizer. Maybe the others would have
accepted their meals, but Di, who is deep into her third Michelob, insists
that everything else go back while they work on their starters. Meanwhile,
the yuppies are waving me down for more decaf and the black couple looks
ready to summon the NAACP.

Much of what happens next is lost in the fog of war. Jesus starts going   19
under. The little printer in front of him is spewing out orders faster than
he can rip them off, much less produce the meals. A menacing restless-
ness rises from the tables, all of which are full. Even the invincible Ellen
is ashen from stress. I take table 24 their reheated main courses, which
they immediately reject as either too cold or fossilized by the microwave.
When I return to the kitchen with their trays (three trays in three trips) Joy
confronts me with arms akimbo: "What *is* this?" She means the food—the
plates of rejected pancakes, hash browns in assorted flavors, toasts, burgers, sausages, eggs. "Uh, scrambled with cheddar," I try, "and that's—"
"*No*," she screams in my face, "is it a traditional, a super-scramble, an
eye-opener?" I pretend to study my check for a clue, but entropy has been
up to its tricks, not only on the plates but in my head, and I have to admit
that the original order is beyond reconstruction. "You don't know an eye-
opener from a traditional?" she demands in outrage. All I know, in fact, is
that my legs have lost interest in the current venture and have announced
their intention to fold. I am saved by a yuppie (mercifully not one of mine)
who chooses this moment to charge into the kitchen to bellow that his
food is twenty-five minutes late. Joy screams at him to get the hell out of
her kitchen, *please*, and then turns on Jesus in a fury, hurling an empty tray
across the room for emphasis.

I leave. I don't walk out, I just leave. I don't finish my side work or   20
pick up my credit card tips, if any, at the cash register or, of course, ask Joy's
permission to go. And the surprising thing is that you *can* walk out without
permission, that the door opens, that the thick tropical night air parts to let
me pass, that my car is still parked where I left it. There is no vindication
in this exit, no fuck-you surge of relief, just an overwhelming dank sense
of failure pressing down on me and the entire parking lot. I had gone into
this venture in the spirit of science, to test a mathematical proposition, but
somewhere along the line, in the tunnel vision imposed by long shifts and
relentless concentration, it became a test of myself, and clearly I have failed.
Not only had I flamed out as a housekeeper/server, I had forgotten to give
George my tips, and, for reasons perhaps best known to hardworking, generous people like Gail and Ellen, this hurts. I don't cry, but I am in a position
to realize, for the first time in many years, that the tear ducts are still there
and still capable of doing their job.

When I moved out of the trailer park, I gave the key to number 46 to   21
Gail and arranged for my deposit to be transferred to her. She told me that
Joan was still living in her van and that Stu had been fired from the Hearthside. According to the most up-to-date rumors, the drug he ordered from
the restaurant was crack and he was caught dipping into the cash register to
pay for it. I never found out what happened to George.

Questions for Close Reading

MyWritingLab

1. What is the selection's thesis? Locate the sentence(s) in which Ehrenreich states her
   main idea. If she doesn't state her thesis explicitly, express it in your own words.
2. What sort of restaurant is Jerry's? What happens to the author's plan to work two
   jobs? Why?
3. The author describes several people that she works with at Jerry's. Who are these
   people? Who becomes her "saving human connection"? Why?
4. What factors contribute to the author's leaving her job at Jerry's? How does her
   relationship with George change? What is the "perfect storm"? Why does the author feel she has "failed" a test?

Questions About the Writer's Craft

1. **The pattern.** How strong is the narrative focus? What narrative techniques does
   the author use to keep the story compelling for the reader? Give some examples.
2. **Other patterns.** The selection opens, in paragraphs 1 and 2, with a *description* of
   Jerry's. What do you think is the author's purpose? Is she successful?
3. Throughout the selection, Ehrenreich uses a wide-ranging vocabulary, from
   formal language, to conversational language, to slang and even vulgarities. Find
   some examples of the different types of language used. What is the effect of this
   type of diction?

4. Ehrenreich uses comparisons in several places. For example, in paragraph 1, she compares the kitchen to a "stomach leading to a lower intestine that is the garbage and dishwashing area." Find at least two other comparisons the author makes. How effective are these comparisons?

Writing Assignments Using Narration as a Pattern of Development

1. Ehrenreich is unprepared for the exhaustion and hard work involved in waitressing at Jerry's. Think of a situation in which you expected a task—for example, caring for a friend's pet or throwing a surprise party—to be easier than it turned out to be. Write an essay in which you narrate what happened. Be sure to use time signals to keep the story focused. Your essay may be serious or humorous in tone.
2. The author gives a lot of detail about the beginning of her job at Jerry's. Think of your own experience with starting a new job, attending classes at a new school, taking a vacation to a new place, or some similar situation. How helpful were the people you encountered? In an essay, tell the story of what happened on your first day. Use present tense verbs and include dialogue.

Writing Assignment Combining Patterns of Development

3. Research the job of server in your state. How much do servers earn? What labor regulations apply to them? What employment benefits do serving jobs typically offer? If possible, interview a waiter about what he or she likes about the job. Write an essay in which you *compare* the pros and cons of working as a server. Use facts from your research to *illustrate* your ideas.

▼ *Additional Writing Topics*

NARRATION

MyWritingLab

General Assignments

Using narration, develop one of these topics into an essay.

1. An emergency that brought out the best or worst in you
2. The hazards of taking children out to eat
3. An incident that made you believe in fate
4. Your best or worst day at school or work
5. An important learning experience
6. A narrow escape
7. Your first date or first day on the job
8. A memorable childhood experience
9. An unpleasant confrontation
10. An imagined meeting with a historical figure

Assignments Using Visuals

Use the suggested visuals to help develop a narrative essay on one of these topics:

1. The best (or worst) vacation of your life (photos)
2. A school experience that had a positive impact on you (sketches or photos)
3. A family outing with an unexpected outcome (photos)
4. Something you did that you wish you could undo (diagram, photo)
5. A civic event you participated in (photos and/or web links)

Assignments with a Specific Purpose, Audience, and Point of View

1. **Academic life.** Write an article for your old high school newspaper. The article will be read primarily by seniors who are planning to go away to college next year. In the article, narrate a story that points to some truth about the "breaking away" stage of life.
2. **Academic life.** A friend of yours has seen someone cheat on a test, plagiarize an entire paper, or seriously violate some other academic policy. In a letter, convince this friend to inform the instructor or a campus administrator by narrating an incident in which a witness did (or did not) speak up in such a situation. Tell what happened as a result.
3. **Civic activity.** You have had a disturbing encounter with one of the people who seems to have "fallen through the cracks" of society—a street person, an unwanted child, or anyone else who is alone and abandoned. Write a letter to the local newspaper describing this encounter. Your purpose is to arouse people's indignation and compassion and to get help for such unfortunates.
4. **Civic activity.** Your younger brother, sister, relative, or neighborhood friend can't wait to be your age. Write a letter in which you narrate a dramatic story that shows the young person that your age isn't as wonderful as he or she thinks. Be sure to select a story that the person can understand and appreciate.
5. **Workplace action.** As fund-raiser for a particular organization (for example, Red Cross, SPCA, Big Brothers/Big Sisters), you're sending a newsletter to contributors. Support your cause by telling the story of a time when your organization made all the difference—the blood donation that saved a life, the animal that was rescued from abuse, and so on.
6. **Workplace action.** A customer has written a letter to you (or your boss) telling about a bad experience that he or she had with someone in your workplace. On the basis of that single experience, the customer now regards your company and its employees with great suspicion. It's your job to respond to this complaint. Write a letter to the customer balancing his or her negative picture by narrating a story that shows the "flip side" of your company and its employees.

MyWritingLab Visit Chapter 4, "Narration," in MyWritingLab to complete the chapter activities, Pre-Reading Journal Entry activities, Questions for Close Reading, and Additional Writing Topics assignments and to test your understanding of the chapter objectives.

□ fat?
□ fit?

EXEMPLIFICATION

In this chapter, you will learn:

5.1 To use the pattern of exemplification to develop your essays.

5.2 To consider how exemplification can fit your purpose and audience.

5.3 To develop strategies for using exemplification in an essay.

5.4 To develop strategies for revising an exemplification essay.

5.5 To analyze how exemplification is used effectively in student-written and professionally authored selections.

5.6 To write your own essays using exemplification as a strategy.

WHAT IS EXEMPLIFICATION?

If someone asked you, "Have you been to any good restaurants lately?" you probably wouldn't answer "Yes" and then immediately change the subject. Most likely, you would go on to illustrate with *examples*. Perhaps you'd give the names of restaurants you've enjoyed and talk briefly about the specific things you liked: the attractive prices, the tasty main courses, the pleasant service, the tempting desserts. Such examples and details are needed to convince others that your opinion—in this or any matter—is valid. Similarly, when you talk about larger and more important issues, people won't pay much attention to your opinion if all you do is string together vague generalizations: "We have to do something about acid rain. It's had disastrous consequences for the environment. Its negative effects increase every year. Action must be taken to control the problem." To be taken seriously and

165

to convince others that your point is well-founded, you must provide specific supporting examples: "The forests in the Adirondacks are dying"; "Yesterday's rainfall was fifty times more acidic than normal"; "Pine Lake, in the northern part of the state, was once a great fishing spot but now has no fish population."

Examples are equally important when you write an essay. It's not fuzzy generalities and lofty abstractions that make writing impressive. Just the opposite is true. Facts, anecdotes, statistics, details, opinions, and observations are at the heart of effective writing, giving your work substance and solidity.

HOW EXEMPLIFICATION FITS YOUR PURPOSE AND AUDIENCE

The wording of assignments and essay exam questions may signal the need for specific examples:

> Soap operas, whether shown during the day or in the evening, are among the most popular television programs. Why do you think this is so? Provide specific examples to support your position.

> Some observers claim that college students are less interested in learning than in getting ahead in their careers. Cite evidence to support or refute this claim.

> A growing number of people feel that parents should not allow young children to participate in highly competitive team sports. Basing your conclusion on your own experiences and observations, indicate whether you think this point of view is reasonable.

Such phrases as "Provide specific examples," "Cite evidence," and "Basing your conclusion on your own experiences and observations" signal that each essay should be developed through examples.

Usually, though, you won't be told so explicitly to provide examples. Instead, as you think about the best way to achieve your essay's purpose, you'll see the need for illustrative details—no matter which patterns of development you use. For instance, to *persuade* skeptical readers of the value of the Patient Protection and Affordable Care Act of 2010, you might mention specific cases—such as a family bankrupted by medical bills or a chronically ill person denied insurance because of a pre-existing condition—and explain how the law would ameliorate these situations. Similarly, you would supply examples in a *causal analysis* speculating on the likely impact of a proposed tuition hike at your college. To convince the college administration of the probable negative effects of such a hike, you might cite the following examples: articles reporting a nationwide upswing in student transfers to less expensive schools; statistics indicating a significant drop in grades among already employed students forced to work more hours to pay increased tuition costs; interviews with students too financially strapped to continue their college education.

Examples make writing *interesting*. Assume you're writing an essay showing that television commercials are biased against women. Your essay would be lifeless and boring if all it did was repeat, in a general way, that commercials present stereotyped views of women.

> An anti-female bias is rampant in television commercials. It is very much alive, yet most viewers seem to take it all in stride. Few people protest the obviously sexist characters and statements in such commercials. Surely, these commercials misrepresent the way most of us live.

Without interesting particulars, readers may respond, "Who cares?" But if you provide specific examples, you'll attract your readers' attention:

> Sexism is rampant in television commercials. Although millions of women hold responsible jobs outside the home, commercials continue to portray women as simple creatures who spend most of their time thinking about wax buildup, cottony-soft bathroom tissue, and static-free clothes. Men, apparently, have better things to do than fret over such mundane household matters. How many commercials can you recall that depict men proclaiming the virtues of squeaky-clean dishes or sparkling bathrooms? Not many.

Examples also make writing *persuasive*. Most writing conveys a point, but many readers are reluctant to accept someone else's point of view unless evidence demonstrates its validity. Imagine you're writing an essay showing that latchkey children are more self-sufficient and emotionally secure than children who return to a home where a parent awaits them. Without specific examples—from your own experience, personal observations, or research studies—your readers would undoubtedly question your position's validity.

Further, examples *help explain* difficult, abstract, or unusual ideas. Suppose you're assigned an essay on a complex subject such as inflation, zero population growth, or radiation exposure. As a writer, you have a responsibility to your readers to make these difficult concepts concrete and understandable. If writing an essay on radiation exposure in everyday life, you might start by providing specific examples of home appliances that emit radiation—color televisions, computers, and microwave ovens—and tell exactly how much radiation we absorb in a typical day from such equipment.

Finally, examples *help prevent unintended ambiguity*. All of us have experienced the frustration of having someone misinterpret what we say.

In face-to-face communication, we can provide on-the-spot clarification. In writing, however, instantaneous feedback isn't available, so it's crucial that meaning be as unambiguous as possible. Examples will help.

STRATEGIES FOR USING EXEMPLIFICATION IN AN ESSAY

The suggestions here and in Figure 5.1 will be helpful whether you use examples as a dominant or a supportive pattern of development.

FIGURE 5.1
Development Diagram: Writing an Exemplification Essay

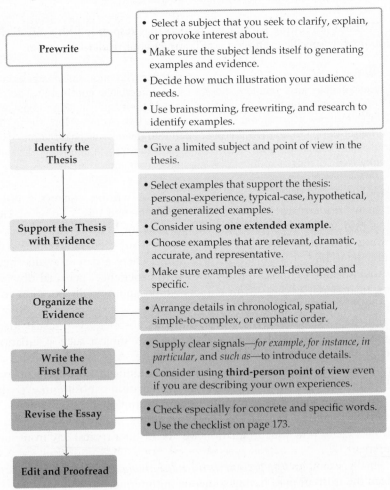

Prewrite
- Select a subject that you seek to clarify, explain, or provoke interest about.
- Make sure the subject lends itself to generating examples and evidence.
- Decide how much illustration your audience needs.
- Use brainstorming, freewriting, and research to identify examples.

Identify the Thesis
- Give a limited subject and point of view in the thesis.

Support the Thesis with Evidence
- Select examples that support the thesis: personal-experience, typical-case, hypothetical, and generalized examples.
- Consider using **one extended example**.
- Choose examples that are relevant, dramatic, accurate, and representative.
- Make sure examples are well-developed and specific.

Organize the Evidence
- Arrange details in chronological, spatial, simple-to-complex, or emphatic order.

Write the First Draft
- Supply clear signals—*for example, for instance, in particular*, and *such as*—to introduce details.
- Consider using **third-person point of view** even if you are describing your own experiences.

Revise the Essay
- Check especially for concrete and specific words.
- Use the checklist on page 173.

Edit and Proofread

1. Generate examples. The first batch of examples is generated during the prewriting stage. With your purpose and thesis in mind, you make a broad sweep for examples, using brainstorming, freewriting, the mapping technique—whichever prewriting technique you prefer. You may also read through your journal for relevant specifics, interview other people, or conduct other research.

Examples can take several forms, including specific names (of people, places, products, and so on), anecdotes, personal observations, expert opinion, as well as facts, statistics, and case studies gathered through research. While prewriting, try to generate more examples than you think you'll need. Starting with abundance—and then picking out the strongest examples—will give you a firm base on which to build the essay. If you have a great deal of trouble finding examples to support your thesis, you may need to revise the thesis. On the other hand, while prewriting, you may unearth numerous examples but find that many of them contradict the point you started out to support. If that happens, don't hesitate to recast your central point.

2. Select the examples to include. Once you've used prewriting to generate as many examples as possible, you're ready to limit your examples to the strongest ones. Keeping your purpose, thesis, and audience in mind, ask yourself several key questions: "Which examples support my thesis? Which do not? Which are most convincing? Which are most likely to interest readers and clarify meaning?"

You may include several brief examples within a single sentence:

> The French people's fascination with some American literary figures, such as Poe and Hawthorne, is understandable, but their great respect for "artists" like comedian Jerry Lewis is a mystery.

Or you may develop a paragraph with a number of "for instances":

> A uniquely American style of movie-acting reached its peak in the 1950s. Certain charismatic actors completely abandoned the stage techniques and tradition that had been the foundation of acting up to that time. Instead of articulating their lines clearly, the actors mumbled; instead of making firm eye contact with their colleagues, they hung their heads, shifted their eyes, even talked with their eyes closed. Marlon Brando, Montgomery Clift, and James Dean were three actors who exemplified this new trend.

As the preceding paragraph shows, *several examples* are usually needed to make a point. An essay with the thesis "Hip hop videos are dangerously violent" wouldn't be convincing if you gave only one example of a violent hip hop video. Several strong examples would be needed for readers to feel you had illustrated your point sufficiently.

As a general rule, you should strive for variety in the kinds of examples you include. For instance, you might choose a *personal-experience example* drawn from your own life or from the life of someone you know. Such examples pack the wallop of personal authority and lend drama to writing. Or you might include a *typical-case example,* an actual event or situation that did occur—but not to you or to anyone you know. The objective nature of such cases makes them especially convincing. You might also include a speculative or *hypothetical example* ("Imagine how difficult it must be for an elderly person to carry bags of groceries from the market to a bus stop several blocks away"). You'll find that hypothetical cases are effective for clarifying and dramatizing key points, but be sure to acknowledge that the example is indeed invented. Finally, you might create a *generalized example*—one that is a composite of the typical or usual. Such generalized examples are often signaled by words that involve the reader ("*All of us,* at one time or another, have been driven to distraction by a trivial annoyance like the buzzing of a fly or the sting of a paper cut"), or they may refer to humanity in general ("When *most people* get a compliment, they perk up, preen, and think the praise-giver is blessed with astute powers of observation").

Occasionally, *one extended example,* fully developed with many details, can support an essay. It might be possible, for instance, to support the thesis "States should raise the legal driving age to eighteen" with a single compelling, highly detailed example of the effects of one sixteen-year-old's high-speed driving spree.

The examples you choose must also be *relevant;* that is, they must have direct bearing on the point you want to make. You would have a hard time convincing readers that Americans have callous attitudes toward the elderly if you described the wide range of new programs, all staffed by volunteers, at a well-financed center for senior citizens. Because these examples *contradict,* rather than support, your thesis, readers are apt to dismiss what you have to say.

Make certain, too, that your examples are *accurate.* Exercise special caution when using statistics. An old saying warns that there are lies, damned lies, and statistics—meaning that statistics can be misleading. A commercial may claim, "In a taste test, 80 percent of those questioned indicated that they preferred Fizzy Cola." Impressed? Don't be—at least, not until you find out how the test was conducted.

Finally, select *representative* examples. Picking the oddball, one-in-a-million example to support a point—and passing it off as typical—is dishonest. Consider an essay with the thesis "Part-time jobs contribute to academic success." Citing only one example of a student who works at a job twenty-five hours a week while earning straight A's isn't playing fair. Why not? You've made a *hasty generalization* based on only one case. To be convincing, you need to show how holding down a job affects *most* students' academic performance. (For more on hasty generalizations, see Chapter 11.)

3. Develop your examples sufficiently.   To ensure that you get your ideas across, your examples must be *specific*. An essay on the types of heroes in American movies wouldn't succeed if you simply strung together a series of undeveloped examples in paragraphs like this one:

Heroes in American movies usually fall into types. One kind of hero is the tight-lipped loner, played by actors like Clint Eastwood and Humphrey Bogart. Another movie hero is the quiet, shy, or fumbling type who has appeared in movies since the beginning. The main characteristic of this hero is lovableness, as seen in actors like Jimmy Stewart. Perhaps the most one-dimensional and predictable hero is the tough guy who battles seemingly impossible odds. This kind of hero is aptly illustrated by Sylvester Stallone as Rocky and by Vin Diesel as Dominic Toretto and Riddick.

If you developed the essay in this way—if you moved from one undeveloped example to another—you would be doing little more than making a list. To be effective, key examples must be expanded in sufficient detail. The examples in the preceding paragraph could be developed in paragraphs of their own. You could, for instance, develop the first example this way:

Heroes can be tight-lipped loners who appear out of nowhere, form no permanent attachments, and walk, drive, or ride off into the sunset. In many of his westerns, from the low-budget "spaghetti westerns" of the 1960s to *Unforgiven* in 1992, *Million Dollar Baby* in 2004, and *Gran Torino* in 2008, Clint Eastwood personifies this kind of hero. He is remote, mysterious, and not talkative. Yet he guns down an evil sheriff, runs other villains out of town, helps a handicapped girl, reluctantly trains a young female fighter, and even more reluctantly helps a young Hmong refugee—acts that cement his heroic status. The loner might also be Sam Spade as played by Humphrey Bogart. Spade solves the crime and sends the guilty off to jail, yet he holds his emotions in check and has no permanent ties beyond his faithful secretary and shabby office. One gets the feeling that he could walk away from these, too, if necessary. Even in *The Right Stuff,* an account of the United States' early astronauts, the scriptwriters mold Chuck Yeager, the man who broke the sound barrier, into a classic loner. Yeager, portrayed by the aloof Sam Shepard, has a wife, but he is nevertheless insular. Taking mute pride in his ability to distance himself from politicians, bureaucrats, even colleagues, he soars into space, dignified and detached.

(For hints on ways to make writing specific, see Chapter 2.)

4. Organize the examples.   If, as is usually the case, several examples support your point, be sure that you present the examples in an *organized* manner. Often you'll find that other patterns of development (cause-effect, comparison-contrast, definition, and so on) suggest ways to sequence

examples. Let's say you're writing an essay showing that stay-at-home vacations offer numerous opportunities to relax. You might begin the essay
with examples that *contrast* stay-at-home and get-away vacations. Then
you might move to a *process analysis* that illustrates different techniques for
unwinding at home. The essay might end with examples showing the *effect*
of such leisurely at-home breaks.

Finally, you need to select an *organizational approach consistent* with
your *purpose* and *thesis*. Imagine you're writing an essay about students' adjustment during the first months of college. The supporting examples could
be arranged *chronologically*. You might start by illustrating the ambivalence
many students feel the first day of college when their parents leave for home;
you might then offer an anecdote or two about students' frequent calls to
Mom and Dad during the opening weeks of the semester; the essay might
close with an account of students' reluctance to leave campus at the midyear
break.

Similarly, an essay demonstrating that a room often reflects the character of its occupant might be organized *spatially:* from the empty soda
cans on the floor to the spitballs on the ceiling. In an essay illustrating the
kinds of skills taught in a composition course, you might move from *simple*
to *complex* examples: starting with relatively matter-of-fact skills such as
spelling and punctuation and ending with more conceptually difficult skills
such as formulating a thesis and organizing an essay. Last, the *emphatic
sequence*—in which you lead from your first example to your final, most
significant one—is another effective way to organize an essay with many
examples.

5. Choose a point of view.   Many essays developed by illustration place
the subject in the foreground and the writer in the background. Such an
approach calls for the *third-person point of view*. For example, even if you
draw examples from your own personal experience, you can present them
without using the *first-person* "I." You might convert such personal material into generalized examples (see page 170), or you might describe the
personal experience as if it happened to someone else. If your professor
allows the use of "I," you may use the first person if that will make the example more believable and dramatic. But remember: Just because an event
happened to you personally doesn't mean you have to use the first-person
point of view.

REVISION STRATEGIES

Once you have a draft of the essay, you're ready to revise. The following
checklist will help you and those giving you feedback apply to exemplification some of the revision techniques discussed in Chapter 2.

☑ EXEMPLIFICATION: A REVISION/PEER REVIEW CHECKLIST

Revise Overall Meaning and Structure

❏ What thesis is being advanced? Which examples don't support the thesis? Should these examples be deleted, or should the thesis be reshaped to fit the examples? Why?

❏ Which patterns of development and methods of organization (chronological, spatial, simple-to-complex, emphatic) provide the essay's framework? Would other ordering principles be more effective? If so, which ones?

Revise Paragraph Development

❏ Which paragraphs contain too many or too few examples? Which contain examples that are too brief or too extended? Which include insufficiently or overly detailed examples?

❏ Which paragraphs contain examples that could be made more compelling?

❏ Which paragraphs include examples that are atypical or incorrect?

Revise Sentences and Words

❏ What signal devices introduce examples and clarify the line of thought? Where are there too many or too few of these devices?

❏ Where would more varied sentence structure heighten the essay's illustrations?

❏ Where would more concrete and specific words make the examples more effective?

STUDENT ESSAY

The following student essay was written by Charlene Adams in response to this assignment.

> In "Tweens: Ten Going on Sixteen," Kay Hymowitz provides examples of the ways our culture pushes children to grow up too fast, incorporating information from a variety of sources to support her thesis. Write an essay in which you explore another cultural phenomenon that affects young people. Provide examples that support a claim you consider important, using information from at least three outside sources, including both personal interviews and published works, to substantiate your claim.

While reading Charlene's essay, try to determine how effectively it applies the principles of exemplification. The annotations on Charlene's composition and the commentary following it will help you look at the essay more closely.

Professors Open Up About the Benefits of a College Degree
by Charlene Adams

Introduction

Thesis ——————

Interview quote, which serves as a topic sentence to introduce the first major point

Paragraph with specific example to support first major point

Topic sentence ——————

Paragraph with specific example to support first major point

Topic sentence that starts with a transition

First of three paragraphs with specific examples to support second major point

Second paragraph with specific examples to support second major point

1   It's no secret that for the past few years the American economy has been in less-than-perfect condition. With the cost of a college education going up and the possibility of finding a well-paying job seemingly going down, the benefits of a college education seem to be dwindling; however, things are not always what they seem. A college education is more important today than ever before.

2   "The people who are more likely to be employed are people with college degrees," says David Loomis, Indiana University of Pennsylvania (IUP) journalism professor. "How much more likely? Twice as likely as people who have only a high school education," Loomis adds. To back up this assertion, Loomis points to a January 2013 *New York Times* article, "Benefits of College Degree in Recession Are Outlined," which reports that although almost everyone has taken an economic hit from the recession, college graduates have fared and continue to fare the best (Pérez-Peña A15).

3   *The New York Times* article uses data from the Pew Economic Mobility Project to illustrate employment trends. Richard Pérez-Peña, the author of *The New York Times* article, states that according to the Pew report, "People with four-year college degrees saw a 5 percent drop in wages, compared with a 12 percent decrease for their peers with associate's degrees, and a 10 percent decline for high school graduates." (See Fig. 1.)

4   The financial perks of a college education are obvious; however, financial benefits aren't the only advantages college graduates experience. Patrice Douglas, a junior at IUP majoring in management information systems, says that college is a huge help in this troubled economy because of the "unlimited exposure and opportunities." Douglas goes on to state the following: "The benefits of a college education include educating yourself on other cultures and people in the diverse college atmosphere. College students benefit from the numerous leadership, travel, and networking opportunities which aren't so easily accessed without being in a college or university."

5   IUP journalism professor Patricia Heilman adds that, contrary to popular belief, "The purpose of a college education is not just to get a job." Heilman goes on to state that

AVERAGE WEEKLY WAGE

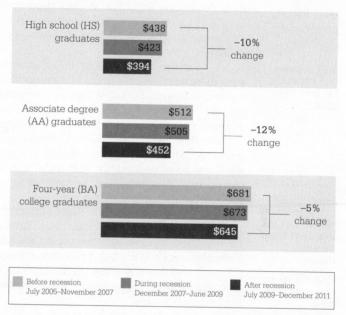

Notes: The percentage change is calculated with unrounded estimates and may not reproduce the percentage change exactly based on the rounded estimates presented here. All statistics are weight-adjusted for probability of selection and household non-response. All differences are significant at the 1 percent level or lower with the exception of the percent change between the high school and associate degree groups.

Source: Current Population Survey (CPS), 2005–2011

Graphic to offer additional support to first major point

FIG. 1

Associate Degree and High School Graduate Wage Declines Were Two Times Higher. From *Current Population Survey* (CPS), 2005-2011 (qtd. in Pew 16).

"the real purpose of a college education is to expand students' minds—to introduce them to other cultures and other schools of thought. And [the hope is that] when they graduate college, they will have learned how much they don't know. So for the rest of their lives, they are continuing to study and to learn, and that makes them better citizens." Professor Heilman adds that because "college graduates are more knowledgeable about other cultures, they do not approach people from other cultures with a preconceived set of prejudices because, at almost all colleges, [students] have probably had classes with people who were from other parts of the world."

Third paragraph with specific examples to support second major point

Professor Heilman believes that the benefits of a college education are so tremendous that to simply limit them to money or a job is "closing the door to all the experiences

6

individuals could have that would affect them for the rest of their lives." She adds that studies show that college graduates are more likely to vote in elections, so they're "more active in the political process" than people who did not attend college.

Topic sentence that introduces the third major point

In addition to increasing financial stability and exposure to other cultures, a third advantage of having a college education is what Professor Loomis refers to as the "habit of learning." He says that whether students attend a university, a community college, or a technical school, they are likely to acquire this invaluable habit. "Institutions of higher learning systematize this habit of learning in a way that makes it almost impossible to forget," he adds. "It's the way that an individual approaches input, any kind of input, that is one of the great advantages of higher education."   7

Two concluding paragraphs that elaborate on the thesis and bring the article to closure

The benefits of a college degree are many. From increasing the likelihood of financial stability, to becoming more familiar with other cultures, and developing the habit of learning, a college education is a gift that will undoubtedly keep on giving.   8

Final closing quote that emphasizes the thesis

Professor Loomis sums up the benefits of having a college degree with his comment: "The more education you get, the better off you are."   9

Works Cited

Douglas, Patrice. Personal interview. 3 Feb. 2013.

Heilman, Patricia. Personal interview. 5 Feb. 2013.

Loomis, David. Personal interview. 30 Jan. 2013.

Pérez-Peña, Richard. "Benefits of College Degree in Recession Are Outlined." *The New York Times,* 10 Jan. 2013, p. A15.

Pew Economic Mobility Project. *How Much Protection Does a College Degree Afford? The Impact of the Recession on Recent College Graduates.* The Pew Charitable Trusts, 10 Jan. 2013.

COMMENTARY

Thesis. In "Professors Open Up About the Benefits of a College Degree," Charlene Adams explores the various ways that having a college degree can positively affect an individual's life. She begins by pointing out a widely held assumption: "With the cost of a college education going up and the possibility of finding a well-paying job seemingly going down, the benefits of a college education seem to be dwindling...." This reference allows her to offer a contrast ("however, things are not always what they seem") to the assumption and then state the main idea she is communicating: "A college education is more important today than ever before." With this statement she makes it clear to her readers that she believes earning a college degree is beneficial, even in depressed economic conditions.

Evidence.   Support for the thesis consists of numerous examples gathered from personal interviews, a *New York Times* article and a Pew report. These examples are organized around the three major points Charlene makes in her essay. She elaborates on these points throughout her essay and summarizes them explicitly as she brings her essay to close: "From increasing the likelihood of financial stability, to becoming more familiar with other cultures, and developing the habit of learning, a college education is a gift that will undoubtedly keep on giving." Charlene uses two paragraphs and a visual to develop her first point, three paragraphs to develop her second point, and one short paragraph to develop her third point.

Organizational strategies.   Although Charlene includes two paragraphs and an illustration to support her first point, followed by three paragraphs to support her second point, she uses only one paragraph to support the third point; this structure implies that she is using reverse *emphatic order.* The first point—that a college education increases the likelihood of financial stability—is a claim that would grab the attention of many readers, and perhaps that is the reason Charlene decided to make it her first point. It could also be considered her strongest point because she uses three of her five sources to support the claim. To support her second point—that a college education increases exposure to other cultures—Charlene uses quotes from Patrice Douglas, a student she interviewed, as well as quotes from Patricia Heilman. In contrast, the final point she makes in her essay—that a college education helps individuals develop a "habit of learning"—is supported by quotes from only one source, David Loomis, whom she quoted previously in her essay in support of her first point.

When reading the essay, you probably felt that there was an easy flow from one major point to the next. To help her achieve *coherence between paragraphs,* Charlene uses sentences that link back to the preceding points: "*The financial perks of a college education are obvious;* however, financial benefits aren't the only advantages college graduates experience," and "*In addition to increasing financial stability and exposure to other cultures,* a third advantage of having a college education is what Professor Loomis refers to as the 'habit of learning.'" These links to previous points serve to remind readers of what they have just read and to introduce new information that follows.

Problems with paragraph development.   You probably recall that an essay developed primarily through exemplification must include examples that are *relevant, interesting, convincing, representative, accurate,* and *specific.* On the whole, Charlene's examples meet these requirements. Paragraphs 2 and 3, especially along with the graph, include information that shows how a college education can increase an individual's likelihood of financial stability. Incorporating examples not only from a college professor but also from highly regarded published sources makes her first point compelling.

The second and third points, however, are underdeveloped. To make these points more convincing, Charlene could incorporate specific examples, perhaps from television documentaries or journal articles focusing on the advantages of a college education. For example, in paragraph 6, Charlene states: "Studies show that college graduates are more likely to vote in elections, so they're 'more active in the political process' [quoting Heilman] than people who did not attend college." This statement could have been much stronger had Charlene added specific information from the "studies" to which Heilman refers. The same holds true for the final point in paragraph 7 regarding how a college education helps an individual develop the "habit of learning." Additional support for these examples would give the essay the solidity it now lacks.

Revising the first draft.   Although the final version of the essay could be strengthened by incorporating more examples, especially in support of the second and third major points, it's stronger than Charlene's first draft. One major addition Charlene made to the final draft was to include a visual to support her first point. This visual draws the reader's attention and clearly illustrates that wage declines were higher among those with an associate degree or high school education than they were among college graduates.

Another revision Charlene made as she worked on her essay was to strengthen transitions from one major point to another. For example, in her rough draft, she moves directly from paragraph 6, the final paragraph in support of her second point, to paragraph 7, in which she uses quotes from Professor Loomis regarding what he calls the "habit of learning." To see how Charlene revised this section of her essay, compare her essay's sixth and seventh paragraphs with her draft version reprinted here.

Original Version of the Sixth and Seventh Paragraphs

Professor Heilman believes that the benefits of a college education are so tremendous that to simply limit them to money or a job is "closing the door to all the experiences an individual could have that would affect them for the rest of their lives." She adds that studies show that college graduates are more likely to vote in elections, so they're "more active in the political process" than people who did not attend college.

Loomis believes that a perk of college education is what he refers to as the "habit of learning." He says that whether students attend a university, a community college, or a technical school, they are likely to acquire this invaluable habit. "Institutions of higher learning systematize this habit of learning in a way that makes it almost impossible to forget," he adds. "It's the way that an individual approaches input, any kind of input, that is one of the great advantages of higher education."

When Charlene looked more closely at her draft, she realized that she had provided no transition to help ease her readers from the second major point of her essay to the third. As she worked on her essay, she revised the opening sentence of the seventh paragraph to read, "In addition to increasing financial stability and exposure to other cultures, a third advantage of having a college education is what Professor Loomis refers to as the 'habit of learning.'" With the addition of this transitional sentence, Charlene reminds her readers of what came before and introduces them to what is yet to come.

Like most pieces of writing, Charlene's essay could be made stronger with additional revisions, but as is almost always the case, writers come to a point when they have to let their writing go, even though they know further revisions could improve the final product. Even so, the experience of writing this essay taught Charlene much that she could use to strengthen her writing in the future.

Activities: Exemplification
Prewriting Activities

MyWritingLab

1. Imagine you're writing two essays: One is a serious paper analyzing the factors that *cause* large numbers of public school teachers to leave the profession each year; the other is a light essay *defining* "preppie," "head banger," or some other slang term used to describe a kind of person. Jot down ways you might use examples in each essay.

2. Use mapping or another prewriting technique to gather examples illustrating the truth of *one* of the following familiar sayings. Then, using the same or a different prewriting technique, accumulate examples that counter the saying. Weigh both sets of examples to determine the saying's validity. After developing an appropriate thesis, decide which examples you would elaborate in an essay.

   a. Haste makes waste.
   b. There's no use crying over spilled milk.
   c. A bird in the hand is worth two in the bush.

Revising Activities

3. The following paragraph is from the first draft of an essay about the decline of small-town shopping districts. The paragraph is meant to show what small towns can do to revitalize business. Revise the paragraph, strengthening it with specific and convincing examples.

(continued)

> A small town can compete with a large new mall for shoppers. But merchants must work together, modernizing the stores and making the town's main street pleasant, even fun, to walk. They should also copy the malls' example by including attention-getting events as often as possible.

4. Reprinted here is a paragraph from the first draft of a light-spirited essay showing that Americans' pursuit of change for change's sake has drawbacks. The paragraph is meant to illustrate that infatuation with newness costs consumers money yet leads to no improvement in product quality. How effective is the paragraph? Which examples are specific and convincing? Which are not? Do any seem non-representative, offensive, or sexist? How could the paragraph's organization be improved? Consider these questions as you rewrite the paragraph. Add specific examples where needed. Depending on the way you revise, you may want to break this one paragraph into several.

> We end up paying for our passion for the new and improved. Trendy clothing styles convince us that last year's outfits are outdated, even though our old clothes are fine. Women are especially vulnerable in this regard. What, though, about items that have to be replaced periodically, like shampoo? Even slight changes lead to new formulations requiring retooling of the production process. That means increased manufacturing costs per item—all of which get passed on to us, the consumer. Then there are those items that tout new, trendsetting features that make earlier versions supposedly obsolete. Some manufacturers, for example, boast that their sound systems transmit an expanded-frequency range. The problem is that humans can't even hear such frequencies. But the high-tech feature dazzles men who are too naive to realize they're being hoodwinked.

Kay S. Hymowitz

A senior fellow at the Manhattan Institute and a contributing editor of the urban-policy magazine *City Journal,* Kay S. Hymowitz (1948–) writes on education and childhood in America. A native of Philadelphia, Hymowitz received graduate degrees from Tufts University and Columbia University. She has taught English literature and composition at Brooklyn College and at Parsons School of Design. Hymowitz is the author of *Liberation's Children: Parents and Kids in a Postmodern Age* (2003) and *Ready or Not: Why Treating Our Children as Small Adults Endangers Their Future and Ours* (1999) and is a principal contributor to *Modern Sex: Liberation and Its Discontents* (2001). In 2006, she published *Marriage and Caste in America: Separate and Unequal Families in a Post-Marital Age,* a collection of her *City Journal* essays. Her latest book is *Manning Up: How the Rise of Women Is Turning Men into Boys* (2011). Her work has appeared in publications including *The New York Times, The Washington Post,* and the *New Republic.* The following essay appeared in the Autumn 1998 issue of *City Journal.*

For ideas about how this exemplification essay is organized, see Figure 5.2 page 186.

Pre-Reading Journal Entry

MyWritingLab

Think back on your childhood. What were some possessions and activities that you cherished and enjoyed? Freewrite for a few moments in your pre-reading journal about these beloved objects and/or pastimes. What exactly were they? Why did you enjoy them so much? Did your feelings about them change as you matured into adolescence?

Tweens: Ten Going On Sixteen

During the past year my youngest morphed from child to teenager. 1 Down came the posters of adorable puppies and the drawings from art class; up went the airbrushed faces of Leonardo di Caprio and Kate Winslet. CDs of Le Ann Rimes and Paula Cole appeared mysteriously, along with teen fan magazines featuring glowering movie and rock-and-roll hunks.... She started reading the newspaper—or at least the movie ads—with all the intensity of a Talmudic scholar, scanning for glimpses of her beloved Leo or, failing that, Matt Damon. As spring approached and younger children skipped past our house on their way to the park, she swigged from a designer water bottle, wearing the obligatory tank top and denim shorts as she whispered on the phone to friends about games of Truth or Dare. The last rites for her childhood came when, embarrassed at reminders of her foolish past, she pulled a sheet over her years-in-the-making American Girl doll collection, now dead to the world.

So what's new in this dog-bites-man story? Well, as all this was going   2
on, my daughter was ten years old and in the fourth grade.

Those who remember their own teenybopper infatuation with Elvis or   3
the Beatles might be inclined to shrug their shoulders as if to say, "It was
ever thus." But this is different. Across class lines and throughout the country, elementary and middle-school principals and teachers, child psychologists and psychiatrists, marketing and demographic researchers all confirm
the pronouncement of Henry Trevor, middle-school director of the Berkeley
Carroll School in Brooklyn, New York: "There is no such thing as preadolescence anymore. Kids are teenagers at ten."

Marketers have a term for this new social animal, kids between eight   4
and 12: they call them "tweens." The name captures the ambiguous reality:
though chronologically midway between early childhood and adolescence,
this group is leaning more and more toward teen styles, teen attitudes, and,
sadly, teen behavior at its most troubling.

The tween phenomenon grows out of a complicated mixture of biology,   5
demography, and the predictable assortment of Bad Ideas. But putting aside
its causes for a moment, the emergence of tweendom carries risks for both
young people and society. Eight- to 12-year-olds have an even more wobbly
sense of themselves than adolescents; they rely more heavily on others to tell
them how to understand the world and how to place themselves in it. Now,
for both pragmatic and ideological reasons, they are being increasingly "empowered" to do this on their own, which leaves them highly vulnerable both
to a vulgar and sensation-driven marketplace and to the crass authority of
their immature peers. In tweens, we can see the future of our society taking
shape, and it's not at all clear how it's going to work.

Perhaps the most striking evidence for the tweening of children comes   6
from market researchers. "There's no question there's a deep trend, not a
passing fad, toward kids getting older younger," says research psychologist
Michael Cohen of Arc Consulting, a public policy, education, and marketing research firm in New York. "This is not just on the coasts. There are
no real differences geographically." It seems my daughter's last rites for her
American Girl dolls were a perfect symbol not just for her own childhood
but for childhood, period. The Toy Manufacturers of America Factbook
states that, where once the industry could count on kids between birth and
14 as their target market, today it is only birth to ten. "In the last ten years
we've seen a rapid development of upper-age children," says Bruce Friend,
vice president of worldwide research and planning for Nickelodeon, a cable
channel aimed at kids. "The 12- to 14-year-olds of yesterday are the ten to
12s of today." The rise of the preteen teen is "the biggest trend we've seen."

Scorning any symbols of their immaturity, tweens now cultivate a self-image   7
that emphasizes sophistication. The Nickelodeon-Yankelovich Youth Monitor
found that by the time they are 12, children describe themselves as "flirtatious,

sexy, trendy, athletic, cool." Nickelodeon's Bruce Friend reports that by 11, children in focus groups say they no longer even think of themselves as children.

They're very concerned with their "look," Friend says, even more so   8
than older teens. Sprouting up everywhere are clothing stores like the chain Limited Too and the catalog company Delia, geared toward tween girls who scorn old-fashioned, little-girl flowers, ruffles, white socks, and Mary Janes[1] in favor of the cool—black mini-dresses and platform shoes.... Teachers complain of ten- or 11-year-old girls arriving at school looking like madams, in full cosmetic regalia, with streaked hair, platform shoes, and midriff-revealing shirts. Barbara Kapetanakes, a psychologist at a conservative Jewish day school in New York, describes her students' skirts as being about "the size of a belt." Kapetanakes says she was told to dress respectfully on Fridays, the eve of the Jewish Sabbath, which she did by donning a long skirt and a modest blouse. Her students, on the other hand, showed their respect by looking "like they should be hanging around the West Side Highway," where prostitutes ply their trade.

Lottie Sims, a computer teacher in a Miami middle school, says that the   9
hooker look for tweens is fanning strong support for uniforms in her district. But uniforms and tank-top bans won't solve the problem of painted young ladies. "You can count on one hand the girls not wearing makeup," Sims says. "Their parents don't even know. They arrive at school with huge bags of lipstick and hair spray, and head straight to the girls' room."

Though the tweening of youth affects girls more visibly than boys, espe-   10
cially since boys mature more slowly, boys are by no means immune to these obsessions. Once upon a time, about ten years ago, fifth- and sixth-grade boys were about as fashion-conscious as their pet hamsters. But a grow-ing minority have begun trading in their baseball cards for hair mousse and baggy jeans. In some places, $200 jackets, emblazoned with sports logos like the warm-up gear of professional athletes, are *de rigueur;* in others, the preppy look is popular among the majority, while the more daring go for the hipper style of pierced ears, fade haircuts, or ponytails. Often these tween peacocks strut through their middle-school hallways taunting those who have yet to catch on to the cool look....

Those who seek comfort in the idea that the tweening of childhood is   11
merely a matter of fashion—who maybe even find their lip-synching, hip-swaying little boy or girl kind of cute—might want to think twice. There are disturbing signs that tweens are not only eschewing the goody-goody child-hood image but its substance as well....

The clearest evidence of tweendom's darker side concerns crime.   12
Although children under 15 still represent a minority of juvenile arrests, their

---

[1]Trademark name of patent-leather shoes for girls, usually having a low heel and a strap that fastens at the side (editors' note).

numbers grew disproportionately in the past 20 years. According to a report by the Office of Juvenile Justice and Delinquency Prevention, "offenders under age 15 represent the leading edge of the juvenile crime problem, and their numbers are growing." Moreover, the crimes committed by younger teens and preteens are growing in severity. "Person offenses,[2] which once constituted 16 percent of the total court cases for this age group," continues the report, "now constitute 25 percent." Headline grabbers—like Nathaniel Abraham of Pontiac, Michigan, an 11-year-old who stole a rifle from a neighbor's garage and went on a shooting spree in October 1997, randomly killing a teenager coming out of a store; and 11-year-old Andrew Golden, who, with his 13-year-old partner, killed four children and one teacher at his middle school in Jonesboro, Arkansas—are extreme, exceptional cases, but alas, they are part of a growing trend toward preteen violent crime....

The evidence on tween sex presents a troubling picture, too. Despite a   13
decrease among older teens for the first time since records have been kept, sexual activity among tweens increased during that period. It seems that kids who are having sex are doing so at earlier ages. Between 1988 and 1995, the proportion of girls saying they began sex before 15 rose from 11 percent to 19 percent. (For boys, the number remained stable, at 21 percent.) This means that approximately one in five middle-school kids is sexually active. Christie Hogan, a middle-school counselor for 20 years in Louisville, Kentucky, says: "We're beginning to see a few pregnant sixth-graders." Many of the principals and counselors I spoke with reported a small but striking minority of sexually active seventh-graders....

Certainly the days of the tentative and giggly preadolescent seem to   14
be passing. Middle-school principals report having to deal with miniskirted 12-year-olds "draping themselves over boys" or patting their behinds in the hallways, while 11-year-old boys taunt girls about their breasts and rumors about their own and even their parents' sexual proclivities. Tweens have even given new connotations to the word "playground": one fifth-grade teacher from southwestern Ohio told me of two youngsters discovered in the bushes during recess.

Drugs and alcohol are also seeping into tween culture. The past six   15
years have seen more than a doubling of the number of eighth-graders who smoke marijuana (10 percent today) and those who no longer see it as dangerous. "The stigma isn't there the way it was ten years ago," says Dan Kindlon, assistant professor of psychiatry at Harvard Medical School and co-author with Michael Thompson of *Raising Cain.* "Then it was the fringe group smoking pot. You were looked at strangely. Now the fringe group is using LSD."

---

[2]Crimes against a person. They include assault, robbery, rape, and homicide (editors' note).

Aside from sex, drugs, and rock and roll, another teen problem—eating   16
disorders—is also beginning to affect younger kids. This behavior grows out
of premature fashion-consciousness, which has an even more pernicious effect
on tweens than on teens, because, by definition, younger kids have a more
vulnerable and insecure self-image. Therapists say they are seeing a growing
number of anorexics and obsessive dieters even among late-elementary-
school girls. "You go on Internet chat rooms and find ten- and 11-year-olds
who know every [fashion] model and every statistic about them," says Nancy
Kolodny, a Connecticut-based therapist and author of *When Food's a Foe:
How You Can Confront and Conquer Your Eating Disorder*. "Kate Moss is
their god. They can tell if she's lost a few pounds or gained a few. If a powerful kid is talking about this stuff at school, it has a big effect."

What change in our social ecology has led to the emergence of tweens?   17
Many note that kids are reaching puberty at earlier ages, but while earlier
physical maturation may play a small role in defining adolescence down,
its importance tends to be overstated. True, the average age at which girls
begin to menstruate has fallen from 13 to between 11 and $12\frac{1}{2}$ today, but
the very gradualness of this change means that 12-year-olds have been living
inside near-adult bodies for many decades without feeling impelled to build
up a cosmetics arsenal or head for the bushes at recess. In fact, some experts
believe that the very years that have witnessed the rise of the tween have also
seen the age of first menstruation stabilize. Further, teachers and principals
on the front lines see no clear correlation between physical and social maturation. Plenty of budding girls and bulking boys have not put away childish
things, while an abundance of girls with flat chests and boys with squeaky
voices ape the body language and fashions of their older siblings....

Of course, the causes are complex, and most people working with   18
tweens know it. In my conversations with educators and child psychologists
who work primarily with middle-class kids nationwide, two major and fairly
predictable themes emerged: a sexualized and glitzy media-driven marketplace and absentee parents. What has been less commonly recognized is that
at this age, the two causes combine to augment the authority of the peer
group, which in turn both weakens the influence of parents and reinforces
the power of the media. Taken together, parental absence, the market, and
the peer group form a vicious circle that works to distort the development of
youngsters....

Questions for Close Reading   MyWritingLab

1. What is the selection's thesis? Locate the sentence(s) in which Hymowitz states her
   main idea. If she doesn't state the thesis explicitly, express it in your own words.
2. According to Hymowitz, what self-image do tweens cultivate? How do they "project" this image to others?

FIGURE 5.2
Essay Structure Diagram: "Tweens: Ten Going On Sixteen" by
Kay S. Hymowitz

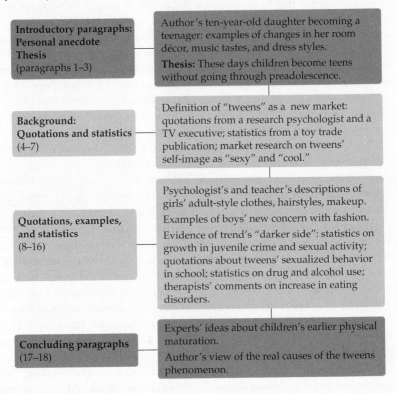

Introductory paragraphs:
Personal anecdote
Thesis
(paragraphs 1–3)

Author's ten-year-old daughter becoming a teenager: examples of changes in her room décor, music tastes, and dress styles.
Thesis: These days children become teens without going through preadolescence.

Background:
Quotations and statistics
(4–7)

Definition of "tweens" as a new market: quotations from a research psychologist and a TV executive; statistics from a toy trade publication; market research on tweens' self-image as "sexy" and "cool."

Quotations, examples, and statistics
(8–16)

Psychologist's and teacher's descriptions of girls' adult-style clothes, hairstyles, makeup. Examples of boys' new concern with fashion. Evidence of trend's "darker side": statistics on growth in juvenile crime and sexual activity; quotations about tweens' sexualized behavior in school; statistics on drug and alcohol use; therapists' comments on increase in eating disorders.

Concluding paragraphs
(17–18)

Experts' ideas about children's earlier physical maturation.
Author's view of the real causes of the tweens phenomenon.

3. What physically dangerous behavioral trends does Hymowitz link to the tween phenomenon?
4. According to Hymowitz, what are the primary causes of the tween phenomenon?

Questions About the Writer's Craft

1. **The pattern.** Hymowitz opens her essay with an anecdotal example of tweenhood—her daughter's. What does this example add to her essay?
2. **The pattern.** What types of examples does Hymowitz provide in her essay? (See pages 169–170 for a discussion of the various forms that examples can take.) Cite at least one example of each type. How does each type of example contribute to her thesis?
3. How would you characterize Hymowitz's tone in the selection? Cite vocabulary that conveys this tone.
4. **Other patterns.** In paragraph 8, Hymowitz uses clothing as a means of presenting an important *contrast*. What does she contrast in these paragraphs? How does this contribute to her thesis?

Writing Assignments Using Exemplification as a Pattern of Development

1. Hymowitz is troubled and perplexed by her daughter's behavior. Think about an older person, such as a parent or another relative, who finds *your* behavior troubling and perplexing. Write an essay in which you illustrate why your behavior distresses this person. (Or, conversely, think of an elder whose behavior *you* find problematic, and write an essay illustrating why that person evokes this response in you.) You might structure your essay by picking the two or three most irksome characteristics or habits and developing supporting paragraphs around each of them. However you choose to organize your essay, be sure to provide abundant examples throughout.

2. The cultivation of a sophisticated self-image is, according to Hymowitz, a hallmark of tweenhood. Think back to when you were around that age. What was your self-image at that time? Did you think of yourself as worldly or inexperienced? Cool or awkward? Attractive or unappealing? In your journal, freewrite about the traits that you would have identified in yourself as either a tween or an adolescent. Write an essay in which you illustrate your self-image at that age, focusing on two to three dominant characteristics you associated with yourself. It's important that you illustrate each trait with examples of when and how you displayed it. For example, if you saw yourself as "dorky," you might recall an embarrassing time when you tripped and fell in the middle of your school lunchroom. Conclude your essay by reflecting on whether the way you saw yourself at the time was accurate, and whether your feelings about yourself have changed since then.

Writing Assignment Combining Patterns of Development

3. Hymowitz advances a powerful argument about the alarming contemporary trend of tweenhood. But many would disagree with her entirely pessimistic analysis. Write an essay in which you *argue*, contrary to Hymowitz, that tweens today actually exhibit several *positive* characteristics. You might say, for example, that tweens today are more independent or more socially conscious than kids in the past. To develop your argument, you'll need to show how each characteristic you're discussing *contrasts* favorably with that characteristic in a previous generation of kids. Be sure, too, to acknowledge opposing arguments as you proceed. Research conducted in the library or on the Internet might help you develop your pro-tween argument.

Temple Grandin

Known as "the face of autism," Temple Grandin earned her Ph.D. in Animal Sciences and is a professor at Colorado State University. She is responsible for the development of livestock handling facility designs that decrease pain and fear for animals and are widely used across the United States today. The 2010 HBO movie *Temple Grandin*, winner of five Emmys, is based on her life story. Grandin's publications include three books: *Thinking in Pictures: My Life with Autism* (2010), *The Way I See*

It: A Personal Look at Autism and Aspergers (2011), and *The Autistic Brain: Helping Different Kinds of Minds Succeed* (2014). The essay that follows was written for and first appeared in the National Public Radio series *This I Believe* on August 16, 2006.

Pre-Reading Journal

MyWritingLab

Autism is one of many qualities that can set a person off from others. Think of other qualities—physical attributes or handicaps, mental or psychological abilities, personality characteristics—that can affect individuals' lives for better or worse. Use your journal to explore these qualities and their effects in people you know.

Seeing in Beautiful, Precise Pictures

Because I have autism, I live by concrete rules instead of abstract beliefs.   1
And because I have autism, I think in pictures and sounds. I don't have the ability to process abstract thought the way that you do. Here's how my brain works: It's like the search engine Google for images. If you say the word "love" to me, I'll surf the Internet inside my brain. Then, a series of images pops into my head. What I'll see, for example, is a picture of a mother horse with a foal, or I think of "Herbie the Lovebug," scenes from the movie *Love Story* or the Beatles song, "Love, love, love...."

When I was a child, my parents taught me the difference between good   2
and bad behavior by showing me specific examples. My mother told me that you don't hit other kids because you would not like it if they hit you. That makes sense. But if my mother told me to be "nice" to someone, it was too vague for me to comprehend. But if she said that being nice meant delivering daffodils to a next-door neighbor, that I could understand.

I built a library of experiences that I could refer to when I was in a new   3
situation. That way, when I confronted something unfamiliar, I could draw on the information in my homemade library and come up with an appropriate way to behave in a new and strange situation.

When I was in my 20s, I thought a lot about the meaning of life. At the   4
time, I was getting started in my career, designing more humane facilities for animals at ranches and slaughterhouses. Many people would think that to even work at a slaughterhouse would be inhumane, but they forget that every human and animal eventually dies. In my mind, I had a picture of a way to make that dying as peaceful as possible.

I believe that doing practical things can make the world a better place.   5
And one of the features of being autistic is that I'm good at synthesizing lots of information and creating systems out of it.

When I was creating my first corral back in the 1970s, I went to 50 dif-   6
ferent feedlots and ranches in Arizona and Texas and helped them work cattle. In my mind, I catalogued the parts of each facility that worked effectively

and assembled them into an ideal new system. I get great satisfaction when a rancher tells me that my corral design helps cattle move through it quietly and easily. When cattle stay calm, it means they are not scared. And that makes me feel I've accomplished something important.

Some people might think if I could snap my fingers I'd choose to be 7 "normal." But I wouldn't want to give up my ability to see in beautiful, precise pictures. I believe in them.

Questions for Close Reading

MyWritingLab

1. What is the selection's thesis? Locate the sentence(s) in which Grandin states her main idea. If she doesn't state her thesis explicitly, express it in your own words.
2. How does Grandin describe the way her brain works? In what specific way does she say her brain works differently from other people's?
3. Why does Grandin see her autism as an asset in her work to make ranch and slaughterhouse conditions more humane?
4. Grandin says that if given the opportunity to be "normal," she would choose to remain the way she is. Why does she feel this way?

Questions About the Writer's Craft

1. **The pattern.** What metaphor does Grandin use to explain how she says her brain works? What examples does she provide to illustrate her metaphor?
2. **The pattern.** What example does Grandin use to show how she learned "the difference between good and bad behavior"? Which examples in the essay most clearly helped you understand the affects of autism?
3. **Other patterns.** In what ways does Grandin use elements of narration and description in her essay? Provide specific examples. How does her use of narration and description make her writing more effective?
4. How does the title of Grandin's essay, "Seeing in Beautiful, Precise Pictures," capture or fail to capture the essence of the message she is trying to convey to her readers?

Writing Assignments Using Exemplification as a Pattern of Development

1. In her essay, Grandin provides examples of how autism has played a major role in shaping her life. Write an essay in which you provide examples of how something in your life affects or affected who you are today. You might write about a traumatic experience in your life—perhaps a divorce in your family, a car accident, or a serious illness. Or you might write about a positive experience, such as a meaningful relationship, the birth of a child, or an acceptance from the college you wanted to attend. Explain how the experience has played in a role in making you the person you have become. Focus on providing examples that illustrate the experience and its influence.
2. Grandin, widely referred to as "the face of autism," believes that her autism is an asset—that being autistic allows her to see life in a way that would not be possible if she were "normal." Write an essay in which you provide examples of how

another public figure turned what might be considered a handicap into an asset. For example, you might conduct research on Franklin D. Roosevelt, the thirty-second president of the United States, and how the polio he contracted at the age of thirty-nine played a role in making him the man he was. Or you might write about the actor Michael J. Fox and how his experience with Parkinson's disease has helped others who are dealing with the condition. Conduct research as needed to discover information that can help you write an effective essay.

Writing Assignment Combining Patterns of Development

3. Conduct research to learn more about how Temple Grandin developed a design for more humane livestock-handling facilities. Write an essay that documents her *process* and *explains* how her designs are now being used, with positive *results*, in facilities across the United States.

Brent Staples

After earning a Ph.D. in psychology from the University of Chicago, Brent Staples (1951–) soon became a nationally recognized essayist. He has worked on numerous newspapers and is now an Editorial Board member of *The New York Times*. Staples's autobiography, *Parallel Time: Growing Up in Black and White*, was published in 1995. This selection first appeared in slightly different form in *Ms.* magazine (1986) and then in *Harper's* (1987).

Pre-Reading Journal Entry

MyWritingLab

In recent years, racial profiling—targeting people for investigation based on their race or ethnicity—has become a controversial issue. What is your opinion of this practice? Is racial profiling ever acceptable? Freewrite on these questions in your journal.

Black Men and Public Space

My first victim was a woman—white, well dressed, probably in her early   1
twenties. I came upon her late one evening on a deserted street in Hyde Park, a relatively affluent neighborhood in an otherwise mean, impoverished section of Chicago. As I swung onto the avenue behind her, there seemed to be a discreet, uninflammatory distance between us. Not so. She cast back a worried glance. To her, the youngish black man—a broad six feet two inches with a beard and billowing hair, both hands shoved into the pockets of a bulky military jacket—seemed menacingly close. After a few more quick glimpses, she picked up her pace and was soon running in earnest. Within seconds she disappeared into a cross street.

That was more than a decade ago. I was twenty-two years old, a gradu-   2
ate student newly arrived at the University of Chicago. It was in the echo

of that terrified woman's footfalls that I first began to know the unwieldy inheritance I'd come into—the ability to alter public space in ugly ways. It was clear that she thought herself the quarry of a mugger, a rapist, or worse. Suffering a bout of insomnia, however, I was stalking sleep, not defenseless wayfarers. As a softy who is scarcely able to take a knife to a raw chicken— let alone hold one to a person's throat—I was surprised, embarrassed, and dismayed all at once. Her flight made me feel like an accomplice in tyranny. It also made it clear that I was indistinguishable from the muggers who occasionally seeped into the area from the surrounding ghetto. That first encounter, and those that followed, signified that a vast, unnerving gulf lay between nighttime pedestrians—particularly women—and me. And I soon gathered that being perceived as dangerous is a hazard in itself. I only needed to turn a corner into a dicey situation, or crowd some frightened, armed person in a foyer somewhere, or make an errant move after being pulled over by a policeman. Where fear and weapons meet—and they often do in urban America—there is always the possibility of death.

In that first year, my first away from my hometown, I was to become   3 thoroughly familiar with the language of fear. At dark, shadowy intersec-tions, I could cross in front of a car stopped at a traffic light and elicit the *thunk, thunk, thunk, thunk* of the driver—black, white, male, or female— hammering down the door locks. On less traveled streets after dark, I grew accustomed to but never comfortable with people crossing to the other side of the street rather than pass me. Then there were the standard unpleasant-ries with policemen, doormen, bouncers, cabdrivers, and others whose busi-ness it is to screen out troublesome individuals *before* there is any nastiness.

I moved to New York nearly two years ago and I have remained an   4 avid night walker. In central Manhattan, the near-constant crowd cover minimizes tense one-on-one street encounters. Elsewhere—in SoHo, for ex-ample, where sidewalks are narrow and tightly spaced buildings shut out the sky—things can get very taut indeed.

After dark, on the warrenlike streets of Brooklyn where I live, I often see   5 women who fear the worst from me. They seem to have set their faces on neu-tral, and with their purse straps strung across their chests bandolier-style, they forge ahead as though bracing themselves against being tackled. I understand, of course, that the danger they perceive is not a hallucination. Women are particularly vulnerable to street violence, and young black males are drastically overrepresented among the perpetrators of that violence. Yet these truths are no solace against the kind of alienation that comes of being ever the suspect, a fearsome entity with whom pedestrians avoid making eye contact.

It is not altogether clear to me how I reached the ripe old age of twenty-   6 two without being conscious of the lethality nighttime pedestrians attributed to me. Perhaps it was because in Chester, Pennsylvania, the small, angry industrial town where I came of age in the 1960s, I was scarcely noticeable against a backdrop of gang warfare, street knifings, and murders. I grew up one of the good boys, had perhaps a half-dozen fistfights. In retrospect, my shyness of combat has clear sources.

As a boy, I saw countless tough guys locked away; I have since buried sev-   7
eral, too. They were babies, really—a teenage cousin, a brother of twenty-two, a childhood friend in his mid-twenties—all gone down in episodes of bravado played out in the streets. I came to doubt the virtues of intimidation early on. I chose, perhaps unconsciously, to remain a shadow—timid, but a survivor.

The fearsomeness mistakenly attributed to me in public places often   8
has a perilous flavor. The most frightening of these confusions occurred in the late 1970s and early 1980s, when I worked as a journalist in Chicago. One day, rushing into the office of a magazine I was writing for with a dead-line story in hand, I was mistaken for a burglar. The office manager called security and, with an ad hoc posse, pursued me through the labyrinthine halls, nearly to my editor's door. I had no way of proving who I was. I could only move briskly toward the company of someone who knew me.

Another time I was on assignment for a local paper and killing time   9
before an interview. I entered a jewelry store on the city's affluent Near North Side. The proprietor excused herself and returned with an enor-mous red Doberman pinscher straining at the end of a leash. She stood, the dog extended toward me, silent to my questions, her eyes bulging nearly out of her head. I took a cursory look around, nodded, and bade her good night.

Relatively speaking, however, I never fared as badly as another black   10
male journalist. He went to nearby Waukegan, Illinois, a couple of sum-mers ago to work on a story about a murderer who was born there. Mistaking the reporter for the killer, police officers hauled him from his car at gunpoint and but for his press credentials would probably have tried to book him. Such episodes are not uncommon. Black men trade tales like this all the time.

Over the years, I learned to smother the rage I felt at so often being   11
taken for a criminal. Not to do so would surely have led to madness. I now take precautions to make myself less threatening. I move about with care, particularly late in the evening. I give a wide berth to nervous people on subway platforms during the wee hours, particularly when I have exchanged business clothes for jeans. If I happen to be entering a building behind some people who appear skittish, I may walk by, letting them clear the lobby be-fore I return, so as not to seem to be following them. I have been calm and extremely congenial on those rare occasions when I've been pulled over by the police.

And on late-evening constitutionals I employ what has proved to be an   12
excellent tension-reducing measure: I whistle melodies from Beethoven and

Vivaldi and the more popular classical composers. Even steely New Yorkers hunching toward nighttime destinations seem to relax, and occasionally they even join in the tune. Virtually everybody seems to sense that a mugger wouldn't be warbling bright, sunny selections from Vivaldi's *Four Seasons*. It is my equivalent of the cowbell that hikers wear when they know they are in bear country.

Questions for Close Reading   `MyWritingLab`

1. What is the selection's thesis? Locate the sentence(s) in which Staples states his main idea. If he doesn't state the thesis explicitly, express it in your own words.
2. How did Staples first learn that he was considered a threat by many people? How did this discovery make him feel?
3. What are some of the dangers that Staples has encountered because of his race? How has he handled each dangerous situation?
4. What "precautions" does Staples take to appear nonthreatening to others? Why do these precautions work?

Questions About the Writer's Craft

1. **The pattern.** Brent Staples reveals both causes and effects of people's reacting with fear to a Black male. Does the essay end with a discussion of causes or of effects? Why do you suppose Staples concludes the essay as he does?
2. **Other patterns.** Why do you think Staples opens the piece with such a dramatic, yet intentionally misleading, *narrative*? What *effect* does he achieve?
3. Is Staples writing primarily for whites, Blacks, or both? How do you know?
4. What is Staples's tone? Why do you think he chose this tone?

Writing Assignments Using Cause-Effect as a Pattern of Development

1. Write an essay showing how your or someone else's entry into a specific public space influenced other people's behavior. Identify the possible reasons that others reacted as they did, and explain how their reactions, in turn, affected the newcomer. Use your analysis to reach some conclusions about human nature.
2. Staples describes circumstances that often result in fear. Focusing on a more positive emotion, like admiration or contentment, illustrate the situations that tend to elicit that emotion in you. Discuss why these circumstances have the effect they do.

Writing Assignment Combining Patterns of Development

3. When he encounters a startled pedestrian, Staples feels some fear but manages to control it. Write an essay showing the *steps* you took one time when you felt afraid but, like Staples, remained in control and got through safely. *Illustrate* your initial fear, your later relief, and any self-discovery that *resulted* from the experience.

Beth Johnson

Beth Johnson (1956–) is a writer, occasional college teacher, and freelance editor. A graduate of Goshen College and Syracuse University, Johnson is the author of numerous inspirational real-life accounts, including *Facing Addiction* (2006) and *Surviving Abuse* (2006) as well as several college texts, including *Everyday Heroes* (1996) and *Reading Changed My Life* (2003); she also coauthored *Voices and Values* (2002) and *English Essentials* (2004). Containing profiles of men and women who have triumphed over obstacles to achieve personal and academic success, the books have provided a motivational boost to college students nationwide. She lives with her husband and three children in Lederach, Pennsylvania. The following piece is one of several that Johnson has written about the complexities and wonders of life.

Pre-Reading Journal Entry

MyWritingLab

When you were young, did adults acknowledge the existence of life's tragedies, or did they deny such harsh truths? In your journal, list several difficult events that you observed or experienced firsthand as a child. How did the adults in your life explain these hardships? In each case, do you think the adults acted appropriately? If not, how should they have responded?

Bombs Bursting in Air

It's Friday night and we're at the Olympics, the Junior Olympics, that   1
is. My son is on a relay-race team competing against fourth-graders from all over the school district. His little sister and I sit high in the stands, trying to pick Isaac out from the crowd of figures milling around on the field during these moments of pre-game confusion. The public address system sputters to life and summons our attention. "And now," the tinny voice rings out, "please join together in the singing of our national anthem."

"Oh saaay can you seeeeee," we begin. My arm rests around Maddie's   2
shoulders. I am touching her a lot today, and she notices. "Mom, you're *squishing* me," she chides, wriggling from my grip. I content myself with stroking her hair. News that reached me today makes me need to feel her near. We pipe along, squeaking out the impossibly high note of "land of the freeeeeeeee." Maddie clowns, half-singing, half-shouting the lyrics, hitting the "b's" explosively on "bombs bursting in air."

Bombs indeed, I think, replaying the sound of my friend's voice over the   3
phone that afternoon: "Bumped her head sledding. Took her in for an x-ray, just to make sure. There was something strange, so they did more tests ... a brain tumor...Children's Hospital in Boston Tuesday ... surgery, yes, right away...." Maddie's playmate Shannon, only five years old. We'd last seen her at Halloween, dressed in her blue princess costume, and we'd talked of

Furby and Scooby-Doo and Tootsie Rolls. Now her parents were hurriedly learning a new vocabulary—CAT scans, glioma, pediatric neurosurgery, and frontal lobe.[1] A bomb had exploded in their midst, and, like troops under attack, they were rallying in response.

The games over, the children and I edge our way out of the school park- 4
ing lot, bumper to bumper with other parents ferrying their families home. I tell the kids as casually as I can about Shannon. "She'll have to have an opera-tion. It's lucky, really, that they found it by accident this way while it's small."

"I want to send her a present," Maddie announces. "That'd be nice," I 5
say, glad to keep the conversation on a positive note.

But my older son is with us now. Sam, who is thirteen, says, "She'll be 6
OK, though, right?" It's not a question, really; it's a statement that I must either agree with or contradict. I want to say yes. I want to say of course she'll be all right. I want them to inhabit a world where five-year-olds do not develop silent, mysterious growths in their brains, where "malignancy" and "seizure" are words for *New York Times* crossword puzzles, not for little girls. They would accept my assurance; they would believe me and sleep well tonight. But I can't; the bomb that exploded in Shannon's home has sent splinters of shrapnel into ours as well, and they cannot be ignored or lied away. "We hope she'll be just fine," I finally say. "She has very good doctors. She has wonderful parents who are doing everything they can. The tumor is small. Shannon's strong and healthy."

"*She'll* be OK," says Maddie matter-of-factly. "In school we read about 7
a little boy who had something wrong with his leg and he had an operation and got better. Can we go to Dairy Queen?"

Bombs on the horizon don't faze Maddie. Not yet. I can just barely 8
remember from my own childhood the sense that still surrounds her, that feeling of being cocooned within reassuring walls of security and order. Back then, Monday meant gym, Tuesday was pizza in the cafeteria, Wednesday brought clarinet lessons. Teachers stood in their familiar spots in the class-rooms, telling us with reassuring simplicity that World War II happened because Hitler, a very bad man, invaded Poland. Midterms and report cards, summer vacations and new notebooks in September gave a steady rhythm to the world. It wasn't all necessarily happy—through the years there were poor grades, grouchy teachers, exclusion from the desired social group, dateless weekends when it seemed the rest of the world was paired off—but it was familiar territory where we felt walled off from the really bad things that hap-pened to other people.

---

[1]A CAT scan is a computerized cross-sectional image of an internal body structure; a glioma is a tumor in the brain or spinal cord; pediatric neurosurgery is surgery performed on the nerves, brain, or spinal cord of a child; the frontal lobe is the largest section of the brain (editors' note).

There were hints of them, though, even then. Looking back, I recall 9
the tiny shock waves, the tremors from far-off explosions that occasionally
rattled our shelter. There was the little girl who was absent for a week and
when she returned wasn't living with her mother and stepfather anymore.
There was a big girl who threw up in the bathroom every morning and then
disappeared from school. A playful, friendly custodian was suddenly fired,
and it had something to do with an angry parent. A teacher's husband had a
heart attack and died. These were interesting tidbits to report to our families
over dinner, mostly out of morbid interest in seeing our parents bite their
lips and exchange glances.

As we got older, the bombs dropped closer. A friend's sister was arrested 10
for selling drugs; we saw her mother in tears at church that Sunday. A boy I
thought I knew, a school clown with a sweet crooked grin, shot himself in
the woods behind his house. A car full of senior boys, going home from a
dance where I'd been sent into ecstasy when the cutest of them all greeted
me by name, rounded a curve too fast and crashed, killing them. We wept
and hugged each other in the halls. Our teachers listened to us grieve and
tried to comfort us, but their words came out impatient and almost angry.
I realize now that what sounded like anger was a helplessness to teach us
lessons we were still too young or too ignorant to learn. For although our
sorrow was real, we still had some sense of a protective curtain between us
and the bombs. If only, we said. If only she hadn't used drugs. If only he'd
told someone how depressed he was. If only they'd been more careful. *We*
weren't like them; we were careful. Like magical incantations, we recited the
things that we would or wouldn't do in order to protect ourselves from such
sad, unnecessary fates.

And then my best friend, a beautiful girl of sixteen, went to sleep one 11
January night and never woke up. I found myself shaken to the core of
my being. My grief at the loss of my vibrant, laughing friend was great.
But what really tilted my universe was the nakedness of my realization that
there was no "if only." There were no drugs, no careless action, no crime,
no accident, nothing I could focus on to explain away what had happened.
She had simply died. Which could only mean that there was no magic barrier separating me and my loved ones from the bombs. We were as vulnerable as everyone else. For months the shock stayed with me. I sat in class
watching my teachers draw diagrams of Saturn, talk about Watergate,[2]

[2]In June 1972, supporters of Republican President Richard Nixon were caught breaking into
the Democratic campaign headquarters in the Watergate office complex in Washington, D.C.
The resulting investigation of the White House connection to the break-in led to President
Nixon's eventual resignation in August 1974 (editors' note).

multiply fractions, and wondered at their apparent cheer and normalcy. Didn't they *know* we were all doomed? Didn't they know it was only a matter of time until one of us took a direct hit? What was the point of anything?

But time moved on, and I moved with it. College came and went, graduate school, adulthood, middle age. My heightened sense of vulnerability began to subside, though I could never again slip fully into the soothing security of my younger days. I became more aware of the intertwining threads of joy, pain, and occasional tragedy that weave through all our lives. College was stimulating, exciting, full of friendship and challenge. I fell in love for the first time, reveled in its sweetness, then learned the painful lesson that love comes with no guarantee. A beloved professor lost two children to leukemia, but continued with skill and passion to introduce students to the riches of literature. My father grew ill, but the last day of his life, when I sat by his bed holding his hand, remains one of my sweetest memories. The marriage I'd entered into with optimism ended in bitter divorce, but produced three children whose existence is my daily delight. At every step along the way, I've seen that the most rewarding chapters of my life have contained parts that I not only would not have chosen, but would have given much to avoid. But selecting just the good parts is not an option we are given.   12

The price of allowing ourselves to truly live, to love and be loved, is (and it's the ultimate irony) the knowledge that the greater our investment in life, the larger the target we create. Of course, it is within our power to refuse friendship, shrink from love, live in isolation, and thus create for ourselves a nearly impenetrable bomb shelter. There are those among us who choose such an existence, the price of intimacy being too high. Looking about me, however, I see few such examples. Instead, I am moved by the courage with which most of us, ordinary folks, continue soldiering on. We fall in love, we bring our children into the world, we forge our friendships, we give our hearts, knowing with increasing certainty that we do so at our own risk. Still we move ahead with open arms, saying yes, yes to life.   13

Shannon's surgery is behind her; the prognosis is good. Her mother reports that the family is returning to its normal routines, laughing again and talking of ordinary things, even while they step more gently, speak more quietly, are more aware of the precious fragility of life and of the blessing of every day that passes without explosion.   14

Bombs bursting in air. They can blind us, like fireworks at the moment of explosion. If we close our eyes and turn away, all we see is their fiery image. But if we have the courage to keep our eyes open and welcoming, even bombs finally fade against the vastness of the starry sky.   15

Questions for Close Reading

MyWritingLab

1. What is the selection's thesis? Locate the sentence(s) in which Johnson states her main idea. If she doesn't state the thesis explicitly, express it in your own words.
2. In paragraph 2, Johnson describes her "need to feel her [daughter] near." What compels her to want to be physically close to her daughter? Why do you think Johnson responds this way?
3. In describing her family's responses to Shannon's illness, Johnson presents three reactions: Maddie's, Sam's, and her own. How do these responses differ? In what ways do Maddie's, Sam's, and Johnson's reactions typify the age groups to which they belong?
4. In paragraph 13, Johnson describes two basic ways people respond to life's inevitable "bombs." What are these ways? Which response does Johnson endorse?

Questions About the Writer's Craft

1. **The pattern.** Although Johnson provides many examples of life's "bombs," she gives more weight to some examples than to others. Which examples does she emphasize? Which ones receive less attention? Why?
2. **Other patterns.** What important *contrast* does Johnson develop in paragraph 6? How does this contrast reinforce the essay's main idea?
3. Writers generally vary sentence structure in an effort to add interest to their work. But in paragraphs 9 and 10, Johnson employs a repetitive sentence structure. Where is the repetition in these two paragraphs? Why do you think she uses this technique?
4. Johnson develops her essay by means of an extended metaphor (see Chapter 3), using bombs as her central image. Identify all the places where Johnson draws upon language and imagery related to bombs and battles. What do you think Johnson hopes to achieve with this sustained metaphor?

Writing Assignments Using Exemplification as a Pattern of Development

1. In paragraphs 9 and 10, Johnson catalogues a number of events that made her increasingly aware of life's bombs. Write an essay of your own, illustrating how you came to recognize the inevitability of painful life events. Start by listing the difficult events you've encountered. Select the three most compelling occurrences, and do some freewriting to generate details about each. Before writing, decide whether you will order your examples chronologically or emphatically; use whichever illustrates more effectively your dawning realization of life's complexity. End with some conclusions about your ability to cope with difficult times.
2. Johnson describes her evolving understanding of life. In an essay of your own, show the way several events combined to change your understanding of a specific aspect of your life. Perhaps a number of incidents prompted you to reconsider career choices, end a relationship, or appreciate the importance of family. Cite

only those events that illustrate your emerging understanding. Your decision to use either chronological or emphatic sequence depends on which illustrates more dramatically the change in your perception.

Writing Assignment Combining Patterns of Development

3. Johnson explores the lasting impact the death of her friend had on her life. Write an essay about the *effect* of a *single* "bomb" on your life. You might *recount* getting left back in school, losing a loved one, seeing the dark side of someone you admired, and so on. Your causal analysis should make clear how the event affected your life. Perhaps the event had painful short-term consequences but positive long-term repercussions.

Chitra Banerjee Divakaruni

Chitra Banerjee Divakaruni was born in Calcutta, India, in 1956. After receiving a B.A. from the University of Calcutta, she came to the United States, earning a master's degree in English from Wright State University and, in 1976, a Ph.D. from the University of California–Berkeley. Divakaruni currently teaches in the creative writing program at the University of Houston. Her work is widely published, including in *The New Yorker* and *The Atlantic Monthly*, and she has won an American Book Award for her short story collection *Arranged Marriage* (1995), as well as other awards. In addition to stories, young adult fiction, and poetry, Divakaruni has published several novels, including *The Mistress of Spices* (1997), *Sister of My Heart* (1999), *Queen of Dreams* (2004), and most recently *One Amazing Thing* (2010). The following essay appeared in Salon.com on June 26, 1997.

Pre-Reading Journal Entry

MyWritingLab

Like distinctive smells, other sensory experiences can also evoke specific memories or feelings. For example, a particular song might remind you of a past romance. Do some freewriting in your journal about sensory experiences that evoke strong memories or feelings for you.

Common Scents: The Smell of Childhood Never Fades

It's a cool December morning halfway across the world in Gurap, a little   1
village outside Calcutta where we've come to visit my mother. I sit on the veranda and watch my little boys, Anand and Abhay, as they play on the dirt road. They have a new cricket bat and ball, a gift from their grandma, but soon they abandon these to feed mango leaves to the neighbor's goat, which has wandered over. Abhay, who is 2, wants to climb onto the goat's back.

Anand, who is 5 and very much the big brother, tells him it's not a good idea, but Abhay doesn't listen.

Behind me the door opens. Even before I hear the flap-flap of her leather 2 chappals,[1] I know who it is. My mother, fresh from her bath, heralded by the scent of the sandalwood soap she has been using ever since I can remember. Its clean, familiar smell pulls me back effortlessly into my childhood.

When I was young, my mother and I had a ritual every evening. She 3 would comb my hair, rub in hibiscus oil and braid it into thick double plaits. It took a long time—there were a lot of knots to work through. But I was rarely impatient. I loved the sleepy fragrance of the oil (the same oil she used, which she sometimes let me rub into her hair). I loved, too, the rhythm of her hands, and the stories (each with its not-so-subtle moral) that she told me as she combed. The tale of Sukhu and Dukhu, the two sisters. The kind one gets the prince, the greedy one is eaten up by a serpent. Or the tale of the little cowherd boy who outwits the evil witch. Size and strength, after all, are no match for intelligence.

What is it about smells that lingers in our subconscious, comforting and 4 giving joy, making real what would otherwise be wooden and wordy? I'm not sure. But I do know this: Every lesson that I remember from my childhood, from my mother, has a smell at its center.

The smell of turmeric, which she made into a paste with milk and 5 rubbed into my skin to take away blemishes, reminds me to take pride in my appearance, to make the best of what nature has given me.

The smell of the rosewater-scented rice pudding she always made 6 for New Year is the smell of hope. It reminds me to never give up. Who knows—something marvelous may be waiting just around the bend.

Even the smell of the iodine she dabbed on my scraped knees and 7 elbows, which I so hated then, is one I now recall with wry gratitude. Its stinging, bitter-brown odor is that of love, love that sometimes hurts while it's doing its job.

Let me not mislead you. I wasn't always so positively inclined toward my 8 mother's lessons—or the smells that accompanied them. When I first moved to the United States, I wanted to change myself, completely. I washed every last drop of hibiscus oil from my hair with Vidal Sassoon shampoo. I traded in my saris for Levis and tank tops. I danced the night away in discos and returned home in the bleary-eyed morning smelling of vodka and sweat and cigarettes, the perfume of young America.

But when Anand was born, something changed. They say you begin to 9 understand your mother only when you become a mother yourself. Only then do you appreciate all the little things about her that you took for granted. Maybe that's true. Otherwise, that morning in the hospital, looking

---

[1]Sandals (editors' note).

down at Anand's fuzzy head, why did I ask my husband to make a trip to the Indian store and bring me back a bar of sandalwood soap?

I have my own rituals now, with my boys, my own special smells that are 10 quite different. (I learned early that we can't be our mothers. Most times, it's better to not even try.)

On weekends I make a big chicken curry with turmeric and cloves. 11 Anand helps me cut up the tomatoes into uneven wedges; Abhay finger-shreds the cilantro with great glee. As the smell of spices fills the house, we sing. Sometimes it's a song from India: *Ay, ay, Chanda mama*—Come to me, Uncle Moon. Sometimes it's "Old MacDonald Had a Farm."

When the children are sick, I sprinkle lavender water on a handkerchief 12 and lay it on their foreheads to fend off that other smell, hot and metallic: the smell of fever and fear.

If I have a special event coming up, I open the suitcase my mother gave 13 me at my wedding and let them pick out an outfit for me, maybe a gold-embroidered kurta² or a silk shawl. The suitcase smells of rose potpourri. The boys burrow into it and take deep, noisy breaths.

Am I creating memories for them? Things that will comfort them in the 14 dark, sour moments that must come to us all at some time? Who knows—there is so much out of my own childhood that I've forgotten that I can only hope so.

"Watch out!" says my mother now, but it's too late. The goat, having 15 eaten enough mango leaves, has decided to move on. He gives a great shrug, and Abhay comes tumbling off his back. He lies on the dirt for a moment, his mouth a perfect O of surprise, then runs crying to me. A twinge goes through me even as I hide my smile. A new lesson, this, since mother-hood: how you can feel someone else's pain so sharply, like needles, in your own bones.

When I pick him up, Abhay buries his face in my neck and stays there a 16 long time, even after the tears have stopped. Is he taking in the smell of my body? Is he going to remember the fragrance of the jabakusum³ oil that I asked my mother to rub into my hair last night, for old time's sake? I'm not sure. But I do know this—I've just gained something new, something to add to my scent-shop of memories: the dusty, hot smell of his hair, his hands pungent with the odor of freshly-torn mango leaves.

---

²A long shirt or blouse that is worn over pants (editors' note).
³Hibiscus (editors' note).

Questions for Close Reading   MyWritingLab

1. What is the selection's thesis? Locate the sentence(s) in which Divakaruni states her main idea. If she doesn't state her thesis explicitly, express it in your own words.

2. Identify the author's initial inspiration for her main idea. What specific life lessons does the author say she learned from her mother?
3. What two occurrences prompt reversals in the author's feelings about her mother? Describe the two scents the author associates with these reversals.
4. What scent-memories does the author hope to pass along to her own children? How does the meaning of these scent-memories differ from the meaning of memories she has of her mother?

Questions About the Writer's Craft

1. **The pattern.** What kind of examples does the author mostly give—personal experience, typical-case, hypothetical, or generalized? Is her choice effective in supporting her main point? What other types of evidence might she have included?
2. **Other patterns.** In what way does the author use *narrative* devices to draw in the reader? Explain.
3. **Other patterns.** In what way does the author use *description* to draw in the reader? Gives some examples of descriptive language. What tone does the description give to the essay?
4. The author uses a number of Hindi (or Hindi-derived) terms (*chappals, kurta, jabakusum*) that she does not define, and she refers to children's songs and stories that American audiences may not know. What effect does this produce?

Writing Assignments Using Exemplification as a Pattern of Development

1. Divakaruni gives a number of life lessons she learned from her mother. Think of positive life lessons that you learned from your parents, grandparents, or other people you admire. Choose one or two lessons and give *examples* of how those teachings influenced your behavior or the choices you have made in your life.
2. In the essay, *veranda* is an example of a Hindi word that has become a common English word. Research some other terms that have come into English from Hindi or another Indian language. Write an essay in which you give *examples* of some words, including if possible how their meanings have changed. Explain whether you think the effect of that language on English is beneficial, detrimental, or neutral.

Writing Assignment Combining Patterns of Development

3. Do you think parents can deliberately create good memories for their children, or do you think it's impossible to predict which experiences will give children their most cherished memories? Write an essay in which you *argue* for one side or the other. Remember to give *examples* from your own experience or from the experiences of people you know.

Additional Writing Topics

EXEMPLIFICATION

MyWritingLab

General Assignments

Using illustration, develop one of these topics into an essay.

1. Today's drivers' dangerous habits
2. Taking care of our neighborhoods
3. The best things in life: definitely not free
4. The importance of part-time jobs for college students
5. How cell phones have changed communication
6. Learning about people from what they wear
7. Americans' obsession with or neglect of physical fitness
8. How to avoid bad eating habits
9. Eliminating obstacles faced by people with handicaps
10. _____ (someone you know) as a_____ (reliable, open-minded, dishonest, pushy, etc.) person

Assignments Using Visuals

Use the suggested visuals to help develop an illustration essay on one of these topics:

1. How cell phones have changed our lives (photos and/or charts)
2. The benefits of a college education (graphs and/or charts)
3. How the Internet has affected society (slide show)
4. Characteristics of college students with high GPAs (charts or cartoons)
5. How a hobby such as hiking or singing can expand our horizons (web links)

Assignments with a Specific Purpose, Audience, and Point of View

1. **Academic life.** Lately, many people at your college have been experiencing stress. As a member of the Student Life Committee, you've been asked to prepare a pamphlet illustrating strategies for reducing different kinds of stress. Decide which stresses to discuss and explain coping strategies for each, providing helpful examples as you go.
2. **Academic life.** A friend of yours will be going away to college in an unfamiliar environment—in a bustling urban setting or in a quiet rural one. To help your friend prepare for this new environment, write a letter giving examples of what life

on an urban or a rural campus is like. You might focus on the benefits and dangers with which your friend is unlikely to be familiar.

3. **Civic activity.** Shopping for a new car, you become annoyed at how many safety features are available only as expensive options. Write a letter of complaint to the auto manufacturer, citing at least three examples of such options. Avoid sounding hostile.

4. **Civic activity.** A pet food company is having an annual contest to choose a new animal to feature in its advertising. To win the contest, you must convince the company that your pet is personable, playful, and unique. Write an essay giving examples of your pet's special qualities.

5. **Workplace action.** Assume that you're an elementary school principal planning to give a speech in which you'll try to convince parents that television distorts children's perceptions of reality. Write the speech, illustrating your point with vivid examples.

6. **Workplace action.** The online publication you work for has asked you to write an article on what you consider to be the "three best consumer products of the past twenty-five years." Support your opinion with lively, engaging specifics that are consistent with the website's offbeat and slightly ironic tone.

MyWritingLab Visit Chapter 5, "Exemplification," in MyWritingLab to complete the chapter activities, Pre-Reading Journal Entry activities, Questions for Close Reading, and Additional Writing Topics assignments and to test your understanding of the chapter objectives.

DIVISION-CLASSIFICATION

In this chapter, you will learn:

6.1 To use the pattern of division-classification to develop your essays.

6.2 To consider how division-classification can fit your purpose and audience.

6.3 To develop strategies for using division-classification in an essay.

6.4 To develop strategies for revising a division-classification essay.

6.5 To analyze how division-classification is used effectively in student-written and professionally authored selections.

6.6 To write your own essays using division-classification as a strategy.

WHAT IS DIVISION-CLASSIFICATION?

Imagine what life would be like if this is how an average day unfolded:

> You go to the supermarket for only five items, but your marketing takes more than an hour because all the items in the store are jumbled together. Clerks put new shipments anywhere they please; the milk might be with the vegetables on Monday but with hair products on Thursday. Next, you go to the drugstore to pick up the prescription your doctor called in for you. You don't have time, though, to wait while the pharmacist roots through the large box into which all of the filled prescriptions have been thrown. You leave to go visit a friend

in the hospital with the flu. There you find your friend in a room with three other patients: a middle-aged man with a heart problem, a young boy ready to have his tonsils removed, and a woman in labor.

Such a muddled world, lacking the most basic forms of organization, would make daily life chaotic. All of us instinctively look for ways to order our environment. Without sorting mechanisms, we'd be overwhelmed by life's complexity. An organization such as a university, for example, is made manageable by being divided into various schools (Liberal Arts, Performing Arts, Engineering, and so on). The schools are then separated into departments (English, History, Political Science), and each department's offerings are grouped into categories—English, for instance, into Literature and Composition—before being further divided into specific courses.

The kind of ordering system we've been discussing is called *division-classification*, a logical way of thinking that allows us to make sense of a complex world. Division and classification, though separate processes, are often used together as complementary techniques. *Division* involves taking a single unit or concept, breaking the unit down into its parts, and then analyzing the connections among the parts and between the parts and the whole. For instance, if we wanted to organize the chaotic hospital described at the start of the chapter, we might think about how the single concept "a hospital" could be broken down into its components. We might come up with the following breakdown: pediatric wing, cardiac wing, maternity wing, and so on.

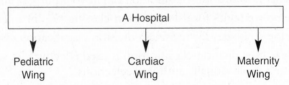

What we have just done involves division: We've taken a single entity (a hospital) and divided it into some of its component parts (wings), each with its own facilities and patients.

In contrast, *classification* brings two or more related items together and categorizes them according to type or kind. If the disorganized supermarket described previously were to be restructured, the clerks would have to classify the separate items arriving at the loading dock. Cartons of lettuce, tomatoes, cucumbers, butter, yogurt, milk, shampoo, conditioner, and styling gel would be assigned to the appropriate categories:

HOW DIVISION-CLASSIFICATION FITS YOUR PURPOSE AND AUDIENCE

The reorganized hospital and supermarket show the way division and classification work in everyday life. But division and classification also come into play during the writing process. Because division involves breaking a subject into parts, it can be a helpful strategy during prewriting, especially if you're analyzing a broad, complex subject: the structure of a film; the motivation of a character in a novel; the problem your community has with vandalism; the controversy surrounding school prayer.

Classification can be useful for imposing order on ideas generated during prewriting. You examine that material to see which of your rough ideas are alike, so that you can cluster related items in the same category. You might, for instance, use classification in a paper showing that Americans are undermining their health through their obsessive pursuit of various diets. Perhaps you begin by brainstorming all the diets that have gained popularity in recent years (Atkins, South Beach, Zone, whatever). Then you categorize the diets according to type: high-fiber, low-protein, high-carbohydrate, and so on. Once the diets are grouped, you can discuss the problems within each category, demonstrating to readers why some of the diets may not be safe or effective.

Division-classification can be crucial when responding to college assignments like the following:

> From your observations, what kinds of appeals do television advertisers use when selling automobiles? In your view, are any of these appeals morally irresponsible?
>
> Analyze the components of effective parenting. Indicate those you consider most vital for raising confident, well-adjusted children.
>
> Describe the hierarchy of the typical high school clique, identifying the various parts of the hierarchy. Use your analysis to support or refute the view that adolescence is a period of rigid conformity.
>
> Many social commentators have observed that discourtesy is on the rise. Indicate whether you think this is a valid observation by characterizing the types of everyday encounters you have with people.

These assignments suggest division-classification through the use of such words as *kinds, components, parts,* and *types.* Generally, though, you won't receive such clear signals to use division-classification. Instead, the broad purpose of the essay—and the point you want to make—will lead you to the analytical thinking characteristic of division-classification.

Sometimes division-classification will be the dominant technique for structuring an essay; other times it will be used as a supplemental pattern in an essay organized primarily according to another pattern of development. Say you want to write an essay *explaining a process.* You could *divide* the process into parts or stages, showing, for instance, that the Heimlich maneuver is an easily mastered skill that readers should acquire. Or perhaps you plan to write a light-spirited essay analyzing the *effect* that increased awareness of sexual stereotypes has had on college students' social lives. In such a case, you might use *classification.* To show readers that shifting gender roles make young people comically self-conscious, you could categorize the places where students scout each other out: in class, at the library, at parties, in dorms. You could then show how students approach each other with laughable tentativeness in these four environments.

Now imagine that you're writing an *argumentation-persuasion* essay urging that the federal government prohibit the use of growth-inducing antibiotics in livestock feed. The paper could begin by *dividing* the antibiotics cycle into stages: the effects of antibiotics on livestock; the short-term effects on humans who consume the animals; the possible long-term effects of consuming antibiotic-tainted meat. To increase readers' understanding of the problem, you might also discuss the antibiotics controversy in terms of an even larger issue: the dangerous ways food is treated before being consumed. In this case, you would consider the various procedures (use of additives, preservatives, artificial colors, and so on), *classifying* these treatments into several types—from least harmful (some additives or artificial colors, perhaps) to most harmful (you might slot the antibiotics here). Such an essay would be developed using both division *and* classification: first, the division of the antibiotics cycle and then the classification of the various food treatments. Frequently, this interdependence will be reversed, and classification will precede rather than follow division.

STRATEGIES FOR USING DIVISION-CLASSIFICATION IN AN ESSAY

The suggestions here and in Figure 6.1 will be helpful whether you use division-classification as a dominant or a supportive pattern of development.

1. Select a principle of division-classification consistent with your purpose. Most subjects can be divided or classified according to a *number of different principles.* For example, when writing about an ideal vacation, you could divide your subject according to any of these principles: location, cost, recreation available. Similarly, when analyzing students at your college, you could base your classification on a variety of principles: students' majors, their racial or ethnic background, whether they belong to a fraternity or sorority. In all cases, though, the principle of division-classification must help you meet your overall purpose and reinforce your central point.

When you write an essay that uses division-classification as its primary method of development, a *single principle* of division-classification provides the foundation for each major section of the paper. Imagine you're writing

FIGURE 6.1
Development Diagram: Writing a Division-Classification Essay

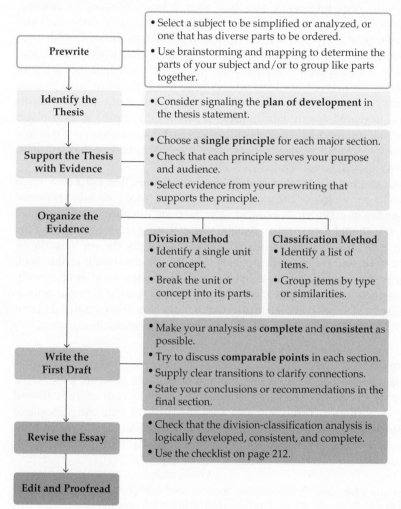

Prewrite	• Select a subject to be simplified or analyzed, or one that has diverse parts to be ordered. • Use brainstorming and mapping to determine the parts of your subject and/or to group like parts together.
Identify the Thesis	• Consider signaling the **plan of development** in the thesis statement.
Support the Thesis with Evidence	• Choose a **single principle** for each major section. • Check that each principle serves your purpose and audience. • Select evidence from your prewriting that supports the principle.
Organize the Evidence	

Division Method
• Identify a single unit or concept.
• Break the unit or concept into its parts.

Classification Method
• Identify a list of items.
• Group items by type or similarities.

Write the First Draft	• Make your analysis as **complete** and **consistent** as possible. • Try to discuss **comparable points** in each section. • Supply clear transitions to clarify connections. • State your conclusions or recommendations in the final section.
Revise the Essay	• Check that the division-classification analysis is logically developed, consistent, and complete. • Use the checklist on page 212.
Edit and Proofread	

an essay showing that the success of contemporary music groups has less to do with talent than with the groups' ability to market themselves to distinct audiences. To develop your point, you might categorize several performers according to the age ranges they appeal to (preteens, adolescents, people in their late twenties) and then analyze the marketing strategies the musicians use to gain their fans' support. The essay's logic would be undermined if you switched, in the middle of your analysis, to another principle of classification—say, the influence of earlier groups on today's music scene.

2. Apply the principle of division-classification logically. You need to demonstrate to readers that your analysis is the result of careful thought. First of all, your division-classification should be as *complete* as possible. Your analysis should include—within reason—all the parts into which you can divide your subject, or all the types into which you can categorize your subjects. Let's say you're writing an essay showing that where college students live is an important factor in determining how satisfied they are with college life. You classify students according to where they live: with parents, in dorms, in fraternity and sorority houses. But what about all the students who live in rented apartments, houses, or rooms off campus? If these places of residence are ignored, your classification won't be complete; you will lose credibility with your readers because they'll probably realize that you have overlooked several important considerations.

Your division-classification should also be *consistent:* The parts into which you break your subject or the groups into which you place your subjects should be as mutually exclusive as possible. The parts or categories should not be mixed, nor should they overlap. Assume you're writing an essay describing the animals at the zoo in a nearby city. You decide to describe the zoo's mammals, reptiles, birds, and endangered species. But such a classification is inconsistent. You begin by categorizing the animals according to scientific class (mammals, birds, reptiles), then switch to another principle when you classify some animals according to whether they are endangered. Because you drift over to a different principle of classification, your categories are no longer mutually exclusive.

3. Prepare an effective thesis. If your essay uses division-classification as its dominant method of development, it might be helpful to prepare a thesis that does more than signal the paper's subject and suggest your attitude toward that general subject. You might also want the thesis to state the principle of division-classification at the heart of the essay. Furthermore, you might want the thesis to reveal which part or category you regard as most important.

Consider the two thesis statements that follow:

> As the observant beachcomber moves from the tidal area to the upper beach to the sandy dunes, rich variations in marine life become apparent.

> Although most people focus on the dangers associated with the disposal of toxic waste in the land and ocean, the incineration of toxic matter may pose an even more serious threat to human life.

The first thesis statement makes clear that the writer will organize the paper by classifying forms of marine life according to location. Because the purpose of the essay is to inform as objectively as possible, the thesis doesn't suggest the writer's opinion about which category is most significant.

The second thesis signals that the essay will divide the issue of toxic waste by methods of disposal. Moreover, because the essay takes a stance on a controversial subject, the thesis is worded to reveal which aspect of the topic the writer considers most important. Such a clear statement of the writer's position is an effective strategy in an essay of this kind.

You may have noted that each thesis statement also signals the essay's plan of development. The first essay, for example, will use specific facts, examples, and details to describe the kinds of marine life found in the tidal area, upper beach, and dunes. However, thesis statements in essays developed primarily through division-classification don't have to be so structured. If an essay is well written, your principle of division-classification, your opinion about which part or category is most important, and the essay's plan of development will become apparent as the essay unfolds.

4. Organize the essay logically.   Whether your essay is developed wholly or in part by division-classification, it should have a logical structure. As much as possible, try to discuss *comparable points* in each section of the essay. In the essay on seashore life, for example, you might describe life in the tidal area by discussing the mollusks, crustaceans, birds, and amphibians that live or feed there. You would then follow through, as much as you could, with this arrangement in the essay's other sections (upper beach and dune). Not describing the bird life thriving in the dunes, especially when you had discussed bird life in the tidal and upper-beach areas, would compromise the essay's structure. Of course, perfect parallelism is not always possible—there are no mollusks in the dunes, for instance.

You should also use *signal devices* to connect various parts of the essay: "*Another* characteristic of marine life battered by the tides"; "A *final* important trait of both tidal and upper-beach crustaceans"; "*Unlike* the creatures of the tidal area and the upper beach." Such signals clarify the connections among the essay's ideas.

5. State any conclusions or recommendations in the essay's final section.   The analytic thinking that occurs during division-classification often leads to surprising insights. Such insights may be introduced early on, or they may be reserved for the end, where they are stated as conclusions or recommendations. An essay might categorize different kinds of coaches—from inspiring to incompetent—and make the point that athletes learn a great deal about human relations simply by having to get along with their coaches, regardless of the coaches' skills. Such a paper might conclude that participation in a team sport teaches more about human nature than several courses in psychology. Or the essay might end with a proposal: Rookies and seasoned team members should be paired so that novice players can get advice on dealing with coaching eccentricities.

REVISION STRATEGIES

Once you have a draft of the essay, you're ready to revise. The following checklist will help you and those giving you feedback apply to division-classification some of the revision techniques discussed in Chapter 2.

☑ DIVISION-CLASSIFICATION: A REVISION/PEER REVIEW CHECKLIST

Revise Overall Meaning and Structure

❏ What is the principle of division-classification at the heart of the essay? How does this principle contribute to the essay's overall purpose and thesis?

❏ Does the thesis state the essay's principle of division-classification? Should it? Does the thesis signal which part or category is most important? Should it? Does the thesis reveal the essay's plan of development? Should it?

❏ Is the essay organized primarily through division, classification, or a blend of both?

❏ If the essay is organized mainly through division, is the subject sufficiently complex to be broken down into parts? What are the parts?

❏ If the essay is organized mainly through classification, what are the categories? How does this categorizing reveal similarities and/or differences that would otherwise not be apparent?

Revise Paragraph Development

❏ Are comparable points discussed in each of the essay's sections? What are these points?

❏ In which paragraphs does the division-classification seem illogical, incomplete, or inconsistent? In which paragraphs are parts or categories not clearly explained?

❏ Are the subject's different parts or categories discussed in separate paragraphs? Is there any overlap among categories?

Revise Sentences and Words

❏ What signal devices help integrate the essay? Are there enough signals? Too many?

❏ Where should sentences and words be made more specific to clarify the parts and categories being discussed?

STUDENT ESSAY

The following student essay was written by Catherine Gispert in response to this assignment:

In "College Pressures," William Zinsser discusses the various kinds of pressures students encounter, a subject with which he has much personal experience. Choose a group of individuals about whom you are knowledgeable, and write an essay in which you divide the group into types. For example, you might write about various types of parents, teachers, friends, or students. Be sure to include specific details that bring the various groups to life for your intended audience.

Catherine, who was double majoring in music and English, decided to write about a subject she knew quite well: the various types of students who use "the dreaded practice rooms."

The Benchers, the Nappers, the Jellyfish, and the Musicians
by Catherine Gispert

First of two introductory paragraphs

As if getting into college and deciding where to go wasn't hard enough, now you have to pick a major. It's a little overwhelming. Should you pick the easy route and check "Undecided," or just write down the first thing that comes to mind? Or maybe you're one of the lucky ones and you know what you want to do. If not, how about the arts? Painting, dancing, and acting might be a little daunting, but almost everyone can sing a bit or play "Hot Cross Buns" on the recorder. So maybe music is your thing. 1

Transition to focus on an issue music majors have to deal with

Second of two introductory paragraphs

Be careful, though. As a music major, you'll find there is one thing that everyone underestimates: the amount of time you'll spend locked up in a small room with only a piano, your sheet music, and a couple of chairs for company. Yes, these are the dreaded practice rooms. Never heard of them? If you choose to become a music major, not only will you quickly learn what they are; most of your life will revolve around trying to find a practice room with a tuned piano, a nicely situated mirror so that you can check your posture and technique, or quite simply, one that's empty—because more often than not, at least during peak practicing times (think lunch time to early afternoon, when sane people are eating and enjoying the sunshine), you won't be able to find an empty practice room. Is this because everyone in the School of Music has the same idea as you: to hone his or her music craft? No, unfortunately, 2

Thesis

that is not the case. You see, there are four types of people in those occupied rooms, and only one of them is actually practicing.

First heading—
informs the
reader of the first
type of practice
room user

Topic sentence

The Benchers

Benchers are the first type of practice room occupi-   3
ers. These are the social butterflies of the major. They're all friends with each other and enthusiastically gossip about conductors and teachers. Instead of practicing, they're gathered around the benches outside the hallway, blocking traffic. This is perfect, right? If they're out socializing, that means there must be a lot of rooms open. Alas, wrong again. The Benchers have all left their book bags and instruments in practice rooms (probably one of the rooms you wanted, too), saving the room for later. Whether "later" is in a couple of minutes or hours is uncertain. Of course, you could take matters into your own hands and knock on closed doors, but you might disturb the second practice room occupant on this list—the Nappers.

Second heading—
informs the reader
of the second type
of practice room
user

The Nappers

Let's not kid ourselves; everyone is a Napper at one time   4
or another. Even you will fall victim to the occasional nap in a practice room. It's really only a matter of time before your fingers grow tired from plucking notes, or your eyelids start to droop after a long day of Sight Singing 101, Music Theory 202, and Music History 303. You'll close your eyes only for a minute, you tell yourself. Just a quick rest before you start on the next exercise in your music. That is, of course, until you are jolted awake by the rapping on the door from a fellow music major, wondering why she can't hear music coming from within. (*Ugh, another Bencher?* she's wondering.) "Taken!" you blurt out, while standing up to set the motion-sensing lights back on. You make a promise not to let them turn off again, but it's a losing battle.

Third heading—
informs the reader
of the third type of
practice room user

Topic sentence

The first of three
paragraphs on
the third type of
practice room user

The Jellyfish

If you've managed to avoid being a Bencher or a Napper,   5
you could very likely end up a Jellyfish—immobilized by fear. Welcome to college, where every exam and final can make or break you—or so the Jellyfish believes. Dramatic? Yeah, but not exactly false, either. As a music major, you will face your very own set of final exams, called "juries." Your fate in the music program depends on your passing them. So, naturally, you will spend all year preparing for them: learning your major and minor scales to perfection, reciting your Italian and German lyrics until you hate both languages, and memorizing music you don't even like. But there will

come a time when even all this won't be enough. Cue the existential crisis.

The second of three paragraphs on the third type of practice room user

6 "What am I doing with my life?" you'll ask yourself, staring blankly at your music, panicking alone in a practice room. "How am I supposed to do this? I'm going to fail, get kicked out of the music school, and end up destitute on the streets."

The third of three paragraphs on the third type of practice room user

7 Yes, no, perhaps. Most likely, you just have pre-performance jitters, and even if that's not the case, maybe it's some comfort to know that you'll probably end up destitute on the streets whether you pass your juries or not. The stereotype isn't "starving musicians" for nothing!

Fourth heading—informs the reader of the fourth type of practice room user

<u>The Musicians</u>

The first of two paragraphs on the fourth type of practice room user

8 At last, there are the real music majors—the Musicians. They will actually be using practice rooms for their intended purpose: practicing. You might every so often hear a curse word or two and the slamming of piano keys, but not to worry; that means the music "genius" is flowing. The Musicians might leave their rooms, but it's generally only to get sheet music from their lockers or use the facilities.

The second of two paragraphs on the fourth type of practice room user

9 These are the people you should aspire to be. They essentially live in the practice rooms and will never have to worry about failing a jury. Benchers? Not a chance. They only socialize when filling their water bottles, and the conversation is usually about what they're practicing. And napping isn't an option; that would take away practice time, after all. What about panicking over their musical future? No time for that. They're too busy creating that future.

Conclusion

10 So if you decide to become a music major, at least you'll know from the start how difficult it is to acquire a practice room. Snagging one won't be easy, but practicing in one of them sure beats getting yelled at by the other students in your dorm or receiving noise complaints from the neighbors next door. Make sure the piano's tuned and still has all its keys, check the mirror for cracks and scratches, and find a good piano bench or chair. And finally, make sure the room just feels right. After all, you'll be spending the next few hours trapped inside, playing the same piece over and over. But that's okay. It's all in pursuit of the musical dream—right?

COMMENTARY

Introduction and thesis. As Catherine Gispert thought about a possible topic for her classification essay, she decided that she would probably write a stronger essay if she wrote about a subject she knew well. As a music major, she spent lots of time in practice rooms, and she had already been doing some thinking about the different types of students who used the rooms, so she decided that might be a good topic for her essay.

As Catherine thought about an imagined audience for her essay, she decided to write for college students who had not yet decided on a major or who were thinking about switching majors. She wanted to engage her readers, and she knew that most of them would never have heard of "practice rooms." She also knew that if her readers were bored with her introduction, they would probably read no further. So as she worked on her essay, Catherine tried to write an introduction that would interest all students—no matter what major they were considering. She also tried to use an informal, playful tone, something that can be difficult to achieve. Catherine thought that an informal tone would help engage her audience and make them want to keep reading. That tone is evident in her thesis: "You see, there are four types of people in those occupied rooms, and only one of them is actually practicing." Catherine does a nice job of crafting a thesis that draws her imagined readers into her essay and makes them want to read on.

Purpose.   Catherine's purpose in writing this essay was to share with her readers one of the challenges they would face if they became music majors—a challenge she faces almost every day: finding a place to practice. She realizes that her audience knows nothing about the topic and that unless she writes an engaging, well-organized, entertaining essay, they will not read it.

Categories and topic sentences.   To make her essay easier to follow, Catherine decided to use a technique she had never used before in an essay: headings. She knew that as a reader, headings helped her navigate difficult texts, and although the subject matter of her essay would not be considered "difficult," it was one that some readers might easily lose interest in, so she thought the headings might help keep them engaged.

As Catherine composed her essay, she realized that the topic sentences she was accustomed to using at the beginning of paragraphs to signal to her readers that she was transitioning to a new point could be repetitive in some cases; often, the headings themselves would signal the moves. So she focused on developing interesting headings that captured the essence of the various types of practice room users ("The Benchers," "The Nappers," "The Jellyfish," and "The Musicians"), as well as supporting paragraphs that described the various types of practice room users and brought them to life for her readers.

Overall organization and paragraph structure.   Catherine made a smart decision when she decided to use headings to help her organize her essay. Although this technique is certainly not appropriate for all essays, it works well in Catherine's informal, playful piece of writing and allows her to shift easily from one type of practice room user to the next.

She also does a good job of balancing the information she provides on the four types of practice room users. Each of the four sections is roughly the same length and provides readers with just enough (but not too much) information to help them picture the types of individuals Catherine is describing. She uses one paragraph (3) to describe the "Benchers," one paragraph (4) to describe the "Nappers," three (5–7) to describe "The Jellyfish," and two (8–9) to describe "The Musicians."

Catherine keeps her paragraphs relatively short and lively with imagined conversations ("'Taken!' you blurt out, while standing up to set the motion-sensing lights back on"—paragraph 4; "'What am I doing with my life?' you'll ask yourself, staring blankly at your music"—paragraph 6), and she provides specific details that allow her readers to know how music majors spend their days ("It's really only a matter of time before your fingers grow tired from plucking notes, or your eyelids start to droop after a long day of Sight Singing 101, Music Theory 202, and Music History 303"—paragraph 4; "...you'll spend all year...learning your major and minor scales to perfection, reciting your Italian and German lyrics until you hate both languages, and memorizing music you don't even like"—paragraph 5).

Although the overall development is balanced and strong, the introduction seems to be long in relation to the rest of the essay. In her eagerness to draw the reader in, Catherine might have focused too much on elaborating her introduction. For example, one parenthetical aside—"(think lunch time to early afternoon, when sane people are eating and enjoying the sunshine)"—introduces humor at the expense of lengthening the introduction with an awkwardly constructed sentence.

Tone.   Although it is often difficult to achieve a humorous tone, Catherine knew before she ever began writing the first draft of her essay that a serious tone would have been off-putting for readers who knew nothing about the lives of music majors and had no particular interest in learning more about them. She decided early in the writing process to use a light, friendly, playful tone that would be more likely to engage readers than would a serious tone. We hear this conversational tone throughout her essay: "So maybe music is your thing" (1); "This is perfect, right?" (3); "Welcome to college, where every exam and final can make or break you—or so the Jellyfish believes. Dramatic? Yeah, but not exactly false, either" (5); "Snagging [a practice room] won't be easy, but practicing in one of them sure beats getting yelled at by the other students in your dorm or receiving noise complaints from the neighbors next door" (10).

Combining patterns of development. Catherine uses a few examples that employ *cause-effect* reasoning: "If they're out socializing, that means there must be a ton of rooms open. Alas, wrong again" (3) and "'How am I supposed to do this? I'm going to fail, get kicked out of the music school, and end up destitute on the streets'" (6). Introducing these patterns of development adds variety to her essay.

Revising the first draft. Before she started drafting her essay, Catherine thought carefully about what she wanted to say and how she wanted to say it. She decided on her intended audience (college students who had not yet decided on a major or were considering switching from one major to another), an essay structure (classification—with headings for the four categories); and an appropriate tone (conversational, informal, and playful). With her audience, structure, and intended tone in mind, Catherine began writing.

As is often the case for writers at all levels, the most difficult part of writing an essay is getting started, and this was true for Catherine as she began typing this one. She struggled to find a way into her topic that captured the tone she wanted to use and engaged her readers. Printed here is the original version of Catherine's opening paragraph.

Original Version of the Opening Paragraph

Congrats! You're in college. All right—enough celebrating. Now you must decide what you want to do with the rest of your life. Thankfully, there are a few options: "Undecided," a freshman favorite, "Biology," something you'll probably change halfway through the year: or "The Arts," the best and worst decision you can make—music, especially.

When Catherine shared her first draft with her peer review group, she let them know that it was not complete—she had not yet written a conclusion—and that she was not at all happy with the opening paragraph and would appreciate any advice they had to offer on how she might revise it. Both members of her group, Shaina and Ed, told her that they liked the informal voice she had used but that she had not come across as especially friendly near the beginning when she stated, "All right—enough celebrating. Now you must decide what you want to do with the rest of your life." Shaina told Catherine that she sounded almost bossy in the opening paragraph, even though she knew that's not the way Catherine intended to come across. Ed agreed and pointed out that her tone softened by the time she got to the second paragraph and that she sounded much friendlier and playful from that point on.

A couple of days had passed since Catherine had written the first draft that she was sharing with Shaina and Ed, and that time away from her writing provided her with the distance she needed to more objectively review what she had written. She realized that Shaina and Ed were right and that the tone she used in the opening paragraph was not what she had intended.

Later that day she returned to her draft, deleted the opening paragraph and completely revised it, using a friendlier, kinder tone. Then she wrote a conclusion that maintained the tone she had used throughout her essay, summarized the virtues of practice rooms despite their handicaps, and brought the essay back to the issue addressed in the introduction—readers' concern with choosing a major.

Activities: Division-Classification

MyWritingLab

Prewriting Activities

1. Imagine you're writing two essays: One is a humorous paper outlining a *process* for impressing college instructors; the other is a serious essay examining the *causes* of the recent rise in volunteerism. What about the topics might you divide and/or classify?

2. Use group brainstorming to identify three principles of division for *one* of the topics in Set A below. Focusing on one of the principles, decide what your thesis might be if you were writing an essay. That done, use group brainstorming to identify three principles of classification that might provide the structure for *one* of the topics in Set B. Focusing on one of the principles, decide what your thesis might be if you were writing an essay.

Set A
- Rock music
- A shopping mall
- A good horror movie

Set B
- Why people get addicted to social networking sites
- How fast-food restaurants affect family life
- Why long-term relationships break up

Revising Activities

3. Following is a scratch outline for an essay developed through division-classification. On what principle of division-classification is the essay based? What problem do you see in the way the principle is applied? How could the problem be remedied?

Thesis: The same experience often teaches opposite things to different people.

- What working as a fast-food cook teaches: Some learn responsibility; others learn to take a "quick and dirty" approach.
- What a negative experience teaches optimists: Some learn from their mistakes; others continue to maintain a positive outlook.

(continued)

Activities: Division-Classification (*continued*)

- What a difficult course teaches: Some learn to study hard; others learn to avoid demanding courses.
- What the breakup of a close relationship teaches: Some learn how to negotiate differences; others learn to avoid intimacy.

4. Following is a paragraph from the first draft of an essay urging that day-care centers adopt play programs tailored to children's developmental needs. What principle of division-classification focuses the paragraph? Is the principle applied consistently and logically? Are parts/categories developed sufficiently? Revise the paragraph, eliminating any problems you discover and adding specific details where needed.

Within a few years, preschool children move from self-absorbed to interactive play. Babies and toddlers engage in solitary play. Although they sometimes prefer being near other children, they focus primarily on their own actions. This is very different from the highly interactive play of the elementary school years. Sometime in children's second year, solitary play is replaced by parallel play, during which children engage in similar activities near one another. However, they interact only occasionally. By age three, most children show at least some cooperative play, a form that involves interaction and cooperative role-taking. Such role-taking can be found in the "pretend" games that children play to explore adult relationships (games of "Mommy and Daddy") and anatomy (games of "Doctor"). Additional signs of youngsters' growing awareness of peers can be seen at about age four. At this age, many children begin showing a special devotion to one other child and may want to play only with that child. During this time, children also begin to take special delight in physical activities such as running and jumping, often going off by themselves to expend their abundant physical energy.

Amy Tan

The American writer Amy Tan was born in 1952, a few years after her parents had emigrated from China. Tan grew up in California and Switzerland, and she earned a master's degree in linguistics from San José State University. Her first novel, *The Joy Luck Club* (1987), won a National Book Award. Her other novels include *The Kitchen God's Wife* (1991), *The Bonesetter's Daughter* (2000), *Saving Fish from Drowning* (2005), *The Hundred Secret Senses* (2010), and *The Valley of Amazement* (2013). The following essay, first published in *The Threepenny Review*, is from her memoir *The Opposite of Fate: A Book of Musings* (2003).

Pre-Reading Journal Entry

MyWritingLab

Most people have different ways of speaking in different situations. Think of how you talk to your parents and other relatives; to children; to friends; to colleagues at work; to professors, doctors, and other professionals; and to your spouse or partner. Write down in your journal some examples of how you speak in various situations.

For ideas on how this division-classification essay is organized, see Figure 6.2 on page 226.

Mother Tongue

I am not a scholar of English or literature. I cannot give you much more than personal opinions of the English language and its variations in this country or others. 1

I am a writer. And by that definition, I am someone who has always loved language. I am fascinated by language in daily life. I spend a great deal of my time thinking about the power of language—the way it can evoke an emotion, a visual image, a complex idea, or a simple truth. Language is the tool of my trade. And I use them all—all the Englishes I grew up with. 2

Recently, I was made keenly aware of the different Englishes I do use. I was giving a talk to a large group of people, the same talk I had already given to half a dozen other groups. The nature of the talk was about my writing, my life, and my book, *The Joy Luck Club*. The talk was going along well enough, until I remembered one major difference that made the whole talk sound wrong. My mother was in the room. And it was perhaps the first time she had heard me give a lengthy speech, using the kind of English I have never used with her. I was saying things like, "The intersection of memory upon imagination" and "There is an aspect of my fiction that relates to thus-and-thus"—a speech filled with carefully wrought grammatical phrases, burdened, it suddenly seemed to me, with nominalized forms, past perfect tenses, conditional phrases, all the forms of standard English that I had learned in school and through books, the forms of English I did not use at home with my mother. 3

Just last week, I was walking down the street with my mother, and   4
I again found myself conscious of the English I was using, and the English
I do use with her. We were talking about the price of new and used furniture
and I heard myself saying this: "Not waste money that way." My husband
was with us as well, and he didn't notice any switch in my English. And then
I realized why. It's because over the twenty years we've been together I've
often used the same kind of English with him, and sometimes he even uses it
with me. It has become our language of intimacy, a different sort of English
that relates to family talk, the language I grew up with.

So you'll have some idea of what this family talk I heard sounds like, I'll   5
quote what my mother said during a recent conversation which I videotaped
and then transcribed. During this conversation, my mother was talking
about a political gangster in Shanghai who had the same last name as her
family's, Du, and how the gangster in his early years wanted to be adopted
by her family, which was rich by comparison. Later, the gangster became
more powerful, far richer than my mother's family, and one day showed up
at my mother's wedding to pay his respects. Here's what she said in part:

"Du Yusong having business like fruit stand. Like off the street kind.   6
He is Du like Du Zong—but not Tsung-ming Island people. The
local people call putong, the river east side, he belong to that side
local people. The man want to ask Du Zong father take him in like
become own family. Du Zong father wasn't look down on him, but
didn't take seriously, until the man big like become a mafia. Now
important person, very hard to inviting him. Chinese way, came
only to show respect, don't stay for dinner. Respect for making big
celebration, he shows up. Mean gives lots of respect. Chinese custom. Chinese social life that way. If too important won't have to stay
too long. He come to my wedding. I didn't see, I heard it. I gone
to boy's side, they have YMCA dinner. Chinese age I was nineteen."

You should know that my mother's expressive command of English belies   7
how much she actually understands. She reads the Forbes report, listens to *Wall
Street Week,* converses daily with her stockbroker, reads all of Shirley MacLaine's
books with ease—all kinds of things I can't begin to understand. Yet some of
my friends tell me they understand 50 percent of what my mother says. Some
say they understand 80 to 90 percent. Some say they understand none of it, as
if she were speaking pure Chinese. But to me, my mother's English is perfectly
clear, perfectly natural. It's my mother tongue. Her language, as I hear it, vivid,
direct, full of observation and imagery. That was the language that helped shape
the way I saw things expressed things, made sense of the world.

Lately, I've been giving more thought to the kind of English my mother   8
speaks. Like others, I have described it to people as "broken" or "fractured"

English. But I wince when I say that. It has always bothered me that I can think of no way to describe it other than "broken," as if it were damaged and needed to be fixed, as if it lacked a certain wholeness and soundness. I've heard other terms used, "limited English," for example. But they seem just as bad, as if everything is limited, including people's perceptions of the limited English speaker.

I know this for a fact, because when I was growing up, my mother's "limited" English limited *my* perception of her. I was ashamed of her English. I believed that her English reflected the quality of what she had to say. That is, because she expressed them imperfectly her thoughts were imperfect. And I had plenty of empirical evidence to support me: the fact that people in department stores, at banks, and at restaurants did not take her seriously, did not give her good service, pretended not to understand her, or even acted as if they did not hear her.

My mother has long realized the limitations of her English as well. When I was fifteen, she used to have me call people on the phone to pretend I was she. In this guise, I was forced to ask for information or even to complain and yell at people who had been rude to her. One time it was a call to her stockbroker in New York. She had cashed out her small portfolio and it just so happened we were going to go to New York the next week, our very first trip outside California. I had to get on the phone and say in an adolescent voice that was not very convincing, "This is Mrs. Tan."

And my mother was standing in back whispering loudly, "Why he don't send me check, already two weeks late. So mad he lie to me, losing me money."

And then I said in perfect English, "Yes, I'm getting rather concerned. You had agreed to send the check two weeks ago, but it hasn't arrived."

Then she began to talk more loudly. "What he want, I come to New York tell him front of his boss, you cheating me?" And I was trying to calm her down, make her be quiet, while telling the stockbroker, "I can't tolerate any more excuses. If I don't receive the check immediately, I am going to have to speak to your manager when I'm in New York next week." And sure enough, the following week there we were in front of this astonished stockbroker, and I was sitting there red-faced and quiet, and my mother, the real Mrs. Tan, was shouting at his boss in her impeccable broken English.

We used a similar routine just five days ago, for a situation that was far less humorous. My mother had gone to the hospital for an appointment, to find out about a benign brain tumor a CAT scan had revealed a month ago. She said she had spoken very good English, her best English, no mistakes. Still, she said, the hospital did not apologize when they said they had lost the CAT scan and she had come for nothing. She said they did not seem to have any sympathy when she told them she was anxious to know the exact diagnosis, since her husband and son had both died of brain tumors. She said they would not give her any more information until the next time and she would have to make another appointment for that. So she said she

9

10

11

12

13

14

would not leave until the doctor called her daughter. She wouldn't budge. And when the doctor finally called her daughter, me, who spoke in perfect English—lo and behold—we had assurances the CAT scan would be found, promises that a conference call on Monday would be held, and apologies for any suffering my mother had gone through for a most regrettable mistake.

I think my mother's English almost had an effect on limiting my pos-   15 sibilities in life as well. Sociologists and linguists probably will tell you that a person's developing language skills are more influenced by peers. But I do think that the language spoken in the family, especially in immigrant families which are more insular, plays a large role in shaping the language of the child. And I believe that it affected my results on achievement tests, IQ tests, and the SAT. While my English skills were never judged as poor, compared to math, English could not be considered my strong suit. In grade school I did moderately well, getting perhaps B's, sometimes B-pluses, in English and scoring perhaps in the sixtieth or seventieth percentile on achievement tests. But those scores were not good enough to override the opinion that my true abilities lay in math and science, because in those areas I achieved A's and scored in the ninetieth percentile or higher.

This was understandable. Math is precise; there is only one correct   16 answer. Whereas, for me at least, the answers on English tests were always a judgment call, a matter of opinion and personal experience. Those tests were constructed around items like fill-in-the-blank sentence completion, such as, "Even though Tom was _____, Mary thought he was _____." And the correct answer always seemed to be the most bland combinations of thoughts, for example, "Even though Tom was shy, Mary thought he was charming," with the grammatical structure "even though" limiting the correct answer to some sort of semantic opposites, so you wouldn't get answers like, "Even though Tom was foolish, Mary thought he was ridiculous." Well, according to my mother, there were very few limitations as to what Tom could have been and what Mary might have thought of him. So I never did well on tests like that.

The same was true with word analogies, pairs of words in which you   17 were supposed to find some sort of logical, semantic relationship—for example, "*Sunset* is to *nightfall* as _____ is to _____." And here you would be presented with a list of four possible pairs, one of which showed the same kind of relationship: *red* is to *stoplight, bus* is to *arrival, chills* is to *fever, yawn* is to *boring.* Well, I could never think that way. I knew what the tests were asking, but I could not block out of my mind the images already created by the first pair, "*sunset* is to *nightfall*"—and I would see a burst of colors against a darkening sky, the moon rising, the lowering of a curtain of stars. And all the other pairs of words—red, bus, stoplight, boring—just threw up a mess of confusing images, making it impossible for me to sort out something as logical as saying: "A sunset precedes nightfall" is the same as "a chill precedes a fever." The only way I would have gotten that answer right would have been to imagine an associative situation, for example, my being disobedient and staying out past sunset, catching a chill at night, which turns into feverish pneumonia as punishment, which indeed did happen to me.

I have been thinking about all this lately, about my mother's English, 18 about achievement tests. Because lately I've been asked, as a writer, why there are not more Asian Americans represented in American literature. Why are there few Asian Americans enrolled in creative writing programs? Why do so many Chinese students go into engineering? Well, these are broad socio-logical questions I can't begin to answer. But I have noticed in surveys—in fact, just last week—that Asian students, as a whole, always do significantly better on math achievement tests than in English. And this makes me think that there are other Asian-American students whose English spoken in the home might also be described as "broken" or "limited." And perhaps they also have teachers who are steering them away from writing and into math and science, which is what happened to me.

Fortunately, I happen to be rebellious in nature and enjoy the challenge 19 of disproving assumptions made about me. I became an English major my first year in college, after being enrolled as pre-med. I started writing nonfic-tion as a freelancer the week after I was told by my former boss that writing was my worst skill and I should hone my talents toward account management.

But it wasn't until 1985 that I finally began to write fiction. And at first 20 I wrote using what I thought would be wittily crafted sentences, sentences that would finally prove I had mastery over the English language. Here's an example from the first draft of a story that later made its way into *The Joy Luck Club*, but without this line: "That was my mental quandary in the nascent state." A terrible line, which I can barely pronounce.

Fortunately, for reasons I won't get into today, I later decided I should 21 envision a reader for the stories I would write. And the reader I decided upon was my mother, because these were stories about mothers. So with this reader in mind—and in fact she did read my early drafts—I began to write stories using all the Englishes I grew up with: the English I spoke to my mother, which for lack of a better term might be described as "simple"; the English she used with me, which for lack of a better term might be described as "broken"; my translation of her Chinese, which could certainly be described as "watered down"; and what I imagined to be her translation of her Chinese if she could speak in perfect English, her internal language, and for that I sought to pre-serve the essence, but neither an English nor a Chinese structure. I wanted to capture what language ability tests can never reveal: her intent, her passion, her imagery, the rhythms of her speech and the nature of her thoughts.

Apart from what any critic had to say about my writing, I knew I had 22 succeeded where it counted when my mother finished reading my book and gave me her verdict: "So easy to read."

FIGURE 6.2

Essay Structure: "Mother Tongue" by Amy Tan

Introductory paragraphs **Background** **Thesis** (paragraphs 1–2)	Identification as a writer, not a scholar **Thesis:** "Language is the tool of my trade. And I use them all–all the Englishes I grew up with."
Background: **examples** (3–7)	Examples of Tan's use of the language (speaking to a group about her writing, writing a novel, talking with family members) Examples of Tan's mother's "broken" English (conversing about a political gangster, talking with a stockbroker, trying to obtain information about her CAT scan)
Causes and effects: **examples** (8–20)	Reflections the author makes about • the *effects* of describing forms of English as "broken" or "limited"; • ways that using "sub-standard" English *affects* students' academic test results; and • how students' use of "limited" English can *cause* teachers to steer them away from writing and towards math and science
Additional details of **classification with** **examples (21)**	Types of English Tan grew up using: • Simple–English Tan spoke to her mother • Broken–English Tan's mother used with her • Watered down–Tan's translation of her mother's Chinese • Tan's mother's internal language–what Tan imagined to be her mother's translation of her mother's Chinese if her mother could speak in perfect English What language ability tests cannot reveal: • Intent • Passion • Imagery • Rhythms of speech • Nature of thoughts
Concluding paragraph (22)	Author's closing comment on how she knew she had succeeded as a writer

Questions for Close Reading

MyWritingLab

1. What is the selection's thesis? Locate the sentence(s) in which Tan states her main idea. If she doesn't state her thesis explicitly, express it in your own words.
2. Describe the particular event that prompted the author to think about her use of language. What does she mean by "different Englishes"? What are these "different Englishes"?
3. What questions has Tan been asked "as a writer"? What survey information does she use in formulating her response? Is the survey information valid? How does Tan use it to support personal information she gives in the essay?
4. How have Tan's feelings about her mother's command of English changed over the years?

Questions About the Writer's Craft

1. **The pattern.** What principle of classification does the author use to identify the "different Englishes" she describes? How is that principle reflected in the different types of English Tan mentions?
2. In paragraph 6, the author gives an extended example of her mother's speech. Why does she do this? What is the effect of having this quotation in the essay? How easy do you think it is to follow Tan's mother's speech?
3. **Other patterns.** The author uses personal anecdotes about her relationship with her mother to illustrate some important points. Identify at least two anecdotes. What points do they support? How effective are they? Why?
4. In paragraph 20, the author quotes a line that she wrote but ultimately did not include in the final version of her novel. Why does she call it a "terrible line," and why do you think she included it? How does the English in that line compare with the English in the excerpt of her mother's speech?

Writing Assignments Using Classification-Division as a Pattern of Development

1. Like the author, you probably do different kinds of writing. You might write e-mails at work, academic papers in class, text messages to friends, and journal or diary entries. You might also compose song lyrics, poems, or other kinds of creative writing. Write an essay in which you classify the types of writing you do. Choose an appropriate principle of classification, and then show how the types of writing are similar and dissimilar. Use examples, including excerpts from your writing, to illustrate the points you make.
2. Tan classifies types of English, but there are other types of expression that can be classified. For example, you can classify manners, modes of dress, facial expressions, and kinds of greetings. Choose one of these topics or another such subject, and write an essay in which you classify types in this group. Decide whether you wish to inform or entertain, and develop a principle of classification that suits your purpose. Remember to include relevant examples.

Writing Assignment Combining
Patterns of Development

3. The author mentions surveys showing how Asian Americans perform on standardized tests, such as the SAT. Proponents of standardized tests believe the tests hold
all students to the same objective standard. Opponents believe some tests are un-
intentionally biased against one or more groups of students. Do some research on
one standardized test. Develop a position about the test, and *argue* your position
in an essay. Include the results of *relevant studies* and the opinions of *experts* as
evidence for your views.

Stephanie Ericsson

Stephanie Ericsson (1953–) is a writer, screenwriter, and ad copywriter who often
uses her own life experiences as starting points for her deeply personal work. She
wrote *Companion Through the Darkness: Inner Dialogues on Grief* (1993) in response
to her husband's sudden death while she was pregnant, and she chronicled her strug-
gles with substance abuse in both *Shamefaced* (1985) and *Women of AA: Recovering
Together* (1986). Ericsson's latest book is *Companion into the Dawn: Inner Dialogues
on Loving* (1994). A frequent speaker on the subject of loss, she lives in Minneapolis,
Minnesota. "The Ways We Lie" was originally published in the *Utne Reader* in 1992.

Pre-Reading Journal Entry   My WritingLab

Something that everyone is guilty of, but may not want to admit to, is lying. Think
for a moment about times when you told a lie. In your pre-reading journal, begin by
listing any episodes of lying you can recall. Then go back and freewrite to a greater
extent about these incidents. In each case, why did you tell the lie—what were the
circumstances? What was the outcome? Do you now regret having lied, or are you
thankful you did it?

The Ways We Lie

The bank called today and I told them my deposit was in the mail, even   1
though I hadn't written a check yet. It'd been a rough day. The baby I'm
pregnant with decided to do aerobics on my lungs for two hours, our three-
year-old daughter painted the living room couch with lipstick, the IRS put me
on hold for an hour, and I was late to a business meeting because I was tired.

I told my client that traffic had been bad. When my partner came home,   2
his haggard face told me his day hadn't gone any better than mine, so when
he asked, "How was your day?" I said, "Oh, fine," knowing that one more
straw might break his back. A friend called and wanted to take me to lunch. I
said I was busy. Four lies in the course of a day, none of which I felt the least
bit guilty about.

We lie. We all do. We exaggerate, we minimize, we avoid confrontation, 3
we spare people's feelings, we conveniently forget, we keep secrets, we justify
lying to the big-guy institutions. Like most people, I indulge in small false-
hoods and still think of myself as an honest person. Sure I lie, but it doesn't
hurt anything. Or does it?

I once tried going a whole week without telling a lie, and it was paralyzing. 4
I discovered that telling the truth all the time is nearly impossible. It means living with some serious consequences: The bank charges me $60 in overdraft
fees, my partner keels over when I tell him about my travails, my client fires me
for telling her I didn't feel like being on time, and my friend takes it personally
when I say I'm not hungry. There must be some merit to lying.

But if I justify lying, what makes me any different from slick politicians 5
or the corporate robbers who raided the S&L industry?[1] Saying it's okay to
lie one way and not another is hedging. I cannot seem to escape the voice
deep inside me that tells me: When someone lies, someone loses.

What far-reaching consequences will I, or others, pay as a result of my 6
lie? Will someone's trust be destroyed? Will someone else pay *my* penance
because I ducked out? We must consider the *meaning of our actions*.
Deception, lies, capital crimes, and misdemeanors all carry meanings.
Webster's definition of *lie* is specific:

> 1: a false statement or action especially made with the intent to de-
> ceive; 2: anything that gives or is meant to give a false impression.

A definition like this implies that there are many, many ways to tell a lie. 7
Here are just a few.

The White Lie

A man who won't lie to a woman has very little consideration for her feelings.
—Bergen Evans

The white lie assumes that the truth will cause more damage than a sim- 8
ple, harmless untruth. Telling a friend he looks great when he looks like hell
can be based on a decision that the friend needs a compliment more than a
frank opinion. But, in effect, it is the liar deciding what is best for the lied to.
Ultimately, it is a vote of no confidence. It is an act of subtle arrogance for
anyone to decide what is best for someone else.

Yet not all circumstances are quite so cut-and-dried. Take, for instance, 9
the sergeant in Vietnam who knew one of his men was killed in action but

---

[1]Reference to the savings and loan scandal of the 1980s, in which corrupt owners of bank-like
institutions defrauded the federal government of vast amounts of money (editors' note).

listed him as missing so that the man's family would receive indefinite compensation instead of the lump-sum pittance the military gives widows and children. His intent was honorable. Yet for twenty years this family kept their hopes alive, unable to move on to a new life.

Façades

Et tu, Brute?
—Caesar

We all put up façades to one degree or another. When I put on a suit   10
to go to see a client, I feel as though I am putting on another face, obeying the expectation that serious businesspeople wear suits rather than sweatpants. But I'm a writer. Normally, I get up, get the kid off to school, and sit at my computer in my pajamas until four in the afternoon. When I answer the phone, the caller thinks I'm wearing a suit (though the UPS man knows better).

But façades can be destructive because they are used to seduce others   11
into an illusion. For instance, I recently realized that a former friend was a liar. He presented himself with all the right looks and the right words and offered lots of new consciousness theories, fabulous books to read, and fascinating insights. Then I did some business with him, and the time came for him to pay me. He turned out to be all talk and no walk. I heard a plethora of reasonable excuses, including in-depth descriptions of the big break around the corner. In six months of work, I saw less than a hundred bucks. When I confronted him, he raised both eyebrows and tried to convince me that I'd heard him wrong, that he'd made no commitment to me. A simple investigation into his past revealed a crowded graveyard of disenchanted former friends.

Ignoring the Plain Facts

Well, you must understand that Father Porter is only human . . . .
—A Massachusetts priest

In the '60s, the Catholic Church in Massachusetts began hearing complaints that Father James Porter was sexually molesting children. Rather   12
than relieving him of his duties, the ecclesiastical authorities simply moved him from one parish to another between 1960 and 1967, actually providing him with a fresh supply of unsuspecting families and innocent children to abuse. After treatment in 1967 for pedophilia, he went back to work, this time in Minnesota. The new diocese was aware of Father Porter's obsession with children, but they needed priests and recklessly believed treatment had

cured him. More children were abused until he was relieved of his duties a year later. By his own admission, Porter may have abused as many as a hundred children.

Ignoring the facts may not in and of itself be a form of lying, but consider the context of this situation. If a lie is *a false action done with the intent to deceive,* then the Catholic Church's conscious covering for Porter created irreparable consequences. The church became a co-perpetrator with Porter.   13

Deflecting

When you have no basis for an argument, abuse the plaintiff.

—Cicero

I've discovered that I can keep anyone from seeing the true me by being selectively blatant. I set a precedent of being up-front about intimate issues, but I never bring up the things I truly want to hide; I just let people assume I'm revealing everything. It's an effective way of hiding.   14

Any good liar knows that the way to perpetuate an untruth is to deflect attention from it. When Clarence Thomas[2] exploded with accusations that the Senate hearings were a "high-tech lynching," he simple switched the focus from a highly charged subject to a radioactive subject. Rather than defending himself, he took the offensive and accused the country of racism. It was a brilliant maneuver. Racism is now politically incorrect in official circles—unlike sexual harassment, which still rewards those who can get away with it.   15

Some of the most skillful deflectors are passive-aggressive[3] people who, when accused of inappropriate behavior, refuse to respond to the accusations. This you-don't-exist stance infuriates the accuser, who, understandably, screams something obscene out of frustration. The trap is sprung and the act of deflection successful, because now the passive-aggressive person can indignantly say, "Who can talk to someone as unreasonable as you?" The real issue is forgotten and the sins of the original victim become the focus. Feeling guilty of name-calling, the victim is fully tamed and crawls into a hole, ashamed. I have watched this fighting technique work thousands of times in disputes between men and women, and what I've learned is that the real culprit is not necessarily the one who swears the loudest.   16

---

[2]Nominated to the Supreme Court in 1993, Clarence Thomas, an African American jurist, was accused by former colleague Anita Hill of sexual harassment. Much of Thomas's confirmation hearing, televised nationwide, focused on this issue (editors' note).

[3]A psychological pattern in which hostility is expressed through an infuriating detachment and nonresponsiveness (editors' note).

Omission

The cruelest lies are often told in silence.

—R. L. Stevenson

Omission involves telling most of the truth minus one or two key facts   17
whose absence changes the story completely. You break a pair of glasses that
are guaranteed under normal use and get a new pair, without mentioning
that the first pair broke during a rowdy game of basketball. Who hasn't tried
something like that? But what about omission of information that could
make a difference in how a person lives his or her life?

For instance, one day I found out that rabbinical legends tell of another   18
woman in the Garden of Eden before Eve. I was stunned. The omission
of the Sumerian goddess Lilith from Genesis—as well as her demonization
by ancient misogynists as an embodiment of female evil—felt like spiritual
robbery. I felt like I'd just found out my mother was really my stepmother.
To take seriously the tradition that Adam was created out of the same mud
as his equal counterpart, Lilith, redefines all of Judeo-Christian history.

Some renegade Catholic feminists introduced me to a view of Lilith that   19
had been suppressed during many centuries when this strong goddess was
seen only as a spirit of evil. Lilith was a proud goddess who defied Adam's
need to control her, attempted negotiations, and when this failed, said adios
and left the Garden of Eden.

This omission of Lilith from the Bible was a patriarchal strategy to keep   20
women weak. Omitting the strong-woman archetype of Lilith from Western
religions and starting the story with Eve the Rib has helped keep Christian
and Jewish women believing they were the lesser sex for thousands of years.

Stereotypes and Clichés

*Where opinion does not exist, the status quo becomes
stereotyped and all originality is discouraged.*

—Bertrand Russell

Stereotype and cliché serve a purpose as a form of shorthand. Our need   21
for vast amounts of information in nanoseconds has made the stereotype
vital to modern communication. Unfortunately, it often shuts down original
thinking, giving those hungry for the truth a candy bar of misinformation
instead of a balanced meal. The stereotype explains a situation with just
enough truth to seem unquestionable.

All the "isms"—racism, sexism, ageism, et al.—are founded on and fueled   22
by the stereotype and the cliché, which are lies of exaggeration, omission, and
ignorance. They are always dangerous. They take a single tree and make it a

landscape. They destroy curiosity. They close minds and separate people. The single mother on welfare is assumed to be cheating. Any black male could tell you how much of his identity is obliterated daily by stereotypes. Fat people, ugly people, beautiful people, old people, large-breasted women, short men, the mentally ill, and the homeless all could tell you how much more they are like us than we want to think. I once admitted to a group of people that I had a mouth like a truck driver. Much to my surprise, a man stood up and said, "I'm a truck driver, and I never cuss." Needless to say, I was humbled.

Groupthink

Who is more foolish, the child afraid of the dark,
or the man afraid of the light?

—Maurice Freehill

Irving Janis, in *Victims of Group Think,* defines this sort of lie as a psy-   23
chological phenomenon within decision-making groups in which loyalty to the group has become more important than any other value, with the result that dissent and the appraisal of alternatives are suppressed. If you've ever worked on a committee or in a corporation, you've encountered groupthink. It requires a combination of other forms of lying—ignoring facts, selective memory, omission, and denial, to name a few.

The textbook example of groupthink came on December 7, 1941. From   24
as early as the fall of 1941, the warnings came in, one after another, that Japan was preparing for a massive military operation. The Navy command in Hawaii assumed Pearl Harbor was invulnerable—the Japanese weren't stupid enough to attack the United States' most important base. On the other hand, racist stereotypes said the Japanese weren't smart enough to invent a torpedo effective in less than 60 feet of water (the fleet was docked in 30 feet); after all, U.S. technology hadn't been able to do it.

On Friday, December 5, normal weekend leave was granted to all the   25
commanders at Pearl Harbor, even though the Japanese consulate in Hawaii was busy burning papers. Within the tight, good-ole-boy cohesiveness of the U.S. command in Hawaii, the myth of invulnerability stayed well entrenched. No one in the group considered the alternatives. The rest is history.

Out-and-Out Lies

The only form of lying that is beyond reproach is lying for its own sake.

—Oscar Wilde

Of all the ways to lie, I like this one the best, probably because I get tired   26
of trying to figure out the real meanings behind things. At least I can trust the

bald-faced lie. I once asked my five-year-old nephew, "Who broke the fence?" (I had seen him do it.) He answered, "The murderers." Who could argue?

At least when this sort of lie is told it can be easily confronted. As the person who is lied to, I know where I stand. The bald-faced lie doesn't toy with my perceptions—it argues with them. It doesn't try to refashion reality, it tries to refute it. *Read my lips...* No sleight of hand.[4] No guessing. If this were the only form of lying, there would be no such things as floating anxiety[5] or the adult, children-of-alcoholics movement.   27

Dismissal

Pay no attention to that man behind the curtain! I am the Great Oz!
—The Wizard of Oz

Dismissal is perhaps the slipperiest of all lies. Dismissing feelings, perceptions, or even the raw facts of a situation ranks as a kind of lie that can do as much damage to a person as any other kind of lie.   28

The roots of many mental disorders can be traced back to the dismissal of reality. Imagine that a person is told from the time she is a tot that her perceptions are inaccurate. *"Mommy, I'm scared."* "No you're not, darling." *"I don't like that man next door, he makes me feel icky."* "Johnny, that's a terrible thing to say, of course you like him. You go over there right now and be nice to him."   29

I've often mused over the idea that madness is actually a sane reaction to an insane world. Psychologist R. D. Laing supports this hypothesis in *Sanity, Madness and the Family,* an account of his investigations into the families of schizophrenics. The common thread that ran through all of the families he studied was a deliberate, staunch dismissal of the patient's perceptions from a very early age. Each of the patients started out with an accurate grasp of reality, which, through meticulous and methodical dismissal, was demolished until the only reality the patient could trust was catatonia.   30

Dismissal runs the gamut. Mild dismissal can be quite handy for forgiving the foibles of others in our day-to-day lives. Toddlers who have just learned to manipulate their parents' attention sometimes are dismissed out of necessity. Absolute attention from the parents would require so much energy that no one would get to eat dinner. But we must be careful and attentive about how far we take our "necessary" dismissals. Dismissal is a dangerous tool, because it's nothing less than a lie.   31

[4]A phrase used by presidential candidate George H. W. Bush during the 1988 campaign (and often parodied thereafter): "Read my lips.... No new taxes" (editors' note).
[5]A psychological condition in which a person feels generalized anxiety for no specific reason (editors' note).

Delusion

We lie loudest when we lie to ourselves.

—Eric Hoffer

I could write the book on this one. Delusion, a cousin of dismissal, is 32 the tendency to see excuses as facts. It's a powerful lying tool because it filters out information that contradicts what we want to believe. Alcoholics who believe that the problems in their lives are legitimate reasons for drinking rather than results of the drinking offer the classic example of deluded thinking. Delusion uses the mind's ability to see things in myriad ways to support what it wants to be the truth.

But delusion is also a survival mechanism we all use. If we were to fully 33 contemplate the consequences of our stockpiles of nuclear weapons or global warming, we could hardly function on a day-to-day level. We don't want to incorporate that much reality into our lives because to do so would be paralyzing.

Delusion acts as an adhesive to keep the status quo intact. It shamelessly 34 employs dismissal, omission, and amnesia, among other sorts of lies. Its most cunning defense is that it cannot see itself.

● ● ●

The liar's punishment... is that he cannot believe anyone else.

—George Bernard Shaw

These are only a few of the ways we lie. Or are lied to. As I said earlier, 35 it's not easy to entirely eliminate lies from our lives. No matter how pious we may try to be, we will still embellish, hedge, and omit to lubricate the daily machinery of living. But there is a world of difference between telling functional lies and living a lie. Martin Buber[6] once said, "The lie is the spirit committing treason against itself." Our acceptance of lies becomes a cultural cancer that eventually shrouds and reorders reality until moral garbage becomes as invisible to us as water is to a fish.

How much do we tolerate before we become sick and tired of being sick 36 and tired? When will we stand up and declare our *right* to trust? When do we stop accepting that the real truth is in the fine print? Whose lips do we read this year when we vote for president? When will we stop being so reticent about making judgments? When do we stop turning over our personal power and responsibility to liars?

[6]A German Jewish scholar and philosopher (1878–1965) (editors' note).

Maybe if I don't tell the bank the check's in the mail I'll be less tolerant   37
of the lies told me every day. A country song I once heard said it all for me:
"You've got to stand for something or you'll fall for anything."

Questions for Close Reading

MyWritingLab

1. What is the selection's thesis? Locate the sentence(s) in which Ericsson states her main idea. If she doesn't state the thesis explicitly, express it in your own words.
2. What did Ericsson discover when she tried to go a whole week without lying?
3. Ericsson classifies as "lies" some behaviors not always considered dishonest. How can "ignoring the plain facts," "deflecting," and "omission" be types of lies? How do "stereotypes and clichés" and "groupthink" qualify as lies?
4. Why doesn't Ericsson easily accept the fact that lies are a necessary part of her life and that of most people?

Questions About the Writer's Craft

1. **The pattern.** In paragraph 6, Ericsson asserts that we "must consider the *meaning of our actions*" when deciding whether or not we have lied. How does this principle of classification help her show that each category of behavior discussed is a type of lying?
2. **Other patterns.** In the body of her essay, Ericsson draws upon both personal experience and third-person material to make her point. Her introduction, though, includes only a first-person *narrative*. Why do you suppose Ericsson decided to open the essay with this brief first-person account?
3. Despite the seriousness of her subject, Ericsson's overall tone is informal—almost conversational. Identify at least five instances of this informality. Why do you suppose Ericsson adopted such a tone?
4. **Other patterns.** In her concluding paragraphs (35–37), Ericsson *contrasts* two broad types of lies, saying that "there is a world of difference between telling functional lies and living a lie." How does this contrast help her sum up the essay?

Writing Assignments Using Division-Classification as a Pattern of Development

1. Ericsson takes an often used, seemingly simple word and, by categorizing its various manifestations, shows that it represents a complex phenomenon. Choose another frequently used word—such as *loyalty, excellence, arrogance,* or *hypocrisy*—and show its complexity by categorizing its different types. Before presenting your categories, offer a definition, either yours or the dictionary's, of the word; then provide dramatic examples to illustrate the various categories.
2. In paragraph 23, Ericsson cites Irving Janus's definition of "groupthink." Using this definition as a starting point, analyze several situations involving groupthink that you have observed or heard about. Classify the kinds of groupthink that are revealed in these situations, illustrating each type with at least one vivid example.

Writing Assignment Combining Patterns of Development

3. Many social commentators call attention, as Ericsson does in paragraph 15, to the growing tendency of individuals to absolve themselves from responsibility for something they've done by claiming that *they* are actually the victims. Gain some background on the issue of victimization by brainstorming with others and locating relevant material in the library or on the Internet. Then write an essay *arguing* that we are or are not becoming a nation of victims and crybabies. Discredit the opposing viewpoint as much as possible by drawing on your own and other people's experiences, as well as the outside sources you've read. And, in the course of your essay, speculate about the *causes* of the behavior you have identified.

William Zinsser

In addition to having taught at both the Columbia University Graduate School of Journalism, and the New School in New York City, William Zinsser has written news journalism, drama criticism, magazine columns, a memoir, and several books on U.S. culture. Born in 1922 in New York, Zinsser worked for *The New York Herald Tribune* and *Life*. In 1970, Zinsser designed a course in nonfiction writing for Yale University. Using what he learned at Yale about the way college students approach the writing process, Zinsser wrote the popular guide *On Writing Well* (1976), now in its seventh edition. His other books include *The City Dwellers* (1962), *Pop Goes America* (1966), *The Lunacy Boom* (1970), *Writing with a Word Processor* (1982), *American Places: A Writer's Pilgrimage to 15 of This Country's Most Visited and Cherished Sites* (1992), *Speaking of Journalism* (1994), and *Writing About Your Life* (2004). He also edited seven books on writing, including *Inventing the Truth: The Art & Craft of Memoir* (1995). The following essay first appeared in the magazine *Country Journal* in 1979.

Pre-Reading Journal Entry

MyWritingLab

Many students feel pressured by college graduation requirements. Do you? What courses are you required to take that you wouldn't ordinarily choose? What courses would you like to take but don't have time for? Should colleges require students to take courses that aren't part of their majors? Why or why not? Use your journal to respond to these questions.

College Pressures

Dear Carlos: I desperately need a dean's excuse for my chem midterm which will begin in about 1 hour. All I can say is that I totally blew it this week. I've fallen incredibly, inconceivably behind.

Carlos: Help! I'm anxious to hear from you. I'll be in my room and won't leave it until I hear from you. Tomorrow is the last day for...

Carlos: I left town because I started bugging out again. I stayed up all night to finish a take-home make-up exam & am typing it to hand in on the 10th. It was due on the 5th. P.S. I'm going to the dentist. Pain is pretty bad.

Carlos: Probably by Friday I'll be able to get back to my studies. Right now I'm going to take a long walk. This whole thing has taken a lot out of me.

Carlos: I'm really up the proverbial creek. The problem is I really *bombed* the history final. Since I need that course for my major I...

Carlos: Here follows a tale of woe. I went home this weekend, had to help my Mom, & caught a fever so didn't have much time to study. My professor...

Carlos: Aargh! Trouble. Nothing original but everything's piling up at once. To be brief, my job interview...

Hey Carlos, good news! I've got mononucleosis.

Who are these wretched supplicants, scribbling notes so laden with anxiety, seeking such miracles of postponement and balm? They are men and women who belong to Branford College, one of the twelve residential colleges at Yale University, and the messages are just a few of the hundreds that they left for their dean, Carlos Hortas—often slipped under his door at 4 A.M.—last year.

But students like the ones who wrote those notes can also be found on campuses from coast to coast—especially in New England and at many other private colleges across the country that have high academic standards and highly motivated students. Nobody could doubt that the notes are real. In their urgency and their gallows humor they are authentic voices of a generation that is panicky to succeed.

My own connection with the message writers is that I am master of Branford College. I live in its Gothic quadrangle and know the students well. (We have 485 of them.) I am privy to their hopes and fears—and also to their stereo music and their piercing cries in the dead of the night ("Does anybody *ca-a-are?*"). If they went to Carlos to ask how to get through tomorrow, they come to me to ask how to get through the rest of their lives.

Mainly I try to remind them that the road ahead is a long one and that 4
it will have more unexpected turns than they think. There will be plenty of
time to change jobs, change careers, change whole attitudes and approaches.
They don't want to hear such liberating news. They want a map—right
now—that they can follow unswervingly to career security, financial security,
Social Security and, presumably, a prepaid grave.

What I wish for all students is some release from the clammy grip of 5
the future. I wish them a chance to savor each segment of their education
as an experience in itself and not as a grim preparation for the next step.
I wish them the right to experiment, to trip and fall, to learn that defeat is as
instructive as victory and is not the end of the world.

My wish, of course, is naïve. One of the few rights that America does 6
not proclaim is the right to fail. Achievement is the national god, vener-
ated in our media—the million-dollar athlete, the wealthy executive—and
glorified in our praise of possessions. In the presence of such a potent state
religion, the young are growing up old.

I see four kinds of pressure working on college students today: eco- 7
nomic pressure, parental pressure, peer pressure, and self-induced pressure.
It is easy to look around for villains—to blame the colleges for charging too
much money, the professors for assigning too much work, the parents for
pushing their children too far, the students for driving themselves too hard.
But there are no villains; only victims.

"In the late 1960s," one dean told me, "the typical question that I got 8
from students was 'Why is there so much suffering in the world?' or 'How
can I make a contribution?' Today it's 'Do you think it would look better
for getting into law school if I did a double major in history and political
science, or just majored in one of them?'" Many other deans confirmed this
pattern. One said: "They're trying to find an edge—the intangible something that will look better on paper if two students are about equal."

Note the emphasis on looking better. The transcript has become a sacred 9
document, the passport to security. How one appears on paper is more important than how one appears in person. *A* is for Admirable and *B* is for
Borderline, even though, in Yale's official system of grading, *A* means "excellent" and *B* means "very good." Today, looking very good is no longer
good enough, especially for students who hope to go on to law school or
medical school. They know that entrance into the better schools will be an
entrance into the better law firms and better medical practices where they
will make a lot of money. They also know that the odds are harsh. Yale Law
School, for instance, matriculates 170 students from an applicant pool of
3,700; Harvard enrolls 550 from a pool of 7,000.

It's all very well for those of us who write letters of recommendation for 10
our students to stress the qualities of humanity that will make them good lawyers or doctors. And it's nice to think that admission officers are really reading

our letters and looking for the extra dimension of commitment or concern. Still, it would be hard for a student not to visualize these officers shuffling so many transcripts studded with *A*s that they regard a *B* as positively shameful.

The pressure is almost as heavy on students who just want to graduate   11 and get a job. Long gone are the days of the "gentleman's *C*," when students journeyed through college with a certain relaxation, sampling a wide variety of courses—music, art, philosophy, classics, anthropology, poetry, religion—that would send them out as liberally educated men and women. If I were an employer I would rather employ graduates who have this range and curiosity than those who narrowly pursued safe subjects and high grades. I know countless students whose inquiring minds exhilarate me. I like to hear the play of their ideas. I don't know if they are getting *A*s or *C*s, and I don't care. I also like them as people. The country needs them, and they will find satisfying jobs. I tell them to relax. They can't.

Nor can I blame them. They live in a brutal economy. Tuition, room,   12 and board at most private colleges now comes to at least $7,000 [in 1979], not counting books and fees. This might seem to suggest that the colleges are getting rich. But they are equally battered by inflation. Tuition covers only 60 percent of what it costs to educate a student, and ordinarily the remainder comes from what colleges receive in endowments, grants, and gifts. Now the remainder keeps being swallowed by the cruel costs—higher every year—of just opening the doors. Heating oil is up. Insurance is up. Postage is up. Health-premium costs are up. Everything is up. Deficits are up. We are witnessing in America the creation of a brotherhood of paupers—colleges, parents, and students, joined by the common bond of debt.

Today it is not unusual for a student, even if he works part time at college   13 and full time during the summer, to accrue $5,000 in loans after four years— loans that he must start to repay within one year after graduation. Exhorted at commencement to go forth into the world, he is already behind as he goes forth. How could he not feel under pressure throughout college to prepare for this day of reckoning? I have used "he," incidentally, only for brevity. Women at Yale are under no less pressure to justify their expensive education to themselves, their parents, and society. In fact, they are probably under more pressure. For although they leave college superbly equipped to bring fresh leadership to traditionally male jobs, society hasn't yet caught up with this fact.

Along with economic pressure goes parental pressure. Inevitably, the   14 two are deeply intertwined.

I see many students taking pre-medical courses with joyless tenacity.   15 They go off to their labs as if they were going to the dentist. It saddens me because I know them in other corners of their life as cheerful people.

"Do you want to go to medical school?" I ask them.   16

"I guess so," they say, without conviction, or "Not really."   17

"Then why are you going?" 18
"Well, my parents want me to be a doctor. They're paying all this 19
money and..."

Poor students, poor parents. They are caught in one of the oldest webs 20
of love and duty and guilt. The parents mean well; they are trying to steer
their sons and daughters toward a secure future. But the sons and daughters
want to major in history or classics or philosophy—subjects with no "practical" value. Where's the payoff on the humanities? It's not easy to persuade
such loving parents that the humanities do indeed pay off. The intellectual
faculties developed by studying subjects like history and classics—an ability to synthesize and relate, to weigh cause and effect, to see events in
perspective—are just the faculties that make creative leaders in business or
almost any general field. Still, many fathers would rather put their money
on courses that point toward a specific profession—courses that are pre-law,
pre-medical, pre-business, or, as I sometimes heard it put, "pre-rich."

But the pressure on students is severe. They are truly torn. One part 21
of them feels obligated to fulfill their parents' expectations; after all, their
parents are older and presumably wiser. Another part tells them that the
expectations that are right for their parents are not right for them.

I know a student who wants to be an artist. She is very obviously an art- 22
ist and will be a good one—she has already had several modest local exhibits.
Meanwhile she is growing as a well-rounded person and taking humanistic
subjects that will enrich the inner resources out of which her art will grow.
But her father is strongly opposed. He thinks that an artist is a "dumb"
thing to be. The student vacillates and tries to please everybody. She keeps
up with her art somewhat furtively and takes some of the "dumb" courses
her father wants her to take—at least they are dumb courses for her. She is
a free spirit on a campus of tense students—no small achievement in itself—
and she deserves to follow her muse.

Peer pressure and self-induced pressure are also intertwined, and they 23
begin almost at the beginning of freshman year.

"I had a freshman student I'll call Linda," one dean told me, "who came 24
in and said she was under terrible pressure because her roommate, Barbara,
was much brighter and studied all the time. I couldn't tell her that Barbara
had come in two hours earlier to say the same thing about Linda."

The story is almost funny—except that it's not. It's symptomatic of all 25
the pressures put together. When every student thinks every other student is
working harder and doing better, the only solution is to study harder still.
I see students going off to the library every night after dinner and coming
back when it closes at midnight. I wish they would sometimes forget about
their peers and go to a movie. I hear the clacking of typewriters in the hours
before dawn. I see the tension in their eyes when exams are approaching and
papers are due: *"Will I get everything done?"*

Probably they won't. They will get sick. They will get "blocked." They   26
will sleep. They will oversleep. They will bug out. *Hey, Carlos, help!*

Part of the problem is that they do more than they are expected to do. A   27
professor will assign five-page papers. Several students will start writing ten-
page papers to impress him. Then more students will write ten-page papers,
and a few will raise the ante to fifteen. Pity the poor student who is still just
doing the assignment.

"Once you have twenty or thirty percent of the student population   28
deliberately overexerting," one dean points out, "it's bad for everybody.
When a teacher gets more and more effort from his class, the student who
is doing normal work can be perceived as not doing well. The tactic works,
psychologically."

Why can't the professor just cut back and not accept longer papers?   29
He can, and he probably will. But by then the term will be half over and
the damage done. Grade fever is highly contagious and not easily reversed.
Besides, the professor's main concern is with his course. He knows his students only in relation to the course and doesn't know that they are also overexerting in their other courses. Nor is it really his business. He didn't sign
up for dealing with the student as a whole person and with all the emotional
baggage the student brought along from home. That's what deans, masters,
chaplains, and psychiatrists are for.

To some extent this is nothing new: a certain number of professors have   30
always been self-contained islands of scholarship and shyness, more comfortable with books than with people. But the new pauperism has widened the gap
still further, for professors who actually like to spend time with students don't
have as much time to spend. They are also overexerting. If they are young,
they are busy trying to publish in order not to perish, hanging by their fingernails onto a shrinking profession. If they are old and tenured, they are buried
under the duties of administering departments—as departmental chairmen or
members of committees—that have been thinned out by the budgetary axe.

Ultimately it will be the students' own business to break the circles in which   31
they are trapped. They are too young to be prisoners of their parents' dreams
and their classmates' fears. They must be jolted into believing in themselves as
unique men and women who have the power to shape their own future.

"Violence is being done to the undergraduate experience," says Carlos   32
Hortas. "College should be open-ended: at the end it should open many,
many roads. Instead, students are choosing their goal in advance, and their
choices narrow as they go along. It's almost as if they think that the country
has been codified in the type of jobs that exist—that they've got to fit into
certain slots. Therefore, fit into the best-paying slot.

"They ought to take chances. Not taking chances will lead to a life of   33
colorless mediocrity. They'll be comfortable. But something in the spirit will
be missing."

I have painted too drab a portrait of today's students, making them 34
seem a solemn lot. That is only half of their story; if they were so dreary
I wouldn't so thoroughly enjoy their company. The other half is that they
are easy to like. They are quick to laugh and to offer friendship. They are not
introverts. They are unusually kind and are more considerate of one another
than any student generation I have known.

Nor are they so obsessed with their studies that they avoid sports and 35
extracurricular activities. On the contrary, they juggle their crowded hours
to play on a variety of teams, perform with musical and dramatic groups, and
write for campus publications. But this in turn is one more cause of anxiety.
There are too many choices. Academically, they have 1,300 courses to select
from; outside class they have to decide how much spare time they can spare
and how to spend it.

This means that they engage in fewer extracurricular pursuits than their 36
predecessors did. If they want to row on the crew and play in the symphony
they will eliminate one; in the '60s they would have done both. They
also tend to choose activities that are self-limiting. Drama, for instance, is
flourishing in all twelve of Yale's residential colleges as it never has before.
Students hurl themselves into these productions—as actors, directors,
carpenters, and technicians—with a dedication to create the best possible
play, knowing that the day will come when the run will end and they can get
back to their studies.

They also can't afford to be the willing slave of organizations like the 37
Yale Daily News.... At the one-hundredth anniversary banquet of that
paper—whose past chairmen include such once and future kings as Potter
Stewart, Kingman Brewster, and William F. Buckley, Jr.—much was made
of the fact that the editorial staff used to be small and totally committed and
that "newsies" routinely worked fifty hours a week. In effect they belonged
to a club; Newsies is how they defined themselves at Yale. Today's student
will write one or two articles a week, when he can, and he defines himself as
a student. I've never heard the word Newsie except at the banquet.

If I have described the modern undergraduate primarily as a driven 38
creature who is largely ignoring the blithe spirit inside who keeps trying to
come out and play, it's because that's where the crunch is, not only at Yale
but throughout American education. It's why I think we should all be worried about the values that are nurturing a generation so fearful of risk and so
goal-obsessed at such an early age.

I tell students that there is no one "right" way to get ahead—that each 39
of them is a different person, starting from a different point and bound for a
different destination. I tell them that change is a tonic and that all the slots
are not codified nor the frontiers closed. One of my ways of telling them is
to invite men and women who have achieved success outside the academic

world to come and talk informally with my students during the year. They are heads of companies or ad agencies, editors of magazines, politicians, public officials, television magnates, labor leaders, business executives, Broadway producers, artists, writers, economists, photographers, scientists, historians—a mixed bag of achievers.

I ask them to say a few words about how they got started. The students   40
assume that they started in their present profession and knew all along that it was what they wanted to do. Luckily for me, most of them got into their field by a circuitous route, to their surprise, after many detours. The students are startled. They can hardly conceive of a career that was not pre-planned. They can hardly imagine allowing the hand of God or chance to nudge them down some unforeseen trail.

Questions for Close Reading

MyWritingLab

1. What is the selection's thesis? Locate the sentence(s) in which Zinsser states his main idea. If he doesn't state the thesis explicitly, express it in your own words.
2. According to Zinsser, why are the pressures on college students so harmful?
3. Zinsser says that some of the pressures are "intertwined." What does he mean? Give examples from the essay.
4. What actions or attitudes on the part of students can help free them from the pressures that Zinsser describes?

Questions About the Writer's Craft

1. **The pattern.** When analyzing a subject, writers usually try to identify divisions and classifications that are—within reason—mutually exclusive. But Zinsser acknowledges that the four pressures he discusses can be seen as two distinct pairs, with each pair consisting of two "deeply intertwined" pressures. How does this overlapping of categories help Zinsser make his point?
2. **Other patterns.** In addition to using classification in this essay, what other pattern of development does Zinsser use? How does this additional pattern help him make his point?
3. Why do you suppose Zinsser uses the notes to Carlos as his essay's introduction? What profile of college students does the reader get from these notes?
4. In paragraph 4, the author writes that students want a map "they can follow unswervingly to career security, financial security, Social Security and, presumably, a prepaid grave." What tone is Zinsser using here? Where else does he use this tone?

Writing Assignments Using Division-Classification as a Pattern of Development

1. Zinsser writes as if all students are the same—panicky, overwrought, and materialistic. Take a position counter to his, and write an essay explaining that campuses contain many students different from those Zinsser writes

about. To support your point, categorize students into types, giving examples of what each type is like. Be sure that the categories you identify refute Zinsser's analysis of the typical student. The tone of your essay may be serious or playful.

2. Is economic security the only kind of satisfaction that college students should pursue? Write an essay classifying the various kinds of satisfactions that students could aim for. At the end of the essay, include brief recommendations about ways that students could best spend their time preparing for these different kinds of satisfactions.

Writing Assignment Combining Patterns of Development

3. Using Zinsser's analysis of the pressures on college students, write an essay explaining how these pressures can be reduced or eliminated. Give *practical suggestions* showing how students can avoid or get around the pressures. Also, indicate what society, parents, and college staff can do to help ease students' anxieties. You might benefit from gathering *examples* of and information on this topic in the library and/or on the Internet before writing.

David Brooks

David Brooks is a syndicated columnist whose work appears in newspapers throughout the nation. Born in 1961, Brooks began his journalism career as a police reporter for the City News Bureau in Chicago and then spent nine years at *The Wall Street Journal* as a critic, foreign correspondent, and op-ed page editor. In 1995 he joined *The Weekly Standard* at its inception, and in 2003 he began to write a regular column for *The New York Times*. Brooks is interested in cultural as well as political issues. He often is on National Public Radio, including *The Diane Rehm Show*, as an analyst, and is a commentator on the *PBS NewsHour* (Public Broadcasting Service). He has written three books, *Bobos in Paradise: The New Upper Class and How They Got There* (2000), *On Paradise Drive: How We Live Now (and Always Have) in the Future Tense* (2004), and *The Social Animal: The Hidden Sources of Love, Character, and Achievement* (2011). He is editor of the anthology *Backward and Upward: The New Conservative Writing*. This column was published in *The New York Times* on November 13, 2005.

Pre-Reading Journal Entry

MyWritingLab

When you are a student, it's natural to think of success and failure simply in terms of grades. However, academic accomplishment is not the only measure of success in one's life. What are your own strengths and successes in life, beyond what you may have achieved in school? Who or what has inspired you to undertake each of these pursuits? Take a few minutes to respond to these questions in your journal.

Psst! "Human Capital"

Help! I'm turning into the "plastics" guy from *The Graduate*.[1] I'm pull-   1
ing people aside at parties and whispering that if they want to understand the
future, it's just two words: "Human Capital."

If we want to keep up with the Chinese and the Indians, we've got   2
to develop our Human Capital. If we want to remain a just, fluid society:
Human Capital. If we want to head off underclass riots: Human Capital.

As people drift away from me at these parties by pretending to recognize   3
long-lost friends across the room, I'm convinced that they don't really understand what human capital is.

Most people think of human capital the way economists and policy   4
makers do—as the skills and knowledge people need to get jobs and thrive
in a modern economy. When President [George W.] Bush proposed his
big education reform, he insisted on tests to measure skills and knowledge.
When commissions issue reports, they call for longer school years, revamped
curriculums and more funds so teachers can transmit skills and knowledge.

But skills and knowledge—the stuff you can measure with tests—is only   5
the most superficial component of human capital. U.S. education reforms
have generally failed because they try to improve the skills of students without addressing the underlying components of human capital.

These underlying components are hard to measure and uncomfortable   6
to talk about, but they are the foundation of everything that follows.

There's cultural capital: the habits, assumptions, emotional dispositions   7
and linguistic capacities we unconsciously pick up from families, neighbors
and ethnic groups—usually by age 3. In a classic study, James S. Coleman
found that what happens in the family shapes a child's educational achievement more than what happens in school. In more recent research, James
Heckman and Pedro Carneiro found that "most of the gaps in college atten-
dance and delay are determined by early family factors."

There's social capital: the knowledge of how to behave in groups and   8
within institutions. This can mean, for example, knowing what to do if your
community college loses your transcript. Or it can mean knowing the basic
rules of politeness. The University of North Carolina now offers seminars to
poorer students so they'll know how to behave in restaurants.

---

[1]Refers to an oft-cited scene in the 1967 film, *The Graduate*. The main character, Benjamin
Braddock, has just graduated college and feels adrift about the future. At a family party, the
character of Mr. McGuire cryptically "tips off" Benjamin about the plastics industry. He says,
"There's a great future in plastics. Think about it. Will you think about it?...Shh! Enough said."
(editors' note).

There's moral capital: the ability to be trustworthy. Students who drop 9
out of high school, but take the G.E.D. exam, tend to be smarter than high
school dropouts. But their lifetime wages tend to be no higher than they
are for those with no high school diplomas. That's because many people
who pass the G.E.D. are less organized and less dependable than their less
educated peers—as employers soon discover. Brains and skills don't matter if
you don't show up on time.

There's cognitive capital. This can mean pure, inherited brainpower. 10
But important cognitive skills are not measured by IQ tests and are not
fixed. Some people know how to evaluate themselves and their abilities,
while others with higher IQ's are clueless. Some low-IQ people can sense
what others are feeling, while brainier peers cannot. Such skills can be
improved over a lifetime.

Then there's aspirational capital: the fire-in-the-belly ambition to 11
achieve. In his book *The Millionaire Mind*, Thomas J. Stanley reports that
the average millionaire had a B-minus collegiate G.P.A.—not very good.
But millionaires often had this experience: People told them they were
too stupid to achieve something, so they set out to prove the naysayers
wrong.

Over the past quarter-century, researchers have done a lot of work 12
trying to understand the different parts of human capital. Their work has
been almost completely ignored by policy makers, who continue to treat
human capital as just skills and knowledge. The result? A series of expensive
policy failures.

We now spend more per capita on education than just about any other 13
country on earth, and the results are mediocre. No Child Left Behind treats
students as skill-acquiring cogs in an economic wheel, and the results have
been disappointing. We pour money into Title 1 and Head Start, but the
long-term gains are insignificant.

These programs are not designed for the way people really are. The only 14
things that work are local, human-to-human immersions that transform
the students down to their very beings. Extraordinary schools, which create
intense cultures of achievement, work. Extraordinary teachers, who inspire
students to transform their lives, work. The programs that work touch all
the components of human capital.

There's a great future in Human Capital, buddy. Enough said. 15

Questions for Close Reading

1. What is the selection's thesis? Locate the sentence(s) in which Brooks states his main idea. If he doesn't state his thesis explicitly, express it in your own words.
2. According to Brooks, why do policies that focus on teaching children skills and knowledge ultimately fail to develop human capital? What policies does he use as examples of such failure?

3. In Brooks's view, what role does the family play in the development of human capital?
4. What type of human capital do many millionaires possess, and how did they acquire it?

Questions About the Writer's Craft

1. Brooks opens this essay by comparing himself to a character in the 1967 movie *The Graduate*. What are the benefits and risks of using such a reference to frame the contents of an essay? In your opinion, is this a successful opening? Why or why not?
2. **The pattern.** How does Brooks organize his explanation of what human capital really consists of? What cues guide the reader in following Brooks's discussion?
3. **Other patterns.** In paragraphs 7 through 11, Brooks develops his ideas about the components of human capital. What patterns does he use in each of these paragraphs?
4. This essay was published as a newspaper op-ed column, a type of writing that is relatively short—about 750 words. How does the limited length of the piece affect the development of Brooks's ideas and evidence? If the piece were longer, how could Brooks strengthen its argument?

Writing Assignments Using Division-Classification as a Pattern of Development

1. Choose one of the elements of human capital that Brooks describes, and write an essay in which you analyze it further into its component parts. For example, if you choose cognitive capital, you can write about specific cognitive skills such as memorizing, learning, problem solving, and creativity.
2. According to economists, capital is any human-made resource used to produce goods and services. For example, capital includes buildings, factories, machinery, equipment, parts, tools, roads, and railroads. Do some research on the concept of capital as used by economists, and write an essay explaining how economists categorize various types of capital, including the human capital Brooks discusses in his essay.

Writing Assignment Combining Patterns of Development

3. Brooks's concept of moral capital is closely tied to the moral values that society holds important and that children learn from their families and others with whom they interact. Write an essay in which you *narrate* the story of a moral issue you have faced, *comparing* and *contrasting* the choices you had. Explain the *process* you went through to resolve the problem.

Bianca Bosker

Princeton University graduate Bianca Bosker is Executive Tech Editor for *The Huffington Post*, an online news website and blog that covers U.S. politics, world news, entertainment, and style. Bosker's publications have appeared in *The Wall Street Journal*, *Condé Nast Traveler*, and the *Far Eastern Economic Review*. She is the co-author of *Bowled Over: A Roll Down Memory Lane*, a tribute to the tradition and culture of bowling. The following article was published on *The Huffington Post* website on May 21, 2013.

Pre-Reading Journal Entry

MyWritingLab

In what ways do you make use of social media sites such as *Facebook*, *Twitter*, *Instagram*, and *MySpace*? How have the ways you use these sites changed over the past several years? If you don't use any of these sites, why not? Why do you think they are a major part of the lives of millions? Explore these ideas in your journal.

How Teens Are Really Using *Facebook*:
It's a "Social Burden," Pew Study Finds

The *Facebook* generation is fed up with *Facebook*.   1

That's according to a report released Tuesday by the Pew Research   2
Center, which surveyed 802 teens between the ages of 12 and 17 [in September 2012] to produce a 107-page report on their online habits.

Pew's findings suggest teens' enthusiasm for *Facebook* is waning, lending   3
credence to concerns, raised by the company's investors and others, that the social network may be losing a crucial demographic that has long fueled its success ("Facebook's CEO").

Facebook has become a "social burden" for teens, write the authors of   4
the Pew report. "While *Facebook* is still deeply integrated in teens' everyday lives, it is sometimes seen as a utility and an obligation rather than an exciting new platform that teens can claim as their own" (Madden et al. 18).

Teens aren't abandoning *Facebook*—deactivating their accounts would   5
mean missing out on the crucial social intrigues that transpire online— and 94 percent of teenage social media users still have profiles on the site, Pew's report notes. But they're simultaneously migrating to *Twitter* and *Instagram*, which teens say offer a parent-free place where they can better express themselves. Eleven percent of teens surveyed had *Instagram* accounts, while the number of teen *Twitter* users climbed from 16 percent in 2011 to 24 percent in 2012. Five percent of teens have accounts on *Tumblr*, which was just purchased by Yahoo for $1.1 billion, while 7 percent have accounts on *MySpace* (Kleinman).

Where teens have social media profiles or accounts
% of teen social media users who use the following sites...

	2011	2012
Facebook	93%	94%
Twitter	12	26
Instagram	n/a	11
MySpace	24	7
YouTube	6	7
Tumblr	2	5
Google Plus	n/a	3
Yahoo (unspecified)	7	2
myYearbook	2	*
Pinterest	n/a	1
Gmail	n/a	1
Meet Me	n/a	1
Other	8	6
Don't know / Don't have own profile	2	1

Source: Madden et al., p. 24.

Facebook, teens say, has been overrun by parents, fuels unnecessary social   6
"drama" and gives a mouthpiece to annoying oversharers who drone on
about inane events in their lives.

"Honestly, *Facebook* at this point, I'm on it constantly but I hate it   7
so much," one 15 year-old girl told Pew during a focus group (Madden
et al. 38).

"I got mine [*Facebook* account] around sixth grade. And I was really ob-   8
sessed with it for a while," another 14 year-old said. "Then towards eighth
grade, I kind of just—once you get into *Twitter*, if you make a *Twitter* and
an *Instagram*, then you'll just kind of forget about *Facebook*, is what I did"
(Madden et al. 27).

On the whole, teens' usage of social media seems to have plateaued, and   9
the fraction of those who check social sites "several times a day" has stayed
steady at around 40 percent since 2011 (Madden et al. 22).

Female (age 19): "Yeah, that's why we go on *Twitter* and *Instagram*
[instead of *Facebook*]. My mom doesn't have that."

Female (age 15): "If you are on *Facebook*, you see a lot of drama."

Female (age 14): "OK, here's something I want to say. I think *Facebook* can be fun, but also it's drama central. On *Facebook*, people imply things and say things, even just by a like, that they wouldn't say in real life."

Male (age 18): "It's because [*Facebook*] it's where people post unnecessary pictures and they say unnecessary things, like saying he has a girlfriend, and a girl will go on and tag him in the picture like, me and him in the sun having fun. Why would you do that?" (Madden et al. 26)

Asked about teens' *Facebook* habits during a recent earnings call with investors, Facebook's chief financial officer answered that the company "remain[s] really pleased with the high level of engagement on *Facebook* by people of all ages around the world" and called younger users "among the most active and engaged users that we have on *Facebook*" ("Facebook's CEO"). 10

Here's what that "high level of engagement" really looks like, according to Pew: 11

They're deleting, lying and blocking: Some three-quarters of *Facebook* users have purged friends on *Facebook*, 58 percent have edited or deleted content they've shared and 26 percent have tried to protect their privacy by sharing false information. Among all teens online (not just *Facebook* users), 39 percent have lied about their age. The report also notes, "Girls are more likely than boys to delete friends from their network (82 percent vs. 66 percent) and block people (67 percent vs. 48 percent)."

Superusers on *Facebook* are superusers on other social sites: Teens with large friend networks on *Facebook* are more likely than their peers to have profiles on other social media sites: 46 percent of teens with over 600 *Facebook* friends have a *Twitter* profile, and 12 percent of such users have an *Instagram* account. By comparison, just 21 percent and 11 percent of teens who have 150 to 300 friends have *Twitter* and *Instagram* accounts, respectively.

Teens have hundreds of friends, but they haven't met them all: The typical *Facebook*-using teen has 300 friends, though girls are more likely to have more friends (the median is 350) than boys (300). Seventy percent of teens are friends with their parents, 30 percent are friends with teachers or coaches, and 33 percent are friends with people they've never met in person.

It turns out parents actually do see what their kids are posting: Just 5 percent of teens tweak their privacy to limit what their parents see.

They're watching out for their privacy: Sixty percent of teens on *Facebook* say they've checked their privacy settings in the past month—a third of them within the past seven days. The majority (60 percent) of teens have their profiles set to private, while 14 percent have profiles that are completely public.

But yes, they are sharing personal details: Teens with more *Facebook* friends are more likely to share a greater variety of personal details about themselves online. Among all teens on *Facebook*, 21 percent share their cell phone number, 63 percent share their relationship status and 54 percent share their email address.

Seventeen percent of teens on *Facebook* will automatically share their location in their posts, and 18 percent say they've shared something they later regret posting.

They're enjoying themselves, but they've been contacted by creeps: Among all teens surveyed by Pew, 17 percent have been contacted by strangers in a way that made them "scared or uncomfortable." However, 57 percent of social media-using teens said they've had an experience online that "made them feel good about themselves," and 37 percent say social media has made them feel more connected to someone else.

Works Cited

"Facebook's CEO Discusses Q1 2013 Results—Earnings Call Transcript." *Seeking Alpha*, 29 Jan. 2014, seekingalpha.com/article/1392101-facebooks-ceo-discusses-q1-2013-results-earnings-call-transcript.

Kleinman, Alexis. "Yahoo Tumblr Deal Is Officially Announced." *The Huffington Post*, 20 May 2013, www.huffingtonpost.com/2013/05/20/yahoo-tumblr-deal_n_3305953.html.

Madden, Mary, et al. *Teens, Social Media, and Privacy.* Pew Research Center, 21 May 2013, www.pewinternet.org/files/2013/05/PIP_TeensSocialMediaandPrivacy_PDF.pdf.

Questions for Close Reading

MyWritingLab

1. **Thesis.** What is the selection's thesis? Locate the sentence(s) that state the main idea. If she doesn't state it explicitly, express it in your own words.
2. According to the Pew report by Madden et al. that Bosker references in her article, in what ways has *Facebook* become a "social burden" for many users?
3. The chart from the Pew report that is included in this reading shows the percentage of teens using various social media sites. According to the chart,

which two show the largest increases in use and which two the greatest decreases?

4. The phrase "high level of engagement" appears in paragraphs 10 and 11 of the article. How does Facebook's chief financial officer's use of the term differ from the way, according to Bosker, the Pew report interprets "what that 'high level of engagement' really looks like"?

Questions About the Writer's Craft

1. **The pattern.** In what ways does Bosker's article classify teens' use of social media sites? Does the classification scheme seem reasonable to you? Why or why not?
2. **Other patterns.** In addition to classifying the ways teens use social media sites, Bosker provides examples that *illustrate* the points she is making. List three of the examples she uses that you think work especially well to support her thesis.
3. Bosker references three sources in her article. Which one does she rely most heavily on and why? How does the use of the other sources enrich her article?
4. Why do you think Bosker decided to include a chart from the Pew report in her article? In what ways does the chart add to the effectiveness of her article?

Writing Assignments Using Division-Classification as a Pattern of Development

1. The authors of the Pew report gathered information on the online habits of teens between the ages of 12 and 17. Conduct your own research by designing a questionnaire on the online habits of another group—perhaps the students in your composition class or the members of another group or community to which you belong. Write an essay in which you present the information you gathered, classifying the ways the members of your research group use online media sites. Consider designing a chart similar to the one in the Bosker article, and include it in your composition to illustrate the various sites where the members of your research group have social media profiles or accounts.
2. Write an essay in which you classify the types of music most popular today among a particular demographic. You might rely on secondary sources for the information you include in your essay—as Bosker did in hers—or you might conduct your own primary research using questionnaires or surveys that you design. Consider using visuals such as charts or graphs to clearly present your findings to your readers.

Writing Assignment Combining Patterns of Development

3. Write an essay in which you *compare* and *contrast* various social media sites. For example, you might compare *Facebook*, *Twitter*, and *Instagram* and explore what the sites have in common as well as how they differ from one another. You might also include quotes from individuals you interview to *illustrate* what these social media users consider to be advantages and disadvantages of the various sites.

Additional Writing Topics

DIVISION-CLASSIFICATION

MyWritingLab

General Assignments

Using division-classification, develop one of these topics into an essay.

Division	Classification
1. A shopping mall	1. Commercials
2. A video system	2. Holidays
3. A particular kind of team	3. Roommates
4. A school library	4. Summer movies
5. A college campus	5. Internet surfers

Assignments Using Visuals

Use the suggested visuals to help develop a division-classification essay on one of these topics:

1. Types of friends and the roles they play in our lives (slide show or cartoons)
2. Novels made into movies in the past two years (web links to movie trailers)
3. Various parenting styles by period or region (charts)
4. This year's most popular TV shows (links to websites or *YouTube* videos)
5. Personality types identified by psychologists (charts or graphs)

Assignments with a Specific Purpose, Audience, and Point of View

1. **Academic life.** You're a dorm counselor. During orientation week, you'll be talking to students on your floor about the different kinds of problems they may have with roommates. Write out what you plan to say, describing each kind of problem and explaining how to cope.
2. **Academic life.** As your college newspaper's TV critic, you plan to write a review of the fall shows, most of which—in your opinion—lack originality. To show how stereotypical the programs are, select one type (for example, situation comedies or crime dramas). Then use a specific division-classification principle to illustrate that the same stale formulas are trotted out from show to show.
3. **Academic life.** Asked to write an editorial for the campus paper, you decide to do a half-serious piece on taking "mental health" days off from classes. Structure your essay around three kinds of occasions when "playing hooky" is essential for maintaining sanity.

4. **Civic activity.** Your favorite magazine runs an editorial asking readers to send in what they think are the main challenges facing their particular gender group. Write a letter to the editor in which you identify at least three categories of problems that your sex faces. Be sure to provide lively, specific examples to illustrate each category. In your letter, you may adopt a serious or lighthearted tone, depending on your overall subject matter.

5. **Workplace action.** As a driving instructor, you decide to prepare a lecture on the types of drivers that your students are likely to encounter on the road. In your lecture, categorize drivers according to a specific principle and show the behaviors of each type.

6. **Workplace action.** A seasoned camp counselor, you've been asked to prepare, for new counselors, an informational sheet on children's emotional needs. Categorizing those needs into types, explain what counselors can do to nurture youngsters emotionally.

MyWritingLab Visit Chapter 6, "Division-Classification," in MyWritingLab to complete the chapter activities, Pre-Reading Journal Entry activities, Questions for Close Reading, and Additional Writing Topics assignments and to test your understanding of the chapter objectives.

PROCESS ANALYSIS

In this chapter, you will learn:

7.1 To use the pattern of process analysis to develop your essays.

7.2 To consider how process analysis can fit your purpose and audience.

7.3 To develop strategies for using process analysis in an essay.

7.4 To develop strategies for revising a process analysis essay.

7.5 To analyze how process analysis is used effectively in student-written and professionally authored selections.

7.6 To write your own essays using process analysis as a strategy.

WHAT IS PROCESS ANALYSIS?

We spend a good deal of our lives learning—everything from speaking our first word to registering for our first college courses. Indeed, the milestones in our lives are often linked to the processes we have mastered: how to cross the street alone; how to drive a car; how to make a speech without being paralyzed by fear.

Process analysis, a technique that explains the steps or sequence involved in doing something, satisfies our need to learn as well as our curiosity about how the world works. All the self-help books continually flooding the market are examples of process analysis. The instructions on the federal tax form and the recipes in a cookbook are also process analyses. Several television shows also capitalize on our desire to learn how things happen: *Nature* shows how animals and ecosystems survive, and *CSI: Crime Scene Investigation* details how investigators gather evidence and use crime lab techniques to catch criminals. Process analysis can be more than merely interesting or entertaining, though; it can be of critical importance. Consider a waiter hurriedly skimming the "Choking Aid" instructions posted on a restaurant wall or an air-traffic controller following emergency procedures in an effort to prevent a midair collision. In these last examples, the consequences could be fatal if the process analyses were slipshod, inaccurate, or confusing.

Undoubtedly, all of us have experienced less dramatic effects of poorly written process analyses. Perhaps you've tried to assemble a bicycle and spent hours sorting through a stack of parts, only to end up with one or two extra pieces never mentioned in the instructions. No wonder many people stay clear of anything that actually admits "assembly required."

HOW PROCESS ANALYSIS FITS YOUR PURPOSE AND AUDIENCE

You will use process analysis in two types of writing situations: (1) when you want to give step-by-step instructions to readers showing how they can do something, or (2) when you want readers to understand how something happens even though they won't actually follow the steps outlined. The first kind of process analysis is *directional;* the second is *informational.*

Process analysis, both directional and informational, is often appropriate in *problem-solving situations.* In such cases, you say, "Here's the problem and here's what should be done to solve the problem." Indeed, college assignments frequently take the form of problem-solving process analyses. Consider these examples:

> Community officials have been accused of mismanaging recent unrest over the public housing ordinance. Describe the steps the officials took, indicating why you think their strategy was unwise. Then explain how you think the situation should have been handled.

> Over the years, there have been many reports citing the abuse of small children in day-care centers. What can parents do to guard against the mistreatment of their children?

> Because many colleges have changed the eligibility requirements for financial aid, fewer students can depend on loans or scholarships. How can students cope with the rising costs of higher education?

Note that the first assignment asks students to explain what's wrong with the current approach before they present their own step-by-step solution. Problem-solving process analyses are often organized in this way. You may also have noted that none of the assignments explicitly requires an essay response using process analysis. However, the wording of the assignments—"*Describe* the *steps*," "*What* can parents *do*," "*How* can students *cope*,"—suggests that process analysis would be an appropriate strategy for developing the responses.

Assignments don't always signal the use of process analysis so clearly. But during the prewriting stage, you'll often realize that you can best achieve your purpose by developing the essay using process analysis. Sometimes process analysis will be the primary strategy for organizing an essay; other times it will help make a point in an essay organized according to another pattern of development. Let's look at process analysis as a supporting strategy.

Assume that you're writing a *causal analysis* examining the impact of television commercials on people's buying behavior. To help readers see that commercials create a need where none existed before, you might describe the various stages of an advertising campaign to pitch a new, completely frivolous product. In an essay *defining* a good boss, you could convey the point that effective managers must be skilled at settling disputes by explaining the steps your boss took to resolve a heated disagreement between two employees. If you write an *argumentation-persuasion* paper urging the funding of programs to ease the plight of the homeless, to dramatize the tragedy of these people's lives, you could explain how the typical street person goes about the desperate jobs of finding a place to sleep and getting food to eat.

STRATEGIES FOR USING PROCESS ANALYSIS IN AN ESSAY

The suggestions here and in Figure 7.1 will be helpful whether you use process analysis as a dominant or a supportive pattern of development.

1. Identify the desired outcome of the process analysis.   Many essays developed primarily through process analysis have a clear-cut purpose—simply to *inform* readers as objectively as possible about a process: "Here's a way of making french fries at home that will surpass the best served in your favorite fast-food restaurant." But a process analysis essay may also have a *persuasive* edge, with the writer advocating a point of view about the process, perhaps even urging a course of action: "If you don't want your arguments to deteriorate into ugly battles, you should follow a series of foolproof steps for having disagreements that leave friendships intact." Before starting to write, you need to decide if the essay is to be purely factual or if it will include this kind of persuasive dimension.

2. Formulate a thesis that clarifies your attitude toward the process.   Like the thesis in any other essay, the thesis in a process analysis should do more than announce your subject. ("Here's how the college's work-study program

FIGURE 7.1
Development Diagram: Writing a Process Analysis Essay

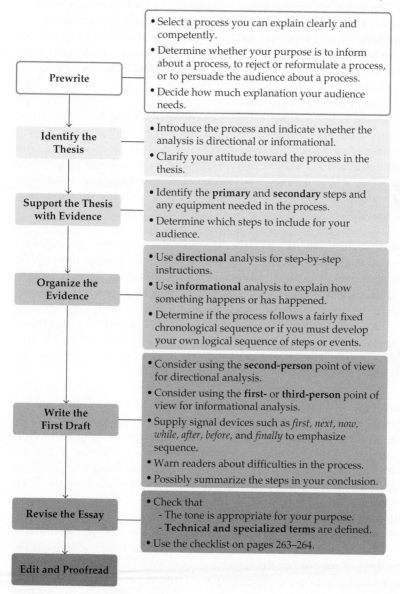

Prewrite

- Select a process you can explain clearly and competently.
- Determine whether your purpose is to inform about a process, to reject or reformulate a process, or to persuade the audience about a process.
- Decide how much explanation your audience needs.

Identify the Thesis

- Introduce the process and indicate whether the analysis is directional or informational.
- Clarify your attitude toward the process in the thesis.

Support the Thesis with Evidence

- Identify the **primary** and **secondary** steps and any equipment needed in the process.
- Determine which steps to include for your audience.

Organize the Evidence

- Use **directional** analysis for step-by-step instructions.
- Use **informational** analysis to explain how something happens or has happened.
- Determine if the process follows a fairly fixed chronological sequence or if you must develop your own logical sequence of steps or events.

Write the First Draft

- Consider using the **second-person** point of view for directional analysis.
- Consider using the **first-** or **third-person** point of view for informational analysis.
- Supply signal devices such as *first, next, now, while, after, before,* and *finally* to emphasize sequence.
- Warn readers about difficulties in the process.
- Possibly summarize the steps in your conclusion.

Revise the Essay

- Check that
  - The tone is appropriate for your purpose.
  - **Technical and specialized terms** are defined.
- Use the checklist on pages 263–264.

Edit and Proofread

operates.") It should also state or imply your attitude toward the process: "Enrolling in the college's work-study program has become unnecessarily complicated. The procedure could be simplified if the college adopted the helpful guidelines prepared by the Student Senate."

3. Keep your audience in mind.   Suppose you've been asked to write an article informing students of the best way to use the university computer center. The article will be published in a newsletter for information technology majors. You would seriously misjudge your audience—and probably put them to sleep—if you explained in detail how to transfer files to a cloud or how to delete information from a file. However, an article on the same topic prepared for a general audience—your composition class, for instance— might require such detailed instructions.

To determine how much explanation is needed, put yourself in your readers' shoes. Don't assume readers will know something just because you do. Ask questions such as these about your audience: "Will my readers need some background about the process before I describe it in depth?" "Are there technical terms I should define?" "If my essay is directional, should I specify near the beginning the ingredients, materials, and equipment needed to perform the process?" (For more help in analyzing your audience, see the checklist "Analyzing Your Audience" in Chapter 2.)

4. Use prewriting to identify the steps in the process.   To explain a sequence to your readers, you need to think through the process thoroughly, identifying its major parts and subparts, locating possible missteps or trouble spots. With your purpose, thesis, and audience in mind, use the appropriate prewriting techniques (brainstorming and mapping should be especially helpful) to break down the process into its component parts. In prewriting, it's a good idea to start by generating more material than you expect to use. Then the raw material can be shaped and pruned to fit your purpose and the needs of your audience.

5. Identify the directional and informational aspects of the process analysis.   Directional and informational process analyses are not always distinct. In fact, they may be complementary. Your prewriting may reveal that you'll need to provide background information about a process before outlining its steps. For example, in a paper describing a step-by-step approach for losing weight, you might first need to explain how the body burns calories.

The kind of process analysis chosen has implications for the way you will relate to your reader. When the process analysis is *directional,* the reader is addressed in the *second person:* "You should first rinse the residue from the radiator by...," or "Wrap the injured person in a blanket and then...." (In the second example, the pronoun *you* is implied.)

If the process analysis has an *informational* purpose, you won't address the reader directly but will choose from a number of other options. For example, you might use the *first-person* point of view. In a humorous essay explaining how not to prepare for finals, you could cite your own disastrous study habits: "Filled with good intentions, I sit on my bed, get in a comfortable position, open my textbook, and promptly fall asleep." The *third-person singular or plural* can also be used in informational process essays: "The spelling bee finalist walks up to the podium, heart pounding, more than a bit nervous, but also challenged by the prospect of winning the competition." Whether you use the first, second, or third person, avoid shifting point of view midstream.

6. Explain the process, one step at a time.   At times your purpose will be to explain a process with a *fairly fixed chronological sequence:* how to make pizza, how to pot a plant, how to change a tire. In such cases, you should include all necessary steps, in the correct chronological order. However, if a strict chronological ordering of steps means that a particularly important part of the sequence gets buried in the middle, the sequence probably should be juggled so that the crucial step receives the attention it deserves.

Other times your goal will be to describe a process having *no commonly accepted sequence*. For example, in an essay explaining how to discipline a child or how to pull yourself out of a blue mood, you will have to come up with your own definition of the key steps and then arrange those steps in some logical order. You may also use process analyses to *reject* or *reformulate* a traditional sequence. In this case, you would propose a more logical series of steps: "Our system for electing congressional representatives is inefficient and undemocratic; it should be reformed in the following ways."

Whether the essay describes a generally agreed-on process or one that is not commonly accepted, you must provide all the details needed to explain the process. Your readers should be able to understand, even visualize, the process. There should be no fuzzy patches or confusing cuts from one step to another.

It's not unusual, especially in less defined sequences, for some steps in a process to occur simultaneously and overlap. When this happens, you should present the steps in the most logical order, being sure to tell your readers that several steps are not perfectly distinct and may merge.

7. Provide readers with the help they need to follow the sequence.   As you move through the steps of a process analysis, don't forget to *warn readers about difficulties* they might encounter. For example, when writing a paper on the artistry involved in butterflying a shrimp, you might say something like this:

Next, make a shallow cut with your sharpened knife along the convex curve of the shrimp's intestinal tract. The tract, usually a thin black line along the outside curve of the shrimp, is faintly visible beneath the translucent flesh. But some shrimp have a thick orange, blue, or gray line instead of a thin black one. In all cases, be careful not to slice too deeply, or you will end up with two shrimp halves instead of one butterflied shrimp.

Transitional words and phrases are also critical in helping readers understand the order of the steps being described. Time signals such as *first, next, now, while, after, before,* and *finally* provide readers with a clear sense of the sequence. Entire sentences can also be used to link parts of the process, reminding your audience of what has already been discussed and indicating what will now be explained: "Once the panel of experts finishes its evaluation of the exam questions, randomly selected items are field-tested in schools throughout the country."

8. Maintain an appropriate tone.   When writing a process analysis essay, be sure your tone is consistent with your purpose, your attitude toward your subject, and the effect you want to have on the reader. When explaining how fraternities and sororities recruit new members, do you want to use an objective, nonjudgmental tone? To decide, take into account readers' attitudes toward your subject. Does your audience have a financial or emotional investment in the process being described? Does your own interest in the process coincide or conflict with that of your audience? Awareness of your readers' stance can be crucial. Consider another example: Assume you're writing a letter to the director of the student health center proposing a new system to replace the currently chaotic one. You'd do well to be tactful in your criticisms. Offend your reader, and your cause is lost. If, however, the letter is slated for the college newspaper and directed primarily to other students, you could adopt a more pointed, even sarcastic tone. Readers, you would assume, will probably share your view and favor change.

Once you settle on the essay's tone, maintain it throughout. If you're writing a light piece on the way the Internet is taking over our lives, you wouldn't include a grim step-by-step analysis of the way confidential information entered on websites may become public.

9. Open and close the process analysis effectively.   An essay developed primarily through process analysis should have a strong beginning. The introduction should state the process to be described and imply whether the essay has an informational or directional intent.

If you suspect readers are indifferent to your subject, use the introduction to motivate them, telling them how important the subject is:

Do you enjoy the salad bars found in many restaurants? If you do, you probably have noticed that the vegetables are always crisp and fresh—no matter how many hours they have been exposed to the air. What are the restaurants doing to make the vegetables look so inviting? There's a simple answer. Many restaurants spray the vegetables with, or dip them into, potent chemicals to make them appetizing.

If you think your audience may be intimidated by your subject (perhaps because it's complex or relatively obscure), the introduction is the perfect spot to reassure them that the process being described is not beyond their grasp:

Studies show that many people willingly accept a defective product just so they won't have to deal with the uncomfortable process of making a complaint. But once a few easy-to-learn basics are mastered, anyone can register a complaint that gets results.

Most process analysis essays don't end as soon as the last step in the sequence is explained. Instead, they usually include some brief final comments that round out the piece and bring it to a satisfying close. This final section of the essay may summarize the main steps in the process—not by repeating the steps verbatim but by rephrasing and condensing them in several concise sentences. The conclusion can also be an effective spot to underscore the significance of the process, recalling what may have been said in the introduction about the subject's importance. Or the essay can end by echoing the note of reassurance that may have been included at the start.

REVISION STRATEGIES

Once you have a draft of the essay, you're ready to revise. The following checklist will help you and those giving you feedback apply to process analysis some of the revision techniques discussed in Chapter 2.

☑ PROCESS ANALYSIS: A REVISION/PEER REVIEW CHECKLIST

Revise Overall Meaning and Structure

❏ What purpose does the process analysis serve—to inform, to persuade, or to do both?

❏ Is the process analysis primarily *directional* or *informational*? How can you tell?

(*continued*)

Process Analysis: A Revision/Peer Review Checklist (*continued*)

❑ Where does the process seem confusing? Where have steps been left out? Which steps need simplifying?

❑ What is the essay's tone? Is the tone appropriate for the essay's purpose and readers? Where are there distracting shifts in tone?

Revise Paragraph Development

❑ Does the introduction specify the process to be described? Does it provide an overview? Should it?

❑ Which paragraphs are difficult to follow? Have any steps or materials been omitted or explained in too much or too little detail? Which paragraphs should warn readers about potential trouble spots or overlapping steps?

❑ Where are additional time signals needed to clarify the sequence within and between paragraphs? Where does overreliance on time signals make the sequence awkward and mechanical?

❑ Which paragraph describes the most crucial step in the sequence? How has the step been highlighted?

❑ How could the conclusion be more effective?

Revise Sentences and Words

❑ What technical or specialized terms appear in the essay? Have they been sufficiently explained? Where could simpler, less technical language be used?

❑ Are there any places where the essay's point of view awkwardly shifts? How could this problem be corrected?

❑ Does the essay use correct verb tenses—the past tense for completed events, the present tense for habitual or ongoing actions?

❑ Where does the essay use the passive voice ("The hole is dug")? Would the active voice ("You dig the hole") be more effective?

STUDENT ESSAY

The following student essay was written by Jared Mosley in response to this assignment:

Alex Horton, a military veteran, provides other military veterans with a plan for college in "On Getting By." Serving a fifteen-month tour in Iraq, returning to the United States, and becoming a college student provided Horton with the experience he needed to help others who could benefit from what he had learned. Write an essay in which you present a *process analysis* of how to do something with which you have experience and consider yourself knowledgeable.

Jared, an English major, a lover of poetry, and a writer of poems, decided to write an essay that could help other students understand how they, too, could become poets.

Don't Write Poetry—Be a Poet
by Jared Mosley

Introduction

The mention of poetry in a college class tends to strike 1
fear into the heart of anyone who's not an English major. But
poetry isn't as scary as it often seems. Poems don't have to be
fancy or complicated, and they are a wonderful way to express
Start of two- yourself. Many forms of artistic expression require learning
sentence thesis new skills. Poetry doesn't; all you need to get started are the
Topic sentence words and ideas you already know.
introducing the To write poetry successfully, you must first learn how 2
first stage to be a poet. In other words, you must develop the habits of
(developing a poet. There are two habits that successful poets constantly
habits) keep in mind. The great news is that you can start practicing
them today.
Topic sentence The first essential habit for poets is reading. A poet's 3
introducing the main tools are words and ideas. More importantly, the poet
first habit specializes in arranging these words and ideas in a meaningful way. Reading helps in two ways: it teaches you how
to use the tools (words and ideas) you already have, and it
introduces you to new ones. If you want to write poems but
you don't know where to start, just read everything you can
find. The material you read doesn't need to be academic or
literary. You can read news sources, popular magazines, your
favorite fiction series, or even comics. Whatever you're pas-
sionate about, read it more often. Once you've got that down,
try reading something you don't know much about; that will
help broaden your understanding of the world. And read other
poets too; that will deepen your ideas about how to make your
poems effective and meaningful.
Two-sentence Understanding the world is very important for poets. 4
introduction That's why the other habit any aspiring poet must have
to the second is thinking. This doesn't mean that you must know all the
habit (thinking), answers to everything. Instead, it means that you must
functioning as a learn as much as you can (through experience, books, mov-
topic sentence ies, whatever) and spend time figuring out what this new
information means to you—because that's what poetry is:
your personal reflection of the world around you.

Supporting ————→ Thinking is easier for some people than for others.   5
paragraph topic   It comes naturally to certain personality types, and for others,
sentence   spending time inside their own minds can be a real struggle.
                     Our modern world of distractions (like the Internet) makes it
                     hard to find time to think. Many individuals actively avoid
                     deep thought because it makes them feel uncomfortable or
                     uneasy. But if you want to be a poet, it is essential to figure
                     out how you feel about yourself and everything else in the
                     universe. So start thinking! Think about what makes you mad,
                     what makes you sad, what you love, hate, or want to change.
Sentence providing   Think about what's funny, fascinating, brilliant, or stupid. And
transition to second when you're ready, you can start writing—unless you come
stage (fighting   up against what is commonly referred to as "writer's block,"
writer's block)   which just means that you feel unable to keep on writing.

Topic sentence ————→ To defeat writer's block, there are some things you need   6
                     to know. The poet's worst enemy is herself. Even the most
                     veteran writers are stricken with writer's block. The only
                     difference is that they're able to overcome it. The first thing
                     to realize is that writer's block usually comes from insecu-
Second stage   rity. Writer's block cleverly disguises itself in many forms,
in process   but the reason the plague strikes in the first place almost
                     always comes down to your not believing you can write
                     something. Writer's block can be especially hard for poets to
                     overcome, because they're often trying to transfer their inner-
                     most thoughts onto the page, which is hard enough without
                     writer's block.

Supporting ————→ The good news is that you always have one sure way to   7
paragraph topic   defeat writer's block: writing. No matter how much you feel
sentence   that you can't write or your work won't be good, write anyway.
                     Write whatever you think of. Nobody has to see it; nobody
                     cares if it is terrible. Let your words be your canvas or your
                     punching bag, and write whatever you want. Don't follow rules
                     if you don't want to. You will be amazed at how freeing this ac-
                     tivity can be, and your writer's block will suddenly disappear.

Topic sentence ————→ Now you know how to develop the habits of a poet and   8
                     how to fight writer's block, but how do you actually write
Third stage in   poems? The answer to that question varies greatly depend-
process   ing on whom you ask, and there is no one right way to do it.
(writing poems)   Poetry is subjective and doesn't have many strict rules. That
                     said, here are five important tips to help you get started.

Five supporting   1. Poems don't need to rhyme. Really. Poems that are good
tips   and that rhyme are a pleasure to read and can be fun to
                       write. But way too many good ideas are ruined because the
                       poet tried to force a rhyming pattern. Don't limit yourself.

                     2. Use sensory details. Keep your poems out of abstract la-la-
                       land by grounding them in the real world with the five senses.

3. When learning about poetry, you'll hear a lot about rhythm. It's true that rhythm is very important, but you don't have to worry too much about technical details. Focus on whether your poem sounds good when it's read aloud; that's all that matters.

4. Not all poems have to be deep or depressing. They can cover the entire range of human emotions. Humorous poems are a lot of fun to write—and to read!

5. Line breaks are more important than you think. When a poem is read aloud, a new line signals a brief pause, so write accordingly. Try to begin and end lines with important words.

Conclusion

Don't be discouraged as you begin your journey as a poet. 9 It is important for you always to remember that your poetry belongs to you. Don't get caught up in trivial things like spelling errors or punctuation; these are the easiest things for you to go back and fix later on. They matter, but only technically. Much more important are the ideas that only you, with your individual mind, can express. Too many people think poetry is a mystical art designed to torture them with confusion. It's not. Instead,

Closing statements it's a beautiful and limitless form of expression. Get your ideas out there. Let your voice be heard.

COMMENTARY

Purpose, thesis.   Jared's essay is an example of *directional process analysis*; his purpose, as is made clear in his title, is to help other students understand how they can become poets. The first sentence of the essay establishes Jared's awareness of many students' attitudes toward poetry; he knows that "the mention of poetry in a college class tends to strike fear into the heart of anyone who's not an English major" (paragraph 1). He continues to write in a friendly, helpful voice throughout the introductory paragraph as he assures students that "poetry isn't as scary as it often seems" and that it doesn't "have to be fancy or complicated." These reassuring statements lead to his thesis: "Many forms of artistic expression require learning new skills. Poetry doesn't; all you need to get started are the words and ideas you already know."

Tone.   Throughout the essay, Jared continues to use the friendly tone he establishes in the introduction. He knows quite well that his topic—how to become a poet—could be an instant turn-off for many students; consequently, he makes a point of using an informal, helpful tone not only in the opening paragraph but throughout the essay.

When discussing reading, "the first essential habit for poets," he puts readers at ease by advising them to "just read everything [they] can find." He goes on to identify reading material that will be comfortable and familiar: "The material you read doesn't need to be academic or literary. You can read news sources, popular magazines, your favorite fiction series, or even comics" (3). When discussing thinking, the second important habit for poets, he makes his ideas clear without using technical language: "This doesn't mean that you must know all the answers to everything. Instead, it means that you must learn as much as you can (through experience, books, movies, whatever) and spend time figuring out how what this new information means to you ..." (4). Jared maintains this tone in his choice of everyday words, such as the adjectives and verbs in these sentences: "Think about what makes you mad, what makes you sad, what you love, hate, or want to change. Think about what's funny, fascinating, brilliant, or stupid. And when you're ready, you can start writing ..." (5). He also uses contractions (*can't, won't, doesn't*) and second-person (*you*) to reinforce the informal tone.

A little later in his essay when he warns of the plague referred to as "writer's block," he gives his readers reassuring advice: "No matter how much you feel that you can't write or it won't be good, write anyway. Write whatever you think of. Nobody has to see it; nobody cares if it is terrible. Let your words be your canvas or your punching bag and write whatever you want" (7). Then in the next paragraph he provides a list of five tips to help his audience as they get started writing their own poems. The friendly, reassuring tone Jared uses throughout his essay helps dissolve the fear many students feel when they consider the idea of writing poetry.

Organization and topic sentences.   To meet the requirements of the assignment, Jared needed to provide a *step-by-step* explanation of a process. As he drafted his essay, Jared realized that the process of becoming a poet has no commonly accepted sequence and that he would need to come up with his own logical series of stages. He decided to structure the stages as (1) developing the habits of a poet, (2) learning how to defeat writer's block, and (3) getting started writing poetry. He explains the first stage, which includes two important habits, in paragraphs 2–5; the second stage in paragraphs 6–7; and the third stage in paragraph 8, which includes a list of five important tips. Each stage begins with a topic sentence indicating the logical progression from one stage to the next.

Transitions.   As Jared drafted his process analysis essay, he was careful to keep in mind that he needed to provide an easy-to-follow structure; consequently, he included transitions to help his readers easily navigate within and among the stages he describes. Notice the transitional word *first* that Jared uses to introduce his discussions of the first stage ("To write poetry successfully, you must *first* learn how to be a poet") and then the habit of reading ("The *first* essential habit for poets is reading"). Then in the following paragraph he uses another transitional word, *other*: "...the *other* essential habit any aspiring poet must have is thinking." As Jared moves from the first stage in his process to the second, he makes sure his readers understand where his ideas are going. He writes, "And when you're ready, you can start writing—unless you come up against what is commonly referred to as 'writer's block.' To defeat writer's block, there are some things you need to know" (5). He creates a smooth transition from the second stage to the third when he writes, at the start of paragraph 8, "Now you know how to develop the habits of a poet and how to defeat writer's block, but how do you actually write poems?" Jared's use of transitions such as these plays an important role in helping him clearly communicate his ideas to his audience.

Combining patterns of development.   Jared uses some *examples*, as in paragraph 3: "You can read news sources, popular magazines, your favorite fiction series, or even comics." However, he makes the decision not to include the names of poets or lines from poems because he is concerned with keeping the essay accessible to readers who do not have much experience with poetry. He does, however, use *definition* in important ways. In paragraph 4, he defines *thinking*: "[Thinking] doesn't mean that you must know all the answers to everything. Instead, it means that you must learn as much as you can ...and spend time figuring out how what this new information means to you...." In addition, he defines *poetry* for readers: "that's what poetry is: your personal reflection of the world around you" (4). Finally, Jared uses definition for another key term: "what is commonly referred to as 'writer's block,' which just means that you feel unable to keep on writing" (5). In explaining how writers can overcome writer's block, Jared uses *cause-effect* to suggest solutions: "The good news is that you always have one sure way to defeat writer's block: writing" (7).

Revising the first draft.   Jared chose to write about a topic that was important to him—one in which he had a deep interest. Reaching his audience and convincing them that poetry is accessible and that they, too, could become poets, was an idea he wanted to clearly communicate to his readers. Before he sat down with his laptop and began putting words on the screen, he thought carefully about his topic and how he might structure his essay.

When working on the first draft, Jared decided to use headings in much the same way that Alex Horton uses them in his essay "On Getting By." Jared liked the way the headings guided him as he read Horton's essay, and although he had never used this type of structure in an essay before, he thought headings might work well in his piece of writing. In his first draft he included his title, "Don't Write Poetry—Be a Poet," followed by his introduction. Then he included the following headings: "Essential Habits for Poets," "Defeating Writer's Block," "How to Write a Poem," and "Don't Be Discouraged" to segue from one part of the essay to the next.

When he shared his first draft with the two other students in his peer review group, one of the students, Olivia, asked him why he had included the headings. Jared explained that he thought they would help readers make the transition from one main idea to the next and then to the conclusion. Olivia told him that she didn't think he needed the headings—that they were unnecessary because of the transitional sentences he had provided to guide readers. Upon hearing what Olivia had to say and thinking about the advice she offered, Hunter, Jared's other classmate in their group, said he thought she had a good point. At first, Jared was hesitant to cut the headings. He liked the idea of using them to guide readers, and he tried cutting the transitional sentences and leaving the headings. However, as he read back over his essay without the transitional sentences, he felt that he was asking his readers to jump from one idea to the next without any guidance. He came to agree with Olivia and Hunter—that the headings were unnecessary and that his essay would be stronger without them.

Jared made other changes as he revised, constantly keeping his audience in mind. He realized that he had overused the pronoun *it*, a habit he knew he needed to break, and that although his pronoun reference was clear to him, it might not be to his readers. To help eliminate this problem, he revised several of his sentences. For example, he revised—

The first thing to realize is that writer's block usually comes from insecurity. *It* cleverly disguises itself in many forms, but *it* always comes down to your not believing you can write something. *It* can be especially hard for poets to overcome...

so that it read—

The first thing to realize is that writer's block usually comes from insecurity. *Writer's block* cleverly disguises itself in many forms, but the *reason the plague strikes in the first place almost* always comes down to your not believing you can write something. *Writer's block* can be especially hard for poets to overcome...

Revisions such as these improved Jared's essay and allowed him to more effectively communicate his ideas to his audience.

Activities: Process Analysis
MyWritingLab

Prewriting Activities

1. Imagine you're writing two essays: One *defines* the term "comparison shopping"; the other *contrasts* two different teaching styles. Jot down ways you might use process analysis in each essay.

2. Select *one* of the essay topics that follow and determine what your purpose, tone, and point of view would be for each audience indicated in parentheses. Then use brainstorming, questioning, mapping, or another prewriting technique to identify the points you'd cover for each audience. Finally, organize the raw material, noting the differences in emphasis and sequence for each group of readers.

   a. How to buy a car (*young people who have just gotten a driver's license; established professionals*)
   b. How children acquire their values (*first-time parents; elementary school teachers*)
   c. How to manage money (*preteens; college students*)
   d. How loans or scholarships are awarded to incoming students on your campus (*high school graduates applying for financial aid; high school guidance counselors*)
   e. How arguments can strengthen relationships (*preteen children; young adults*)
   f. How to relax (*college students; parents with young children*)

Revising Activities

1. Below is the brainstorming for a brief essay that describes the steps involved in making a telephone sales call. The paper has the following thesis: "Establishing rapport with customers is the most challenging and the most important part of phone sales." Revise the brainstormed material by deleting anything that undermines the essay's unity and organizing the steps in a logical sequence.

   * Keep customers on the phone as long as possible to learn what they need
   * The more you know about customers' needs, the better
   * The tone of the opening comments is very important
   * Gently introduce the product
   * Use a friendly tone in opening comments
   * End on a friendly tone, too
   * Don't introduce the product right away
   * Growing rudeness in society. Some people hang up right away. Very upsetting.
   * Try in a friendly way to keep the person on the phone
   * Many people are so lonely they don't mind staying on the phone so they can talk to someone—anyone
   * How sad that there's so much loneliness in the world
   * Describe the product's advantages—price, convenience, installment plan
   * If person is not interested, try in a friendly way to find out why

(continued)

Activities: Process Analysis (*continued*)

> • Don't tell people that their reasons for not being interested are silly
> • Don't push people if they're not interested
> • Encourage credit card payment—the product will arrive earlier
> • Explain payment—check, money order, or credit card payment

2. Following is a paragraph from the first draft of a humorous essay advising shy college students how to get through a typical day. Written as a process analysis, the paragraph outlines techniques for surviving class. Revise the paragraph, deleting digressions that disrupt the paragraph's unity, eliminating unnecessary repetition, and sequencing the steps in the proper order. Also correct inappropriate shifts in person and add transitions where needed. Feel free to add any telling details.

> Simply attending class can be stressful for shy people. Several strategies, though, can lessen the trauma. Shy students should time their arrival to coincide with that of most other class members—about two minutes before the class is scheduled to begin. If you arrive too early, you may be seen sitting alone, or, even worse, may actually be forced to talk with another early arrival. If you arrive late, all eyes will be upon you. Before heading to class, the shy student should dress in the least conspicuous manner possible—say, in jeans, a T-shirt, and flip-flops that 99.9 percent of your classmates wear. That way you won't stand out from everyone else. Take a seat near the back of the room. Don't, however, sit at the very back since professors often take sadistic pleasure in calling on students back there, assuming they chose those seats because they didn't want to be called on. A friend of mine who is far from shy uses just the opposite ploy. In an attempt to get in good with her professors, she sits in the front row and, incredibly enough, volunteers to participate. However, since shy people don't want to call attention to themselves, they should stifle any urge to sneeze or cough. You run the risk of having people look at you or offer you a tissue or cough drop. And of course, never, ever volunteer to answer. Such a display of intelligence is sure to focus all eyes on you. In other words, make yourself as inconspicuous as possible. How, you might wonder, can you be inconspicuous if you're blessed (or cursed) with great looks? Well,...have you ever considered earning your degree online?

Amy Sutherland was born in 1959 and grew up in suburban Cincinnati, Ohio. She has a B.A. in art history from the University of Cincinnati, and an M.S.J. from the Medill School of Journalism at Northwestern University. After thirteen years as an arts and features reporter for newspapers in Vermont and Maine, Sutherland accompanied a Maine resident to the 2000 Pillsbury Bake-off in San Francisco, an assignment that turned into a book, *Cookoff: Recipe Fever in America* (2003). Her next book, *Kicked, Bitten, and Scratched: Life and Lessons at the Premier School for Exotic Animal Trainers,* was published in 2006 and inspired the essay that follows, which appeared in the *New York Times*. In turn, the essay led to another book, *What Shamu Taught Me About Life, Love, and Marriage* (2008) as well as a movie. In addition to writing, Sutherland teaches journalism at Boston University.

For ideas about how this process analysis essay is organized, see Figure 7.2 on page 277.

Pre-Reading Journal Entry

MyWritingLab

All of us have habits—patterns of behavior that we repeat, sometimes even without being aware that we are performing them. Reflect on your own habits, good and bad, past and present. In your journal, list some of your habits, and describe the situations in which they arise and the patterns of behavior that characterize them.

What Shamu Taught Me About a Happy Marriage

As I wash dishes at the kitchen sink, my husband paces behind me, 1 irritated. "Have you seen my keys?" he snarls, then huffs out a loud sigh and stomps from the room with our dog, Dixie, at his heels, anxious over her favorite human's upset.

In the past I would have been right behind Dixie. I would have turned 2 off the faucet and joined the hunt while trying to soothe my husband with bromides like, "Don't worry, they'll turn up." But that only made him angrier, and a simple case of missing keys soon would become a full-blown angst-ridden drama starring the two of us and our poor nervous dog.

Now, I focus on the wet dish in my hands. I don't turn around. I don't 3 say a word. I'm using a technique I learned from a dolphin trainer.

I love my husband. He's well read, adventurous and does a hysterical 4 rendition of a northern Vermont accent that still cracks me up after 12 years of marriage.

But he also tends to be forgetful, and is often tardy and mercurial. He 5 hovers around me in the kitchen asking if I read this or that piece in *The New Yorker* when I'm trying to concentrate on the simmering pans. He leaves wadded tissues in his wake. He suffers from serious bouts of spousal deafness but never fails to hear me when I mutter to myself on the other side of the house. "What did you say?" he'll shout.

These minor annoyances are not the stuff of separation and divorce, but 6 in sum they began to dull my love for Scott. I wanted—needed—to nudge him a little closer to perfect, to make him into a mate who might annoy me a little less, who wouldn't keep me waiting at restaurants, a mate who would be easier to love.

So, like many wives before me, I ignored a library of advice books and 7 set about improving him. By nagging, of course, which only made his behavior worse: he'd drive faster instead of slower; shave less frequently, not more; and leave his reeking bike garb on the bedroom floor longer than ever.

We went to a counselor to smooth the edges off our marriage. She 8 didn't understand what we were doing there and complimented us repeatedly on how well we communicated. I gave up. I guessed she was right—our union was better than most—and resigned myself to stretches of slow-boil resentment and occasional sarcasm.

Then something magical happened. For a book I was writing about 9 a school for exotic animal trainers, I started commuting from Maine to California, where I spent my days watching students do the seemingly impossible: teaching hyenas to pirouette on command, cougars to offer their paws for a nail clipping, and baboons to skateboard.

I listened, rapt, as professional trainers explained how they taught dolphins 10 to flip and elephants to paint. Eventually it hit me that the same techniques might work on that stubborn but lovable species, the American husband.

The central lesson I learned from exotic animal trainers is that I should 11 reward behavior I like and ignore behavior I don't. After all, you don't get a sea lion to balance a ball on the end of its nose by nagging. The same goes for the American husband.

Back in Maine, I began thanking Scott if he threw one dirty shirt into 12 the hamper. If he threw in two, I'd kiss him. Meanwhile, I would step over any soiled clothes on the floor without one sharp word, though I did sometimes kick them under the bed. But as he basked in my appreciation, the piles became smaller.

I was using what trainers call "approximations," rewarding the small 13 steps toward learning a whole new behavior. You can't expect a baboon to learn to flip on command in one session, just as you can't expect an American husband to begin regularly picking up his dirty socks by praising him once for picking up a single sock. With the baboon you first reward a hop, then a bigger hop, then an even bigger hop. With Scott the husband, I began to praise every small act every time: if he drove just a mile an hour slower, tossed one pair of shorts into the hamper, or was on time for anything.

I also began to analyze my husband the way a trainer considers an exotic   14
animal. Enlightened trainers learn all they can about a species, from anatomy
to social structure, to understand how it thinks, what it likes and dislikes,
what comes easily to it and what doesn't. For example, an elephant is a herd
animal, so it responds to hierarchy. It cannot jump, but can stand on its
head. It is a vegetarian.

The exotic animal known as Scott is a loner, but an alpha male. So hier-   15
archy matters, but being in a group doesn't so much. He has the balance of
a gymnast, but moves slowly, especially when getting dressed. Skiing comes
naturally, but being on time does not. He's an omnivore, and what a trainer
would call food-driven.

Once I started thinking this way, I couldn't stop. At the school in   16
California, I'd be scribbling notes on how to walk an emu or have a wolf
accept you as a pack member, but I'd be thinking, "I can't wait to try this
on Scott."

On a field trip with the students, I listened to a professional trainer   17
describe how he had taught African crested cranes to stop landing on his head
and shoulders. He did this by training the leggy birds to land on mats on the
ground. This, he explained, is what is called an "incompatible behavior," a
simple but brilliant concept.

Rather than teach the cranes to stop landing on him, the trainer taught   18
the birds something else, a behavior that would make the undesirable
behavior impossible. The birds couldn't alight on the mats and his head
simultaneously.

At home, I came up with incompatible behaviors for Scott to keep him   19
from crowding me while I cooked. To lure him away from the stove, I piled
up parsley for him to chop or cheese for him to grate at the other end of the
kitchen island. Or I'd set out a bowl of chips and salsa across the room. Soon
I'd done it: no more Scott hovering around me while I cooked.

I followed the students to SeaWorld San Diego, where a dolphin trainer   20
introduced me to least reinforcing syndrome (L.R.S.). When a dolphin does
something wrong, the trainer doesn't respond in any way. He stands still for
a few beats, careful not to look at the dolphin, and then returns to work.
The idea is that any response, positive or negative, fuels a behavior. If a behavior provokes no response, it typically dies away.

In the margins of my notes I wrote, "Try on Scott!"   21

It was only a matter of time before he was again tearing around the   22
house searching for his keys, at which point I said nothing and kept at what
I was doing. It took a lot of discipline to maintain my calm, but results were
immediate and stunning. His temper fell far shy of its usual pitch and then
waned like a fast-moving storm. I felt as if I should throw him a mackerel.

Now he's at it again; I hear him banging a closet door shut, rustling   23
through papers on a chest in the front hall and thumping upstairs. At the

sink, I hold steady. Then, sure enough, all goes quiet. A moment later, he walks into the kitchen, keys in hand, and says calmly, "Found them."

Without turning, I call out, "Great, see you later."   24

Off he goes with our much-calmed pup.   25

After two years of exotic animal training, my marriage is far smoother,   26
my husband much easier to love. I used to take his faults personally; his dirty clothes on the floor were an affront, a symbol of how he didn't care enough about me. But thinking of my husband as an exotic species gave me the distance I needed to consider our differences more objectively.

I adopted the trainers' motto: "It's never the animal's fault." When   27
my training attempts failed, I didn't blame Scott. Rather, I brainstormed new strategies, thought up more incompatible behaviors and used smaller approximations. I dissected my own behavior, considered how my actions might inadvertently fuel his. I also accepted that some behaviors were too entrenched, too instinctive to train away. You can't stop a badger from digging, and you can't stop my husband from losing his wallet and keys.

Professionals talk of animals that understand training so well they   28
eventually use it back on the trainer. My animal did the same. When the training techniques worked so beautifully, I couldn't resist telling my husband what I was up to. He wasn't offended, just amused. As I explained the techniques and terminology, he soaked it up. Far more than I realized.

Last fall, firmly in middle age, I learned that I needed braces. They were   29
not only humiliating, but also excruciating. For weeks my gums, teeth, jaw and sinuses throbbed. I complained frequently and loudly. Scott assured me that I would become used to all the metal in my mouth. I did not.

One morning, as I launched into yet another tirade about how   30
uncomfortable I was, Scott just looked at me blankly. He didn't say a word or acknowledge my rant in any way, not even with a nod.

I quickly ran out of steam and started to walk away. Then I realized what   31
was happening, and I turned and asked, "Are you giving me an L.R.S.?" Silence. "You are, aren't you?"

He finally smiled, but his L.R.S. has already done the trick. He'd begun   32
to train me, the American wife.

Questions for Close Reading

MyWritingLab

1. What is the selection's thesis? Locate the sentence(s) in which Sutherland states her main idea. If she doesn't state her thesis explicitly, express it in your own words.
2. Sutherland tries a couple of solutions to her problems with her husband before she starts using the behavioral techniques that are the main focus of the essay. What were these initial solutions, and why did they fail to improve her relationship with her husband?

FIGURE 7.2

Essay Structure Diagram: "What Shamu Taught Me About a Happy Marriage" by Amy Sutherland

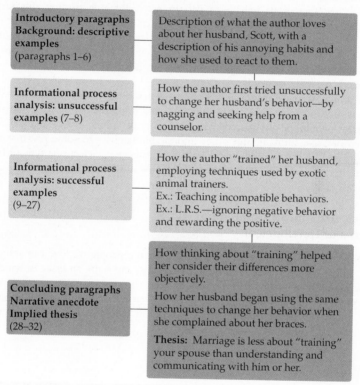

3. What techniques for changing behavior did Sutherland learn from the animal trainers? How did she apply each of these techniques to her husband Scott's behavior?

4. Why did changing her husband's behavior improve Sutherland's marriage?

Questions About the Writer's Craft

1. **The pattern.** What type of process analysis does Sutherland use in this essay? How does the first-person point of view support the pattern of development?

2. What is the tone of Sutherland's essay? What contributes to the tone?

3. **Other patterns.** What pattern of development, besides process analysis, helps organize this essay? What does the other pattern contribute to the essay?

4. Is Sutherland's conclusion effective? How does her conclusion change your response to the essay?

Writing Assignments Using Process Analysis as a Pattern of Development

1. In this essay, Sutherland describes how animal trainers teach cranes, dolphins, and other animals to behave in certain ways. Imagine turning this scenario around, and thinking of animals teaching their human masters how to behave. For example, a cat might train its owner to feed it at 5:00 A.M. by ceasing to howl the second her bowl of food is set on the floor. Write an essay from an animal's point of view in which you explain how the animal trains its human "master" to meet its needs.

2. The animal-training techniques Sutherland describes in this essay are similar to behavioral therapies used by psychologists and other mental health professionals to treat people for phobias, anxiety, and other disorders, and to change specific behaviors, like smoking and other undesirable habits. Do some research in the library and on the Internet about behavioral therapies. Select one type of behavioral therapy and write an essay explaining how it works. Give examples of its use in your essay.

Writing Assignment Combining Patterns of Development

3. Sutherland's essay shows how irritating even the people we love can sometimes be. Select one of your own close relationships, and write an essay in which you *describe* what you find annoying about the other person. Give *examples* of the person's behavior to illustrate your points. What *effects* do this person's annoying traits have on the relationship as a whole? How would you change this person if you could?

Alex Horton

Alex Horton (1985–) is known as "Army of Dude," the title of the blog that he has been keeping since 2006, when he was deployed to Iraq for a fifteen-month tour. He is currently the senior writer for *VAntage Point*, the official blog of the U.S. Department of Veterans Affairs, and is studying writing at Georgetown University in Washington, D.C. His work has appeared in *The Atlantic*, *The New York Times*, and the *St. Petersburg Times*. Horton was a finalist for Weblog Awards for Best Military Blog in 2007 and 2008. The selection that follows was posted on *Army of Dude* on January 13, 2010.

Pre-Reading Journal Entry

MyWritingLab

What do you know about blogs? Have you ever created one or posted to one? If so, what kind(s) of blog(s) did you post to? What is the purpose of a blog? Explore these questions in your journal and use the Internet to find out more about blogs if you are unfamiliar with them.

On Getting By

In my previous post, I outlined some basic principles (Horton) needed   1
to successfully navigate the murky waters of education under the GI Bill.
The challenges in dealing with the VA for education benefits are considerable, yet veterans new to college face an unfamiliar, unpredictable and
strange environment on campus. If taken all at once, these hurdles can
quickly overwhelm a student veteran and distract from the overall goal: to
finish a degree on time with benefits to spare. Next week I will be in class
for my fifth semester of higher education, and in my time I have tinkered
with a system of how to bring up my veteran status, discussing Iraq and
Afghanistan in the classroom and dealing with the myriad reactions fellow
students have had. The system cannot be expected to work for everyone, but
as veterans file into classrooms for the first time this spring, these tips could
help in the development of a coping system better tailored for you. These
should simply help to get you started.

Modesty Is the Best Policy

There are only two kinds of veterans in school: those who prattle   2
on about their time in the military and overseas, and those who do
not. The former will find any opportunity to bring up their time in
Afghanistan or Iraq, even if it is not relevant to class discussion. They forget one of the tenets of military experience—the role of the consummate
professional. Joining the military and serving in a time of war are sacred
acts and carry a certain degree of respect and modesty. We owe it to our
injured buddies and fallen friends not to brag about our exploits overseas.
We have done our fair share of things that set us apart from others in
the classroom, and that is exactly why it is best to retain an understated
presence among others.

This is a difficult situation as it applies to reintegration, as the chasm   3
between veterans and civilians has never been wider. From World War II to
Vietnam, it would have been a difficult task to know someone that neither
served overseas nor had a family member or friend who did. Now there
are whole classrooms filled with those people. As Matthew McConaughey
spoke prophetically in *Dazed and Confused*, "I get older, they stay the
same age." An 18 year old in college this year would have been nine years
old during the invasion of Afghanistan and eleven years old during the invasion of Iraq. They have grown up with war to the point of it becoming
a mind numbingly prosaic concept. It would be a frustrating battle to try
and close the rift with those who don't see a rift at all. The best thing to
do is use your judgment when bringing up your veteran status in the classroom. I've done it just a few times and felt uncomfortable enough to think

twice about the next time. Now I tend to mention it in private conversation, not when I have the floor in public, and even then it is a casual touch on the subject. When you are ready to talk...

...Prepare for a Question Salvo

No matter how much you try to keep it stashed away from students   4
and coworkers, your military experience will come out sooner or later. There are things you simply cannot hide forever, like going to prison or reading *Twilight*. Once you begin to move past casual conversation, it's only a matter of time before that period of your life is visited. It usually begins with a discussion of age. When I tell people I'm 24, the followup questions are almost always, "What have you done since high school?" or, "Why did you wait so long to go to school?" People tend to catch on if you mention extended vacations in the Middle East or recite monologues, so at that point it is best to come clean. However, be prepared for the questions they are more than willing to hurl your way. They might not know anyone who has deployed, but our hyperviolent culture has removed any restraint left in the world and enables them to ask any question that comes to mind. Here is what you can expect, in order of the most frequently asked:

1. What's it like?
2. Was it really hot?
3. Did you kill anyone?
4. Seriously, how hot was it?
5. Do you regret it?
6. Did you see any camel spiders?
7. Were you in Iran?

It's hard to get upset at some of those questions, as I find it difficult to   5
think of what I'd ask if the roles were switched. #3 can be blamed on ignorance and apathy, but #5 is the most troubling I've heard. It suggests that there is something shameful about service, duty and sacrifice. Both questions trivialize an important part of our lives. The best answer to #3 I've heard comes from the The Kitchen Dispatch comment section: "I will forgive you for asking that question if you forgive me for not answering it." Something that personal should never be asked, only told (Fong).

The flip side to some of those cavalier probes are questions that handle   6
the topic with kid gloves. Once a coworker found out I was in the Army, she asked, "Did you go to...one of those places they send people?" It was uncomfortable for her just to utter those dirty "I" and "A" words, like we were speaking about some subversive topic. The kind of questions you will

get will be all over the map, spanning from a place of genuine interest to the depths of sheer morbidity. Be prepared to answer anything, or politely let them know the subject isn't appropriate for casual banter.

Let the Right Ones In

Popular culture is replete with images of the maladjusted veteran, from 7 Rambo to Travis Bickle to Red Forman. These characters are ingrained in our national conscious and typically become placeholders in the event someone doesn't personally know a veteran. When these sources are taken at face value, war veterans are invariably crazy, depressive, easily startled, quick to anger and alcoholics. We come from broken homes, trying to escape jail time and were too dumb or poor to go to college after high school. The best way to combat these silly notions is to let people get to know you, the person, before you, the veteran. Those stereotypes aren't going anywhere soon, so the best idea is to take the concept of guarding your veteran status in the classroom and carry it over to blossoming relationships. That way your service and overseas experience complement your personality and don't define it. Revealing too much at one time can damage a friendship before it takes off. Just like in the classroom, take it slow. If they are worth keeping around, they'll understand why. We have met our lifelong friends already; we can afford to be picky.

Try to Keep a Straight Face

There's a huge disparity between what you have been asked to do in the 8 service and what you will be asked to do in school. At the very basic level you were asked to maintain a clean weapon and uniform. Many of you were tasked with watching the back of your fellow soldiers while in imminent danger or operate complex machinery and vehicles. At school, you'll be held responsible for showing up and turning in work before deadlines. That's it. Like I mentioned in the earlier post, college seems like an insurmountable gauntlet of crushed dreams when you're in the military. Once you transition to civilian life and take a few classes, you'll be astounded at the lack of discipline and drive in some of your classmates. It's a big joke, but try to maintain composure. I'm not saying it's easy the whole way through, but I guarantee you've done something harder than a five page essay. As they say, the rest is downhill.

Find Another Brother

If you were in active duty, the friends you met along the way are now 9 scattered across the country. Perhaps I've always been an introvert, but I don't make friends as easy as some people. I've met just two people in fourteen classes that I consider friends, and one of them is an Afghanistan veteran. It's easy to understand why we get along. Do your best to find other veterans in your class and say hello. Talking to them will come easier than the 18 year old hipster next to you about his passion for ironic hats. Find out if there is a veteran's organization on campus, but be wary of their motives. While some will join to find support and befriend fellow veterans, others will use it for recognition. . . .

Enjoy the Ride

Besides getting a degree or learning new skills, people go to college to meet   10 new people and to experience a different life. If you've served since Sept. 12, 2001, you've already had a bit of each. But don't let that stop you from enjoying everything school has to offer. It's the last time very little will be expected of you, unless you get another government job. Then you're golden.

If you are recently out of the military and on your way to college, these   11 tenets, coupled with the GI Bill pointers, should help you get started in academia ("Post-9/11"). Like most things, your experience may vary, and I would hope you don't safeguard your veteran status like it's a dark secret or the true location of Jimmy Hoffa's body. It's something to be proud of, but not flaunted. It's something to share with your friends who genuinely want to know about the world you lived in, but not with the people who have twisted notions of what you have done overseas. The last thing you want people to know you as is the guy who went to Iraq. You want them to say "Hey, that's Alex, he's good people," and not "I wonder how many ear necklaces he has. I'm betting two." Hopefully these tips will help even just a tiny bit in that regard.

Works Cited

Fong, Kanani. "Seven Things Never to Say to a Veteran." *The Kitchen Dispatch: A View from the Breakfast Table during War,* 3 Jan. 2010, kitchendispatch.blogspot.com/.
Horton, Alex. "Here to There: Tips and Tricks for the Student Veteran." *Army of Dude,* 29 Dec. 2009, armyofdude.blogspot.com/.
"Post-9/11 GI Bill." *United States Department of Veterans Affairs,* www.benefits. va.gov/gibill/post911_gibill.asp. Accessed 13 Jan. 2010.

Questions for Close Reading   MyWritingLab

1. What is the selection's thesis? Locate the sentence(s) in which Horton states his main idea. If he doesn't state the thesis explicitly, express it in your own words.
2. What reason does Horton give veterans for why they should generally avoid talking about their military experiences when they are at school?
3. Of the questions Horton lists as those other students are likely to ask when they discover one of their classmates is a veteran, which one does Horton find most troubling and why?

4. How does Horton compare what former military think college will be like with what he thinks they are likely to discover when they actually go to college?

Questions About the Writer's Craft

1. **The pattern.** How does Horton organize his process analysis? What tool does he use, and how does his strategy make his blog more effective?
2. **The pattern.** Is Horton's process analysis primarily *directional* or *informational*? Explain. To what extent does Horton try to persuade readers that the process he describes should be followed?
3. **Other patterns.** Although Horton organizes his selection as a process analysis, he also weaves in his own experience—his own *narrative* about what he learned when he returned to civilian life and started taking college classes. How does this combination of patterns make Horton's writing stronger than it would be without the inclusion of his own story?
4. Horton's intended audience is those currently or formerly in the military—not students and their teachers. What parts of his essay might some students and instructors find offensive and why?

Writing Assignments Using Process Analysis as a Pattern of Development

1. In his essay Horton, a military veteran, provides other military veterans with a plan for how to "get by" in college. Write an essay in which you present a process analysis of ways a member of a group to which you belong or have belonged can adjust to a particular situation—perhaps an essay written to high school seniors on how to adjust to college life or an essay for new employees on how to adjust to working at your place of employment.
2. Horton is an expert on the subject he addresses. Write an essay in which you present a process analysis that provides both directions and information for an audience unfamiliar with or less experienced than you on a particular subject. For example, if you are an avid gamer, you might write an essay on how to successfully navigate a challenging game such as *Call of Duty, Forza,* or *Portal.* Or if you have learned how to survive as a student on a bare-bones budget, you might write an essay in which you offer tips to college students in a similar situation.

Writing Assignment Combining Patterns of Development

3. In his *process analysis* Horton also tells a story—a *narrative*—about the common societal experience of adjusting to college life. Write an essay in which you examine another common process, for example, applying for a driver's license, or a larger societal process, such as electing a president. Give the process involved, but also include sufficient *description*—for example, of an exam room at the license bureau or the crowds at a political rally—to support your thesis. You might find it helpful to conduct some original research on the subject.

Paul Roberts

Paul Roberts (1917–67) was a scholar of linguistics and a respected teacher whose textbooks helped scores of high school and college students become better writers. Roberts's works include *English Syntax* (1954) and *Patterns of English* (1956). The following selection is from his best-known book, *Understanding English* (1958).

Pre-Reading Journal Entry

MyWritingLab

Many educators argue that first-year college students write bland essays because their high school English classes didn't teach them how to think clearly and creatively. Do you agree? Take some time to reflect in your journal about your best and worst high school English classes. For each class, focus on teaching style, classroom atmosphere, assignments, activities, and so on.

How to Say Nothing in 500 Words

Nothing About Something

It's Friday afternoon, and you have almost survived another week of 1 classes. You are just looking forward dreamily to the weekend when the English instructor says: "For Monday you will turn in a five-hundred-word composition on college football."

Well, that puts a good big hole in the weekend. You don't have any 2 strong views on college football one way or the other. You get rather excited during the season and go to all the home games and find it rather more fun than not. On the other hand, the class has been reading Robert Hutchins in the anthology and perhaps Shaw's "Eighty-Yard Run," and from the class discussion you have got the idea that the instructor thinks college football is for the birds. You are no fool, you. You can figure out what side to take.

After dinner you get out the portable typewriter that you got for 3 high school graduation. You might as well get it over with and enjoy Saturday and Sunday. Five hundred words is about two double-spaced pages with normal margins. You put in a sheet of paper, think up a title, and you're off:

Why College Football Should Be Abolished

College football should be abolished because it's bad for the school 4 and also bad for the players. The players are so busy practicing that they don't have any time for their studies.

This, you feel, is a mighty good start. The only trouble is that it's only thirty-two words. You still have four hundred and sixty-eight to go, and you've pretty well exhausted the subject. It comes to you that you do your best thinking in the morning, so you put away the typewriter and go to the movies. But the next morning you have to do your washing and some math problems, and in the afternoon you go to the game. The English instructor turns up too, and you wonder if you've taken the right side after all. Saturday night you have a date, and Sunday morning you have to go to church. (You shouldn't let English assignments interfere with your religion.) What with one thing and another, it's ten o'clock Sunday night before you get out the typewriter again. You make a pot of coffee and start to fill out your views on college football. Put a little meat on the bones. 5

Why College Football Should Be Abolished

In my opinion, it seems to me that college football should be abolished. The reason why I think this to be true is because I feel that football is bad for the colleges in nearly every respect. As Robert Hutchins says in his article in our anthology in which he discusses college football, it would be better if the colleges had race horses and had races with one another, because then the horses would not have to attend classes. I firmly agree with Mr. Hutchins on this point, and I am sure that many other students would agree too. 6

One reason why it seems to me that college football is bad is that it has become too commercial. In the olden times when people played football just for the fun of it, maybe college football was all right, but they do not play football just for the fun of it now as they used to in the old days. Nowadays college football is what you might call a big business. Maybe this is not true at all schools, and I don't think it is especially true here at State, but certainly this is the case at most colleges and universities in America nowadays, as Mr. Hutchins points out in his very interesting article. Actually the coaches and alumni go around to the high schools and offer the high school stars large salaries to come to their colleges and play football for them. There was one case where a high school star was offered a convertible if he would play football for a certain college. 7

Another reason for abolishing college football is that it is bad for the players. They do not have time to get a college education, because they are so busy playing football. A football player has to practice every afternoon from three to six, and then he is so tired that he can't concentrate on his studies. He just feels like dropping off to sleep after dinner, and then the next day he goes to his classes without having studied and maybe he fails the test. 8

(Good ripe stuff so far, but you're still a hundred and fifty-one words from home. One more push.)

Also I think college football is bad for the colleges and the universi-   9
ties because not very many students get to participate in it. Out of a
college of ten thousand students only seventy-five or a hundred play
football, if that many. Football is what you might call a spectator
sport. That means that most people go to watch it but do not play
it themselves.

(Four hundred and fifteen. Well, you still have the conclusion, and when
you retype it, you can make the margins a little wider.)

These are the reasons why I agree with Mr. Hutchins that college   10
football should be abolished in American colleges and universities.

On Monday you turn it in, moderately hopeful, and on Friday it comes   11
back marked "weak in content" and sporting a big "D."

This essay is exaggerated a little, not much. The English instructor   12
will recognize it as reasonably typical of what an assignment on college
football will bring in. He knows that nearly half of the class will contrive
in five hundred words to say that college football is too commercial and
bad for the players. Most of the other half will inform him that college
football builds character and prepares one for life and brings prestige to
the school. As he reads paper after paper all saying the same thing in almost
the same words, all bloodless, five hundred words dripping out of nothing,
he wonders how he allowed himself to get trapped into teaching English
when he might have had a happy and interesting life as an electrician or a
confidence man.

Well, you may ask, what can you do about it? The subject is one   13
on which you have few convictions and little information. Can you be
expected to make a dull subject interesting? As a matter of fact, this is
precisely what you are expected to do. This is the writer's essential task. All
subjects, except sex, are dull until somebody makes them interesting. The
writer's job is to find the argument, the approach, the angle, the wording that will take the reader with him. This is seldom easy, and it is particularly hard in subjects that have been much discussed: College Football,
Fraternities, Popular Music, Is Chivalry Dead?, and the like. You will feel
that there is nothing you can do with such subjects except repeat the old
bromides. But there are some things you can do which will make your
papers, if not throbbingly alive, at least less insufferably tedious than they
might otherwise be.

Avoid the Obvious Content

Say the assignment is college football. Say that you've decided to be 14
against it. Begin by putting down the arguments that come to your mind: it
is too commercial, it takes the students' minds off their studies, it is hard on
the players, it makes the university a kind of circus instead of an intellectual
center, for most schools it is financially ruinous. Can you think of any more
arguments just off hand? All right. Now when you write your paper, *make
sure that you don't use any of the material on this list.* If these are the points
that leap to your mind, they will leap to everyone else's too, and whether
you get a "C" or a "D" may depend on whether the instructor reads your
paper early when he is fresh and tolerant or late, when the sentence "In my
opinion, college football has become too commercial," inexorably repeated,
has brought him to the brink of lunacy.

Be against college football for some reason or reasons of your own. 15
If they are keen and perceptive ones, that's splendid. But even if they are
trivial or foolish or indefensible, you are still ahead so long as they are not
everybody else's reasons too. Be against it because the colleges don't spend
enough money on it to make it worth while, because it is bad for the characters of the spectators, because the players are forced to attend classes, because
the football stars hog all the beautiful women, because it competes with baseball and is therefore un-American and possibly Communist inspired. There
are lots of more or less unused reasons for being against college football.

Sometimes it is a good idea to sum up and dispose of the trite and con- 16
ventional points before going on to your own. This has the advantage of
indicating to the reader that you are going to be neither trite nor conventional. Something like this:

> We are often told that college football should be abolished because 17
> it has become too commercial or because it is bad for the players.
> These arguments are no doubt very cogent, but they don't really
> go to the heart of the matter.

Then you go to the heart of the matter.

Take the Less Usual Side

One rather simple way of getting interest into your paper is to take 18
the side of the argument that most of the citizens will want to avoid. If the
assignment is an essay on dogs, you can, if you choose, explain that dogs
are faithful and lovable companions, intelligent, useful as guardians of the
house and protectors of children, indispensable in police work—in short,
when all is said and done, man's best friends. Or you can suggest that those
big brown eyes conceal, more often than not, a vacuity of mind and an

inconstancy of purpose; that the dogs you have known most intimately have been mangy, ill-tempered brutes, incapable of instruction; and that only your nobility of mind and fear of arrest prevent you from kicking the flea-ridden animals when you pass them on the street.

Naturally, personal convictions will sometimes dictate your approach. 19 If the assigned subject is "Is Methodism Rewarding to the Individual?" and you are a pious Methodist, you have really no choice. But few assigned subjects, if any, will fall in this category. Most of them will lie in broad areas of discussion with much to be said on both sides. They are intellectual exercises and it is legitimate to argue now one way and now another, as debaters do in similar circumstances. Always take the side that looks to you hardest, least defensible. It will almost always turn out to be easier to write interestingly on that side.

This general advice applies where you have a choice of subjects. If you are 20 to choose among "The Value of Fraternities" and "My Favorite High School Teacher" and "What I Think About Beetles," by all means plump for the beetles. By the time the instructor gets to your paper, he will be up to his ears in tedious tales about the French teacher at Bloombury High and assertions about how fraternities build character and prepare one for life. Your views on beetles, whatever they are, are bound to be a refreshing change.

Don't worry too much about figuring out what the instructor thinks 21 about the subject so that you can cuddle up with him. Chances are his views are no stronger than yours. If he does have convictions and you oppose them, his problem is to keep from grading you higher than you deserve in order to show he is not biased. This doesn't mean that you should always cantankerously dissent from what the instructor says; that gets tiresome too. And if the subject assigned is "My Pet Peeve," do not begin, "My pet peeve is the English instructor who assigns papers on 'my pet peeve.'" This was still funny during the War of 1812, but it has sort of lost its edge since then. It is in general good manners to avoid personalities.

Slip Out of Abstraction

If you will study the essay on college football...you will perceive that one 22 reason for its appalling dullness is that it never gets down to particulars. It is just a series of not very glittering generalities: "football is bad for the colleges," "it has become too commercial," "football is a big business," "it is bad for the players," and so on. Such round phrases thudding against the reader's brain are unlikely to convince him, though they may well render him unconscious.

If you want the reader to believe that college football is bad for the 23 players, you have to do more than say so. You have to display the evil. Take your roommate, Alfred Simkins, the second-string center. Picture poor old Alfy coming home from football practice every evening, bruised and aching, agonizingly tired, scarcely able to shovel the mashed potatoes into his mouth. Let us see him staggering up to the room, getting out his econ textbook, peering desperately at it with his good eye, falling asleep and failing the test in the morning. Let us share his unbearable tension as Saturday draws near. Will he fail, be demoted, lose his monthly allowance, be forced to return to the coal mines? And if he succeeds, what will be his reward? Perhaps a slight ripple of applause when the third-string center replaces him, a moment of elation in the locker room if the team wins, of despair if it loses. What will he look back on when he graduates from college? Toil and torn ligaments. And what will be his future? He is not good enough for pro football, and he is too obscure and weak in econ to succeed in stocks and bonds. College football is tearing the heart from Alfy Simkins and, when it finishes with him, will callously toss aside the shattered hulk.

This is no doubt a weak enough argument for the abolition of college 24 football, but it is a sight better than saying, in three or four variations, that college football (in your opinion) is bad for the players.

Look at the work of any professional writer and notice how constantly 25 he is moving from the generality, the abstract statement, to the concrete example, the facts and figures, the illustration. If he is writing on juvenile delinquency, he does not just tell you that juveniles are (it seems to him) delinquent and that (in his opinion) something should be done about it. He shows you juveniles being delinquent, tearing up movie theatres in Buffalo, stabbing high school principals in Dallas, smoking marijuana in Palo Alto. And more than likely he is moving toward some specific remedy, not just a general wringing of the hands.

It is no doubt possible to be *too* concrete, too illustrative or anecdotal, 26 but few inexperienced writers err this way. For most the soundest advice is to be seeking always for the picture, to be always turning general remarks into seeable examples. Don't say, "Sororities teach girls the social graces." Say "Sorority life teaches a girl how to carry on a conversation while pouring tea, without sloshing the tea into the saucer." Don't say, "I like certain kinds of popular music very much." Say, "Whenever I hear Gerber Spinklittle play 'Mississippi Man' on the trombone, my socks creep up my ankles."

Get Rid of Obvious Padding

The student toiling away at his weekly English theme is too often 27 tormented by a figure: five hundred words. How, he asks himself, is he to achieve this staggering total? Obviously by never using one word when he can somehow work in ten.

He is therefore seldom content with a plain statement like "Fast driv- 28 ing is dangerous." This has only four words in it. He takes thought, and the sentence becomes:

In my opinion, fast driving is dangerous.

Better, but he can do better still:

> In my opinion, fast driving would seem to be rather dangerous.

If he is really adept, it may come out:

> In my humble opinion, though I do not claim to be an expert on this complicated subject, fast driving, in most circumstances, would seem to be rather dangerous in many respects, or at least so it would seem to me.

Thus four words have been turned into forty, and not an iota of content has been added.

Now this is a way to go about reaching five hundred words, and if you are content with a "D" grade, it is as good a way as any. But if you aim higher, you must work differently. Instead of stuffing your sentences with straw, you must try steadily to get rid of the padding, to make your sentences lean and tough. If you are really working at it, your first draft will greatly exceed the required total, and then you will work it down, thus:

> It is thought in some quarters that fraternities do not contribute as much as might be expected to campus life.
> Some people think that fraternities contribute little to campus life.

> The average doctor who practices in small towns or in the country must toil night and day to heal the sick.
> Most country doctors work long hours.

> When I was a little girl, I suffered from shyness and embarrassment in the presence of others.
> I was a shy little girl.

> It is absolutely necessary for the person employed as a marine fireman to give the matter of steam pressure his undivided attention at all times.
> The fireman has to keep his eye on the steam gauge.

You may ask how you can arrive at five hundred words at this rate. Simply. You dig up more real content. Instead of taking a couple of obvious points off the surface of the topic and then circling warily around them for six paragraphs, you work in and explore, figure out the details. You illustrate. You say that fast driving is dangerous, and then you prove it. How long does it take to stop a car at forty and at eighty? How far can you see at night? What happens when a tire blows? What happens in a head-on collision at fifty miles an hour? Pretty soon your paper will be full of broken glass and blood and headless torsos, and reaching five hundred words will not really be a problem.

Call a Fool a Fool

Some of the padding in freshman themes is to be blamed not on anxiety   31
about the word minimum but on excessive timidity. The student writes, "In my opinion, the principal of my high school acted in ways that I believe every unbiased person would have to call foolish." This isn't exactly what he means. What he means is, "My high school principal was a fool." If he was a fool, call him a fool. Hedging the thing about with "in-my-opinion's" and "it-seems-to-me's" and "as-I-see-it's" and "at-least-from-my-point-of-view's" gains you nothing. Delete these phrases whenever they creep into your paper.

The student's tendency to hedge stems from a modesty that in other   32
circumstances would be commendable. He is, he realizes, young and inexperienced, and he half suspects that he is dopey and fuzzy-minded beyond the average. Probably only too true. But it doesn't help to announce your incompetence six times in every paragraph. Decide what you want to say and say it as vigorously as possible, without apology and in plain words.

Linguistic diffidence can take various forms. One is what we call   33
euphemism. This is the tendency to call a spade "a certain garden implement" or women's underwear "unmentionables." It is stronger in some eras than others and in some people than others but it always operates more or less in subjects that are touchy or taboo: death, sex, madness, and so on. Thus we shrink from saying "He died last night" but say instead "passed away," "left us," "joined his Maker," "went to his reward." Or we try to take off the tension with a lighter cliché: "kicked the bucket," "cashed in his chips," "handed in his dinner pail." We have found all sorts of ways to avoid saying *mad:* "mentally ill," "touched," "not quite right upstairs," "feeble-minded," "innocent," "simple," "off his trolley," "not in his right mind." Even such a now plain word as *insane* began as a euphemism with the meaning "not healthy."

Modern science, particularly psychology, contributes many polysyllables   34
in which we can wrap our thoughts and blunt their force. To many writers there is no such thing as a bad schoolboy. Schoolboys are maladjusted or unoriented or misunderstood or in need of guidance or lacking in continued success toward satisfactory integration of the personality as a social unit, but they are never bad. Psychology no doubt makes us better men or women, more sympathetic and tolerant, but it doesn't make writing any easier. Had Shakespeare been confronted with psychology, "To be or not to be" might have come out, "To continue as a social unit or not to do so. That is the personality problem. Whether 'tis a better sign of integration at the conscious

level to display a psychic tolerance toward the maladjustments and repressions induced by one's lack of orientation in one's environment or—" But Hamlet would never have finished the soliloquy.

Writing in the modern world, you cannot altogether avoid modern   35
jargon. Nor, in an effort to get away from euphemism, should you salt your paper with four-letter words. But you can do much if you will mount guard against those roundabout phrases, those echoing polysyllables that tend to slip into your writing to rob it of its crispness and force.

Beware of the Pat Expression

Other things being equal, avoid phrases like "other things being equal."   36
Those sentences that come to you whole, or in two or three doughy lumps, are sure to be bad sentences. They are no creation of yours but pieces of common thought floating in the community soup.

Pat expressions are hard, often impossible, to avoid, because they come   37
too easily to be noticed and seem too necessary to be dispensed with. No writer avoids them altogether, but good writers avoid them more often than poor writers.

By "pat expressions" we mean such tags as "to all practical intents and   38
purposes," "the pure and simple truth," "from where I sit," "the time of his life," "to the ends of the earth," "in the twinkling of an eye," "as sure as you're born," "over my dead body," "under cover of darkness," "took the easy way out," "when all is said and done," "told him time and time again," "parted the best of friends," "stand up and be counted," "gave him the best years of her life," "worked her fingers to the bone." Like other clichés, these expressions were once forceful. Now we should use them only when we can't possibly think of anything else.

Some pat expressions stand like a wall between the writer and thought.   39
Such a one is "the American way of life." Many student writers feel that when they have said that something accords with the American way of life or does not they have exhausted the subject. Actually, they have stopped at the highest level of abstraction. The American way of life is the complicated set of bonds between a hundred and eighty million ways. All of us know this when we think about it, but the tag phrase too often keeps us from thinking about it.

So with many another phrase dear to the politician: "this great land of   40
ours," "the man in the street," "our national heritage." These may prove our patriotism or give a clue to our political beliefs, but otherwise they add nothing to the paper except words.

Colorful Words

The writer builds with words, and no builder uses a raw material more   41
slippery and elusive and treacherous. A writer's work is a constant struggle to get the right word in the right place, to find that particular word that will

convey his meaning exactly, that will persuade the reader or soothe him or startle or amuse him. He never succeeds altogether—sometimes he feels that he scarcely succeeds at all—but such successes as he has are what make the thing worth doing.

There is no book of rules for this game. One progresses through ever-lasting experiment on the basis of ever-widening experience. There are few useful generalizations that one can make about words as words, but there are perhaps a few. 42

Some words are what we call "colorful." By this we mean that they are calculated to produce a picture or induce an emotion. They are dressy instead of plain, specific instead of general, loud instead of soft. Thus, in place of "Her heart beat," we may write "Her heart *pounded, throbbed, fluttered, danced.*" Instead of "He sat in his chair," we may say, "He *lounged, sprawled, coiled.*" Instead of "It was hot," we may say, "It was *blistering, sultry, muggy, suffocating, steamy, wilting.*" 43

However, it should not be supposed that the fancy word is always better. Often it is as well to write "Her heart beat" or "It was hot" if that is all it did or all it was. Ages differ in how they like their prose. The nineteenth century liked it rich and smoky. The twentieth has usually preferred it lean and cool. The twentieth-century writer, like all writers, is forever seeking the exact word, but he is wary of sounding feverish. He tends to pitch it low, to understate it, to throw it away. He knows that if he gets too colorful, the audience is likely to giggle. 44

See how this strikes you: "As the rich, golden glow of the sunset died away along the eternal western hills, Angela's limpid blue eyes looked softly and trustingly into Montague's flashing brown ones, and her heart pounded like a drum in time with the joyous song surging in her soul." Some people like that sort of thing, but most modern readers would say, "Good grief," and turn on the television. 45

Colored Words

Some words we would call not so much colorful as colored—that is, loaded with associations, good or bad. All words—except perhaps structure words—have associations of some sort. We have said that the meaning of a word is the sum of the contexts in which it occurs. When we hear a word, we hear with it an echo of all the situations in which we have heard it before. 46

In some words, these echoes are obvious and discussable. The word *mother,* for example, has, for most people, agreeable associations. When you hear *mother* you probably think of home, safety, love, food, and various other pleasant things. If one writes, "She was like a mother to me," he gets an effect which he would not get in "She was like an aunt to me." The advertiser makes use of the associations of *mother* by working it in when he talks about his product. The politician works it in when he talks about himself. 47

So also with such words as *home, liberty, fireside, contentment, patriot,*   48
tenderness, sacrifice, childlike, manly, bluff, limpid. All of these words
are loaded with favorable associations that would be rather hard to indicate in a straightforward definition. There is more than a literal difference
between "They sat around the fireside" and "They sat around the stove."
They might have been equally warm and happy around the stove, but *fireside* suggests leisure, grace, quiet tradition, congenial company, and *stove*
does not.

Conversely, some words have bad associations. *Mother* suggests pleasant   49
things, but *mother-in-law* does not. Many mothers-in-law are heroically lovable and some mothers drink gin all day and beat their children insensible,
but these facts of life are beside the point. The thing is that *mother* sounds
good and *mother-in-law* does not.

Or consider the word *intellectual.* This would seem to be a compli-   50
mentary term, but in point of fact it is not, for it has picked up associations
of impracticality and ineffectuality and general dopiness. So also with such
words as *liberal, reactionary, Communist, socialist, capitalist, radical, school-
teacher, truck driver, undertaker, operator, salesman, huckster, speculator.*
These convey meanings on the literal level, but beyond that—sometimes, in
some places—they convey contempt on the part of the speaker.

The question of whether to use loaded words or not depends on   51
what is being written. The scientist, the scholar, try to avoid them; for the
poet, the advertising writer, the public speaker, they are standard equipment. But every writer should take care that they do not substitute for
thought. If you write, "Anyone who thinks that is nothing but a Socialist
(or Communist or capitalist)," you have said nothing except that you
don't like people who think that, and such remarks are effective only with
the most naïve readers. It is always a bad mistake to think your readers
more naïve than they really are.

Colorless Words

But probably most student writers come to grief not with words that   52
are colorful or those that are colored but with those that have no color at
all. A pet example is *nice,* a word we would find it hard to dispense with
in casual conversation but which is no longer capable of adding much to a
description. Colorless words are those of such general meaning that in a particular sentence they mean nothing. Slang adjectives, like *cool* ("That's real
cool") tend to explode all over the language. They are applied to everything,
lose their original force, and quickly die.

Beware also of nouns of very general meaning, like *circumstances, cases,*   53
instances, aspects, factors, relationships, attitudes, eventualities, etc. In most
circumstances you will find that those cases of writing which contain too

many instances of words like these will in this and other aspects have factors leading to unsatisfactory relationships with the reader resulting in unfavorable attitudes on his part and perhaps other eventualities, like a grade of "D." Notice also what "etc." means. It means "I'd like to make this list longer, but I can't think of any more examples."

Questions for Close Reading

MyWritingLab

1. What is the selection's thesis? Locate the sentence(s) in which Roberts states his main idea. If he doesn't state the thesis explicitly, express it in your own words.
2. According to Roberts, what do students assume they have to do to get a good grade on an English composition?
3. How do "colorful words," "colored words," and "colorless words" differ? Which should be used in essay writing? Why?
4. What are Roberts's most important pieces of advice for the student writer?

Questions About the Writer's Craft

1. **The pattern.** What two processes does Roberts analyze in this essay? Is each process informational, directional, or a combination of the two?
2. Why do you think Roberts uses the second person "you" throughout the essay? How does this choice of point of view affect your response to the essay?
3. What is Roberts's tone in the essay? Find some typical examples of his tone. How does Roberts achieve this tone? Considering the author's intended audience, is this tone a good choice? Explain.
4. Does Roberts "practice what he preaches" about writing? Review the section headings of the essay and find examples of each piece of advice in the essay.

Writing Assignments Using Process Analysis as a Pattern of Development

1. Write a humorous essay showing how to avoid doing schoolwork, household chores, or anything else most people tend to put off. You may use the second person as Roberts does. Or you may use the first person and describe your typical method of avoidance.
2. Borrowing some of Roberts's lively techniques, make a routine, predictable process interesting to read about. You might choose an activity such as how to register to vote, apply for a driver's license, register for college courses, take care of laundry, play a simple game, study for an exam, or execute some other familiar process.

Writing Assignment Combining Patterns of Development

3. Should a composition course be required of all first-year college students? Write an essay *arguing* the value—or lack of value—of such a course. Follow Roberts's advice for writing a lively composition: avoid obvious padding, choose unusual points and *examples,* avoid abstractions, go to the heart of the matter, use colorful words.

Caroline Rego

Caroline Rego was born in 1950 in Edmond, Oklahoma. A graduate of the University of Oklahoma, she began her journalistic career as a police reporter for a daily newspaper in Montana. Later, while filling in for a vacationing colleague in the features section of another newspaper, she found her true calling: writing consumer-affairs articles that teach readers how to protect themselves against shoddy service, dangerous products, and inefficiency. A sought-after public speaker, Rego talks frequently to students and community groups on strategies for becoming an informed consumer. The following selection is part of a work in progress on consumer empowerment.

Pre-Reading Journal Entry   MyWritingLab

When you're disappointed with someone or something, how do you typically react—passively, assertively, or in some other way? In your journal, list a few disappointments you've experienced. How did you respond on each occasion? In retrospect, are you happy with your responses? Why or why not?

The Fine Art of Complaining

You waited forty-five minutes for your dinner, and when it came it 1
was cold—and not what you ordered in the first place. You washed your
supposedly machine-washable, preshrunk T-shirt (the one the catalogue claimed
was "indestructible"), and now it's the size of a napkin. Your new car broke
down a month after you bought it, and the dealer says the warranty doesn't apply.

Life's annoyances descend on all of us—some pattering down like 2
gentle raindrops, others striking with the bruising force of hailstones. We
dodge the ones we can, but inevitably, plenty of them make contact. And
when they do, we react fairly predictably. Many of us—most of us, probably—grumble to ourselves and take it. We scowl at our unappetizing food
but choke it down. We stash the shrunken T-shirt in a drawer, vowing never
again to order from a catalogue. We glare fiercely at our checkbooks as we
pay for repairs that should have been free.

A few of us go to the other extreme. Taking our cue from the crazed 3
newscaster in the 1976 movie *Network,* we go through life mad as hell and
unwilling to take it anymore. In offices, we shout at hapless receptionists
when we're kept waiting for appointments. In restaurants, we make scenes
that have fellow patrons craning their necks to get a look at us. In stores,
we argue with salespeople for not waiting on us. We may notice after a
while that our friends seem reluctant to venture into public with us, but
hey—we're just standing up for our rights. Being a patsy doesn't get you
anywhere in life.

It's true—milquetoasts live unsatisfying lives. However, people who go   4
through the day in an eye-popping, vein-throbbing state of apoplectic rage
don't win any prizes either. What persons at both ends of the scale need—
what could empower the silent sufferer and civilize the Neanderthal—is a
course in the gentle art of *effective* complaining.

Effective complaining is not apologetic and half-hearted. It's not making   5
one awkward attempt at protest—"Uh, excuse me, I don't think I ordered
the squid and onions"—and then slinking away in defeat. But neither is it
roaring away indiscriminately, attempting to get satisfaction through the
sheer volume of our complaint.

Effective complainers are people who act businesslike and impor-   6
tant. Acting important doesn't mean puffing up your chest and saying,
"Do you know who I am?"—an approach that would tempt anyone to
take you down a peg or two. It doesn't mean shouting and threatening—
techniques that will only antagonize the person whose help you need.
It *does* mean making it clear that you know your request is reasonable
and that you are confident it will be taken care of. People are generally
treated the way they expect to be treated. If you act like someone making
a fair request, chances are that request will be granted. Don't beg, don't
explain. Just state your name, the problem, and what you expect to have
done. Remain polite. But be firm. "My car has been in your garage for
three days, and a mechanic hasn't even looked at it yet," you might say.
"I want to know when it is going to be worked on." Period. Now it is up
to them to give you a satisfactory response. Don't say, "Sorry to bother
you about this, but..." or "I, uh, was sort of expecting...." You're only
asking people to remedy a problem, after all; that is not grounds for
apology.

If your problem requires an immediate response, try to make your   7
complaint in person; a real, live, in-the-flesh individual has to be dealt with
in some way. Complaining over the telephone, by contrast, is much less
effective. When you speak to a disembodied voice, when the person at the
other end of the line doesn't have to face you, you're more likely to get a
runaround.

Most importantly, complain to the right person. One of the greatest   8
frustrations in complaining is talking to a clerk or receptionist who cannot
solve your problem and whose only purpose seems to be to drive you crazy.
Getting mad doesn't help; the person you're mad at probably had nothing
to do with your actual problem. And you'll have to repeat everything you've
said to the clerk once you're passed along to the appropriate person. So
make sure from the start that you're talking to someone who can help—a
manager or supervisor.

If your problem doesn't require an immediate response, complaining   9
by letter is probably the most effective way to get what you want. A letter of

complaint should be brief, businesslike, and to the point. If you have a new vacuum cleaner that doesn't work, don't spend a paragraph describing how your Uncle Joe tried to fix the problem and couldn't. As when complaining in person, be sure you address someone in a position of real authority. Here's an example of an effective letter of complaint.

Ms. Anne Lublin   10
Manager
Mitchell Appliances
80 Front Street
Newton, MA 02159

Dear Ms. Lublin: 11

First section: Explain the problem. Include facts to back up your story.   12

On August 6, I purchased a new Perma-Kool freezer from your store (a copy of   13
my sales receipt is enclosed). In the two weeks I have owned the freezer, I have
had to call your repair department three times in an attempt to get it running
properly. The freezer ran normally when it was installed, but since then it has
repeatedly turned off, causing the food inside to spoil. My calls to your repair
department have not been responded to promptly. After I called the first time,
on August 10, I waited two days for the repair person to show up. It took three
days to get a repair person here after my second call, on August 15. The freezer
stopped yet again on August 20. I called to discuss this recent problem, but no
one has responded to my call.

Second section: Tell how you trust the company and are confident that your   14
reader will fix the problem. This is to "soften up" the reader a bit.

I am surprised to receive such unprofessional service and poor quality from   15
Mitchell Appliances since I have been one of your satisfied customers for fifteen
years. In the past, I have purchased a television, air conditioner, and washing
machine from your company. I know that you value good relations with your
customers, and I'm sure you want to see me pleased with my most recent
purchase.

Third section: Explain exactly what you want to be done—repair, replacement,   16
refund, etc.

Although your repair department initially thought that the freezer needed only   17
some minor adjustments, the fact that no one has been able to permanently

fix the problem convinces me that the freezer has some serious defect. I am understandably unwilling to spend any more time having repairs made. Therefore, I expect you to exchange the freezer for an identical model by the end of this week (August 30). Please call me to arrange for the removal of the defective freezer and the delivery of the new one.

Sincerely,   18

Janice Becker

P.S. (Readers always notice a P.S.) State again when you expect the problem to   19
be taken care of, and what you will do if it isn't.

P.S. I am confident that we can resolve this problem by August 30. If the   20
defective freezer is not replaced by then, however, I will report this incident to
the Better Business Bureau.

Notice that the P.S. says what you'll do if your problem isn't solved.   21
In other words, you make a threat—a polite threat. Your threat must be
reasonable and believable. A threat to burn down the store if your purchase price isn't refunded is neither reasonable nor believable—or if it
were believed, you could end up in jail. A threat to report the store to a
consumer-protection agency, such as the Better Business Bureau, however,
is credible.

Don't be too quick to make one of the most common—and com-   22
monly empty—threats: "I'll sue!" A full-blown lawsuit is more trouble,
and more expensive, than most problems are worth. On the other
hand, most areas have a small-claims court where suits involving modest
amounts of money are heard. These courts don't use complex legal language or procedures, and you don't need a lawyer to use them. A store or
company will often settle with you—if your claim is fair—rather than go
to small-claims court.

Whether you complain over the phone, in person, or by letter, be   23
persistent. One complaint may not get results. In that case, keep on complaining, and make sure you keep complaining to the same person. Chances
are he or she will get worn out and take care of the situation, if only to be
rid of you.

Someday, perhaps, the world will be free of the petty annoyances that   24
plague us all from time to time. Until then, however, toasters will break
down, stores will refuse to honor rainchecks, and bills will include items that
were never purchased. You can depend upon it—there will be grounds for
complaint. You might as well learn to be good at it.

Questions for Close Reading

MyWritingLab

1. What is the selection's thesis? Locate the sentence(s) in which Rego states her main idea. If she doesn't state the thesis explicitly, express it in your own words.
2. In Rego's opinion, what types of actions and statements are *not* helpful when making a complaint?
3. What should be included in a letter of complaint? What should be omitted?
4. What does Rego suggest doing if a complaint is ignored?

Questions About the Writer's Craft

1. **The pattern.** Is Rego's process analysis primarily directional or primarily informational? Explain. To what extent does Rego try to persuade readers to follow her process?
2. **Other patterns.** Where does Rego include *narrative* elements in her essay? What do these brief narratives add to the piece?
3. **Other patterns.** Numerous oppositions occur throughout the essay. How do these *contrasts* enliven the essay and help Rego persuade readers to adopt her suggestions?
4. Reread the essay, noting where Rego shifts point of view. Where does she use the second-person (*you*), the first-person-plural (*we*), and the third-person-plural (*they*) points of view? How does her use of multiple points of view add to the essay's effectiveness?

Writing Assignments Using Process Analysis as a Pattern of Development

1. Write an essay explaining to college students how to register—with someone in a position of authority—an effective complaint about a campus problem. You could show, for example, how to complain to a professor about a course's grading policy, to the bookstore manager about the markup on textbooks, to security about the poorly maintained college parking lots. Feel free to adapt some of Rego's recommendations, but be sure to invent several strategies of your own. In either case, provide—as Rego does—lively examples to illustrate the step-by-step procedure for registering an effective complaint with a specific authority figure on campus.
2. Rego argues that "people who go through the day in an eye-popping, vein-throbbing state of apoplectic rage don't win any prizes." But sometimes, getting mad can be appropriate—even productive. Write an essay explaining the best process for expressing anger effectively. Explain how to vent emotion safely, communicate the complaint in a nonthreatening way, encourage more honest interaction, and prompt change for the better. Illustrate the process by drawing upon your own experiences and observations.

Writing Assignment Combining Patterns of Development

3. Think about a service or product that failed to live up to your expectations. Perhaps you were disgruntled about your mechanic's car repair, a store's return policy, or a hotel's accommodations. Using Rego's suggestions, write a letter of complaint in which you *describe* the problem, convey confidence in the reader's ability to resolve the problem, and state your request for specific action. Remember that a firm but cordial tone will *persuade* your reader that you have legitimate grounds for seeking the resolution you propose.

Werner Gundersheimer

Director emeritus of the Folger Shakespeare Library in Washington, D.C., and former president of the National Humanities Alliance, Werner Gundersheimer has published extensively on Italian Renaissance art and culture. He is a graduate of both Amherst College and Harvard University and has taught at the University of Wisconsin, the University of Pennsylvania, John Hopkins University, and Tel Aviv University. Gundersheimer is a member of the Executive Council of the American Jewish Historical Society and a member of the Board of Trustees for both the British Institute of America and The Medici Foundation.

Pre-Reading Journal Entry

MyWritingLab

In the reading that follows, Gundersheimer shares the process he went through in an effort to discover the secrets his mother kept and to try to understand why she kept those secrets from him. Think about discoveries you have made about people close to you and how you made those discoveries. Choose one such discovery and spend a few minutes writing about what prompted you to uncover the truth and how you found what you were looking for.

A Mother's Secret

We dance round in a ring and suppose,
But the Secret sits in the middle and knows.
    —Robert Frost

More than half a century ago, my mother gave me, as a college graduation present, an album of photographs illustrating my life from infancy through high school. The first page depicts my grandparents—my father's parents, shown together early in their marriage, probably around 1902. In this photo, the young Sophie gazes to her left at her gorgeous new   1

husband, Samuel, resplendent with handlebar mustache and elegant white bow tie, as he looks off to his left into the middle distance. Below them on the page are small, separate images of Mother's parents, Anna and Siegfried Siegel, in middle age, looking directly at the camera, engaging the viewer with their solemn expressions. Their pictures were taken around 1940. The next pages depict a standard middle-class European childhood, except that the scene keeps changing—from Frankfurt to London to a village in the English countryside to Cambridge to Weekapaugh, Rhode Island, then on to Wolfeboro, Ossipee, and Henniker, New Hampshire, and eventually various places in greater Philadelphia.

Surrounding the carefully mounted photographs that chronicle that   2
odyssey are brief texts in my mother's hand. The tone is light and humorous, as if she were describing her own progress toward adulthood in a placid German village. "First sunbath," "Isn't life beautiful?" "You are learning to walk," "What fun with mother's gloves," "We have a picknick," "Your first girlfriend," and so on. It's as if what actually happened had never happened. Reading through this lovingly constructed, almost idyllic narrative of a beautiful childhood, one would be hard-pressed to deduce that our little nuclear family had gotten out of Germany by the skin of our teeth in August 1939, lost just about everything but our lives, lived as transients in England through that first bitter winter of war, arrived in New York in May 1940 with exactly $30; or that in the course of our first American summer,

my parents somehow persuaded themselves to place me in foster care with a Congregational minister in New Hampshire for a year while they went to Pittsburgh, my father as a guest lecturer, my mother as a domestic servant.

I was deeply touched by this gift, so lovingly and thoughtfully constructed. This was the childhood my mother wanted me to think I'd had; and it is indeed a version of my actual childhood. But Mom's own memories were so devastating, and so close to the surface, that I couldn't bring myself to point out to her the irony of creating such a sanitized version of the past for a son who was about to head off to graduate school to become a professional historian, a child who—perhaps because of the denials and evasions of his early attempts to understand things—had an incurable itch to get to the bottom of those things. We all know that memory is selective, and that the mind blots out what it can't bear to retain. But that wasn't Mom's problem. For her, the past was always present, and the only way to keep it at bay was to steer clear of it. 3

That wasn't so obvious to me when I got the album. I saw it as a product of her choice—the way she chose to have me understand my childhood. Only later did I come to recognize that, for her, there had been no choice. She had to bury her past, and mine, along with its grim realities, its dreadful secrets. For example, the album's basic plot line is genealogical—it starts with the "begats." Yet after the first page, the grandparents practically disappear. On page three, there's a passport-size photo of Samuel, and one of Siegfried holding one-year-old me and my teddy bear. A few pages later there's a 16-line poem for my third birthday written and sent to me in England by my mother's parents in Germany. Composed in rhymed couplets, it conveys an almost fatalistic sense of resignation that they might be forgotten, despite the photographs they enclosed with the poem. Indeed, that was their last appearance in the album. They simply vanish, like Grandfather Samuel, who had died in September 1939 of a botched operation at a Jewish hospital in Frankfurt. Grandmother Sophie reappears briefly a bit later, in the fall of 1946, at the age of 71, having spent the intervening years in Jerusalem, now an old lady in black with a somber black hat. That's it for her—she's never mentioned again, nor is there any allusion to the fact that she lived with us for three years and then spent the rest of her life with my aunt and uncle in London. Why had she come, and why did she silently vanish? 4

Some survivors can talk freely about their experiences; others prefer silence. Whether you fall into the first or second group has nothing to do with wanting to get on with your life after the trauma is past. Everyone wants to get on with life, even though the trauma is never past. Mother read Elie Wiesel and Primo Levi,[1] but she couldn't imagine doing what 5

---

[1] Elie Wiesel, a Jewish-American born in Romania in 1928, has written about his experiences as a prisoner in Nazi concentration camps. Primo Levi (1919–1987) was a Jewish-Italian chemist and writer who wrote about his incarceration in the concentration camp at Auschwitz (editors' note).

they did—talking and writing about the experience of having survived, or evoking and re-presenting the attendant losses. Those were her private, even secret, griefs. Had she known them, she might have loved those great lines in *Richard II* in which the king realizes that there's nothing more that anyone can take away from him:

> You may my glories and my state depose,
> But not my griefs; still am I king of those. (4.1.192-93)

Mother got a postcard sometime in 1943. It reported that her mother, 6 whose letters from Frankfurt had stopped coming toward the end of 1941, had died on December 16, 1942, in the Theresienstadt[2] concentration camp. It wasn't until long after the war had ended that Mother found out what had happened to her father. He survived Theresienstadt only to be shipped in a transport to Auschwitz-Birkenau in May 1944. Further details were unavailable.

These are not the kinds of events one would want to incorporate, or 7 even think of including, in a beloved child's photo album. But one might suppose that a moment could arrive—perhaps 30, or 40, or 50 years later— when it would feel right to speak to one's children of these tragic matters. Mother lived to be almost 94, but for her, that moment never came. Hers remained a secret, unshared pain. Over the years, when I asked her about the fate of her parents, she just said that they had died in Theresienstadt. But eventually I went there and found in the archives exactly what had befallen each of them, and when. By then I was in my 50s, and she was about 80. My impression was that Mother wasn't fully apprised of the facts I had turned up and would want to know them. So after my return from the Czech Republic, I told her that I'd found the full documentation for both of my long-deceased grandparents.

"Yes," she said. "I know all that." 8

"Even the train and boxcar numbers of Siegfried's deportation?" 9 I asked.

She thought she had seen that information. It was clear that this wasn't 10 a subject she wished to pursue.

August 7, 2010, would have been mother's 100th birthday. She was born 11 under Kaiser Wilhelm,[3] well before the First World War. When she was a little girl, her father fought in that war and came home to his wholesale wine business

---

[2]Theresienstadt and Auschwitz-Birkenau were two of the World War II Nazi concentration camps in which six million Jews, as well as others considered "undesirable" (for example, gays and lesbians, and Romani people), were exterminated in what came to be known as the Holocaust (editors' note).
[3]Kaiser Wilhelm (1859–1941) served as emperor of Germany from 1888 until the end of World War I (editors' note).

as a decorated veteran. She grew up in Weimar Germany,[4] remembered the great inflation, endured the moment when Jewish girls were segregated out of high school, witnessed the rise of Nazism, suffered the destruction of home and family, married and had a child in the face of all that, and then managed to get out at the urging of her parents, who knew full well there would be no place for themselves outside Germany. That was a burden she would carry in silence all the days of her life, a burden she chose not to share with her children. After her death, I found in the filing cabinet in her apartment a collection of letters from my grandparents to my parents. The series begins on September 15, 1940, and ends with a postcard dated November 24, 1941. There is also a letter from my parents to my grandparents, dated December 19, 1941, which never reached its destination. It was sent back with the notation "Service suspended—return to sender." America had entered the war.[5] There was to be no further contact. Although she preserved them scrupulously, my mother never mentioned these letters. They document the growing hardship, terror, and longing of a single, aging couple in just one German city, a moving folder in the secret archive of this very private woman's past.

Surprisingly, there was an unexpected limit to Mom's secrecy. Among the online resources concerning victims of the Shoah[6] is the website of Yad Vashem, the memorial and research center in Jerusalem. On a historian's hunch, I consulted it not long ago, to see whether its Central Database of Shoah Victims' Names contained any information I hadn't already found on Anna and Siegfried Siegel. They were both there. But to my astonishment, all the basic information on their deportation and their deaths had been supplied not once, but on two occasions seven years apart during the 1980s, by my mother. She had even turned over the photographs my grandparents had enclosed with their poem for my third birthday. The very fact that she had done this was yet another secret she took to her grave.

12

---

[4]The Weimar Republic is the name given by historians to the federal republic that replaced the imperial form of government in Germany after World War I (editors' note).
[5]The United States entered World War II days after the Japanese attack on Pearl Harbor on December 7, 1941 (editors' note).
[6]*Shoah* is the Hebrew name for the Holocaust.

Questions for Close Reading

MyWritingLab

1. **Thesis.** What is the selection's thesis? Locate the sentence(s) in which Gundersheimer states his main idea. If he doesn't state the thesis explicitly, express it in your own words.

2. What photos appear on the first page of the album Gundersheimer's mother gave him as a college graduation present? How do the two sets of photos on the page differ? On the basis of the information included in the essay, what might account for those differences?

3. What does Gundersheimer reveal regarding the relationship between his personal history and his choice of careers?
4. What secret about his mother does Gundersheimer discover after her death?

Questions About the Writer's Craft

1. **The pattern.** What type of process analysis does Gundersheimer use in this essay—directional or informational? How does the first-person point of view support the pattern of development?
2. **The pattern.** Skim back over the essay and make notes as you read to help you chart the process Gundersheimer went through in his efforts to uncover his mother's secrets. As you read, make a list of the discoveries he makes and the order in which he makes them.
3. **Other patterns.** What do you think the author hopes to achieve by starting the essay with a photo and a detailed *description* of the album his mother gave him? Is he successful? What role does *narration* play in the essay?
4. In the second paragraph, Gundersheimer describes the tone his mother used in the brief texts she includes in the album she made for him. How does the tone Gundersheimer uses in his essay differ from that used by his mother in the album?

Writing Assignments Using Process Analysis as a Pattern of Development

1. Gundersheimer shares the process he went through as he set about trying to uncover the secrets his mother kept from him over the years. Think of a time when you were determined to get to the bottom of something that was a mystery to you. For example, perhaps you were determined to find out more about your family tree—to see how far back you could trace your ancestry. Or perhaps you wanted to learn more about your grandfather's experiences when he fought in Vietnam or the great aunt you never met who was rumored to be the black sheep of the family. Write an essay in which you describe the process you went through in an effort to uncover the truth.
2. While those trying to uncover secrets go through a process, so do those who are trying to cover their tracks. Write an essay in which you focus on the steps a public figure took to try to hide the truth about his or her unsavory conduct. If no one immediately comes to mind, a few minutes of research will provide you with a long list of individuals from whom you might choose. Conduct additional research as needed to write an interesting, well-documented essay.

Writing Assignment Combining Patterns of Development

3. Gundersheimer speculates that his mother kept silent about her secret pain because "the only way to keep it at bay was to steer clear of it." On the other hand, he acknowledges that some people find relief in writing or talking about painful events in their lives. In what different ways do people deal with difficult memories? Write an essay in which you give *examples* of different coping techniques. *Describe* one technique and *explain* the effects of using it. If possible, include a brief *narrative* of your or someone else's experience with the technique. Interview friends and family or do Internet research to develop your ideas.

Additional Writing Topics

PROCESS ANALYSIS

MyWritingLab

General Assignments

Using process analysis, develop one of these topics into an essay.

Directional: How to Do Something

1. How to drive defensively
2. How to improve the place where you work or study
3. How to relax
4. How to show appreciation to others
5. How to get through school despite personal problems

Informational: How Something Happens

1. How a student becomes burned out
2. How a dead thing decays (or some other natural process)
3. How humans choose a mate
4. How a bad habit develops
5. How people fall into debt

Assignments Using Visuals

Use the suggested visuals to help develop a process analysis essay on one of these topics:

1. Making it through freshman year without gaining the "Freshman 15" (photos)
2. Juggling school, friends, relationships, and a job (pie chart)
3. Deciding on the right career path to your dream job (web links)
4. The evolution of the national parks system (web links)
5. Becoming a successful entrepreneur (diagrams or links to videos)

Assignments with a Specific Purpose, Audience, and Point of View

1. **Academic life.** As an experienced campus tour guide for prospective students, you've been asked by your school's Admissions Office to write a pamphlet explaining to new tour guides how to conduct a tour of your school's campus. When explaining the process, keep in mind that tour guides need to portray the school in its best light.
2. **Academic life.** You write an "advice to the lovelorn" column for the campus newspaper. A correspondent writes saying that he or she wants to break up with a steady girlfriend/boyfriend but doesn't know how to do it without hurting the person. Give the writer guidance on how to end a meaningful relationship with a minimal amount of pain.

3. **Civic activity.** To help a sixteen-year-old friend learn how to drive, explain a specific driving maneuver one step at a time. You might, for example, describe how to make a three-point turn, parallel park, or handle a skid. Remember, your friend lacks self-confidence and experience.
4. **Civic activity.** Your best friend plans to move into his or her own apartment but doesn't know the first thing about how to choose one. Explain the process of selecting an apartment—where to look, what to investigate, what questions to ask before signing a lease.
5. **Workplace action.** As a staff writer for a consumer magazine, you've been asked to write an article on how to shop for a certain product. Give specific steps explaining how to save money, buy a quality product, and the like.
6. **Workplace action.** An author of books for elementary school children, you want to show children how to do something—take care of a pet, get along with siblings, keep a room clean. Explain the process in terms a child would understand yet not find condescending.

MyWritingLab Visit Chapter 7, "Process Analysis," in MyWritingLab to complete the chapter activities, Pre-Reading Journal Entry activities, Questions for Close Reading, and Additional Writing Topics assignments and to test your understanding of the chapter objectives.

COMPARISON-CONTRAST

In this chapter, you will learn:

8.1 To use the pattern of comparison-contrast to develop your essays.

8.2 To consider how comparison-contrast can fit your purpose and audience.

8.3 To develop strategies for using comparison-contrast in an essay.

8.4 To develop strategies for revising a comparison-contrast essay.

8.5 To analyze how comparison-contrast is used effectively in student-written and professionally authored selections.

8.6 To write your own essays using comparison-contrast as a strategy.

WHAT IS COMPARISON-CONTRAST?

Seeing how things are alike (comparing) and how they are different (contrasting) helps us impose meaning on experiences that otherwise might remain fragmented and disconnected. Barely aware that we're comparing and contrasting, we may think, "I woke up in a great mood this morning, but now I feel uneasy and anxious. I wonder why I feel so different." This inner questioning, which may occur in a flash, is just one example of how we use comparison and contrast to understand ourselves and our world.

Comparing and contrasting also help us make choices. We compare and contrast everything—from two brands of soap we might buy to two colleges we might attend. We listen to a favorite radio station, watch a preferred nightly news show, select a particular dessert from a menu—all because we have done some degree of comparing and contrasting. We often weigh these alternatives in an unstudied, casual manner, as when we flip from one radio station to another. But when we have to make important decisions, we tend to think rigorously about how things are alike or different: Should I live in a dorm or rent an apartment? Should I accept the higher-paying job or the lower-paying one that offers more challenges? Such a deliberate approach to comparison-contrast may also provide us with needed insight into complex contemporary issues: Is television's coverage of political campaigns more or less objective than it used to be? What are the merits of the various positions on abortion?

HOW COMPARISON-CONTRAST FITS YOUR PURPOSE AND AUDIENCE

Comparison-contrast works well if you want to demonstrate any of the following: (1) that one thing is better than another (the first example that follows); (2) that things which seem different are actually alike (the second example that follows); (3) that things which seem alike are actually different (the third example that follows).

> Compare and contrast the way male and female relationships are depicted in *Cosmopolitan, Ms., Playboy,* and *Esquire.* Which publication has the most limited view of men and women? Which has the broadest perspective?

> Football, basketball, and baseball differ in how they appeal to fans. Describe the unique drawing power of each sport, but also reach some conclusions about the appeals the three sports have in common.

> Studies show that both college students and their parents feel that post-secondary education should equip young people to succeed in the marketplace. Yet the same studies report that the two groups have a very different understanding of what it means to succeed. What differences do you think the studies identify?

Other assignments will, in less obvious ways, lend themselves to comparison-contrast. For instance, although terms like *compare, contrast, differ,* and *have in common* don't appear in the following assignments, essay responses could be organized around the comparison-contrast format:

> The emergence of the two-career family is one of the major phenomena of our culture. Discuss the advantages and disadvantages of having both parents work, showing how you feel about such two-career households.

Some people believe that the 1950s, often called the golden age of television, produced several never-to-be-equaled comedy classics. Do you agree that such shows as *I Love Lucy* and *The Honeymooners* are superior to the situation comedies aired on television today?

There has been considerable criticism recently of the news coverage by the city's two leading newspapers, *The Herald* and *The Beacon*. Indicate whether you think the criticism is valid by discussing the similarities and differences in the two papers' news coverage.

Note: The last assignment shows that a comparison-contrast essay may cover similarities *and* differences, not just one or the other.

As you have seen, comparison-contrast can be the key strategy for achieving an essay's purpose. But comparison-contrast can also be a supplemental method used to help make a point in an essay organized chiefly around another pattern of development. A serious, informative essay intended for laypeople might *define* clinical depression by contrasting that state of mind with ordinary run-of-the-mill blues. Writing humorously about the exhausting *effects* of trying to get in shape, you might dramatize your plight for readers by contrasting the leisurely way you used to spend your day with your current rigidly compulsive exercise regimen. Or, in an urgent *argumentation-persuasion* essay on the need for stricter controls over drug abuse in the workplace, you might provide readers with background by comparing several companies' approaches to the problem.

STRATEGIES FOR USING COMPARISON-CONTRAST IN AN ESSAY

The suggestions here and in Figure 8.1 (page 312) will be helpful whether you use comparison-contrast as a dominant or a supportive pattern of development.

1. Be sure your subjects are at least somewhat alike.   Unless you plan to develop an *analogy* (see information on *analogies* that follows in item #2), the subjects you choose to compare or contrast should share some obvious characteristics or qualities. It makes sense to compare different parts of the country, two comedians, or several college teachers. But a reasonable essay wouldn't result from, let's say, a comparison of a television game show with a soap opera. Your subjects must belong to the same general group so that your comparison-contrast stays within good logical bounds and doesn't veer off into pointlessness.

2. Stay focused on your purpose.   When writing, remember that comparison-contrast isn't an end in itself. That is, your objective isn't to turn an essay into a mechanical list of "how A differs from B" or "how A is like B."

FIGURE 8.1
Development Diagram: Writing a Comparison-Contrast Essay

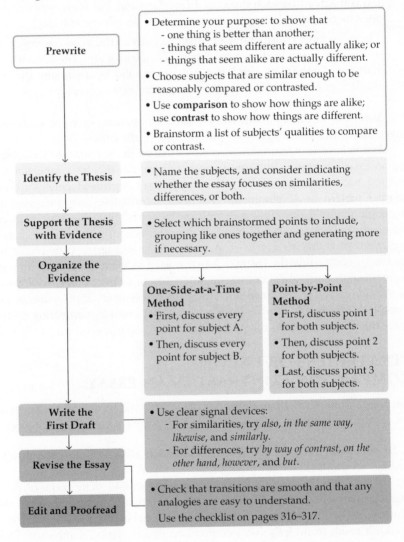

Like the other patterns of development discussed in this book, comparison-contrast is a strategy for making a point or meeting a larger purpose.

Consider the assignment on page 311 about the two newspapers. Your purpose here might be simply to *inform*, to present information as objectively as possible: "This is what *The Herald*'s news coverage is like. This is what *The Beacon*'s news coverage is like."

More frequently, though, you'll use comparison-contrast to *evaluate* your subjects' pros and cons, your goal being to reach a conclusion or make a judgment: "Both *The Herald* and *The Beacon* spend too much time reporting local news," or "*The Herald*'s analysis of the recent hostage crisis was more insightful than *The Beacon*'s." Comparison-contrast can also be used to *persuade* readers to take action: "People interested in thorough coverage of international events should read *The Herald* rather than *The Beacon*." Persuasive essays may also propose a change, contrasting what now exists with a more ideal situation: "For *The Beacon* to compete with *The Herald*, it must assign more reporters to international stories."

Yet another purpose you might have is to *clear up misconceptions* by revealing previously hidden similarities or differences. For example, perhaps your town's two newspapers are thought to be sharply different. A comparison-contrast analysis might reveal that—although one paper specializes in sensationalized stories whereas the other adopts a more muted approach—both resort to biased, emotionally charged analyses of local politics.

Comparing and contrasting also make it possible to *draw an analogy* between two seemingly unrelated subjects. An analogy is an imaginative comparison that delves beneath the surface differences of subjects to expose their significant and often unsuspected similarities or differences. Your purpose may be to show that singles bars and zoos share a number of striking similarities. The analogical approach can make a complex subject easier to understand—as when the national deficit is compared to a household budget gone awry.

3. Formulate a strong thesis.   Your essay should be focused by a solid thesis. Besides revealing your attitude, the thesis may do the following:

- Name the subjects being compared and contrasted.
- Indicate whether the essay focuses on the subjects' similarities, differences, or both.
- State the essay's main point of comparison or contrast.

Not all comparison-contrast essays need thesis statements as structured as those that follow. Even so, these examples can serve as models of clarity. Note that the first thesis statement signals similarities, the second differences, and the last both similarities and differences:

Middle-aged parents are often in a good position to empathize with adolescent children because the emotional upheavals experienced by the two age groups are much the same.

The priorities of most retired people are more conducive to health and happiness than the priorities of most young professionals.

College students in their thirties and forties face many of the same pressures as younger students, but they are better equipped to withstand these pressures.

4. Select the points to be discussed. Once you have identified the essay's subjects, purpose, and thesis, you need to decide which aspects of the subjects to compare or contrast. College professors, for instance, could be compared and contrasted on the basis of their testing methods, ability to motivate students, confidence in front of a classroom, personalities, level of enthusiasm, and so forth.

Brainstorming, freewriting, and mapping are valuable for gathering possible points to cover. Whichever prewriting technique you use, try to produce more raw material than you'll need, so that you have the luxury of narrowing the material down to the most significant points.

When selecting points to cover, be sure to consider your audience. Ask yourself: "Will my readers be familiar with this item? Will I need it to get my message across? Will my audience find this item interesting or convincing?" What your readers know, what they don't know, and what you can predict about their reactions should influence your choices. And, of course, you need to select points that support your thesis. If your essay explains the differences between healthy, sensible diets and dangerous crash diets, it wouldn't be appropriate to talk about aerobic exercise.

5. Organize the points to be discussed. There are two common ways to organize an essay developed wholly or in part by comparison-contrast: the one-side-at-a-time method and the point-by-point method. Although both strategies may be used in a paper, one method usually predominates.

In the *one-side-at-a-time method* of organization, you discuss everything relevant about one subject before moving to another subject. For example, responding to the previous assignment that asked you to analyze the news coverage in two local papers, you might first talk about *The Herald*'s coverage of international, national, and local news; then you would discuss *The Beacon*'s coverage of the same categories. Note that the areas discussed should be the same for both newspapers. Moreover, the areas compared and contrasted should be presented in the same order.

This is how you would organize the essay using the one-side-at-a-time method.

Everything about A   *The Herald*'s news coverage
                            • International
                            • National
                            • Local

Everything about B   *The Beacon's* news coverage
- International
- National
- Local

In the *point-by-point method* of organization, you alternate from one aspect of the first subject to the same aspect of your other subject(s). For example, you would first discuss *The Herald's* international coverage, then *The Beacon's* international coverage; next *The Herald's* national coverage, then *The Beacon's*; and finally, *The Herald's* local coverage, then *The Beacon's*.

Using the point-by-point method, this is how the essay would be organized.

First aspect of A and B   *The Herald:* International coverage
                                 The Beacon: International coverage

Second aspect of A and B   *The Herald:* National coverage
                                 The Beacon: National coverage

Third aspect of A and B   *The Herald:* Local coverage
                                 The Beacon: Local coverage

Deciding which of these two methods of organization to use is largely a personal choice, though there are several factors to consider. The one-side-at-a-time method tends to convey a more unified feeling because it highlights broad similarities and differences. It is, therefore, an effective approach for subjects that are fairly uncomplicated. This strategy also works well when essays are brief; the reader won't find it difficult to remember what has been said about subject A when reading about subject B.

Because the point-by-point method permits more extensive coverage of similarities and differences, it is often a wise choice when subjects are complex. This pattern is also useful for lengthy essays because readers would probably find it difficult to remember, let's say, ten pages of information about subject A while reading the next ten pages about subject B. The point-by-point approach, however, may cause readers to lose sight of the broader picture, so remember to keep them focused on your central point.

6. Supply the reader with clear transitions. Although a well-organized comparison-contrast format is important, it doesn't guarantee that readers will be able to follow your line of thought easily. *Transitions*—especially those signaling similarities or differences—are needed to show readers where they have been and where they are going. Such cues are essential in all writing, but they're especially crucial in a paper using comparison-contrast.

By indicating clearly when subjects are being compared or contrasted, the transitions help weave the discussion into a coherent whole.

The transitions (in boldface) in the following examples would *signal similarities* in an essay on the news coverage in *The Herald* and *The Beacon:*

- *The Beacon* **also** allots only a small portion of the front page to global news.
- **In the same way,** *The Herald* tries to include at least three local stories on the first page.
- **Likewise,** *The Beacon* emphasizes the importance of up-to-date reporting of town meetings.
- *The Herald* is **similarly** committed to extensive coverage of high school and college sports.

The transitions (in boldface) in the following examples would *signal differences:*

- **By way of contrast,** *The Herald'*s editorial page deals with national matters on the average of three times a week.
- **On the other hand,** *The Beacon* does not share *The Herald'*s enthusiasm for interviews with national figures.
- *The Beacon,* **however,** does not encourage its reporters to tackle national stories the way *The Herald* does.
- **But** *The Herald'*s coverage of the Washington scene is much more comprehensive than its competitor's.

REVISION STRATEGIES

Once you have a draft of the essay, you're ready to revise. The following checklist will help you and those giving you feedback apply to comparison-contrast some of the, revision techniques discussed in Chapter 2.

☑ COMPARISON-CONTRAST: A REVISION/PEER REVIEW CHECKLIST

Revise Overall Meaning and Structure

❏ Are the subjects sufficiently alike for the comparison-contrast to be logical and meaningful?

❏ What purpose does the essay serve—to inform, to evaluate, to persuade readers to accept a viewpoint, to eliminate misconceptions, or to draw a surprising analogy?

❏ What is the essay's thesis? How could the thesis be stated more effectively?

❏ Is the overall essay organized primarily by the one-side-at-a-time method or by the point-by-point method? Why is that the best strategy for this essay?

❏ Are the same features discussed for each subject? Are they discussed in the same order?

❏ Which points of comparison and/or contrast need further development? Which points should be deleted? Where do significant points seem to be missing? How has the most important similarity or difference been emphasized?

Revise Paragraph Development

❏ If the essay uses the one-side-at-a-time method, which paragraph marks the switch from one subject to another?

❏ If the essay uses the point-by-point method, do paragraphs consistently alternate between subjects? If this alternation becomes too elaborate or predictable, what could be done to eliminate the problem?

❏ If the essay uses both methods, which paragraph marks the switch from one method to the other? If the switch is confusing, how could it be made less so?

❏ Where would signal devices make it easier to see similarities and differences between the subjects being discussed?

Revise Sentences and Words

❏ Where do too many signal devices make sentences awkward and mechanical?

❏ Which sentences and words fail to convey the intended tone?

STUDENT ESSAY

The following student essay was written by Blake Norman in response to this assignment:

> In "Euromail and Amerimail," Eric Weiner, a former foreign correspondent for NPR who has traveled widely, compares and contrasts European and American e-mail styles. He writes about a subject he knows well from his own experiences, and he also incorporates outside sources to support his assertions. Write an essay about a subject

you are familiar with from your own experience. As Weiner does, incorporate several outside sources into your essay. For example, you might choose to write about a hobby you enjoy, comparing various types of equipment or supplies needed to effectively participate in that pastime, or you might write about a purchase you are considering making and compare your various options, using information from outside sources for added support.

Buying a Cross-Country Mountain Bike
by Blake Norman

Introduction	Cross-country mountain bike racing has become 1 increasingly popular over the past couple of decades. It offers an enjoyable way for people to exercise their heart as well as other muscles. An added benefit is the chance to join a biking club and meet new people. One result of this popularity is that there are more bikes than ever before on the market. There are also many factors that consumers need to consider if they are thinking about purchasing one of them. Consumers should get information about minor features, such as brakes, saddle, seatpost, and stem length. However, to find the right
Thesis	cross-country bike, beginning bikers need to consider how the bike's major features—suspension and wheel size, as well as weight, stiffness, and price—suit their biking habits.
Topic sentence	A bike's suspension determines how smoothly it rides. 2 The Vital MTB website features 926 bikes and explains that
First factor to consider— suspension types compared	cross-country mountain bikes "come in two varieties—full-suspension or hardtail." Full-suspension bikes offer a smoother ride than do hardtail bikes, which have only front suspension. However, many riders claim that hardtail bikes travel faster without the added suspension.
Topic sentence	Wheel size is the next factor to consider in buying a 3 cross-country bike. The Vital MTB website explains that cross-country mountain bikes come in 26-inch and 29-inch wheel
Second factor to consider—wheel sizes compared	sizes and that the tires are "relatively skinny . . . and are made to roll fast." Bikes with larger wheels are more stable than smaller-wheeled bikes, so they tend to climb better and descend better. Also, larger wheels, which are becoming more popular, are less likely than smaller wheels to fall into potholes on a trail.
Topic sentence serving as a transition	In addition to deciding on the type of suspension and 4 wheel size, consumers also need to consider the weight, stiffness, and price of the bike. These features vary by type of
Introduction to third, fourth, and fifth factors to consider	material used in the frame—aluminum alloy, steel, titanium, or carbon fiber. Table 1 compares the different frame materials by weight, stiffness, and price.

Table summarizing
information on
frame material

TABLE 1
Cross-Country Bike Features by Frame Material

Feature	Aluminum alloy	Steel	Titanium	Carbon fiber
Weight	Light	Heaviest; most durable	Light; strong	Lightest; least durable
Stiffness	Moderately stiff	Stiffest	Moderately stiff	Depends on bike design
Price	Moderately expensive	Least expensive	Very expensive	Most expensive
Best use	Popular with a range of riders	Good for entry-level bikers	Used in high-end and custom bikes	Used by serious bikers and racers

Topic sentence ———▸ The weight of a cross-country mountain racing bike   5
is especially important to consider because a heavy bike
will slow bikers down when they are racing. The majority of
Third factor to   cross-country bikes are made of aluminum alloy. It is more
consider—weights   expensive than steel, but it's lighter. Some manufacturers
of frame materials   have higher-end, lighter aluminum frames that are more
compared   expensive. Titanium frames are light and strong, but are very
                       expensive and are used primarily on high-end bikes. Carbon
Evaluative state-   fiber is light and strong, but manufacturing it is very labor-
ment that brings   intensive. Because of this, carbon fiber frames are primarily
the paragraph to   used by enthusiasts and racers. Also carbon-fiber frames are
closure   lighter than all other types of frames.
Topic sentence ———▸ Stiffness is definitely an aspect that individuals need to   6
take into account when deciding on a bike for cross-country
mountain racing because a bike that is stiff will have a better
Fourth factor to   pedaling efficiency. Stiffness controls how much a bike will
consider—stiffness   resist twisting, especially in rough terrain. Aluminum alloy
of frame materials   frames can be very stiff and also light. In comparison, steel
compared   frames are stiff but may be too heavy for experienced riders.
                       Titanium frames can be both stiff and strong, but they are
Evaluative state-   not as strong as steel and are expensive to repair. Carbon-
ment that brings   fiber frames can be the stiffest of all bike frames ("Material").
the paragraph to ——▸ As bikers become more experienced, their appreciation for a
closure   bike frame's stiffness increases.

Topic sentence ──────▸Cross-country mountain bikes come in a wide range of   7
prices. Vital MTB's "Mountain Bike Buyer's Guide" states,
"In general, the more expensive a bike is, the more durable it
will be (at least until you start getting into the high-end where
lightweight construction may reduce durability)." It's important to keep in mind, of course, that one of the main purposes
of the site that makes this claim is to sell bikes and make
Fifth factor to   money; but even so, the claim makes good sense. On the other
consider—prices   hand, there is a lot of truth to the old saying "You get what you
compared   pay for." The site recommends that those who plan to ride on
a regular basis spend a minimum of $900 on a bike. Prices of
bikes they feature range from $330 for the 2013 GT Palomar
GTW model (steel frame, 26-inch tires) to $11,000 for the 2013
Cannondal Scalpel 29er Carbon Ultimate model (carbon frame,
29-inch tires), and there are 924 bikes with prices between
these two extremes.

Topic sentence ──────▸Deciding on the right mountain bike will take some   8
time and effort, but the more thinking and research consumers do before making a purchase, the smarter their choice is
likely to be. Although it appears that the weight and stiffness
of bikes made from carbon fiber make them better choices
than those constructed of aluminum alloy, steel, or tita-
Conclusion   nium, the choice should depend on both the biker's budget
and on how the person plans to use the bike. Readers can
consult the "Best use" row in Table 1, but consumers must
ask themselves these questions: How much can I afford to
spend? How often do I plan to ride? Do I plan to ride in competitive racing events or primarily with friends for fun and
Concluding state-   relaxation? What kinds of trails do I plan to ride on—smooth
ment that brings the or rocky? flat or steep? Once beginning bikers think through
essay to closure ──── these issues and do some research, they will be ready to purchase the cross-country mountain bike that is the best fit.

Works Cited

"Material Assets." *The CARE Exchange*, May 2006, www.
caree.org/bike101framematerials.htm.

"Mountain Bike Buyers Guide." *Vital MTB*, 2014, www.vitalmtb.
com/product/category/Bikes,1.

COMMENTARY

Purpose and thesis. In his essay, Blake compares factors first-time buyers
should consider in buying a cross-country mountain bike—suspension, wheel
size, weight, stiffness, and price—and provides information that is valuable

for someone thinking about purchasing one. The *comparison-contrast* pattern allows him to analyze the drawbacks and merits of the various factors, thus providing the essay with an *evaluative purpose*. Using the title to let readers know that his essay will be useful to anyone interested in purchasing a cross country mountain bike, Blake places the *thesis* at the end of his introductory paragraph: "However, to find the right cross-country bike, beginning bikers need to consider how the bike's major features—suspension and wheel size, as well as weight, stiffness, and price—suit their biking habits." The thesis specifies the five factors to be discussed and indicates why Blake chose to focus on those five areas: they are the "major" features to be considered.

Overall organization.   Blake begins his essay by introducing the advantages of cross-country biking and its growing popularity. He distinguishes between "minor features" and "major features" in bikes and then goes on to state in his thesis statement the five major features that he will discuss. He then discusses the features one by one, comparing options for each feature, starting with two features—suspension and wheel size—that can be dealt with in self-contained paragraphs. Then he focuses on the remaining three features—weight, stiffness, and price, in that order—saving the discussion of price for the end because he thinks that feature will be the most significant one for beginning bikers. Throughout, Blake also uses signal devices ("However"; "in comparison"; "on the other hand") to make comparisons clear to his readers. Blake then moves on to his concluding paragraph and brings his essay to closure.

Paragraph development and sequence of points.   Blake generally uses a *point-by-point comparison method*. Blake's first two supporting paragraphs (paragraphs 2 and 3) are relatively short; each compares the options for a specific point—either suspension or wheel size. Then Blake includes a transitional paragraph in which he explains that he will discuss each remaining point in terms of four newly introduced subjects: "type of material used in the frame—aluminum alloy, steel, titanium, or carbon fiber." Because he must repeat the four subjects for each point, the three supporting paragraphs for weight, stiffness, and price are longer than the previous paragraphs and are of roughly equal length. Blake briefly considered using a *one-side-at-a-time comparison method*—devoting a paragraph to each type of frame material. However, he realized that he would have had difficulty fitting the discussion of suspension and wheel size into that comparison structure.

   In discussing the weight of bikes, Blake first explains why weight is an important factor and then goes on to compare the four types of materials from which cross-country mountain bikes are commonly built. He concludes this section of his essay with an evaluative statement: "carbon fiber frames are primarily used by enthusiasts and racers."

Using a similar structure in the next section of the essay in which he discusses the stiffness of bikes, Blake begins by explaining why stiffness is an important factor and then goes on to compare the four most common types of frame materials. As he did in the previous section, Blake concludes this section of his essay with evaluative statements: "As bikers become more experienced, their appreciation for a bike frame's stiffness increases" (6). He incorporates a quote from a biking website, with a parenthetical reference: ("Material").

The structure of the final supporting paragraph on price is somewhat different. Blake seems to assume that his readers will want to spend their money wisely and that there is no need to begin this paragraph with an explanation of why it is important to consider the price of the bike. Following the topic sentence for paragraph 7, "Cross-country mountain bikes come in a wide range of prices," Blake supplies information from the Vital MTB Mountain Bikes website, which recommends that those who plan to ride on a regular basis spend a minimum of $900 on a bike. Next, Blake indirectly explains why it is important to consider the price of the bike you purchase: "On the other hand, you get what you pay for." He concludes the paragraph with brief descriptions of Vital MTB's least expensive ($330) and most expensive ($11,000) bikes. The concluding paragraph reemphasizes Blake's main point—that consumers new to cross-country biking need to do research before buying—and supplies readers with a list of questions they can ask themselves to determine their biking needs.

Table.   Blake decided that his readers would benefit from a graphic that pulled together the important points he was making. He tried creating a table that included all five features. However, because he was not comparing suspension and wheel size by frame material, he soon realized that he could not include them in the table he had in mind. Blake also thought that the table would be a good place to give his evaluations, so he added a row labeled "Best use." He made sure that the reference to the table preceded the table itself in the essay.

Combining patterns of development.   To illustrate his points, Blake makes extensive use of *exemplification*, and his discussion also has elements typical of *causal analysis*: "Bikes with larger wheels are more stable than smaller-wheeled bikes, so they tend to climb better and descend" (3). In addition, he includes examples of various wheel sizes, frame materials, and prices of bikes, along with examples of the kinds of questions that should be considered before purchasing a cross-country mountain bike. He also traces the effect of various types of materials on the weight, stiffness, and price of bikes.

A problem with structure.   Blake begins the paragraph on price with a rather weak topic sentence ("Cross-country mountain bikes come in a wide range of prices") that says nothing about why it is important to carefully consider the price of bikes. Later in the paragraph, he implies that the buyer should not have high expectations of a less expensive model, but his essay could have been stronger had he begun with a clear explanation of why price is such an important element to consider. Also, although Blake included outside sources, his choice of sources might have been more reliable. One is a commercial website, which he admits has a bias. The other website is not commercial, but it was last updated in 2006. Blake did his own Internet research, but he might have benefitted from a librarian's help in finding sources.

Conclusion.   Blake's final paragraph does a nice job of bringing his essay to closure. Instead of simply restating his thesis and reminding readers of what he stated in his paper, Blake provides a series of questions that, if carefully considered, can help readers make informed, educated choices when buying a cross-country mountain bike: "How much can I afford to spend? How often do I plan to ride? Do I plan to ride in competitive racing events or primarily with friends for fun and relaxation? What kinds of trails do I plan to ride on—smooth or rocky? flat or steep?" These questions should prove most useful to anyone interested in purchasing a cross-country mountain bike, and the final sentence ("Once beginning bikers think through these issues and do some research, they will be ready to purchase the cross-country mountain bike that is the best fit"), should give them confidence that they can make a smart choice.

Revising the first draft.   Parts of Blake's first draft were radically different from the final draft he later submitted for a grade. Upon deciding on a topic for his essay, Blake, an avid cross-country mountain bike racer, thought that because he had purchased several mountain bikes over the years and had done some thinking about how he wanted to organize his essay, he could easily and quickly complete a first draft. Consequently, he did something most writers do at one time or another: He put off the writing until the night before the draft was due. After completing the first draft and quickly reading through it, he felt as if he had done a pretty good job.

The next morning Blake arrived at his classroom a few minutes early and spent the extra minutes reading over his draft again. As he re-read it, he realized that the draft was not as strong as he had thought it was the night before. For example, he realized that his introduction did not do a good job of engaging readers or of explaining the various kinds of issues that need to be considered when deciding what kind of cross-country mountain bike to purchase.

In class that morning, Blake shared his draft with Olivia and Gabby, the two classmates in his peer review group. He told them that he had put off the writing until the last minute, and that as a result, he had not had time to go back and give his essay the attention he knew it needed. You'll get a good sense of the kinds of revisions he made if you compare the original introduction printed here with the final version in the full essay.

Original Version of the Introduction

Cross-country mountain bike racing is one of the most popular forms of mountain bike racing. As a result there are many different types of bikes to choose from. A base-level rider may prefer to ride a fully carbon dual suspension bike whereas a pro-level racer may prefer to use an aluminum hard tail. The most important factors to consider in a bike are weight, stiffness, and price.

Blake already knew that his introduction was weak and that he needed to do a much better job of engaging the reader and explaining the various kinds of issues that need to be considered when deciding on what kind of cross-country mountain bike to purchase, but Olivia and Gabby provided him with additional insights. As the three of them read through the draft together, Olivia and Gabby, who knew very little about cross-country mountain bikes, asked Blake questions about what they would need to know if they were going to purchase a bike. Their questions and the explanations Blake gave them as they talked helped him gain a clearer picture of what he needed to do to make his draft stronger. As he talked with Olivia and Gabby, he explained to them that deciding on the right bike is complicated because there are so many factors to consider: full suspension or hardtail; the type of brakes, saddle, seatpost, and stem length; along with weight, stiffness, and price—which he considered most important of all.

Blake left his classroom that morning with a much clearer idea of the revisions he needed to make to clearly communicate his ideas to his readers. The combination of letting his writing sit for a while and talking about his draft with his Olivia and Gabby was exactly what Blake needed to be ready to improve his essay. His instructor's comments on his draft confirmed his ideas, and he revised his essay considerably before submitting his final draft.

Activities: Comparison-Contrast

MyWritingLab

Prewriting Activities

1. Imagine you're writing two essays: One explores the *effects* of holding a job while in college; the other explains a *process* for budgeting money wisely. Jot down ways you might use comparison-contrast in each essay.

2. Using your journal or freewriting, jot down the advantages and disadvantages of two ways of doing something (for example, watching movies in the theater versus watching them on a laptop; following trends versus ignoring them; dating

one person versus playing the field; and so on). Reread your prewriting and determine what your thesis, purpose, audience, tone, and point of view might be if you were to write an essay. Make a scratch list of the main ideas you would cover. Would a point-by-point or a one-side-at-a-time method of organization work more effectively?

Revising Activities

1. Of the statements that follow, which would *not* make effective thesis statements for comparison-contrast essays? Identify the problem(s) in the faulty statements and revise them accordingly.

   a. Although their classroom duties often overlap, teacher aides are not as equipped as teachers to handle disciplinary problems.
   b. This college provides more assistance to its students than most schools.
   c. During the state's last congressional election, both candidates relied heavily on television to communicate their messages.
   d. There are many differences between American and foreign cars.

2. The following paragraph is from the draft of an essay detailing the qualities of a skillful manager. How effective is this comparison-contrast paragraph? What revisions would help focus the paragraph on the point made in the topic sentence? Where should details be added or deleted? Rewrite the paragraph, providing necessary transitions and details.

   A manager encourages creativity and treats employees courteously, whereas a boss discourages staff resourcefulness and views it as a threat. At the hardware store where I work, I got my boss's approval to develop a system for organizing excess stock in the storeroom. I shelved items in roughly the same order as they were displayed in the store. The system was helpful to all the salespeople, not just to me, because everyone was stymied by the boss's helter-skelter system. What he did was store overstocked items according to each wholesaler, even though most of us weren't there long enough to know which items came from which wholesaler. His supposed system created chaos. When he saw what I had done, he was furious and insisted that we continue to follow the old slapdash system. I had assumed he would welcome my ideas the way my manager did last summer when I worked in a drugstore. But he didn't and I had to scrap my work and go back to his eccentric system. He certainly could learn something about employee relations from the drugstore manager.

Eric Weiner

Eric Weiner (1963–) is a national correspondent for NPR.org, part of National Public Radio. He began his journalism career by reporting on business issues for *The New York Times* and NPR's Washington, D.C., bureau and then spent most of the 1990s reporting on wars and world events from South Asia and the Middle East. A licensed pilot who loves to eat sushi, Weiner occasionally writes lighter pieces drawing on his experience with other cultures. He is the author of *The Geography of Bliss: One Grump's Search for the Happiest Places in the World* (2008). A short version of this piece about e-mail was broadcast on *Day to Day*, a National Public Radio magazine show, on March 24, 2005; the full version, which appears here, was posted on Slate.com the next day.

For ideas about how this comparison-contrast essay is organized, see Figure 8.2 on page 329.

Pre-Reading Journal Entry

MyWritingLab

Just one hundred years ago, people communicated only by speaking face to face or by writing a letter—with an occasional brief telegram in emergencies. Today, technology has given us many ways to communicate. Think over all the different ways you communicate with your family, friends, classmates, instructors, coworkers, and others. What methods of communication do you use with each of these groups? Which forms do you prefer, and why? Use your journal to answer these questions.

Euromail and Amerimail

North America and Europe are two continents divided by a common technology: e-mail. Techno-optimists assure us that e-mail—along with the Internet and satellite TV—make the world smaller. That may be true in a technical sense. I can send a message from my home in Miami to a German friend in Berlin and it will arrive almost instantly. But somewhere over the Atlantic, the messages get garbled. In fact, two distinct forms of e-mail have emerged: Euromail and Amerimail.

Amerimail is informal and chatty. It's likely to begin with a breezy "Hi" and end with a "Bye." The chances of Amerimail containing a smiley face or an "xoxo" are disturbingly high. We Americans are reluctant to dive into the meat of an e-mail; we feel compelled to first inform hapless recipients about our vacation on the Cape which was really excellent except the jellyfish were biting and the kids caught this nasty bug so we had to skip the whale watching trip but about that investors' meeting in New York ... Amerimail is a bundle of contradictions: rambling and yet direct; deferential, yet arrogant. In other words, Amerimail *is* America.

Euromail is stiff and cold, often beginning with a formal "Dear Mr. X" 3
and ending with a brusque "Sincerely." You won't find any mention of kids
or the weather or jellyfish in Euromail. It's also business. It's also slow. Your
correspondent might take days, even weeks, to answer a message. Euromail is
also less confrontational in tone, rarely filled with the overt nastiness that char-
acterizes American e-mail disagreements. In other words, Euromail is exactly
like the Europeans themselves. (I am, of course, generalizing. German e-mail
style is not exactly the same as Italian or Greek, but they have more in common with each other than they do with American mail.)

These are more than mere stylistic differences. Communication matters. 4
Which model should the rest of the world adopt: Euromail or Amerimail?

A California-based e-mail consulting firm called People-onthego sheds 5
some light on the e-mail divide. It recently asked about 100 executives on
both sides of the Atlantic whether they noticed differences in e-mail styles.
Most said yes. Here are a few of their observations:

> "Americans tend to write (e-mails) exactly as they speak."
> "Europeans are less obsessive about checking e-mail."
> "In general, Americans are much more responsive to email—
> they respond faster and provide more information."

One respondent noted that Europeans tend to segregate their e-mail
accounts. Rarely do they send personal messages on their business
accounts, or vice versa. These differences can't be explained merely by
differing comfort levels with technology. Other forms of electronic communication, such as SMS text messaging, are more popular in Europe than
in the United States.

The fact is, Europeans and Americans approach e-mail in a fundamen- 6
tally different way. Here is the key point: For Europeans, e-mail has replaced
the business letter. For Americans, it has replaced the telephone. That's
why we tend to unleash what e-mail consultant Tim Burress calls a "brain
dump": unloading the content of our cerebral cortex onto the screen and
hitting the send button. "It makes Europeans go ballistic," he says.

Susanne Khawand, a German high-tech executive, has been on the 7
receiving end of American brain dumps, and she says it's not pretty. "I feel
like saying, 'Why don't you just call me instead of writing five e-mails
back and forth,'" she says. Americans are so overwhelmed by their bulging
inboxes that "you can't rely on getting an answer. You don't even know if
they read it." In Germany, she says, it might take a few days, or even weeks,
for an answer, but one always arrives.

Maybe that's because, on average, Europeans receive fewer e-mails and 8
spend less time tending their inboxes. An international survey of business
owners in 24 countries (conducted by the accounting firm Grant Thornton)

found that people in Greece and Russia spend the least amount of time dealing with e-mail every day: 48 minutes on average. Americans, by comparison, spend two hours per day, among the highest in the world. (Only Filipinos spend more time on e-mail, 2.1 hours.) The survey also found that European executives are skeptical of e-mail's ability to boost their bottom line.

It's not clear why European and American e-mail styles have evolved   9
separately, but I suspect the reasons lie within deep cultural differences. Americans tend to be impulsive and crave instant gratification. So we send e-mails rapid-fire and get antsy if we don't receive a reply quickly. Europeans tend to be more methodical and plodding. They send (and reply to) e-mails only after great deliberation.

For all their Continental fastidiousness, Europeans can be remarkably   10
lax about e-mail security, says Bill Young, an executive vice president with the Strickland Group. Europeans are more likely to include trade secrets and business strategies in e-mails, he says, much to the frustration of their American colleagues. This is probably because identity theft—and other types of backing—are much less of a problem in Europe than in the United States. Privacy laws are much stricter in Europe.

So, which is better: Euromail or Amerimail? Personally, I'm a convert—   11
or a defector, if you prefer—to the former. I realize it's not popular these days to suggest we have anything to learn from Europeans, but I'm fed up with an inbox cluttered with rambling, barely cogent missives from friends and colleagues. If the alternative is a few stiffly written, politely worded bits of Euromail, then I say ... bring it on.

Questions for Close Reading   MyWritingLab

1. What is the selection's thesis? Locate the sentence(s) in which Weiner states his main idea. If he doesn't state his thesis explicitly, express it in your own words.
2. According to Weiner, what are the main characteristics of American e-mail? What are the main characteristics of European e-mail?
3. When Americans and Europeans e-mail one another for business reasons, frustration often ensues. Why, according to Weiner, is this so? What are some examples of e-mail differences that cause frustration?
4. Which type of e-mail does Weiner favor? Why?

Questions About the Writer's Craft

1. The opening paragraph of this essay is full of technology-related words: *technology, e-mail, techno-optimists, Internet, Satellite TV, technical sense, Euromail,* and *Amerimail.* What is the effect of using all these "techno-terms"? How does the remainder of the essay contrast with the dominant impression of the first paragraph?
2. **The Pattern.** What type of organization does Weiner use for the essay? How else could he have organized the points he makes? Which method of organization do you think is more effective for this essay?

FIGURE 8.2

Essay Structure Diagram: "Euromail and Amerimail" by Eric Weiner

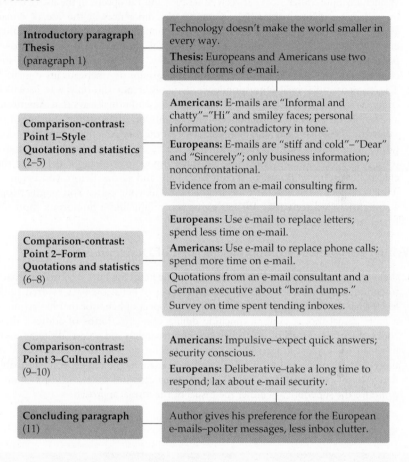

3. **Other patterns.** Identify the transitional expressions that Weiner uses to signal similarities and differences. Why do you think there are so few of these expressions? How might the fact that this essay was meant to be read aloud affect Weiner's transitions between Amerimail and Euromail? (You can listen to the short version of the essay at www.npr.org; search using the key term "Euromail.") Do you think the essay would be better if Weiner had used more transitional expressions? Explain.

4. What type of conclusion does Weiner use? (To review strategies for conclusions, see Chapter 2). What is his concluding point? Were you surprised by this conclusion? Why or why not?

Writing Assignments Using Comparison-Contrast as a Pattern of Development

1. Weiner attributes differences between Americans and Europeans in the use of e-mail to underlying cultural differences. Consider the differences in the use of e-mail among specific sub-groups of Americans, for example, among Americans of different generations, different genders, or different ethnic groups. Drawing on your own personal experience and that of people you know, write an essay comparing and contrasting some of the ways these two different groups of Americans use e-mail.

2. The etiquette of e-mail correspondence certainly is not the only way in which Americans differ from Europeans. Consider some additional ways that Americans as a whole differ from another specific nationality or ethnic group, European or otherwise. Write an essay in which you *contrast* the way Americans and the other group approach at least three cultural practices. You might look at attitudes toward gender roles, child-rearing, personal fitness, treatment of the ill or the elderly, leisure to work ratios, the environment, and so on. Before you begin to write, consider what sort of tone might best suit your essay. You might adopt a straightforward tone (like Weiner's), or you might find a humorous approach better suits your material.

Writing Assignment Combining Patterns of Development

3. Weiner's preference for Euromail indicates that he longs for a more formal approach to communication. Over time, several other types of behaviors have evolved to be less formal than they once were. Select another aspect of behavior that has acquired a more casual mode; examples include dining etiquette, forms of address, dress codes, classroom protocol or student-teacher dynamics, and so on. Write an essay in which you explore at least two to three *causes* for the shift from more formal to more casual expressions of this behavior. As you examine the causes, you'll probably find yourself *contrasting* former and current practices. And your conclusion should *argue* for the superiority of either the casual or the formal approach.

Josie Appleton

Josie Appleton is the director and spokesperson for the Manifesto Club, a British civil liberties campaign group that speaks out against excessive state regulation. As a journalist, Appleton frequently writes for *Spiked* (or *sp!ked*), an online publication based in London. The following article appeared in *Spiked* on July 9, 2003.

Pre-Reading Journal Entry   MyWritingLab

There's no denying the growing popularity of tattoos and piercings. What responses—both positive and negative—might people with tattoos or piercings expect or hope to experience at school, at work, or in other societal situations? Explore these ideas in your journal.

The Body Piercing Project

The opening of a tattoo and piercing section in the up-market London   1
store Selfridges shows that body modification has lost its last trace of taboo.

"Metal Morphosis," nestled in the thick of the ladies clothing section,   2
is a world away from the backstreets of Soho—where the company has its
other branch. Teenagers, middle-aged women, men in suits and young
guys in jeans flock to peer at the rows of tastefully displayed rings and leaf
through the tattoo brochures.

Tattooist Greg said that he had seen a "broad variety" of people: 3
"everything from the girl who turned 18 to the two Philippino cousins who
just turned 40." The piercer, Barry, said that a number of "Sloanies" come
for piercings (the most expensive navel bar retails at £3000 [$4,550], and
there is a broad selection that would set you back several hundred pounds).
A handful of women have even asked to be tattooed with the label of their
favorite bottle of wine (Rumbelow).

This is not just affecting London high-streets. According to current   4
estimates, between 10 and 25 percent of American adolescents have some
kind of piercing or tattoo (Carroll and Anderson 627). And their mothers are
taking it up, too—in the late 1990s, the fastest growing demographic group
seeking tattoo services in America was middle-class suburban women (Levins).

But while tattoos have been taken up by university students and ladies   5
who lunch, more traditional wearers of tattoos—sailors, soldiers, bikers,
gangs—find themselves increasingly censured.

In June 2003, the police rejected an applicant because his tattoos were   6
deemed to have an "implication of racism, sexism or religious prejudice"
("Police"). The US Navy has banned "tattoos/body art/brands that are
excessive, obscene, sexually explicit or advocate or symbolize sex, gender,
racial, religious, ethnic or national origin discrimination" and "symbols
denoting any gang affiliation, supremacist or extremist groups, or drug
use" (Jontz). New-style tattoos are a very different ball-game to their
frowned-upon forebears. While the tattoos of football supporters, sailors and
gang-members tend to be symbols of camaraderie or group affiliation, the
Selfridges brigade are seeking something much more individual.

For some, tattoos and piercing are a matter of personal taste or fashion.   7
"It's purely aesthetic decoration," said 37-year-old Sarah, waiting to get
her navel pierced at Metal Morphosis. The erosion of moral censure on tattooing, and the increasing hygiene of tattoo parlors, has meant that body
modification has become a fashion option for a much wider group of people.

For others, tattooing seems to go more than skin-deep. Tattoo artist   8
Greg thinks that many of those getting tattoos today are looking for "self-
empowerment"—tattoos, he says, are about establishing an "identity for

the self." As a permanent mark on your body that you choose for yourself, a tattoo is "something no one will ever be able to take away from you," that allows you to say *"this is mine."*

Seventeen-year-old Laura said that she got her piercings done because   9
she "wanted to make a statement." When she turned 18, she planned to have "XXX" tattooed on the base of her spine, symbolizing her pledge not to drink, smoke or take drugs. "It's not to prove anything to anyone else," she said: "it's a pact with myself completely."

Sue said that she had her navel pierced on her fortieth birthday to mark a   10
turning point in her life. Another young man planned to have his girlfriend's name, and the dates when they met, tattooed on his arm "to show her that I love her"—and to remind himself of this moment. "The tattoo will be there forever. Whether or not I feel that in the future, I will remember that I felt it at the time, that I felt strong enough to have the tattoo."

The tattoos of bikers, sailors and gang-members would be a kind of   11
social symbol, that would establish them as having a particular occupation or belonging to a particular cultural subgroup. By contrast, Laura's "XXX" symbol is a sign to herself of how she has chosen to live her life; Sue pierced her navel to mark her transition to middle-age. These are not symbols that could be interpreted by anyone else. Even the man who wanted to get tattooed with his girlfriend's name had a modern, personal twist to his tale: the tattoo was less a pact to stay with her forever, than to remind himself of his feelings at this point.

Much new-style body modification is just another way to look good.   12
But the trend also presents a more profound, and worrying, shift: the growing crisis in personal identity.

In his book, *Modernity and Self-Identity* (1991), sociologist Anthony   13
Giddens argues that it is the erosion of important sources of identity that helps to explain the growing focus on the body. Body modification began to really take off and move into the mainstream in the late 1980s and early 1990s. At around this time, personal and community relationships that previously helped to provide people with an enduring sense of self could no longer be depended upon. The main ideological frameworks that provided a system to understand the world and the individual's place in it, such as class, religion, or the work ethic, began to erode.

These changes have left individuals at sea, trying to establish their own   14
sense of who they are. In their piercing or tattooing, people are trying to construct a "narrative of self" on the last thing that remains solid and tangible: their physical bodies. While much about social experience is uncertain and insecure, the body at least retains a permanence and reliability. Making marks upon their bodies is an attempt by people to build a lasting story of who they are.

Many—including, to an extent, Giddens—celebrate modification as a   15
liberating and creative act. "If you want to and it makes you feel good, you

should do it," Greg tells me. Websites such as the *Body Modification Ezine* (*BMEzine*) are full of readers' stories about how their piercing has completely changed their life. One piercer said that getting a piercing "helped me know who I am." Another said that they felt "more complete ... a better, more rounded and fuller person" (qtd. in Featherstone 68). Others even talk about unlocking their soul, or finally discovering that "I AM."

But what these stories actually show is less the virtues of body piercing, than the desperation of individuals' attempts to find a foothold for themselves. There is a notable contrast between the superlatives about discovering identity and Being, and the ultimately banal act of sticking a piece of metal through your flesh.   16

Piercings and tattoos are used to plot out significant life moments, helping to lend a sense of continuity to experience. A first date, the birth of a child, moving house: each event can be marked out on the body, like the notches of time on a stick. One woman said that her piercings helped to give her memory, to "stop me forgetting who I am." They work as a "diary" that "no one can take off you" (qtd. in Featherstone 69).   17

This springs from the fact that there is a great deal of confusion about the stages of life today. Old turning points that marked adulthood—job, marriage, house, kids—have both stopped being compulsory and lost much of their significance. It is more difficult to see life in terms of a narrative, as a plot with key moments of transition and an overall aim. Piercings and tattoos are used to highlight formative experiences and link them together.   18

Some also claim that body modification helps them to feel "comfortable in my own skin," or proud of parts of their body of which they were previously ashamed. The whole process of piercing—which involves caring for the wound, and paying special attention to bodily processes—is given great significance. By modifying a body part, some argue that you are taking possession of it, making it truly yours. "The nipple piercings have really changed my relationship to my breasts," one woman said (qtd. in Siebers 175).   19

This is trying to resolve a sense of self-estrangement—the feeling of detachment from experiences, the feeling that your life doesn't really belong to you. One young woman says how she uses piercing: "[It's been] done at time when I felt like I needed to ground myself. Sometimes I feel like I'm not in my body—then its time" (Holtham).   20

But piercing is trying to deal with the problem at the most primitive and brutal level—in the manner of "I hurt therefore I am." The experience of pain becomes one of the few authentic experiences. It also tries to resolve the crisis in individual identity in relation to my breasts or my navel, rather than in relation to other people or anything more meaningful in the world.   21

Many claims are made as to the transformative and creative potential of body modification. One girl, who had just had her tongue pierced, writes: "I've always been kind of quiet in school and very predictable. . . .   22

I wanted to think of myself as original and creative, so I decided I wanted something pierced.... Now people don't think of me as shy and predictable, they respect me and the person I've become and call me crazily spontaneous" ("My").

Others say they use modification to help master traumatic events. Transforming the body is seen as helping to re-establish a sense of self-control in the face of disrupting or degrading experiences. One woman carved out a Sagittarius symbol on her thigh to commemorate a lover who died. "It was my way of coming to terms with the grief I felt," she said. "It enabled me to always have him with me and to let him go" (Polhemus and Randall 79).   23

Here the body is being modified as a way of trying to effect change in people's lives. It is the way to express creativity, find a challenge, or put themselves through the hoops. "I was ecstatic. I did it!" writes one contributor to *BMEZine*. Instead of a life project, this is a "body project." In the absence of obvious social outlets for creativity, the individual turns back on himself and to the transformation of his own flesh.   24

Body piercing expresses the crisis of social identity—but it actually also makes it worse, too. Focusing on claiming control over my body amounts to making a declaration of independence from everybody else.   25

People with hidden piercings comment on how pleased they were they had something private. One says: "I get so happy just walking along and knowing that I have a secret that no one else could ever guess!" Another said that they now had "something that people could not judge me for, and something that I could hide." Another said that her piercing made her realize that "what other people say or think doesn't matter. The only thing that mattered at that moment was that I was happy with this piercing; I felt beautiful and comfortable in my own skin.... They remind me that I'm beautiful to who it matters... *me*" ("My").   26

Body modification encourages a turn away from trying to build personal identity through relationships with others, and instead tries to resolve problems in relation to one's own body. When things are getting rough, or when somebody wants to change their lives, the answer could be a new piercing or a new tattoo. There is even an underlying element of self-hatred here, as individuals try to deal with their problems by doing violence to themselves. As 17-year-old Laura told me: "You push yourself to do more and more.... You want it to hurt."   27

This means that the biggest questions—of existence, self-identity, life progression, creativity—are being tackled with the flimsiest of solutions. A mark on the skin or a piercing through the tongue cannot genuinely resolve grief, increase creativity, or give a solid grounding to self-identity. For this reason, body modification can become an endless, unfulfilling quest, as one piercing only fuels a desire for another. All the contributions to *BMEZine* start by saying how much their life has been changed—but then   28 promptly go on to plan their next series of piercings. "Piercing can be addictive!" they warn cheerily.

Body modification should be put back in the fashion box. As a way   29
of improving personal appearance, piercing and tattooing are no better or
worse than clothes, makeup or hair gel. It is when body modification is
loaded with existential significance that the problems start.

Works Cited

Carroll, Lynne, and Roxanne Anderson. "Body Piercing, Tattooing, Self-Esteem, and Body Investment in Adolescent Girls." *Adolescence*, vol. 37, no. 147, 2002, pp. 627–37.

Featherstone, Mike, editor. *Body Modification.* Sage Publications, 2000. Theory, Culture, & Society.

Giddens, Anthony. *Modernity and Self-Identity: Self and Society in the Late Modern Age.* Polity Press, 1991.

Holtham, Susan. "Body Piercing in the West: A Sociological Inquiry." *Ambient Inc: Body Art Resources*, www.ambient.ca/bodymod/essay.html. Accessed 8 July 2003.

Jontz, Sandra. "Navy Draws a Line on Some Forms of Body Piercing, Ornamentation, Tattoos." *Stars and Stripes*, 29 Jan. 2003, www.stripes.com/news/navy-draws-a-line-on-some-forms-of-body-piercing-ornamentation-tattoos-1.1390.

Levins, Hoag. "The Changing Cultural Status of the Tattoo Arts in America: As Documented in Mainstream U.S. Reference Works, Newspapers and Magazines." *Tattoo Arts in America*, TattooArtist.com, 1997, tattooartist.com/history.html. Accessed 8 July 2003.

"My Beautiful Piercing." *BME*, BMEZine.com, 30 June 2003, www.bme.com/media/story/854435/?cat=pierce.

Polhemus, Ted, and Housk Randall. *The Customized Body.* 2nd ed., Serpent's Tail, 2000.

"Police Reject Tattooed Applicant." *BBC News*, 16 June 2003, news.bbc.co.uk/go/pr/fr/-/2/hi/uk_news/england/oxfordshire/2995556.stm.

Rumbelow, Helen. "Ladies Who Lunch Get a Tattoo for Starters." *The Times: UK News*, 18 June 2003, www.thetimes.co.uk/tto/news/uk/article1909578.ece.

Siebers, Tobin, editor. *The Body Aesthetic: From Fine Art to Body Modification.* U of Michigan P, 2000.

Questions for Close Reading   MyWritingLab

1. What is the selection's thesis? Locate the sentence(s) in which Appleton states her main idea. If she doesn't state the thesis explicitly, express it in your own words.
2. According to Appleton, what are the two main factors that have made body modifications a fashion option for a growing number of individuals?
3. To what cause does the sociologist Anthony Giddens attribute what Appleton calls "the growing focus on the body"? Do you agree with Giddens's assertion? Explain your response.
4. Think of individuals you know—perhaps yourself, your friends, your family members—who have tattoos or piercings and those individuals' reasons for making these body modifications. In what ways does Appleton's thesis ring true or false when you consider her ideas in relation to those reasons?

Questions About the Writer's Craft

1. **The pattern.** Appleton *compares* and *contrasts* the types of tattoos typical of various demographic groups. She distinguishes between "tattoos of football supporters, sailors and gang-members" whose tattoos "tend to be symbols of camaraderie or group affiliation," with those of "the Selfridges brigade" who "are seeking something much more individual" (paragraph 6). Does this distinction make sense to you? Does it apply when you think of individuals you know with tattoos? Why or why not?
2. **The pattern.** Although most essays state their thesis near the beginning, Appleton saves hers for later in the selection. Why do you think she chose to organize her essay in this manner? Do you think her essay would have been more effective had she stated her thesis in the first or second paragraph? Why or why not?
3. **Other patterns.** Josie Appleton reveals both *causes* and *effects* of body modifications. Do the two next-to-the last paragraphs of the essay (28 and 29) discuss *causes*, *effects*, or both? Why do you suppose Appleton organizes the paragraphs this way?
4. Appleton includes a number of sources in her essay. List the various types of sources she includes. Of those, which ones do you consider most effective in helping her convince readers of her thesis? Why?

Writing Assignments Using Comparison-Contrast as a Pattern of Development

1. Appleton begins her essay with this statement: "The opening of a tattoo and piercing section in the up-market London store Selfridges shows that body modification has lost its last trace of taboo." Write an essay in which you compare and contrast the popularity of and attitudes toward tattoos in the United States in the 1950s with their current popularity and people's attitudes toward them. Consider including one or more images and several outside sources, possibly including personal interviews, to add to the effectiveness of your essay.
2. Write an essay in which you compare and contrast the most popular types of tattoos of various demographic groups in the United States today. You might include some of the groups Appleton mentions in her essay: teenagers, middle-aged women, men in suits, football supporters, sailors, and gang members. Conduct both library and Internet research to identify outside sources of information you can use to enrich your essay.

Writing Assignment Combining Patterns of Development

3. Write a *cause-effect* essay in which you focus on an individual who chose to modify his or her body—perhaps with tattoos or piercing, or perhaps through a surgical procedure. Explore the reasons the person decided to make these changes and the effect of the body modifications. Include information as to whether the modifications brought about the desired results as you share the individual's *narrative*.

Jeffrey N. Wasserstrom

Jeffrey N. Wasserstrom, a member of the faculty at the University of California, Irvine, and a specialist in Chinese history, is especially interested in patterns of student protest and the effects of globalization on urban life and popular culture. His publications include *China in the 21st Century: What Everyone Needs to Know* (2013) and *Global Shanghai, 1850–1990* (2009). "A Mickey Mouse Approach to Globalization" first appeared in *Yale Global Online* and later in *Global Policy Forum*, an independent policy watchdog group that works to encourage accountability in international organizations such as the United Nations.

Pre-Reading Journal

MyWritingLab

How do customs and practices from other cultures around the world influence your life on a daily basis? How are the words you use, the foods you eat, the music you listen to, and the sports you enjoy influenced by other worldwide cultures? Explore these ideas in your journal.

A Mickey Mouse Approach to Globalization

From Buenos Aires to Berlin, people around the world are looking 1 more and more American. They're wearing Levis, watching CNN, buying coffee at interchangeable Starbucks outlets, and generally experiencing life in "very American" ways. Looking only at the surface of this phenomenon, one might erroneously conclude that US cultural products are creating a homogenized global community of consumers. But the cultural aspects of the globalization story are far more complex than might be assumed from looking at just consumer behavior. Even when the same shirt, song, soda, or store is found on all five continents, it tends to mean different things depending on who is doing the wearing, singing, drinking, or shopping. The "strange" fate of global products in China illustrates these points.

Consider, first of all, the Chinese meaning of Big Macs. In *The Lexus* 2 *and the Olive Tree*, Thomas Friedman says he has eaten McDonald's burgers in more countries than he can count and is well qualified to state that they "really do all taste the same." What he actually means, though, is they all taste the same to him. Nearly identical Big Macs may be sold in Boston and Beijing, but as anthropologist Yan Yunxiang has convincingly argued, the experiences of eating them and even the meaning of going to McDonald's in these two locales was very different in the 1990s. In Beijing, but not in Boston, a Big Mac was classified as a snack, not a meal, and university students thought of McDonald's as a good place to go for a romantic night out. To bite into a Big Mac thinking that you are about to do something pleasantly familiar or shamefully plebian—two common American experiences—is one thing. To bite into one imagining you are on the brink of discovering what modernity tastes like—a common Chinese experience—is another thing altogether.

Or take the curious arrival of Mickey Mouse in China, which I wit-   3
nessed firsthand. While living in Shanghai in the mid-1980s, two things I remember seeing are sweatshirts for sale on the streets emblazoned with the face of Disney's most famous creation, and a wall poster showing a stake being driven through Mickey's heart. Were these signs that a big American corporation was extracting profits from a new market and that local people were angered by cultural imperialism? Hardly. Yes, Disney was trying to make money, offering Chinese state television free cartoons to show in the hope that viewers would rush out and buy authorized products. But the plan went astray: the sweatshirts I saw were all knock-offs. The only people making money from them were Chinese entrepreneurs. And the wall poster was, of all things, part of a Communist Party health campaign. A call had just gone out for all citizens to work hard to rid their cities of rats, which are called "laoshu," the same term used for mice. It wasn't long before enterprising local residents put up posters showing various forms of violence being directed at "Mi Laoshu," as Mickey is known in Chinese, not because they hated America but simply because he was the most famous rodent in China.

Flash forward to the year 2000, when Starbucks first opened in both the   4
American town I live in (Bloomington, Indiana) and the Chinese city I study (Shanghai), and we see further evidence of the divergent local meanings of globally familiar icons. In Bloomington, Starbucks triggered mixed reactions. Some locals welcomed its arrival. Others staged non-violent protests or smashed its windows, complaining that the chain's record on environmental and labor issues was abysmal and that Starbucks would drive local coffee shops out of business. In Shanghai, by contrast, there were no demonstrations. The chain's arrival was seen as contributing to, rather than putting a check upon, the proliferation of new independently run coffeehouses.

The local meanings of Shanghai Starbucks do not stop there. For example,   5
when outlets open in Europe, they are typically seen, for understandable reasons, as symbols of creeping—or steam-rolling—Americanization. In Shanghai, though, guidebooks sometimes classify Starbucks as a "European-style" (as opposed to "Japanese-style") foreign coffee house. To further complicate things, the management company that operates the dozens of Shanghai Starbucks outlets is based not in Seattle but in Taiwan.

These examples of American products taking on distinctly new cultural   6
meanings when moved from the US to China are useful in undermining superficial assertions equating globalization with "Americanization." But it

is important not to stop there. The same thing has happened—and continues to happen—with the global meanings of Asian icons in America. Here, again, a Chinese illustration seems apt; that of a Middle Kingdom figure, Chairman Mao, whose face nearly rivals Mickey Mouse's in terms of global recognition.

One indication of the fame and varied meanings of Mao's visage is that in 2002 news stories appeared that told of the simultaneous appearance of the Chairman's image in three totally different national contexts. Representations of Mao showed up in the huts of Nepalese guerrillas; on posters carried by protesting laid-off workers in Northeast China; and in a London art exhibit. In Nepal, Mao was invoked because he endorsed peasant revolt. In Northeast China, his link to the days when Chinese workers had iron rice bowls for life was what mattered. And in London, it was his status as a favorite subject of a pop art pioneer that counted: the exhibit was a Warhol retrospective. 7

There is, in sum, more to keep in mind about globalization than Friedman's divide between the worlds of mass-produced Lexus cars and individuated olive trees. One reason is simply that a Lexus can mean myriad things, depending on where it is. Whether one first encounters it in the showroom or working the assembly line matters. And it makes a difference whether the people who watch it are seeing it whiz by as they walk the streets of Toledo or seeing it crawl as they sit on a Tokyo-bound Bullet Train. It is not just in physics, after all, but also in cultural analysis, that the complex workings of relativity need to be kept in mind. 8

Questions for Close Reading

MyWritingLab

1. What is the selection's thesis? Locate the sentence(s) in which Wasserstrom states his main idea. If he doesn't state his thesis explicitly, express it in your own words.
2. What two images of Mickey Mouse in China in the mid-1980s does Wasserstrom describe and how does he explain the popularity of the images?
3. In his essay Wasserstrom refers to both Thomas Friedman and Yan Yunxiang. What does the essay reveal regarding who these individuals are and how their ideas differ?
4. What three images of Mao Zedong does Wasserstrom describe in his essay, and how does he explain the "fame and varied meanings of Mao's image" (paragraph 7)?

Questions About the Writer's Craft

1. **The pattern.** Does Wasserstrom use the *one-side-at-a-time* or the *point-by-point* method to *compare* and *contrast* ideas and images in his essay? Give examples from the text to back up your assertions. Is his chosen method effective? Why or why not?
2. Wasserstrom uses first-, second-, and third-person point of view in his essay. Give examples of his use of each one and explain why you think he uses all three.

3. Other patterns. In what ways does Wasserstrom use *exemplification* throughout his essay? Give specific examples. How do these examples help convince readers of his *argument* that globalization does not equal Americanization?

4. Wasserstrom refers to Thomas Friedman in his second paragraph and again in his conclusion. Why do you think he uses this strategy? What purpose does it serve?

Writing Assignments Using Comparison-Contrast as a Pattern of Development

1. Wasserstrom notes that university students in China considered a visit to McDonald's "a romantic night out." Think of how different groups within your own community experience various American cultural institutions, such as Thanksgiving Day, Super Bowl Sunday, and high school graduation. The groups can be ethnic, religious, neighborhood, or school groups, or families or groups of friends. Choose one item and compare and contrast how it is treated differently in two or more groups.

2. Wasserstrom references Thomas Friedman and Yan Yunxiang in the second paragraph of his essay and tells us a little about their ideas. Conduct library and Internet research to find out more about these individuals, and then write an essay in which you compare and contrast them and the views they espouse. Alternatively, research the ideas of two other experts on globalization and compare and contrast their views.

Writing Assignment Combining Patterns of Development

3. Using his example of the Andy Warhol retrospective, Wasserstrom claims that other cultures can influence our own American culture. Think of non-American cultural institutions that you are familiar with and that you feel have had an impact on American culture. Some examples might be pizza, salsa music, and manga comic books—or even yoga and soccer. Choose three *examples* and *define* or *describe* them. Then explain how they have influenced American culture. Consider using *narrative* in the form of anecdotes about people you know to illustrate your ideas.

Dave Barry

Pulitzer Prize–winning humorist Dave Barry (1947–) began his writing career covering—as he puts it—"incredibly dull municipal meetings" for the *Daily Local News* of West Chester, Pennsylvania. Next came an eight-year stint trying to teach businesspeople not to write sentences like "Enclosed please find the enclosed enclosures." In 1983, Barry joined the staff of the the *Miami Herald,* where his rib-tickling commentary on the absurdities of everyday life quickly brought him a legion of devoted fans. Barry's column is now syndicated in more than 150 newspapers. A popular guest on television and radio, Barry has written dozens of books, including *Dave Barry's Complete Guide to Guys* (1995), *Dave Barry in Cyberspace*

(1996), *Dave Barry Hits Below the Beltway* (2001), *Boogers Are My Beat* (2003), *Dave Barry's Money Secrets* (2006), *I'll Mature When I'm Dead* (2010), *Insane City* (2013), and *You Can Date Boys When You're Forty* (2014). He has also written the the comic mystery novels *Big Trouble* (1999) and *Tricky Business* (2002). The father of two, Barry lives in Miami with his wife. The following essay, published also under the title "The Ugly Truth About Beauty," first appeared in the *Miami Herald* in 1998.

Pre-Reading Journal Entry

MyWritingLab

To what extent would you say our images of personal attractiveness are influenced by TV commercials and magazine advertisements? Think of commercials and ads you've seen recently. What physical traits are typically identified as attractive in women? In men? List as many as you can. What assumptions does each trait suggest? Use your journal to respond to these questions.

Beauty and the Beast

If you're a man, at some point a woman will ask you how she looks. 1

"How do I look?" she'll ask. 2

You must be careful how you answer this question. The best technique 3 is to form an honest yet sensitive opinion, then collapse on the floor with some kind of fatal seizure. Trust me, this is the easiest way out. Because you will never come up with the right answer.

The problem is that women generally do not think of their looks in the 4 same way that men do. Most men form an opinion of how they look in the seventh grade, and they stick to it for the rest of their lives. Some men form the opinion that they are irresistible stud muffins, and they do not change this opinion even when their faces sag and their noses bloat to the size of eggplants and their eyebrows grow together to form what appears to be a giant forehead-dwelling tropical caterpillar.

Most men, I believe, think of themselves as average-looking. Men will 5 think this even if their faces cause heart failure in cattle at a range of 300 yards. Being average does not bother them; average is fine, for men. This is why men never ask anybody how they look. Their primary form of beauty care is to shave themselves, which is essentially the same form of beauty care that they give to their lawns. If, at the end of his four-minute daily beauty regimen, a man has managed to wipe most of the shaving cream out of his hair and is not bleeding too badly, he feels that he has done all he can, so he stops thinking about his appearance and devotes his mind to more critical issues, such as the Super Bowl.

Women do not look at themselves this way. If I had to express, in three 6 words, what I believe most women think about their appearance, those words would be: "not good enough." No matter how attractive a woman may appear to be to others, when she looks at herself in the mirror, she thinks: woof. She thinks that at any moment a municipal animal-control officer is going to throw a net over her and haul her off to the shelter.

Why do women have such low self-esteem? There are many complex   7 psychological and societal reasons, by which I mean Barbie. Girls grow up playing with a doll proportioned such that, if it were human, it would be seven feet tall and weigh 81 pounds, of which 53 pounds would be bosoms. This is a difficult appearance standard to live up to, especially when you contrast it with the standard set for little boys by their dolls... excuse me, by their action figures. Most of the action figures that my son played with when he was little were hideous-looking. For example, he was very fond of an action figure (part of the He-Man series) called "Buzz-Off," who was part human, part flying insect. Buzz-Off was not a looker. But he was extremely self-confident. You could not imagine Buzz-Off saying to the other action figures: "Do you think these wings make my hips look big?"

But women grow up thinking they need to look like Barbie, which for   8 most women is impossible, although there is a multibillion-dollar beauty industry devoted to convincing women that they must try. I once saw an Oprah show wherein supermodel Cindy Crawford dispensed makeup tips to the studio audience. Cindy had all these middle-aged women applying beauty products to their faces; she stressed how important it was to apply them in a certain way, using the tips of their fingers. All the women dutifully did this, even though it was obvious to any sane observer that, no matter how carefully they applied these products, they would never look remotely like Cindy Crawford, who is some kind of genetic mutation.

I'm not saying that men are superior. I'm just saying that you're   9 not going to get a group of middle-aged men to sit in a room and apply cosmetics to themselves under the instruction of Brad Pitt, in hopes of looking more like him. Men would realize that this task was pointless and demeaning. They would find some way to bolster their self-esteem that did not require looking like Brad Pitt. They would say to Brad: "Oh YEAH? Well what do you know about LAWN CARE, pretty boy?"

Of course many women will argue that the reason they become obsessed   10 with trying to look like Cindy Crawford is that men, being as shallow as a drop of spit, WANT women to look that way. To which I have two responses:

1. Hey, just because WE'RE idiots, that does not mean you have to be; and   11

2. Men don't even notice 97 percent of the beauty efforts you make   12 anyway. Take fingernails. The average woman spends 5,000 hours per year worrying about her fingernails; I have never once, in more than 40 years of listening to men talk about women, heard a man say, "She has a nice set of fingernails!" Many men would not notice if a woman had upward of four hands.

Anyway, to get back to my original point: If you're a man, and a   1 woman asks you how she looks, you're in big trouble. Obviously, you can't say she looks bad. But you also can't say that she looks great, because she'll think you're lying, because she has spent countless hours, with the help of the multibillion-dollar beauty industry, obsessing about the differences between herself and Cindy Crawford. Also, she suspects that you're not qualified to judge anybody's appearance. This is because you have shaving cream in your hair.

Questions for Close Reading

MyWritingLab

1. What is the selection's thesis? Locate the sentence(s) in which Barry states his main idea. If he doesn't state the thesis explicitly, express it in your own words.
2. Barry tells us that most men consider themselves to be "average-looking" (paragraph 5). Why, according to Barry, do men feel this way?
3. When Barry writes that most women think of themselves as "not good enough" (6), what does he mean? What, according to Barry, causes women to develop low opinions of themselves?
4. Barry implies that women could have a more rational response to the "difficult appearance standard" that pervades society (7). What would that response be?

Questions About the Writer's Craft

1. **The pattern.** Which comparison-contrast method of organization (point-by-point or one-side-at-a-time) does Barry use to develop his essay? Why might he have chosen this pattern?
2. Barry uses exaggeration, a strategy typically associated with humorous writing. Locate instances of exaggeration in the selection. Why do you think he uses this strategy?
3. **Other patterns.** Barry demonstrates a series of *cause-effect* chains in his essay. Locate some of the cause-effect series. How do they help Barry reinforce his thesis?
4. How does the essay's title foreshadow the essay's ideas?

Writing Assignments Using Comparison-Contrast as a Pattern of Development

1. Examine the pitches made in magazines and on TV for the male and female versions of *one* kind of grooming product. Possibilities include deodorant, hair dye, soap, and so on. Then write an essay contrasting the persuasive appeals that the product makes to men with those it makes to women. (Don't forget to examine the assumptions behind the appeals.)
2. Barry contrasts women's preoccupation with looking good to men's lack of concern about their appearance. Now consider the flip side—something men care about deeply that women virtually ignore. Write an essay contrasting men's stereotypical fascination with *one* area to women's indifference. You might, for example, examine male and female attitudes toward sports, cars, tools, even lawn care. Following Barry's example, adopt a playful tone in your essay, illustrating the absurdity of the obsession you discuss.

Writing Assignment Combining Patterns of Development

3. Barry implies that most men, unaffected by the "multibillion-dollar beauty industry," are content to "think of themselves as average looking." Do you agree? Conduct your own research into whether or not Barry's assertions about men are true. Begin by interviewing several male friends, family members, and class-mates to see how these men feel about their physical appearance. In addition, in the library or online, research magazines such as *People*, *GQ*, or *Men's Health* for articles describing how everyday men as well as male celebrities view their looks. Then write an essay *refuting* or *defending* the view that being average-looking doesn't bother most men. Start by acknowledging the opposing view; then sup-port your assertion with convincing *examples* and other evidence drawn from your research.

Stephen Chapman

Stephen Chapman was an associate editor for the *New Republic*, the publication for which he wrote "The Prisoner's Dilemma" in 1980. Since then, he has joined the staff of the *Chicago Tribune*, where his twice-weekly syndicated column on national and international affairs originates. Born in Texas in 1954, Chapman graduated *cum laude* from Harvard University in 1976 and did graduate work in business administration at the University of Chicago. He has contributed articles to national magazines including *The Atlantic*, *Harper's*, *Reason*, and *The American Spectator*. Chapman lives with his family outside Chicago.

Pre-Reading Journal Entry   MyWritingLab

Should wrongdoing be punished in public? Why or why not? Use your journal to consider the pros and cons of public punishment for illegal actions. Think of three or four wrongdoings (from lesser offenses like shoplifting to serious crimes like armed robbery). For each offense, list possible forms of public punishment as well as the advantages and disadvantages of each form.

The Prisoner's Dilemma

One of the amusements of life in the modern West is the opportunity   1
to observe the barbaric rituals of countries that are attached to the customs
of the dark ages. Take Pakistan, for example.... President Zia, in harmony
with the Islamic fervor that is sweeping his part of the world, revived the
traditional Moslem practice of flogging lawbreakers in public. In Pakistan,
this qualified as mass entertainment, and no fewer than 10,000 law-abiding
Pakistanis turned out to see justice done to 26 convicts. To Western sensibilities the spectacle seemed barbaric—both in the sense of cruel and
in the sense of pre-civilized. In keeping with Islamic custom each of the

unfortunates—who had been caught in prostitution raids the previous night and summarily convicted and sentenced—was stripped down to a pair of white shorts, which were painted with a red stripe across the buttocks (the target). Then he was shackled against an easel, with pads thoughtfully placed over the kidneys to prevent injury. The floggers were muscular, fierce-looking sorts—convicted murderers, as it happens—who paraded around the flogging platform in colorful loincloths. When the time for the ceremony began, one of the floggers took a running start and brought a five-foot stave down across the first victim's buttocks, eliciting screams from the convict and murmurs from the audience. Each of the 26 received from five to 15 lashes. One had to be carried from the stage unconscious.

Flogging is one of the punishments stipulated by Koranic law, which has   2
made it a popular penological device in several Moslem countries, including Pakistan, Saudi Arabia, and, most recently, the ayatollah's Iran. Flogging, or *ta'zir*, is the general punishment prescribed for offenses that don't carry an explicit Koranic penalty. Some crimes carry automatic *hadd* punishments—stoning or scourging (a severe whipping) for illicit sex, scourging for drinking alcoholic beverages, amputation of the hands for theft. Other crimes—as varied as murder and abandoning Islam—carry the death penalty (usually carried out in public). Colorful practices like these have given the Islamic world an image in the West, as described by historian G. H. Jansen, "of blood dripping from the stumps of amputated hands and from the striped backs of malefactors, and piles of stones barely concealing the battered bodies of adulterous couples." Jansen, whose book *Militant Islam* is generally effusive in its praise of Islamic practices, grows squeamish when considering devices like flogging, amputation, and stoning. But they are given enthusiastic endorsement by the Koran itself.

Such traditions, we all must agree, are no sign of an advanced civiliza-   3
tion. In the West, we have replaced these various punishments (including the death penalty in most cases) with a single device. Our custom is to confine criminals in prison for varying lengths of time. In Illinois, a reasonably typical state, grand theft carries a punishment of three to five years; armed robbery can get you from six to 30. The lowest form of felony theft is punishable by one to three years in prison. Most states impose longer sentences on habitual offenders. In Kentucky, for example, habitual offenders can be sentenced to life in prison. Other states are less brazen, preferring the more genteel sounding "indeterminate sentence," which allows parole boards to keep inmates locked up for as long as life. It was under an indeterminate sentence of one to 14 years that George Jackson served 12 years in California prisons for committing a $70 armed robbery. Under a Texas law imposing an automatic life sentence for a third felony conviction, a man was sent to jail for life last year because of three thefts adding up to less than $300 in property value. Texas also is famous for occasionally imposing extravagantly long

sentences, often running into hundreds or thousands of years. This gives Texas a leg up on Maryland, which used to sentence some criminals to life plus a day—a distinctive if superfluous flourish....

What are the advantages of being a convicted criminal in an advanced   4
culture? First there is the overcrowding in prisons. One Tennessee prison, for example, has a capacity of 806, according to accepted space standards, but it houses 2300 inmates. One Louisiana facility has confined four and five prisoners in a single six-foot-by-six-foot cell. Then there is the disease caused by overcrowding, unsanitary conditions, and poor or inadequate medical care. A federal appeals court noted that the Tennessee prison had suffered frequent outbreaks of infectious diseases like hepatitis and tuberculosis. But the most distinctive element of American prison life is its constant violence. In his book *Criminal Violence, Criminal Justice,* Charles Silberman noted that in one Louisiana prison, there were 211 stabbings in only three years, 11 of them fatal. There were 15 slayings in a prison in Massachusetts between 1972 and 1975. According to a federal court, in Alabama's penitentiaries (as in many others), "robbery, rape, extortion, theft and assault are everyday occurrences."

At least in regard to cruelty, it's not at all clear that the system of punish-   5
ment that has evolved in the West is less barbaric than the grotesque practices of Islam. Skeptical? Ask yourself: would you rather be subjected to a few minutes of intense pain and considerable public humiliation, or be locked away for two or three years in a prison cell crowded with ill-tempered sociopaths? Would you rather lose a hand or spend 10 years or more in a typical state prison? I have taken my own survey on this matter. I have found no one who does not find the Islamic system hideous. And I have found no one who *given the choices* mentioned above, would not prefer its penalties to our own....

Imprisonment is now the universal method of punishing criminals in   6
the United States. It is thought to perform five functions, each of which has been given a label by criminologists. First, there is simple *retribution:* punishing the lawbreaker to serve society's sense of justice and to satisfy the victims' desire for revenge. Second, there is *specific deterrence:* discouraging the offender from misbehaving in the future. Third, *general deterrence:* using the offender as an example to discourage others from turning to crime. Fourth, *prevention:* at least during the time he is kept off the streets, the criminal cannot victimize other members of society. Finally, and most important, there is *rehabilitation:* reforming the criminal so that when he returns to society he will be inclined to obey the laws and able to make an honest living.

How satisfactorily do American prisons perform by these criteria? Well,   7
of course, they do punish. But on the other scores they don't do so well. Their effect in discouraging future criminality by the prisoner or others is the subject of much debate, but the soaring rates of the last 20 years suggest that prisons are not a dramatically effective deterrent to criminal behavior.

Prisons do isolate convicted criminals, but only to divert crime from ordinary citizens to prison guards and fellow inmates. Almost no one contends any more that prisons rehabilitate their inmates. If anything, they probably impede rehabilitation by forcing inmates into prolonged and almost exclusive association with other criminals. And prisons cost a lot of money. Housing a typical prisoner in a typical prison costs far more than a stint at a top university. This cost would be justified if prisons did the job they were intended for. But it is clear to all that prisons fail on the very grounds—humanity and hope of rehabilitation—that caused them to replace earlier, cheaper forms of punishment. . . .

So the debate continues to rage in all the same old ruts. No one, of 8 course, would think of copying the medieval practices of Islamic nations and experimenting with punishments such as flogging and amputation. But let us consider them anyway. How do they compare with our American prison system in achieving the ostensible objectives of punishment? First, do they punish? Obviously they do, and in a uniquely painful and memorable way. Of course any sensible person, given the choice, would prefer suffering these punishments to years of incarceration in a typical American prison. But presumably no Western penologist would criticize Islamic punishments on the grounds that they are not barbaric enough. Do they deter crime? Yes, and probably more effectively than sending convicts off to prison. Now we read about a prison sentence in the newspaper, then think no more about the criminal's payment for his crimes until, perhaps, years later we read a small item reporting his release. By contrast, one can easily imagine the vivid impression it would leave to be wandering through a local shopping center and to stumble onto the scene of some poor wretch being lustily flogged. And the occasional sight of an habitual offender walking around with a bloody stump at the end of his arm no doubt also would serve as a forceful reminder that crime does not pay.

Do flogging and amputation discourage recidivism? No one knows 9 whether the scars on his back would dissuade a criminal from risking another crime, but it is hard to imagine that corporal measures could stimulate a higher rate of recidivism than already exists. Islamic forms of punishment do not serve the favorite new right goal of simply isolating criminals from the rest of society, but they may achieve the same purpose of making further crimes impossible. In the movie *Bonnie and Clyde*, Warren Beatty successfully robs a bank with his arm in a sling, but this must be dismissed as artistic license. It must be extraordinarily difficult, at the very least, to perform much violent crime with only one hand.

Do these medieval forms of punishment rehabilitate the criminal? Plainly 10 not. But long prison terms do not rehabilitate either. And it is just as plain that typical Islamic punishments are no crueler to the convict than incarceration in the typical American state prison.

Of course there are other reasons besides its bizarre forms of punishment   11
that the Islamic system of justice seems uncivilized to the Western mind.
One is the absence of due process. Another is the long list of offenses—such
as drinking, adultery, blasphemy, "profiteering," and so on—that can bring
on conviction and punishment. A third is all the ritualistic mumbo-jumbo in
pronouncements of Islamic law.... Even in these matters, however, a little
cultural modesty is called for. The vast majority of American criminals are
convicted and sentenced as a result of plea bargaining, in which due process
plays almost no role. It has been only half a century since a wave of religious
fundamentalism stirred this country to outlaw the consumption of alcoholic
beverages. Most states also still have laws imposing austere constraints on
sexual conduct. *The Washington Post* reported that the FBI had spent two
and a half years and untold amounts of money to break up a nationwide
pornography ring. Flogging the clients of prostitutes, as the Pakistanis did,
does seem silly. But only a few months ago Mayor Koch of New York was
proposing that clients caught in his own city have their names broadcast by
radio stations. We are not so far advanced on such matters as we often like to
think. Finally, my lawyer friends assure me that the rules of jurisdiction for
American courts contain plenty of petty requirements and bizarre distinc-
tions that would sound silly enough to foreign ears.

Perhaps it sounds barbaric to talk of flogging and amputation, and perhaps   12
it is. But our system of punishment also is barbaric, and probably more so. Only
cultural smugness about their system and willful ignorance about our own
make it easy to regard the one as cruel and the other as civilized. We inflict our
cruelties away from public view, while nations like Pakistan stage them in front
of 10,000 onlookers. Their outrages are visible; ours are not. Most Americans
can live their lives for years without having their peace of mind disturbed by the
knowledge of what goes on in our prisons. To choose imprisonment over flogging and amputation is not to choose human kindness over cruelty, but merely
to prefer that our cruelties be kept out of sight, and out of mind.

Public flogging and amputation may be more barbaric forms of punish-   13
ment than imprisonment, even if they are not more cruel. Society may pay
a higher price for them, even if the particular criminal does not. Revulsion
against officially sanctioned violence and infliction of pain derives from
something deeply ingrained in the Western conscience, and clearly it is
something admirable. Grotesque displays of the sort that occur in Islamic
countries probably breed a greater tolerance for physical cruelty, for example, which prisons do not do precisely because they conceal their cruelties.
In fact it is our admirable intolerance for calculated violence that makes it
necessary for us to conceal what we have not been able to do away with. In a
way this is a good thing, since it holds out the hope that we may eventually
find a way to do away with it. But in another way it is a bad thing, since it
permits us to congratulate ourselves on our civilized humanitarianism while
violating its norms in this one area of our national life.

Questions for Close Reading

MyWritingLab

1. What is the selection's thesis? Locate the sentence(s) in which Chapman states his main idea. If he doesn't state the thesis explicitly, express it in your own words.
2. Chapman calls Islamic punishment practices "barbaric." What are some of these practices? Why would they seem barbaric to most Americans?
3. According to our society's philosophy of punishment, what goals is imprisonment supposed to accomplish? How successful, in Chapman's view, are U.S. prisons in meeting these goals?
4. For Chapman, what is the core difference between the U.S. punishment system and that of Islamic nations like Pakistan? Which system does he find preferable? Why?

Questions About the Writer's Craft

1. **The pattern.** In paragraphs 7 through 10, Chapman contrasts the success of the American and Islamic systems in meeting the five goals of punishment cited in paragraph 6. How does Chapman help readers keep those goals in mind as he develops his contrast?
2. **Other patterns.** In paragraphs 1, 2, and 6, Chapman provides a number of *definitions*. How do these definitions help him convince readers to accept key points in his argument?
3. **Other patterns.** Examine the *examples* that Chapman provides in paragraphs 3 and 4. Why do you think he sequences each set of examples as he does?
4. Examine Chapman's tone, especially in paragraphs 3, 4, 5, and 8 to 9. Where does he shift from a fairly neutral tone to a more sarcastic and mocking one? How does this change help Chapman convince readers of the seriousness of the problems in U.S. justice?

Writing Assignments Using Comparison-Contrast as a Pattern of Development

1. Select one situation in which people are, in your opinion, ineffectively punished for violating a law or regulation. For example, you might focus on the punishment typically imposed for driving while intoxicated, plagiarizing a school paper, or habitually coming to work late. Write an essay describing the violation and its customary punishment. Then contrast this punishment with a more effective way of correcting the offending behavior. Whether you choose the one-side-at-a-time or the point-by-point method, be sure to provide clear signals, as Chapman does, to help readers follow your ideas.
2. Chapman contrasts two cultures' approaches to criminal punishment. Write an essay comparing and/or contrasting two cultures' approaches to another aspect of life. To structure your paper, use either the one-side-at-a-time or point-by-point method of development. The cultures you discuss need not be nationalities or ethnicities. You might, for example, focus on parents' and teenagers' preferences in music, male and female expectations in a relationship, or high school teachers' and college professors' attitudes toward student responsibility. If appropriate, consider using a humorous tone to make fun of both sides—or to convey which side's approach you find preferable.

Writing Assignment Combining Patterns of Development

 3. Chapman states that there is "universal acknowledgment that prisons do not rehabilitate." Conduct research in the library or on the Internet on recent developments in criminal rehabilitation. Bibliographic sources like EBSCOhost, the *Social Sciences Index,* and *Criminal Justice Abstracts* will help you locate relevant information. Then write an essay *refuting* or *defending* the common view that the rehabilitation of prisoners is a futile goal. Start by acknowledging the opposing view, and then support your argument with convincing *examples* and other evidence drawn from your research.

Additional Writing Topics

COMPARISON-CONTRAST   MyWritingLab

General Assignments

Using comparison-contrast, develop one of these topics into an essay.

1. Living at home versus living in an apartment or dorm
2. Two-career family versus one-career family
3. Children's pastimes today and yesterday
4. Neighborhood stores versus shopping malls
5. A sports team then and now
6. Watching a movie on television versus viewing it in a theater
7. Two approaches to parenting
8. Two approaches to studying
9. Marriage versus living together
10. Talking on the phone versus texting

Assignments Using Visuals

Use the suggested visuals to help develop a comparison-contrast essay on one of these topics:

1. Divorce rates of those who marry in their twenties and in their thirties (charts)
2. Owning and maintaining a small versus a large vehicle (photos or web links)
3. Making choices about diet and/or exercise (graphs or cartoons)
4. Advantages and disadvantages of a career in health care (slide show)
5. Working in a fast-food versus a fine dining restaurant (charts)

Assignments with a Specific Purpose, Audience, and Point of View

1. **Academic life.** You would like to change your campus living arrangements. Perhaps you want to move from a dormitory to an off-campus apartment or from home to a dorm. Before you do, though, you'll have to convince your parents (who are paying most of your college costs) that the move will be beneficial. Write out what you would say to your parents. Contrast your current situation with your proposed one, explaining why the new arrangement would be better.
2. **Academic life.** Write a guide on "Passing Exams" for first-year college students, contrasting the right and wrong ways to prepare for and take exams. Although your purpose is basically serious, write the section on how not to approach exams with some humor.
3. **Civic activity.** As president of your local neighbors' association, you're concerned about the way your local government is dealing with a particular situation (for example, an increase in robberies, muggings, graffiti, and so on). Write a letter to your mayor contrasting the way your local government handles the situation with another city or town's approach. In your conclusion, point out the advantages of adopting the other neighborhood's strategy.
4. **Civic activity.** Your old high school has invited you back to make a speech before an audience of seniors. The topic will be "how to choose the college that is right for you." Write your speech in the form of a comparison-contrast analysis. Focus on the choices available (two-year versus four-year schools, large versus small, local versus faraway, and so on), showing the advantages and/or disadvantages of each.
5. **Workplace action.** As a store manager, you decide to write a memo to all sales personnel explaining how to keep customers happy. Compare and/or contrast the needs and shopping habits of several different consumer groups (by age, spending ability, or sex), and show how to make each group comfortable in your store.
6. **Workplace action.** You work as a volunteer for a mental health hot line. Many people call simply because they feel "stressed out." Do some research on the subject of stress management, and prepare a brochure for these people, recommending a "Type B" approach to stressful situations. Focus the brochure on the contrast between "Type A" and "Type B" personalities: the former is nervous, hard-driving, competitive; the latter is relaxed and noncompetitive. Give specific examples of how each "type" tends to act in stressful situations.

MyWritingLab Visit Chapter 8, "Comparison-Contrast," in MyWritingLab to complete the chapter activities, Pre-Reading Journal Entry activities, Questions for Close Reading, and Additional Writing Topics assignments and to test your understanding of the chapter objectives.

CAUSE-EFFECT

In this chapter, you will learn:

9.1 To use the pattern of cause-effect to develop your essays.

9.2 To consider how cause-effect can fit your purpose and audience.

9.3 To develop strategies for using cause-effect in an essay.

9.4 To develop strategies for revising a cause-effect essay.

9.5 To analyze how cause-effect is used effectively in student-written and professionally authored selections.

9.6 To write your own essays using cause-effect as a strategy.

WHAT IS CAUSE-EFFECT?

All of us think in terms of cause and effect, sometimes consciously, sometimes unconsciously: "Why did they give me such an odd look?" we wonder, or "How would I do at another college?" we speculate. This exploration of reasons and results is also at the heart of most professions: "What led to our involvement in Vietnam?" historians question; "What will happen if we administer this experimental drug?" scientists ask.

Cause-effect writing, often called *causal analysis,* is rooted in this elemental need to make connections. Because the drive to understand reasons and results is so fundamental, causal analysis is a common kind of writing. An article analyzing the unexpected outcome of an election, a report linking poor nutrition to low academic achievement, an editorial analyzing the impact of a proposed tax cut—all are examples of cause-effect writing.

Done well, cause-effect pieces can uncover the subtle and often surprising connections between events or phenomena. By determining causes and projecting effects, causal analysis enables us to make sense of our experiences, revealing a universe that is somewhat less arbitrary and chaotic.

HOW CAUSE-EFFECT FITS YOUR PURPOSE AND AUDIENCE

Many assignments and exam questions in college involve writing essays that analyze causes, effects, or both. Sometimes, as in the following examples, you'll be asked to write an essay developed primarily through the cause-effect pattern:

> Although divorces have leveled off in the last few years, the number of marriages ending in divorce is still greater than it was a generation ago. What do you think are the causes of this phenomenon?

> Political commentators were surprised that so few people voted in the last election. Discuss the probable causes of this weak voter turnout.

> Americans never seem to tire of gossip about the rich and famous. What effect has this fascination with celebrities had on U.S. culture?

> The federal government is expected to pass legislation that will significantly reduce the funding of student loans. Analyze the possible effects of such a cutback.

Other assignments and exam questions may not explicitly ask you to address causes and effects, but they may use words that suggest causal analysis would be appropriate. Consider these examples, paying special attention to the words in boldface:

> In contrast to the socially involved youth of the 1960s, many young people today tend to remove themselves from political issues. What do you think are the **sources** of the political apathy found among 18- to 25-year-olds? (*cause*)

> A number of experts forecast that drug abuse will be the most significant factor affecting U.S. productivity in the coming decade. Evaluate the validity of this observation by discussing the **impact** of drugs in the workplace. (*effect*)

> According to school officials, a predictable percentage of entering students drop out of college at some point during their first year. What **motivates** students to drop out? What **happens** to them once they leave? (*cause and effect*)

In addition to serving as the primary strategy for achieving an essay's purpose, causal analysis can also be a supplemental method used to help make a point in an essay developed chiefly through another pattern of development. Assume, for example, that you want to write an essay *defining* the term *the homeless*. To help readers see that unfavorable circumstances can result in nearly anyone becoming homeless, you might discuss some of the unavoidable, everyday factors causing people to live on streets and in subway stations. Similarly, in a *persuasive* proposal urging your college administration to institute an honors program, you would probably spend some time analyzing the positive effect of such a program on students and faculty.

STRATEGIES FOR USING CAUSE-EFFECT IN AN ESSAY

The suggestions here and in Figure 9.1 (page 355) will be helpful whether you use causal analysis as a dominant or a supportive pattern of development.

1. Stay focused on the purpose of your analysis.   When writing a causal analysis, don't lose sight of your overall purpose. Consider, for example, an essay on the causes of widespread child abuse. If you're concerned primarily with explaining the problem of child abuse to your readers, you might take a purely *informative* approach:

> Although parental stress is the immediate cause of child abuse, the more compelling reason for such behavior lies in the way parents were themselves mistreated in their own families.

Or you might want to *persuade* the audience about some point or idea concerning child abuse:

> The tragic consequences of child abuse provide strong support for more aggressive handling of such cases by social workers and judges.

Then again, you could choose a *speculative* approach, your main purpose being to suggest possibilities:

> Psychologists disagree about the potential effect on youngsters of all the media attention to child abuse. Will children exposed to this media coverage grow up assertive, self-confident, and able to protect themselves? Or will they become fearful and distrustful?

These examples illustrate that an essay's causal analysis may have more than one purpose.

FIGURE 9.1
Development Diagram: Writing a Cause-Effect Essay

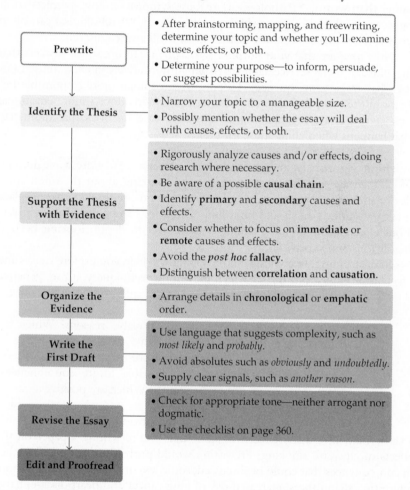

Prewrite
- After brainstorming, mapping, and freewriting, determine your topic and whether you'll examine causes, effects, or both.
- Determine your purpose—to inform, persuade, or suggest possibilities.

Identify the Thesis
- Narrow your topic to a manageable size.
- Possibly mention whether the essay will deal with causes, effects, or both.

Support the Thesis with Evidence
- Rigorously analyze causes and/or effects, doing research where necessary.
- Be aware of a possible **causal chain**.
- Identify **primary** and **secondary** causes and effects.
- Consider whether to focus on **immediate** or **remote** causes and effects.
- Avoid the *post hoc* **fallacy**.
- Distinguish between **correlation** and **causation**.

Organize the Evidence
- Arrange details in **chronological** or **emphatic** order.

Write the First Draft
- Use language that suggests complexity, such as *most likely* and *probably*.
- Avoid absolutes such as *obviously* and *undoubtedly*.
- Supply clear signals, such as *another reason*.

Revise the Essay
- Check for appropriate tone—neither arrogant nor dogmatic.
- Use the checklist on page 360.

Edit and Proofread

2. Adapt content and tone to your purpose and readers. Your purpose and audience determine what supporting material and what tone will be most effective in a cause-effect essay. Assume you want to direct your essay on child abuse to general readers who know little about the subject. To *inform* readers, you might use facts, statistics, and expert opinion to provide an objective discussion of the causes of child abuse. Your analysis might show the following: (1) adults who were themselves mistreated as children tend to abuse their own offspring; (2) marital stress contributes to the mistreatment of children; and (3) certain personality disorders increase the likelihood of child abuse. Sensitive to what your readers would and wouldn't understand, you would stay away from a technical or formal tone. Rather than writing "Pathological preabuse symptomatology predicts adult transference of high aggressivity," you would say "Psychologists can often predict, on the basis of family histories, who will abuse children."

Now imagine that your purpose is to *convince* future social workers that the failure of social service agencies to act authoritatively in child-abuse cases often has tragic consequences. Hoping to encourage more responsible behavior in the prospective social workers, you would adopt a more emotional tone in the essay, perhaps citing wrenching case histories that dramatize what happens when child abuse isn't taken seriously.

3. Think rigorously about causes and effects. To write a meaningful causal analysis, you should do some careful thinking about the often complex relationship between causes and effects. Imprecise thinking has no place in essay writing. You should be willing to dig for causes, to think creatively about effects. You should examine your subject in depth, looking beyond the obvious and superficial.

Brainstorming, freewriting, and mapping will help you explore causes and effects thoroughly. No matter which prewriting technique you use, generate as many explanations as possible by asking yourself questions like these:

Causes: What happened? What are the possible reasons? Which are most likely? Who was involved? Why?

Effects: What happened? Who was involved? What were the observable results? What are some possible future consequences? Which consequences are negative? Which are positive?

If you remain open and look beyond the obvious, you'll discover that a cause may have many effects. Imagine that you're writing a paper on the effects of cigarette smoking. Prewriting would probably generate a number of consequences that could be discussed, some less obvious but perhaps more interesting than others: increased risk of lung cancer and heart disease, harm traced to secondhand smoke, legal battles regarding the rights of smokers and nonsmokers, lower birth weights in babies of mothers who smoke, and developmental problems experienced by such underweight infants.

In the same way, prewriting will help you see that an effect may have multiple causes. An essay analyzing the reasons for world hunger could discuss many causes, again some less evident but perhaps more thought-provoking than others: climatic changes, inefficient use of land, cultural predispositions for large families, and poor management of international relief funds.

Your analysis may also uncover a *causal chain* in which one cause (or effect) brings about another, which, in turn, brings about another, and so on. Here's an example of a causal chain: The Prohibition Amendment to the U.S. Constitution went into effect on January 29, 1920; bootleggers and organized crime stepped in to supply public demand for alcoholic beverages; ordinary citizens began breaking the law by buying illegal alcohol and patronizing speakeasies; disrespect for legal authority became widespread and acceptable. As you can see, a causal chain often leads to interesting points. In this case, the subject of Prohibition leads not just to the obvious (illegal consumption of alcohol) but also to the more complex issue of society's decreasing respect for legal authority.

If your subject involves multiple causes and effects, limit what you'll discuss. Identify which causes and effects are *primary* and which are *secondary*. How extensively you cover secondary factors will depend on your purpose and audience. In an essay intended to inform a general audience about the harmful effects of pesticides, you would most likely focus on everyday dangers—polluted drinking water, residues in food, and the like. You probably wouldn't include a discussion of more long-range consequences (evolution of resistant insects, disruption of the soil's acid-alkaline balance).

Similarly, decide whether to focus on *immediate*, more obvious causes and effects, or on less obvious, more *remote* ones. Or perhaps you need to focus on both. In an essay about a faculty strike at your college, should you attribute the strike simply to the faculty's failure to receive a salary increase? Or should you also examine other factors: the union's failure to accept a salary package that satisfied most professors; the administration's inability to coordinate its negotiating efforts? It may be more difficult to explore more remote causes and effects, but it can also lead to more original and revealing essays.

When developing a causal analysis, be careful to avoid the *post hoc fallacy*. Named after the Latin phrase *post hoc, ergo propter hoc*, meaning "after this, therefore because of this," this kind of faulty thinking occurs when you assume that simply because one event *followed* another, the first event *caused* the second. For example, if the Republicans win a majority of seats in Congress and, several months later, the economy collapses, can you conclude that the Republicans caused the collapse? A quick assumption of "Yes" fails the test of logic because the timing of events could be coincidental and not indicative of any cause-effect relationship. The collapse may have been triggered by uncontrolled inflation that began well before the congressional elections.

Also, be careful not to mistake *correlation* for *causation*. Two events correlate when they occur at about the same time. Such co-occurrence, however, doesn't guarantee a cause-effect relationship. For instance, although the number of ice cream cones eaten and the instances of heat prostration both increase during the summer months, this doesn't mean that eating ice cream causes heat prostration! A third factor—in this case, summer heat—is the actual cause.

4. Write a thesis that focuses the paper on causes, effects, or both.   The thesis in an essay developed through causal analysis often indicates whether the essay will deal with mostly causes, effects, or both causes and effects. Here, for example, are three thesis statements for causal analyses dealing with the public school system. You'll see that each thesis signals that essay's particular emphasis:

> Our school system has been weakened by an overemphasis on trendy electives. (*causes*)
>
> An ineffectual school system has led to crippling teachers' strikes and widespread disrespect for the teaching profession. (*effects*)
>
> Bureaucratic inefficiency has created a school system unresponsive to children's emotional, physical, and intellectual needs. (*causes and effects*)

Note that the thesis statement—in addition to signaling whether the paper will discuss causes or effects or both—may also point to the essay's plan of development. Consider the last thesis statement; it makes clear that the paper will discuss children's emotional needs first, their physical needs second, and their intellectual needs last.

The thesis statement in a causal analysis doesn't have to specify whether the essay will discuss causes, effects, or both. Nor does the thesis have to be worded in such a way that the essay's plan of development is apparent. But when first writing cause-effect essays, you may find that a highly focused thesis will keep your analysis on track.

5. Choose an organizational pattern. There are two basic ways to organize the points in a cause-effect essay: You may use a chronological or an emphatic sequence. If you select a *chronological order,* you discuss causes and effects in the order in which they occur or will occur. Suppose you're writing an essay on the causes for the popularity of imported cars. These causes might be discussed in chronological sequence: American plant workers became frustrated and dissatisfied on the job; some workers got careless whereas others deliberately sabotaged the production of sound cars; a growing number of defective cars hit the market; consumers grew dissatisfied with American cars and switched to imports.

Chronology might also be used to organize a discussion about effects. Imagine you want to write an essay about the need to guard against disrupting delicate balances in the country's wildlife. You might start the essay by discussing what happened when the starling, a non-native bird, was introduced into the American environment. Because the starling had few natural predators, the starling population soared out of control; starlings took over the food sources and habitats of native species; the bluebird, a native species, declined and is now threatened with extinction.

Although a chronological pattern can be an effective way to organize material, a strict time sequence can present a problem if your primary cause or effect ends up buried in the middle of the sequence. In such a case, you might use *emphatic order*, reserving the most significant cause or effect for the end. Emphatic order is an especially effective way to sequence cause-effect points when readers hold what, in your opinion, are mistaken or narrow views about a subject. To encourage readers to look more closely at the issues, you present what you consider the erroneous or obvious views first, show why they are unsound or limited, and then present what you feel to be the actual causes and effects. Such a sequence nudges the audience into giving further thought to the causes and effects you have discovered. Here is an informal outline for a causal analysis using this approach.

Subject: The causes of the riot at the rock concert

1. Some commentators blame the excessively hot weather.
2. Others cite drug use among the concertgoers.
3. Still others blame the beer sold at the concessions.
4. But the real cause of the disaster was poor planning by the concert promoters.

When using emphatic order in a causal analysis, you might want to word the thesis in such a way that it signals which point your essay will stress. Look at the following thesis statements:

Although many immigrants arrive in this country without marketable skills, their most pressing problem is learning how to make their way in a society whose language they don't know.

The space program has led to dramatic advances in computer technology and medical science. Even more important, though, the program has helped change many people's attitudes toward the planet we live on.

These thesis statements reflect an awareness of the complex nature of cause-effect relationships. Although not dismissing secondary issues, the statements establish which points the writer considers most noteworthy.

Whether you use a chronological or emphatic pattern to organize your essay, you'll need to provide clear *signals* to identify when you're discussing causes and when you're discussing effects. Expressions such as "Another reason" and "A final outcome" help readers follow your line of thought.

6. Use language that hints at the complexity of cause-effect relationships. Because it's difficult—if not impossible—to identify causes and effects with certainty, you should avoid such absolutes as "It must be obvious" and "There is no doubt." Instead, try phrases like "Most likely" or "It's probable that." Using such language is not indecisive; rather, it reflects your understanding of the often tangled nature of causes and effects. Be careful, though, of going to the other extreme and being reluctant to take a stand on the issues. If you've thought carefully about causes and effects, you have a right to state your analysis with conviction. Don't undercut the hard work you've done by writing as if your ideas were unworthy of your reader's attention.

REVISION STRATEGIES

Once you have a draft of the essay, you're ready to revise. The following checklist will help you and those giving you feedback apply to cause-effect some of the revision techniques discussed in Chapter 2.

☑ CAUSE-EFFECT: A REVISION/PEER REVIEW CHECKLIST

Revise Overall Meaning and Structure

- ❏ Is the essay's purpose informative, persuasive, speculative, or a combination of these?
- ❏ What is the essay's thesis? Is it stated specifically or implied? Where? Could it be made any clearer? How?
- ❏ Does the essay focus on causes, effects, or both? How do you know?
- ❏ Where has correlation been mistaken for causation? Where is the essay weakened by *post hoc* thinking?
- ❏ Where does the essay distinguish between primary and secondary causes and effects? Do the most critical causes and effects receive special attention?
- ❏ Where does the essay dwell on the obvious?

Revise Paragraph Development

- ❏ Are the essay's paragraphs sequenced chronologically or emphatically? Could they be sequenced more effectively? How?
- ❏ Where would signal devices make it easier to follow the progression of thought within and between paragraphs?
- ❏ Which paragraphs would be strengthened by vivid examples (such as statistics, facts, anecdotes, or personal observations) that support the causal analysis?

Revise Sentences and Words

- ❏ Where do expressions like *as a result, because,* and *therefore* mislead the reader by implying a cause-effect relationship? Would words such as *following* and *previously* eliminate the problem?
- ❏ Do any words or phrases convey an arrogant or dogmatic tone (*there is no question, undoubtedly, always, never*)? What other expressions (*most likely, probably*) would improve credibility?

STUDENT ESSAY

The following student essay was written by Erica Zwieg in response to this assignment:

In "When Will People Help in a Crisis?" John M. Darley and Bibb Latané explore reasons why people sometimes choose not to come to the aid of those in need. Write an essay about a situation in which an individual or a group of individuals chose to reach out and do what they could to help others. Describe both the situation that sparked the acts of kindness and the effects of the decision to help those in need.

Erica Zwieg, a college student who played a leading role in her school's annual Children's Miracle Network (CMN) Dance Marathon, chose to write an essay describing the situation that led to the first CMN Dance Marathon and how that first marathon paved the way for similar events at schools across the United States.

Party with a Purpose
by Erica Zwieg

Introduction and background information

    In 1984, Ryan White, a 13-year-old boy living in Kokomo, Indiana, was diagnosed with HIV/AIDS after receiving a contaminated blood transfusion. His doctors diagnosed him with six months to live. At the time, there was much misinformation surrounding the HIV/AIDS virus. Many people were afraid that they could contract the virus simply by being around others with the disease. This misconception caused Ryan to experience intolerance and prejudice within his community and school after he

First link in causal chain ("banned")

received his diagnosis. He was banned from attending his local middle school—a decision supported and rallied for by parents within the misinformed community who feared that Ryan might infect their children. Though Ryan's doctors confirmed that he was not contagious, he continued to face vicious protests that included gunfire into his home to instill fear within his family. Ryan was fighting for his life within the hospital and on the streets of his own neighborhood (Evans).

Topic sentence

    News about the discrimination Ryan was experiencing quickly spread throughout the United States and beyond. Ryan's physically draining battle with his disease, coupled with prejudice faced within his hometown, sparked the

Second link in causal chain ("media's attention")

media's attention and made him an overnight sensation. Celebrities like Michael Jackson and Elton John became advocates in Ryan's defense, seeking to educate the nation on HIV/AIDS awareness.

1

2

3

Topic sentence ———

Ryan's face and story were soon all of the news, and his responses to interview questions showed the nation what a courageous and giving person he was. When asked how he was coping with all that he was going through, Ryan responded, "I figure...that since this was the way the hand was dealt...then I've got to live with it this way and I'm going to try to help anybody I can" ("Story"). In another interview, Ryan was asked to describe his experience with prejudice and to comment on why he thought he was being treated unfairly. He stated, "In my case, it was fear [that caused people to treat me unfairly], and I suppose because I had something in my body that nobody else had, or very few people had. It was because [I was] different" ("Story"). For five years Ryan did his best to help others understand more about the HIV/AIDS virus and to speak out against intolerance, living much longer that his doctors had thought possible.

Paragraph adding
support to second
link in causal chain

Though friends and family rallied behind his courageous struggle, Ryan lost his battle against HIV/AIDS on April 8, 1990, one year before he planned to enter Indiana University as a freshman. After losing Ryan to the disease, his friends and family were determined to honor his memory and expand the nationwide movement of change he had created. A year after his death, Ryan's friends who were students at the school he had planned to attend founded the Indiana University Dance Marathon (IUDM). The event began as a way for the student body and the community to celebrate Ryan's life, raise awareness about his disease, and generate funds to help children like Ryan who were facing life-threatening diagnoses. At that first marathon in 1991, students and the community stood together for thirty-six hours, dancing and raising money for children's health care. The event served as a way to celebrate the wonderful person Ryan had been and also gave the student body and the community the opportunity to party with a purpose. Since that first marathon, IUDM has raised over $16 million for the Ryan White Center for Infectious Disease at the Riley Hospital for Children in Indianapolis, Indiana ("Story").

4

Topic sentences
(two sentences) ———

Paragraph on third
link in causal chain

Topic sentence ———→

Paragraph on
fourth link in
causal chain

Little did Ryan's friends at Indiana University realize that they had created the foundation for a Dance Marathon movement that would spread throughout the nation and into the hearts of students in over two hundred and fifty universities and high schools. Today these students stand united under one motto: "For the Kids." Students in participating schools spend countless hours planning events similar to the first one at Indiana University. The funds raised are allotted to the local Children's Miracle Network Hospitals within their surrounding areas, in addition to pediatric programs of their choice. These funds are used to help fund items and programs such

5

as advanced medical equipment, pediatric ICUs (intensive care units), cancer and infectious disease research, and diversionary programs for patients and families undergoing long hospital stays ("Miracle Network"). In their description of these marathons and the student volunteers who organize them, the Children's Miracle Network states:

> These students spend a year learning invaluable leadership and life skills while raising funds and interacting with children's hospital patients and families. The year culminates with a 12–40 hour long event where the students stay on their feet through dancing, games and entertainment in celebration of the total amount raised that year. ("Miracle Network")

The Children's Miracle Network goes on to report that the Dance Marathon's movement has raised over $62 million for children across the nation ("Miracle Network").

Conclusion and two-sentence thesis

Start of two-sentence thesis

Ryan White's struggle with HIV/AIDS sparked a desire   6 within his friends to stand in his honor and fight for children facing life-threatening illnesses. His memory serves as the foundation for Dance Marathons across the nation that raise money to provide support, awareness, and medical treatment regardless of race, religion, gender, or what type of disease these children are fighting.

Works Cited

Evans, Tim. "Retro Indy: Ryan White (1971-1990)." *IndyStar*, 8 Apr. 2010, www.indystar.com/story/news/history/retroindy/2014/04/08/ryan-white/7458579/.

"Miracle Network Dance Marathon." *UI Dance Marathon*, 1995-2016, dancemarathon.uiowa.edu/about/miracle-network-dance-marathon/.

"The Story of Dance Marathon." *YouTube*, uploaded by CMN Hospitals, 13 Aug. 2013, www.youtube.com/watch?v=kIHuxf4i6Ms.

COMMENTARY

Title. Erica shared her draft with Sam and Ruben, the two students in her peer review group. She gave each a copy. Then before reading it aloud to them as her teacher had instructed, Erica mentioned she had still not thought of a title. She told them that she often struggled to come up with titles that she thought would interest her readers and make them want to read what she had written. Both classmates said they knew exactly what she was talking about—that they had the same problem. As Erica was reading her paper aloud, a phrase in the fourth paragraph caught her attention: "party with a purpose." After reading those words aloud, she paused, looked at Sam and Ruben, and said, "I think I just found my title." They both thought she had a great idea. Had she not read the paper aloud and heard the spoken phrase, she might have settled, as she often had, for a less effective title.

Purpose and thesis.   Erica's purpose was to write an *informational causal analysis* that informed her readers of Ryan White's experiences with intolerance and prejudice and how he and others reacted to those injustices. She also hoped that her essay would help her readers more clearly understand the importance of coming to the assistance of those in need. Instead of stating her thesis near the beginning of her essay, as she often did, Erica decided to begin by telling Ryan's story and then to go on to describe how his experiences affected others. She saved her thesis for the concluding paragraph, in which she ends her essay by making certain her readers understand the main ideas she is trying to communicate: "Ryan White's struggle with HIV/AIDS sparked a desire within his friends to stand in his honor and fight for children facing life-threatening illnesses. His memory serves as the foundation for Dance Marathons across the nation that raise money to provide support, awareness, and medical treatment regardless of race, religion, gender, or what type of disease these children are fighting."

Combining patterns of development.   Erica draws on various patterns of development to develop her causal analysis. She uses *narration* as she tells Ryan's story in chronological order, beginning with his diagnosis and moving forward. For example, she narrates for her readers the story of how he was treated by parents in his hometown who were afraid he would spread HIV/AIDS to their children if he attended school with them and of how gunshots were fired into his home in an effort to "instill fear within his family." Erica also uses *exemplification* as she includes examples of celebrities such as Michael Jackson and Elton John who stood up for Ryan and tried "to educate the nation on HIV/AIDS awareness" and when she provides examples of the ways in which funds raised in Dance Marathons benefit children with life-threatening conditions. In addition, she uses *description* in paragraph 5, where she provides additional information about the marathons across the country, the work of the student volunteers who organize them, and the funds they have raised for children with life-threatening conditions.

Causal chains.   Erica's essay reveals a causal chain in which one cause (or effect) brings about another, which in turn brings about another, and so on. In the first several sentences of paragraph 1, she clearly states the first cause (Ryan's diagnosis and misconceptions surrounding HIV/AIDS), and she goes on in that same paragraph to reveal the first effect: "This caused Ryan to experience intolerance within his community and school after receiving his diagnosis." Paragraphs 2 and 3 focus on the next link in the causal chain: the media's coverage of Ryan's story and how that led to support from individuals, including Michael Jackson and Elton John, and opportunities for Ryan to tell his story across the country. The attention from the media made students at Indiana University aware of what had happened to Ryan and more likely to participate in the dance marathon held "to celebrate Ryan's life, raise awareness about his disease, and generate funds to help children like Ryan who were facing life-threatening diagnoses" (paragraph 4). This first dance marathon (the third link) led directly to the final link in the causal chain as described in paragraph 5: "a Dance Marathon movement that would spread throughout the nation and into the hearts of students in over two hundred and fifty universities and high schools."

A problem with the essay's close.   When reading the essay, you might have noticed that Erica's conclusion is a bit weak. Although providing a clear statement of her thesis at the end of her essay is a good idea, it's not enough. We learn nothing from reading the final paragraph that we did not already know. Ending an otherwise vigorous essay with such a slight conclusion undercuts the effectiveness of the entire composition. Erica focused so much on developing the body of her essay that she ran out of the time needed to write a more forceful conclusion. Careful budgeting of her time would have allowed her to prepare a stronger concluding paragraph.

Revising the first draft.   As you read the final draft of Erica's essay, you might have noted that the chronological order she uses makes it easy to follow. However, that order did not come as easily as you might assume. You might also have imagined that she easily located effective quotes to use in her essay. That, too, would be incorrect. When Erica shared her early draft with Sam and Ruben, these were issues that needed to be resolved, and the students pointed them out to Erica. Comparing Erica's original version of her second paragraph with paragraphs 2 and 3 in the final version of the essay will show you how she went about revising.

Original Version of the Second Paragraph

During a talk-show interview, Ryan was asked to describe his experience with prejudice and describe where he believes discrimination stems from. He stated, "In my case, it was fear, and I suppose because I had something in my body that nobody else had, or very few people had. It was because [I was] different. I mean, I'm surprised we really have dogs now days because they're different. It's amazing how you can accept a dog into your house. But you can't accept someone because of their race, their color, their religion, or what they have in them," said Ryan ("Story"). He continued to speak out against intolerance for an astonishing five years, surpassing his six-month diagnosis. Celebrities like Michael Jackson and Elton John became advocates in Ryan's defense, seeking to educate the nation on HIV/AIDS awareness. Ryan's physically draining battle with his disease, coupled with prejudice faced within his hometown, sparked the media's attention and made him an overnight sensation.

After sharing her essay with Sam and Ruben, Erica realized that she could make this part of her composition much stronger. She saw that she had jumped from her opening paragraph in which she discussed Ryan's diagnosis, misconceptions surrounding HIV/AIDS, and the ways in which his community treated him, to the next paragraph in which Ryan is suddenly making an appearance on a talk show. That was a huge leap to make—one that was likely to confuse her readers. Sam and Ruben also asked her about the quote in which Ryan comments on how he is "surprised we really have dogs now days because they're different" and goes on to compare the acceptance of dogs with the non-acceptance of people who are different "because of their race, their color, their religion, or what they have in them." Although this is certainly an interesting comment in its own way, one made by a young teenage boy who suddenly finds himself not only with a short time left to live but also having to appear on national television, Sam and Ruben suggested that it might not be the most effective comment for her essay.

As she revised, Erica decided that she needed to begin her second paragraph with a transition statement that would help guide her readers smoothly from her introductory paragraph to the next section of her essay on the effects of media coverage. She accomplished this by beginning her revised second paragraph with the sentence "News about the discrimination Ryan was experiencing quickly spread throughout the United States and beyond." She also realized that before relating quotes Ryan made in interviews, it would make good sense to describe how celebrities became Ryan's advocates and helped spread his story, and to then move on to interview quotes.

Once Erica made those changes, she decided that she needed a separate paragraph for the interview quotes she wanted to include; she wanted those quotes to allow her readers to get to know Ryan better through comments he had made that "showed the nation what a courageous and giving person he was." She did some more research and located an interview quote that does precisely that: "'I figure...that since this was the way the hand was dealt...then I've got to live with it this way and I'm going to try to help anybody I can' ("Story"). She decided to keep the quote in which he commented on his experience with discrimination and its causes but to follow Sam and Ruben's advice to delete the part in which Ryan compared the acceptance of dogs with the non-acceptance of various groups of individuals—though she wasn't entirely sure that was a smart decision. As is often the case, deciding which elements of peer review critique to accept and which to reject can be difficult. As Erica handed her final draft to her teacher, she wondered if her essay would have been stronger had she included those quotes.

Erica worked hard at revising other sections of her paper as well. With the exception of the weak spots already discussed, she made the changes needed to craft a well-written essay that shows the positive effects of helping others.

Activities: Cause-Effect
Prewriting Activities

MyWritingLab

1. Imagine you're writing two essays: One *argues* the need for high school courses in personal finance (how to budget money, balance a checkbook, and the like); the other explains a *process* for showing appreciation. Jot down ways you might use cause-effect in each essay.

2. Use mapping, collaborative brainstorming, or another prewriting technique to generate possible causes and/or effects for *one* of the topics that follows. Be sure to keep in mind the audience indicated in parentheses. Next, devise a thesis and decide whether your purpose would be informative, persuasive, speculative, or some combination of these. Finally, organize your raw material into a brief outline, with related causes and effects grouped in the same section.

   a. Pressure on students to do well (*high school students*)
   b. Children's access to pornography on the Internet (*parents*)
   c. Being physically fit (*those who are out of shape*)
   d. Spiraling costs of a college education (*college officials*)

Revising Activities

3. Explain how the following statements demonstrate *post hoc* thinking and confuse correlation and cause-effect.

   a. Our city now has many immigrants from Latin American countries. The crime rate in our city has increased. Latin American immigrants are the cause of the crime wave.
   b. The divorce rate has skyrocketed. More women are working outside the home than ever before. Working outside the home destroys marriages.
   c. A high percentage of people in Dixville have developed cancer. The landfill, used by XYZ Industries, has been located in Dixville for twenty years. The XYZ landfill has caused cancer in Dixville residents.

(continued)

Activities: Cause-Effect (*continued*)

4. The following paragraph is from the first draft of an essay arguing that techno-
logical advances can diminish the quality of life. How solid is the paragraph's
causal analysis? Which causes and/or effects should be eliminated? Where is the
analysis simplistic? Where does the writer make absolute claims even though
cause-effect relationships are no more than a possibility? Keeping these questions
in mind, revise the paragraph.

How did the banking industry respond to inflation? It simply
introduced a new technology—the automated teller machine (ATM).
By making money more available to the average person, the ATM
gives people the cash to buy inflated goods—whether or not they can
afford them. Not surprisingly, ATMs have had a number of negative
consequences for the average individual. Since people know they can
get cash at any time, they use their lunch hours for something other
than going to the bank. How do they spend this newfound time? They
go shopping, and machine-vended money means more impulse buying,
even more than with a credit card. Also, because people don't need their
checkbooks to withdraw money, they can't keep track of their accounts
and therefore develop a casual attitude toward financial matters. It's no
wonder children don't appreciate the value of money. Another problem
is that people who would never dream of robbing a bank try to trick the
machine into dispensing money "for free." There's no doubt that this kind
of fraud contributes to the immoral climate in the country.

Jane S. Shaw

Jane S. Shaw, born in 1944, received a B.A. in English from Wellesley College and was an associate economics editor at *Business Week*. Currently president of the Pope Center for Higher Education Policy, Shaw was formerly a senior fellow at the Property and Environment Research Center, a nonprofit organization that advocates improving the environment by means of property rights and market forces, rather than by government regulation. Shaw's articles have appeared in publications such as *The Wall Street Journal, The Washington Times, USA Today, Liberty, Public Choice*, and *The Cato Journal*. She is coeditor with Ronald D. Utt of *A Guide to Smart Growth: Shattering Myths and Providing Solutions* (2000). The following selection, adapted from *A Guide to Smart Growth*, was published separately by The Heritage Foundation in 2004. The footnotes are all the author's.

Pre-Reading Journal Entry

MyWritingLab

Encounters with wildlife and other animals can inspire a range of responses. Think of several encounters you have had with animals, for example, spying a deer in your backyard, purchasing a canary as a pet, or catching a fish. How did you feel about these encounters? In your journal make some notes about your experiences.

For ideas on how this cause-effect essay is organized, see Figure 9.2 on page 375.

Nature in the Suburbs

A decade ago, who would have thought that New Jersey would host a   1
black bear hunt—the first in 33 years? Or that Virginia, whose population of bald eagles was once down to 32 breeding pairs, would have 329 known active bald eagle nests? Who would have expected *Metropolitan Home* magazine to be advising its readers about ornamental grasses to keep away white-tailed deer, now found in the millions around the country?

Such incidents illustrate a transformed America. This nation, often con-   2
demned for being crowded, paved over, and studded with nature-strangling shopping malls, is proving to be a haven for wild animals.

It is difficult to ignore this upsurge of wildlife, because stories about   3
bears raiding trashcans and mountain lions sighted in subdivisions frequently turn up in the press or on television. Featured in these stories are animals as large as moose, as well as once-threatened birds such as eagles and falcons and smaller animals like wolverines and coyotes.

One interpretation of these events is that people are moving closer to   4
wilderness and invading the territory of wild animals. But this is only a small part of the story. As this essay will show, wild animals increasingly find suburban life in the United States to be attractive.

The stories, while fascinating, are not all upbeat. Americans are grap-   5
pling with new problems—the growing hazard of automobile collisions

369

with deer, debates over the role of hunting, the disappearance of fragile wild plants gobbled up by hungry ruminants, and even occasional human deaths caused by these animals.

At the same time, the proliferation of wildlife should assure Americans   6 that the claim that urban sprawl is wiping out wildlife is simply poppycock. Human settlement in the early 21st century may be sprawling and suburban—about half the people in this country live in suburbs—but it is more compatible with wildlife than most people think. There may be reasons to decry urban sprawl or the suburbanization of America, but the loss of wildlife is not one of them.

Why So Many Wild Animals?

Two phenomena are fueling this increase in wild animals. One is natural   7 reforestation, especially in the eastern United States. This is largely a result of the steady decline in farming, including cotton farming, a decline that allows forests to retake territory they lost centuries ago. The other is suburbanization, the expansion of low-density development outside cities, which provides a variety of landscapes and vegetation that attract animals. Both trends undermine the claim that wild open spaces are being strangled and that habitat for wild animals is shrinking.

The trend toward regrowth of forest has been well-documented. The   8 percent of forested land in New Hampshire increased from 50 percent in the 1880s to 86 percent 100 years later. Forested land in Connecticut, Massachusetts, and Rhode Island increased from 35 percent to 59 percent over that same period. "The same story has been repeated in other places in the East, the South, and the Lake States," writes forestry expert Roger Sedjo.[1]

Environmentalist Bill McKibben exulted in this "unintentional and   9 mostly unnoticed renewal of the rural and mountainous East" in a 1995 article in *The Atlantic Monthly*. Calling the change "the great environmental story of the United States, and in some ways of the whole world," he added, "Here, where 'suburb' and 'megalopolis' were added to the world's vocabulary, an explosion of green is under way."[2] Along with the reforestation come the animals; McKibben cites a moose "ten miles from Boston," as well as an eastern United States full of black bears, deer, alligators, and perhaps even mountain lions.

This re-greening of the eastern United States explains why some large   10 wild animals are thriving, but much of the wildlife Americans are seeing today is a direct result of the suburbs. Clearly, suburban habitat is not sterile.

---

[1]Roger A. Sedjo, "Forest Resources," in Kenneth D. Frederick and Roger A. Sedjo, eds., *America's Renewable Resources: Historical Trends and Current Challenges* (Washington, D.C.: Resources for the Future, 1991), p. 109.
[2]Bill McKibben, "An Explosion of Green," *Atlantic Monthly*, April 1995, p. 64.

Habitat for Wildlife

When people move onto what once was rural land, they modify the land- 11
scape. Yes, they build more streets, more parking lots, and more buildings.
Wetlands may be drained, hayfields may disappear, trees may be cut down,
and pets may proliferate. At the same time, however, the new residents will
create habitat for wildlife. They will create ponds, establish gardens, plant
trees, and set up bird nesting-boxes. Ornamental nurseries and truck farms
may replace cropland, and parks may replace hedgerows.

This new ecology is different, but it is often friendly to animals, especially 12
those that University of Florida biologist Larry Harris calls "meso-mammals,"
or mammals of medium size.[3] They do not need broad territory for roaming
to find food, as moose and grizzly bears do. They can find places in the suburbs to feed, nest, and thrive, especially where gardens flourish.

One example of the positive impact of growth is the rebound of the 13
endangered Key deer, a small white-tailed deer found only in Florida and
named for the Florida Keys. According to *Audubon* magazine, the Key
deer is experiencing a "remarkable recovery."[4] The news report continues:
"Paradoxically, part of the reason for the deer's comeback may lie in the
increasing development of the area." Paraphrasing the remarks of a university researcher, the reporter says that human development "tends to open
up overgrown forested areas and provide vegetation at deer level—the same
factors fueling deer population booms in suburbs all over the country."

Indeed, white-tailed deer of normal size are the most prominent species 14
proliferating in the suburbs. In *The New York Times*, reporter Andrew C.
Revkin has commented that "suburbanization created a browser's paradise:
a vast patchwork of well-watered, fertilizer-fattened plantings to feed on and
vest-pocket forests to hide in, with hunters banished to more distant woods."[5]

The increase in the number of deer in the United States is so great that 15
many people, especially wildlife professionals, are trying to figure out what to
do about them. In 1997, the Wildlife Society, a professional association of
wildlife biologists, devoted a special 600-page issue of its *Bulletin* to "deer overabundance." The lead article noted, "We hear more each year about the high
costs of crop and tree-seedling damage, deer-vehicle collisions, and nuisance
deer in suburban locales."[6] Insurance companies are worried about the increase
in damage from automobile collisions with deer and similar-sized animals. And
there are fears that the increase in deer in populated areas means that the deer
tick could be causing the increased number of reported cases of Lyme disease.

[3]Larry D. Harris, in e-mail communication with the author, January 16, 2000.
[4]Nancy Klingener, "Doe, Re, Key Deer," *Audubon*, January-February 2000, p. 17.
[5]Andrew C. Revkin, "Out of Control: Deer Send Ecosystem into Chaos," the *New York Times*,
November 12, 2002.
[6]Donald M. Waller and William S. Alverson, "The White-Tailed Deer: A Keystone Herbivore,"
Wildlife Society Bulletin, Vol. 25, No. 2 (Summer 1997), p. 217.

Yes, the proliferation of deer poses problems, as do geese, whose flocks   16
can foul ponds and lawns and are notorious nuisances on golf courses, and
beaver, which can cut down groves of trees. Yet the proliferation of deer is also
a wildlife success story. At least that is the view of Robert J. Warren, editor of
the *Bulletin*, who calls the resurgence of deer "one of the premier examples of
successful wildlife management."[7] Today's deer population in the United States
may be as high as 25 million, says Richard Nelson, writing in *Sports Afield*.[8]

People have mixed feelings about deer. In the *Wildlife Society Bulletin*, Dale   17
R. McCullough and his colleagues reported on a survey of households in El
Cerrito and Kensington, two communities near Berkeley, California. Twenty-
eight percent of those who responded reported severe damage to vegetation by
the deer, and 25 percent reported moderate damage. Forty-two percent liked
having the deer around, while 35 percent disliked them and 24 percent were
indifferent. The authors summarized the findings by saying: "As expected, some
residents loved deer, whereas others considered them 'hoofed rats.'"[9]

James Dunn, a geologist who has studied wildlife in New York State,   18
believes that suburban habitat fosters deer more than forests do. Dunn cites
statistics on the harvest of buck deer reported by the New York State government. Since 1970 the deer population has multiplied 7.1 times in suburban
areas (an increase of 610 percent), but only 3.4 times (an increase of 240
percent) in the state overall.[10]

Dunn explains that the forests have been allowed to regrow without log-   19
ging or burning, so they lack the "edge" that allows sunlight in and encourages
vegetation suitable for deer. In his view, that explains why counties with big cities
(and therefore with suburbs) have seen a greater increase in deer populations than
have the isolated, forested rural counties. Supporting this point, Andrew Revkin
quotes a wildlife biologist at the National Zoo in Washington, D.C. "Deer are an
edge species," he says, "and the world is one big edge now."[11]

Deer are not the only wild animals that turn up on lawns and door-   20
steps, however. James Dunn lists species in the Albany, New York, suburbs in addition to deer: birds such as robins, woodpeckers, chickadees,
grouse, finches, hawks, crows, and nuthatches, as well as squirrels, chip-
munks, opossums, raccoons, foxes, and rabbits.[12] Deer attract coyotes

[7]Robert J. Warren, "The Challenge of Deer Overabundance in the 21st Century," *Wildlife
Society Bulletin*, Vol. 25, No. 2 (Summer 1997), p. 213.
[8]Richard Nelson, "Deer Nation," *Sports Afield*, September 1998, p. 40.
[9]Dale R. McCullough, Kathleen W. Jennings, Natalie B. Gates, Bruce G. Elliott, and Joseph E.
DiDonato, "Overabundant Deer Populations in California," *Wildlife Society Bulletin*, Vol. 25,
No. 2 (1997), p. 481.
[10]James R. Dunn, "Wildlife in the Suburbs," Political Economy Research Center, PERC
Reports, September 1999, pp. 3-5. See also James R. Dunn and John E. Kinney, *Conservative
Environmentalism: Reassessing the Means, Redefining the Ends* (Westport, Conn.: Quorum
Books, 1996).
[11]Revkin, "Out of Control."
[12]Dunn, "Wildlife in the Suburbs," p. 3.

too. According to a 1999 article in *Audubon*, biologists estimate that the coyote population (observed in all states except Hawaii) is about double what it was in 1850.[13]

Joel Garreau, author of *Edge City*, includes black bears, red-tailed hawks, 21 peregrine falcons, and beaver on his list of animals that find suburban niches. Garreau still considers these distant "edge city" towns a "far less diverse ecology than what was there before." However, he writes, "if you measure it by the standard of city, it is a far more diverse ecology than anything humans have built in centuries, if not millennia."[14]

For one reason or another, some environmental activists tend to dismiss 22 the resurgence of deer and other wildlife. In an article criticizing suburban sprawl, Carl Pope, executive director of the Sierra Club, says that the suburbs are "very good for the most adaptable and common creatures—raccoons, deer, sparrows, starlings, and sea gulls" but "devastating for wildlife that is more dependent upon privacy, seclusion, and protection from such predators as dogs and cats."[15]

Yet the suburbs attract animals larger than meso-mammals, and the subur- 23 ban habitat may be richer than what they replace. In many regions, suburban growth comes at the expense of agricultural land that was cultivated for decades, even centuries. Cropland doesn't necessarily provide abundant habitat. Environmental essayist Donald Worster, for example, has little favorable to say about land cultivated for crops or used for livestock grazing. In Worster's view, there was a time when agriculture was diversified, with small patches of different crops and a variety of animals affecting the landscape. Not now. "[T]he trend over the past two hundred years or so," he writes, "has been toward the establishment of monocultures on every continent."[16] In contrast, suburbs are not monocultures.

Even large animals can be found at the edges of metropolitan areas. 24 Early in 2004, a mountain lion attacked a woman riding a bicycle in the Whiting Ranch Wilderness Park in the foothills above populous Orange County, and the same animal may have killed a man who was found dead nearby. According to the *Los Angeles Times*, if the man's death is confirmed as caused by the mountain lion, it would be the first death by a mountain lion in Orange County. The *Times* added, however, that "[m]ountain lions are no strangers in Orange County's canyons and wilderness parks."[17] Indeed, in 1994, mountain lions killed two women in state parks near San Diego and

[13]Mike Finkel, "The Ultimate Survivor," *Audubon*, May-June 1999, p. 58.
[14]Joel Garreau, *Edge City: Life on the New Frontier* (New York: Random House, 1991), p. 57.
[15]Carl Pope, "Americans Are Saying No to Sprawl," Political Economy Research Center, PERC Reports, February 1999, p. 6.
[16]Donald Worster, *The Wealth of Nature: Environmental History and the Ecological Imagination.* (New York: Oxford University Press, 1993), p. 59.
[17]Kimi Yoshino, David Haldane, and Daniel Yi, "Lion Attacks O.C. Biker; Man Found Dead Nearby," *Los Angeles Times*, January 9, 2004.

Sacramento. Deer may be attracting the cats, suggests Paul Beier, a professor at the University of California at Berkeley.[18]...

Sharing Our Turf

The fact that wildlife finds a home in suburban settings does not mean   25
that all wildlife will do so. The greening of the suburbs is no substitute for big stretches of land—both public and private—that allow large mammals such as grizzly bears, elk, antelope, and caribou to roam. The point of this essay is that the suburbs offer an environment that is appealing to many wild animal species.

If the United States continues to prosper, the 21st century is likely to be an   26
environmental century. Affluent people will seek to maintain or, in some cases, restore an environment that is attractive to wildlife, and more parks will likely be nestled within suburban developments, along with gardens, arboreta, and environmentally compatible golf courses. As wildlife proliferates, Americans will learn to live harmoniously with more birds and meso-mammals. New organizations and entrepreneurs will help integrate nature into the human landscape. There is no reason to be pessimistic about the ability of wildlife to survive and thrive in the suburbs.

---

[18]McCullough et al., "Overabundant Deer Populations in California," p. 479.

Questions for Close Reading

MyWritingLab

1. What is the selection's thesis? Locate the sentence(s) in which Shaw states her main idea. If she doesn't state her thesis explicitly, express it in your own words.
2. What evidence does Shaw give to support her assertion, at the beginning of the article and then later on, about an "upsurge in wildlife"?
3. Shaw gives two causes for the increase in wildlife—reforestation and suburbanization. How have these two trends brought about an increase in wildlife? Why does she believe that suburbanization may promote more wildlife than either thick forest growth or cropland?
4. An increase in wildlife, Shaw says, has its negative side. Give at least two examples she uses to prove this point Why do you think Shaw includes these?

Questions About the Writer's Craft

1. **The pattern.** To what extent does the author focus on causes, on effects, or on both causes and effects? Identify at least one causal chain.
2. Is Shaw's purpose to inform, entertain, or persuade? How effective is the author's use of research in achieving this purpose? Identify at least three kinds of sources the author uses, and give an example of each. How credible are the sources (see "Evaluating Source Materials" in Appendix A)?

FIGURE 9.2

Essay Structure Diagram: "Nature in the Suburbs" by Jane S. Shaw

	Examples of proliferation of wild animals in the United States and the problems they cause.
Introductory paragraphs **Examples** **Counterargument Thesis** (paragraphs 1–6)	Counterargument of causes for increase in the number of wild animals: "People are moving closer to wilderness and invading the territory of wild animals."
	Thesis: "There may be reasons to decry urban sprawl or the suburbanization of America, but the loss of wildlife is not one of them."
Two prime causes (with examples in parentheses) (7–10)	**Cause 1:** Natural reforestation (Examples: increases in forested land in New Hampshire, Connecticut, Massachusetts, Rhode Island, and other places in the East, the South, and the Lake States.)
	Cause 2: Suburbanization (Examples: suburbanization from the Florida Keys to New York to California.)
Causal chain for suburbanization cause (with examples in parentheses) (11–24)	**First causal link:** Some changes make land less habitable for wild animals (constructing streets, parking lots, buildings; clearing land; bringing in pets). However, other changes make land more habitable for and attractive to wild animals (creating ponds and parks, planting gardens and trees).
	Second causal link: Increase in wild animals causes problems (deer damage crops and tree seedlings and cause vehicle collisions, possibly increase Lyme disease; geese contaminate ponds and lawns; beaver cut down trees).
	Third causal link: Even large mammals (coyotes and mountain lions) are attracted to the rich, diverse environment of the suburbs and may endanger people's lives.
Concluding paragraphs (25–26)	Closing restates the thesis and looks to the future of environment restoration: "As wildlife proliferates, Americans will learn to live more harmoniously with birds and meso-mammals."

3. **Other patterns.** At different points, Shaw states objections to her main ideas and then refutes those objections. Find at least two instances of this *argument* technique.
4. The selection opens with a series of questions. What do you think is the author's purpose in posing these questions? How effective do you think the questions are?

Writing Assignments Using Cause-Effect as a Pattern of Development

1. Just as cropland can become suburbs, other environments can also change. Think of a place you know that has been changed by human activity. Maybe a polluted stream has been cleaned up and filled with fish, or an abandoned lot has become a vibrant neighborhood park. In an essay, show either what *caused* the change or what *effects* the change has had. Use your personal experiences as examples to support your ideas.
2. Like environmental changes made by people, human inventions can also have unintended consequences. Write an essay showing how an innovation may have had unintended *effects*. For example, the automobile makes travel easy, but it may also lead to a sedentary lifestyle. If possible, include a relevant causal chain. Be sure to add specific details to support your ideas.

Writing Assignment Combining Patterns of Development

3. Wild animals can be dangerous. Yet many people acquire animals such as tigers, cobras, and chimpanzees as pets. In an essay, *define* what "pet" means to you. Then *compare* the pros and cons of wild animals and domestic animals as pets. Include examples to *illustrate* your ideas.

Leila Ahmed

Leila Ahmed is a member of the faculty at Harvard Divinity School, where she became the first women's studies professor. Her research and publications focus primarily on issues relating to Islam and Islamic feminism. She is the author of *Women and Gender in Islam: The Historical Roots of a Modern Debate* (1993), *A Border Passage: From Cairo to America—A Woman's Journey* (2000), and *A Quiet Revolution: The Veil's Resurgence, from the Middle East to America* (2011), as well as many articles, including "Reinventing the Veil," which was first published in *Financial Times* on May 20, 2011.

Pre-Reading Journal

MyWritingLab

In the essay that follows, Ahmed explores how her ideas about wearing a *hijab*—a veil that covers the head and chest—have changed over the years. Think of something about which your ideas have changed as you've grown older and thought more about the subject. Take a few minutes to write in your journal and explore your ideas about how and why that change might have occurred.

Reinventing the Veil

I grew up in Cairo, Egypt. Through the decades of my childhood and   1
youth—the 1940s, 1950s and 1960s—the veil was a rarity not only at home
but in many Arab and Muslim-majority cities. In fact, when Albert Hourani,
the Oxford historian, surveyed the Arab world in the mid-1950s, he predicted that the veil would soon be a thing of the past.

Hourani's prophecy, made in an article called *The Vanishing Veil:*   2
A Challenge to the Old Order, would prove spectacularly wrong, but his piece
is nevertheless a gem because it so perfectly captures the ethos of that era.
Already the veil was becoming less and less common in my own country,
and, as Hourani explains, it was fast disappearing in other "advanced Arab
countries," such as Syria, Iraq and Jordan as well. An unveiling movement
had begun to sweep across the Arab world, gaining momentum with the
spread of education.

In those days, we shared all of Hourani's views and assumptions, includ-   3
ing the connections he made between unveiling, "advancement" and education (and between veiling and "backwardness"). We believed the veil was
merely a cultural habit, of no relevance to Islam or to religious piety. Even
deeply devout women did not wear a hijab. Being unveiled simply seemed
the modern "advanced" way of being Muslim.

Consequently the veil's steady "return" from the mid-1980s, and its   4
growing adoption, disturbed us. It was very troubling for people like me
who had been working for years as feminists on women and Islam. Why
would educated women, particularly those living in free western societies
where they could dress as they wished, be willing (apparently) to take on this
symbol of patriarchy and women's oppression?

The appearance of the hijab in my own neighborhood of Cambridge,   5
Massachusetts, in the late 1990s was the trigger that launched my own
studies into the phenomenon. I well remember the very evening that generated that spark. While I was walking past the common with a friend, a well-
known feminist who was visiting from the Arab world, we saw a large crowd
with all the women in hijab. At the time, this was still an unusual sight and,
frankly, it left us both with distinct misgivings.

While troubling on feminist grounds, the veil's return also disturbed me   6
in other ways. Having settled in the US, I had watched from afar through
the 1980s and 1990s as cities back home that I had known as places where
scarcely anyone wore hijab were steadily transformed into streets where the
vast majority of women now wore it.

This visually dramatic revolution in women's dress changed, to my eyes,   7
the very look and atmosphere of those cities. It had come about as a result of
the spread of Islamism in the 1970s, a very political form of Islam that was
worlds away from the deeply inward, apolitical form that had been common

in Egypt in my day. Fueled by the Muslim Brotherhood, the spread of Islamism always brought its signature emblem: the hijab.

Those same decades were marked in Egypt by rising levels of violence   8
and intellectual repression. In 1992, Farag Foda, a well-known journalist and critic of Islamism, was gunned down. Nasr Hamid Abu Zayd, a professor at Cairo University, was brought to trial on grounds of apostasy and had to flee the country. Soon after, Naguib Mahfouz, the Egyptian novelist and Nobel Laureate, was stabbed by an Islamist who considered his books blasphemous. Such events seemed a shocking measure of the country's descent into intolerance.

The sight of the hijab on the streets of America brought all this to mind.   9
Was its growing presence a sign that Islamic militancy was on the rise here too? Where were these young women (it was young women in particular who wore it) getting their ideas? And why were they accepting whatever it was they were being told, in this country where it was entirely normal to challenge patriarchal ideas? Could the Muslim Brotherhood have somehow succeeded in gaining a foothold here?

My instinctive readings of the Cambridge scene proved correct in some   10
ways. The Brotherhood, as well as other Islamist groups, had indeed established a base in America. While most immigrants were not Islamists, those who were quickly set about founding mosques and other organizations. Many immigrants who grew up as I did, without veils, sent their children to Islamic Sunday schools where they imbibed the Islamist outlook—including the hijab.

The veiled are always the most visible, but today Islamist-influenced   11
people make up no more than 30 to 40 percent of American Muslims. This is also roughly the percentage of women who veil as opposed to those who do not. This means of course that the majority of Muslim American women do not wear the veil, whether because they are secular or because they see it as an emblem of Islamism rather than Islam.

My research may have confirmed some initial fears, but it also chal-   12
lenged my assumptions. As I studied the process by which women had been persuaded to veil in Egypt in the first place, I came to see how essential women themselves had been in its promotion and the cause of Islamism. Among the most important was Zainab al-Ghazali, the "unsung mother" of the Muslim Brotherhood and a forceful activist who had helped keep the organization going after the death of its founder.

For these women, adopting hijab could be advantageous. Joining   13
Islamist groups and changing dress sometimes empowered them in relation to their parents; it also expanded job and marriage possibilities. Also, since the veil advertised women's commitment to conservative sexual mores, wearing it paradoxically increased their ability to move freely in public space—allowing them to take jobs in offices shared with men.

My assumptions about the veil's patriarchal meanings began to un- 14
ravel in the first interviews I conducted. One woman explained that she
wore it as a way of raising consciousness about the sexist messages of our
society. (This reminded me of the bra-burning days in America when
some women refused to shave their legs in a similar protest.) Another
wore the hijab for the same reason that one of her Jewish friends wore a
yarmulke: this was religiously required dress that made visible the presence
of a minority who were entitled, like all citizens, to justice and equality.
For many others, wearing hijab was a way of affirming pride and rejecting
negative stereotypes (like the Afros that flourished in the 1960s among
African-Americans).

Both Islamist and American ideals—including American ideals of gen- 15
der justice—seamlessly interweave in the lives of many of this younger
generation. This has been a truly remarkable decade as regards Muslim
women's activism. Perhaps the post-9/11 atmosphere in the west, which
led to intense criticism of Islam and its views of women, spurred Muslim
Americans into corrective action. Women are reinterpreting key religious
texts, including the Koran, and they have now taken on positions of leadership in Muslim American institutions: Ingrid Mattson, for example, was
twice elected president of the Islamic Society of North America. Such female
leadership is unprecedented in the home countries: even al-Ghazali, vital as
she was to the Brotherhood, never formally presided over an organization
which included men.

Many of these women—although not all—wear hijab. Clearly here 16
in the west, where women are free to wear what they want, the veil can
have multiple meanings. These are typically a far cry from the old notions
which I grew up with, and profoundly different from the veil's ancient
patriarchal meanings, which are still in full force in some countries. Here
in the west—embedded in the context of democracy, pluralism and a
commitment to gender justice—women's hijabs can have meanings that
they could not possibly have in countries which do not even subscribe to
the idea of equality.

But things are changing here as well. Interestingly, the issue of hijab 17
and whether it is religiously required or not is now coming under scrutiny
among women who grew up wearing it. Some are re-reading old texts and
concluding that the veil is irrelevant to Islamic piety. They cast it off even as
they remain committed Muslims.

It is too soon to tell whether this development, emerging most particu- 18
larly among intellectual women who once wore hijab, will gather force and
become a new unveiling movement for the 21st century: one that repeats,
on other continents and in completely new ways, the unveiling movement of
the early 20th century. Still, in a time when a number of countries have tried
banning the hijab and when typically such rules have backfired, it is worth

noting that here in America, where there are no such bans, a new movement may be quietly getting under way, a movement led this time by committed Muslim women who once wore hijab and who, often after much thought and study, have taken the decision to set it aside.

Occasionally now, although less so than in the past, I find myself nos- 19 talgic for the Islam of my childhood and youth, an Islam without veils and far removed from politics. An Islam which people seemed to follow not in the prescribed, regimented ways of today but rather according to their own inner sense, and their own particular temperaments, inclinations and the shifting vicissitudes of their lives.

I think my occasional yearning for that now bygone world has abated 20 (not that it is entirely gone) for a number of reasons. As I followed, a little like a detective, the extraordinary twists and turns of history that brought about this entirely unpredicted and unlikely "return" of the veil, I found the story itself so absorbing that I seemed to forget my nostalgia. I also lost the vague sense of annoyance, almost of affront, that I'd had over the years at how history had, seemingly so casually, set aside the entirely reasonable hopes and possibilities of that brighter and now vanished era.

In the process I came to see clearly what I had long known abstractly: 21 that living religions are by definition dynamic. Witness the fact that today we have women priests and rabbis—something unheard of just decades ago. As I followed the shifting history of the veil—a history which had reversed directions twice in one century—I realized that I had lived through one of the great sea changes now overtaking Islam. My own assumptions and the very ground they stood on had been fundamentally challenged. It now seems absurd that we once labeled people who veiled "backward" and those who did not "advanced," and that we thought that it was perfectly fine and reasonable to do so. Seeing one's own life from a new perspective can be unsettling, of course—but it is also quite bracing, and even rather exciting.

Questions for Close Reading   MyWritingLab

1. What is the selection's thesis? Locate the sentence(s) in which Ahmed states her main idea. If she doesn't state her thesis explicitly, express it in your own words.
2. According to her essay, what event "generated [the] spark" that caused Ahmed to explore the reason educated women were wearing what she thought of as a "symbol of patriarchy and women's oppression"?
3. According to Ahmed, how is Islamism different from Islam, and what examples does she provide of violent acts attributed to the spread of Islamism in Egypt towards the end of the twentieth century?
4. Who are Zainab al-Ghazali and Ingrid Mattson, and what roles have they played?

Questions About the Writer's Craft

1. The pattern. Does Ahmed's causal analysis have an essentially informative, speculative, or persuasive purpose? What makes you think so?

2. Other patterns. Ahmed *compares* and *contrasts* attitudes toward wearing hijabs. How do these comparisons and contrasts reinforce her thesis?

3. Other patterns. Ahmed incorporates several *narratives* into her essay. Identify the narratives she includes and comment on the purpose they serve.

4. How would you describe the tone Ahmed uses in her essay? Do you think the tone she uses is effective? Why or why not?

Writing Assignments Using Cause-Effect as a Pattern of Development

1. In her essay, Ahmed explores the ways in which ideas about "the veil" have changed in recent years and what caused those changes—a topic that clearly engages her for both personal and philosophical reasons. Write an essay in which you explore the causes and/or the effects of changes in attitude toward an issue that interests you. For example, you might explore the causes and/or effects of changes in attitude toward smoking, profanity, or obesity. Consider using outside sources and/or images to strengthen your essay.

2. Ahmed states, "The appearance of the hijab in my own neighborhood of Cambridge, Massachusetts, in the late 1990s was the trigger that launched my own studies into the phenomenon." What she saw that evening caused her to want to more clearly understand why an increasing number of women were wearing the veil. Think of an event that caused you to change your thinking about something. Maybe you read a news article about hungry children in your community and decided to volunteer at a food bank. Or maybe you witnessed a lifeguard rescuing a swimmer and decided to improve your own swimming skills. Write an essay in which you explain the event and why you changed your behavior as a result of it.

Writing Assignments Combining Patterns of Development

3. Ahmed references Albert Hourani, "the Oxford historian [who] surveyed the Arab world in the mid-1950s and predicted that the veil would soon become a thing of the past"—a prediction which proved to be incorrect. What other predictions can you think of (or identify after doing some research) that seemed likely to come true—at least at the time they were made—but later proved inaccurate. For example, as the year 2000 approached, many computer experts predicted widespread chaos, anticipating that computer clocks would automatically reset to 1900 rather than advance to the next millennium. Yet, as January 1, 2000, came and went, it became clear that these predictions were inaccurate and alarmist. Write an essay in which you not only *describe* the incorrect prediction and what prompted it but also *compare* and *contrast* the predicted outcome with what actually transpired.

Jacques D'Amboise

When Jacques D'Amboise (1934–) was growing up in a tough, gang-infested New York City neighborhood, his French-Canadian mother wanted to give her children a glimpse into a world of beauty. She enrolled D'Amboise's sister in a ballet class and, hoping to protect her son from the dangers of street life, insisted that her son take the class, too. It was there that D'Amboise discovered his love of dance. While still in his teens, D'Amboise joined the New York City Ballet and became one of the foremost dancers of his day. He appeared in several films, including *Seven Brides for Seven Brothers* (1954) and *Carousel* (1956). In 1976, he founded the National Dance Institute (NDI), which offers dance classes to public school students, most from underprivileged backgrounds. Through NDI, hundreds of children have experienced the joy and discipline of dance. D'Amboise's NDI experience provided the basis of a book he coauthored, *Teaching the Magic of Dance* (1983), and his contributions to the arts led to his being honored at the Kennedy Center in 1995. In 2011, he published his memoir, *I Was a Dancer*. The following selection originally appeared in *Parade* magazine in 1989.

Pre-Reading Journal Entry   MyWritingLab

While you were growing up, to what extent were you exposed to the arts: music, dance, drawing, painting, and so forth? Looking back, do you think that this exposure—or lack of exposure—worked to your advantage or to your disadvantage? Use your journal to respond to these questions.

Showing What Is Possible

When I was 7 years old, I was forced to watch my sister's ballet classes. 1 This was to keep me off the street and away from my pals, who ran with gangs like the ones in *West Side Story*. The class was taught by Madame Seda, a Georgian-Armenian[1] who had a school at 181st Street and St. Nicholas Avenue in New York City. As she taught the little girls, I would sit, fidget and diabolically try to disrupt the class by making irritating little noises.

But she was very wise, Madame Seda. She let me get away with it, ignor- 2 ing me until the end of the class, when everybody did the big jumps, a series of leaps in place, called *changements.*

At that point, Madame Seda turned and, stabbing a finger at me, said, 3 "All right, little brother, if you've got so much energy, get up and do these jumps. See if you can jump as high as the girls." So I jumped. And loved it. I felt like I was flying. And she said, "Oh, that was wonderful! From now on, if you are quiet during the class, I'll let you join in the *changements.*"

[1]A person from the neighboring republics of Georgia and Armenia, formerly of the Soviet Union (editors' note).

After that, I'd sit quietly in the class and wait for the jumps. A few   4
classes later, she said, "You've got to learn how to jump and not make any
noise when you come down. You should learn to do the *pliés* [graceful knee
bends] that come at the beginning of the class." So I would do *pliés*, then
wait respectfully for the end of class to do the jumps.

Finally she said, "You jump high, and you are landing beautifully, but   5
you look awful in the air, flaying your arms about. You've got to take the
rest of the class and learn how to do beautiful hands and arms."

I was hooked.   6

An exceptional teacher got a bored little kid, me, interested in ballet.   7
How? She challenged me to a test, complimented me on my effort and then
immediately gave me a new challenge. She set up an environment for the
achievement of excellence and cared enough to invite me to be part of it.
And, without realizing it fully at the time, I made an important discovery.

Dance is the most immediate and accessible of the arts because it in-   8
volves your own body. When you learn to move your body on a note of
music, it's exciting. You have taken control of your body and, by learning to
do that, you discover that you can take control of your life.

I took classes with Madame Seda for six months, once a week, but at   9
the end of spring, in June 1942, she called over my mother, my sister and
me and did an unbelievably modest and generous thing. She said, "You and
your sister are very talented. You should go to a better teacher." She sent us
to George Balanchine's school—the School of American Ballet.

Within a few years, I was performing children's roles. At 15, I became   10
part of a classical ballet company. What an extraordinary thing for a street
boy from Washington Heights, with friends in gangs. Half grew up to
become policemen and the other half gangsters—and I became a ballet
dancer!

I had dreamed of being a doctor or an archaeologist or a priest. But   11
by the time I was 17, I was a principal dancer performing major roles in
the ballets, and by the time I was 21, I was doing movies, Broadway shows
and choreography. I then married a ballerina from New York City Ballet,
Carolyn George, and we were (and still are) blessed with two boys and twin
daughters.

It was a joyful career that lasted four decades. That's a long time to   12
be dancing and, inevitably, a time came when I realized that there were
not many years left for me as a performer. I wasn't sure what to do next,
but then I thought about how I had become a dancer, and the teachers
who had graced my life. Perhaps I could engage young children, especially
boys, in the magic of the arts—in dance in particular. Not necessarily to
prepare them to be professional performers, but to create an awareness by
giving them a chance to experience the arts. So I started National Dance
Institute.

That was 13 years ago. Since then, with the help of fellow teachers and   13
staff at NDI, I have taught dance to thousands of inner-city children. And in
each class, I rediscover why teaching dance to children is so important.

Each time I can use dance to help a child discover that he can control   14
the way he moves, I am filled with joy. At a class I recently taught at P.S. 59
in Brooklyn, there was one boy who couldn't get from his right foot to his
left. He was terrified. Everyone was watching. And what he had to do was
so simple: take a step with his left foot on a note of music. All his classmates
could do it, but he couldn't.

He kept trying, but he kept doing it wrong until finally he was frozen,   15
unable to move at all. I put my arm around him and said, "Let's do it together. We'll do it in slow motion." We did it. I stepped back and said,
"Now do it alone, and fast." With his face twisted in concentration, he
slammed his left foot down correctly on the note. He did it!

The whole class applauded. He was so excited. But I think I was even   16
happier, because I knew what had taken place. He had discovered he could
take control of his body, and from that he can learn to take control of his life.
If I can open the door to show a child that that is possible, it is wonderful.

Dance is the art to express time and space. That is what our universe is   17
about. We can hardly make a sentence without signifying some expression
of distance, place or time: "See you later." "Meet you at the corner in five
minutes."

Dance is the art that human beings have developed to express that we   18
live, right now, in a world of movement and varying tempos.

Dance, as an art, has to be taught. However, when teaching, it's im-   19
portant to set up an environment where both the student and teacher can
discover together. Never teach something you don't love and believe in. But
how to set up that environment?

When I have a new group of young students and I'm starting a class, I   20
use Madame Seda's technique. I say, "Can you do this test? I'm going to
give all 100 of you exactly 10 seconds to get off your seats and be standing
and spread out all over the stage floor. And do it silently. Go!" And I start a
countdown. Naturally, they run, yelling and screaming, and somehow arrive
with several seconds to spare. I say, "Freeze. You all failed. You made noise,
and you got there too soon. I said 'exactly 10 seconds'—not 6 or 8 or 11.
Go back to your seats, and we'll do it again. And if you don't get it, we'll go
back and do it again until you do. And if, at the end of the hour, you still
haven't gotten it, I'm not going to teach you."

They usually get it the second time. Never have I had to do it more   21
than three.

Demand precision, be clear and absolutely truthful. When they re-   22
spond—and they will—congratulate them on the extraordinary control they
have just exhibited. Why is that important? Because it's the beginning of

knowing yourself, knowing that you can manage yourself if you want. And it's the beginning of dance. Once the children see that we are having a class of precision, order and respect, they are relieved, and we have a great class.

I've taught dance to Russian children, Australian children, Indian chil- 23
dren, Chinese children, fat children, skinny children, handicapped children, groups of Australian triathletes, New York City police, senior citizens and 3-year-olds. The technique is the same everywhere, although there are cultural differences.

For example, when I was in China, I would say to the children, "I want 24
everybody to come close and watch what I am going to do." But in China they have had to deal with following a teacher when there are masses of them. And they discovered that the way to see what the teacher does is not to move close but to move away. So 100 people moved back to watch the one—me.

I realized they were right. How did they learn that? Thousands of years 25
of masses of people having to follow one teacher.

There are cultural differences and there are differences among people. 26
In any group of dancers, there are some who are ready and excel more than others. There are many reasons—genetic, environment, the teachers they had. People blossom at different times.

But whatever the differences, someone admiring you, encouraging you 27
works so much better than the reverse. "You can do it, you are wonderful," works so much better than, "You're no good, the others are better than you, you've got to try harder." That never works.

I don't think there are any untalented children. But I think there are 28
those whose talents never get the chance to flower. Perhaps they were never encouraged. Perhaps no one took the time to find out how to teach them. That is a tragedy.

However, the single most terrible thing we are doing to our children, 29
I believe, is polluting them. I don't mean just with smog and crack, but by not teaching them the civilizing things we have taken millions of years to develop. But you cannot have a dance class without having good manners, without having respect. Dance can teach those things.

I think of each person as a trunk that's up in the attic. What are you go- 30
ing to put in the trunk? Are you going to put in machine guns, loud noises, foul language, dirty books and ignorance? Because if you do, that's what is going to be left after you, that's what your children are going to have, and that will determine the world of the future. Or are you going to fill that trunk with music, dance, poetry, literature, good manners and loving friends?

I say, fill your trunk with the best that is available to you from the wealth 31
of human culture. Those things will nourish you and your children. You can clean up your own environment and pass it on to the next generation. That's why I teach dance.

Cause-Effect

Questions for Close Reading

1. What is the selection's thesis? Locate the sentence(s) in which D'Amboise states his main idea. If he doesn't state the thesis explicitly, express it in your own words.
2. In paragraph 2, D'Amboise says that Madame Seda "was very wise." In what ways was she wise?
3. D'Amboise believes that dance has to be taught in a particular kind of environment. What, according to D'Amboise, are the most important qualities of that environment?
4. What does D'Amboise mean in paragraph 29 when he says that we pollute our children? What does D'Amboise consider the possible consequences of such pollution?

Questions About the Writer's Craft

1. **The pattern.** Writers often organize cause-effect pieces using either a chronological or an emphatic sequence—or perhaps a combination of the two. Identify the organizational pattern that D'Amboise uses.
2. **Other patterns.** D'Amboise begins his essay with a *narrative* that tells the story of his first experience with Madame Seda. What is the purpose of this opening narrative? How does it prepare readers for what follows?
3. Reread paragraphs 20–21. The two short sentences in paragraph 21 could have concluded paragraph 20. Why do you think D'Amboise placed these two sentences in a separate paragraph?
4. In the last two paragraphs, D'Amboise uses an *analogy* (a comparison between two objects or people that seem to have little in common). Identify the analogy, and explain its relevance to the essay's central idea.

Writing Assignments Using Cause-Effect as a Pattern of Development

1. According to D'Amboise, a good teacher is one who provides a classroom of precision and order. Without structure and clear expectations, D'Amboise suggests, children will not flourish in the classroom. Do you think the same might be said of children in the home? Write a paper analyzing the effect on children of *one* of the following: a parenting style that imposes a reasonable number of boundaries, one that imposes too many limits, one that imposes too few restrictions. When writing, draw upon your own experiences and observations as well as those of friends, classmates, and family members.
2. D'Amboise asserts that "the single most terrible thing we are doing to our children...is polluting them...by not teaching them the civilizing things we have taken millions of years to develop." Among the pollutants he lists are drugs, violence, and pornography. Select one of these negative influences (or another you consider important), and write an essay analyzing how it pollutes children. You might show how this factor affects children's behavior, self-concept, and attitudes toward others. Before preparing your paper, interview classmates, friends, and family members to learn in what ways they think this factor influences children.

Writing Assignment Combining Patterns of Development

3. D'Amboise's opening narrative *illustrates* how he became interested in dance. Consider the career path you have chosen or are thinking about choosing. What experiences pointed you in that direction? Write an essay in which you explain why you are interested in that particular career. *Recount* at least two experiences that helped you feel this work would be interesting and rewarding. Use vivid dialogue to dramatize the intensity of the experiences.

Juan Williams

Juan Williams was born in 1954, the year of the historic U.S. Supreme Court decision in *Brown v. Board of Education*. Williams and his family emigrated to the United States from Panama in 1958, and Willliams, who attended New York City public schools for many years, went on to earn a B.A. in philosophy from Haverford College. During the course of his career, Williams has written for many prominent media outlets, including *The New York Times, The Washington Post*, and National Public Radio. In addition, he is the author of a number of books, including *Eyes on the Prize: America's Civil Rights Years, 1954–1965*. He currently works for Fox News Channel. The following selection was first published in the April 2004 issue of the *American School Board Journal*.

Pre-Reading Journal Entry

MyWritingLab

Like legal rulings, personal decisions can have far-reaching or unintended consequences. Think of decisions you have made, for example, deciding where to go to college, whom to have as a roommate, or whether to take (or quit) a job. Were the results of those decisions what you expected? Jot down some notes in your journal about those decisions.

The Ruling That Changed America

Fifty years later, the *Brown*[1] decision looks different. At a distance   1
from the volcanic heat of May 17, 1954, the real impact of the legal, political, and cultural eruption that changed America is not exactly what it first appeared to be.

On that Monday in May, the high court's ruling outlawing school seg-   2
regation in the United States generated urgent news flashes on the radio and frenzied black headlines in special editions of afternoon newspapers. One

---

[1]In the legal case *Brown v. Board of Education*, the U.S. Supreme Court ruled that separation of schools and other public facilities by race (known as the "separate but equal" doctrine) violated the Constitution (editors' note).

swift and unanimous decision by the top judges in the land was going to end segregation in public schools. Southern politicians reacted with such fury and fear that they immediately called the day "Black Monday."

South Carolina Gov. James Byrnes, who rose to political power with pas-   3 sionate advocacy of segregation, said the decision was "the end of civilization in the South as we have known it." Georgia Gov. Herman Talmadge struck an angry tone. He said Georgia had no intention of allowing "mixed race" schools as long as he was governor. And he touched on Confederate pride from the days when the South went to war with the federal government over slavery by telling supporters that the Supreme Court's ruling was not law in his state; he said it was "the first step toward national suicide." The *Brown* decision should be regarded, he said, as nothing but a "mere scrap of paper."

Meanwhile, newspapers for black readers reacted with exultation.   4 "The Supreme Court decision is the greatest victory for the Negro people since the Emancipation Proclamation,"[2] said Harlem's *Amsterdam News*. A writer in the *Chicago Defender* explained, "[N]either the atomic bomb nor the hydrogen bomb will ever be as meaningful to our democracy." And Thurgood Marshall,[3] the NAACP lawyer who directed the legal fight that led to *Brown,* predicted the end of segregation in all American public schools by the fall of 1955.

Slow Progress, Backward Steps

Ten years later, however, very little school integration had taken place.   5 True to the defiant words of segregationist governors, the Southern states had hunkered down in a massive resistance campaign against school integration. Some Southern counties closed their schools instead of allowing blacks and whites into the same classrooms. In other towns, segregationist academies opened, and most if not all of the white children left the public schools for the racially exclusive alternatives. And in most places, the governors, mayors, and school boards found it easy enough to just ask for more time before integrating schools.

That slow-as-molasses approach worked. In 1957. President Eisenhower   6 had to send troops from the 101st Airborne into Little Rock just to get nine black children safely into Central High School. Only in the late '60s, under the threat of losing federal funding, did large-scale school integration begin in Southern public schools. And in many places, in both the North and the South, black and white students did not go to school together until a federal court ordered schoolchildren to ride buses across town to bring the races together.

[2]On January 1, 1863, President Abraham Lincoln issued an executive order, known as the Emancipation Proclamation, freeing most slaves in the states and territories (editors' note).
[3]Thurgood Marshall went on to become the first African-American Supreme Court justice, serving from 1967 to 1991 (editors' note).

Today, 50 years later, a study by the Civil Rights Project at Harvard   7
University finds that the percentage of white students attending public
schools with Hispanic or black students has steadily declined since 1988.
In fact, the report concludes that school integration in the United States is
"lower in 2000 than in 1970, before busing for racial balance began." In the
South, home to the majority of America's black population, there is now less
school integration than there was in 1970. The Harvard report concluded,
"At the beginning of the 21st century, American schools are now 12 years
into the process of continuous resegregation."

Today, America's schools are so heavily segregated that more than two-   8
thirds of black and Hispanic students are in schools where a majority of the
students are not white. And today, most of the nation's white children attend
a school that is almost 80 percent white. Hispanics are now the most segregated group of students in the nation because they live in highly concentrated
clusters.

At the start of the new century, 50 years after *Brown* shook the nation,   9
segregated housing patterns and an increase in the number of black and
brown immigrants have concentrated minorities in impoverished big cities
and created a new reality of public schools segregated by race and class.

The Real Impact of *Brown*

So, if *Brown* didn't break apart school segregation, was it really the   10
earth-quake that it first appeared to be?

Yes. Today, it is hard to even remember America before *Brown* because   11
the ruling completely changed the nation. It still stands as the laser beam
that first signaled that the federal government no longer gave its support to
racial segregation among Americans.

Before *Brown*, the federal government lent its power to enforcing the   12
laws of segregation under an 1896 Supreme Court ruling that permitted
"separate but equal" treatment of blacks and whites. Blacks and whites who
tried to integrate factories, unions, public buses and trains, parks, the military, restaurants, department stores, and more found that the power of the
federal government was with the segregationists.

Before *Brown*, the federal government had struggled even to pass a law   13
banning lynching.

But after the Supreme Court ruled that segregation in public schools   14
was a violation of the Constitution, the federal attitude toward enforcing
second-class citizenship for blacks shifted on the scale of a change in the
ocean's tide or a movement in the plates of the continents. Once the highest
court in the land said equal treatment for all did not allow for segregation,
then the lower courts, the Justice Department, and federal prosecutors, as
well as the FBI, all switched sides They didn't always act to promote integration, but they no longer used their power to stop it.

An irreversible shift had begun, and it was the direct result of the *Brown*   15
decision.

The change in the attitude of federal officials created a wave of antici-   16
pation among black people, who became alert to the possibility of achieving the long-desired goal of racial equality. There is no way to offer a hard
measure of a change in attitude. But the year after *Brown*, Rosa Parks
refused to give up her seat to a white man on a racially segregated bus
in Montgomery, Ala. That led to a yearlong bus boycott and the emergence of massive, nonviolent protests for equal rights. That same year,
Martin Luther King Jr. emerged as the nation's prophet of civil rights for
all Americans.

Even when a black 14-year-old, Emmit Till, was killed in Mississippi for   17
supposedly whistling at a white woman, there was a new reaction to old racial brutality. One of Till's elderly relatives broke with small-town Southern
tradition and dared to take the witness stand and testify against the white
men he saw abduct the boy. Until *Brown*, the simple act of a black man
standing up to speak against a white man in Mississippi was viewed as futile
and likely to result in more white-on-black violence.

The sense among black people—and many whites as well—that a   18
new era had opened created a new boldness. Most black parents in Little
Rock did not want to risk harm to their children by allowing them to
join in efforts to integrate Central High. But working with local NAACP
officials, the parents of nine children decided it was a new day and time to
make history. That same spirit of new horizons was at work in 1962 when
James Meredith became the first black student to enroll at the University
of Mississippi. And in another lurch away from the traditional support
of segregation, the federal government sent troops as well as Justice
Department officials to the university to protect Meredith's rights.

The next year, when Alabama Gov. George Wallace felt the political   19
necessity of making a public stand against integration at the University of
Alabama, he stood only briefly in the door to block black students and then
stepped aside in the face of federal authority. That was another shift toward
a world of high hopes for racial equality; again, from the perspective of the
21st century, it looks like another aftershock of the *Brown* decision.

The same psychology of hope infected young people, black and white,   20
nationwide in the early '60s. The Freedom Rides, lunch-counter sit-ins, and
protest marches for voting rights all find their roots in *Brown*. So, too, did
the racially integrated 1963 March on Washington at which Martin Luther
King Jr. famously said he had a vision of a promised land where the sons of
slaves and the sons of slave owners could finally join together in peace. The
desire for change became a demand for change in the impatient voice of
Malcolm X, the militant Black Muslim who called for immediate change by
violent means if necessary.

In 1964, a decade after *Brown*, the Civil Rights Act[4] was passed by a   21
Congress beginning to respond to the changing politics brought about by
the landmark decision. The next year, 1965, the wave of change had swelled
to the point that Congress passed the Voting Rights Act.[5]

Closer to the Mountaintop

This sea change in black and white attitudes toward race also had an   22
impact on culture. Churches began to grapple with the Christian and Jewish
principles of loving thy neighbor, even if thy neighbor had a different color
skin. Major league baseball teams no longer feared a fan revolt if they allowed
more than one black player on a team. Black writers, actors, athletes, and musicians—ranging from James Baldwin to the Supremes and Muhammad Ali—
began to cross over into the mainstream of American culture.

The other side of the change in racial attitudes was white support for   23
equal rights. College-educated young white people in the '60s often defined
themselves by their willingness to embrace racial equality. Bob Dylan sang
about the changing times as answers "blowing in the wind." Movies like
"Guess Who's Coming to Dinner"[6] found major audiences among all races.
And previously all white private colleges and universities began opening
their doors to black students. The resulting arguments over affirmative action in college admissions led to the Supreme Court's 1978 decision in the
Bakke[7] case, which outlawed the use of quotas, and its recent ruling that the
University of Michigan can take race into account as one factor in admitting
students to its law school. The court has also had to deal with affirmative action in the business world, in both hiring and contracts—again as a result of
questions of equality under the Constitution raised by *Brown*.

But the most important legacy of the *Brown* decision, by far, is the   24
growth of an educated black middle class. The number of black people
graduating from high school and college has soared since *Brown*, and the
incomes of blacks have climbed steadily as a result. Home ownership and
investment in the stock market among black Americans have rocketed since
the 1980s. The political and economic clout of that black middle class

[4]Civil Rights Act of 1964 essentially prohibits discrimination against people on the basis of race,
color, religion, sex, or national origin (editors' note).
[5]The National Voting Rights Act of 1965 outlaws any voting requirements, such as literacy
tests, that have the effect of preventing people, especially minorities, from exercising their right
to vote (editors' note).
[6]In the movie, which stars Sidney Poitier, a young white woman from a liberal family brings her
black fiancé home to introduce to her parents (editors' note).
[7]The U.S. Supreme Court decided, in the case *Regents of the University of California v. Bakke*,
that racial quotas were illegal in college admissions, but that race could be used as one factor in
deciding on an applicant's admission (editors' note).

continues to bring America closer to the mountaintop vision of racial equality that Dr. King might have dreamed of 50 years ago.

The Supreme Court's May 17, 1954, ruling in *Brown* remains a landmark legal decision. But it is much more than that. It is the "Big Bang" of all American history in the 20th century.   25

Questions for Close Reading   MyWritingLab

1. What is the selection's thesis? Locate the sentence(s) in which Williams states his main idea. If he doesn't state his thesis explicitly, express it in your own words.
2. According to Williams, what were the two contrasting types of reactions to the Supreme Court decision in the *Brown* case?
3. What does Williams say about the ultimate effect of the *Brown* decision on school integration? What evidence does he provide to support his point of view?
4. How does Williams characterize the effect of the *Brown* decision on American culture? What examples does he use to support his view?

Questions About the Writer's Craft

1. **The pattern.** In the section headed "The Real Impact of *Brown*," the author establishes a causal chain. Identify the components of the chain. Does the author's analysis seem well supported?
2. The author uses section headings in his essay. What effect does this have? What do the headings reflect about the essay's organization? How is information organized within each section?
3. **Other patterns.** Williams uses illustration and comparison to educate readers about the realities of segregation. Where is comparison used most effectively in the essay? What are some metaphors Williams uses to describe the *Brown* decision?
4. Williams gives many examples and quotations to support his thesis. He also cites a study. What study is this? How is the study used? Do you think the study offers reliable proof?

Writing Assignments Using Cause-Effect as a Pattern of Development

1. Williams asserts that the *Brown* decision eventually led to the passage of important federal civil rights legislation. Think of a federal law that has had a big impact on Americans' civil liberties. Some possibilities are the Americans with Disabilities Act, the Individuals with Disabilities Education Act, Title IX (sports education for girls and women), and the Indian Civil Rights Act. Do some research and write an essay explaining the effects of the law. Include any relevant personal examples.
2. The author ascribes much of the progress in civil rights to a "change in racial attitudes." Think of a law, custom, or societal attitude that you feel should be changed. For example, you might think that attitudes toward consumerism need to change. Brainstorm a list of possible actions that could cause the attitude change and possible consequences of a successful attitude change. Write an essay in which you focus on causes, effects, or both. Remember to use specific examples to support your points.

Writing Assignment Combining Patterns of Development

3. The author mentions two examples of art that express changed racial attitudes: Bob Dylan's song "Blowin' in the Wind" and the movie *Guess Who's Coming to Dinner,* starring Sidney Poitier. Identify two other works of art—movies, books, plays, and so on—that express a change in cultural attitudes. For example, the movies *Brokeback Mountain* and *Dallas Buyers Club* might reflect a change in attitudes toward homosexuality. *Describe* the works and explain how they *illustrate* cultural change.

John M. Darley & Bibb Latané

Harvard graduate John M. Darley (1938–) is professor of psychology at Princeton University, where he studies the principles of moral judgment in children and adults. Bibb Latané (1937–) has been chair of the Psychology Department at Florida Atlantic University, director of the Institute for Research in Social Science at the University of North Carolina, and director of the Behavioral Science Laboratory at Ohio State University. Currently head of the Center for Human Science in Chapel Hill, North Carolina, Latané is interested in how groups of people change and interact. Darley and Latané are coauthors of *The Unresponsive Bystander: Why Doesn't He Help?* (1970) and *Help in a Crisis: Bystander Response to an Emergency* (1976). Based on their research into the origins of noninvolvement, "When Will People Help in a Crisis?" (1968) was awarded an essay prize from the American Association for the Advancement of Science.

Pre-Reading Journal Entry

MyWritingLab

Faced with a challenging or difficult situation, people sometimes choose *not* to get involved—and then later regret this decision. Such situations might include, for example, helping an injured stranger, standing up for someone being bullied, and letting in a stray animal on a cold day. In your journal, write about one or more times when you faced a difficult situation and failed to respond in a way that you now believe you should have.

When Will People Help in a Crisis?

Kitty Genovese is set upon by a maniac as she returns home from work at 3 A.M. Thirty-eight of her neighbors in Kew Gardens, N.Y., come to their windows when she cries out in terror; not one comes to her assistance, even though her assailant takes half an hour to murder her. No one so much as calls the police. She dies. 1

Andrew Mormille is stabbed in the head and neck as he rides in a New York City subway train. Eleven other riders flee to another car as the 2

Source: Reprinted with Permission from *Psychology Today* Magazine, (Copyright © 1968 Sussex Publishers, LLC.).

17-year-old boy bleeds to death; not one comes to his assistance, even though his attackers have left the car. He dies.

Eleanor Bradley trips and breaks her leg while shopping on New York   3
City's Fifth Avenue. Dazed and in shock, she calls for help, but the hurrying stream of people simply parts and flows past. Finally, after 40 minutes, a taxi driver stops and helps her to a doctor.

How can so many people watch another human being in distress and do   4
nothing? Why don't they help?

Since we started research on bystander responses to emergencies, we   5
have heard many explanations for the lack of intervention in such cases. "The megalopolis in which we live makes closeness difficult and leads to the alienation of the individual from the group," says the psychoanalyst. "This sort of disaster," says the sociologist, "shakes the sense of safety and sureness of the individuals involved and causes psychological withdrawal." "Apathy," say others. "Indifference."

All of these analyses share one characteristic: they set the indifferent wit-   6
ness apart from the rest of us. Certainly not one of us who reads about these incidents in horror is apathetic, alienated or depersonalized. Certainly these terrifying cases have no personal implications for us. We needn't feel guilty, or re-examine ourselves, or anything like that. Or should we?

If we look closely at the behavior of witnesses to these incidents, the   7
people involved begin to seem less inhuman and a lot more like the rest of us. They were not indifferent. The 38 witnesses of Kitty Genovese's murder, for example, did not merely look at the scene once and then ignore it. They continued to stare out of their windows, caught, fascinated, distressed, unwilling to act but unable to turn away.

Why, then, didn't they act?   8

There are three things the bystander must do if he is to intervene in an   9
emergency: *notice* that something is happening; *interpret* that event as an emergency; and decide that he has *personal responsibility* for intervention. As we shall show, the presence of other bystanders may at each stage inhibit his action.

The Unseeing Eye

Suppose that a man has a heart attack. He clutches his chest, staggers to   10
the nearest building and slumps sitting to the sidewalk. Will a passerby come to his assistance? First, the bystander has to notice that something is happening. He must tear himself away from his private thoughts and pay attention. But Americans consider it bad manners to look closely at other people in public. We are taught to respect the privacy of others, and when among strangers we close our ears and avoid staring. In a crowd, then, each person is less likely to notice a potential emergency than when alone.

Experimental evidence corroborates this. We asked college students to 11
an interview about their reactions to urban living. As the students waited to
see the interviewer, either by themselves or with two other students, they
filled out a questionnaire. Solitary students often glanced idly about while
filling out their questionnaires: those in groups kept their eyes on their
own papers.

As part of the study, we staged an emergency: smoke was released into 12
the waiting room through a vent. Two thirds of the subjects who were alone
noticed the smoke immediately, but only 25 percent of those waiting in
groups saw it as quickly. Although eventually all the subjects did become
aware of the smoke—when the atmosphere grew so smoky as to make them
cough and rub their eyes—this study indicates that the more people present, the slower an individual may be to perceive an emergency and the more
likely he is not to see it at all.

Seeing Is Not Necessarily Believing

Once an event is noticed, an onlooker must decide if it is truly an emer- 13
gency. Emergencies are not always clearly labeled as such; "smoke" pouring
into a waiting room may be caused by fire, or it may merely indicate a leak in
a steam pipe. Screams in the street may signal an assault or a family quarrel.
A man lying in a doorway may be having a coronary—or he may simply be
sleeping off a drunk.

A person trying to interpret a situation often looks at those around him 14
to see how he should react. If everyone else is calm and indifferent, he will
tend to remain so; if everyone else is reacting strongly, he is likely to become
aroused. This tendency is not merely slavish conformity; ordinarily we derive
much valuable information about new situations from how others around us
behave. It's a rare traveler who, in picking a roadside restaurant, chooses to
stop at one where no other cars appear in the parking lot.

But occasionally the reactions of others provide false information. The 15
studied nonchalance of patients in a dentist's waiting room is a poor indication of their inner anxiety. It is considered embarrassing to "lose your cool"
in public. In a potentially acute situation, then, everyone present will appear
more unconcerned that he is in fact. A crowd can thus force inaction on its
members by implying, through its passivity, that an event is not an emergency. Any individual in such a crowd fears that he may appear a fool if he
behaves as though it were.

To determine how the presence of other people affects a person's inter- 16
pretation of an emergency, Latané and Judith Rodin set up another experiment. Subjects were paid $2 to participate in a survey of game and puzzle
preferences conducted at Columbia University by the Consumer Testing
Bureau. An attractive young market researcher met them at the door and

took them to the testing room, where they were given questionnaires to fill out. Before leaving, she told them that she would be working next door in her office, which was separated from the room by a folding room-divider. She then entered her office, where she shuffled papers, opened drawers and made enough noise to remind the subjects of her presence. After four minutes she turned on a high-fidelity tape recorder.

On it, the subjects heard the researcher climb up on a chair, perhaps to   17
reach for a stack of papers on the bookcase. They heard a loud crash and a scream as the chair collapsed and she fell, and they heard her moan, "Oh, my foot…I…I…can't move it Oh, I…can't get this…thing off me." Her cries gradually got more subdued and controlled.

Twenty-six people were alone in the waiting room when the "accident"   18
occurred. Seventy percent of them offered to help the victim. Many pushed back the divider to offer their assistance; others called out to offer their help.

Among those waiting in pairs, only 20 percent—8 out of 40—offered   19
to help. The other 32 remained unresponsive. In defining the situation as a nonemergency, they explained to themselves why the other member of the pair did not leave the room; they also removed any reason for action themselves. Whatever had happened, it was believed to be not serious. "A mild sprain," some said. "I didn't want to embarrass her." In a "real" emergency, they assured us, they would be among the first to help.

The Lonely Crowd

Even if a person defines an event as an emergency, the presence of   20
other bystanders may still make him less likely to intervene. He feels that his responsibility is diffused and diluted. Thus, if your car breaks down on a busy highway, hundreds of drivers whiz by without anyone's stopping to help—but if you are stuck on a nearly deserted country road, whoever passes you first is likely to stop.

To test this diffusion-of-responsibility theory, we simulated an emer-   21
gency in which people overheard a victim calling for help. Some thought they were the only person to hear the cries; the rest believed that others heard them, too. As with the witnesses to Kitty Genovese's murder, the subjects could not *see* one another or know what others were doing. The kind of direct group inhibition found in the other two studies could not operate.

For the simulation, we recruited 72 students at New York University   22
to participate in what was referred to as a "group discussion" of personal problems in an urban university. Each student was put in an individual room equipped with a set of headphones and a microphone. It was explained that this precaution had been taken because participants might feel embarrassed about discussing their problems publicly. Also, the experimenter said that he

would not listen to the initial discussion, but would only ask for reactions later. Each person was to talk in turn.

The first to talk reported that he found it difficult to adjust to New York and his studies. Then, hesitantly and with obvious embarrassment, he mentioned that he was prone to nervous seizures when he was under stress. Other students then talked about their own problems in turn. The number of people in the "discussion" varied. But whatever the apparent size of the group—two, three or six people—only the subject was actually present; the others, as well as the instructions and the speeches of the victim-to-be, were present only on a pre-recorded tape. 23

When it was the first person's turn to talk again, he launched into the following performance, becoming louder and having increasing speech difficulties: "I can see a lot of er of er how other people's problems are similar to mine because er I mean er they're not er e-easy to handle sometimes and er I er um I think I I need er if if could er er somebody er er er give me give me a little er give me a little help here because er I er *uh* I've got a a one of the er seiz-er er things coming *on* and and er uh uh (choking sounds)..." 24

Eighty-five percent of the people who believed themselves to be alone with the victim came out of their room to help. Sixty-two percent of the people who believed there was *one* other bystander did so. Of those who believed there were four other bystanders, only 31 percent reported the fit. The responsibility-diluting effect of other people was so strong that single individuals were more than twice as likely to report the emergency as those who thought other people also knew about it. 25

The Lesson Learned

People who failed to report the emergency showed few signs of the apathy and indifference thought to characterize "unresponsive bystanders." When the experimenter entered the room to end the situation, the subject often asked if the victim was "all right." Many of them showed physical signs of nervousness; they often had trembling hands and sweating palms. If anything, they seemed more emotionally aroused than did those who reported the emergency. Their emotional behavior was a sign of their continuing conflict concerning whether to respond or not. 26

Thus, the stereotype of the unconcerned, depersonalized *homo urbanus,* blandly watching the misfortunes of others, proves inaccurate. Instead, we find that a bystander to an emergency is an anguished individual in genuine doubt, wanting to do the right thing but compelled to make complex decisions under pressure of stress and fear. His reactions are shaped by the actions of others—all too frequently by their inaction. 27

And we are that bystander. Caught up by the apparent indifference of others, we may pass by an emergency without helping or even realizing 28 that help is needed. Once we are aware of the influence of those around us, however, we can resist it. We can choose to see distress and step forward to relieve it.

Questions for Close Reading

MyWritingLab

1. What is the selection's thesis? Locate the sentence(s) in which Darley and Latané state their main idea. If they don't state the thesis explicitly, express it in your own words.
2. According to the authors, what three factors prevent people in a crowd from helping victims during an emergency?
3. Why did Darley and Latané isolate the subjects in separate rooms during the staged emergency described in paragraphs 21–26?
4. What kind of person, according to the authors, would tend to ignore or bypass a person experiencing a problem? What might encourage this person to act more responsibly?

Questions About the Writer's Craft

1. **The pattern.** What techniques do Darley and Latané use to help readers focus on the causes of people's inaction during an emergency?
2. **Other patterns.** The three brief *narratives* that open the essay depict events that happened well before Darley and Latané wrote their essay. Why might the authors have chosen to recount these events in the present tense rather than in the past tense?
3. Locate places where Darley and Latané describe the experiments investigating bystander behavior. How do the authors show readers the steps—and the implications—of each experiment?
4. What purpose do you think the authors had in mind when writing the selection? How do you know?

Writing Assignments Using Cause-Effect as a Pattern of Development

1. Write an essay showing the "responsibility-diluting effect" that can occur when several people witness a critical event. Brainstorm with others to gather examples of this effect; then select two or three dramatic situations as the basis of your essay. Be sure to acknowledge other factors that may have played a role in inhibiting people's ability to act responsibly.
2. Although Darley and Latané focus on times when individuals fail to act responsibly, people often respond with moral heroism during difficult situations. Brainstorm with others to identify occasions in which people have taken the initiative to avert a crisis. Focusing on two or three compelling instances, write an essay in which you analyze the possible motives for people's responsible behavior. Also show how their actions affected the other individuals involved.

Writing Assignment Combining Patterns of Development

3. How could families or schools or communities or religious organizations encourage children to act rather than withdraw when confronted by someone in difficulty? Focusing on *one* of these situations, talk with friends, classmates, and family members to gather their experiences and recommendations. Then consider doing some research on this subject in the library and/or on the Internet. Select the most provocative ideas, and write an essay explaining the *steps* that this particular institution could take to help develop children's sense of responsibility to others. Develop your points with specific *examples* of what has been done and what could be done.

Additional Writing Topics

CAUSE-EFFECT

MyWritingLab

General Assignments

Using cause-effect, develop one of these topics into an essay.

1. Sleep deprivation
2. Having the parents you have
3. Lack of communication in a relationship
4. Overexercising or not exercising
5. Traveling or living in a foreign country

6. Skill or ineptitude in sports
7. A major life decision
8. Changing attitudes toward the environment
9. Voter apathy
10. An act of violence or cruelty

Assignments Using Visuals

Use the suggested visuals to help develop a cause-effect essay on one of these topics:

1. Sleep deprivation and its effects (slide show)
2. Giving children responsibilities and holding them accountable (web links)
3. Stress and its impact on the human body (charts and/or graphs)
4. The consequences of texting while driving (graphs)
5. The effects of stereotyping by gender, race, or disability (web links)

Assignments with a Specific Purpose, Audience, and Point of View

1. **Academic life.** A debate about the prominence of athletics at colleges and universities is going to be broadcast on the local cable station. For this debate, prepare a speech pointing out either the harmful or the beneficial effects of "big-time" college athletic programs.

2. **Academic life.** Why do students "flunk out" of college? Write an article for the campus newspaper outlining the main causes of failure. Your goal is to steer students away from dangerous habits and situations that lead to poor grades or dropping out.

3. **Civic activity.** Write a letter to the editor of your favorite newspaper analyzing the causes of the country's current "trash crisis." Be sure to mention the nationwide love affair with disposable items and the general disregard of the idea of thrift. Conclude by offering brief suggestions for how people in your community can begin to remedy this problem.

4. **Civic activity.** Write a letter to the mayor of your town or city suggesting a "Turn Off the TV" public relations effort, convincing residents to stop watching television for a month. Cite the positive effects that "no TV" would have on parents, children, and the community in general.

5. **Workplace action.** As the manager of a store or office, you've noticed that a number of employees have negative workplace habits and/or attitudes. Write a memo for your employees in which you identify these negative behaviors and show how they affect the workplace environment. Be sure to adopt a tone that will sound neither patronizing nor overly harsh.

6. **Workplace action.** Why do you think teenage suicide is on the rise? You're a respected psychologist. After performing some research, write a fact sheet for parents of teenagers and for high school guidance counselors describing the factors that could make a young person desperate enough to attempt suicide. At the end, suggest what parents and counselors can do to help confused, unhappy young people.

MyWritingLab Visit Chapter 9, "Cause-Effect," in MyWritingLab to complete the chapter activities, Pre-Reading Journal Entry activities, Questions for Close Reading, and Additional Writing Topics assignments and to test your understanding of the chapter objectives.

10

DEFINITION

In this chapter, you will learn:

10.1 To use the pattern of definition to develop your essays.

10.2 To consider how definition can fit your purpose and audience.

10.3 To develop strategies for using definition in an essay.

10.4 To develop strategies for revising a definition essay.

10.5 To analyze how definition is used effectively in student-written and professionally authored selections.

10.6 To write your own essays using definition as a strategy.

WHAT IS DEFINITION?

For language to communicate, words must have accepted *definitions*. Dictionaries, the sourcebooks for accepted definitions, are compilations of current word meanings, enabling speakers of a language to understand one another. But as you might suspect, things are not as simple as they first appear. We all know that a word like *discipline* has a standard dictionary definition. We also know, though, that parents argue over what constitutes "discipline" and that controversies about the meaning of "discipline" rage within school systems year after year. Moreover, many of the wrenching moral debates of our time also boil down to questions of definition. Much of the controversy over abortion, for instance, centers on what is meant by "life" and when it "begins."

Words can, in short, be slippery. Each of us has unique experiences, attitudes, and values that influence the way we use words and the way we interpret the words of others. In addition, some words may shift in meaning over time. The word *pedagogue*, for instance, originally meant "a teacher or leader of children." However, with time, *pedagogue* has come to mean "a dogmatic, pedantic teacher." And, of course, we invent other words (*sexting, selfie, defriend*) as the need arises.

Writing a definition, then, is no simple task. Primarily, the writer tries to answer basic questions: "What does _____ mean?" and "What is the special or true nature of _____?" As you will see, there are various strategies for expanding definitions far beyond the single-word synonyms or brief phrases that dictionaries provide.

HOW DEFINITION FITS YOUR PURPOSE AND AUDIENCE

Many times, short-answer exam questions call for definitions. Consider the following examples:

Define the term *mob psychology*.

What is the difference between a metaphor and a simile?

How would you explain what a religious cult is?

In such cases, a good response might involve a definition of several sentences or several paragraphs.

Other times, definition may be used in an essay organized mainly around another pattern of development. In this situation, all that's needed is a brief formal definition or a short definition given in your own words. For instance, a *process analysis* showing readers how computers have revolutionized the typical business office might start with a textbook definition of the term *artificial intelligence*. In an *argumentation-persuasion* paper urging students to support recent efforts to abolish fraternities and sororities, you could refer to the definitions of *blackballing* and *hazing* found in the university handbook. Or your personal definition of *hero* could be the starting point for a *causal analysis* that explains to readers why there are few real heroes in today's world.

But the most complex use of definition, and the one we are primarily concerned with in this chapter, involves exploring a subject through an *extended definition*. Extended definition allows you to apply a personal interpretation to a word, to make a case for a revisionist view of a commonly accepted meaning, to analyze words representing complex or controversial issues. "Pornography," "gun control," "secular humanism," and "right-to-life" would be excellent subjects for extended definition—each is multifaceted, often misunderstood, and fraught with emotional meaning.

STRATEGIES FOR USING DEFINITION IN AN ESSAY

The suggestions here and in Figure 10.1 will be helpful whether you use definition as a dominant or a supportive pattern of development.

1. Stay focused on the essay's purpose, audience, and tone. Because your purpose for writing an extended definition shapes the entire essay, you need to keep that objective in mind when developing your definition. Suppose you decide to write an essay defining *jazz*. The essay could be purely *informative* and discuss the origins of jazz, its characteristic tonal patterns, and some of the great jazz musicians of the past. Or the essay could move beyond pure information and take on a *persuasive* edge.

FIGURE 10.1
Development Diagram: Writing a Definition Essay

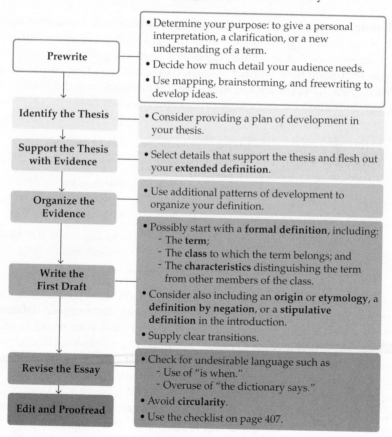

It might, for example, argue that jazz is the only contemporary form of music worth considering seriously.

Just as your purpose in writing will vary, so will your tone. A strictly informative definition will generally assume a detached, objective tone ("Apathy is an emotional state characterized by listlessness and indifference"). By way of contrast, a definition essay with a persuasive slant might be urgent in tone ("To combat student apathy, we must design programs that engage students in campus life"), or it might take a satiric approach ("An apathetic stance is a wise choice for any thinking student").

As you write, keep thinking about your audience as well. Not only do your readers determine what terms need to be defined (and in how much detail), but they also keep you focused on the essay's purpose and tone. For instance, you probably wouldn't write a serious, informative piece for the college newspaper about the "mystery meat" served in the campus cafeteria. Instead, you would adopt a light tone as you defined the culinary horror and might even make a persuasive pitch about improving the food prepared on campus.

2. Formulate an effective definition.   A definition essay sometimes begins with a brief *formal definition*—the dictionary's, a textbook's, or the writer's—and then expands that initial definition with supporting details. Formal definitions are traditionally worded as three-part statements that consist of the following: the *term,* the *class* to which the term belongs, and the *characteristics* that distinguish the term from other members of its class.

Term	Class	Characteristics
The peregrine falcon,	an endangered bird,	is the world's fastest flyer.
A bodice-ripper	is a paperback book	that deals with highly charged romance in exotic places and faraway times.
Back to basics	is a trend in education	that emphasizes skill mastery through rote learning.

A definition that meets these guidelines will clarify what your subject *is* and what it *is not.* These guidelines also establish the boundaries of your definition, removing unlike items from consideration in your (and your reader's) mind. For example, defining "back to basics" as a trend that emphasizes rote learning signals a certain boundary; it lets readers know that other educational trends, such as those that emphasize children's social or emotional development, will not be part of the essay's definition.

If you decide to include a formal definition, avoid tired openers such as "the dictionary says" or "according to *Webster's.*" Such weak starts are just plain boring and often herald an unimaginative essay. You should also keep in mind that a strict dictionary definition may actually confuse readers.

You should also stay clear of ungrammatical "is when" definitions: "Blind ambition is when you want to get ahead, no matter how much other people are hurt." Instead, write "Blind ambition is wanting to get ahead, no matter how much other people are hurt." A final pitfall to avoid in writing formal definitions is *circularity*, saying the same thing twice and therefore defining nothing: "A campus tribunal is a tribunal composed of various members of the university community." Circular definitions like this often repeat the term being defined (*tribunal*) or use words having the same meaning (*campus; university community*).

3. Develop the extended definition. You can choose from a variety of patterns when formulating an extended definition. Description, narration, process analysis, and comparison-contrast can be used—alone or in combination. Imagine that you're planning to write an extended definition of "robotics." You might develop the term by providing *examples* of the ways robots are currently being used in scientific research; by *comparing* and *contrasting* human and robot capabilities; or by *classifying* robots, starting with the most basic and moving to the most advanced or futuristic models.

Which patterns of development to use will often become apparent during the prewriting stage. Here is a list of prewriting questions as well as the pattern of development implied by each question.

Question	Pattern of Development
How does X look, taste, smell, feel, and sound?	Description
What does X do? When? Where?	Narration
What are some typical instances of X?	Exemplification
What are X's component parts? What different forms can X take?	Division-classification
How does X work?	Process analysis
What is X like or unlike?	Comparison-contrast
What leads to X? What are X's consequences?	Cause-effect

Those questions yielding the most material often suggest the effective pattern(s) for developing an extended definition.

4. Organize the material that develops the definition. If you use a single pattern to develop the extended definition, apply the principles of organization suited to that pattern, as described in the appropriate chapter of this book. Assume that you're defining "fad" by means of *process analysis*. You might organize your paragraphs according to the steps in the process: a fad's slow start as something avant-garde or eccentric; its wildfire acceptance by the general public; the fad's demise as it becomes familiar or tiresome. If you want to define "character" by means of a single *narration*, you would probably organize paragraphs chronologically.

5. Write an effective introduction.   It can be helpful to provide—near the beginning of a definition essay—a brief formal definition of the term you're going to develop in the rest of the essay. You might explain the *origin* of the term being defined: "Acid rock is a term first coined in the 1960s to describe music that was written or listened to under the influence of the drug LSD." Similarly, you could explain the *etymology*, or linguistic origin, of the key word that focuses the paper.

You may also use the introduction to clarify what the subject is *not*. Such *definition by negation* can be an effective strategy at the beginning of an essay, especially if readers don't share your view of the subject. In such a case, you might write something like this: "The gorilla, far from being the vicious killer of jungle movies and popular imagination, is a sedentary, gentle creature living in a closely knit family group." Such a statement provides the special focus of your essay and signals some of the misconceptions or fallacies soon to be discussed.

In addition, you may include in the introduction a *stipulative definition*, one that puts special restrictions on a term: "Strictly defined, a mall refers to a one- or two-story enclosed building containing a variety of retail shops and at least two large anchor stores. Highway-strip shopping centers or downtown centers cannot be considered true malls." When a term has multiple meanings, or when its meaning has become fuzzy through misuse, a stipulative definition sets the record straight right at the start, so that readers know exactly what is, and is not, being defined.

Finally, the introduction may end with a *plan of development* that indicates how the definition essay will unfold. A student who returned to school after having raised a family decided to write a paper defining the *midlife crisis* that led to her enrollment in college. After providing a brief formal definition of "midlife crisis," the student rounded off her introduction with this sentence: "Such a midlife crisis starts with vague misgivings, turns into depression, and ends with a significant change in lifestyle."

REVISION STRATEGIES

Once you have a draft of the essay, you're ready to revise. The following checklist will help you and those giving you feedback apply to definition some of the revision techniques discussed in Chapter 2.

> ☑ DEFINITION: A REVISION/PEER REVIEW CHECKLIST
>
> *Revise Overall Meaning and Structure*
>
> ❏ Is the essay's purpose informative, persuasive, or both?
> ❏ Is the term being defined clearly distinguished from similar terms?
> ❏ Where does a circular definition cloud meaning? Where are technical, nonstandard, or ambiguous terms a source of confusion?
> ❏ Where would a word's historical or linguistic origin clarify meaning? Where would a formal definition, stipulative definition, or definition by negation help?
> ❏ Which patterns of development are used to develop the definition? How do these help the essay achieve its purpose?
> ❏ If the essay uses only one pattern, is the essay's method of organization suited to that pattern (step-by-step for process analysis, chronological for narration, and so on)?
> ❏ Where could a dry formal definition be deleted without sacrificing overall clarity?
>
> *Revise Paragraph Development*
>
> ❏ If the essay uses several patterns of development, where would separate paragraphs for different patterns be appropriate?
> ❏ Which paragraphs are flat or unconvincing? How could they be made more compelling?
>
> *Revise Sentences and Words*
>
> ❏ Which sentences and words are inconsistent with the essay's tone?
> ❏ Where should overused phrases like "the dictionary says" and "according to *Webster's*" be replaced by more original wording?
> ❏ Have "is when" definitions been avoided?

STUDENT ESSAY

The following student essay was written by Olivia Fletcher in response to this assignment:

> In "Beyond the Pleasure Principle," Ann Hulbert explores the characteristics of "Gen Nexters," a term that did not exist until the late 1900s. Write an essay in which you identify a word that has existed for years but has recently taken on new meanings. Explore both the original meaning of the word and the new meaning or meanings, as well as occurrences that resulted in the new definition.

Olivia Fletcher, who was enrolled in a first-year college composition course, decided to write her essay about a word used to refer to something that she and her friends do almost every day: *tweet*.

"Tweet, Tweedle-lee-dee" (118 Characters Left)
by Olivia Fletcher

Introduction   Once upon a time, the word *tweet* simply referred to   1
                       the sharp, trilling sound a bird makes, and some folks can
Original definition   still remember Bobby Day's 1958 song, "Rockin' Robin," with
                       its chorus "Tweet, tweedle-lee-dee" ("Rockin' Robin"). Since
                       those days, *tweet* has morphed into a word whose meaning
Thesis   your great grandfather could have never imagined when he
                       was listening to Day's hit on *Billboard*'s Hot 100.
Topic sentence   Jack Dorsey's creation of a new social networking   2
                       site called *Twitter* in March 2006 soon led to a new defini-
                       tion for the word *tweet*. Dorsey wanted to share his text
Start of a series of   messages and updates with all of his friends, but in those
causes and effects   days, some of his friends didn't have phones with texting
                       abilities but did spend significant amounts of time on
                       their home computers. So Dorsey invented *Twitter*, the
                       social networking site that uses what came to be known
New definition   as *tweets*, messages composed of 140 or fewer characters
                       to share updates, thus eliminating the need to contact
                       each person individually (Bellis). Before the word *tweet*
                       came into existence, individuals posting to *Twitter* were
                       referred to as "twitter-ers" and their posts were called
                       "twits"—both rather awkward-sounding terms. Then in
                       January 2007, in an e-mail Blaine Cook, a founding en-
                       gineer at *Twitter*, sent to Craig Hockenberry, a software
                       designer and creator of the *Twitter* app, Cook asks, "How
                       about changing 'twit' to 'tweet'...?" Commenting on the
                       exchange with Cook in his blog post, "The Origin of the Word
                       Tweet," Hockenberry writes, "It's rare to have unanimous
                       agreement when naming things in software, but in this
                       case *everyone* loved the word 'tweet.'" Hockenberry also
                       states in his 2013 blog post that the word had recently been
                       added to the *Oxford English Dictionary*. He goes on to quote
                       John Simpson, chief editor of the *OED*: "This breaks at least
                       one *OED* rule, namely that a new word needs to be current
                       for ten years before consideration for inclusion." The new
                       word caught on so quickly and was used so widely that the
                       OED made an exception for it.
Topic sentence   Today, a tweet is a thought brought to the social table   3
                       of all thoughts imaginable. The tweet has to be 140 or fewer
Start of a series   characters, which forces users to be concise, something they
of contrasts

don't need to consider when posting on *Facebook*, a site that allows users to include an unlimited number of characters. *Twitter* was designed for social-networking users who are on the go and do not have time to read four paragraphs about what is going on in their friends' lives.

Start of a series of negative examples In the days since Dorsey sent the first "twit" in 2006, **4** tweets have become more and more infamous. Celebrities such as Miley Cyrus, Justin Bieber, Perez Hilton, and John Mayer, along with many others, have shared and continue to share their thoughts in 140 or fewer characters in the form of tweets. Some celebrities, along with thousands of not-so-famous individuals, have used tweets to share personal thoughts better left unsaid. People can do as much damage in 140 or fewer characters as they can in four paragraphs.

Topic sentence → A few years ago the blogger Perez Hilton and the singer **5** John Mayer got into a "*Twitter* war." They carefully, or not **Continuation of a series of negative examples** so carefully, crafted their personal thoughts of each other in 140 or fewer characters and shared them publicly on the World Wide Web via *Twitter*. Their tweets were not only insulting but also devious, in that they posted the tweets without using each other's actual usernames; that meant the person being insulted could not see the "subtweet" in his or her *Twitter* timeline. This, of course, created even more drama and more subtweets back and forth between the two individuals. This *Twitter* war between Hilton and Mayer provides a perfect example of how ridiculous amounts of drama have been introduced into society with a simple tweet. In his *Elite Daily* article, "Top 10 Celebrity *Twitter* Feuds," Robert Anthony, a New York-based writer, had the following to say about the Hilton-Mayer feud, which, by the way, he ranked number one among the top ten feuds:

> "People don't want to see you hurt, they want to see you experience something equalizing," tweeted Mayer, presumably as an act of revenge for all of Hilton's web-based attacks on Mayer over the years. Hilton, ever the martyr, whined that Mayer's tweets weren't funny and that "karma would be me losing my site and going bankrupt." (Anthony)

Topic sentence → While used all too often to insult others, tweets can be **6** used positively, especially in educational settings. Huge **Start of a series of positive examples** screens at the front of every meeting room, dining room, and classroom were set up at a scholarship competition at the University of West Florida on the third weekend of January 2014. The rising seniors who attended the event could tweet anything with the "hashtag" (another word that has been incorporated into the tweeting world) #UWFadmissions, and it would appear on the screen. One hilarious incident took place at the competition when one student tweeted, "Having fun at this scholaship competition #UWFadmissions," and another quickly tweeted back, "This guy can't even spell *scholarship*. That's a bad sign. #UWFadmissions." The crowd erupted with laughter at the witty remark and from that moment on, every few seconds a tweet discussing the events of the "scholaship" competition would appear on the white screens at the front of the rooms (Williams).

Topic sentence ⟶ Another example of tweets being used positively   7
in academic settings is described in Mackenzie Ryan's article "Florida School Engaging Students through *Twitter*," which explains how teachers and students at Holy Trinity
Continuation of Episcopal Academy, a college-prep school in Melbourne,
series of positive Florida, have incorporated *Twitter* into the classroom with
examples ⟶ positive outcomes. "The children are learning how to use social media appropriately. They're learning how what they post on *Twitter* and other social media sites can be viewed by literally the whole world," says Susan Bearden, the school's director of information technology and a nationally recognized leader on the value of incorporating social media into classroom activities. "That's such an important concept for kids to understand," Bearden goes on to say. "When [students] realize there's a broader audience...they really up their game."

"*Twitter* has helped give quieter students a voice," adds   8
Continuation of Valerie Williams, a teacher who works with Bearden at Holy
series of positive Trinity. Many students who are hesitant to participate in
examples ⟶ classroom discussions are happy to tweet their ideas to others in the classroom and beyond. Giselle Spicer, a fourteen-year-old student in Williams's class who is usually reluctant to enter traditional classroom discussions, comments, "It feels like I can be part of the conversation without having to talk" (Ryan).

The word *tweet* has taken on an entirely new mean-   9
ing since its first known use in 1851 ("Tweet"). While a small bird's chirping sound is still considered a tweet, the word is now used to describe a powerful tool that can help
Conclusion friends stay connected, make friendships, break up friendships, and serve as an educational tool. While tweets are sometimes used negatively, they are increasingly being used as positive tools. The word has come a long way since Bobby Day recorded his "Rockin' Robin" classic, "Tweet, tweedle-lee-dee."

Works Cited

MLA documentation

Anthony, Robert. "Top 10 Celebrity *Twitter* Feuds." *Elite Daily*, 2 Apr. 2012, elitedaily.com/entertainment/celebrity/top-ten-celebrity-twitter-feuds/.

Bellis, Mary. "What Is *Twitter*? Who Invented It?" *About.com*, inventors.about.com/od/tstartinventions/a/Twitter.htm. Accessed 19 Jan. 2014.

Hockenberry, Craig. "The Origin of the Word *Tweet*." *Furbo*, 28 June 2013, furbo.org/2013/06/28/the-origin-of-tweet/.

"Rockin' Robin (Original)." *YouTube*, uploaded by Buddha Mist, 11 Feb. 2011, www.youtube.com/watch?v=PcmvwFcfWmY.

Ryan, Mackenzie. "Florida School Engaging Students through *Twitter*." *10News: Tampa Bay Sarasota*, 21 Sept. 2014, legacy.wtsp.com/story/news/local/2014/09/21/twitter-classroom-twitter/16004283/.

"Tweet." *Merriam-Webster*, 2014, www.merriam-webster.com/dictionary/tweet.

Williams, Tiffany. Personal interview. 25 Jan. 2014.

COMMENTARY

Title, introduction, and thesis.   Olivia and her friends regularly posted tweets, so she decided to write about the word *tweet*. As she thought about the word and its original meaning, Michael Jackson's recording of "Rockin' Robin," with its chorus of "Tweet, tweedle-lee-dee," came to mind. Then she discovered through an Internet search that the song was first recorded by Bobby Day in 1958. As Olivia listened to the song on *YouTube* and watched Day's performance, she understood why the song had been a hit. The lyrics were catchy, and the song had a great beat.

As she sat down to begin drafting her essay, Olivia already knew that she wanted to use words from the song as the title of her essay. As she was typing "Tweet, Tweedle-lee-dee" at the top of the page, she realized that by adding "(118 Characters Left)" to the title, she could provide readers with an additional hint regarding her essay's subject. Then as she began composing the introduction, Olivia decided to refer to the title of the song in her introductory paragraph as well. She thought that the title did a nice job of illustrating the original definition of *tweet* and would allow her to juxtapose that early definition with the new one that she would define and explore in her essay. The reference to the title of the 1958 hit song led to the point she wanted to communicate in her thesis: "Since those days, *tweet* has morphed into a word whose meaning your great grandfather could have never imagined when he was listening to Day's hit on *Billboard*'s Hot 100." Although Olivia's introductory paragraph is brief, it does a nice job of engaging the reader and introducing the topic to be discussed.

Organization.   Olivia organizes the body of her essay into three parts. First, she devotes paragraphs 2 and 3 to providing information about the new definition of the word *tweet*, circumstances that led to its creation, and a comparison of *Twitter* and *Facebook*. Next, in paragraphs 4 and 5, she discusses negative ways tweets are used and gives an extended block quote to illustrate a negative example. Then in paragraphs 6-8, she focuses on positive ways tweets are being used in educational settings.

A definite organizational strategy determines the sequence of the three major sections of Olivia's essay, and the essay moves smoothly from one section to another. Olivia begins the first section with the topic sentence "Jack Dorsey's creation of a new social networking site called *Twitter* in March 2006 soon led to a new definition for the word *tweet*." She transitions to the second section of her essay with the topic sentence "In the days since Dorsey sent the first 'twit' in 2006, tweets have become more and more infamous," providing a clear message for her readers of what's to come. And then she moves from the second section to the third with the topic sentence "While used all too often to insult others, tweets can be used positively, especially in educational settings." Olivia does a nice job of providing smooth, clear topic sentences that also function as transitional statements for her readers as they navigate her essay.

Combining patterns of development.   In addition to *defining* the original meaning of *tweet*, along with the new, additional meaning, Olivia draws on several other patterns of development in her essay. She uses *causal analysis* in paragraph 2 to explain the circumstances that led to the need for a new word and its evolution from *twit* to *tweet*. She uses *comparison-contrast* in paragraph 3 as she compares *Twitter* with *Facebook*, contrasting the ways in which the two social networking sites are used. Olivia goes on to use *exemplification* as a pattern of development in paragraphs 4 to 8, as she provides examples of negative and positive ways in which tweets are used. This combination of various patterns of development allows her to explore not only the two definitions of the word *tweet* but also how the word came into being and how tweets can be both harmful and beneficial.

A weak example.   As you read Olivia's essay, you might have noticed that one example of the supposedly positive effects of tweeting in paragraph 6 is not the strongest or most effective example she might have chosen to include. She provides the example of a university scholarship competition where students' tweets appeared on a screen for everyone to see.

The purpose of allowing the students to tweet during the competition is never made clear. Although some might assume that the purpose of allowing students to tweet at the scholarship competition was to help build a sense of camaraderie among the students, that idea is never stated. Moreover, Olivia describes how one student's misspelling of the word *scholarship* in his tweet was ridiculed in subsequent tweets. Though Olivia refers to one tweet as a "witty remark" that prompted other tweets "discussing the events of the 'scholaship' competition" (paragraph 6), many would consider the tweet making fun of a typo to be more thoughtless and inconsiderate than "witty." The essay would be stronger if this example were replaced with one that clearly demonstrates a positive effect of tweeting in educational settings.

Conclusion.   Olivia's *conclusion* rounds off the essay nicely and brings it to a satisfying close. In addition to restating her thesis, Olivia adds a new detail: The first known use of the word *tweet* was in 1851. This new detail lets her readers know that for more than 150 years, the only definition of *tweet* was the chirping sound of a small bird. She brings her essay full circle with her closing reference to words from "Rockin' Robin" that she used in her title: "Tweet, tweedle-lee-dee."

Revising the first draft.   As Olivia reread her first draft, she realized that she had some work to do. When writing that early draft, she did not have a clear organizational pattern in view. Her goal was to write down everything that came to mind that she might want to include in her essay and worry about matters of structure later. The introduction in that early draft included not only information about the original meaning of the word *tweet*, but also information about the founding of *Twitter* and the new, additional meaning of the word. Then in the second paragraph of the first draft, she had focused on the two definitions of the word. The first draft of that second paragraph is reprinted here:

Original Version of the Second Paragraph

    The *Merriam-Webster* online dictionary offers two definitions of the word *tweet*: "Tweet: noun, 1. A chirping note. 2. A post made on the Twitter online message service" ("Tweet"). The online dictionary also notes that the first known use of the word *tweet* was used in 1851, so the first definition has actually been used for a much longer period of time than the modern definition. The word *tweet* used to have only one definition, however, and it was a very simple one. The only definition that it had before 2006 was a sharp chirping sound made by a small bird. One could hear it outside her window on a bright summer morning, on a walk down a trail in the woods, and some would say it was one of the most beautiful musical instruments of nature. It still is all of those things, but now "tweets" can be found other places. In fact, the most popular place they can found today is in nature's archenemy—the Internet.

After allowing her first draft to sit for a couple of days to gain some distance from what she had written, Olivia realized that her second paragraph was confusing and disordered. At the beginning of the paragraph she had focused on dictionary definitions that weren't really needed. In the first sentence of her essay, she had provided the original definition of the word, and so to include a dictionary definition from *Merriam-Webster* in the following paragraph was redundant. She also realized that in the last part of the first paragraph of her rough draft, she had provided the new, additional meaning of the word. As she looked closely at the rest of her second paragraph, she saw other places where she had repeated herself and had made rambling comments that did nothing to make her essay stronger. In fact, the only detail she thought worth saving in the entire paragraph was the one about the first known use of the word *tweet* in 1851. Olivia knew that her essay would be more effective if she cut the entire paragraph and saved the one interesting detail to possibly include somewhere else.

After making that decision and taking time to think about the overall structure of her essay, Olivia decided to move information regarding the new definition of the word *tweet* and the events that led to its creation from the first paragraph to the second and third paragraphs. After revising the structure of her essay so that one section led logically to the next, Olivia continued to critically read her essay and to eliminate the clutter: anything that was redundant or did not support the major points she was trying to communicate. For example, in her first draft, toward the end of the third paragraph in which she compares *Twitter* with *Facebook*, she had included the following sentences: "Going back to the original meaning of the word, a bird's *tweet* is short, sharp, and full of beautiful sound depending on who is listening. A *tweet* off of *Twitter* is short, to the point, and can be considered very creative, colorful, and powerful, depending on who the reader is." As she reread what she had written, Olivia realized that although the similarities between the original and new meanings of *tweet* were interesting, they had no place in the paragraph, so she cut them.

As Olivia revised her essay, she realized that her practice of writing down everything that came to mind that she might want to include in her essay was more like freewriting that drafting. Although the approach definitely generated lots of ideas, she still had the task of organizing her thoughts and identifying her main points. Then she had to be willing to look at her writing objectively and cut ideas that did not support her main points. She decided that thinking of her initial work as prewriting would make it easier for her to organize her ideas and cut unnecessary material.

Although Olivia had to make extensive changes as she revised her first draft, the final product is an effective piece of writing of which she can be proud. She does a good job of exploring the new definition of *tweet*, the circumstances that led to its creation, and both the negative of positive effects of tweeting.

Activities: Definition

MyWritingLab

Prewriting Activities

1. Imagine you're writing two essays: one explains the *process* for registering a complaint that gets results; the other *contrasts* the styles of two stand-up comics. Jot down ways you might use definition in each essay.

2. Select a term whose meaning varies from person to person or one for which you have a personal definition. Some possibilities include:

success	femininity	a liberal
patriotism	affirmative action	a housewife
individuality	pornography	intelligence

Brainstorm with others to identify variations in the term's meaning. Then examine your prewriting material. What thesis comes to mind? If you were writing an essay, would your purpose be informative, persuasive, or both? Finally, prepare a scratch list of the points you might cover.

Revising Activities

3. Explain why each of the following is an effective or ineffective definition. Rewrite those you consider ineffective.
   a. *Passive aggression* is when people show their aggression passively.
   b. A *terrorist* tries to terrorize people.
   c. *Being assertive* means knowing how to express your wishes and goals in a positive, noncombative way.
   d. *Pop music* refers to music that is popular.
   e. *Loyalty* is when someone stays by another person during difficult times.

4. The following introductory paragraph is from the first draft of an essay contrasting walking and running as techniques for reducing tension. Although intended to be a definition paragraph, it actually doesn't tell us anything we don't already know. It also relies on the old-hat "*Webster's* says." Rewrite the paragraph so it is more imaginative. You might use a series of anecdotes or one extended example to define *tension* and introduce the essay's thesis more gracefully.

According to *Webster's*, tension is "mental or nervous strain, often accompanied by muscular tightness or tautness." Everyone feels tense at one time or another. It may occur when there's a deadline to meet. Or it could be caused by the stress of trying to fulfill academic, athletic, or social goals. Sometimes it comes from criticism by family, bosses, or teachers. Such tension puts wear and tear on our bodies and on our emotional well-being. Although some people run to relieve tension, research has found that walking is a more effective tension reducer.

Ann Hulbert

Writer Ann Hulbert was born in 1956 and attended Harvard College and Cambridge University. Her work has appeared in many publications, including *Slate*, *The New York Times Book Review*, *The New York Review of Books*, and *The New Republic*. Hulbert is the author of *The Interior Castle: The Art and Life of Jean Stafford* and *Raising America: Experts, Parents, and a Century of Advice About Children*. This article was published on March 11, 2007, in *The New York Times Magazine*.

Pre-Reading Journal Entry

MyWritingLab

One of the benefits of family life is getting to know people of other generations. What generations are represented by the people in your extended family? What generation do you belong to? What generation do your parents and your children, if any, belong to? How do the generations in your family differ? Use your journal to answer these questions.

For ideas on how this definition essay is organized, see Figure 10.2 on page 418.

Beyond the Pleasure Principle

It is a point of pride among baby boomers that after our kids leave home, 1 we enjoy a continuing closeness with them that our parents rarely had with us. We certainly do keep in touch: 80 percent of 18- to 25-year-olds had talked to their parents in the past day, according to "A Portrait of Generation Next," a recent study conducted by the Pew Research Center in tandem with MacNeil/Lehrer Productions. Yet if the survey is any guide, Gen Nexters aren't getting the credit they deserve for being—as many of them told pollsters they felt they were—"unique and distinct." It is not easy carving out your niche in the shadow of parents who still can't get over what an exceptional generation they belong to.

So what is special about Gen Nexters? Don't count on them to capture 2 their own quintessence. "The words and phrases they used varied widely," the Pew researchers noted, "ranging from 'lazy' to 'crazy' to 'fun.'" But if you look closely, what makes Gen Nexters *sui generis*—and perhaps more mysterious than their elders appreciate—are their views on two divisive social topics, abortion and gay marriage. On the by-now-familiar red-and-blue map of the culture wars, positions on those issues are presumed to go hand in hand: those on the right oppose both as evidence of a promiscuous society and those on the left embrace them as rights that guarantee privacy and dignity. Yet as a group, Gen Nexters seem to challenge the package deals.

Young Americans, it turns out, are unexpectedly conservative on abortion 3 but notably liberal on gay marriage. Given that 18- to 25-year-olds are the least Republican generation (35 percent) and less religious than their elders (with 20 percent of them professing no religion or atheism or agnosticism), it

416

is curious that on abortion they are slightly to the right of the general public. Roughly a third of Gen Nexters endorse making abortion generally available, half support limits and 15 percent favor an outright ban. By contrast, 35 percent of 50- to 64-year-olds support readily available abortions. On gay marriage, there was not much of a generation gap in the 1980s, but now Gen Nexters stand out as more favorably disposed than the rest of the country. Almost half of them approve, compared with under a third of those over 25.

It could simply be, of course, that some young people are pro-gay marriage 4 and others are pro-life and that we can expect more of the same old polarized culture warfare ahead of us. But what if Gen Nexters, rather than being so, well, lazy, are forging their own new crossover path? When I contacted John Green, an expert on religious voters who is currently working at the Pew Forum on Religion and Public Life, he said that pollsters hadn't tackled that question. But after crunching some numbers, he suggested that there might indeed be a middle way in the making. Many individual Gen Nexters hold what seem like divergent views on homosexuality and government involvement with morality—either liberal on one while being conservative on the other or else confirmed in their views on one question while ambivalent on the other.

Oh, how these young people can confound us! All this could amount to 5 no more than what the experts call a "life-cycle effect": Gen Nexters may hold heterogeneous views now because they are exploring diverse values that may congeal in more conventional ways as they get older. But a more intriguing possibility is that it is a "cohort effect," a distinctive orientation that will stick with them. Liberals could take heart that perhaps homosexual marriage has replaced abortion as the new "equality issue" for Gen Nexters, suggested John Russonello, a Washington pollster whose firm is especially interested in social values; Gen Nexters may have grown up after the back-alley abortion era, but they haven't become complacent about sexual rights. Conservatives might take comfort from a different hypothesis that Green tried out: maybe Gen Nexters have been listening to their parents' lectures about responsibility. Don't do things that make you have an abortion, young people may have concluded, and do welcome everyone into the social bulwark of family responsibility.

Put the two perspectives together, and an ethos emerges that looks at 6 once refreshingly pragmatic and yet still idealistic. On one level, Gen Nexters sound impatient with a strident stalemate between entrenched judgments of behavior; after all, experience tells them that in the case of both abortion and gay rights, life is complicated and intransigence has only impeded useful social and political compromises. At the same time, Gen Nexters give every indication of being attentive to the moral issues at stake: they aren't willing to ignore what is troubling about abortion and what is equally troubling about intolerant exclusion. A hardheadedness, but also a high-mindedness and softheartedness, seems to be at work.

And to risk what might be truly wishful thinking, maybe there are signs 7 here that Gen Nexters are primed to do in the years ahead what their elders have so signally failed to manage: actually think beyond their own welfare to worry about—of all things—the next generation. For when you stop to consider it, at the core of Gen Nexters' seemingly discordant views on these hot-button issues could be an insistence on giving priority to children's interests. Take seriously the lives you could be creating: the Gen Next wariness of abortion sends that message. Don't rule out for any kid who is born the advantage of being reared by two legally wedded parents: that is at least one way to read the endorsement of gay marriage. However you end up sorting out the data, fun or crazy wouldn't be how I would describe the Gen Next mix. Judged against the boomers' own past or present, though, the outlook definitely looks unique.

FIGURE 10.2
Essay Structure: "Beyond the Pleasure Principle" by Ann Hulbert

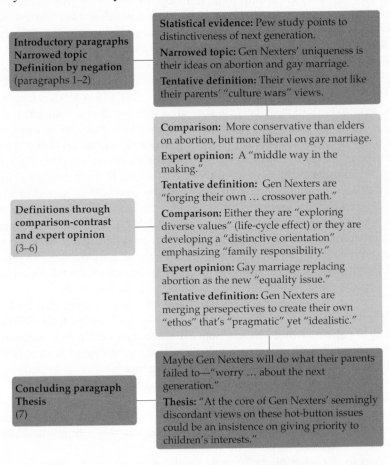

Introductory paragraphs
Narrowed topic
Definition by negation
(paragraphs 1–2)

Statistical evidence: Pew study points to distinctiveness of next generation.

Narrowed topic: Gen Nexters' uniqueness is their ideas on abortion and gay marriage.

Tentative definition: Their views are not like their parents' "culture wars" views.

Definitions through comparison-contrast and expert opinion
(3–6)

Comparison: More conservative than elders on abortion, but more liberal on gay marriage.

Expert opinion: A "middle way in the making."

Tentative definition: Gen Nexters are "forging their own ... crossover path."

Comparison: Either they are "exploring diverse values" (life-cycle effect) or they are developing a "distinctive orientation" emphasizing "family responsibility."

Expert opinion: Gay marriage replacing abortion as the new "equality issue."

Tentative definition: Gen Nexters are merging persepectives to create their own "ethos" that's "pragmatic" yet "idealistic."

Concluding paragraph
Thesis
(7)

Maybe Gen Nexters will do what their parents failed to—"worry ... about the next generation."

Thesis: "At the core of Gen Nexters' seemingly discordant views on these hot-button issues could be an insistence on giving priority to children's interests."

Questions for Close Reading

MyWritingLab

1. What is the selection's thesis? Locate the sentence(s) in which Hulbert states her main idea. If she doesn't state her thesis explicitly, express it in your own words.
2. What statistics about Gen Nexters are the basis for much of the extended definition in this article?
3. What is the difference between a "life-cycle effect" and a "cohort effect"? Which type of effect does Hulbert claim her essay is about?
4. According to Hulbert, what has the elder generation—the baby boomers—failed to do?

Questions About the Writer's Craft

1. What is Hulbert's underlying purpose in defining the characteristics of Gen Nexters? Is her purpose mainly informative, speculative, or persuasive? How can you tell?
2. **The pattern.** Hulbert uses the "definition by negation" strategy throughout this essay. Identify examples of this strategy in the article and evaluate how well it works.
3. **Other patterns.** Hulbert also uses the compare-contrast strategy at many points in her article. What signal devices does she use to signal when she is comparing and contrasting?
4. What is the effect of the delayed thesis on the reader's experience of this article? Is the delayed thesis effective? Do you think Hulbert should have stated her thesis at the beginning of the essay?

Writing Assignments Using Definition as a Pattern of Development

1. In her essay, Hulbert presents an extended definition of Gen Nexters, Americans born in the 1980s. Write an essay in which you define the key characteristics of another generation. You might, for example, write an essay defining the characteristics of baby boomers (born from 1946 through the early 1960s), Generation Xers (born from 1965 to 1980), or the Millennials, those born in the 1990s or later. If you choose to define the youngest generation, be sure to give it an "official" name. Before you write, decide whether your tone will be serious or humorous.
2. In her article, Hulbert mentions the current polarization of Americans—liberals versus conservatives and blue states versus red states. The meanings of these four terms can vary widely, however, often depending on the viewpoint of the writer. Write an essay in which you define what you think it means to be a liberal or a conservative, or to live in a red state or a blue state. What are the key characteristics of the term you chose? What are the values and attitudes associated with the term? Discussing these issues with friends and family might help you clarify your ideas before you write.

Writing Assignment Combining
Patterns of Development

3. In paragraph 5, Hulbert mentions the "life-cycle effect," which refers to the way people's values and behaviors change as they pass from one stage of life to the next—from adolescence to adulthood, for example. Some of these life-cycle effects are marked by ritual. For example, there are many coming-of-age rites of passage, such as graduation, bar or bat mitzvah, confirmation, the debutante's ball, the *quinceañera*, and getting a driver's license. Choose one of your own life's rites of passage and write an essay about it. Narrate what happened, describe the *process* you went through, and give *examples* of how your life changed as a result.

Keith Johnson

Keith Johnson, born in 1972, was educated at the University of Georgia, where he earned a B.A. in history and an M.A. in Spanish literature. Early in his career, he joined *The Wall Street Journal,* where he continues to work as a journalist. Between 1998 and 2001, as a news assistant, Johnson mostly reported on technology and politics. Then, as a staff reporter from 2001 to 2007, he covered Spain, terrorism, airlines, and energy, including reporting on the Iraqi oil industry in the summer of 2003. Johnson went on to run the *Journal*'s blog *Environmental Capital,* which focuses on energy and the environment, from 2008 to early 2010. Currently, he is part of the newspaper's national security team, for which he reports on areas such as homeland security, domestic and transnational terrorism, piracy, and energy security, as well as on some Latin American issues. The following article was published in *The Wall Street Journal* on August 20, 2010.

Pre-Reading Journal Entry   MyWritingLab

Pirates have been romanticized in movies such as *Pirates of the Caribbean* and *The Sea Hawk* and in novels such as *Treasure Island.* Why do you think pirates are such glamorous figures? What other kinds of villains have been treated similarly? Do some freewriting in your journal on this subject.

Who's a Pirate? In Court, A Duel over Definitions

Not since Lt. Robert Maynard of the Royal Navy sailed back tri-   1
umphantly to nearby Hampton Roads in 1718 with the severed head of
Blackbeard[1] swinging from his bowsprit has this Navy town been so em-
broiled in the fight against piracy.

---

[1]Blackbeard is the pseudonym of an infamous British pirate who operated off the Eastern Coast of the United States (editors' note).

Prosecuting pirates, rather than hanging them from the yardarm, is the   2
modern world's approach to the scourge of Somali piracy that has turned
huge swathes of the Indian Ocean into a no-go zone for commercial vessels.

But there's a problem: Some 2,000 years after Cicero[2] defined pirates as   3
the "common enemy of all," nobody seems able to say, legally, exactly what
a pirate is.

U.S. law long ago made piracy a crime but didn't define it. International   4
law contains differing, even contradictory, definitions. The confusion threat-
ens to hamstring U.S. efforts to crack down on modern-day Blackbeards.

The central issue in Norfolk: If you try to waylay and rob a ship at sea—   5
but you don't succeed—are you still a pirate?

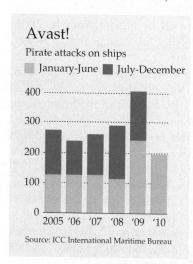

Avast!

Pirate attacks on ships

■ January-June   ■ July-December

Source: ICC International Maritime Bureau

It may seem strange there should   6
be doubt about an offense as old as this
one. Piracy was the world's first crime
with universal jurisdiction, meaning that
any country had the right to apprehend
pirates on the high seas.

The Romans took piracy so seri-   7
ously they overrode a cautious Senate
and gave near-dictatorial powers to an
up-and-coming general named Pompey,[3]
who soon swept away piracy in the
Mediterranean.

In more recent centuries, European   8
countries such as Britain cracked down on
pirates—except when busy enlisting certain
ones, dubbed "privateers," to help them
fight their wars by raiding enemy ships.

Pirates even spurred the creation   9
of the U.S. Navy, after Thomas Jefferson erupted over the cost of paying
tribute to the Barbary Corsairs[4] for safe passage of U.S. merchant ships. At
the time, the U.S. was paying about one-tenth of the federal budget to the
pirates. Supplied with warships, President Jefferson waged war on the
Barbary pirates (whence the line "to the shores of Tripoli" in the Marines'
Hymn). By 1815, the North African pirate kingdoms had been subdued.

When Congress dealt with piracy in a statute four years later, the crime   10
was so easy to recognize that legislators didn't bother to describe it, just

---

[2]Cicero (106–43 BCE) was a philosopher and statesman in ancient Rome (editors' note).
[3]Pompey (106–48 BCE) was a statesman and great military leader in ancient Rome
(editors' note).
[4]The Barbary Corsairs were Muslim pirates or privateers who operated out of North Africa
(editors' note).

the punishment. The 1819 statute that made piracy a capital offense (since changed to mandatory life in prison) simply deferred to "the law of nations." That legal punt has kept American jurists scrambling ever since.

The stage was set for the Norfolk trial on April 10 of this year [2010] 11
when the *USS Ashland*, cruising in the Gulf of Aden about 330 miles off Djibouti, was fired upon at 5 A.M. by Somali men in a small skiff. The Navy vessel, an amphibious dock landing ship, returned fire with 25-mm cannon, wrecking the 18-foot skiff and sending its six occupants overboard.

The *Ashland* sent a search boat to recover the Somalis and photograph 12
the smoking hulk of the skiff, which contained at least one weapon and what looked like a grappling hook or anchor. Though that boat was blasted to pieces, even when pirate skiffs survive, the ships they target are often loath to bring the skiffs aboard. One captured by a Navy force in 2006, according to the judge advocate's testimony in a subsequent trial in Kenya, was crawling with "roaches the size of leopards."

In Norfolk, the prosecution has begun its effort to convince the U.S. 13
District Court for the Eastern District of Virginia that the quickly foiled Somalis are guilty not just of lesser charges they face but of the main charge of piracy.

"Violent attacks on the high seas without lawful authority have always 14
been piracy under the law of nations, in 1819 and today," said the lead prosecutor, Benjamin Hatch, at a pretrial hearing last month [July 2010].

"So if one ship fires a bow-and-arrow," asked Judge Raymond Jackson, 15
rubbing his brow, "or a slingshot, or a rock, those are all acts of violence, and thus piracy?" The prosecutor nodded.

The public defender, Geremy Kamens, weighed in. "That a slingshot 16
fired upon another ship would expose the defendant to a mandatory life sentence shows the absurd result of this reading," he said. The defense added that under this broad definition, Greenpeace[5] activists could be considered pirates for their anti-whaling antics on the seas.

The defense lawyers trawled through history books, coming to rest 17
upon an obscure 1820 Supreme Court ruling.

"We have, therefore, no hesitation in declaring that piracy, by the law of 18
nations, is robbery upon the sea," Justice Joseph Story wrote for the majority in the case of *United States v. Smith.*

That gave the defense lawyers their main argument: Piracy is robbery on 19
the high seas; it isn't merely attempted robbery at sea, which is covered by a separate statute that the Somalis are charged with as well.

Since the attack on the *Ashland* clearly failed, it wasn't piracy, the de- 20
fense argues, and therefore, the most serious charge should be dropped.

---

[5]Greenpeace, an activist environmental organization, is known for putting its ships between "whales and harpoons," as its website notes, on the high seas to deter whaling (editors' note).

But the prosecutors, too, have probed early sources—17th-century   21
Dutch jurists, 18th-century British writers, 19th-century maritime cases,
an 1800 speech by then-congressman John Marshall, and a slew of international treaties.

The prosecution has leaned heavily on a 1934 ruling by Britain's Privy   22
Council,[6] which pondered the case of a similarly failed attack at sea, near
Hong Kong. In that case, the jury found the defendants guilty, but said its
verdict was subject to the question of whether it's really piracy if no actual
robbery occurs. The court in Hong Kong said it isn't, and acquitted the
attackers.

The Privy Council members, however, after hacking through thickets   23
of legal technicalities, ultimately reached a different conclusion. "Actual
robbery is not an essential element in the crime of piracy," they said; "A frustrated attempt to commit piratical robbery is equally piracy."

Troubled Waters

Attacks on ships in the first   Boarding or hijacking
half of 2010, by region   Failed attack

AFRICA: 114
EAST: Gulf of Aden,
Red Sea, Somalia,
Tanzania

WEST: Cameroon,
Congo, Republic of
Congo, Guinea, Ivory
Coast, Liberia, Nigeria

SOUTHEAST ASIA: 30
Indonesia, Malacca
Straits, Malaysia,
Philippines, Singapore
Straits, Thailand

FAR EAST: 23
China, Vietnam

AMERICAS: 15
Colombia, Ecuador,
Guyana, Haiti, Peru,
Venezuela

**INDIAN
SUB-CONTINENT: 12**
Bangladesh, India

ARABIAN SEA: 2   Source: ICC International
                                      Maritime Bureau

[6]The Privy Council, formerly very powerful, is a group of advisors to the British sovereign
(editors' note).

They added, with more than a hint of exasperation: "Their Lordships   24
are almost tempted to say that a little common sense is a valuable quality in
the interpretation of international law."

Beyond the legal wrangling and obscure historical references, the   25
implications of the case in Norfolk are serious. Piracy's golden age may have
passed two centuries ago, but it remains a scourge in places like the Strait of
Malacca in Indonesia and Malaysia, off the coast of Nigeria, and above all
off the east coast of Africa, where the disintegration of Somalia has led to a
major resurgence.

The first half of 2010 saw about 200 raids and unsuccessful attacks on   26
ships at sea worldwide, the bulk of them off Somalia. In early August, two
cargo ships were hijacked. In all, an estimated 18 ships and their crews are
currently [as of August 2010] being held for ransom.

To fight the problem, the U.S. and the United Nations are count-   27
ing on prosecuting pirates. Some U.N. officials dream of establishing an
international piracy tribunal, similar to the one for war crimes in The
Hague.

In the meantime, the U.S. and other countries have helped Kenya,   28
the closest stable country to the source, to put scores of pirates on
trial. But Kenyan law is cumbersome, requiring witnesses to testify on
three separate occasions, a tough order logistically for merchant sailors. The European Union is now trying to jump-start Kenya's pirate
prosecutions—the first sentence will come later this month—but progress is slow.

As a result, attackers captured by European warships in the Indian   29
Ocean often are let go for lack of any real legal recourse. A Spanish warship
caught seven Somali pirates red-handed in early August, men who had been
trying to waylay a Norwegian chemical tanker. The Spanish frigate immediately released them because it would have been difficult to prosecute them,
the EU naval force off Somalia said.

That leaves courtrooms like the one in Norfolk as among the best hopes   30
for bringing pirates to justice and deterring future ones. But even seemingly
clear-cut cases don't necessarily pass muster in court.

After a celebrated incident in April 2009, when U.S. Navy Seals   31
snipers killed three Somali men holding an American captain hostage on a
small boat after a raid, rescuing him, the lone Somali survivor of that attack
on the *Maersk Alabama* pleaded guilty to lesser charges in New York, not
to piracy.

Indeed, the last U.S. piracy conviction was in 1861, of a Confederate   32
blockade runner.

Now the court in Norfolk must contend with the defense motion to   33
dismiss the piracy charge, which would leave only such lesser charges as
attempted plunder.

The prosecution argues that U.S. courts should defer to international   34
law, especially an 1982 U.N. Law of the Sea treaty the U.S. never ratified.
Aping the 1958 Geneva Convention,[7] it offers an expansive definition of
piracy as any illegal acts of violence, detention or depredation committed for
private ends on the high seas.

Defense lawyers balk at that suggestion. "We do not interpret U.S. law   35
based on U.N. resolutions, but rather what Congress meant at the time,"
says the public defender, Mr. Kamens.

Judge Jackson is expected to rule soon.[8]   36

---

[7]The Geneva Convention of April 29, 1958, sets forth internationally agreed-upon rules for
conduct on the high seas, for example, fishing rights (editors' note).
[8]The Norfolk court ultimately ruled against trying the men on the charge of piracy (editors' note).

Questions for Close Reading

`MyWritingLab`

1. What is the selection's thesis? Locate the sentence(s) in which Johnson states his
   main idea. If he doesn't state his thesis explicitly, express it in your own words.
2. What, according to the author, is the essential issue with defining *piracy*? What
   does the author have to say about the history of piracy before this century?
3. What were the prosecution's arguments in favor of trying the defendants for
   piracy? What arguments did the defense put forth?
4. Two graphs accompany the article. What information do the graphs supply? How
   do they support Johnson's point that it is important to resolve the definition of
   piracy at this time?

Questions About the Writer's Craft

1. **The pattern.** What are the term, class, and characteristics involved in the definition of *piracy*? In what way does the selection focus on definition by negation?
2. Does the author intend to inform, entertain, or persuade the reader? What is the
   selection's tone? Is it suitable to his purpose? How are the two graphs relevant, or
   not relevant, to the author's purpose?
3. What historical anecdote does Johnson use to open his article? What is the effect
   of this opening? Describe the two current-day piracy anecdotes, besides that of
   the Norfolk trial, that the author relates.
4. The author refers to a number of legal rulings and often gives technical terms for
   parts of ships. What language techniques does he use to keep the selection interesting and accessible to the average reader? Give some examples.

Writing Assignments Using Definition
as a Pattern of Development

1. The Geneva Convention sets forth rules for treating noncombatants during war-
   time. One major controversy today concerns how to treat captured terrorists. Do
   some research, and write an essay in which you define *terrorism*. In your definition

include your view of whether a non-U.S. citizen on trial for terrorism should be treated as a civilian or an enemy combatant.

2. *Piracy* has come to mean acts such as downloading music from the Internet without permission, knocking off designer handbags, or bootlegging copies of movies. Write an essay in which you establish a definition of *piracy* that focuses on these kinds of acts. Decide whether these acts should be considered theft.

Writing Assignment Combining Patterns of Development

3. Should crimes against humanity have universal jurisdiction, as piracy does? For example, in 1998 the Chilean dictator Augusto Pinochet was indicted by a magistrate in Spain for human rights violations committed in Chile. He was arrested in London, but then ultimately released and allowed to return to Chile. Do some research on how human rights crimes are prosecuted internationally. Write an essay in which you *describe* and *compare* the possibilities for prosecution of human rights violations.

Laura Fraser

Laura Fraser, born in 1961, is a San Francisco-based journalist and novelist whose work has appeared in a wide variety of publications including *Food and Wine, The New York Times, Salon, Health, O: The Oprah Magazine,* and *Mother Jones.* She is the author of *The New York Times* bestseller *An Italian Affair* (2001) and, more recently, of *All Over the Map* (2010), a travel memoir and sequel to her bestseller. Much of her writing focuses on women's health issues, travel, and cultural aspects of food. The essay that follows, adapted from Fraser's first book, *Losing It: America's Obsession with Weight and the Industry That Feeds on It* (1997), appeared in the 2009 book *The Fat Studies Reader,* edited by Esther Rothblum and Sondra Solovay.

Pre-Reading Journal Entry

MyWritingLab

Our ideas of what we think beautiful people should look like are influenced to a large extent by the culture in which we live. How similar or dissimilar is your concept of beauty from what you see in movies, fashion, and advertisements? What factors have contributed to your sense of what the word *beauty* means? Explore these ideas in your journal.

The Inner Corset

Once upon a time, a man with a thick gold watch swaying from a   1
big, round paunch was the very picture of American prosperity and vigor. Accordingly, a hundred years ago, a beautiful woman had plump cheeks and arms, and she wore a corset and even a bustle to emphasize her full, substantial hips. Women were *sexy* if they were heavy. In those days,

The thin ideal that developed in the United States from the 1880s to 1920s can be traced through the evolution of three ideal types: the plump Victorian woman (*top left*), the athletic but curvaceous Gibson Girl (*top right*), and the boyishly straight-bodied flapper (*bottom*).

Americans knew that a layer of fat was a sign that you could afford to eat well and that you stood a better chance of fighting off infectious diseases than most people. If you were a woman, having that extra adipose blanket also meant that you were probably fertile, and warm to cuddle up next to on chilly nights.

Between the 1880s and 1920s, that pleasant image of fat thoroughly   2
changed in the United States. Some began early on to hint that fat was a health risk. In 1894, Woods Hutchinson, a medical professor who wrote for women's magazines, defended fat against this new point of view. "Adipose," he wrote, "while often pictured as a veritable Frankenstein, born of and breeding disease, sure to ride its possessor to death sooner or later, is really a most harmless, healthful, innocent tissue" ("Fat and Its Follies"). Hutchinson reassured his *Cosmopolitan* readers that fat was not only benign, but also attractive, and that if a poll of beautiful women were taken in any city, there would be at least three times as many plump ones as slender ones. He advised them that no amount of starving or exercise—which were just becoming popular as means of weight control—would change more than 10 percent of a person's body size anyway. "The fat man tends to remain fat, the thin woman to stay thin—and both in perfect health—in spite of everything they can do," he said in that article.

But by 1926, Hutchinson, who was by then a past president of the   3
American Academy of Medicine, had to defend fat against fashion, too, and he was showing signs of strain. "In this present onslaught upon one of the most peaceable, useful and law-abiding of all our tissues," he told readers of *The Saturday Evening Post*, "fashion has apparently the backing of grave physicians, of food reformers and physical trainers, and even of great insurance companies, all chanting in unison the new commandment of fashion: 'Thou shalt be thin!'" ("Fat and Fashion").

Hutchinson mourned this trend, and was dismayed that young girls   4
were ridding themselves of their roundness and plumpness of figure. He tried to understand the new view that people took toward fat: "It is an outward and visible sign of an inward and spiritual disgrace, of laziness, of self-indulgence," he explained in that article, but he remained unconvinced. Instead, he longed for a more cheerful period in the not-so-distant past when a little fat never hurt anyone, and he darkly warned that some physicians were deliberately underfeeding girls and young women solely for the purpose of giving them a more svelte figure. "The longed-for slender and boyish figure is becoming a menace," Hutchinson wrote, "not only to the present, but also the future generations" ("Fat and Fashion").

And so it would. But why did the fashion for plumpness change so   5
dramatically during those years? What happened that caused Americans to alter their tastes, not only to admire thinner figures for a time, but for

the next century, culminating in fin de siècle extremes of thinness, where women's magazines in the 1990s would print ads featuring gaunt models side-by-side with photo essays on anorexia?

Many things were happening at once, and with dizzying speed. Foremost was a changing economy: In the late 1800s, for the first time, ample amounts of food were available to more and more people who had to do less and less work to eat. The agricultural economy, based on family farms and home workshops, shifted to an industrial one. A huge influx of immigrants—many of them genetically shorter and rounder than the earlier American settlers—fueled the industrial machine. People moved to cities to do factory work and service jobs, stopped growing their own food, and relied more on store-bought goods. Large companies began to process food products, distribute them via railroads, and use refrigeration to keep perishables fresh. Food became more accessible and convenient to all but the poorest families. People who once had too little to eat now had plenty, and those who had a tendency to put on weight began to do so. When it became possible for people of modest means to become plump, being fat no longer was a sign of prestige. Well-to-do Americans of northern European extraction wanted to be able to distinguish themselves, physically and racially, from stockier immigrants. As anthropologist Margaret Mackenzie notes, the status symbols flipped: it became chic to be thin and all too ordinary to be overweight. 6

In this new environment, older cultural undercurrents suspicious of fat began to surface. Europeans had long considered slenderness a sign of class distinction and finer sensibilities, and Americans began to follow suit. In Europe, during the late 18th and early 19th centuries, many artists and writers—the poets John Keats and Percy Bysshe Shelley, and authors Emily Brontë, Edgar Allan Poe, and Anton Chekhov—had tuberculosis, which made them sickly thin. Members of the upper classes believed that having tuberculosis, and being slender itself, were signs that one possessed a delicate, intellectual, and superior nature. "For snobs and parvenus and social climbers, TB was the one index of being genteel, delicate, [and] sensitive," writes essayist Susan Sontag in *Illness as Metaphor* (28). "It was glamorous to look sickly." So interested was the poet Lord Byron in looking as fashionably ill as the other Romantic poets that he embarked on a series of obsessive diets, consuming only biscuits and water, or vinegar and potatoes, and succeeded in becoming quite thin. Byron—who, at five feet six inches tall, with a clubfoot that prevented him from walking much, weighed over two hundred pounds in his youth—disdained fat in others. "A woman," he wrote, "should never be seen eating or drinking, unless it be *lobster salad* and *champagne*, the only truly feminine and becoming viands" (qtd. in Schwartz 38). Aristocratic European women, thrilled with the romantic figure that Byron cut, took his diet advice 7 and despaired of appearing fat. Aristocratic Americans, trying to imitate Europeans, adopted their enthusiasm for champagne and slenderness.

Americans believed that it was not only a sign of class to be thin, but   8 also a sign of morality. There was a long tradition in American culture that suggested that indulging the body and its appetites was immoral, and that denying the flesh was a sure way to become closer to God. Puritans such as the minister Cotton Mather frequently fasted to prove their worthiness and to cleanse themselves of their sins. Benjamin Franklin, in his *Poor Richard's Almanack*, chided his readers to eat lightly to please not only God, but also a new divinity, Reason: "Wouldst thou enjoy a long life, a healthy Body, and a Vigorous Mind, and be acquainted also with the wonderful works of God? Labour in the first place to bring thy Appetite into Subjection to Reason" (238). Franklin's attitude toward food not only reveals a puritanical distrust of appetite as overly sensual, but also presaged diets that would attempt to bring eating in line with rational, scientific calculations. "The Difficulty lies, in finding out an exact Measure;" he wrote, "but eat for Necessity, not Pleasure, for Lust knows not where Necessity ends" (238).

At the end of the 19th century, as Hutchinson observed, science was   9 also helping to shape the new slender ideal. Physicians came to believe that they were able to arrive at an exact measure of human beings; they could count calories, weigh people on scales, calculate "ideal" weights, and advise those who deviated from that ideal that they could change themselves. Physicians were both following and encouraging the trend for thinness. In the 1870s, after all, when plumpness was in vogue, physicians had encouraged people to *gain* weight. Two of the most distinguished doctors of the age, George Beard and S. Weir Mitchell, believed that excessive thinness caused American women to succumb to a wide variety of nervous disorders, and that a large number of fat cells was absolutely necessary to achieve a balanced personality (Banner 113). But when the plump figure fell from favor, physicians found new theories to support the new fashion. They hastily developed treatments—such as thyroid, arsenic, and strychnine—to prescribe to their increasing numbers of weight loss patients, many of whom were not exactly corpulent, but who were more than willing to part with their pennies along with their pounds.

As the 20th century got underway, other cultural changes made slen-   10 derness seem desirable. When many women ventured out of their homes and away from their strict roles as mothers, they left behind the plump and reproductive physique, which began to seem old-fashioned next to a thinner, freer, more modern body. The new consumer culture encouraged the trend toward thinness with fashion illustrations and ads featuring slim models; advertisers learned early to offer women an unattainable dream of thinness and beauty to sell more products. In short, a cultural obsession with weight became firmly established in the United States when several disparate factors that favored a desire for thinness—economic status symbols, morality, medicine, modernity, changing women's roles, and consumerism—all collided at once.

Thinness is, at its heart, a peculiarly American preoccupation. Europeans admire slenderness, but without our Puritanism they have more relaxed and moderate attitudes about food, eating, and body size (the British are most like us in both being heavy and fixating on weight loss schemes). In countries where people do not have quite enough to eat, and where women remain in traditional roles, plumpness is still widely admired. Other westernized countries have developed a slender ideal, but for the most part they have imported it from the United States. No other culture suffers from the same wild anxieties about weight, dieting, and exercise as we do because they do not share our history.

The thin ideal that developed in the United States from the 1880s to 1920s was not just a momentary shift in fashion; it was a monumental turning point in the way that women's bodies were appraised by men and experienced by women. The change can be traced through the evolution of three ideal types: the plump Victorian woman, the athletic but curvaceous Gibson Girl, and the boyishly straight-bodied flapper. By 1930, American women knew how very important it was for them to be thin. From then on, despite moments when voluptuousness was admired again (e.g., Marilyn Monroe), American women could never be too thin.

Works Cited

Banner, Lois. *American Beauty.* U of Chicago P, 1983.

Franklin, Benjamin. *The Complete Poor Richard Almanacks.* Vol. 1, Barre, Imprint Society, 1970.

Hutchinson, Woods. "Fat and Fashion." *The Saturday Evening Post,* 21 Aug. 1926, p. 60.

---. "Fat and Its Follies." *Cosmopolitan,* June 1894, p. 395.

Mackenzie, Margaret. Letter to the author. 12 June 1996.

Schwartz, Hillel. *Never Satisfied: A Cultural History of Diets, Fantasies, and Fat.* Free Press, 1986.

Sontag, Susan. *Illness as Metaphor.* Farrar, 1978.

Questions for Close Reading

MyWritingLab

1. **Thesis.** What is the selection's thesis? Locate the sentence(s) in which Fraser states her main idea. If she doesn't state the thesis explicitly, express it in your own words.
2. What information does Fraser include in her essay to explain the influence of tuberculosis on Americans' fixation on being thin?

3. How does Fraser explain the change in America's definition of what it means to be beautiful? What six factors does she consider responsible for America's switch from a preference for plumpness to a desire to look almost anorexic?

4. According to Fraser, how is America's attitude toward thinness different from the attitude in most of Europe? In what parts of the world is plumpness still admired?

Questions About the Writer's Craft

1. **The pattern.** Why do you think Fraser chose to begin her essay by focusing on what many would consider to be overweight individuals? What might have been her purpose?

2. **The pattern.** Look closely at the manner in which Fraser structures her essay. How would you describe the order in which she presents the factors she believes are responsible for America's current definition of beauty? Why might she have organized her essay this way?

3. **Other patterns.** Although Fraser's essay focuses on the change in America's *definition* of what it means to be beautiful, she also incorporates other organizational patterns. What other patterns does she make use of and how?

4. How would you describe Fraser's tone in this essay? Why do you think she chose to address readers in this way? Do the photos add to our understanding of Fraser's thesis, or are they unnecessary?

Writing Assignments Using Definition as a Pattern of Development

1. Fraser's essay explores the changing definition of what it means to be beautiful. Think of another term that is used to describe or label individuals—a term whose definition has changed over the last century. Write an essay in which you explore how the changing definition has affected the way individuals think about themselves and others, as well as how they live their lives. For example, you might consider the changing definition of terms such as *educated, successful, middle-class,* or *well-traveled.*

2. In her essay, Fraser mentions that ideas about what it means to be healthy have changed since the early 1900s. Write an essay in which you focus on the differences between what it meant to be healthy a century ago, and what the term *healthy* means today. Consider using a variety of sources, ranging from personal interviews to published sources on the subject, along with charts or graphs that reference and support ideas and statistics in your essay.

Writing Assignment Combining Patterns of Development

3. Fraser's essay focuses on how and why the definition of beauty has changed. Write an essay in which you focus on the *effects* of the new definition. As you plan your essay about the *effects* of the pressure to be thin, consider *narrating* the stories of particular individuals and the lengths they have gone to in an effort to lose weight.

Lillian Comas-Díaz

Lillian Comas-Díaz, an ethnic minority psychologist, was born in Chicago but moved to her parents' native Puerto Rico at the age of six and lived there until she was in her twenties. Her research focuses primarily on issues of social justice, intersecting identities, and ethnocultural approaches to mental health. Comas-Díaz's publications include *Ethnocultural Psychotherapy* (2007) and *Multicultural Care in Practice* (2013), along with many articles, including the one that follows, which was published in *The Journal on Cultural Diversity and Ethnic Minority Psychology*.

Pre-Reading Journal

MyWritingLab

In the essay that follows, Comas-Díaz explores how our identity can be expressed in the names we choose for ourselves. Think of labels you have used for yourself—for example, *first-generation American, romantic, patriot, pragmatist,* or *free spirit.* In your journal, write down what you think the labels convey about you to other people. How important are the labels you choose to your ability to define yourself and your identity?

Hispanics, Latinos, or Americanos: The Evolution of Identity

Identity is the number-one national problem here.
(Hoffman, 1989, p. 262)

One of the fastest growing ethnic minority groups in the United States is in search of a name. Or so it appears, given the multiple terms used for its designation. Historically, such an amalgamation of people was referred to as Spanish speaking, a current misnomer, given that a significant segment of this population is English dominant. Hispanics, Latinos, Hispanos, Latins, Central Americans, and South Americans—to name a few—are some of the general terms used to designate this diverse ethnic collage. Many individuals prefer to politically affirm their ethnic identity by using terms such as Chicanos, Xicanos, Ricans, or Boricuas, whereas others affirm their national origins by using terms such as Mexicans or Mexican Americans, Cubans or Cuban Americans, Colombians, Dominicans, Peruvians, Salvadorans, or Venezuelans, among many others.

Encased within historical eras, ethnic self-designation reflects the dialectics between dominance and self-determination. Because the systematic negation and oppression of people of color result in pervasive identity conflicts (Fanon, 1967), Latinos' power to name themselves advances liberation by rejecting colonization (Castillo, 1994). Searching for a name to designate this heterogeneous group can be a challenging and confusing ordeal. Because self- and other identification is a developmental process, naming evolves in response to psychosocial and geopolitical factors.

In this essay I present a brief taxonomy of terms in an attempt to clarify   3 the complexity of ethnic identification. Such presentation is situated within the current historical and political context. As Hispanic/Latinos bear a plural identity, ethnic names that are appropriate today may be obsolete or even offensive tomorrow. The mediating factors in self-designation are gaining a voice and power to name one's identity and define one's reality. I conclude with a discussion of the evolution of the Latino identity.

A Taxonomic Panorama

I offer a taxonomy of ethnic terms used to designate the generic Hispanic/   4 Latino population in addition to specific names used to designate distinct groups. Besides the references cited, the interested reader can consult Internet resources, such as the Chicano-Latino Network (CLNET), accessible through the University of California, Los Angeles gopher server, the Encyclopedia. com, and The Hispano Crypto-Jewish Resource Center (located at the Ira M. Beck Memorial Archives, University of Denver Main Campus, Penrose Library Special Collections, Denver, Colorado), and other related links.

Generic Terms

Hispanic

The generic term *Hispanic* was officially created by the United States   5 Bureau of the Census to designate people of Spanish origin who identified themselves as such in the 1970 census (COSSMHO, 1986). Often used to refer collectively to all Spanish speakers, it connotes a lineage or cultural heritage related to Spain. Indeed, the term Hispanic can be related to internalized colonization because it is strongly supported by politically conservative groups who regard their European ancestry as superior to the conquered indigenous peoples of the Americas (Falicov, 1998). An example of identity imperialism, the term Hispanic is inaccurate, incorrect, and often offensive as a collective name for all Spanish speakers or Latinos. Many millions of Spanish-speaking people—such as Native Americans—are not of true Spanish descent, and millions of Latin Americans do not speak Spanish or claim Spanish heritage (e.g., Brazilians); therefore, they are not Hispanics.

Latino(a)

Recognizing the diversity of this ethnic minority group, *Latino* (male) or   6 *Latina* (female) is used to refer to people originating from or having a heritage related to Latin America. Acting as a superset of many nationalities, *Latino* is preferred by many over the term Hispanic because it excludes Europeans such as Spaniards from being identified as ethnic minorities in the United States while it includes Brazilians, who do not qualify as Hispanics because their mother tongue is Portuguese. Many politically correct people prefer Latino because it reaffirms their native pre-Hispanic identity (Falicov, 1998). The term *Latin* comes into use as the least common denominator for all peoples of Latin America in recognition of the fact that some romance language (Spanish, Portuguese, French) is the native tongue of the majority of Latin Americans. Shorris (1992) argued that the term Latino is linguistically correct in Spanish because it has gender, contrary to the term Hispanic that follows the English usage of nongendered grammar. However, as the current term used to designate the vast majority of this ethnic group, Latino(a) is not appropriate for the millions of Native Americans who inhabit the Americas.

La Raza

La Raza (literally meaning "the race") is a widespread term in use among Spanish speaking and Spanish-surnamed people in the United States. La Raza emerges as a designation acceptable to many Latino, Caribbean, Chicano, and Mexican Americans born in the United States or Latin America. The term La Raza has been intricately involved in political activism. In the 1960s and 1970s, The Brown Power [movement] grew politically active, demanding equal opportunities and rights. Cesar Chavez organized the United Farm Workers in 1962, obtaining victories against large California growers. Although La Raza Unida, a party formed in 1970, has won local elections, greater political success has come to Mexican Americans in mainstream U.S. political parties.

Hispano(a)

The term *Hispano* or *Hispana* comprises those individuals who trace their history to the Spanish conquistadores and settlers who arrived in 1494 and occupied and dominated what is known today as Mexico, California, Texas, Florida, New Mexico, and Arizona in the 1600s to the 1800s (COSSMHO, 1986). Comprising the Creole Spanish–Native American race, Hispanos tend to identify with their Spanish heritage as opposed to the Mexican settlers. A traditionally closed and conservative group, evidence suggests that many Hispanos may be descendants of persecuted Jews who fled Spain during the 16th and 17th centuries seeking refuge in what were then the farthest reaches of the known world. They survived by minimizing their contact with outsiders and by hiding or disguising their religious and cultural identities as much as possible. They are what historical researchers call "cryptic or crypto Jews," meaning hidden Jews (Bloom & Bloom, 1993).

"Spanish People"

This term is frequently used in the United States to refer indiscriminately to any person who speaks Spanish. As an ethnic term, "Spanish people" is imprecise and often inappropriate in that it includes people from the American continents, the Caribbean, and Spain. The term, however, is a proper designation for the people of Spain, as some Spaniards, or native people of Spain, do reside in the United States. Nonetheless, some of the "Spaniards" living in the United States, such as Basques, Catalonians, and Spanish gypsies, do not consider themselves Spaniards. As an illustration, Basques and Catalonians each have a different culture and language from Spain, in addition to separatist political movements to become independent republics. The originators of flamenco, *gitanos* or Spanish gypsies, do not consider themselves Spaniards, and many call themselves the Roma people.

Americano(a)

This term is traditionally used to designate Americans who are not of   10
Hispanic/Latino extraction. However, it has been used recently to designate Latinos living in the United States. The term *Americano* embraces and celebrates the diversity and energy of the contemporary Latin American community wedded through a wealth of nationalities (Olmos, Ybarra, & Monterey, 1999). Moreover, Americano describes a group of people bound together by their languages and traditions, as varied as America itself.

Specific or National Terms

Mexican

The nationality of the inhabitants of Mexico, *Mexicans* is the term   11
used appropriately for Mexican citizens who visit or work in the United States. However, it is an ineffective name to designate those people who are citizens of the United States—either born in the United States or naturalized citizens of the United States who are of Mexican ancestry. Some Mexicans maintain strong family ties in Mexico (by visiting periodically and by investing economically and emotionally in Mexico), and they usually intend to return to Mexico provided they can become economically secure. Therefore, these people maintain and nurture their offspring in their language, religion, and culture.

Mexican American

Following the pattern sometimes used to identify the extraction of   12
other ethnic Americans (African American, Italian American, etc.), *Mexican American* refers to those individuals of Mexican descent who are U.S. citizens. This term is acceptable to many Mexican descendants, with the exception of those who do not identify with a Mexican heritage but rather with a Spanish heritage (such as Hispanos). Also, for those who do not view themselves as "Americans" by choice, this designation is problematic, and still others reject a hyphenated identity.

Chicano(a)

Used to describe Mexican Americans, *Chicano* (male) and *Chicana*   13
(female) was originally pejorative. Brown Power movement activists of
the 1960s and 1970s in the United States adopted this designation with
a sense of pride. One theory of its etymology traces its origin to the
1930s and 1940s period when poor, rural, indigenous Mexicans came to
the United States as seasonal migrant workers. The term seems to have
come into first use in the fields of California in derision of the inability of
native Nahuatl speakers to refer to themselves as "Mexicanos" and instead
spoke of themselves as "Mesheecanos," in accordance with the pronunciation rules of their language. Another theory of the etymology of Chicano is
that in vulgar Spanish it is common for Mexicans to use the "ch" conjunction in place of certain consonants to create a term of endearment. Among
some Mexican Americans, the term still retains an offensive connotation,
particularly because it is used by activists and by those who seek to create
a new identity for their culture rather than to subsume it under the mainstream culture.

Xicano(a)

Like Chicano(a), the word *Xicano* derives from the Nahautl pronunciation   14
of *Mexica* or *Mexicanos,* the group of indigenous people commonly referred
to as the Aztecs. In using Xicano, which replaces the "ch" in Chicano with the
"x," the person affirms his or her indigenous heritage (Castillo, 1994).

Boricua

This Taino name refers to the inhabitants of Borinquen, the island   15
that became Puerto Rico, a colony of Spain, in 1493. Neither a state nor
a republic, Puerto Rico is a free-associated state, an American commonwealth, whereby political power remains with the United States government
(Comas-Diaz, Lykes, & Alarcon, 1998). The island has limited political
self-determination because of its colonial status. The terms used by Puerto
Ricans for self-designation tend to reflect an identity crisis borne by their
country's uncertain political status. *Boricua* emphasizes a political identification with a Spanish-speaking Latin American identity, as opposed to
an English-speaking United States one. During the late 1960s and 1970s,
the phrase *"Boricua, defiende lo tuyo"* (Boricua, defend what is yours) was
used as a revolutionary cry. *Boricua* is also an endearing expression used by
Puerto Ricans to designate each other.

Nuyorican

This term refers to Puerto Ricans born in the continental United   16
States, particularly in New York City. A separate ethnic identity from
island Puerto Ricans who are members of a majority group, many

Nuyoricans' identity is colored by being an ethnic minority population (Algarin & Pinero, 1975). Indeed, some Nuyoricans are politically radicalized within their experiences as people of color in the United States society. Continental Puerto Ricans are also born outside of New York; therefore, the collective term used to designate them is *Ricans*. As an illustration, whereas a Nuyorican is a Rican born and raised in New York, a Chicagorican is a Rican born and raised in Chicago.

Rican

Rican refers to the second- and third-generation Puerto Ricans on the   17
U.S. mainland. Like Nuyoricans, many Ricans maintain close contact with island Puerto Rican communities through migration and reverse migration. Regardless of their birthplace, Puerto Ricans are United States citizens since 1917. Ricans embrace a cultural identity different from Puerto Ricans. Like Spanglish,[1] Rican culture synthesizes Puerto Rican and United States cultures into a brand new one. For instance, contrary to the dominant ideology on Puerto Rico, which has deemphasized the role of slavery in Puerto Rican history and the presence of African traits and cultural elements, many Ricans tend to underline their debt to Africa, affirming their Black heritage (Klor de Alva, 1997).

LatiNegro(a)

This term was coined to designate the African Latino(a) who is perceived   18
beyond any doubt as Black by both the North American and the Latino communities (Comas-Diaz, 1994). This term avoids the partial or total negation of the Latinness in African Latinos by the Latino community. The offspring of African American (Caribbean or North, Central, and South American) and Latino parents, some LatiNegros are immersed in the African American community. Also known as Afro Latinos, this segment of the Latino population bears a racial identification based on the combined and class discrimination they experience from the mainstream society as well as from the Hispanic/Latino community.

Caribeno(a)

This term refers to the Latinos from the Caribbean. Acknowledging   19
that the Caribbean region provides a specific worldview, many Spanish-speaking Caribbean groups, such as Cubans, Dominicans, and Puerto Ricans, are additionally using this self-designation, recognizing their emotional-geographic locale. The term *Caribeno(a)* also embraces the psychology of being an islander.

---

[1] *Spanglish* refers to a version of the Spanish language that incorporates many English words (editors' note).

Epilogue or Prelude: La Raza Cósmica/The Cosmic Race

The Latino mosaic reflects a pluralistic, dynamic, and evolving transforma- 20
tion. An apt metaphor for the development of the United States, Latino identity evolution offers a parallel to the collective identity redefinition. Historically,
some Latinos were indigenous to this land, whereas others arrived searching for
the immigrant's golden dream of opportunities, and still others continue to be
washed up on American shores searching for freedom and political asylum.

The high rate of Latin American immigration, [high] Latino birth 21
[rates], and growing numbers of mixed marriages accentuate the emerging
Latino preponderance in the United States. No longer "strangers among
us," Latinos transform the North American ethnic makeup and economy
(Suro, 1999). As both outsiders and insiders, many Latinos live in the
hyphen (Stavans, 1996), creating a space whereby transculturation changes
both the Latino and mainstream cultures. The concept of transculturation
involves an adaptive, dynamic, evolutionary, and dialectical process (Comas-
Diaz, 1987). It differs from acculturation in that it gives birth to a distinct
culture emerging from conflicting cultural values (De Granda, 1968).

Likewise, Latino identity evolution underscores *mestizaje*, or the mixing 22
of races to produce a new one. As early as 1925, José Vasconcelos (1997), a
Mexican philosopher, presented his racial theory of the cosmic race—the future
of humankind—as emanating out of the synthesis of Indian, White, "Mongol,"[2]
and African races. Arguing that *mestizaje* promoted civilization, Vasconcelos
believed that the Spanish Empire in Europe, the Americas, and the Philippines
connected, for the first time, all of the major racial groups. Contrary to other
Christian religions, he asserted the Spanish Catholic Church enhanced racial
unification by including the Indians through religious conversion and education.

Regardless of calling themselves Hispanics, Latinos, Americanos, or 23
la Raza Cósmica, this ethnic group continues searching for the evolution of
identity. As people of all colors, they transform every inch of the Americas'
spiritual, physical, and emotional geography.

References

Algarin, M., & Piñero, M. (Eds.). (1975). *Nuyorican poetry: An anthology of Puerto Rican words and feelings.* New York: William Morrow.
Bloom, L. G., & Bloom, D. A. (1993, Fall). The Crypto-Jews: An ancient heritage comes alive again. *The Leona G and David A Bloom Southwest Jewish Archives,* 2(1, Whole issue).
Castillo, A. (1994). *Massacre of the dreamers: Essays on Xicanisma.* New York: Plume (Penguin Books).

[2] *Mongol* refers to the people of Mongolia and was used by Vasconcelos to refer to East Asians (editors' note).

440   Definition

Comas-Díaz, L. (1987). Feminist therapy with Puerto Rican women. *Psychology of Women Quarterly, 11,* 461–474.

Comas-Díaz, L. (1994). LatiNegra: Mental health needs of African Latinas. *Journal of Feminist Family Therapy, 5,* 35–74.

Comas-Díaz, L., Lykes, M. B., & Alarcón, R. (1998). Ethnic conflict and psychology of liberation in Guatemala, Perú, and Puerto Rico. *American Psychologist, 53,* 778–792.

COSSMHO (National Coalition of Hispanic Health and Human Services Organizations). (1986). *Delivering preventive health care to Hispanics: A manual for providers.* Washington, DC: Author.

De Granda, G. (1968). *Transculturación e interferencia lingüística en el Puerto Rico contemporáneo* [Transculturation and linguistic interference in contemporary Puerto Rico]. Bogotá, Colombia: Ediciones Bogotá.

Falicov, C. J. (1998). *Latino families in therapy: A guide to multicultural practice.* New York: Guilford Press.

Fanon, F. (1967). *Black skin, White masks.* New York: Grove Press.

Hoffman, E. (1989). *Lost in translation: A life in a new language.* New York: Penguin Books.

Klor de Alva, J. J. (1997). The invention of ethnic origins and the negotiation of Latino identity, 1969–1981. In M. Romero, P. Hondagneu-Sotelo, & V. Ortiz (Eds.), *Challenging fronteras: Structuring Latina and Latino lives in the U.S.* (pp. 55–74). New York: Routledge.

Olmos, E. J., Ybarra, L., & Monterey, M. (Eds.). (1999). *Americanos: Latino life in the United States/La vida Latina en los Estados Unidos.* New York: Little Brown.

Shorris, E. (1992). *Latinos: A biography of a people.* New York: Norton.

Stavans, L. (1996). *The Hispanic condition: Reflections on culture and identity in America.* New York: HarperPerennial.

Suro, R. (1999). *Strangers among us: Latinos' lives in a changing America.* New York: Vintage Books.

Vasconcelos. J. (1997). *The cosmic race/La raza cósmica* (D. T. Jaén, Trans.). Baltimore: Johns Hopkins University Press.

Questions for Close Reading   MyWritingLab

1. What is the selection's thesis? Locate the sentence(s) in which Comas-Díaz states her main idea. If she doesn't state her thesis explicitly, express it in your own words.
2. In what she refers to as "a taxonomy of ethnic terms," Comas-Díaz defines six words used to label the "generic" Hispanic/Latino population. List the words and provide a brief definition for each one.
3. According to Comas-Díaz, where does the generic term *Hispanic* come from, and why is it considered "inaccurate, incorrect, and often offensive as a collective name for all Spanish speakers or Latinos"?
4. Comas-Díaz describes nine words that are used to designate specific groups. Based on the background information on Comas-Díaz that precedes the essay and the information the author provides in her essay, how would Comas-Díaz be likely to identify the specific group to which she belongs? What various qualities define members of this particular group?

Questions About the Writer's Craft

1. **The pattern.** Comas-Díaz makes extensive use of headings and subheadings to assist in defining the various terms in her essay. Why might she have decided to use this type of structure? Do you think this type of structure is appropriate for her essay? Why?
2. **Other Patterns.** Although *definition* is the primary pattern of development used in the essay, *exemplification*, *comparison-contrast*, and *classification* are also employed. Find places in the text where you see these other patterns of development used. Does the use of these patterns make the essay more effective? Why or why not?
3. As she defines various words that are used to label "an amalgamation of people" that were, in the past, "referred to as Spanish speaking," Comas-Díaz includes information from numerous outside sources. What do you think was her purpose in deciding to include so many references? Do the references contribute to her essay's effectiveness? Why or why not?
4. Comas-Díaz's essay was first published in *The Journal on Cultural Diversity and Ethnic Minority Psychology*, a scientific journal of the American Psychological Association. What does this imply about her intended audience? How might her essay have been different had she been writing for a popular magazine or newspaper? What challenges (if any) did the essay present for you as you read it?

Writing Assignments Using Definition as a Pattern of Development

1. In her essay, Comas-Díaz defines the various terms that are used to refer to a particular ethnic minority group in the United States. Write an essay in which you provide a definition for another group—perhaps one to which you belong. For example, if your field is communications, you might define a typical communications major. Or you might define what it means to be a serious athlete or good driver or a model dorm resident. Be sure to give the *term* you are defining, the *class* to which the term belongs, and the *defining characteristics* of the term.
2. Comas-Díaz believes that it is important for individuals to name their own "identity" and define their own "reality." However, she does not define *identity* and *reality*, nor does she define other critical terms, such as *ethnic, race, community*, and *self-determination*. Choose one of these terms or another significant term from the reading, and write an essay in which you define what the term means for you in your own life. Include how your definition may have changed over the years and what it might contribute to the future life you hope to create for yourself.

Writing Assignment Combining Patterns of Development

3. Comas-Díaz explains that the labels used to name groups are frequently "imprecise and often inappropriate." Sometimes a label can unfairly stereotype a person without acknowledging the person's individuality. Write a *narrative* essay in which you tell the story of someone who exceeded the expectations implied by a label. For example, you might write about someone who was hired for a rewarding job despite being labeled "mentally challenged." Or you might write about someone who defied the label "little old lady" by running a marathon. As you tell the story, be sure to describe both the *cause* and the *effects* of the labeling or stereotyping.

William Raspberry

Journalist William Raspberry (1935–2012) was born in Okolona, Mississippi. From his mother, an English teacher and poet, Raspberry learned to care "about the rhythm and grace of words." His father, a shop teacher, taught him "that neither end tables nor arguments are worthwhile unless they stand solidly on all four legs." Raspberry graduated from Indiana Central College and later joined the staff of the Indianapolis *Recorder* as a reporter and editor. Following a two-year stint in the army, he was hired by *The Washington Post*, where his nationally syndicated column ran from 1971 to 2005. His coverage of the Watts race riots in 1965 won him the Capital Press Club Journalist of the Year award, and he later went on to win the Pulitzer Prize for commentary in 1994. *Looking Backward at Us*, a collection of Raspberry's columns, was published in 1991. The following selection appeared in Raspberry's *Washington Post* column in 1982.

Pre-Reading Journal Entry   MyWritingLab

Which do you think plays a more important role in determining what a person accomplishes: innate talent or belief in oneself? Take a few minutes to respond to this question in your journal, jotting down examples drawn from your experiences and observations.

The Handicap of Definition

I know all about bad schools, mean politicians, economic deprivation   1
and racism. Still, it occurs to me that one of the heaviest burdens black
Americans—and black children in particular—have to bear is the handicap of
definition: the question of what it means to be black.

Let me explain quickly what I mean. If a basketball fan says that the   2
Boston Celtics' Larry Bird plays "black," the fan intends it—and Bird
probably accepts it—as a compliment. Tell pop singer Tom Jones he
moves "black" and he might grin in appreciation. Say to Teena Marie or
the Average White Band that they sound "black" and they'll thank you.

But name one pursuit, aside from athletics, entertainment or sexual   3
performance, in which a white practitioner will feel complimented to be
told he does it "black." Tell a white broadcaster he talks "black" and he'll
sign up for diction lessons. Tell a white reporter he writes "black" and he'll
take a writing course. Tell a white lawyer he reasons "black" and he might
sue you for slander.

What we have here is a tragically limited definition of blackness, and it   4
isn't only white people who buy it.

Think of all the ways black children can put one another down with   5
charges of "whiteness." For many of these children, hard study and hard
work are "white." Trying to please a teacher might be criticized as acting

"white." Speaking correct English is "white." Scrimping today in the interest of tomorrow's goals is "white." Educational toys and games are "white."

An incredible array of habits and attitudes that are conducive to success   6
in business, in academia, in the nonentertainment professions are likely to be thought of as somehow "white." Even economic success, unless it involves such "black" undertakings as numbers banking, is defined as "white."

And the results are devastating. I wouldn't deny that blacks often are   7
better entertainers and athletes. My point is the harm that comes from too narrow a definition of what is black.

One reason black youngsters tend to do better at basketball, for in-   8
stance, is that they assume they can learn to do it well, and so they practice constantly to prove themselves right.

Wouldn't it be wonderful if we could infect black children with the no-   9
tion that excellence in math is "black" rather than white, or possibly Chinese? Wouldn't it be of enormous value if we could create the myth that morality, strong families, determination, courage and love of learning are traits brought by slaves from Mother Africa and therefore quintessentially black?

There is no doubt in my mind that most black youngsters could develop   10
their mathematical reasoning, their elocution and their attitudes, the way they develop their jump shots and their dance steps: by the combination of sustained, enthusiastic practice and the unquestioned belief that they can do it.

In one sense, what I am talking about is the importance of developing   11
positive ethnic traditions. Maybe Jews have an innate talent for communication; maybe the Chinese are born with a gift for mathematical reasoning; maybe blacks are naturally blessed with athletic grace. I doubt it. What is at work, I suspect, is assumption, inculcated early in their lives, that this is a thing our people do well.

Unfortunately, many of the things about which blacks make this as-   12
sumption are things that do not contribute to their career success—except for that handful of the truly gifted who can make it as entertainers and athletes. And many of the things we concede to whites are the things that are essential to economic security.

So it is with a number of assumptions black youngsters make about what   13
it is to be a "man": physical aggressiveness, sexual prowess, the refusal to submit to authority. The prisons are full of people who, by this perverted definition, are unmistakably men.

But the real problem is not so much that the things defined as "black"   14
are negative. The problem is that the definition is much too narrow.

Somehow, we have to make our children understand that they are intel-   15
ligent, competent people, capable of doing whatever they put their minds to and making it in the American mainstream, not just in a black subculture.

What we seem to be doing, instead, is raising up yet another generation   16
of young blacks who will be failures—by definition.

Questions for Close Reading

MyWritingLab

1. What is the selection's thesis? Locate the sentence(s) in which Raspberry states his main idea. If he doesn't state the thesis explicitly, express it in your own words.
2. In paragraph 14, Raspberry emphasizes that the word *black* presents a problem not because it's negative but because it has become "much too narrow." According to Raspberry, what limitations have become associated with the term *black?* What negative consequences does he see resulting from these limitations?
3. In paragraph 11, Raspberry talks about "positive ethnic traditions." What does he mean by this term? What examples does he provide?
4. In Raspberry's opinion, what needs to be done to ensure the future success of African-American children?

Questions About the Writer's Craft

1. **The pattern.** Raspberry is primarily concerned with showing how limited the definition of *black* has come to be in our society. In the course of the essay, though, he also defines three other terms. Locate these terms and their definitions. How do the definitions and the effects of the definitions help Raspberry make his point about the narrowness of the term *black?*
2. **Other patterns.** In his opening paragraph, Raspberry uses the *argumentation* technique of refutation. What does he refute? What does he achieve by using this strategy at the very beginning of the essay?
3. A black journalist, Raspberry wrote, for many years, a nationally syndicated column that originated in *The Washington Post,* a major newspaper serving the nation's capital and the nation as a whole. Consider these facts when examining Raspberry's use of the pronouns *I, we,* and *our* in the essay. What do these pronouns seem to imply about Raspberry's intended audience? What is the effect of these pronouns?
4. Raspberry has chosen a relatively abstract topic to write about—the meaning of the term *black.* What techniques does he use to draw in readers and keep them engaged? Consider his overall tone, choice of examples, and use of balanced sentence structure.

Writing Assignments Using Definition as a Pattern of Development

1. Raspberry points out how restrictive the definitions of *black* and *white* can be. Do you think that the definitions of *male* and *female* can be equally restrictive? Focusing on the term *male* or *female,* write an essay showing how the term was defined as you were growing up. Considering the messages conveyed by your family, the educational system, and society at large, indicate whether you came to perceive the term as limiting or liberating.
2. In paragraph 15, Raspberry seems to define *success* as "making it in the American mainstream," but not everyone would agree that this is what constitutes success. Write an essay in which you offer your personal definition of *success.* You might contrast what you consider success with what you consider failure. Or you might narrate the success story of a person you respect highly. No matter how you proceed, be sure to provide telling specifics that support your definition.

Writing Assignment Combining
Patterns of Development

3. In his conclusion, Raspberry makes a plea for providing the younger generation with a more positive, more expansive definition of *black*. Consider the beliefs and principles that today's older generation seems to impart to the younger generation. Write an essay *arguing* which aspects of this value system seem helpful and valid and which do not. Also explain what additional values and convictions the older generation should be passing on, providing *examples* along the way. How should parents, teachers, and others convey these precepts?

Additional Writing Topics

DEFINITION

MyWritingLab

General Assignments

Using definition, develop one of these topics into an essay.

1. Fads
2. Helplessness
3. An epiphany
4. A workaholic
5. A Pollyanna

6. Inner peace
7. Obsession
8. Generosity
9. Depression
10. Greed

11. Exploitation
12. A double bind
13. A conflict of interest
14. An ethical quandary
15. A win-win situation

Assignments Using Visuals

Use the suggested visuals to help develop a definition essay on one of these topics:

1. Masculinity and how it is presented in ads (photos or web links to ads)
2. Discrimination in the United States today (charts or graphs)
3. Various definitions of *success* and which one most resonates with you (photos)
4. What it means to be middle class (graphs or charts)
5. New technologies over the past 500 years (photos and web links)

Assignments with a Specific Purpose, Audience, and Point of View

1. Academic life. You've been asked to write part of a pamphlet for students who come to the college health clinic. For this pamphlet, define *one* of the following conditions and its symptoms: *depression, stress, burnout, test anxiety, addiction* (to alcohol, drugs, or TV), *workaholism*. Part of the pamphlet should describe ways to cope with the condition described.

2. **Academic life.** One of your responsibilities as a peer counselor in the student counseling center involves helping students communicate more effectively. To assist students, write a definition of some term that you think represents an essential component of a strong interpersonal relationship. You might, for example, define *respect, sharing, equality,* or *trust.* Part of the definition should employ definition by negation, a discussion of what the term is *not.*

3. **Civic activity.** *Newsweek* magazine runs a popular column called "My Turn," consisting of readers' opinions on subjects of general interest. Write a piece for this column defining *today's college students.* Use the piece to dispel some negative stereotypes (for example, that college students are apathetic, ill-informed, self-centered, and materialistic).

4. **Civic activity.** In your apartment building, several residents have complained about their neighbors' inconsiderate and rude behavior. You're president of the residents' association, and it's your responsibility to address this problem at your next meeting. Prepare a talk in which you define *courtesy,* the quality you consider most essential to neighborly relations. Use specific examples of what courtesy is and isn't to illustrate your definition.

5. **Workplace action.** You're an attorney arguing a case of sexual harassment—a charge your client has leveled against an employer. To win the case, you must present to the jury a clear definition of exactly what *sexual harassment* is and isn't. Write such a definition for your opening remarks in court.

6. **Workplace action.** A new position has opened in your company. Write a job description to be sent to employment agencies that will screen candidates. Your description should define the job's purpose, state the duties involved, and outline essential qualifications.

MyWritingLab Visit Chapter 10, "Definition," in MyWritingLab to complete the chapter activities, Pre-Reading Journal Entry activities, Questions for Close Reading, and Additional Writing Topics assignments and to test your understanding of the chapter objectives.

Regulation of Genetically Engineered Animals

The Food and Drug Administration (FDA) has issued final guidance on its approach to regulating genetically engineered (GE) animals.

The guidance, issued Jan. 15, 2009, is aimed at industry; however, FDA believes the guidance may also help the public gain a better understanding of this important and developing area.

FDA invited public comments for 60 days after the release of its draft guidance on regulating GE animals in September 2008. The agency received comments from groups and individuals ranging from consumers and animal advocates, to food producers and trade associations, to academics and researchers. FDA considered the approximately 28,000 public comments in producing the final guidance.

Genetic Engineering
Genetic engineering is a process in which scientists use recombinant DNA (rDNA) technology to introduce desirable traits into an organism. DNA is the chemical inside the nucleus of a cell that carries the genetic instructions for making living organisms. Scientists use rDNA techniques to manipulate DNA molecules.

ARGUMENTATION-PERSUASION

In this chapter, you will learn:

11.1 To use the pattern of argumentation-persuasion to develop your essays.

11.2 To consider how argumentation-persuasion can fit your purpose and audience.

11.3 To develop strategies for using argumentation-persuasion in an essay.

11.4 To develop strategies for revising an argumentation-persuasion essay.

11.5 To analyze how argumentation-persuasion is used effectively in student-written and professionally authored selections.

11.6 To write your own essays using argumentation-persuasion as a strategy.

WHAT IS ARGUMENTATION-PERSUASION?

"You can't possibly believe what you're saying."
"Look, I know what I'm talking about, and that's that."

Does this heated exchange sound familiar? Probably. When we hear the word *argument,* most of us think of a verbal battle propelled by stubbornness and irrational thought, with one person pitted against the other.

447

Argumentation in writing, though, is a different matter. Using clear thinking and logic, the writer tries to convince readers of the soundness of a particular opinion on a controversial issue. If, while trying to convince, the writer uses emotional language and dramatic appeals to readers' concerns, beliefs, and values, then the piece is called *persuasion*. Besides encouraging acceptance of an opinion, persuasion often urges readers (or another group) to commit themselves to a course of action. Assume you're writing an essay protesting the federal government's policy of offering aid to those suffering from hunger in other countries while many Americans go hungry. If your purpose is to document, coolly and objectively, the presence of hunger in the United States, you would prepare an argumentation essay. Such an essay would be filled with statistics, report findings, and expert opinion to demonstrate how widespread hunger is nationwide. If, however, your purpose is to shake up readers, even motivate them to write letters to their congressional representatives and push for a change in policy, you would write a persuasive essay. In this case, your essay might contain emotional accounts of undernourished children, ill-fed pregnant women, and nearly starving elderly people.

Because people respond rationally *and* emotionally to situations, argumentation and persuasion are usually *combined*. Suppose you decide to write an article for the campus newspaper advocating a pre-Labor Day start for the school year. Your audience includes the college administration, students, and faculty. The article might begin by *arguing* that several schools starting the academic year earlier were able to close for the month of January and thus reduce heating and other maintenance expenses. Such an argument, supported by documented facts and figures, would help convince the administration. To gain student and faculty support for your idea, you might argue further that the proposed change would mean that students and faculty could leave for winter break with the semester behind them—papers written, exams taken, grades calculated and recorded. To make this part of your argument especially compelling, you could adopt a *persuasive* strategy by using emotional appeals and positively charged language.

When argumentation and persuasion blend in this way, emotion *supports* rather than *replaces* logic and sound reasoning. Although some writers resort to emotional appeals to the exclusion of rational thought, when you prepare argumentation-persuasion essays, you should advance your position through a balanced appeal to reason and emotion.

HOW ARGUMENTATION-PERSUASION FITS YOUR PURPOSE AND AUDIENCE

Your own writing involves argumentation-persuasion. When you prepare a *causal analysis, descriptive piece, narrative,* or *definition essay,* you advance a specific point of view: MTV has a negative influence on teens' views of sex;

Cape Cod in winter is imbued with a special kind of magic; a disillusioning experience can teach people much about themselves; *character* can be defined as the willingness to take unpopular positions on difficult issues. Indeed, an essay organized around any of the patterns of development described in this book may have a persuasive intent. You might, for example, encourage readers to try out a *process* you've explained, or to see one of the two movies you've *compared*.

Argumentation-persuasion, however, involves more than presenting a point of view and providing evidence. Unlike other forms of writing, it assumes controversy and addresses opposing viewpoints. Consider the following assignments, all of which require the writer to take a position on a controversial issue:

In parts of the country, communities established for older citizens or childless couples have refused to rent to families with children. How do you feel about this situation? What do you think are the rights of the parties involved?

Citing the fact that the highest percentage of automobile accidents involve young men, insurance companies consistently charge their highest rates to young males. Is this policy fair? Why or why not?

Some colleges and universities have instituted a "no pass, no play" policy for athletes. Explain why this practice is or is not appropriate.

It's impossible to predict with absolute certainty what will make readers accept the view you advance or take the action you propose. But the ancient Greeks, who formulated our basic concepts of logic, isolated three factors crucial to the effectiveness of argumentation-persuasion: *logos, pathos,* and *ethos.*

Your main concern in an argumentation-persuasion essay should be with the *logos,* or soundness, of your argument: the facts, statistics, examples, and authoritative statements you gather to support your viewpoint. This supporting evidence must be unified, specific, adequate, accurate, and representative (see Chapter 2). Imagine, for instance, you want to convince people that a popular charity misappropriates the money it receives from the public. Your readers, inclined to believe in the good works of the charity, will probably dismiss your argument unless you can substantiate your claim with valid, well-documented evidence that enhances the *logos* of your position.

Sensitivity to *pathos,* or the emotional power of language, is another key consideration for writers of argumentation-persuasion essays. *Pathos* appeals to readers' needs, values, and attitudes, encouraging them to commit themselves to a viewpoint or course of action. The *pathos* of a piece derives partly from the writer's language. *Connotative* language—words with strong emotional overtones—can move readers to accept a point of view and may even spur them to act.

Advertising and propaganda generally rely on *pathos* to the exclusion of logic, using emotion to influence and manipulate. Consider the following pitches for a man's cologne and a woman's perfume. The language—and the attitudes to which it appeals—is different in each case:

> Brawn: Experience the power. Bold. Yet subtle. Clean. Masculine. The scent for the man who's in charge.

> Black Lace is for you—the woman who dresses for success but who dares to be provocative, slightly naughty. Black Lace. Perfect with pearls by day and with diamonds by night.

The appeal to men plays on the impact that terms like *Brawn, bold, power,* and *in charge* may have for some males. Similarly, the charged words *Black Lace, provocative, naughty,* and *diamonds* are intended to appeal to business women who—in the advertiser's mind, at least—may be looking for ways to reconcile sensuality and professionalism.

Like an advertising copywriter, you must select language that reinforces your message. In an essay supporting an expanded immigration policy, you might use evocative phrases like "land of liberty," "a nation of immigrants," and "America's open-door policy." However, if you were arguing for strict immigration quotas, you might use language such as "save jobs for unemployed Americans," "flood of unskilled labor," and "illegal aliens." Remember, though: Such language should support, not supplant, clear thinking.

Finally, whenever you write an argumentation-persuasion essay, you should establish your *ethos,* or credibility and integrity. You cannot expect readers to accept or act on your viewpoint unless you convince them that you know what you're talking about and that you're worth listening to. Be sure, then, to tell readers about any experiences you've had that make you knowledgeable about the issue being discussed. You will also come across as knowledgeable and trustworthy if you present a logical, reasoned argument that takes opposing views into account. And make sure that your appeals to emotion aren't excessive. Overwrought emotionalism undercuts credibility. Remember, too, that *ethos* isn't constant. A writer may have credibility on one subject but not on another: An army general might be a reliable source for information on military preparedness but not for information on federal funding of day care.

Writing an effective argumentation-persuasion essay involves an interplay of *logos, pathos,* and *ethos.* The exact balance among these factors is determined by your audience and purpose (that is, whether you want the audience simply to agree with your view or whether you also want them to take action). More than any other kind of writing, argumentation-persuasion requires that you *analyze your readers* and tailor your approach to them. You need to determine how much they know about the issue, how they feel about you and your position, what their values and attitudes are, what motivates them.

In general, most readers will fall into one of three broad categories: supportive, wavering, or hostile. Each type of audience requires a different blend of *logos, pathos,* and *ethos* in an argumentation-persuasion essay.

1. A supportive audience. If your audience agrees with your position and trusts your credibility, you don't need a highly reasoned argument dense with facts, examples, and statistics. Although you may want to solidify support by providing additional information (*logos*), you can rely primarily on *pathos*—a strong emotional appeal—to reinforce readers' commitment to your shared viewpoint. Assume that you belong to a local fishing club and have volunteered to write an article encouraging members to support threatened fishing rights in state parks. You might begin by stating that fishing strengthens the fish population by thinning out overcrowded streams. Because your audience would certainly be familiar with this idea, you wouldn't need to devote much discussion to it. Instead, you would attempt to move them emotionally. You might evoke the camaraderie in the sport, the pleasure of a perfect cast, the beauty of the outdoors, and perhaps conclude with "If you want these enjoyments to continue, please make a generous contribution to our fund."

2. A wavering audience. At times, readers may be open to what you have to say but may not be committed fully to your viewpoint. Or perhaps they're not as informed about the subject as they should be. In either case, you don't want to risk alienating them with a heavy-handed emotional appeal. Concentrate instead on *ethos* and *logos*, bolstering your image as a reliable source and providing the evidence needed to advance your position. If you want to convince an audience of high school seniors to take a year off to work between high school and college, you might establish your credibility by recounting the year you spent working and by showing the positive effects it had on your life (*ethos*). In addition, you could cite studies indicating that delayed entry into college is related to higher grade point averages. A year's savings, you would explain, allows students to study when they might otherwise need to hold down a job to earn money for tuition (*logos*).

3. A hostile audience. An apathetic, skeptical, or hostile audience is obviously most difficult to convince. With such an audience, you should avoid emotional appeals because they might seem irrational, sentimental, or even comical. Instead, weigh the essay heavily in favor of logical reasoning and hard-to-dispute facts (*logos*). Assume your college administration is working to ban liquor from the student pub. You plan to submit to the campus newspaper an open letter supporting this generally unpopular effort. To sway other students, you cite the positive experiences of schools that have gone dry. Many colleges, you explain, have found their tavern revenues actually increase because all students—not just those of drinking age—can now support the pub. With the greater revenues, some schools have upgraded the food served in the pubs and have hired disc jockeys or musical groups to provide entertainment. Many schools have also seen a sharp reduction in alcohol-related vandalism. Readers may not be won over to your side, but your sound, logical argument may encourage them to be more tolerant of your viewpoint. Indeed, such increased receptivity may be all you can reasonably expect from a hostile audience. (For more help in analyzing your audience, see Chapter 2.)

STRATEGIES FOR USING ARGUMENTATION-PERSUASION IN AN ESSAY

The suggestions here and in Figure 11.1 on page 453 will be helpful for writing an argument-persuasion essay.

1. At the beginning of the essay, identify the controversy surrounding the issue and state your position in the thesis.   Your introduction should clarify the controversy about the issue. In addition, it should provide as much background information as your readers are likely to need.

The thesis of an argumentation-persuasion essay is often called the *assertion* or *proposition*. Occasionally, the proposition appears at the essay's end, but it is usually stated at the beginning. If you state the thesis right away, your audience knows where you stand and is better able to evaluate the evidence presented.

Be sure your proposition focuses on a controversial issue and indicates your view. Avoid a proposition that is merely factual; what is demonstrably true allows little room for debate. To see the difference between a factual statement and an effective thesis, examine the two statements that follow:

> *Fact:* In the past decade, the nation's small farmers have suffered financial hardships.
>
> *Thesis:* Inefficient management, rather than competition from agricultural conglomerates, is responsible for the financial plight of the nation's small farmers.

The first statement is certainly true. It would be difficult to find anyone who believes that these are easy times for small farmers. Because the statement invites little opposition, it can't serve as the focus of an

FIGURE 11.1
Development Diagram: Writing an Argumentation-Persuasion Essay

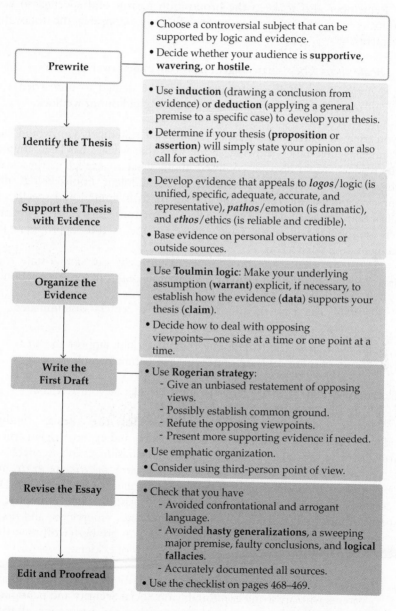

Prewrite
- Choose a controversial subject that can be supported by logic and evidence.
- Decide whether your audience is **supportive, wavering,** or **hostile.**

Identify the Thesis
- Use **induction** (drawing a conclusion from evidence) or **deduction** (applying a general premise to a specific case) to develop your thesis.
- Determine if your thesis (**proposition** or **assertion**) will simply state your opinion or also call for action.

Support the Thesis with Evidence
- Develop evidence that appeals to *logos*/logic (is unified, specific, adequate, accurate, and representative), *pathos*/emotion (is dramatic), and *ethos*/ethics (is reliable and credible).
- Base evidence on personal observations or outside sources.

Organize the Evidence
- Use **Toulmin logic:** Make your underlying assumption (**warrant**) explicit, if necessary, to establish how the evidence (**data**) supports your thesis (**claim**).
- Decide how to deal with opposing viewpoints—one side at a time or one point at a time.

Write the First Draft
- Use **Rogerian strategy:**
  - Give an unbiased restatement of opposing views.
  - Possibly establish common ground.
  - Refute the opposing viewpoints.
  - Present more supporting evidence if needed.
- Use emphatic organization.
- Consider using third-person point of view.

Revise the Essay
- Check that you have
  - Avoided confrontational and arrogant language.
  - Avoided **hasty generalizations,** a sweeping major premise, faulty conclusions, and **logical fallacies.**
  - Accurately documented all sources.

Edit and Proofread
- Use the checklist on pages 468–469.

argumentation-persuasion essay. The second statement, though, takes a controversial stance on a complex issue. Such a proposition is a valid starting point for an essay intended to argue and persuade.

Remember also to keep the proposition narrow and specific, so you can focus your thoughts in a purposeful way. Consider the following statements:

> *Broad thesis:* The welfare system has been abused over the years.
>
> *Narrow thesis:* Welfare payments should be denied to unmarried teenage girls who have more than one child out of wedlock.

If you tried to write an essay based on the first statement, you would face an unmanageable task—showing all the ways that welfare has been abused. Your readers would also be confused about what to expect in the essay: Will it discuss unscrupulous bureaucrats, fraudulent bookkeeping, dishonest recipients? In contrast, the revised thesis is limited and specific. It signals that the essay will propose severe restrictions on welfare payments. Such a proposal will surely have opponents and is thus appropriate for argumentation-persuasion.

The thesis in an argumentation-persuasion essay can simply state your opinion about an issue, or it can go a step further and call for some action:

> *Opinion:* The lack of affordable day-care centers discriminates against lower-income families.
>
> *Call for action:* The federal government should support the creation of more day-care centers in low-income neighborhoods.

In either case, your stand on the issue must be clear to your readers.

2. Provide readers with strong support for the thesis. Finding evidence that relates to the readers' needs, values, and experience is a crucial part of writing an effective argumentation-persuasion essay. Readers will be responsive to evidence that is *unified, adequate, specific, accurate,* and *representative.* It might consist of personal experiences or observations. Or it could be gathered from outside sources—statistics; facts; examples; or expert authority taken from books, articles, reports, interviews, and documentaries. An essay arguing that elderly Americans are better off than they used to be might incorporate the following kinds of evidence:

- *Personal observation or experience:* A description of the writer's grandparents who are living comfortably on Social Security and pensions.
- *Statistics from a report:* A statement that the per capita after-tax income of older Americans is $335 greater than the national average.

- *Fact from a newspaper article:* The point that the majority of elderly Americans do not live in nursing homes or on the streets; rather, they have their own houses or apartments.
- *Examples from interviews:* Accounts of several elderly couples living comfortably in well-managed retirement villages in Florida.
- *Expert opinion cited in a documentary:* A statement by Dr. Marie Sanchez, a specialist in geriatrics: "An over-sixty-five American today is likely to be healthier, and have a longer life expectancy, than a fifty-year-old living only a decade ago."

As you seek outside evidence, you may—perhaps to your dismay—come across information that undercuts your argument. Resist the temptation to ignore such material; instead, use the evidence to arrive at a more balanced, perhaps somewhat qualified viewpoint. Conversely, don't blindly accept points made by sources agreeing with you. Retain a healthy skepticism, analyzing the material as rigorously as if it were advanced by the opposing side.

Also, keep in mind that outside sources aren't infallible. They may have biases that cause them to skew evidence. So be sure to evaluate your sources. If you're writing an essay supporting a woman's right to abortion, the National Abortion Rights Action League (NARAL) can supply abundant statistics, case studies, and reports. But realize that NARAL most likely won't give you the complete picture; it will probably present evidence that supports its "pro-choice" position only. To counteract such bias, you should review what those with differing opinions have to say. You should, for example, examine material published by such "pro-life" organizations as the National Right-to-Life Committee—keeping in mind, of course, that this material is also bound to present support for its viewpoint only. Remember, too, that there are more than two sides to a complex issue. To get as broad a perspective as possible, you should also track down sources that have no axe to grind—that is, sources that make a deliberate effort to examine all sides of the issue.

Whatever sources you use, be sure to *document* (give credit to) that material. Otherwise, readers may dismiss your evidence as nothing more than your subjective opinion, or they may conclude that you have *plagiarized*—tried to pass off someone else's ideas as your own. (Documentation isn't necessary when material is commonly known or is a matter of historical or scientific record.) In brief informal essays, documentation may consist of simple citations like "In 'The Dilemma of the Depressed Mother-to-Be,' Lia Grainger discusses the pros and cons of taking antidepressant medications during pregnancy" or "An *Atlantic* article by Lia Grainger (August 4, 2014) explains some of the negative effects of antidepressant medication on fetuses." (See Appendix A, "A Guide to Using Sources.")

3. Seek to create goodwill.   To avoid alienating readers with views different from your own, stay away from condescending expressions like "Anyone can see that..." or "It's obvious that..." Also, guard against personalizing the debate and being confrontational: "*My opponents* find the law ineffective" sounds adversarial, whereas "*Those opposed* to the law find it ineffective" or "*Opponents* of the law find it ineffective" is more evenhanded. The last two statements also focus—as they should—on the issue, not on the people involved in the debate.

Goodwill can also be established by finding a *common ground*—some points on which all sides can agree, despite their differences. Assume a township council has voted to raise property taxes. The additional revenues will be used to preserve, as parkland, a wooded area that would otherwise be sold to developers. Before introducing its tax-hike proposal, the council would do well to remind homeowners of everyone's shared goals: maintaining the town's beauty and preventing the community's overdevelopment. This reminder of the common values shared by the town council and homeowners will probably make residents more receptive to the tax hike. (For more on establishing common ground, see pages 457–459.)

4. Organize the supporting evidence.   The support for an argumentation-persuasion essay can be organized in a variety of ways. Any of the patterns of development described in this book (description, narration, definition, causal analysis, and so on) may be used—singly or in combination—to develop the essay's proposition. Imagine you're writing an essay arguing that car racing should be banned from television. Your essay might contain a *description* of a horrifying accident that was televised in graphic detail; you might devote part of the paper to a *causal analysis* showing that the broadcast of such races encourages teens to drive carelessly; you could include a *process analysis* to explain how young drivers "soup up" their cars in a dangerous attempt to imitate the racers seen on television. If your essay includes several patterns, you may need a separate paragraph for each.

When presenting evidence, arrange it so you create the strongest possible effect. In general, you should end with your most compelling point, leaving readers with dramatic evidence that underscores your proposition's validity.

5. Use Rogerian strategy to acknowledge differing viewpoints.   A good argument seeks out and acknowledges conflicting viewpoints. Such a strategy strengthens your argument in several ways. It helps you anticipate objections, alerts you to flaws in your own position, and makes you more aware of the other sides' weaknesses. Further, by acknowledging dissenting views, you come across as reasonable and thorough—qualities that may disarm readers and leave them more receptive to your argument. You may not convince them to surrender their views, but you can enlarge their perspectives and encourage them to think about your position.

Psychologist Carl Rogers took the idea of acknowledging contrary viewpoints a step further. He believed that argumentation's goal should be to *reduce conflict*, rather than to produce a "winner" and a "loser." But he recognized that people identify so strongly with their opinions that they experience any challenge to those opinions as an attack on their very identity. And what's the characteristic response to such a perceived attack? People become defensive; they dig in their heels and become more adamant than ever about their position. Indeed, when confronted with solid information that calls their opinion into question, they devalue that evidence rather than allow themselves to be persuaded. Experiments show that after people form a first impression of another person, they are unlikely to let future conflicting information affect that impression. If, for example, they initially perceive someone to be unpleasant and disagreeable, they tend to reject subsequent evidence that casts the person in a more favorable light.

For these reasons, Rogerian strategy rejects any adversarial approach and adopts, instead, a respectful, conciliatory posture that demonstrates a real understanding of opposing views and emphasizes shared interests and values. The ideal is to negotiate differences and arrive at a synthesis: a new position that both parties find at least as acceptable as their original positions. What follows are three basic Rogerian strategies to keep in mind as you write.

First, you may acknowledge the opposing viewpoint in a two-part proposition consisting of a subordinate clause followed by a main clause. The *first part of the proposition* (the subordinate clause) *acknowledges opposing opinions;* the *second part* (the main clause) *states your opinion* and implies that your view stands on more solid ground. The following thesis illustrates this strategy (the opposing viewpoint is underlined once; the writer's position is underlined twice):

<u>Although some instructors think that standardized finals restrict academic freedom,</u> <u>such exams are preferable to those prepared by individual professors.</u>

Second, *in the introduction,* you may provide—separate from the proposition—a *one- or two-sentence summary of the opposing viewpoint.* Suppose you're writing an essay advocating a ten-day waiting period before an individual can purchase a handgun. Before presenting your proposition at the end of the introductory paragraph, you might include sentences like these: "Opponents of the waiting period argue that the ten-day delay is worthless without a nationwide computer network that can perform background checks. Those opposed also point out that only a percentage of states with a waiting period have seen a reduction in gun-related crime."

Third, you can take *one or two body paragraphs* near the beginning of the essay to *present in greater detail arguments raised by opposing viewpoints.* After that, you *grant* (when appropriate) the validity of some of those points ("It may be true that...," "Granted,..."). Then you go on to *present evidence* for your position ("Even so...," "Nevertheless..."). Imagine you're preparing an editorial for your student newspaper arguing that fraternities and sororities on your campus should be banned. You "research" the opposing viewpoint by seeking out supporters of Greek organizations and listening respectfully to the points they raise. When it comes time to write the editorial, you start by summarizing the points made by those supporting fraternities and sororities. You might, for example, mention their argument that Greek organizations build college spirit, contribute to worthy community causes, and provide valuable contacts for entry into the business world. Following this summary of the opposing viewpoint, you might concede that the point about the Greeks' contributions to community causes is especially valid; you could then reinforce this conciliatory stance by stressing some common ground you share—perhaps that enjoyable social activities with like-minded people are an important part of campus life. Having done all that, you would be in a good position to present arguments why you nevertheless think fraternities and sororities should be banned.

6. **Refute differing viewpoints.** There will be times, though, that acknowledging opposing viewpoints and presenting your own case won't be enough. Particularly when an issue is complex and when readers strongly disagree with your position, you may have to refute all or part of the *dissenting views. Refutation* means pointing out the problems with opposing viewpoints, thereby highlighting your own position's superiority. You may focus on the opposing sides' inaccurate or inadequate evidence, or you may point to their faulty logic. (Some common types of illogical thinking are discussed on pages 460–463, and 466–467.)

Let's consider how you could refute a competing position in an essay you're writing that supports sex education in public schools. Adapting the Rogerian approach to suit your purposes, you might start by acknowledging the opposing viewpoint's key argument: "Sex education should be the prerogative of parents." After granting the validity of this view in an ideal world, you might show that many parents don't provide such education. You could present statistics on the number of parents who avoid discussing sex with their children because the subject makes them uncomfortable; you could cite studies revealing that children in single-parent homes are apt to receive even less parental guidance about sex; and you could give examples of young people whose parents provided sketchy, even misleading information.

You may refute opposing views *one side at a time* or *one point at a time*. When using the one-side-at-a-time approach, you cite all the points raised by the opposing side and then present your counterargument to each point. When using the one-point-at-a-time strategy, you mention the first point made by the opposing side, refute that point, then move on to the second point and refute that, and so on. (For more on comparing and contrasting the sides of an issue, see Chapter 8.)

Throughout the essay, be sure to provide clear signals so that readers can distinguish your arguments from the other side's: "Despite the claims of those opposed to the plan, many think that..." and "Those not in agreement think that...."

7. Use induction or deduction to think logically about your argument.   There are two basic ways to think about a subject: *inductively* and *deductively.* Though the following discussion treats induction and deduction as separate processes, the two often overlap and complement each other.

Inductive Reasoning   *Inductive reasoning* involves examination of specific cases, facts, or examples. Based on these specifics, you then draw a conclusion or make a generalization. This is the kind of thinking scientists use when they examine evidence (the results of experiments, for example) and then draw a *conclusion:* "Smoking increases the risk of cancer." All of us use inductive reasoning in everyday life. We might think the following: "My head is aching" (evidence); "My nose is stuffy" (evidence); "I'm coming down with a cold" (conclusion). Based on the conclusion, we might go a step further and take some action: "I'll take a cold remedy."

Let's suppose that you're writing a paper about a crime wave in the small town where you live. You might use inductive thinking to structure the essay's argument:

Several people were mugged last month while shopping in the center of town. (*evidence*)

Several homes and apartments were burglarized in the past few weeks. (*evidence*)

Several cars were stolen from people's driveways over the weekend. (*evidence*)

The police force hasn't adequately protected town residents. (*conclusion, or proposition, for an argumentation essay with probable elements of persuasion*)

The police force should take steps to upgrade its protection of town residents. (*conclusion, or proposition, for an argumentation essay with a clearly persuasive intent*)

This inductive sequence highlights a possible structure for the essay. After providing a clear statement of your proposition, you might detail recent muggings, burglaries, and car thefts. Then you could move to the opposing viewpoint: a description of the steps the police say they have taken to protect town residents. At that point, you would refute the police's claim, citing additional evidence that shows the measures taken have not been sufficient. Finally, if you wanted your essay to have a decidedly persuasive purpose, you could end by recommending specific action the police department should take to improve its protection of the community.

As in all essays, your evidence should be *specific, unified, adequate,* and *representative.* These last two characteristics are critical when you think inductively; they guarantee that your conclusion would be equally valid even if other evidence were presented. Insufficient or atypical evidence often leads to *hasty generalizations* that mar the essay's logic. For example, you might think the following: "Some elderly people are very wealthy and do not need Social Security checks" (evidence), and "Some Social Security recipients illegally collect several checks" (evidence). If you then conclude "Social Security is a waste of taxpayers' money," your conclusion is invalid and hasty because it's based on only a few atypical examples. Millions of Social Security recipients aren't wealthy and don't abuse the system. If you've failed to consider the full range of evidence, any action you propose ("The Social Security system should be disbanded") will probably be considered suspect by thoughtful readers. It's possible, of course, that Social Security should be disbanded, but the evidence leading to such a conclusion must be sufficient and representative.

When reasoning inductively, you should also be careful that the evidence you collect is both *recent* and *accurate.* No valid conclusion can result from dated or erroneous evidence. To ensure that your evidence is sound, you also need to evaluate the reliability of your sources. When a person who is legally drunk claims to have seen a flying saucer, the evidence is shaky, to say the least. But if two respected scientists, both with 20/20 vision, saw the saucer, their evidence is worth considering.

Finally, it's important to realize that there's always an element of uncertainty in inductive reasoning. The conclusion can never be more than an *inference,* involving what logicians call an *inductive leap.* There could be other explanations for the evidence cited and thus other positions to take and actions to advocate. For example, given a small town's crime wave, you might conclude not that the police force has been remiss but that residents are careless about protecting themselves and their property. In turn, you might call for a different kind of action—perhaps that the police conduct public workshops in self-defense and home security. In an inductive argument, your task is to weigh the evidence, consider alternative explanations, then choose the conclusion and course of action that seem most valid.

Deductive Reasoning Unlike inductive reasoning, which starts with a specific case and moves toward a generalization or conclusion, *deductive reasoning* begins with a generalization that is then applied to a specific case. This movement from general to specific involves a three-step form of reasoning called a *syllogism*. The first part of a syllogism is called the *major premise*, a general statement about an entire group. The second part is the *minor premise*, a statement about an individual within that group. The syllogism ends with a *conclusion* about that individual.

Just as you use inductive thinking in everyday life, you use deductive thinking—often without being aware of it—to sort out your experiences. When trying to decide which car to buy, you might think as follows:

Major premise: In an accident, large cars are safer than small cars.

Minor premise: The Turbo Titan is a large car.

Conclusion: In an accident, the Turbo Titan will be safer than a small car.

Based on your conclusion, you might decide to take a specific action, buying the Turbo Titan rather than the smaller car you had first considered.

To create a valid syllogism and thus arrive at a sound conclusion, you need to avoid two major pitfalls of deductive reasoning. First, be sure not to start with a *hasty generalization* (see page 460) as your *major premise*. Second, don't accept as truth a *faulty conclusion*. Let's look at each problem.

Sweeping major premise.   Perhaps you're concerned about a trash-to-steam incinerator scheduled to open near your home. Your thinking about the situation might follow these lines:

Major premise: Trash-to-steam incinerators have had serious problems and pose significant threats to the well-being of people living near the plants.

Minor premise: The proposed incinerator in my neighborhood will be a trash-to-steam plant.

Conclusion: The proposed trash-to-steam incinerator in my neighborhood will have serious problems and pose significant threats to the well-being of people living near the plant.

Having arrived at this conclusion, you might decide to join organized protests against the opening of the incinerator. But your thinking is somewhat illogical. Your *major premise* is a *sweeping* one because it indiscriminately groups all trash-to-steam plants into a single category. It's unlikely that you're familiar with the operations of all trash-to-steam incinerators in this country and abroad; it's probably not true that *all* such plants have had serious difficulties that endangered the public. For your argument to reach a

462   Argumentation-Persuasion

valid conclusion, the major premise must be based on repeated observations or verifiable facts. You would have a better argument, and thus reach a more valid conclusion, if you restricted or qualified the major premise, applying it to some, not all, of the group.

> *Major premise:*   A number of trash-to-steam incinerators have had serious problems and posed significant threats to the well-being of people living near the plants.
>
> *Minor premise:*   The proposed incinerator in my neighborhood will be a trash-to-steam plant.
>
> *Conclusion:*   It's possible that the proposed trash-to-steam incinerator in my neighborhood will run into serious problems and pose significant threats to the well-being of people living near the plant.

This new conclusion, the result of more careful reasoning, would probably encourage you to learn more about trash-to-steam incinerators in general and about the proposed plant in particular. If further research still left you feeling uncomfortable about the plant, you would probably decide to join the protest. On the other hand, your research might convince you that the plant has incorporated into its design a number of safeguards that have been successful at other plants. This added information could reassure you that your original fears were unfounded. In either case, the revised deductive process would lead to a more informed conclusion and course of action.

Faulty conclusion.   Your syllogism—and thus your reasoning—would also be invalid if your *conclusion reverses the "if...then" relationship implied in the major premise.* Assume you plan to write a letter to the college newspaper urging the resignation of the student government president. Perhaps you pursue a line of reasoning that goes like this:

> *Major premise:*   Students who plagiarize papers must appear before the Faculty Committee on Academic Policies and Procedures.
>
> *Minor premise:*   Yesterday, Jennifer Kramer, president of the student government, appeared before the Faculty Committee on Academic Policies and Procedures.
>
> *Conclusion:*   Jennifer must have plagiarized a paper.
>
> *Action:*   Jennifer should resign her position as president of the student government.

Such a chain of reasoning is illogical and unfair. Here's why. *If* students plagiarize their papers and are caught, *then* they must appear before the committee. However, the converse isn't necessarily true—that *if* students appear before the committee, *then* they must have plagiarized. In other words, not *all* students appearing before the committee have been called up on plagiarism charges. For example, Jennifer could have been speaking on behalf of another student; she could have been protesting some action taken by the committee; she could have been seeking the committee's help on an article she plans to write about academic honesty. The conclusion doesn't allow for other possible explanations.

Now that you're aware of potential problems associated with deductive reasoning, let's look at the way you can use a syllogism to structure an argumentation-persuasion essay. Suppose you decide to write an essay advocating support for a projected space mission. You know that controversy surrounds the manned space program, especially since seven astronauts died in a 1986 launch and another crew of seven died in a shuttle reentry accident in 2003. Confident that these tragedies have led to more rigorous controls, you want to argue that the benefits of an upcoming mission outweigh its risks. A deductive pattern could be used to develop your argument. In fact, outlining your thinking as a syllogism might help you formulate a proposition, organize your evidence, deal with opposing viewpoints, and—if appropriate—propose a course of action:

Major premise:	Space programs in the past have led to important developments in technology, especially in medical science.
Minor premise:	The Cosmos Mission is the newest space program.
Proposition (essay might be persuasive):	The Cosmos Mission will most likely lead to important developments in technology, especially in medical science.
Proposition (essay clearly is persuasive):	Congress should continue its funding of the Cosmos Mission.

Having outlined the deductive pattern of your thinking, you might begin by stating your proposition and then discuss some new procedures developed to protect the astronauts and the rocket system's structural integrity. With that background established, you could detail the opposing claim that little of value has been produced by the space program so far. You could then move to your refutation, citing significant medical advances derived from former space missions. Finally, the paper might conclude on a persuasive note, with a plea to Congress to continue funding the latest space mission.

8. Use Toulmin logic to establish a strong connection between your evidence and your thesis. Whether you use an essentially inductive or deductive approach, your argument depends on strong evidence. In *The Uses of Argument*, Stephen Toulmin describes a useful approach for strengthening the connection between evidence and thesis. Toulmin divides a typical argument into three parts:

- **Claim**—The thesis, proposition, or conclusion.
- **Data**—The evidence (facts, statistics, examples, observations, expert opinion) used to convince readers of the claim's validity.
- **Warrant**—The underlying assumption that justifies moving from evidence to claim.

The train engineer was under the influence of drugs when the train crashed.

(Data)

Transportation employees entrusted with the public's safety should be tested for drug use.

(Claim)

Transportation employees entrusted with the public's safety should not be allowed on the job if they use drugs.

(Warrant)

As Toulmin explains in his book, readers are more apt to consider your argument valid if they know what your warrant is. Sometimes your warrant will be so obvious that you won't need to state it explicitly; an *implicit warrant* will be sufficient. Assume you want to argue that the use of live animals to test product toxicity should be outlawed. To support your claim, you cite the following evidence: first, current animal tests are painful and usually result in the animal's death; second, human cell cultures frequently offer more reliable information on how harmful a product may be to human tissue; and third, computer simulations often can more accurately rate a substance's toxicity. Your warrant, although not explicit, is nonetheless clear: "It is wrong to continue product testing on animals when more humane and valid test methods are available."

Other times, you'll do best to make your warrant *explicit*. Suppose you plan to argue that students should be involved in deciding which faculty members are granted tenure. To develop your claim, you present some evidence. You begin by noting that, currently, only faculty members and administrators review candidates for tenure. Next, you call attention to the controversy surrounding two professors, widely known by students to be poor teachers, who were nonetheless granted tenure. Finally, you cite a decision, made several years ago, to discontinue using student evaluations as part of the tenure process; you emphasize that since that time complaints about teachers' incompetence have risen dramatically. Some readers, though, still might wonder how you got from your evidence to your claim. In this case, your argument could be made stronger by stating your warrant explicitly: "Since students are as knowledgeable as the faculty and administrators about which professors are competent, they should be involved in the tenure process."

The more widely accepted your warrant, Toulmin explains, the more likely it is that readers will accept your argument. If there's no consensus about the warrant, you'll probably need to *back it up*. For the preceding example, you might mention several reports that found students evaluate faculty fairly (most students don't, for example, use the ratings to get back at professors against whom they have a personal grudge); further, students' ratings correlate strongly with those given by administrators and other faculty.

Toulmin describes another way to increase receptivity to an argument: *qualify the claim*—that is, explain under what circumstances it might be invalid or restricted. For instance, you might grant that most students know little about their instructors' research activities, scholarly publications, or participation in professional committees. You could, then, qualify your claim this way: "Because students don't have a comprehensive view of their instructors' professional activities, they should be involved in the tenure process but play a less prominent role than faculty and administrators."

As you can see, Toulmin's approach provides strategies for strengthening an argument. So, when prewriting or revising, take a few minutes to ask yourself the questions listed here.

☑ QUESTIONS FOR USING TOULMIN LOGIC: A CHECKLIST

❑ What data (*evidence*) should I provide to support my claim (*thesis*)?
❑ Is my warrant clear? Should I state it explicitly? What backup can I provide to justify my warrant?
❑ Would qualifying my claim make my argument more convincing?

Your responses to these questions will help you structure a convincing and logical argument.

9. Recognize logical fallacies.   When writing an argumentation-persuasion essay, you need to recognize *logical fallacies* both in your own argument and in points raised by opposing sides. Work to eliminate such gaps in logic from your own writing and, when they appear in opposing arguments, try to expose them in your refutation. Logicians have identified many logical fallacies—including the sweeping or hasty generalization and the faulty conclusion discussed on pages 460 and 462. Other logical fallacies are described in the paragraphs that follow.

Post Hoc Thinking.   The *post hoc fallacy* (short for a Latin phrase meaning "after this, therefore because of this") occurs when you conclude that a cause-effect relationship exists simply because one event preceded another. Let's say you note the growing number of immigrants settling in a nearby city, observe the city's economic decline, and conclude that the immigrants' arrival caused the decline. Such a chain of thinking is faulty because it assumes a cause-effect relationship based purely on co-occurrence. Perhaps the immigrants' arrival was a factor in the economic slump, but there could also be other reasons: the lack of financial incentives to attract business to the city, restrictions on the size of the city's manufacturing facilities, citywide labor disputes that make companies leery of settling in the area. Your argument should also consider these possibilities. (For more on the *post hoc* fallacy, see Chapter 9.)

Non Sequiturs.   The *non sequitur fallacy* (Latin for "it does not follow") is an even more blatant muddying of cause-effect relationships. In this case, a conclusion is drawn that has no logical connection to the evidence cited: "Millions of Americans own cars, so there is no need to fund public transportation." The faulty conclusion disregards the millions of Americans who don't own cars; it also ignores pollution and road congestion, both of which could be reduced if people had access to safe, reliable public transportation.

Ad Hominem Arguments.   An *ad hominem argument* (from the Latin meaning "to the man") occurs when someone attacks a person rather than a point of view. Suppose your college plans to sponsor a physicians' symposium on the abortion controversy. You decide to write a letter to the school paper opposing the symposium. Taking swipes at two of the invited doctors who disapprove of abortion, you mention that one was recently involved in a messy divorce and that the other is alleged to have a drinking problem. By hurling personal invective, you avoid discussing the issue. Mudslinging is a poor substitute for reasoned argument.

Questionable Authority. *Appeals to questionable or faulty authority* also weaken an argument. Most of us have developed a healthy suspicion of phrases like *sources close to, an unidentified spokesperson states, experts claim,* and *studies show.* If these people and reports are so reliable, they should be clearly identified.

Begging the Question. *Begging the question* involves failure to establish proof for a debatable point. The writer expects readers to accept as given a premise that's actually controversial. For instance, you would have trouble convincing readers that prayer should be banned from public schools if you based your argument on the premise that school prayer violates the U.S. Constitution. If the Constitution does, either explicitly or implicitly, prohibit prayer in public education, your essay must demonstrate that fact. You can't build a strong argument if you pretend there's no controversy surrounding your premise.

False Analogies. A *false analogy* wrongly implies that because two things share *some* characteristics, they are therefore *alike in all respects.* You might, for example, compare nicotine and marijuana. Both, you could mention, involve health risks and have addictive properties. If, however, you go on to conclude, "Driving while smoking a cigarette isn't illegal, so driving while smoking marijuana shouldn't be illegal either," you're employing a false analogy. You've overlooked a major difference between nicotine and marijuana: Marijuana impairs perception and coordination—important aspects of driving—whereas there's no evidence that nicotine does the same.

Either/or Fallacies. The *either/or fallacy* occurs when you assume that a particular viewpoint or course of action can have only one of two diametrically opposed outcomes—either totally this or totally that. Say you argue as follows: "Unless colleges continue to offer scholarships based solely on financial need, no one who is underprivileged will be able to attend college." Such a statement ignores the fact that bright, underprivileged students could receive scholarships based on their potential or their demonstrated academic excellence.

Red Herring Arguments. Finally, a *red herring argument* is an intentional digression from the issue—a ploy to deflect attention from the matter being discussed. Imagine that you're arguing that condoms shouldn't be dispensed to high school students. You would introduce a red herring if you began to rail against parents who fail to provide their children with any information about sex. Most people would agree that parents *should* provide such information. However, the issue being discussed is not parents' irresponsibility but the pros and cons of schools' distributing condoms to students.

REVISION STRATEGIES

Once you have a draft of the essay, you're ready to revise. The following checklist will help you and those giving you feedback apply to argumentation-persuasion some of the revision techniques discussed in Chapter 2.

☑ ARGUMENTATION-PERSUASION: A REVISION/PEER REVIEW CHECKLIST

Revise Overall Meaning and Structure

❑ What issue is being discussed? What is controversial about it?

❑ What is the essay's thesis? How does it differ from a generalization or mere statement of fact?

❑ What is the essay's purpose—to win readers over to a point of view, to spur readers to some type of action?

❑ For what audience is the essay written? What strategies are used to make readers receptive to the essay's thesis?

❑ What tone does the essay project? Is the tone likely to win readers over?

❑ If the essay's argument is essentially deductive, is the major premise sufficiently restricted? What evidence is the premise based on? Are the minor premise and conclusion valid? If not, how could these problems be corrected?

❑ Where is the essay weakened by hasty generalizations, a failure to weigh evidence honestly, or a failure to draw the most valid conclusion?

❑ Where does the essay commit any of the following logical fallacies: Concluding that a cause-effect relationship exists simply because one event preceded another? Attacking a person rather than an issue? Drawing a conclusion that isn't logically related to the evidence? Failing to establish proof for a debatable point? Relying on questionable or vaguely specified authority? Drawing a false analogy? Resorting to *either/or* thinking? Using a *red herring* argument?

Revise Paragraph Development

❑ How apparent is the link between the evidence (data) and the thesis (claim)? How could an explicit warrant clarify the connection? How would supporting the warrant or qualifying the claim strengthen the argument?

❑ Which paragraphs lack sufficient evidence (facts, examples, statistics, and expert opinion)?

❑ Which paragraphs lack unity? How could they be made more focused? In which paragraph(s) does evidence seem bland, overly general, unrepresentative, or inaccurate?

❏ Which paragraphs take opposing views into account? Are these views refuted? How? Which counterarguments are ineffective?

❏ Where do outside sources require documentation?

Revise Sentences and Words

❏ What words and phrases help readers distinguish the essay's arguments from those advanced by the opposing side?

❏ Which words carry strong emotional overtones? Is this connotative language excessive? Where does emotional language replace rather than reinforce clear thinking?

❏ Where might dogmatic language ("Anyone can see that..." and "Obviously,...") alienate readers?

STUDENT ESSAY

The following student essay was written by Lydia Gumm in response to this assignment:

> In "What Causes Weight Gain," television personality and cookbook author Mark Bittman, widely known for his stance on the importance of avoiding hyperprocessed foods, addresses a health issue he considers important. Think of an issue about which you have strong feelings and write an argumentation-persuasion essay in which you take a stand on the issue. Decide on a specific purpose and audience for your essay, and tailor your approach for that purpose and audience. Incorporate a variety of credible outside sources (both print and online) to add support to your argument.

Upon receiving this assignment, Lydia, a member of her university's women's golf team, knew exactly what she wanted to write about.

Your instructor may not ask you to include research in your essay. But, if you're asked—as Lydia was—to research your essay and to provide *formal documentation*, you'll want to pay special attention to the way Lydia credits her sources. (In *your* essay, the Works Cited list should be double-spaced— along with the rest of the essay—and placed at the end on a separate page.) You'll also find it helpful to refer to Appendix A, "A Guide to Using Sources." If your instructor wants you to research your essay but will accept *informal documentation*, the material on pages 454–455 should come in handy.

Whether or not you include research in your paper, the annotations on Lydia's essay and the comments following it will help you determine how well it applies the principles of argumentation-persuasion.

Gumm 1

Lydia Gumm

Professor Bruce Bowles

English 1102

1 December 2014

It's About Time, Augusta!

Center title and double-space all text.

Introduction

Sports fans across the nation, even those who are not avid golfers, are familiar with Augusta National Golf Club. Augusta National is the home of what many consider to be the most prestigious golf tournament in the United States—The Masters. Augusta National is one of the most perfectly designed, best maintained, and absolutely gorgeous golf courses in the world. Its visitors find not a single divot that needs to be replaced or one blade of grass leaning in the wrong direction. It's a sight that amazes almost every individual who sets foot on its grounds. Augusta might be the most beautiful golf course in all of America, but the stubbornness of the board and the history of the club have proven to people all over the world that discrimination is alive and well in our country. While Augusta National Golf Club has taken steps in the right direction, its members still have a long way to go if they want to improve the club's tarnished reputation.

Thesis

Topic sentence

While many like to think that gender inequality is a thing of the past, Augusta National Golf Club is living proof that it is still very much alive. In many respects, equality for females has progressed significantly since 1920, when American women fought for their right to vote. Indeed, sports has been an agent for change for women in many ways: "Women's desire to play golf not only forced men to accommodate them, but also forced restrictive and antiquated clothing into the closet" (Knott 176). Today, more women than ever before not only play golf, but are active in a wide variety of sports, have fulfilling careers, and hold positions of leadership throughout our country. For most Americans, the idea that women are "the weaker

Common knowledge. No need to document.

Parenthetical citation for a specific page of a source

1

2

Gumm 2

sex" and undeserving of all the rights that men enjoy is largely a thing of the past. However, things have not changed so dramatically at Augusta. To this day, female memberships at the club are few and far between, and the fact that they did not allow one female member inside the gates of their immaculate grounds until August 2012 is inexcusable. The presence of women at Augusta has been such an anomaly that during the 2010 Masters, a female reporter was stopped by a guard when she and her male colleague were walking into a room to interview a player. It took a moment for the guard to rethink the situation and realize that for this particular occasion, it was actually okay for the female to be in the room (Plaschke).

Many people wonder how on earth such a renowned club could get away with such blatant discrimination of females. It makes no sense that in 2012, there were still rooms at Augusta other than restrooms with signs on the door that read "Males Only." Were people still that prejudiced? Augusta was. At Augusta National, the members make the rules. In her *New York Times* article that was published the day the club finally admitted its first female members, columnist Karen Crouse says, "Augusta National conducts business on its own terms, long responding to questions about its policies by saying that it is a private club and that membership issues are a private matter" (A1). In other words, the all-male members owned the club, and they could do whatever they wanted. What they wanted was to deny membership to women.

Gender inequality is not the first publicized discrimination issue that Augusta National has faced. Racism at Augusta is an issue that the entire nation became aware of in 1990. Augusta National Golf Club was established in 1933 as an "all-white" club, and it took members fifty-eight years to finally admit their first African American male member, twenty-six years after the Civil Rights Act was passed (McCarthy and Brady). This is another example of the members of

Annotations (left margin):

common knowledge. No need to document.

Parenthetical citation for source having one author. No page even since electronic text is unpaged.

Topic sentence

Attribution giving author's full name and title of newspaper

Annotations (right margin):

3

Full-sentence quotation is preceded by a comma and begins with a capital letter.

4

Parenthetical citation for a source with two authors

Gumm 3

the club doing exactly what they wanted to do. In their *USA Today*
article, Michael McCarthy and Erik Brady do a good job of describing
the members of the club: "Members at Augusta National are not
accustomed to being told what to do. These are the guys who tell
others what to do: Augusta's 300 or so members are a who's who of
corporate power and old money." Had Augusta National not been
pressured by the Professional Golf Association, the members might
have never integrated the club. In 1990, the PGA Championship was
hosted at Shoal Creek Country Club in Alabama, which at the time
was an all-white golf club. The PGA announced that it would no longer
host tournaments, not even the prestigious Masters, at all-white clubs.
It is no coincidence that three weeks after this announcement was
made, Augusta welcomed its first African American member (Juckett).

It took threats from the PGA for Augusta to finally integrate in   5
1990, and similarly, it took threats from IBM, one of the main sponsors
of the Masters, as well as threats from CBS, the main network that
broadcasts the tournament, for Augusta National to finally allow
women to become members (Crouse B9). For years, IBM had very
close ties with the club. In fact, until 2012, the four previous CEOs
of IBM had been invited to be members. However, in 2012, IBM
hired a new CEO, Virginia Rometty, and Augusta did not send her
an invitation. This did not go over well at IBM, and the company
threatened to no longer sponsor the event. Media outlets including
ESPN and The Golf Channel learned of the story and publicized it
widely. News of Augusta's discriminatory practices quickly spread
across the nation, and organizations, sponsors, and partners of The
Masters began questioning whether they would maintain connections
with Augusta. CBS threatened to no longer cover the event. The issue
was quickly becoming a nationwide topic that was bringing much
criticism and negative publicity to Augusta (Crouse B9).

Full-sentence introduction to a quotation ends with a colon.

Topic sentence

Gumm 4

As in 1990, when Augusta changed its "all-white" male   6
member policy, the club finally gave in to the pressure of
supporters, the media, and society and did away with its "no
female" policy. On August 20, 2012, Billy Payne, Augusta National
chairman, made an announcement that pleased many golfers,
sports fans, and women across America: Augusta National Golf
Club would no longer exclude females from its premises and female
memberships would be allowed. While Payne called the big news
a "joyous occasion," many doubted his sincerity (Meece). Still, the
announcement was a milestone for women.

On that same day, two females were added to the   7
exclusive list of members of the Augusta National Golf Club:
former Secretary of State Condoleezza Rice and private
investment firm partner of Rainwater, Inc., Darla Moore. The
two women made history. Some wonder why these two females
in particular were chosen to become the first female members.
When asked that question, Billy Payne responded with the
following statement:

> We are fortunate to consider many qualified candidates for
> membership at Augusta National. Consideration with regard
> to any candidate is deliberate, held in strict confidence and
> always takes place over an extended period of time. The
> process for Condoleezza and Darla was no different. These ac-
> complished women share our passion for the game of golf and
> both are well known and respected by our membership. It will
> be a proud moment when we present Condoleezza and Darla
> their green jackets.... (qtd. in Meece)

While many regarded Payne's remarks as highly hypocritical,   8
the fact that two females were admitted into Augusta was a milestone
for women. Martha Burk, former chair of the National Council of

Gumm 5

Women's Organizations had the following to say when she learned of the change in policy and that Rice and Moore had become members: "It's about ten years too late for the boys to come into the 20th century, never mind the 21st century. But it's a milestone for women in business" (qtd. in Crouse B9). Burk had led a "highly publicized protest of the club," including putting pressure on corporate sponsors, to "force a change" in Augusta's policy (Hudson 119). Unfortunately, two years later, Rice and Moore remain the only two females on the list of around three hundred members at Augusta.

> Parenthetical citation for a quotation cited in a secondary source.

> Parenthetical citation of a specific page of a source

> Conclusion

Not integrating the club until 1990 was indecent, and to deny women memberships until 2012 indicates a lack of integrity. It is time for Augusta National Golf Club to prove to the country that it has moved beyond its discriminating policies. One way the club could begin to improve its tarnished image is by inviting additional female members to join the club, and another is by hosting an LPGA tournament. Come on, Augusta. It's time for you to prove to America that you have moved beyond your discriminating policies of the past.

9

> Start on a new page, double-spaced, no extra space after heading or between entries. Each entry begins flush left. Indent successive lines half an inch.

Gumm 6

Works Cited

Crouse, Karen. "Host to Masters Drops a Barrier with Its First 2 Female Members." *The New York Times*, 21 Aug. 2012, pp. A1+.

> Article with a single author in a print newspaper

Hudson, David L. *Women in Golf: The Players, the History, and the Future of the Sport.* Praeger, 2008.

> Print book by a single author

Juckett, Ron. "3 Reasons Why Augusta National Waited So Long to Admit Women." *Bleacher Report*, 20 Aug. 2012, bleacherreport.com/articles/1304349-3-reasons-why-augusta-national-waited-so-long-to-admit-women.

> Article in an online newsletter

Knott, Rick. Review of *Golf and the American Country Club*, by Richard J. Moss. *Journal of Sport History*, vol. 37, no. 1, 2010, pp. 176-77.

McCarthy, Michael, and Erik Brady. "Privacy Becomes Public at Augusta." *USA Today*, 27 Sept. 2002, usatoday30.usatoday.com/sports/golf/masters/2002-09-27-augusta_x.htm.

Meece, Mickey. "History Is Made at Augusta with the Admission of Condoleezza Rice and Darla Moore." *Forbes*, 20 Aug. 2012, www.forbes.com/sites/mickeymeece/2012/08/20/history-is-made-at-augusta-national-golf-club/#3211015b4c27.

Plaschke, Bill. "Augusta Does the Right Thing ... but What Took So Long?" *Los Angeles Times*, 21 Aug. 2012, articles.latimes.com/2012/aug/21/sports/la-sp-plaschke-augusta-20120821.

Book review in a print journal

Article with two authors in an online newspaper

Article in an online magazine

Article in an online newspaper

COMMENTARY

Blend of argumentation and persuasion.   Tackling a controversial issue, Lydia takes the position that Augusta National Golf Club should be ashamed of the discriminatory policies it upheld for far too long and that the club is still a long way from proving it has moved beyond its unfair membership practices. Lydia's essay is a good example of how *argumentation* and *persuasion* often mix: Although Lydia presents her position in a logical, well-reasoned manner (argumentation), she also appeals to readers' personal values and suggests a course of action (persuasion).

Audience analysis.   When planning the essay, Lydia carefully considered how her audience—the students in her composition class—was likely to respond to her argument. Lydia was enrolled in a themed composition class, "Writing about Sports," and many of her classmates had been actively engaged in playing sports for most of their lives. Even so, she thought that some of her classmates would initially disagree with her argument that Augusta National had not done enough to convince Americans that it had turned from its discriminatory ways. She knew that some of her classmates would need to be persuaded that although Augusta National had taken steps in the right direction, it still had a long way to go toward proving that it had abandoned its discriminatory

476 Argumentation-Persuasion

policies. She also knew that some of her classmates might think that because Augusta National is privately owned by its members, the club has the right to make whatever policies it wants to make, even if they are discriminatory.

Introduction and thesis. Lydia introduces her subject by describing Augusta National Golf Club as "the home of what many consider to be the most prestigious golf tournament in the United States—The Masters." She goes on to explain that "Augusta National is one of the most perfectly designed, best maintained, and absolutely gorgeous golf courses in the world," and then she juxtaposes the beauty of the grounds with the ugliness of the discriminatory policies the club embraced for years. These comments lead to her thesis at the end of the introduction: "While Augusta National Golf Club has taken steps in the right direction, its members still have a long way to go if they want to improve the club's tarnished reputation" (paragraph 1).

Toulmin logic and inductive reasoning. Using *Toulmin logic* to establish a strong connection between her evidence and thesis, Lydia devotes the body of her essay to providing *data* for her *claim* that Augusta National has not done enough to convince the public that it welcomes a diverse membership. Her evidence is in the form of public knowledge about the policies of Augusta National and specific quotations concerning when and how the policy changed so that two women—but no more than two—were eventually admitted as members. Although Lydia does not explicitly state her warrant, it is nonetheless clear: "It is wrong to discriminate against individuals on the basis of their gender or race, even if doing so in a private club is not illegal."

Lydia arrives at her position *inductively*, through a series of *inferences* or *inductive leaps*. She provides specific cases, facts, and examples that lead readers to draw a conclusion. She provides examples of gender inequality and racism at Augusta National, as well as specific cases and facts from a variety of outside sources. She also provides facts which indicate that the club finally changed its discriminatory policies only because of threats from its major sponsors, and that years after it invited its first two female members, those two women remained the only female members at Augusta National.

Use of outside sources Throughout her body paragraphs, Lydia brings in a variety of outside sources to convince readers of her claim's validity. She uses seven outside sources—a book review published in a journal (Knott, paragraph 2); an online *Los Angeles Times* article (Plaschke, paragraph 2); a print *New York Times* article (Crouse, paragraphs 3, 5, and 8); an online *USA Today* article (McCarthy and Brady, paragraph 4); a sports newsletter website (Juckett, paragraph 4); an online *Forbes* article (Meece, paragraphs

6 and 7); and a book, *Women in Golf: The Players, the History, and the Future of the Sport* (Hudson, paragraph 8)—to provide her readers with strong support that is unified, adequate, specific, accurate, and representative. The *data* she provides makes her readers aware of the discriminatory policies Augusta National enforced for years and points to her *warrant*—the underlying assumption that justifies moving from evidence to claim.

Acknowledging and refuting opposing viewpoints.   Although never pretending to respect the opposing views, Lydia does acknowledge them. In paragraph 3, she points out the first opposing view—that the club's members are free to make their own rules. She cites Crouse who says, "Augusta National conducts business on its own terms, long responding to questions about its policies by saying that it is a private club and that membership issues are a private matter." Lydia also mentions the second opposing viewpoint—that the "joyous occasion," of admitting two women to Augusta is a policy change borne out of a desire to do the right thing.

Against the first view, Lydia implies that the legality of an action does not make it right. "In other words, the all-male members owned the club, and they could do whatever they wanted. And what they wanted was to deny membership to women," she says disdainfully, letting her tone carry her implied criticism. For the second opposing viewpoint, Lydia provides a pointed *refutation*. She cites Martha Burk, former chair of the National Council of Women's Organizations, on the club's sincerity: "It's about ten years too late for the boys to come into the 20th century, never mind the 21st century," and she cites evidence suggesting that it was outside pressure, rather than moral conviction, that forced August National to admit women. She also makes the point that two years after Augusta's change in policy, Rice and Moore remained the club's only female members.

With these refutations, Lydia firmly establishes her *claim* that Augusta National did not suddenly have a change of heart and make the decision to abandon its racist, prejudiced attitudes. Instead, the club finally let go of its discriminatory policies because of threats from the PGA and leading sponsors of the Masters such as IBM and CBS.

Combining patterns of development.   To develop her argument, Lydia draws on several patterns of development. She uses *description* as she conveys to readers the beauty of the golf course, and she employs *exemplification* as she provides examples of Augusta National's discriminatory practices. Lydia includes *process analysis* when she explains the sequence of events that led to the club's finally changing its membership rules and allowing non-white and then female members. She draws on *cause-effect* as she explains how threats from leading sponsors led to the club's change in its membership policies.

Conclusion.   Although Lydia relied on *logos* throughout much of her essay as she provided facts, statistics, and examples to convince readers of her claim, in the closing paragraph she relies heavily on *pathos*, the emotional power of language. She appeals to her readers' values in the opening sentence of the conclusion, where she says, "Not integrating the club until 1990 was indecent, and to deny women memberships until 2012 indicates a lack of integrity." That done, she restates her thesis: "It is time for Augusta National Golf Club to prove to the country that it has moved beyond its discriminating policies," and then she goes on to suggest specific steps the club should take to improve its "tarnished reputation." She ends her essay with a call to action: "Come on, Augusta. It's time for you to prove to America that you have moved beyond your discriminating policies of the past."

Revising the first draft.   Given the complex nature of the assignment, Lydia found that she had to revise her essay several times. One way to illustrate some of the changes she made is to compare her final conclusion with the original draft printed here:

Original Version of the Conclusion

Augusta is such a prominent golf course that it is a shame the women on the LPGA tour have never been able to experience it. Although women are now allowed as members, there still has not been an LPGA tournament hosted at Augusta. Augusta would make so much money from hosting an LPGA event, especially if it were to host a major. At The Masters, the average ticket price is $250, and during the tournament there are 50,000 patrons. Just in ticket sales, Augusta makes $12,500,000. That doesn't even include merchandise sales, television earnings, or sponsorships. Obviously, an LPGA major tournament wouldn't bring in that much money, but it would bring in enough money to definitely make a large profit. It would also be good for Augusta to host an LPGA event just to show society that it actually has a heart. There might be only two female members at the moment, but things are definitely moving in the right direction. August 20, 2012, was a day that changed history, and the day that Augusta National Golf Club finally woke up from its dreams of the twentieth century. It's about time, Augusta!

When Lydia met with her classmate, Lamarcus, for a peer review session, she found that he had a number of helpful suggestions for revising various sections of the essay. But Lydia's partner focused most of his comments on the essay's conclusion because he felt it needed special attention. Following Lamarcus's suggestion, Lydia completely revised her conclusion. She realized that the original focus on the idea that Augusta should host an LPGA event because it would "make so much money" was problematic for several reasons. Hosting an LPGA tournament so that the club could add more money to its coffers is hardly an admirable reason to admit female members and certainly was not the principled rationale that Lydia felt would add force to her argument. In addition, when Lamarcus asked Lydia where she found the information about the average ticket price at The Masters and the number of patrons attending, she told him that she had family members who had attended and they told her they paid $250 for their tickets and that they heard there were around 50,000 attendees. She realized that she could not formally document that information as she would need to do in a well-written research essay, and consequently, she knew she should not include it. In addition, after talking with Lamarcus and reading over her original conclusion, she realized that the ideas she had presented did not support her claim that Augusta still had a long way to go if it wanted to "improve its tarnished image." Instead of supporting her thesis, the statement in the original conclusion that "there might be only two female members at the moment, but things are definitely moving in the right direction" contradicted the main argument she was trying to make.

As Lydia revised her conclusion, she focused on bringing her essay to closure by appealing to her readers' sense of values and by suggesting a specific course of action the club could take to prove to Americans that it rejects discrimination and values diversity.

These are just a few of the many changes Lydia made while reworking her essay. Because she budgeted her time carefully, she was able to revise thoroughly and create an essay that is well-reasoned and convincing.

MLA format. Lydia followed the style given in the *MLA Handbook*, 8th ed. (2016). to format her paper. For more guidance on styling in-text references and Works-Cited lists, see Appendix A.

Activities: Argumentation-Persuasion   MyWritingLab
Prewriting Activities

1. Following are several thesis statements for argumentation-persuasion essays. For each thesis, determine whether the three audiences indicated in parentheses are apt to be supportive, wavering, or hostile. Then select *one* thesis and use group brainstorming to identify, for each audience, specific points you would make to persuade each group.

   a. Students should not graduate from college until they have passed a comprehensive exam in their majors (*college students, their parents, college officials*).
   b. Abandoned homes owned by the city should be sold to low-income residents for a nominal fee (*city officials, low-income residents, general citizens*).

(continued)

Activities: Argumentation-Persuasion (*continued*)

   c. The town should pass a law prohibiting residents who live near the reservoir from using pesticides on their lawns (*environmentalists, homeowners, members of the town council*).

   d. Faculty advisors to college newspapers should have the authority to prohibit the publication of articles that reflect negatively on the school (*alumni, college officials, student journalists*).

Revising Activities

2. Following is the introduction from the first draft of an essay advocating the elimination of mandatory dress codes in public schools. Revise the paragraph, being sure to consider these questions: How effectively does the writer deal with the opposing viewpoint? Does the paragraph encourage those who might disagree with the writer to read on? Why or why not? Do you see any logical fallacies in the writer's thinking? Where? Does the writer introduce anything that veers away from the point being discussed? Where? Before revising, you may find it helpful to do some brainstorming—individually or in a group—to find ways to strengthen the paragraph.

    After reworking the paragraph, take a few minutes to consider how the rest of the essay might unfold. What persuasive strategies could be used? How could Rogerian argument win over readers? What points could be made? What action could be urged in the effort to build a convincing argument?

    In three nearby towns recently, high school administrators joined forces to take an outrageously strong stand against students' constitutional rights. Acting like fascists, they issued an edict in the form of a preposterous dress code that prohibits students from wearing expensive jewelry, designer jeans, leather jackets—anything that the administrators, in their supposed wisdom, consider ostentatious. Perhaps the next thing they'll want to do is forbid students to play rock music at school dances. What prompted the administrators' dictatorial prohibition against certain kinds of clothing? Somehow or other, they got it into their heads that having no restrictions on the way students dress creates an unhealthy environment, where students vie with each other for the flashiest attire. Students and parents alike should protest this and any other dress code. If such codes go into effect, we might as well throw out the Constitution.

Stanley Fish

Stanley Fish is best known as a scholar of the English poet John Milton and as a literary theorist. He was born in Providence, Rhode Island, in 1938. Fish has taught English at the University of California at Berkeley, Johns Hopkins University, and Duke University. From 1999 to 2004 he was dean of the College of Liberal Arts and Sciences at the University of Illinois at Chicago, and in 2005 he became a professor of humanities and law at Florida International University. In 2013 he joined the faculty at Cardoza Law School in New York City as Floersheimer Visiting Professor of Law. His best-known work on Milton is *Surprised by Sin: The Reader in Paradise Lost* (1967). In addition to his distinguished academic career and more than 200 scholarly publications, Fish is also a leading public intellectual. He has written and lectured about many issues, including the politics of the university. His books on current political and cultural issues include *There's No Such Thing as Free Speech...and It's a Good Thing, Too* (1994), *The Trouble with Principle* (1999), and *Save the World on Your Own Time* (2008). This article was published in *The Chronicle of Higher Education,* for which Fish writes a regular column on campus politics and academic careers, on June 13, 2003.

For ideas about how this argumentation-persuasion essay is organized, see Figure 11.2 on page 486.

Pre-Reading Journal Entry

MyWritingLab

How do you feel about freedom of speech on campus? In your journal, list several controversial issues that might be debated in a college setting. For each issue, indicate whether you feel that divergent, even inflammatory views should have an opportunity to be heard on campus—for example, in class, in the college newspaper, or in a lecture series. Reflect in your journal on why you feel as you do.

Free-Speech Follies

The modern American version of crying wolf is crying First Amendment.[1] If you want to burn a cross on a black family's lawn or buy an election by contributing millions to a candidate or vilify Jerry Falwell and his mother in a scurrilous "parody," and someone or some government agency tries to stop you, just yell "First Amendment rights" and you will stand a good chance of getting to do what you want to do.   1

In the academy,[2] the case is even worse: Not only is the First Amendment pressed into service at the drop of a hat (especially whenever anyone is disciplined for anything), it is invoked ritually when there are no First Amendment issues in sight.   2

[1]The relevant part of the First Amendment of the U.S. Constitution reads: "Congress shall make no law...abridging the freedom of speech, or of the press; or the right of the people peaceably to assemble, and to petition the Government for a redress of grievances" (editors' note).

[2]Refers to institutions of higher learning (editors' note).

Take the case of the editors of college newspapers who will always cry   3
First Amendment when something they've published turns out to be the
cause of outrage and controversy. These days the offending piece or editorial
or advertisement usually involves (what is at least perceived to be) an attack
on Jews. In January of this year, the *Daily Illini,* a student newspaper at the
University of Illinois at Urbana-Champaign, printed a letter from a resident
of Seattle with no university affiliation. The letter ran under the headline
"Jews Manipulate America" and argued that because their true allegiance is
to the state of Israel, the president should "separate Jews from all government
advisory positions"; otherwise, the writer warned, "the Jews might face
another Holocaust."

When the predictable firestorm of outrage erupted, the newspaper's edi-   4
tor responded by declaring, first, that "we are committed to giving all people
a voice"; second, that, given this commitment, "we print the opinions of others with whom we do not agree"; third, that to do otherwise would involve
the newspaper in the dangerous acts of "silencing" and "self-censorship";
and, fourth, that "what is hate speech to one member of a society is free
speech to another."

Wrong four times.   5

I'll bet the *Daily Illini* is not committed to giving all people a voice—the   6
KKK? man-boy love? advocates of slavery? would-be Unabombers? Nor do
I believe that the editors sift through submissions looking for the ones they
disagree with and then print those. No doubt they apply some principles of
selection, asking questions like, Is it relevant, or Is it timely, or Does it get the
facts right, or Does it present a coherent argument?

That is, they exercise judgment, which is quite a different thing from   7
silencing or self-censorship. No one is silenced because a single outlet
declines to publish him; silencing occurs when that outlet (or any other)
is forbidden by the state to publish him on pain of legal action; and that is
also what censorship is.

As for self-censoring, if it is anything, it is what we all do whenever we   8
decide it would be better not to say something or cut a sentence that went
just a little bit too far or leave a manuscript in the bottom drawer because
it is not yet ready. Self-censorship, in short, is not a crime or a moral failing;
it is a responsibility.

And, finally, whatever the merits of the argument by which all assertions   9
are relativised—your hate speech is my free speech—this incident has nothing to do with either hate speech or free speech and everything to do with
whether the editors are discharging or defaulting on their obligations when
they foist them off on an inapplicable doctrine, saying in effect, "The First
Amendment made us do it."

More recently, the same scenario played itself out at Santa Rosa Junior   10
College. This time it was a student who wrote the offending article. Titled

"Is Anti-Semitism Ever the Result of Jewish Behavior?" it answered the question in the affirmative, creating an uproar that included death threats, an avalanche of hate mail, and demands for just about everyone's resignation. The faculty adviser who had approved the piece said, "The First Amendment isn't there to protect agreeable stories."

He was alluding to the old saw that the First Amendment protects   11
unpopular as well as popular speech. But what it protects unpopular speech *from* is abridgment by the government of its free expression; it does not protect unpopular speech from being rejected by a newspaper, and it confers no positive obligation to give your pages over to unpopular speech, or popular speech, or any speech.

Once again, there is no First Amendment issue here, just an issue of   12
editorial judgment and the consequences of exercising it. (You can print anything you like; but if the heat comes, it's yours, not the Constitution's.)

In these controversies, student editors are sometimes portrayed, or   13
portray themselves, as First Amendment heroes who bravely risk criticism and censure in order to uphold a cherished American value. But they are not heroes; they are merely confused and, in terms of their understanding of the doctrine they invoke, rather hapless.

Not as hapless, however, as the Harvard English department, which made   14
a collective fool of itself three times when it invited, disinvited and then reinvited poet Tom Paulin to be the Morris Gray lecturer. Again the flash point was anti-Semitism. In his poetry and in public comments, Paulin had said that Israel had no right to exist, that settlers on the West Bank "should be shot dead," and that Israeli police and military forces were the equivalent of the Nazi SS. When these and other statements came to light shortly before Paulin was to give his lecture, the department voted to rescind the invitation. When the inevitable cry of "censorship, censorship" was heard in the land, the department flip-flopped again, and a professor-spokesman declared, "This was a clear affirmation that the department stood strongly by the First Amendment."

It was of course nothing of the kind; it was a transparent effort of a bunch   15
that had already put its foot in its mouth twice to wriggle out of trouble and regain the moral high ground by striking the pose of First Amendment defender. But, in fact, the department and its members were not First Amendment defenders (a religion they converted to a little late), but serial bunglers.

What should they have done? Well, it depends on what they wanted to   16
do. If they wanted to invite this particular poet because they admired his poetry, they had a perfect right to do so. If they were aware ahead of time of Paulin's public pronouncements, they could have chosen either to say something by way of explanation or to remain silent and let the event speak for itself; either course of action would have been at once defensible and productive of risk. If they knew nothing of Paulin's anti-Israel sentiments (difficult to believe of a gang of world-class researchers) but found out about

them after the fact, they might have said, "Oops, never mind" or toughed it out—again alternatives not without risk. But at each stage, whatever they did or didn't do would have had no relationship whatsoever to any First Amendment right—Paulin had no right to be invited—or obligation—there was no obligation either to invite or disinvite him, and certainly no obligation to reinvite him, unless you count the obligations imposed on yourself by a succession of ill-thought-through decisions. Whatever the successes or failures here, they were once again failures of judgment, not doctrine.

In another case, it looked for a moment that judgment of an appropri-   17
ate kind was in fact being exercised. The University of California at Berkeley houses the Emma Goldman Papers Project, and each year the director sends out a fund-raising mailer that always features quotations from Goldman's work. But this January an associate vice chancellor edited the mailer and removed two quotations that in context read as a criticism of the Bush administration's plans for a war in Iraq. He explained that the quotations were not randomly chosen and were clearly intended to make a "political point, and that is inappropriate in an official university situation."

The project director (who acknowledged that the quotes were selected   18
for their contemporary relevance) objected to what she saw as an act of censorship and a particularly egregious one given Goldman's strong advocacy of free expression.

But no one's expression was being censored. The Goldman quotations   19
are readily available and had they appeared in the project's literature in a setting that did not mark them as political, no concerns would have been raised. It is just, said the associate vice chancellor, that they are inappropriate in this context, and, he added, "It is not a matter of the First Amendment."

Right, it's a matter of whether or not there is even the appearance of the   20
university's taking sides on a partisan issue; that is, it is an empirical matter that requires just the exercise of judgment that associate vice chancellors are paid to perform. Of course he was pilloried by members of the Berkeley faculty and others who saw First Amendment violations everywhere.

But there were none. Goldman still speaks freely through her words.   21
The project director can still make her political opinions known by writing letters to the editor or to everyone in the country, even if she cannot use the vehicle of a university flier to do so. Everyone's integrity is preserved. The project goes on unimpeded, and the university goes about its proper academic business. Or so it would have been had the administration stayed firm. But it folded and countermanded the associate vice chancellor's decision.

At least the chancellor had sense enough to acknowledge that no one's   22
speech had been abridged. It was just, he said, an "error in judgment." Aren't they all?

Are there then no free-speech issues on campuses? Sure there are; there   23
just aren't very many. When Toni Smith, a basketball player at Manhattanville

College, turned her back to the flag during the playing of the national anthem in protest against her government's policies, she was truly exercising her First Amendment rights, rights that ensure that she cannot be compelled to an affirmation she does not endorse.... And as she stood by her principles in the face of hostility, she truly was (and is) a First Amendment hero, as the college newspaper editors, the members of the Harvard English department, and the head of the Emma Goldman Project are not. The category is a real one, and it would be good if it were occupied only by those who belong in it.

Questions for Close Reading

MyWritingLab

1. What is the selection's thesis? Locate the sentence(s) in which Fish states his main idea. If he doesn't state his thesis explicitly, express it in your own words.
2. What does Fish mean by "Self-censorship, in short, is not a crime or a moral failing; it is a responsibility" (paragraph 8)?
3. In paragraph 15, Fish refers to the Harvard English department as "serial bunglers." What does he mean by this?
4. According to Fish, why aren't the editors of student newspapers that publish inflammatory material First Amendment heroes? Who does he believe are the true First Amendment heroes?

Questions About the Writer's Craft

1. **The pattern.** Fish presents the viewpoint that self-censorship is not a violation of the First Amendment. What strategies does Fish use to deal with this view and to present his own argument?
2. **Other patterns.** All the examples that Fish uses to support his argument are related to anti-Semitism. If Fish had broadened the examples to include instances of speech that defamed groups other than Jews, would the essay have been more or less effective? Support your answer.
3. Paragraph 5 is just "Wrong four times." What is the effect of this brevity?
4. Most readers of *The Chronicle of Higher Education,* where this essay was first published, are academics—administrators, faculty, and graduate students—or those with a professional interest in higher education. They are likely to know Fish by reputation, especially because he publishes a regular column. Given this, how would you assess Fish's *ethos*? How effective is his use of *logos* in this argument? How effective is his use of *pathos*?

Writing Assignments Using Argumentation-Persuasion as a Pattern of Development

1. Fish gives an example of a controversy surrounding an anti-Semitic letter to the editor published in a campus student newspaper. Because publications print letters to the editor to open up their pages to public opinion and dissent, one might argue that the criteria for printing letters to the editor should be quite broad—much broader than the criteria the publication uses for its own articles—to give members of the public an opportunity to air their views. Write an essay in which

FIGURE 11.2
Essay Structure Diagram: "Free-Speech Follies" by Stanley Fish

Introductory paragraphs:
Thesis
(paragraphs 1–2)

Invoking the First Amendment has become a way of "crying wolf."

Thesis: In the academy, the First Amendment is invoked often in situations that don't really concern free speech.

Opposing and supporting arguments illustrated by examples
(3–22)

Example: Anti-Semitic letter in University of Illinois newspaper.

Opposing arguments: (1) Editors have an obligation to give all people a voice. (2) Editors have an obligation to print views they don't agree with. (3) Not to publish is "silencing" and self-censorship. (4) Hate speech to one person is free speech to another. First Amendment protects all speech, not just agreeable speech.

Supporting arguments: (1) Editors must use some selection criteria—for writing quality and content. (2) Exercising judgment is not the same as silencing because writers are free to publish elsewhere. (3) Self-censorship is not a crime; it's a responsibility. (4) The incident did not concern hate speech vs. free speech, but rather whether editors discharged their responsibilities.

Example: Anti-Semitic article in a Santa Rosa Junior College newspaper.
(Opposing and supporting arguments given.)

Example: Harvard English department invites, then uninvites, then reinvites a poet who had expressed anti-Semitic views.
(Opposing and supporting arguments given.)

Example: Quotations critical of the Bush administration deleted from a University of California at Berkeley exhibit flyer.
(Opposing and supporting arguments given.)

Concluding paragraph
(23)

Example of a true First Amendment hero: College basketball player turning her back on the flag during the national anthem to protest government policies.

you *argue* that letters to the editor should (or should not) be printed with the aim of giving all readers an opportunity to state their opinions. Don't forget to acknowledge (and, if possible, to refute) opposing viewpoints.

2. Many colleges and universities have limited controversial speech to designated "free-speech zones," areas on campus where speeches, rallies, and pamphleteering are permitted. Elsewhere free speech is subject to tight administration control. Proponents argue that universities have a right to control activities that interfere with their operation; opponents argue that free-speech zones are unconstitutional. Conduct library and/or Internet research on free speech zones, and write an essay *arguing* that free-speech zones are (or are not) a legitimate way to manage free-speech issues on campus. If your own campus has free-speech zones, use it as an example to support your argument. Use other colleges and universities as examples as well. Conclude your essay with a call to action.

Writing Assignment Combining Patterns of Development

3. What procedures has your college or university established so that people can file grievances if they feel they have been the targets of hate speech or have been discriminated against in some way? In an essay, describe this *process* and indicate whether you feel it is adequate and appropriate. If it isn't, explain what steps need to be taken to improve the procedures. Provide *examples* to illustrate your point of view.

Mary Sherry

Following her graduation from Dominican University in 1962 with a degree in English, Mary Sherry (1940–) wrote freelance articles and advertising copy while raising her family. Over the years, a love of writing and an interest in education have been integral to all that Sherry does professionally. Founder and owner of a small research and publishing firm in Minnesota, she has taught creative and remedial writing to adults for more than twenty years. The following selection first appeared as a 1991 "My Turn" column in *Newsweek*.

Pre-Reading Journal Entry

MyWritingLab

Imagine you had a son or daughter who didn't take school seriously. How would you go about motivating the child to value academic success? Would your strategies differ depending on the age and gender of the child? If so, how and why? What other factors might influence your approach? Use your journal to respond to these questions.

In Praise of the "F" Word

Tens of thousands of 18-year-olds will graduate this year and be handed meaningless diplomas. These diplomas won't look any different from those awarded their luckier classmates. Their validity will be questioned only when their employers discover that these graduates are semiliterate.   1

Eventually a fortunate few will find their way into educational repair   2
shops—adult-literacy programs, such as the one where I teach basic grammar and writing. There, high-school graduates and high-school dropouts
pursuing graduate-equivalency certificates will learn the skills they should
have learned in school. They will also discover they have been cheated by
our educational system.

As I teach, I learn a lot about our schools. Early in each session I ask   3
my students to write about an unpleasant experience they had in school. No
writers' block here! "I wish someone would have had made me stop doing
drugs and made me study." "I liked to party and no one seemed to care."
"I was a good kid and didn't cause any trouble, so they just passed me along
even though I didn't read well and couldn't write." And so on.

I am your basic do-gooder, and prior to teaching this class I blamed   4
the poor academic skills our kids have today on drugs, divorce and other
impediments to concentration necessary for doing well in school. But, as I
rediscover each time I walk into the classroom, before a teacher can expect
students to concentrate, he has to get their attention, no matter what distractions may be at hand. There are many ways to do this, and they have
much to do with teaching style. However, if style alone won't do it, there is
another way to show who holds the winning hand in the classroom. That is
to reveal the trump card[1] of failure.

I will never forget a teacher who played that card to get the attention   5
of one of my children. Our youngest, a world-class charmer, did little to develop his intellectual talents but always got by. Until Mrs. Stifter.

Our son was a high-school senior when he had her for English. "He   6
sits in the back of the room talking to his friends," she told me. "Why don't
you move him to the front row?" I urged, believing the embarrassment
would get him to settle down. Mrs. Stifter looked at me steely-eyed over
her glasses. "I don't move seniors," she said. "I flunk them." I was flus-
tered. Our son's academic life flashed before my eyes. No teacher had ever
threatened him with that before. I regained my composure and managed
to say that I thought she was right. By the time I got home I was feeling
pretty good about this. It was a radical approach for these times, but, well,
why not? "She's going to flunk you," I told my son. I did not discuss it any
further. Suddenly English became a priority in his life. He finished out the
semester with an A.

I know one example doesn't make a case, but at night I see a parade   7
of students who are angry and resentful for having been passed along until they could no longer even pretend to keep up. Of average intelligence
or better, they eventually quit school, concluding they were too dumb to

---

[1]In cards, an advantage held in reserve until it's needed (editors' note).

finish. "I should have been held back" is a comment I hear frequently. Even sadder are those students who are high-school graduates who say to me after a few weeks of class, "I don't know how I ever got a high-school diploma."

Passing students who have not mastered the work cheats them and the employers who expect graduates to have basic skills. We excuse this dishonest behavior by saying kids can't learn if they come from terrible environments. No one seems to stop to think that—no matter what environments they come from—most kids don't put school first on their list unless they perceive something is at stake. They'd rather be sailing.   8

Many students I see at night could give expert testimony on unemployment, chemical dependency, abusive relationships. In spite of these difficulties, they have decided to make education a priority. They are motivated by the desire for a better job or the need to hang on to the one they've got. They have a healthy fear of failure.   9

People of all ages can rise above their problems, but they need to have a reason to do so. Young people generally don't have the maturity to value education in the same way my adult students value it. But fear of failure, whether economic or academic, can motivate both.   10

Flunking as a regular policy has just as much merit today as it did two generations ago. We must review the threat of flunking and see it as it really is—a positive teaching tool. It is an expression of confidence by both teachers and parents that the students have the ability to learn the material presented to them. However, making it work again would take a dedicated, caring conspiracy between teachers and parents. It would mean facing the tough reality that passing kids who haven't learned the material—while it might save them grief for the short term—dooms them to long-term illiteracy. It would mean that teachers would have to follow through on their threats, and parents would have to stand behind them, knowing their children's best interests are indeed at stake. This means no more doing Scott's assignments for him because he might fail. No more passing Jodi because she's such a nice kid.   11

This is a policy that worked in the past and can work today. A wise teacher, with the support of his parents, gave our son the opportunity to succeed—or fail. It's time we return this choice to all students.   12

Questions for Close Reading

MyWritingLab

1. What is the selection's thesis? Locate the sentence(s) in which Sherry states her main idea. If she doesn't state the thesis explicitly, express it in your own words.
2. Sherry opens her essay with these words: "Tens of thousands of 18-year-olds will graduate this year and be handed meaningless diplomas." Why does Sherry consider these diplomas meaningless?

3. According to Sherry, what justification do many teachers give for "passing students who have not mastered the work" (paragraph 8)? Why does Sherry think that it is wrong to pass such students?
4. What does Sherry think teachers should do to motivate students to focus on school despite the many "distractions...at hand" (4)?

Questions About the Writer's Craft

1. **The pattern.** To write an effective argumentation-persuasion essay, writers need to establish their credibility. How does Sherry convince readers that she is qualified to write about her subject? What does this attempt to establish credibility say about Sherry's perception of her audience's point of view?
2. Sherry's title is deliberately misleading. What does her title lead you to believe the essay will be about? Why do you think Sherry chose this title?
3. Why do you suppose Sherry quotes her students rather than summarizing what they had to say? What effect do you think Sherry hopes the quotations will have on readers?
4. **Other patterns.** What *example* does Sherry provide to show that the threat of failure can work? How does this example reinforce her case?

Writing Assignments Using Argumentation-Persuasion as a Pattern of Development

1. Like Sherry, write an essay arguing your position on a controversial school-related issue. Possibilities include but need not be limited to the following: College students should *or* should not have to fulfill a physical education requirement; high school students should *or* should not have to demonstrate computer proficiency before graduating; elementary school students should *or* should not be grouped according to ability; a course in parenting should *or* should not be a required part of the high school curriculum. Once you select a topic, brainstorm with others to gather insight into varying points of view. When you write, restrict your argument to one level of education, and refute as many opposing arguments as you can.
2. Sherry acknowledges that she used to blame students' poor academic skills on "drugs, divorce and other impediments." To what extent should teachers take these and similar "impediments" into account when grading students? Are there certain situations that call for leniency, or should out-of-school forces affecting students not be considered? To gain perspective on this issue, interview several friends, classmates, and instructors. Then write an essay in which you argue your position. Provide specific examples to support your argument, being sure to acknowledge and—when possible—to refute opposing viewpoints.

Writing Assignment Combining Patterns of Development

3. Where else, besides in the classroom, do you see people acting irresponsibly, expending little effort, and taking the easy way out? You might consider the workplace, a school-related club or activity, family life, or interpersonal relationships. Select *one* area and write an essay *illustrating* the *effects* of this behavior on everyone concerned.

Wendell Berry

A widely respected American writer, Wendell Berry, born in 1934, earned a B.A. and an M.S. in English from the University of Kentucky, where he returned to teach creative writing for extended periods between 1964 and 1993. In 1965, Berry purchased a farm, Lane's Landing, where he continues to farm to this day. He has published numerous books of poetry and fiction, as well as many essays, primarily on approaches to agriculture, and has won numerous awards for his writing. The following essay is from his collection *Another Turn of the Crank* (1996).

Pre-Reading Journal Entry

MyWritingLab

Think of areas—for example, education, communications, transportation, and medicine—in which technology has brought about major change. Was the change ultimately positive or negative? In your journal, take some notes on your ideas.

Farming and the Global Economy

We have been repeatedly warned that we cannot know where we wish to go if we do not know where we have been. And so let us start by remembering a little history. 1

As late as World War II, our farms were predominantly solar powered. That is, the work was accomplished principally by human beings and horses and mules. These creatures were empowered by solar energy, which was collected, for the most part, on the farms where they worked and so was pretty cheaply available to the farmer. 2

However, American farms had not become as self-sufficient in fertility as they should have been—or many of them had not. They were still drawing, without sufficient repayment, against an account of natural fertility accumulated over thousands of years beneath the native forest trees and prairie grasses. 3

The agriculture we had at the time of World War II was nevertheless often pretty good, and it was promising. In many parts of our country we had begun to have established agricultural communities, each with its own local knowledge, memory, and tradition. Some of our farming practices had become well adapted to local conditions. The best traditional practices of the Midwest, for example, are still used by the Amish[1] with considerable success in terms of both economy and ecology. 4

[1]Members of the Amish Church, a Christian denomination, believe in living simply and avoiding modern technology; Amish farmers typically use horses, rather than tractors, and cow manure, rather than synthetic fertilizers, for farm work (editors' note).

Now that the issue of sustainability has arisen so urgently, and in fact   5
so transformingly, we can see that the correct agricultural agenda following
World War II would have been to continue and refine the already established connection between our farms and the sun and to correct, where
necessary, the fertility deficit. There can be no question, now, that that is
what we should have done.

It was, notoriously, not what we did. Instead, the adopted agenda called   6
for a shift from the cheap, clean, and, for all practical purposes, limitless energy of the sun to the expensive, filthy, and limited energy of the fossil fuels.
It called for the massive use of chemical fertilizers to offset the destruction
of topsoil and the depletion of natural fertility. It called also for the displace-
ment of nearly the entire farming population and the replacement of their
labor and good farming practices by machines and toxic chemicals. This
agenda has succeeded in its aims, but to the benefit of no one and nothing
except the corporations that have supplied the necessary machines, fuels, and
chemicals—and the corporations that have bought cheap and sold high the
products that, as a result of this agenda, have been increasingly expensive for
farmers to produce.

The farmers have not benefited—not, at least, as a class—for as a result   7
of this agenda they have become one of the smallest and most threatened of
all our minorities. Many farmers, sad to say, have subscribed to this agenda
and its economic assumptions, believing that they would not be its victims.
But millions, in fact, have been its victims—not farmers alone but also their
supporters and dependents in our rural communities.

The people who benefit from this state of affairs have been at pains to   8
convince us that the agricultural practices and policies that have almost an-
nihilated the farming population have greatly benefited the population of
food consumers. But more and more consumers are now becoming aware
that our supposed abundance of cheap and healthful food is to a considerable extent illusory. They are beginning to see that the social, ecological,
and even the economic costs of such "cheap food" are, in fact, great. They
are beginning to see that a system of food production that is dependent on
massive applications of drugs and chemicals cannot, by definition, produce
"pure food." And they are beginning to see that a kind of agriculture that
involves unprecedented erosion and depletion of soil, unprecedented waste
of water, and unprecedented destruction of the farm population cannot by
any accommodation of sense or fantasy be called "sustainable."

From the point of view, then, of the farmer, the ecologist, and the con-   9
sumer, the need to reform our ways of farming is now both obvious and
imperative. We need to adapt our farming much more sensitively to the nature of the places where the farming is done. We need to make our farming
practices and our food economy subject to standards set not by the industrial
system but by the health of ecosystems and of human communities.

The immediate difficulty in even thinking about agricultural reform   10
is that we are rapidly running out of farmers. The tragedy of this decline
is not just in its numbers; it is also in the fact that these farming people,
assuming we will ever recognize our need to replace them, cannot be
replaced anything like as quickly or easily as they have been dispensed
with. Contrary to popular assumption, good farmers are not in any simple
way part of the "labor force." Good farmers, like good musicians, must be
raised to the trade.

The severe reduction of our farming population may signify nothing   11
to our national government, but the members of country communities
feel the significance of it—and the threat of it—every day. Eventually
urban consumers will feel these things, too. Every day farmers feel the
oppression of their long-standing problems: overproduction, low prices,
and high costs. Farmers sell on a market that because of overproduction is
characteristically depressed, and they buy their supplies on a market that is
characteristically inflated—which is necessarily a recipe for failure, because
farmers do not control either market. If they will not control production
and if they will not reduce their dependence on purchased supplies, then
they will keep on failing.

The survival of farmers, then, requires two complementary efforts.   12
The first is entirely up to the farmers, who must learn—or learn again—to
farm in ways that minimize their dependence on industrial supplies. They
must diversify, using both plants and animals. They must produce, on their
farms, as much of the required fertility and energy as they can. So far as they
can, they must replace purchased goods and services with natural health and
diversity and with their own intelligence. To increase production by increasing costs, as farmers have been doing for the last half century, is not only
unintelligent; it is crazy. If farmers do not wish to cooperate any longer in
their own destruction, then they will have to reduce their dependence on
those global economic forces that intend and approve and profit from the
destruction of farmers, and they will have to increase their dependence on
local nature and local intelligence.

The second effort involves cooperation between local farmers and   13
local consumers. If farmers hope to exercise any control over their
markets, in a time when a global economy and global transportation make
it possible for the products of any region to be undersold by the products
of any other region, then they will have to look to local markets. The
long-broken connections between towns and cities and their surrounding
landscapes will have to be restored. There is much promise and much hope
in such a restoration. But farmers must understand that this requires an
economics of cooperation rather than competition. They must understand
also that such an economy sooner or later will require some rational means
of production control.

If communities of farmers and consumers wish to promote a sustainable, 14
safe, reasonably inexpensive supply of good food, then they must see that the
best, the safest, and most dependable source of food for a city is not the global
economy, with its extreme vulnerabilities and extravagant transportation costs,
but its own surrounding countryside. It is, in every way, in the best interest of
urban consumers to be surrounded by productive land, well farmed and well
maintained by thriving farm families in thriving farm communities.

If a safe, sustainable local food economy appeals to some of us as a goal 15
that we would like to work for, then we must be careful to recognize not
only the great power of the interests arrayed against us but also our own
weakness. The hope for such a food economy as we desire is represented
by no political party and is spoken for by no national public officials of any
consequence. Our national political leaders do not know what we are talking
about, and they are without the local affections and allegiances that would
permit them to learn what we are talking about.

But we should also understand that our predicament is not with- 16
out precedent; it is approximately the same as that of the proponents of
American independence at the time of the Stamp Act—and with one difference in our favor: in order to do the work that we must do, we do not
need a national organization. What we must do is simple: we must shorten
the distance that our food is transported so that we are eating more and
more from local supplies, more and more to the benefit of local farmers,
and more and more to the satisfaction of local consumers. This can be
done by cooperation among small organizations: conservation groups,
churches, neighborhood associations, consumer co-ops, local merchants,
local independent banks, and organizations of small farmers. It also can
be done by cooperation between individual producers and consumers.
We should not be discouraged to find that local food economies can
grow only gradually; it is better that they should grow gradually. But as
they grow they will bring about a significant return of power, wealth, and
health to the people.

One thing at least should be obvious to us all: the whole human popula- 17
tion of the world cannot live on imported food. Some people somewhere are
going to have to grow the food. And wherever food is grown, the growing
of it will raise the same two questions: How do you preserve the land in use?
And how do you preserve the people who use the land?

The farther the food is transported, the harder it will be to answer those 18
questions correctly. The correct answers will not come as the inevitable by-
products of the aims, policies, and procedures of international trade, free or
unfree. They cannot be legislated or imposed by international or national
or state agencies. They can only be supplied locally, by skilled and highly
motivated local farmers meeting as directly as possible the needs of informed
local consumers.

Questions for Close Reading

MyWritingLab

1. What is the selection's thesis? Locate the sentence(s) in which Berry states his main idea. If he doesn't state his thesis explicitly, express it in your own words.
2. What does Berry think of farming practices up until the first half of the twentieth century? What changes have happened to farming since World War II? What does he say are the negative effects of those changes? How are consumers responding?
3. What does Berry see as the major immediate obstacle to changing the food production system? What two solutions does he offer for overcoming this obstacle?
4. How does Berry suggest his solutions can be implemented? Ultimately, who can supply the correct answers to questions about land use?

Questions About the Writer's Craft

1. **The pattern.** Do you think the audience for this essay is supportive, wavering, or hostile (see pages 451–452)? What makes you say so? What is the author's purpose?
2. Berry uses two analogies to communicate ideas about farmers and about changing the current food production system. What are those analogies? What do they imply? How valid are they? How effective?
3. **Other patterns.** The author uses comparison-contrast at the beginning of the essay. What does he compare? Give some details of the comparison.
4. The very first word of the essay is "We," and Berry continues to use the third-person plural throughout. Who is "we"? What does Berry accomplish by writing from this point of view? Give some examples of how Berry uses "we."

Writing Assignments Using Argumentation-Persuasion as a Pattern of Development

1. Berry argues that the growth of local food economies will ultimately bring "power, wealth, and health to the people." Think of foods you like that do not grow in your region. Write an essay in which you *argue* that the global food marketplace enhances quality of life by making a wide variety of foods available at low prices. You might visit your local supermarket for examples to support your ideas.
2. The author opposes large agricultural corporations. Yet he also seems against ask- ing "national political leaders" for help. Do some research on the federal regulation of agriculture. Write an essay in which you *argue* for or against additional federal regulation. For what purpose? Include examples to illustrate your points.

Writing Assignment Combining Patterns of Development

3. Some advocates of large-scale mechanized farming say that it enables the produc- tion of surplus food that can be sent to poor countries. Do some research about food aid at organizations like the United Nations and the U.S. Department of Agriculture. Write an essay in which you *describe* efforts to relieve hunger worldwide and *categorize* the types of aid programs available. Include statistics and other facts that you uncover.

Mark Twain

Mark Twain is a central figure in American literature. Published in 1884, *The Adventures of Huckleberry Finn*, Twain's finest work, recounts a journey down the Mississippi by two memorable figures: a white boy and a black slave. Twain was born Samuel Langhorne Clemens in 1835 and was raised in Hannibal, Missouri. During his early years, he worked as a riverboat pilot, newspaper reporter, printer, and gold prospector. Although his popular image is as the author of such comic works as *The Adventures of Tom Sawyer* (1876), *Life on the Mississippi* (1883), and *The Prince and the Pauper* (1882), Twain had a darker side that may have resulted from the bitter experiences of his life: financial failure and the deaths of his wife and daughter. His last writings are savage, satiric, and pessimistic. The following selection is taken from *Letters From the Earth*, one of Twain's later works.

Pre-Reading Journal Entry   MyWritingLab

What would you identify as the major differences between human beings and other animals? What are the similarities? In your journal, list as many items for each as you can, from the obvious to the subtle. Be as specific as you can.

The Damned Human Race

I have been studying the traits and dispositions of the "lower animals" (so-called), and contrasting them with the traits and dispositions of man. I find the result humiliating to me. For it obliges me to renounce my allegiance to the Darwinian theory of the Ascent of Man from the Lower Animals; since it now seems plain to me that the theory ought to be vacated in favor of a new and truer one, this new and truer one to be named the *Descent* of Man from the Higher Animals.

In proceeding toward this unpleasant conclusion I have not guessed or speculated or conjectured, but have used what is commonly called the scientific method. That is to say, I have subjected every postulate that presented itself to the crucial test of actual experiment, and have adopted it or rejected it according to the result. Thus I verified and established each step of my course in its turn before advancing to the next. These experiments were made in the London Zoological Gardens, and covered many months of painstaking and fatiguing work.

Before particularizing any of the experiments, I wish to state one or two things which seem to more properly belong in this place than further along. This in the interest of clearness. The massed experiments established to my satisfaction certain generalizations, to wit:

1. That the human race is of one distinct species. It exhibits slight variations—in color, stature, mental caliber, and so on—due to climate,

environment, and so forth; but it is a species by itself, and not to be confounded with any other.

2. That the quadrupeds are a distinct family, also. This family exhibits variations—in color, size, food preferences and so on; but it is a family by itself.

3. That the other families—the birds, the fishes, the insects, the reptiles, etc.—are more or less distinct, also. They are in the procession. They are links in the chain which stretches down from the higher animals to man at the bottom.

Some of my experiments were quite curious. In the course of my read-   4
ing I had come across a case where, many years ago, some hunters on our Great Plains organized a buffalo hunt for the entertainment of an English earl—that, and to provide some fresh meat for his larder. They had charming sport. They killed seventy-two of those great animals; and ate part of one of them and left the seventy-one to rot. In order to determine the difference between an anaconda and an earl—if any—I caused seven young calves to be turned into the anaconda's cage. The grateful reptile immediately crushed one of them and swallowed it, then lay back satisfied. It showed no further interest in the calves, and no disposition to harm them. I tried this experiment with other anacondas; always with the same result. The fact stood proven that the difference between an earl and an anaconda is that the earl is cruel and the anaconda isn't; and that the earl wantonly destroys what he has no use for, but the anaconda doesn't. This seemed to suggest that the anaconda was not descended from the earl. It also seemed to suggest that the earl was descended from the anaconda, and had lost a good deal in the transition.

I was aware that many men who have accumulated more millions of   5
money than they can ever use have shown a rabid hunger for more, and have not scrupled to cheat the ignorant and the helpless out of their poor servings in order to partially appease that appetite. I furnished a hundred different kinds of wild and tame animals the opportunity to accumulate vast stores of food, but none of them would do it. The squirrels and bees and certain birds made accumulations, but stopped when they had gathered a winter's supply, and could not be persuaded to add to it either honestly or by chicanery. In order to bolster up a tottering reputation the ant pretended to store up supplies, but I was not deceived. I know the ant. These experiments convinced me that there is this difference between man and the higher animals: he is avaricious and miserly, they are not.

In the course of my experiments I convinced myself that among the   6
animals man is the only one that harbors insults and injuries, broods over them, waits till a chance offers, then takes revenge. The passion of revenge is unknown to the higher animals.

Roosters keep harems, but it is by consent of their concubines; therefore   7
no wrong is done. Men keep harems, but it is by brute force, privileged by
atrocious laws which the other sex were allowed no hand in making. In this
matter man occupies a far lower place than the rooster.

Cats are loose in their morals, but not consciously so. Man, in his   8
descent from the cat, has brought the cat's looseness with him but has left
the unconsciousness behind—the saving grace which excuses the cat. The
cat is innocent, man is not.

Indecency, vulgarity, obscenity—these are strictly confined to man; he   9
invented them. Among the higher animals there is no trace of them. They
hide nothing; they are not ashamed. Man, with his soiled mind, covers himself. He will not even enter a drawing room with his breast and back naked,
so alive are he and his mates to indecent suggestion. Man is "The Animal that
Laughs." But so does the monkey, as Mr. Darwin pointed out; and so does
the Australian bird that is called the laughing jackass. No—Man is the Animal
that Blushes. He is the only one that does it—or has occasion to.

At the head of this article[1] we see how "three monks were burnt to   10
death" a few days ago, and a prior "put to death with atrocious cruelty."
Do we inquire into the details? No; or we should find out that the prior was
subjected to unprintable mutilations. Man—when he is a North American
Indian—gouges out his prisoner's eyes; when he is King John, with a
nephew to render untroublesome, he uses a red-hot iron; when he is a religious zealot dealing with heretics in the Middle Ages, he skins his captive
alive and scatters salt on his back; in the first Richard's time he shuts up a
multitude of Jew families in a tower and sets fire to it; in Columbus's time
he captures a family of Spanish Jews and—but *that* is not printable; in our
day in England a man is fined ten shillings for beating his mother nearly to
death with a chair, and another man is fined forty shillings for having four
pheasant eggs in his possession without being able to satisfactorily explain
how he got them. Of all the animals, man is the only one that is cruel. He is
the only one that inflicts pain for the pleasure of doing it. It is a trait that is
not known to the higher animals. The cat plays with the frightened mouse;
but she has this excuse, that she does not know that the mouse is suffering.
The cat is moderate—unhumanly moderate: she only scares the mouse,
she does not hurt it; she doesn't dig out its eyes, or tear off its skin, or drive
splinters under its nails—man-fashion; when she is done playing with it she
makes a sudden meal of it and puts it out of its trouble. Man is the Cruel
Animal. He is alone in that distinction.

The higher animals engage in individual fights, but never in organized   11
masses. Man is the only animal that deals in that atrocity of atrocities, War.

---

[1]Twain originally began his article with newspaper clippings containing telegrams that reported
atrocities in Crete (editors' note).

He is the only one that gathers his brethren about him and goes forth in cold blood and with calm pulse to exterminate his kind. He is the only animal that for sordid wages will march out, as the Hessians did in our Revolution, and as the boyish Prince Napoleon did in the Zulu war, and help to slaughter strangers of his own species who have done him no harm and with whom he has no quarrel.

Man is the only animal that robs his helpless fellow of his country—takes 12 possession of it and drives him out of it or destroys him. Man has done this in all the ages. There is not an acre of ground on the globe that is in possession of its rightful owner, or that has not been taken away from owner after owner, cycle after cycle, by force and bloodshed.

Man is the only Slave. And he is the only animal who enslaves. He has 13 always been a slave in one form or another, and has always held other slaves in bondage under him in one way or another. In our day he is always some man's slave for wages, and does that man's work; and this slave has other slaves under him for minor wages, and they do *his* work. The higher animals are the only ones who exclusively do their own work and provide their own living.

Man is the only Patriot. He sets himself apart in his own country, under 14 his own flag, and sneers at the other nations, and keeps multitudinous uniformed assassins on hand at heavy expense to grab slices of other people's countries, and keep *them* from grabbing slices of *his*. And in the intervals between campaigns he washes the blood off his hands and works for "the universal brotherhood of man"—with his mouth.

Man is the Religious Animal. He is the only Religious Animal. He is 15 the only animal that has the True Religion—several of them. He is the only animal that loves his neighbor as himself, and cuts his throat if his theology isn't straight. He has made a graveyard of the globe in trying his honest best to smooth his brother's path to happiness and heaven. He was at it in the time of the Caesars, he was at it in Mahomet's time, he was at it in the time of the Inquisition, he was at it in France a couple of centuries, he was at it in England in Mary's day, he has been at it ever since he first saw the light, he is at it today in Crete—as per the telegrams quoted above[2]—he will be at it somewhere else tomorrow. The higher animals have no religion. And we are told that they are going to be left out, in the Hereafter. I wonder why? It seems questionable taste.

Man is the Reasoning Animal. Such is the claim. I think it is open 16 to dispute. Indeed, my experiments have proven to me that he is the Unreasoning Animal. Note his history, as sketched above. It seems plain to me that whatever he is he is *not* a reasoning animal. His record is the fantastic record of a maniac. I consider that the strongest count against

[2]See note, page 498 (editors' note).

his intelligence is the fact that with that record back of him he blandly sets himself up as the head animal of the lot: whereas by his own standards he is the bottom one.

In truth, man is incurably foolish. Simple things which the other animals   17
easily learn, he is incapable of learning. Among my experiments was this. In an hour I taught a cat and a dog to be friends. I put them in a cage. In another hour I taught them to be friends with a rabbit. In the course of two days I was able to add a fox, a goose, a squirrel and some doves. Finally a monkey. They lived together in peace; even affectionately.

Next, in another cage I confined an Irish Catholic from Tipperary,   18
and as soon as he seemed tame I added a Scotch Presbyterian from Aberdeen. Next a Turk from Constantinople; a Greek Christian from Crete; an Armenian; a Methodist from the wilds of Arkansas; a Buddhist from China; a Brahman from Benares. Finally, a Salvation Army Colonel from Wapping. Then I stayed away two whole days. When I came back to note results, the cage of Higher Animals was all right, but in the other, there was but a chaos of gory odds and ends of turbans and fezzes and plaids and bones and flesh—not a specimen left alive. These Reasoning Animals had disagreed on a theological detail and carried the matter to a Higher Court.

One is obliged to concede that in true loftiness of character, Man can-   19
not claim to approach even the meanest of the Higher Animals. It is plain that he is constitutionally incapable of approaching that altitude; that he is constitutionally afflicted with a Defect which must make such approach forever impossible, for it is manifest that this defect is permanent in him, indestructible, ineradicable.

I find this Defect to be *the Moral Sense*. He is the only animal that   20
has it. It is the secret of his degradation. It is the quality *which enables him to do wrong*. It has no other office. It is incapable of performing any other function. It could never have been intended to perform any other. Without it, man could do no wrong. He would rise at once to the level of the Higher Animals.

Since the Moral Sense has but the one office, the one capacity—to en-   21
able man to do wrong—it is plainly without value to him. It is as valueless to him as is disease. In fact, it manifestly *is* a disease. *Rabies* is bad, but it is not so bad as this disease. Rabies enables a man to do a thing which he could not do when in a healthy state: kill his neighbor with a poisonous bite. No one is the better man for having rabies: The Moral Sense enables a man to do wrong. It enables him to do wrong in a thousand ways. Rabies is an innocent disease, compared to the Moral Sense. No one, then, can be the better man for having the Moral Sense. What, now, do we find the Primal Curse to have been? Plainly what it was in the beginning: the infliction upon man of the Moral Sense; the ability to distinguish good from evil; and with

it, necessarily, the ability to *do* evil; for there can be no evil act without the presence of consciousness of it in the doer of it.

And so I find that we have descended and degenerated, from some far ancestor—some microscopic atom wandering at its pleasure between the mighty horizons of a drop of water perchance—insect by insect, animal by animal, reptile by reptile, down the long highway of smirchless innocence, till we have reached the bottom stage of development—namable as the Human Being. Below us—nothing. 22

Questions for Close Reading

MyWritingLab

1. What is the selection's thesis? Locate the sentence(s) in which Twain states his main idea. If he doesn't state the thesis explicitly, express it in your own words.
2. Because of their intelligence, humans are usually called the highest animal. What, according to Twain, are the specific traits that make humans the lowest animal?
3. How does the story of the earl who hunted down seventy-two buffalo show that an anaconda is superior to an earl?
4. What does Twain mean when he points out that humankind is the only animal that "has occasion to" blush? What are some of the occasions for blushing that he highlights in the essay?

Questions About the Writer's Craft

1. **The pattern.** Most writers don't tell the reader outright the reasoning process they used to arrive at their essay's proposition. But Twain claims that he reached his conclusion about human beings inductively—through the use of the "scientific method." Why does Twain make this claim?
2. Where in the essay does Twain try to shock the audience? Why do you think he adopts this technique?
3. **Other patterns.** In some paragraphs, Twain provides numerous *examples* of political and religious atrocities. Why do you suppose he supplies so many examples?
4. Black humor is defined as "the use of the morbid and the absurd for comic purposes." What elements of the morbid and the absurd do you find in Twain's essay? Would you say "The Damned Human Race" is an example of black humor? Explain.

Writing Assignments Using Argumentation-Persuasion as a Pattern of Development

1. In an essay, argue that human beings are worthy of being considered the "highest animal." The paper should acknowledge and then refute Twain's charges that people are miserly, vengeful, foolish, and so on. To support your proposition, use specific examples of how human beings can be kind, caring, generous, and peace-loving.
2. Write an essay agreeing with Twain that it is our everyday meannesses, unkindnesses, and cruelties that make us the "lowest animal." Use compelling examples

to support your argument, including description and dialogue whenever appropriate. You might focus on one of the following topics:

Violence toward children
Abuse of animals
Hurtful sarcasm
Insults of a racial, sexist, or religious nature
Indifference to the unfortunate

Somewhere in the essay, you should acknowledge the view that humans are capable of considerable kindness and compassion.

Writing Assignment Combining Patterns of Development

3. How could humans become less cruel? Write an essay outlining a new *process* for raising children or "re-civilizing" adults—a process that, if instituted, would have a clearly beneficial *effect* on human morality.

Anna Quindlen

Writer Anna Quindlen was born in Philadelphia, Pennsylvania, in 1952, and now lives in New York City. While attending Barnard College, she worked as a copy girl at *The New York Times*. After graduating, Quindlen was a reporter for *The New York Post* before returning to the *Times* in 1977. At the *Times* she eventually became a regular op-ed columnist, winning the Pulitzer Prize for Commentary in 1992. In 1995 Quindlen left newspaper work and devoted herself primarily to fiction. She has written novels, nonfiction, self-help books, and children's books. Quindlen also wrote regularly for *Newsweek,* where this article appeared on June 11, 2007.

Pre-Reading Journal Entry   MyWritingLab

Getting a driver's license is an important rite of passage for young people in the United States. It's often preceded by a highly stressful process of learning to drive. Recall your own driving lessons and licensing tests. Who taught you to drive? What were the lessons like? What emotions did you experience while learning to drive and taking your driving test? If you do not know how to drive, why not? How do you feel about not having a driver's license? Use your journal to answer these questions.

Driving to the Funeral

The four years of high school grind inexorably to a close, the milestones   1
passed. The sports contests, the SATs, the exams, the elections, the dances, the proms. And too often, the funerals. It's become a sad rite of passage in many American communities, the services held for teenagers killed in auto

accidents before they've even scored a tassel to hang from the rearview mirror. The hearse moves in procession followed by the late-model compact cars of young people, boys trying to control trembling lower lips and girls sobbing into one another's shoulders. The yearbook has a picture or two with a black border. A mom and dad rise from their seats on the athletic field or in the gym to accept a diploma posthumously.

It's simple and inarguable: car crashes are the No. 1 cause of death   2
among 15- to 20-year-olds in this country. What's so peculiar about that fact is that so few adults focus on it until they are planning an untimely funeral. Put it this way: if someone told you that there was one single behavior that would be most likely to lead to the premature death of your kid, wouldn't you try to do something about that? Yet parents seem to treat the right of a 16-year-old to drive as an inalienable one, something to be neither questioned nor abridged.

This makes no sense unless the argument is convenience, and often it   3
is. In a nation that developed mass-transit amnesia and traded the exurb for the small town, a licensed son or daughter relieves parents of a relentless roundelay of driving. Soccer field, Mickey Ds, mall, movies. Of course, if that's the rationale, why not let 13-year-olds drive? Any reasonable person would respond that a 13-year-old is too young. But statistics suggest that that's true of 16-year-olds as well. The National Highway Traffic Safety Administration has found that neophyte drivers of 17 have about a third as many accidents as their counterparts only a year younger.

In 1984 a solution was devised for the problem of teenage auto acci-   4
dents that lulled many parents into a false sense of security. The drinking age was raised from 18 to 21. It's become gospel that this has saved thousands of lives, although no one actually knows if that's the case; fatalities fell, but the use of seat belts and airbags may have as much to do with that as penalties for alcohol use. And there has been a pronounced negative effect on college campuses, where administrators describe a forbidden-fruit climate that encourages binge drinking. The pitchers of sangria and kegs of beer that offered legal refreshment for 18-year-olds at sanctioned campus events 30 years ago have given way to a new tradition called "pre-gaming," in which dry college activities are preceded by manic alcohol consumption at frats, dorms and bars.

Given the incidence of auto-accident deaths among teenagers despite   5
the higher drinking age, you have to ask whether the powerful lobby Mothers Against Drunk Driving simply targeted the wrong D. In a survey of young drivers, only half said they had seen a peer drive after drinking. Nearly all, however, said they had witnessed speeding, which is the leading factor in fatal crashes by teenagers today. In Europe, governments are relaxed about the drinking age but tough on driving regulations and licensing provisions; in most countries, the driving age is 18.

In America some states have taken a tough-love position and bumped   6
up the requirements for young drivers: longer permit periods, restrictions
or bans on night driving. Since the greatest danger to a teenage driver is
another teenager in the car—the chance of having an accident doubles with
two teenage passengers and skyrockets with three or more—some new rules
forbid novice drivers from transporting their peers.

In theory this sounds like a good idea; in fact it's toothless. New Jersey   7
has some of the most demanding regulations for new drivers in the nation,
including a provision that until they are 18 they cannot have more than one
nonfamily member in the car. Yet in early January three students leaving school
in Freehold Township died in a horrific accident in which the car's 17-year-old
driver was violating that regulation by carrying two friends. No wonder he took
the chance: between July 2004 and November 2006, only 12 provisional drivers
were ticketed for carrying too many passengers. Good law, bad enforcement.

States might make it easier on themselves, on police officers and on   8
teenagers, too, if instead of chipping away at the right to drive they merely
raised the legal driving age wholesale. There are dozens of statistics to back
up such a change: in Massachusetts alone, one third of 16-year-old drivers
have been involved in serious accidents. Lots and lots of parents will tell
you that raising the driving age is untenable, that the kids need their freedom and their mobility. Perhaps the only ones who wouldn't make a fuss
are those parents who have accepted diplomas at graduation because their
children were no longer alive to do so themselves, whose children traded
freedom and mobility for their lives. They might think it was worth the wait.

Questions for Close Reading   MyWritingLab

1. What is the selection's thesis? Locate the sentence(s) in which Quindlen states her
   main idea. If she doesn't state her thesis explicitly, express it in your own words.
2. According to Quindlen, what solutions to the problem of teenage auto accidents
   have not worked over the last twenty five years?
3. What approach to young adults' drinking and driving do European nations take?
4. According to Quindlen, what would be a more effective solution to the problem
   of teen auto accidents?

Questions About the Writer's Craft

1. **The pattern.** What type of audience—supportive, wavering, or hostile (see page
   451–452)—does Quindlen seem to be addressing? How can you tell?
2. **The pattern.** How effective are the statistics in this essay? Use the criteria for
   sound evidence to evaluate Quindlen's use of statistics.
3. **Other patterns.** What other patterns does Quindlen use in this essay? Where?
   What purpose do these passages serve?
4. **The pattern.** What appeals to *pathos* (see pages 450–451) does Quindlen use?
   How effective are they?

Writing Assignments Using Argumentation-Persuasion as a Pattern of Development

1. In paragraph 4 of her essay, Quindlen claims that raising the drinking age from 18 to 21 has had an unintended negative effect on college campuses, where binge drinking has become commonplace. Many college administrators agree with her. In fact, a hundred college and university presidents launched the Amethyst Initiative in 2008, calling for "an informed and dispassionate public debate over the effects of the 21-year-old drinking age." Although the college presidents did not actually call for lowering the drinking age, they argued that the current drinking age simply drives drinking underground, where it is more tempting for students and harder to control. Do you agree with the college presidents that the current drinking age of 21 should be reexamined and possibly lowered? Or do you disagree? Do some research on the Amethyst Initiative and the drinking age issue, and then write an essay in which you argue that the current drinking age should be lowered or should remain the same. Be sure to support your position with sound evidence.

2. Quindlen supports raising the legal driving age to decrease teen auto accidents, indicating that the main arguments for a low legal driving age are that it "relieves parents of an endless roundelay of driving" (paragraph 3) and that "the kids need their freedom and their mobility" (paragraph 8). Are there any other reasons that might support a low legal driving age? Write an essay opposing Quindlen's argument for a higher driving age and supporting a legal driving age of 16, with or without restrictions, depending on your view. Be sure to support your argument with reasons and examples.

Writing Assignment Combining Patterns of Development

3. Provisional driver's licenses vary from state to state, but all are designed to decrease teen auto accidents by restricting driving privileges among the youngest drivers and gradually allowing them more freedom as they get older and remain accident-free. Develop your own rules for a fair and effective provisional driver's license, and write a *process analysis* essay explaining your system. Indicate what drivers are allowed to do at various ages until they are granted full driving privileges as well as the penalties you would impose for infractions and accidents, and give *examples* to illustrate the provisions. In support of your plan, explain the beneficial *effects* that your provisional license would have on teen driving.

Michael Marlow & Sherzod Abdukadirov

Michael Marlow and Sherzod Abdukadirov are researchers at the Mercatus Center at George Mason University, a nonprofit research center and think tank. Marlow, also a professor of economics at California Polytechnic State University, earned his Ph.D. in economics from Virginia Polytechnic Institute in 1978 and is widely published in scholarly journals. Abdukadirov holds a Ph.D. from George Mason. The essay that follows was originally published in *U.S. News and World Report* on June 5, 2012.

Pre-Reading Journal   MyWritingLab

There is no denying the fact that obesity has become a serious problem in the United States. Think of people you know who are dangerously obese. How does their size affect their lifestyle? Why do you think they are unable to control their weight? What kinds of programs, if any, do you think might actually help them lose weight and keep it off? Explore these ideas in your journal.

Government Intervention Will Not Solve Our Obesity Problem

It is clear the United States is facing a rising obesity problem. But   1
the challenge remains: We have yet to determine a successful way to tackle it. According to the National Center for Health Statistics, the prevalence of obesity among adults more than doubled from 13.4 percent in 1960 to 34.3 percent in 2008 (Ogden and Carroll). A new report...by the *American Journal of Preventive Medicine* predicts that by 2030, 42 percent of Americans will be obese and 11 percent will be severely obese, or 100 pounds overweight (Finkelstein, Khavjou et al. 563).

Despite the myriad of studies showing American obesity is increasing,   2
research does not clearly support that government can solve this complex problem. And yet, government solutions that provide information the public already knows—weight gain occurs when we eat too much and exercise too little—have been the focus to eliminate this epidemic.

Not only is this method not solving the problem, we may actually   3
be increasing the social stigma associated with weight gain. Rather than pursuing a one-size-fits-all solution, we need to push back against government intervention, and allow people to find the solution that best meets their needs.

One popular government solution requires restaurant chains to post   4
calorie counts on their menus to prevent citizens from underestimating their caloric intakes. A recent study examined the impact of New York City's 2008 law requiring restaurant chains to post calorie counts. While 28 percent of patrons said the information influenced their choices, researchers could not detect a change in calories purchased after the law (Elbel et al.). A different study in Seattle found similar evidence that their mandatory menu labeling did little to change fast food purchasing behavior (Finkelstein, Strombotne et al. 122).

Another government favorite, taxing sugary drinks, does more to shore   5
up government coffers than to reduce obesity. A few studies examined the impact of increasing sugary drinks taxes by 20 percent or more. They find that higher taxes do reduce obesity, but the effect is rather limited (Lin et al. 329;

Trends in overweight, obesity, and extreme obesity among adults aged
20–74 years: United States, 1960–2008

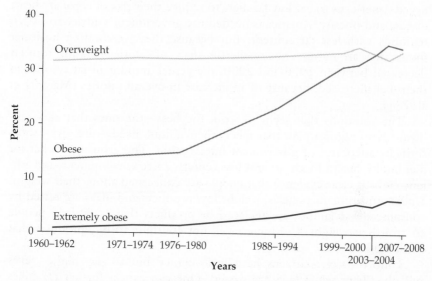

Notes: Age adjusted by the direct method to the 2000 U.S. Census population using age groups 20–39, 40–59,
and 60–74. Pregnant females were excluded. Overweight is a body mass index (BMI) of 25 kg/m² or greater but
less than 30 kg/m²; obesity is a BMI greater than or equal to 30 kg/m²; and extreme obesity is a BMI greater
than or equal to 40 kg/m².

Sources: CDC/NCHS, National Health Examination Survey I 1960–1962; National Health and Nutrition
Examination Survey (NHANES) I 1971–1974; NHANES II 1976–1980; NHANES III 1988–1994;
NHANES 1999–2000, 2001–2002, 2003–2004, 2005–2006, 2007–2008, and 2009–2010. In Cynthia L.
Ogden and Margaret D. Carroll, "Prevalence of Overweight, Obesity, and Extreme Obesity Among Adults:
United States, Trends 1960–1962 Through 2007–2008," *Health E-Stats* (Centers for Disease Control and
Prevention / National Center for Health Statistics, June 2010).

Fletcher 23). Interestingly, soda taxes mostly cause people without weight
problems to cut back their consumption, even though they are not the intended targets of the policy. Meanwhile, frequent soda drinkers buy lower-
priced soda, engage in bulk discounted purchases, and brew more sweetened
ice tea.

Beyond being ineffective, there are serious harms from these state   6
interventionist polices. Government policies are subject to intense
lobbying by well-heeled interest groups, which can lead to results that are
counterproductive to the problems they are trying to solve. In one case,
Congress effectively declared pizza a vegetable under the intense pressure
from agricultural business lobby. This allowed Congress to block attempts
by the U.S. Department of Agriculture to replace pizza, which is classified as
a vegetable because it contains tomato paste, with more vegetables.

Government policies may also lead to unintended consequences. 7
Since the 1970s, Department of Agriculture dietary guidelines have
urged Americans to eat low fat diets to reduce their risk of coronary heart
disease and obesity. Americans heeded the government's advice to switch
to foods with less fat content. But because they were eating healthier
foods, they ate more. Thus, while the share of calories coming from fat
decreased between 1970 and 2000, the actual amount of fat calories in
their diet increased, because of an increase in overall calories (Marantz et
al. 234).

The solutions that seem to work the best—the ones that allow in- 8
dividuals to tailor a plan that meets their unique needs—are given short
shrift by advocates of government intervention. The growing market for
diet books, health foods, weight loss centers, exercise equipment, and athletic clubs is clear evidence that people are concerned about their weight.
Unlike government policies, weight loss products and ideas are tested by
consumers and failures are replaced by products that really help people
control their weight. Consumers will not continue to buy products that
don't work.

Unfortunately, citizens have little choice but to pay higher taxes 9
and obey bans when laws are passed. One can expect further tax hikes
and bans as policymakers conclude that their well-intentioned policies failed simply because they were not harsh enough, but pushing
more stringent, failed policies will not improve public health. Instead of
wasting resources on inadequate solutions, consumers should return to
the market for the innovative solutions, like healthy foods, gyms, and
nutrition centers.

Works Cited

Elbel, Brian, et al. "Calorie Labeling and Food Choices: A First Look at the Effects
on Low-Income People in New York City." *Health Affairs*, vol. 28, no. 6, doi:
10.1377/hlthaff.28.6.w1110.

Finkelstein, Eric, Kiersten Strombotne, et al. "Mandatory Menu Labeling in One
Fast-Food Chain in King County, Washington." *American Journal of Preventive
Medicine*, Feb. 2011, pp. 122–27.

Finkelstein, Eric, Olga Khavjou, et al. "Obesity and Severe Obesity Forecasts through
2030." *American Journal of Preventive Medicine*, June 2012, pp. 563–70.

Fletcher, Jason, et al. "Can Soft Drink Taxes Reduce Population Weight?" *Contemporary Economic Policy*, Jan. 2010, pp. 23–35.

Lin, B. H., et al. "Measuring Weight Outcomes for Obesity Intervention Strategies: The Case of a Sugar-Sweetened Beverage Tax." *Economics and Human Biology*, Dec. 2011, pp. 329–41.

Marantz, Paul, et al. "A Call for Higher Standards of Evidence for Dietary Guidelines." *American Journal of Preventive Medicine*, Mar. 2008, pp. 234–40.

Ogden, Cynthia, and Margaret Carroll. *Prevalence of Overweight, Obesity, and Extreme Obesity among Adults: United States, Trends 1960–1962 through 2007–2008. Health E-Stats*, Centers for Disease Control and Prevention / National Center for Health Statistics, June 2010, www.cdc.gov/nchs/data/hestat/obesity_adult_07_08/obesity_adult_07_08.htm.

Questions for Close Reading

MyWritingLab

1. What is the selection's thesis? Locate the sentence(s) in which Marlow and Abdukadirov state their main idea. If they don't state the thesis explicitly, express it in your own words.
2. According to evidence cited by Marlow and Abdukadirov, what has been the effect of posting calorie counts on restaurant menus and taxing sugary drinks in an effort to change purchasing behavior and help control obesity?
3. According to the reading, what harmful and unintended consequences have resulted from government interventionist policies?
4. What solution does the reading offer, instead of government regulation, to help combat our nation's obesity problem?

Questions About the Writer's Craft

1. **The pattern.** Do Marlow and Abdukadirov use *inductive* or *deductive* reasoning (pages 459–462) to develop their argument and persuade their readers? Provide evidence from the reading to support your answer.
2. What does the argument put forth by Marlow and Abdukadirov have in common with the argument put forth by Bittman in the next reading? In what ways do the arguments differ? In your opinion, which argument is more convincing and why?
3. **The pattern.** To what extent do Marlow and Abdukadirov employ the Rogerian strategy outlined previously in this chapter (page 456–458)? In your opinion, is the strategy effective? Does it help them establish a strong argument that is likely to convince their readers? Do you think their essay would have been more effective if they had adhered more strictly to the Rogerian strategy? Why or why not?
4. The essay by Marlow and Abdukadirov is accompanied by a visual component—a graph that illustrates trends in overweight, obese, and extremely obese adults in the United States. What does the graph add to the essay?

Writing Assignments Using Argument-Persuasion as a Pattern of Development

1. In their essay, Marlow and Abdukadirov attempt to persuade their readers that government intervention is not the answer to our nation's obesity problem, and they employ a modified Rogerian strategy. Write an essay about an issue that is important to you, and use the Rogerian strategy to acknowledge differing viewpoints, point out areas of common ground, and finally, present evidence for your position. You might address an issue such as requiring all students at your school to live on campus during their first year, or banning freshmen and sophomores from having cars on campus. Or you might address a more widespread issue such as providing birth control without parental consent to people aged eleven to seventeen, or requiring all public school students to wear uniforms.

2. Marlow and Abdukadirov take a stand against government intervention to help control obesity. Many others, however, including Bittman, maintain an opposing view. Write an essay in which you argue that in light of the seriousness of the obesity problem in the United States, government intervention is both appropriate and necessary. Research specific evidence to support your position, and include at least one image to strengthen your argument.

Writing Assignment Combining Patterns of Development

3. In their argumentation-persuasion essay, Marlow and Abdukadirov state in the opening paragraph that although "it is clear the United States is facing a rising obesity problem…we have yet to determine a successful way to tackle it." Write an essay in which you *define* obesity and then *illustrate* possible solutions to this problem. You might interview one or more individuals who were once obese but managed to get their weight under control to find out how they accomplished the feat. You might also conduct research to find out more about programs such as Weight Watchers, Medifast, and Nutrisystem that claim to help individuals lose weight and keep it off. You could also explore how operations such as gastric bypass and gastric banding help some individuals control their weight.

Mark Bittman

Lead food columnist for *The New York Times*, Mark Bittman is also a popular television personality and an award-winning best-selling cookbook author. His publications include *How to Cook Everything* (1998), *How to Cook Everything Vegetarian* (2007), *Food Matters: A Guide to Conscious Eating* (2008), and *VB6: Eat Vegan Before 6:00 to Lose Weight and Restore Your Health…for Good* (2013). The essay that follows was first published in the online *New York Times* on June 10, 2014.

Pre-Reading Journal   MyWritingLab

Our nation's obesity problem has been the recent subject of countless talk shows, news broadcasts, and magazine articles. How has all of the "buzz" surrounding this issue affected you? Are you more conscious of how much you weigh and of what you eat than you were a few years ago? Do you see correlations in your own life among your health, your weight, and the food you consume? Explore these ideas in your journal.

What Causes Weight Gain

If I ask you what constitutes "bad" eating, the kind that leads to obe-   1
sity and a variety of connected diseases, you're likely to answer, "Salt, fat and sugar." This trilogy of evil has been drilled into us for decades, yet that's not an adequate answer.

We don't know everything about the dietary links to chronic disease,   2
but the best-qualified people argue that real food is more likely to promote health and less likely to cause disease than hyperprocessed food. And we can further refine that message: Minimally processed plants should dominate our diets. (This isn't just me saying this; the Institute of Medicine and the Department of Agriculture agree.)

And yet we're in the middle of a public health emergency that isn't   3
being taken seriously enough. We should make it a national priority to create two new programs, a research program to determine precisely what causes diet-related chronic illnesses (on top of the list is "Just how bad is sugar?"), and a program that will get this single, simple message across: Eat Real Food.

Real food solves the salt/fat/sugar problem. Yes, excess salt may cause or   4
exacerbate high blood pressure, and lowering sodium intake in people with high blood pressure helps. But salt is only one of several risk factors in devel-oping high blood pressure, and those who eat a diverse diet and few processed foods—which supply more than 80 percent of the sodium in typical American diets—need not worry about salt intake (Nestle).

"Fat" is a loaded word and a complicated topic, and the jury is still out.   5
Most naturally occurring fats are probably essential, but too much of some fats—and, again, it may be the industrially produced fats used in hyperpro-cessed foods—seems harmful. Eat real food and your fat intake will probably be fine.

"Sugar" has come to represent (or it should) the entire group of pro-   6
cessed, nutritionally worthless caloric sweeteners, including table sugar, high fructose corn syrup and so-called healthy alternatives like agave syrup, brown rice syrup, reduced fruit juice and a dozen others.

All appear to be damaging because they're *added* sugars, as opposed to   7
naturally occurring ones, like those in actual fruit, which are not problem-atic. And although added fructose may be more harmful than the others, it could also be that those highly refined carbohydrates that our bodies rapidly

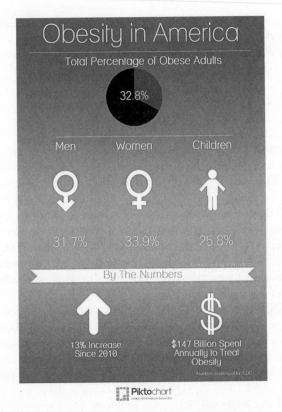

Source: "America Tops List of 10 Most Obese Countries" by Amir Khan, *US News: Health and Wellness*, May 28, 2014. Based on figures from the CDC.

break down to sugar—white bread, for example—are equally unhealthy. Again: These are hyperprocessed foods.

In sum: Sugar is not the enemy, or not the only enemy. The enemy is hyperprocessed food, including sugar.   8

In the United States—the world's most obese country—the most recent number for the annual cost of obesity is close to $200 billion (Khan).   9

(Obesity-related costs are incalculable but could easily exceed $1 trillion annually. Wanna balance the budget? Eat real food.) The amount the National Institutes of Health expends for obesity-related research is less than $1 billion annually, and there is no single large, convincing study (and no small study will do) that proposes to solve the underlying causes of obesity ("Estimates"). If the solution were as simple as "salt, fat, sugar" or the increasingly absurd-sounding "calories in, calories out," surely we'd have made some progress by now.   10

We know that eating real food is a general solution, but a large part of 11
our dietary problems might stem from something as simple as the skyrock-
eting and almost unavoidable consumption of caloric sweeteners and/or
hyperprocessed carbs, which are in 80 percent of our food products ("Why
Katie Couric").

Or it could be those factors in tandem with others, like the degradation 12
of our internal networks of bacteria, which in turn could be caused by the
overuse of antibiotics or other environmental issues. Or it could be even
more complex.

The point is we need to know for certain, because until we have an 13
actual smoking gun, it's difficult to persuade lawmakers to enact needed
policies. (Smoking gun studies are difficult in the diet world, but throwing
up our hands in the face of complexity serves the interests of processed-food
pushers.) Look no further than the example of tobacco.

Meanwhile, if we had to pick one target in the interim, caloric sweeteners 14
are unquestionably it; they're well correlated with weight gain (and their reduction equally well correlated with weight loss), Type 2 diabetes and many
other problems (Johnson et al.). How to limit the intake of sugar? A soda
tax is a start, proper labeling would be helpful, and—quite possibly most
important, because it's going to take us a generation or two to get out of
this mess—restrictions on marketing sweet "food" to children.

There's no reason to delay action on those kinds of moves. But let's 15
get the science straight so that firm, convincing, sound, evenhanded recommendations can be made based on the best possible evidence. And
meanwhile, let's also get the simple message straight: It's "Eat Real Food."

Works Cited

"Estimates of Funding for Various Research, Condition, and Disease Categories
(RCDC)." *National Institutes of Health: Research Portfolio Online Reporting
Tools*, United States Department of Health and Human Services, 7 Mar. 2014,
report.nih.gov/categorical_spending.aspx.

Johnson, Rachel K., et al. "Dietary Sugars Intake and Cardiovascular Health: A
Scientific Statement from the American Heart Association." *Circulation*, vol.
120, 2009, doi:10.1161/CIRCULATIONAHA.109.192627.

Khan, Amir. "America Tops List of 10 Most Obese Countries." *US News and
World Report*, 28 May 2014, health.usnews.com/health-news/health-wellness/
articles/2014/05/28/america-tops-list-of-10-most-obese-countries.

Nestle, Marion. "Interview with Scientific American on the Complexities of
Salt Science." *Food Politics*, 15 July 2011, www.foodpolitics.com/2011/07/
interview-with-scientific-american-on-the-complexities-of-salt-science/.

"Why Katie Couric Wants You to Get 'Fed Up,' Take a Sugar Challenge." *ABC
News*, 8 May 2014, abcnews.go.com/blogs/health/2014/05/08/why-katie-
couric-wants-you-to-get-fed-up-take-a-sugar-challenge/.

Questions for Close Reading

MyWritingLab

1. What is the selection's thesis? Locate the sentence(s) in which Bittman states his main idea. If he doesn't state his thesis explicitly, express it in your own words.
2. Bittman states that the creation of two new programs should be a national priority. What are those two programs, and why does he believe they are so important?
3. Bittman believes that hyperprocessed food is the leading cause of obesity in the United States. How does he define the term *hyperprocessed food*? What examples of hyperprocessed foods does he provide?
4. What specific legislative action does Bittman recommend to "limit the intake of sugar"? Why does he target sugar?

Questions About the Writer's Craft

1. **The pattern.** For argumentation-persuasion essays to be effective, writers need to make sure that their audiences believe they know what they are talking about and that they are worth listening to. Has Bittman succeeded in establishing his authority on the subject about which he writes? Why or why not?
2. Bittman's title, "What Causes Weight Gain," includes no question mark. Do you think the mark of punctuation was intentionally left out, or do you think its omission was a careless error? Explain your reasoning.
3. **Other patterns.** Bittman uses *causal analysis* throughout his essay. For example, early on, he indicates that "real food" results in better health and less disease than hyperprocessed food. Provide several other examples that illustrate his use of *causal analysis*.
4. How would you describe the tone Bittman uses in his writing? Why do you think he decided to use this tone? Do you think it's effective? Why or why not?

Writing Assignments Using Argumentation-Persuasion as a Pattern of Development

1. In his essay, Bittman argues that "Minimally processed plants should dominate our diets." Write an essay in which you either agree or disagree with his position and provide evidence from outside sources to support your claim. In addition to library and Internet sources, consider incorporating information from personal interviews. Also consider using images such as charts or diagrams to add to the effectiveness of your essay.
2. Bittman clearly feels strongly regarding the health issue about which he is writing. Think of a health issue about which you have strong feelings and write an argumentation-persuasion essay in which you make effective use of *logos, pathos,* and *ethos*. For example, you might write about the building of public exercise facilities such as ball courts, the requirements for childhood vaccinations, or laws governing the use of tobacco, alcohol, or marijuana. Decide on a specific purpose and audience for your essay, and tailor your approach for that purpose and audience. You might talk to classmates and friends outside class to make sure your topic is sufficiently narrow. Then develop a thesis that contains a *claim* for which you can provide evidence. Consider using images such as charts or diagrams as well as other outside sources to add to the effectiveness of your essay.

Writing Assignment Combining Patterns of Development

3. In his argumentation-persuasion essay, Bittman states, "'Fat' is a loaded word and a complicated topic, and the jury is still out." Write an essay in which you explore the *definition* of the word *fat*, the power of the word, and how the word is used in our culture today. What *effect* does the word have on people? Include *examples* from your own experience or the experiences of people you know.

Gerry Garibaldi

Writer and teacher Gerry Garibaldi was born in 1951, grew up in San Francisco, and attended San Francisco State University. Following college, he worked for Paramount Pictures first as a reader and eventually as a vice-president of production, which involved working with writers and directors. For the next twenty-five years he worked as an executive, a freelance writer for film studios, and a journalist. Then Garibaldi changed careers, moving to Connecticut, with his wife and children, to teach high school English. This article was published in *City Journal,* an urban policy quarterly, in summer 2006.

Pre-Reading Journal Entry

MyWritingLab

Think back to your own high school days. Recall how boys and girls were treated in school and how they behaved. Did you notice any differences in the way boys and girls were treated by teachers? In the way they behaved in class? In your journal, record some of the differences between the sexes that you noted. To what extent was your own behavior as a high school student influenced by your gender?

How the Schools Shortchange Boys

In the newly feminized classroom, boys tune out.   1

Since I started teaching several years ago, after 25 years in the movie   2
business, I've come to learn firsthand that everything I'd heard about the
feminization of our schools is real—and far more pernicious to boys than I
had imagined. Christina Hoff Sommers was absolutely accurate in describing, in her 2000 bestseller, *The War Against Boys,* how feminist complaints
that girls were "losing their voice" in a male-oriented classroom have
prompted the educational establishment to turn the schools upside down to
make them more girl-friendly, to the detriment of males.

As a result, boys have become increasingly disengaged. Only 65 percent   3
earned high school diplomas in the class of 2003, compared with 72 percent
of girls, education researcher Jay Greene recently documented. Girls now so
outnumber boys on most university campuses across the country that some
schools, like Kenyon College, have even begun to practice affirmative action
for boys in admissions. And as in high school, girls are getting better grades
and graduating at a higher rate.

As Sommers understood, it is boys' aggressive and rationalist nature—   4
redefined by educators as a behavioral disorder—that's getting so many of them
in trouble in the feminized schools. Their problem: they don't want to be girls.

Take my tenth-grade student Brandon. I noted that he was on the no-   5
pass list again, after three consecutive days in detention for being disruptive.
"Who gave it to you this time?" I asked, passing him on my way out.

"Waverly," he muttered into the long folding table.   6

"What for?"   7

"Just asking a question," he replied.   8

"No," I corrected him. "You said"—and here I mimicked his voice—   9
"'Why do we have to do this crap anyway?' Right?"

Brandon recalls one of those sweet, ruby-cheeked boys you often see   10
depicted on English porcelain.

He's smart, precocious, and—according to his special-education   11
profile—has been "behaviorally challenged" since fifth grade. The special-ed
classification is the bane of the modern boy. To teachers, it's a yellow flag
that snaps out at you the moment you open a student's folder. More than
any other factor, it has determined Brandon's and legions of other boys'
troubled tenures as students.

Brandon's current problem began because Ms. Waverly, his social stud-   12
ies teacher, failed to answer one critical question: What was the point of the
lesson she was teaching? One of the first observations I made as a teacher
was that boys invariably ask this question, while girls seldom do. When a
teacher assigns a paper or a project, girls will obediently flip their notebooks
open and jot down the due date. Teachers love them. God loves them. Girls
are calm and pleasant. They succeed through cooperation.

Boys will pin you to the wall like a moth. They want a rational explanation   13
for everything. If unconvinced by your reasons—or if you don't bother to offer
any—they slouch contemptuously in their chairs, beat their pencils, or watch
the squirrels outside the window. Two days before the paper is due, girls are
handing in the finished product in neat vinyl folders with colorful clip-art title
pages. It isn't until the boys notice this that the alarm sounds. "Hey, you never
told us 'bout a paper! What paper?! I want to see my fucking counselor!"

A female teacher, especially if she has no male children of her own, I've   14
noticed, will tend to view boys' penchant for challenging classroom assignments as disruptive, disrespectful—rude. In my experience, notes home and
parent-teacher conferences almost always concern a boy's behavior in class,
usually centering on this kind of conflict. In today's feminized classroom,
with its "cooperative learning" and "inclusiveness," a student's demand for
assurance of a worthwhile outcome for his effort isn't met with a reasonable
explanation but is considered inimical to the educational process. Yet it's this
very trait, innate to boys and men, that helps explain male success in the hard
sciences, math, and business.

The difference between the male and female predilection for hard proof 15
shows up among the teachers, too. In my second year of teaching, I attended
a required seminar on "differentiated instruction," a teaching model that is
the current rage in the fickle world of pop education theory. The method
addresses the need to teach all students in a classroom where academic abilities
vary greatly—where there is "heterogeneous grouping," to use the ed-school
jargon—meaning kids with IQs of 55 sit side by side with the gifted. The theory
goes that the "least restrictive environment" is best for helping the intellectually
challenged. The teacher's job is to figure out how to dice up his daily lessons to
address every perceived shortcoming and disability in the classroom.

After the lecture, we broke into groups of five, with instructions to work 16
cooperatively to come up with a model lesson plan for just such a classroom
situation. My group had two men and three women. The women immediately
set to work; my seasoned male cohort and I reclined sullenly in our chairs.

"Are the women going to do all the work?" one of the women inquired 17
brightly after about ten minutes.

"This is baloney," my friend declared, yawning, as he chucked the semi- 18
nar handout into a row of empty plastic juice bottles. "We wouldn't have
this problem if we grouped kids by ability, like we used to."

The women, all dedicated teachers, understood this, too. But that 19
wasn't the point. Treating people as equals was a social goal well worth pursuing. And we contentious boys were just too dumb to get it.

Female approval has a powerful effect on the male psyche. Kindness, 20
consideration, and elevated moral purpose have nothing to do with an
irreducible proof, of course. Yet we male teachers squirm when women
point out our moral failings—and our boy students do, too. This is the
virtue that has helped women redefine the mission of education.

The notion of male ethical inferiority first arises in grammar school, 21
where women make up the overwhelming majority of teachers. It's here
that the alphabet soup of supposed male dysfunctions begins. And make no
mistake: while girls occasionally exhibit symptoms of male-related disorders
in this world, females diagnosed with learning disabilities simply don't exist.

For a generation now, many well-meaning parents, worn down by their 22
boy's failure to flourish in school, his poor self-esteem and unhappiness, his
discipline problems, decide to accept administration recommendations to
have him tested for disabilities. The pitch sounds reasonable: admission into
special ed qualifies him for tutoring, modified lessons, extra time on tests
(including the SAT), and other supposed benefits. It's all a hustle, Mom and
Dad privately advise their boy. Don't worry about it. We know there's nothing wrong with you.

To get into special ed, however, administrators must find something 23
wrong. In my four years of teaching, I've never seen them fail. In the first
IEP (Individualized Educational Program) meeting, the boy and his parents

learn the results of disability testing. When the boy hears from three smiling adults that he does indeed have a learning disability, his young face quivers like Jell-O. For him, it was never a hustle. From then on, however, his expectations of himself—and those of his teachers—plummet.

Special ed is the great spangled elephant in the education parade. Each   24 year, it grows larger and more lumbering, drawing more and more boys into the procession. Since the publication of Sommers's book, it has grown tenfold. Special ed now is the single largest budget item, outside of basic operations, in most school districts across the country.

Special-ed boosters like to point to the success that boys enjoy after   25 they begin the program. Their grades rise, and the phone calls home cease. Anxious parents feel reassured that progress is happening. In truth, I have rarely seen any real improvement in a student's performance after he's become a special-ed kid. On my first day of teaching, I received manila folders for all five of my special-ed students—boys all—with a score of modifications that I had to make in each day's lesson plan.

I noticed early on that my special-ed boys often sat at their desks with   26 their heads down or casually staring off into space, as if tracking motes in their eyes, while I proceeded with my lesson. A special-ed caseworker would arrive, take their assignments, and disappear with the boys into the resource room. The students would return the next day with completed assignments.

"Did you do this yourself?" I'd ask, dubious.   27

They assured me that they did. I became suspicious, however, when I   28 noticed that they couldn't perform the same work on their own, away from the resource room. A special-ed caseworker's job is to keep her charges from failing. A failure invites scrutiny and reams of paperwork. The caseworkers do their jobs.

Brandon has been on the special-ed track since he was nine. He knows   29 his legal rights as well as his caseworkers do. And he plays them ruthlessly. In every debate I have with him about his low performance, Brandon delicately threads his response with the very sinews that bind him. After a particularly easy midterm, I made him stay after class to explain his failure.

"An 'F'?!" I said, holding the test under his nose.   30

"You were supposed to modify that test," he countered coolly. "I only   31 had to answer nine of the 27 questions. The nine I did are all right."

His argument is like a piece of fine crystal that he rolls admiringly in his   32 hand. He demands that I appreciate the elegance of his position. I do, particularly because my own is so weak.

Yet while the process of education may be deeply absorbing to Brandon,   33 he long ago came to dismiss the content entirely. For several decades, white Anglo-Saxon males—Brandon's ancestors—have faced withering assault from feminism- and multiculturalism-inspired education specialists. Armed with a spiteful moral rectitude, their goal is to sever his historical reach, to defame, cover over, dilute . . . and then reconstruct.

In today's politically correct textbooks, Nikki Giovanni and Toni Morrison stand shoulder-to-shoulder with Mark Twain, William Faulkner, and Charles Dickens, even though both women are second-raters at best. But even in their superficial aspects, the textbooks advertise publishers' intent to pander to the prevailing PC[1] attitudes. The books feature page after page of healthy, exuberant young girls in winning portraits. Boys (white boys in particular) will more often than not be shunted to the background in photos or be absent entirely or appear sitting in wheelchairs.   34

The underlying message isn't lost on Brandon. His keen young mind reads between the lines and perceives the folly of all that he's told to accept. Because he lacks an adult perspective, however, what he cannot grasp is the ruthlessness of the war that the education reformers have waged. Often when he provokes, it's simple boyish tit for tat.   35

A week ago, I dispatched Brandon to the library with directions to choose a book for his novel assignment. He returned minutes later with his choice and a twinkling smile.   36

"I got a grreat book, Mr. Garibaldi!" he said, holding up an old, bleary, clothbound item. "Can I read the first page aloud, pahlease?"   37

My mind buzzed like a fly, trying to discover some hint of mischief.   38

"Who's the author?"   39

"Ah, Joseph Conrad," he replied, consulting the frontispiece. "Can I? Huh, huh, huh?"   40

"I guess so."   41

Brandon eagerly stood up before the now-alert class of mostly black and Puerto Rican faces, adjusted his shoulders as if straightening a prep-school blazer, then intoned solemnly: "*The Nigger of the 'Narcissus'*"—twinkle, twinkle, twinkle. "Chapter one. . . ."   42

Merry mayhem ensued. Brandon had one of his best days of the year.   43

Boys today feel isolated and outgunned, but many, like Brandon, don't lack pluck and courage. They often seem to have more of it than their parents, who writhe uncomfortably before a system steeled in the armor of "social conscience." The game, parents whisper to themselves, is to play along, to maneuver, to outdistance your rival. Brandon's struggle is an honest one: to preserve truth and his own integrity.   44

Boys who get a compartment on the special-ed train take the ride to its end without looking out the window. They wait for the moment when they can step out and scorn the rattletrap that took them nowhere. At the end of the line, some, like Brandon, may have forged the resiliency of survival. But that's not what school is for.   45

[1]Short for "politically correct," usually used pejoratively (editors' note).

Questions for Close Reading

MyWritingLab

1. What is the selection's thesis? Locate the sentence(s) in which Garibaldi states his main idea. If he doesn't state his thesis explicitly, express it in your own words.
2. According to Garibaldi, how do boys and girls—and men and women—react to being given an assignment?
3. Why are so many boys tested for disabilities, according to Garibaldi?
4. How does Garibaldi's student Brandon take advantage of his special education designation?

Questions About the Writer's Craft

1. **The pattern.** What types of evidence does Garibaldi use in this essay? How effective is his evidence in supporting his argument?
2. **Other patterns.** Garibaldi uses a lot of cause-effect, comparison-contrast, and process analysis in this essay. Identify passages in which these patterns are used.
3. The first sentence in the essay is a strongly worded declaration: "In the newly feminized classroom, boys tune out." Where else does Garibaldi use such strongly worded statements? What is the effect of this style?
4. Where does Garibaldi use vulgar or offensive language? What effect, if any, does this have on his argument?

Writing Assignments Using Argumentation-Persuasion as a Pattern of Development

1. Read Michael Kimmel's "A War Against Boys?" (page 521), an essay that takes exception to Garibaldi's view of boys' education. Decide which writer presents his case more convincingly. Then write an essay arguing that the *other writer* has trouble making a strong case for his position. Consider the merits and flaws (including any logical fallacies) in the argument, plus such issues as the writer's credibility, strategies for dealing with the opposing view, and use of emotional appeals. Throughout, support your opinion with specific examples drawn from the selection. Keep in mind that you are critiquing the effectiveness of the writer's argument. It's not appropriate, then, simply to explain why you agree or disagree with the writer's position or merely to summarize what the writer says.
2. Although Garibaldi argues forcefully that boys are shortchanged by the "feminization" of education and the special education system, he does not propose any changes to improve the way boys are educated. How might public elementary, middle, and high school education be changed so that boys flourish? What activities or subjects would help boys in school? Using Garibaldi's essay as a take-off point, write an essay in which you argue for changes in education that would benefit boys.

Writing Assignment Combining Patterns of Development

3. In paragraph 34, Garibaldi refers to "politically correct textbooks" and "PC attitudes." What does the phrase "politically correct" mean to you? What are its connotations? Write an essay in which you *define* "political correctness." Be sure to give examples to support your definition. Before you start, decide whether the purpose of your essay is to inform, persuade, or entertain, and approach your definition accordingly.

Michael Kimmel

Michael Kimmel is a professor of sociology at State University of New York at Stonybrook and one of the world's leading researchers in gender studies. Born in New York City in 1951, he attended Vassar College and received a master's degree from Brown University and a Ph.D. from the University of California at Berkeley. He is the author or editor of more than twenty volumes on men and masculinity, including *Manhood in America: A Cultural History* (1996) and his latest work, *Guyland: The Perilous World Where Boys Become Men* (2008). His articles appear in dozens of magazines, newspapers, and scholarly journals, and he lectures extensively. The following piece was excerpted from an article published in the Fall 2006 issue of *Dissent Magazine*.

Pre-Reading Journal Entry

MyWritingLab

The phrase "boys will be boys" is often cited to explain certain types of male behavior. What kinds of actions typically fall in this category? List a few of them in your journal. Which behaviors are positive? Why? Which are negative? Why?

A War Against Boys?

Doug Anglin isn't likely to flash across the radar screen at an Ivy League 1 admissions office. A seventeen-year-old senior at Milton High School, a suburb outside Boston, Anglin has a B-minus average and plays soccer and baseball. But he's done something that millions of other teenagers haven't: he's sued his school district for sex discrimination.

Anglin's lawsuit, brought with the aid of his father, a Boston 2 lawyer, claims that schools routinely discriminate against males. "From the elementary level, they establish a philosophy that if you sit down, follow orders, and listen to what they say, you'll do well and get good grades," he told a journalist. "Men naturally rebel against this." He may have a point: overworked teachers might well look more kindly on classroom docility and decorum. But his proposed remedies—such as raising boys' grades retroactively—are laughable.

And though it's tempting to parse the statements of a mediocre high 3 school senior—what's so "natural" about rebelling against blindly following orders, a military tactician might ask—Anglin's apparent admissions angle is but the latest skirmish of a much bigger battle in the culture wars. The current salvos concern boys. The "trouble with boys" has become a staple on talk-radio, the cover story in *Newsweek*, and the subject of dozens of columns in newspapers and magazines. And when the First Lady offers a helping hand to boys, you know something political is in the works. "Rescuing" boys actually translates into bashing feminism.

There is no doubt that boys are not faring well in school. From elemen-   4
tary schools to high schools they have lower grades, lower class rank, and
fewer honors than girls. They're 50 percent more likely to repeat a grade
in elementary school, one-third more likely to drop out of high school, and
about six times more likely to be diagnosed with attention deficit and hyper-
activity disorder (ADHD).

College statistics are similar—if the boys get there at all. Women now   5
constitute the majority of students on college campuses, having passed men in
1982, so that in eight years women will earn 58 percent of bachelor's degrees
in U.S. colleges. One expert, Tom Mortensen, warns that if current trends
continue, "the graduation line in 2068 will be all females." Mortensen may be
a competent higher education policy analyst, but he's a lousy statistician. His
dire prediction is analogous to predicting forty years ago that, if the enrollment
of black students at Ol' Miss was one in 1964, and, say, two hundred in 1968
and one thousand in 1976, then "if present trends continue" there would be
no white students on campus by 1982. Doomsayers lament that women now
outnumber men in the social and behavioral sciences by about three to one,
and that they've invaded such traditionally male bastions as engineering (where
they now make up 20 percent) and biology and business (virtually par).

These three issues—declining numbers, declining achievement, and increas-   6
ingly problematic behavior—form the empirical basis of the current debate. But
its political origins are significantly older and ominously more familiar. Peeking
underneath the empirical façade helps explain much of the current lineup.

Why now?   7

If boys are doing worse, whose fault is it? To many of the current critics,   8
it's women's fault, either as feminists, as mothers, or as both. Feminists, we
read, have been so successful that the earlier "chilly classroom climate" has
now become overheated to the detriment of boys. Feminist-inspired programs have enabled a whole generation of girls to enter the sciences, medicine, law, and the professions; to continue their education; to imagine careers
outside the home. But in so doing, these same feminists have pathologized
boyhood. Elementary schools are, we read, "anti-boy"—emphasizing reading
and restricting the movements of young boys. They "feminize" boys, forcing
active, healthy, and naturally exuberant boys to conform to a regime of obe-
dience, "pathologizing what is simply normal for boys," as one psychologist
puts it. Schools are an "inhospitable" environment for boys, writes Christina
Hoff Sommers, where their natural propensities for rough-and-tumble play,
competition, aggression, and rambunctious violence are cast as social problems in the making. Michael Gurian argues in *The Wonder of Boys*, that, with
testosterone surging through their little limbs, we demand that they sit still,
raise their hands, and take naps. We're giving them the message, he says, that
"boyhood is defective." By the time they get to college, they've been steeped
in anti-male propaganda. "Why would any self-respecting boy want to attend

one of America's increasingly feminized universities?" asks George Gilder in *National Review*. The American university is now a "fluffy pink playpen of feminist studies and agitprop 'herstory,' taught amid a green goo of eco-motherism..." [author's ellipsis].

Such claims sound tinnily familiar. At the turn of the last century, cultural critics were concerned that the rise of white-collar businesses meant increasing indolence for men, whose sons were being feminized by mothers and female teachers. Then, as now, the solutions were to find arenas in which boys could simply be boys, and where men could be men as well. So fraternal lodges offered men a homo-social sanctuary, and dude ranches and sports provided a place where these sedentary men could experience what Theodore Roosevelt called the strenuous life. Boys could troop off with the Boy Scouts, designed as a fin-de-siècle "boys' liberation movement." Modern society was turning hardy, robust boys, as Boy Scouts' founder Ernest Thompson Seton put it, into "a lot of flat chested cigarette smokers with shaky nerves and doubtful vitality." Today, women teachers are once again to blame for boys' feminization. "It's the teacher's job to create a classroom environment that accommodates both male and female energy, not just mainly female energy," explains Gurian.

What's wrong with this picture? Well, for one thing, it creates a false opposition between girls and boys, assuming that educational reforms undertaken to enable girls to perform better hinder boys' educational development. But these reforms—new classroom arrangements, teacher training, increased attentiveness to individual learning styles—actually enable larger numbers of boys to get a better education. Though the current boy advocates claim that schools used to be more "boy friendly" before all these "feminist" reforms, they obviously didn't go to school in those halcyon days, the 1950s, say, when the classroom was far more regimented, corporal punishment common, and teachers far more authoritarian; they even gave grades for "deportment." Rambunctious boys were simply not tolerated; they dropped out.

Gender stereotyping hurts both boys and girls. If there is a zero-sum game, it's not because of some putative feminization of the classroom. The net effect of the No Child Left Behind Act has been zero-sum competition, as school districts scramble to stretch inadequate funding, leaving them little choice but to cut noncurricular programs so as to ensure that curricular mandates are followed. This disadvantages "rambunctious" boys, because many of these programs are after-school athletics, gym, and recess. And cutting "unnecessary" school counselors and other remedial programs also disadvantages boys, who compose the majority of children in behavioral and remedial educational programs. The problem of inadequate school funding lies not at feminists' door, but in the halls of Congress. This is further compounded by changes in the insurance industry, which often pressure therapists to put children on medication for ADHD rather than pay for expensive therapy.

Another problem is that the frequently cited numbers are misleading. **12** More people—that is, males and females—are going to college than ever before. In 1960, 54 percent of boys and 38 percent of girls went directly to college; today the numbers are 64 percent of boys and 70 percent of girls. It is true that the rate of increase among girls is higher than the rate of increase among boys, but the numbers are increasing for both.

The gender imbalance does not obtain at the nation's most elite col- **13** leges and universities, where percentages for men and women are, and have remained, similar. Of the top colleges and universities in the nation, only Stanford sports a fifty-fifty gender balance. Harvard[1] and Amherst enroll 56 percent men, Princeton and Chicago 54 percent men, Duke and Berkeley 52 percent, and Yale 51 percent. In science and engineering, the gender imbalance still tilts decidedly toward men: Cal Tech is 65 percent male and 35 percent female; MIT is 62 percent male, 38 percent female.

And the imbalance is not uniform across class and race. It remains the **14** case that far more working-class women—of all races—go to college than do working-class men. Part of this is a seemingly rational individual decision: a college-educated woman still earns about the same as a high-school educated man, $35,000 to $31,000. By race, the disparities are more starkly drawn. Among middle-class, white, high school graduates going to college this year, half are male and half are female. But only 37 percent of black college students and 45 percent of Hispanic students are male. The numerical imbalance turns out to be more a problem of race and class than gender. It is what Cynthia Fuchs Epstein calls a "deceptive distinction"—a difference that appears to be about gender, but is actually about something else.

Why don't the critics acknowledge these race and class differences? To **15** many who now propose to "rescue" boys, such differences are incidental because, in their eyes, all boys are the same aggressive, competitive, rambunctious little devils. They operate from a facile, and inaccurate, essentialist dichotomy between males and females. Boys must be allowed to be boys—so that they grow up to be men.

This facile biologism leads the critics to propose some distasteful remedies **16** to allow these testosterone-juiced boys to express themselves. Gurian, for example, celebrates all masculine rites of passage, "like military boot camp, fraternity hazings, graduation day, and bar mitzvah" as "essential parts of every boy's life." He also suggests reviving corporal punishment, both at home and at school—but only when administered privately with cool indifference and never in the heat of adult anger. He calls it "spanking responsibly," though I suspect school boards and child welfare agencies might have another term for it.

But what boys need turns out to be pretty much what girls need. In **17** their best-selling *Raising Cain*, Michael Thompson and Dan Kindlon

[1]Harvard University now enrolls more women than men (author's note).

describe boys' needs: to be loved, get sex, and not be hurt. Parents are counseled to allow boys their emotions; accept a high level of activity; speak their language; and treat them with respect. They are to teach the many ways a boy can be a man, use discipline to guide and build, and model manhood as emotionally attached. Aside from the obvious tautologies, what they advocate is exactly what feminists have been advocating for girls for some time....

How does a focus on the ideology of masculinity explain what is happening to boys in school? Consider the parallel for girls. Carol Gilligan's work on adolescent girls describes how these assertive, confident, and proud young girls "lose their voices" when they hit adolescence. At that same moment, Pollack[2] notes, boys become more confident, even beyond their abilities. You might even say that boys find their voices, but it is the inauthentic voice of bravado, posturing, foolish risk-taking, and gratuitous violence. He calls it "the boy code." The boy code teaches them that they are supposed to be in power, and so they begin to act as if they are. They "ruffle in a manly pose," as William Butler Yeats[3] once put it, "for all their timid heart." 18

In adolescence, both boys and girls get their first real dose of gender inequality: girls suppress ambition, boys inflate it. Recent research on the gender gap in school achievement bears this out. Girls are more likely to undervalue their abilities, especially in the more traditionally "masculine" educational arenas such as math and science. Only the most able and most secure girls take courses in those fields. Thus, their numbers tend to be few, and their mean test scores high. Boys, however, possessed of this false voice of bravado (and facing strong family pressure) are likely to overvalue their abilities, to remain in programs though they are less capable of succeeding. 19

This difference, and not some putative discrimination against boys, is the reason that girls' mean test scores in math and science are now, on average, approaching that of boys. Too many boys remain in difficult math and science courses longer than they should; they pull the boys' mean scores down. By contrast, the smaller number of girls, whose abilities and self-esteem are sufficient to enable them to "trespass" into a male domain, skew female data upward. 20

A parallel process is at work in the humanities and social sciences. Girls' mean test scores in English and foreign languages, for example, outpace those of boys. But this is not the result of "reverse discrimination"; it is because the boys bump up against the norms of masculinity. Boys regard English as a "feminine" subject. Pioneering research by Wayne Martino in Australia and Britain found that boys avoid English because of what it might say about their (inauthentic) masculine pose. "Reading is lame, sitting down and looking at words is pathetic," commented one boy. "Most guys who 21

[2]William Pollack, author of *Real Boys* (editors' note).
[3]Yeats (1865–1939) was a major Irish poet and playwright (editors' note).

like English are faggots." The traditional liberal arts curriculum, as it was before feminism, is seen as feminizing. As Catharine Stimpson[4] recently put it, "Real men don't speak French."

Boys tend to hate English and foreign languages for the same reasons   22
that girls love them. In English, they observe, there are no hard-and-fast rules, one expresses one's opinion about the topic and everyone's opinion is equally valued. "The answer can be a variety of things, you're never really wrong," observed one boy. "It's not like maths and science where there is one set answer to everything." Another boy noted:

> I find English hard. It's because there are no set rules for reading   23
> texts...[author's ellipsis]. English isn't like maths where you have
> rules on how to do things and where there are right and wrong an-
> swers. In English you have to write down how you feel and that's
> what I don't like.

Compare this to the comments of girls in the same study: 24

> I feel motivated to study English because...[author's ellipsis]   25
> you have freedom in English—unlike subjects such as maths and
> science—and your view isn't necessarily wrong. There is no defi-
> nite right or wrong answer, and you have the freedom to say what
> you feel is right without it being rejected as a wrong answer.

It is not the school experience that "feminizes" boys, but rather the ideology   26
of traditional masculinity that keeps boys from wanting to succeed. "The work you do here is girls' work," one boy commented to a researcher. "It's not real work."

"Real work" involves a confrontation—not with feminist women, whose   27
sensible educational reforms have opened countless doors to women while clos-ing off none to men—but with an anachronistic definition of masculinity that stresses many of its vices (anti-intellectualism, entitlement, arrogance, and ag-gression) but few of its virtues. When the self-appointed rescuers demand that we accept boys' "hardwiring," could they possibly have such a monochromatic and relentlessly negative view of male biology? Maybe they do. But simply shrugging our collective shoulders in resignation and saying "boys will be boys" sets the bar much too low. Boys can do better than that. They can be men.

Perhaps the real "male bashers" are those who promise to rescue boys   28
from the clutches of feminists. Are males not also "hardwired" toward com-passion, nurturing, and love? If not, would we allow males to be parents? It

---

[4]Stimpson, a professor of English at New York University, has written about women in culture and society (editors' note).

is never a biological question of whether we are "hardwired" for some behavior; it is, rather, a political question of which "hardwiring" we choose to respect and which we choose to challenge....

Questions for Close Reading

`MyWritingLab`

1. What is the selection's thesis? Locate the sentence(s) in which Kimmel states his main idea. If he doesn't state his thesis explicitly, express it in your own words.
2. How does Kimmel interpret the statistics that show that more girls than boys go to college?
3. According to Kimmel, how do girls and boys change when they reach adolescence?
4. What does Kimmel mean by the phrase " 'the boy code' " (paragraph 18)?

Questions About the Writer's Craft

1. **The pattern.** What strategy does Kimmel use in the opening paragraphs of his essay? Is it effective?
2. **The pattern.** What is the purpose of paragraphs 4–6? Paragraphs 7–9? Where does Kimmel start presenting his own view of the causes of boys' difficulty in school?
3. **Other patterns.** What is the main pattern, other than argumentation-persuasion, that is used in this essay? Give specific examples.
4. Reread the biographical sketch of Kimmel on page 521. How does Kimmel's background contribute to the *ethos* of this argument? Does it influence your response to his claims?

Writing Assignments Using Argumentation-Persuasion as a Pattern of Development

1. Both Garibaldi and Kimmel focus primarily on how gender inequality affects boys, but gender inequality affects girls as well (see Kimmel, paragraphs 19 and following). Write an essay in which you argue that gender roles and norms limit (or do not limit) what women can accomplish in school and in their careers.
2. Kimmel criticizes those who claim that biology, or inborn traits, are primarily responsible for shaping gender differences. He believes that biological differences may exist, but that the environment, including political and cultural forces, have a strong influence. Write an essay arguing your own position about the role that biology and environment play in determining sex-role attitudes and behaviors. Remember to acknowledge opposing views and to defend your own position with examples based on your experiences and observations.

Writing Assignment Combining Patterns of Development

3. Feminism is mentioned throughout Garibaldi's and Kimmel's essays, but neither of them defines the term. Do some research in the library and/or on the Internet about the history of feminism. Brainstorm with others—both men and women—about the topic, and write an essay in which you *define* feminism. Be sure to give *examples* of what you mean by feminism, either from your own experience or from history.

Alexander T. Tabarrok

Canadian economist Alexander Tabarrok, born in 1966, received his Ph.D. from George Mason University. He is an associate professor of economics at George Mason University and holds the Bartley J. Madden Chair in Economics at the Mercatus Center. He has also taught at the University of Virginia and Ball State University. Tabarrok's writings on a range of economic issues have appeared in *The Journal of Law and Economics, Public Choice, Economic Inquiry, Journal of Health Economics, Journal of Theoretical Politics, The American Law and Economics Review,* and *Kyklos* as well as in magazines and newspapers. He is research director for The Independent Institute, a public policy research group, and assistant editor of the organization's *Independent Review.* The following selection appeared as a *Newsroom* article on the Independent Institute's website on February 19, 2001.

Pre-Reading Journal Entry   MyWritingLab

How persuasive do you find economic principles? In your own life, do you tend to make decisions on a financial basis or do you have other criteria for making decisions? What kinds of decisions are these? Jot down some notes in your journal on these ideas.

A Moral Solution to the Organ Shortage

Thousands of people will die this year while they wait helplessly for an   1
organ transplant. Tragically, these deaths could be avoided if only more people signed their organ donor cards. Yet every year the organ shortage tends to become worse as medical technology increases the number of potential beneficiaries while social apathy and fear keep the number of donors relatively constant. Today, roughly 60,000 people are waiting for organ transplants, while less than 10,000 will become donors. Despite a prominent advertising campaign with Michael Jordan as spokesperson, and a national campaign of pastors, rabbis and other clergy supporting donation, the supply of donors remains far below that necessary to save everyone on the waiting list.

Nobel Prize–winning economist Gary Becker has suggested that one   2
possible solution to the crisis is to increase the incentive to donate organs by paying donors. One system, for example, would let organ procurement organizations pay the funeral expenses of organ donors.

Economists argue that anytime the price of a good or service is held be-   3
low its market demand, a shortage develops. Just as government-mandated rent controls imposed in New York and other cities have led to a shortage of housing, government rules that outlaw buying or selling organs on the open market hold the price of organs at zero and make an organ shortage inevitable. Lift the restrictions, Becker and others say, and the shortage will end.

To some, this analysis may sound shocking, but these ideas are now so   4
familiar to economists that at least one well-known textbook—Pindyck and

Rubinfeld's *Microeconomics*—uses the organ shortage to illustrate the effect of price controls more generally. Nonetheless, many people may still be uncomfortable with the idea of human organs for sale. And for better or worse, few politicians are likely to take up the banner of laissez-faire when it comes to human organs. Fortunately, there is another possible solution.

I propose that the United Network for Organ Sharing (UNOS) con-   5
sider restricting organ transplants to those who previously agreed to be organ donors; in short, a "no-give no-take" rule. While it is understandable that some people may have misgivings about becoming donors for personal or religious reasons, why should someone who was not willing to give an organ be allowed to take an organ?

Signing your organ donor card should be thought of as entry into a   6
club, the club of potential organ recipients. Current UNOS policy is that organs are a "national resource." This is wrong. Organs should be the resource of potential organ donors, and signing an organ donor card should be tantamount to buying insurance. Being willing to give up an organ, should it no longer be of use to you, is the premium to be paid for the right to receive someone else's organ if one of yours fails.

How would the "no-give no-take" rule work in practice? Anyone could   7
sign an organ donor card at any time and be registered as a potential donor. Most people would sign their cards when they receive their driver's license, as occurs today. Children would be automatically eligible to receive organs until the age of 16, when they would have the option of signing their card. To prevent someone from signing after learning they were in need, there would be a mandatory waiting period of at least one year before the right to receive an organ took effect.

Organs are now allocated on the basis of a point system in which   8
medical need, the probability that the transplant would be effective, and the length of time already spent on the waiting list all play a role. A modest version of the "no-give no-take" rule could be implemented by stating that, henceforth, points should also be awarded for previously having signed one's organ donor card.

While this change may result in some people losing the chance to receive   9
a transplant, far more people will be able to be served because there will be many more potential organ donors. If enough people sign their donor cards, this plan could even produce a surplus of organs.

What is needed to end the shortage of human organs, and to save the   10
thousands of individuals who die because of the shortage, is a rethinking of the moral basis of organ collection and donation. Organs should not be owned by the nation as a whole, but rather by you and I and every other potential organ donor. We may still disagree on whether organs should be commodities traded on the open market, but few could argue with the notion that those who are willing to give should be the first to receive.

Questions for Close Reading

MyWritingLab

1. What is the selection's thesis? Locate the sentence(s) in which Tabarrok states his main idea. If he doesn't state his thesis explicitly, express it in your own words.
2. What problem does the author see in the current procedures for obtaining organ transplants? What evidence does he give for his view?
3. The author suggests that one way of bettering the organ shortage is to allow donors to be paid. What arguments does he offer in support of this view? What arguments does he give in opposition to it?
4. What solution does Tabarrok advocate? Why does he say his solution is fair? What essential premise is his solution based on?

Questions About the Writer's Craft

1. **The pattern.** What types of evidence does Tabarrok use? Why or why not is the evidence persuasive?
2. **Other patterns.** The author uses exemplification throughout the essay. Give two instances of exemplification. How effective are these?
3. What is the metaphor that Tabarrok uses to describe his proposal? Is the metaphor effective? Why or why not?
4. Who is the audience for this essay? Do you think it is aimed at medical personnel? People waiting on transplant lists? Politicians? The general public?

Writing Assignments Using Argumentation-Persuasion as a Pattern of Development

1. Tabarrok's thesis requires society to change how we view organs—from seeing them as a "national resource" to thinking of them as "the resource of potential organ donors." How would making such a change in our basic assumption about organ donation affect our feelings about the sale of organs? Formulate a thesis in response to that question, and write an essay in which you support your thesis. For evidence, draw on Tabarrok's essay and also on "Need Transplant Donors? Pay Them" (page 531), by Virginia Postrel, which also advocates a change in the organ donation system.
2. Tabarrok argues in favor of an economic solution to the inadequacy of the organ donation system. Think of another societal issue—for example, our dependency on imported oil—that might benefit from an economic approach. You may wish to do some research on your subject. Then write an essay in which you suggest a possible economic action. Make sure to give both the pros and cons in your argument.

Writing Assignment Combining Patterns of Development

3. Health care reform is a serious concern today. Do you know someone who needs an organ transplant or who has had a serious illness or injury? Was the person's experience with medical professionals and institutions mostly positive or mostly negative? Write an essay in which you *narrate* the person's story, including *descriptive* details and *examples* to support your ideas.

Virginia Postrel

Virginia Postrel (1960–) graduated Phi Beta Kappa from Princeton University with a degree in English literature. She worked as a reporter for *The Wall Street Journal* and as a columnist for *Forbes*. Postrel was an economics columnist for *The New York Times* business section for six years before working as a columnist for *The Atlantic* from 2006 to 2009. An award-winning writer, Postrel writes on cultural and economic subjects and has published articles in a wide range of publications. Her work has been featured in *The Best American Science and Nature Writing 2004* and *The Best American Science and Nature Writing 2009*. Postrel is the author of three books—*The Future and Its Enemies* (1999), *The Substance of Style* (2004), and *The Power of Glamour* (2013). The following selection is excerpted from an article published in the *Los Angeles Times* on June 10, 2006.

Pre-Reading Journal Entry

MyWritingLab

Like the author of this essay, many of us have performed a selfless act for the benefit of others, whether it was to save a life as Postrel did or simply to volunteer at a local charity or help a neighbor. Think about altruistic acts you have performed. What motivated you? How did you feel afterward? If you had received payment or a reward for the action, would your feelings and behavior have been different? Take notes on your ideas.

Need Transplant Donors? Pay Them

...Our national transplant system is broken: it spends too much time coping   1 with an ever-growing, life-threatening organ shortage rather than finding ways to reduce or end it. More than 66,000 Americans are languishing on the national waiting list for kidneys—10 times the number of kidneys transplanted from deceased donors each year. And the list keeps growing, with a queue of more than 100,000 expected by 2010.

Kidney patients literally live or die by where they are on the waiting list.   2 While getting progressively sicker, they must spend several hours at least three times a week hooked up to a dialysis machine,[1] the kidney-disease equivalent of an iron lung[2] (it prolongs your life but imposes a physically debilitating prison sentence).

Increasing the supply of deceased donors, while desirable, is difficult—   3 organ donors have to die healthy and in exactly the right circumstances. But

---

[1] A dialysis machine filters a person's blood to cleanse it of waste (editors' note).
[2] The iron lung, used mainly in the first half of the twentieth century, is a metal machine that helps people to breathe when their chest muscles are paralyzed; most of the person's body is placed in the machine, with only the head and neck remaining free (editors' note).

even if every eligible cadaver were harvested, it wouldn't fill the gap. We
need more kidney donors, lots more. And they need to be alive.

Unfortunately, our laws and culture discourage healthy people from do-   4
nating organs, as I learned this spring when I gave a kidney to a friend.

My parents were appalled. My doctor told me, "You know you can   5
change your mind." Many people couldn't understand why I didn't at least
wait until my friend had been on dialysis for a while.

This pervasive attitude not only pressures donors to back out, it shapes   6
policies that deter them. Some transplant centers require intrusive, demeaning psychological probes that scare people off. Some bioethicists suspect
that donors suffer from a mental disorder, as opposed to being motivated by
benevolence or religious conviction.

The scrutiny is particularly nasty when healthy people want to give their   7
organs to strangers—not truly unknown people, mind you, but patients they
have gotten to know through Internet sites or press coverage.

Many transplant centers flatly refuse "directed donations" to specific   8
strangers. Some argue that it's "unfair" for patients to jump the queue with
personal initiative and an appealing story; others insist that such donors
aren't to be trusted (they must be either criminal or crazy). Posters at living-
donorsonline.org warn givers to never even mention the Internet, lest their
good intentions be thwarted.

Sandra Grijalva, a San Francisco woman with polycystic kidney disease,[3]   9
asked Kaiser[4] officials if she could find a donor online—after having one of
her friends disqualified because of high blood pressure. "They said absolutely not," she says. The donor, Kaiser maintained, might someday try to
extort money. (So might your cousin, but at least you'd be alive.)

Instead of dire possibilities, consider a cold reality: Without tens of   10
thousands of new living donors, most of the people on that very long waiting list are going to suffer and die on dialysis. The transplant community's
top priority should be increasing the supply of willing donors.

The most obvious way to increase the supply of any scarce commodity—   11
paying more for it—is illegal. Federal law blocks transplant centers, patients
and insurers from compensating donors in an above-board process, with full
legal and medical protections. The growing and inevitable "transplant tour-
ism" industry, and even shadier organ brokers, are the kidney equivalents of
back-alley abortionists.

Legalized financial incentives would encourage more people to volunteer   12
their organs. Donors would probably still be relatively rare, just as surrogate

---

[3]Polycystic kidney disease is a genetic disease that leads to kidney failure; the disease affects
nearly 1 in 1,000 Americans (editors' note).
[4]Kaiser Permanente is a major health management organization based in California but
operating in regions throughout the United States (editors' note).

mothers[5] are. Many, like me, would still help out without payment, just as some people get paid for giving blood or fighting fires while others do it for free.

Paying donors need not hurt the poor, any more than paying dialysis   13 centers does. Compensation could, in fact, help low-income Americans, who are disproportionately likely to suffer from kidney disease. A one-year tax holiday for donors would nudge rich people to help. A pool to make up for lost wages (legal, but rare today) would enable many otherwise willing friends and relatives to contribute.

But even talking about incentives is taboo to some self-styled patient   14 advocates.

In 2006, the American Enterprise Institute held a conference in   15 Washington on incentive-based transplant reforms. (It was organized by my kidney recipient, a physician and health-policy scholar at the institute.) When the National Kidney Foundation heard about the conference, its chief executive, John Davis, complained to the institute's president, "We don't see how an AEI forum would contribute substantively to debate on this issue."

Davis' group adamantly opposes donor compensation, lobbying against   16 even experimental programs and small tax credits. It's as though the National Parkinson Foundation opposed stem cell research, or thought researchers should work for free.

Even a limited market in kidneys would transfer power from the rationing   17 establishment to kidney patients and supportive communities. It would give patients more options. Grijalva, who works with developmentally disabled seniors, would welcome the shift.

"My biggest fear and my biggest feeling," she says, "is that I'm totally   18 out of control, that these people have the control and they are making all the decisions, and I have absolutely no input whatsoever."

---

[5]A surrogate mother is a woman who agrees to become pregnant and give birth to a child for a couple to adopt and raise; the surrogate may or may not be the genetic mother of the child (editors' note).

Questions for Close Reading

MyWritingLab

1. What is the selection's thesis? Locate the sentence(s) in which Postrel states her main idea. If she doesn't state her thesis explicitly, express it in your own words.
2. What does the author tell us about the state of kidney donations? What evidence does she use to support her assertion?
3. What is the author's personal experience with kidney transplants? What does she say is society's view of living donors? Identify at least three examples the author gives to support her assessment.
4. What consequences will result if donors are paid for their kidney donations, in the author's view? Do her conclusions about consequences make her argument more or less convincing? Why?

Questions About the Writer's Craft

1. **The pattern.** What claim about the transplant community's obligations does the author ask us to accept? What does she say about other claims that might be the reasons for readers' hesitation to accept her proposal?
2. **The pattern.** Is the essay based primarily on the appeal of *ethos*, *pathos*, or *logos* (see pages 449–452)? In what ways?
3. **Other patterns.** The author makes a number of comparisons throughout the essay. Identify at least two comparisons. What do you think is the intended effect? Are the comparisons convincing?
4. Who do you think is the audience for this essay—the general public? Medical professionals? Patients? Possible voluntary donors? Why?

Writing Assignments Using Argumentation-Persuasion as a Pattern of Development

1. Some of the most profound ethical issues involve how we treat human life. Postrel refers to two—abortion and stem-cell research. But individuals can hold seemingly inconsistent views on these issues. For example, a person who is opposed to abortion might be in favor of capital punishment, or a person who supports stem-cell research might be a pacificist. Write an essay in which you *argue* that consistency on these kinds of ethical issues is either crucial or irrelevant. Remember to give examples to support your view.
2. The author says that "increasing the supply of willing donors" should be the "top priority" of the organ transplant community. Do you agree? Or do you think that another goal—for example, ensuring the fair distribution of organs or preventing the exploitation of living donors—should be the highest priority? Do some research on the bioethics of organ donation. Then write an essay in which you *argue* a position on this issue, using expert opinion to support your own views.

Writing Assignment Combining Patterns of Development

3. Read Alexander Tabarrok's essay "A Moral Solution to the Organ Shortage" (page 528). In what ways is the concept of compensation the same or different in these two selections? Write an essay in which you *compare* Tabarrok's idea of rewarding people who sign organ donor cards with Postrel's idea of allowing "[e]ven a limited market in kidneys." Support your argument with examples from the readings.

Additional Writing Topics

ARGUMENTATION-PERSUASION

MyWritingLab

General Assignments

Using argumentation-persuasion, develop one of these topics into an essay.

1. Hiring or college admissions quotas
2. Giving birth control to teenagers
3. Prayer in the schools
4. Same-sex marriage
5. Reinstating the military draft
6. Penalties for plagiarism
7. Increasing the retirement age
8. Spouses sharing housework equally
9. Smoking in public places
10. Big-time sports in college

Assignments Using Visuals

Use the suggested visuals to help develop an argumentation-persuasion essay on one of these topics:

1. AIDS-prevention education and a decline in AIDS cases (graphs)
2. The influences of ethnic cultures on American culture (photos)
3. Societally beneficial uses of public lands (graphs and photos)
4. Bicycle-riding campaigns and the quality of life in cities (photos)
5. The financial expectations of college and high school graduates (graphs).

Assignments with a Specific Purpose, Audience, and Point of View

1. **Academic.** Your college's financial aid department has decided not to renew your scholarship, citing a drop in your grades and an unenthusiastic recommendation from an instructor. Write a letter to the Director of Financial Aid arguing for the renewal of your scholarship.
2. **Academic.** You strongly believe that a particular policy or regulation on campus is unreasonable or unjust. Write a letter to the Dean of Students (or other appropriate administrator) arguing that the policy needs to be, if not completely revoked, amended in some way. Support your contention with specific examples showing how the regulation has gone wrong. End by providing constructive suggestions for how the policy problem can be solved.

3. **Civic activity.** You and your family don't agree on some aspect of your romantic life (you want to live with your boyfriend/girlfriend and they don't approve; you want to get married and they want you to wait). Write a letter explaining why your preference is reasonable. Try hard to win your family over to your side.

4. **Civic activity.** Assume you're a member of a racial, ethnic, religious, or social minority. You might, for example, be a Native American, an elderly person, a female executive. On a recent television show or in a TV commercial, you saw something that depicts your group in an offensive way. Write a letter (to the network or the advertiser) expressing your feelings and explaining why you feel the material should be taken off the air.

5. **Workplace action.** As a staff writer for an online pop-culture magazine, you've been asked to nominate the "Most Memorable TV Moment of the Last 50 Years" to be featured as the magazine's lead article. Write a letter to your supervising editor in support of your nominee.

6. **Workplace action.** As a high school teacher, you support some additional restriction on students. The restriction might be "no cell phones in school," "no T-shirts," "no food in class," "no smoking on school grounds." Write an article for the school newspaper justifying this new rule to the student body.

MyWritingLab Visit Chapter 11, "Argumentation-Persuasion," in MyWritingLab to complete the chapter activities, Pre-Reading Journal Entry activities, Questions for Close Reading, and Additional Writing Topics assignments and to test your understanding of the chapter objectives.

COMBINING THE PATTERNS

In this chapter, you will learn:

12.1 To use different patterns of development during the writing process.

12.2 To analyze how different patterns of development are used effectively in a student-written essay.

12.3 To analyze how different patterns of development are used effectively in a professionally authored selection.

Throughout this book, you've studied the patterns of development—narration, process analysis, definition, and so on—in depth. You've seen how the patterns are used as strategies for generating, developing, and organizing ideas for essays. You've also learned that, in practice, most types of writing combine two or more patterns. The two sections that follow provide additional information about these important points. The rest of the chapter then gives you an opportunity to look more closely at the way several writers use the patterns of development in their work.

THE PATTERNS IN ACTION: DURING THE WRITING PROCESS

The patterns of development come into play throughout the composing process. In the prewriting stage, awareness of the patterns encourages you to think about your subject in fresh, new ways. Assume, for example, that you've been asked to write an essay about the way children are disciplined in school. However, you draw a blank as soon as you try to limit this general subject. To break the logjam, you could apply one or more patterns of development to your subject. *Comparison-contrast* might prompt you to write an essay investigating the differences between your parents' and your own feelings about school discipline. *Division-classification* might lead you to another paper—one that categorizes the kinds of discipline used in school. And *cause-effect* might point to still another essay—one that explores the way students react to being suspended.

Further along in the writing process—after you've identified your limited subject and your thesis—the patterns of development can help you generate your essay's evidence. Imagine that your thesis is "Teachers shouldn't discipline students publicly just to make an example of them." You're not sure, though, how to develop this thesis. Calling upon the patterns might spark some promising possibilities. *Narration* might encourage you to recount the disastrous time you were singled out and punished for the misdeeds of an entire class. Using *definition,* you might explain what is meant by an *autocratic* disciplinary style. *Argumentation-persuasion* might prompt you to advocate a new plan for disciplining students fairly and effectively.

The patterns of development also help you organize your ideas by pointing the way to an appropriate framework for an essay. Suppose you plan to write an essay for the campus newspaper about the disturbingly high incidence of shoplifting among college students; your purpose is to persuade young people not to get involved in this tempting, supposedly victimless crime. You believe that many readers will be deterred from shoplifting if you tell them about the harrowing *process* set in motion once a shoplifter is detected. With this step-by-step explanation in mind, you can now map out the essay's content: what happens when a shoplifter is detained by a salesperson, questioned by store security personnel, led to a police car, booked at the police station, and tried in a courtroom.

THE PATTERNS IN ACTION: IN AN ESSAY

Although this book devotes a separate chapter to each of the nine patterns of development, all chapters emphasize the same important point: Most writing consists of several patterns, with the dominant pattern providing the piece's organizational framework. To reinforce this point, each chapter contains a section, "How [the Pattern] Fits Your Purpose and Audience," that shows how a writer's purpose often leads to a blending of patterns. Also, the commentary following each student essay talks about the way the essay mixes patterns. Similarly, at least one of the questions in the "Questions About the Writer's Craft" section following each professional selection asks you to analyze the piece's combination of patterns. Further, the assignments in "Writing Assignment Combining Patterns of Development" encourage you to experiment with mixing patterns in your own writing. In short, all through *The Longman Reader* we emphasize that the patterns of development are far from being mechanical formulas. On the contrary: They are practical strategies that open up options in every stage of the composing process.

Now you'll have a chance to focus on the way student and professional writers combine patterns in their essays. In the pages ahead, you'll find one student essay and four professional selections, one by each of the following writers: Hillary Rodham Clinton; Martin Luther King, Jr.; Joan Didion; and Jonathan Swift. As you read each essay, ask yourself these questions:

1. What are the writer's *purpose* and *thesis?*
2. What *pattern of development dominates* the essay? How does this pattern help the writer support the essay's thesis and fulfill the essay's purpose?
3. What *other patterns appear* in the essay? How do these secondary patterns help the writer support the essay's thesis and fulfill the essay's purpose?

Your responses to these three questions will reward you with a richer understanding of the way writers work. To give you an even clearer sense of how writers mix patterns, we have annotated the student essay (Houston Barber's "Dating Then and Now: A Convoluted Mess") and the first professional essay (Hillary Rodham Clinton's "Remarks to the United Nations Fourth World Conference on Women" on page 546). The preceding three questions served as our guide when we prepared the annotations. By making your own annotations on these essays and then comparing them to ours, you can measure your ability to analyze writers' use of the patterns. You can further evaluate your analysis of the pieces by answering the three questions on your own and then comparing your responses to ours on pages 544–545 and 553–556.

STUDENT ESSAY

The following student essay was written by Houston Barber in response to this assignment:

In her essay, "Tweens: Ten Going On Sixteen," Kay S. Hymowitz discusses how consumer culture influences her daughter's development. Think of other ways in which cultural developments have influenced how people conduct their lives. Write an essay in which you explore a significant life event, such a choosing a college, buying a car, or arranging a wedding, and how it has been affected by a contemporary phenomenon such as social media use, high college tuition rates, or environmental concerns over energy use.

The annotations on the essay will help you look at the way Houston uses various patterns of development to achieve his purpose and develop his thesis.

Title implies *comparison* of dating in the past with dating in the present

Dating Then and Now: A Convoluted Mess

by Houston Barber

Introduction

Contrast between what dating used to be and what it is today

Thesis: Dating has changed from a "simple process" to one that leaves "everyone feel[ing] miserable."

The twelve years of dating that my parents went through before they got married is a part of their lives that I never thought much about until recently. I thought that by the time I had been dating for a few years, I would be getting better and better at it. Let's just say that's not exactly how things are turning out. So lately, I've been doing a lot of thinking about how my generation has ruined the whole concept of dating. What used to be a simple process of small, social interactions designed to allow two people to get to know each other has devolved into a convoluted mess designed to make everyone involved feel miserable.

1

Process analysis of how dating used to work

From what I've gleaned from 1990s sitcoms, this is how dating used to work: You're out in public and you see someone who looks interesting, so you decide to walk up and start a conversation with the person. If everything goes well, you call and ask the person out for coffee or lunch, and if that goes well, you do it again. This process repeats until you become exclusive and a relationship forms. Life would be so simple if that's how dating still worked today, and I guess for some people, it does. But for most of us, that process does not sound at all familiar.

2

Beginning of *process analysis* of how dating works today

Exemplification of author's viewpoint

I would like to break down step-by-step how dating works today, but before I do that, I should probably clarify that my neurotic, misanthropic perception of dating will probably not be true for everyone. I haven't watched enough episodes of *Girls* to proclaim that I'm the voice of my generation, so if you can't relate to any of what I'm saying, feel free to just laugh at how weird and clueless I am; that way we can all have a good time.

3

Step 1 in *Process Analysis*: meeting someone to date

First, how do people meet? The concept of approaching complete strangers with the intention of dating them is such a foreign concept to me that it's not even something I've ever considered. If I'm going to try to talk or flirt with someone,

4

it will most likely be a person that I know or am friends with already. This generation gets criticized a lot for a lack of ability to hold face-to-face conversations and just being generally anti-social, and I would have to admit that for the most part that criticism is legitimate. I guess before I was born, everyone was constantly going up to strangers and holding deep, insightful conversations. I'm sorry I missed it. But for now I'm happy with the friends that I have.

This, unfortunately, brings us to one of my generation's worst contributions to society, the concept of the "friend zone." I think when historians look back, they will mostly blame *500 Days of Summer* for this—a movie with an impact similar to that of cigarettes: it seemed cool at first, but no one had any idea the harm it would cause until years later. If you are lucky enough not to know about the term *friend zone,* let me explain: it's a situation in which a person, usually a guy, blames his inability to date the girl he wants on the fact that she only wants to be friends, when in reality, the girl probably wants nothing to do with him. It's pretty pathetic, and it's also the plot of *500 Days of Summer.*

5

Definition of friend zone

But let's say you find someone that you want to start a relationship with. What's the next step? Since you're friends, you have the person's number and so begins the texting stage, a complete waste of time in my opinion. I hate texting more than pretty much anything in the world. Unfortunately, one of the only things I hate more is talking on the phone, so texting is a necessary evil. When I think back to how much of my youth I've wasted waiting for someone to text me back, I want to start crying. One of the worst things about texting, besides everything, is that it completely strips you of all personality. Who I am through text and who I am in real life are so totally different that if those two people ever met, they wouldn't even be friends. The worst part is that texting seems to form the foundation of most modern-day relationships, which leads to some serious problems.

6

Stage 2 in process analysis: texting each other

Effect of loss of personality in texting

Contrast of texting image with real person

When I was at orientation before freshman year, I met a girl that I became friends with, and we spent that entire summer texting each other. By the time school started in the fall, I felt not only that we were already in a semi-relationship, but that I knew everything about this girl. Then one day when I was walking across campus, I saw her up ahead, for the first time since orientation, and I suddenly realized I did not know anything about this girl at all. The thought of having a real-life conversation with her freaked me out so much that we walked past each other without any acknowledgment whatsoever. As awkward as that was for me, it must have been even worse for her because I haven't seen her since.

7

Exemplification used to provide an example of the shortcomings of texting

Narrative of negative encounter with a texting friend

Texting is especially awful for anyone with any amount   8
of paranoia, because when someone doesn't text back, the
immediate reaction is that you've done something to deeply
offend the person and your friendship is now over, when in
reality they're probably just watching a movie or something.

Third step in process   The texting stage can last indefinitely, but at some   9
analysis: "hanging   point, if things go well, texting transitions into hanging out.
out"   It's important not to get "hanging out" confused with "going
Comparison of   out." Going out is dinner and a movie. Hanging out is going to
"hanging out" and   the Greek food festival with her and her friends. Hanging
"going out," along   out is basically a way of saying, "Hey, I like you and want to
with *definitions* of   spend time with you, but it has to be with my friends, and
each term   I'm going to spend the majority of the time talking to them."
Exemplification   It's usually during the hanging out stage when one or both
used to provide an   people involved realize the big mistake they have made.
example of possible   I once invited a girl to go with me and my roommates to see
problems associated   former President Bill Clinton speak on campus, because noth-
with "hanging out"   ing says romance like a good political rally. It started off nicely
but ended abruptly when she didn't even want to be near
me because I was cheering too loudly at everything Clinton
was saying. I feel that story sums up what this stage of dating
is like.

Contrast of the   But there's a soft spot in my heart for the hanging out   10
negative aspects of   phase; it's a sort of preview of what life together might be like.
hanging out with   You get to share interests and show a true personality for the
the positive aspects   first time, and if everything keeps going well, things get taken
up a notch and you progress to the stage where you spend
your first time alone together. On the other hand, if you want
to back out, now is your time to do that because after this it's
a one-way ticket to "Relationshiptown, Population: 2."

That's a brief, ideal overview of what the modern dating   11
scene is. It is pretty much the system that has been created
over the last ten years or so, and it's what members of my gen-
Description of   eration have all gotten used to. But there's a monster lurking
mobile dating apps   beneath that wants to undo all of this, referred to unaffection-
that further compli-   ately as "mobile dating apps." Apps come in a wide array of
cate dating today   styles and creepiness, but there's no denying the massive
Classification of   impact they have had. Some apps started out as dating web-
dating apps   sites (Match.com, eHarmony, OkCupid) that charge a fee and
supposedly match people up "scientifically." Others put some
kind of twist on the process, like letting users suggest a possible activity for a date (How About We) or setting up group
dates (Grouper). And many apps pretty much act as photo
Exemplification   albums—giving minimal information about people that you
used to provide   can connect with, often, on the spot (Blendr).
an example of a   At the moment, the most popular one of the photo-album   12
specific mobile   types seems to be Tinder, a word I almost feel dirty just
dating app

saying. At this point I wish I could say that I have no experience with this whatsoever and everything I know about it is either conjecture or hearsay. But unfortunately, I'm staring at the app on my phone right now. I guess I keep it there to be routinely humiliated and ripped of any self-esteem.

Definition of *Tinder*

For the unfamiliar, Tinder is an app that allows you to   13
upload a picture of yourself and then scroll through other people's pictures one at a time, marking each one as to whether or not you're interested in that person. The people you see are all within a hundred miles of you at the time, so you can easily meet if you want to. It's perfect for people who have the desire to judge another human being completely on the basis of one picture. If you get matched with someone else, then you gain the ability to talk with the person, an art I have not mastered to say the least.

Narrative used to provide an *example* of the way mobile dating apps further complicate dating today

I've met one person on Tinder. We talked on the app for   14
a day or so and decided to meet at a coffee shop. I was pretty nervous because I had never had a first date with someone I'd never met face to face. But surprisingly, the date actually went really well, at least for a while. We spent over two hours talking about our lives and just having a rare twenty-first-century face-to-face conversation. As we were leaving she said, "Hey, do you want to come over to my apartment and help me study for chemistry?" To which I replied with complete honesty, "Oh I'm not really good at chemistry. You should probably find someone else." That was the last I ever heard from her, and I'll admit that was pretty much my fault. Later on, I realized the invitation to study was really an invitation to get to know each other better. Now she's added to my ever-increasing list of people to avoid for the rest of my life.

When I think of the twelve years that my parents dated,   15
I wonder what those years were like for them, and I think about how difficult dating is for me today. It's easy to think

Conclusion includes *narrative* and *descriptive* elements

that our generation has ruined dating. But if my parents dated for twelve years, I guess that means dating wasn't so simple back then either. Dating is absurd; it's ridiculous. More often than not, it leads to misery. That's probably why my parents never tell me anything about the time they dated. There's no way I would tell my kids any of my dating stories. I'm sure the twelve years my parents dated were filled with all the embarrassment and confusion that I am experiencing, but without those twelve years, they wouldn't be getting ready to celebrate the twenty-five. So yes, we've ruined dating, and texting is the pits, and Zooey Deschanel is annoying, but in the end it's all worth it for just the hope that one day we'll find someone to share our lives with and laugh at the next generation while they laugh at us.

The following answers to the questions on page 539 will help you analyze Houston Barber's use of the patterns of development in his essay "Dating Then and Now: A Convoluted Mess."

1. What are the writer's purpose and thesis?

The general purpose of Houston's essay is to compare dating in the past with dating in the present and to explore the reasons dating has changed so much over the years. He expresses his thesis in the final statement of the introductory paragraph: "What used to be a simple process of small, social interactions designed to allow two people to get to know each other has devolved into a convoluted mess designed to make everyone involved feel miserable."

2. What pattern of development dominates the essay? How does this pattern help the writer support the essay's thesis and fulfill the essay's purpose?

Houston uses *process analysis* as his essay's principal pattern of development. In paragraph 2 he explains the dating process of yesteryear, which, as he understands it, involved only a few simple steps: meeting someone you found interesting, talking with that person, asking him or her out for coffee or lunch, and then repeating the coffee or lunch step as needed until the two of you became a couple. Houston then moves on to an analysis of the present-day dating process, one that he considers much more complicated and which he spends most of the rest of the essay exploring. In short, the steps are as follows: becoming interested in someone whom you probably already know (which is complicated by the "friend zone" phenomenon); texting that individual (a period that can go on indefinitely); "hanging out" with that person (not to be confused with "going out"); and finally, spending time alone together and establishing a relationship. The entire process is further complicated by what Houston considers to be the "monster lurking beneath the surface" that can completely ruin the dating process: the use of "mobile dating apps."

3. What other patterns appear in the essay? How do these secondary patterns help the writer support the essay's thesis and fulfill the essay's purpose?

Although Houston's essay is primarily a process analysis, it contains elements of each of the other eight patters of development. Houston uses *comparison-contrast* in several parts of his essay: in his title, where he implies that in his essay he'll *compare* dating in the past with dating in the present; in his thesis, where he states that "what used to be a simple process...has devolved into a convoluted mess"; in paragraph 6, where he *compares* his texting image with his real-life image; in paragraph 9, where he *compares* "hanging out" with "going out"; and in paragraph 10, where he *contrasts* the negative and positive aspects of "hanging out."

Houston also makes frequent use of *exemplification*: in paragraph 3, where he provides an *example* of his "neurotic, misanthropic" viewpoint; in paragraph 7, where he gives an *example* of the shortcomings of texting; in paragraph 9, where he provides an *example* of possible problems associated with "hanging out"; and in paragraph 12, where he gives an *example* of a specific mobile dating app.

In addition to these patterns of development, Houston draws on *narration*: in paragraph 7, where he *tells* about a negative encounter with a girl he had texted after orientation; in paragraph 14, to explain the way mobile dating apps complicate dating today; and in the conclusion, where he talks about his parents who are about to celebrate their twenty-fifth wedding anniversary.

Other patterns of development Houston draws on include *cause-effect* in paragraph 6, where he states that "one of the worst things about texting…is that it completely strips you of all personality"; *definition* in paragraphs 5 and 13, where he defines *friend zone* and *Tinder*; *classification* in paragraph 11, where he categorizes the various dating apps; and *description* in the essay's conclusion, where he offers a depiction of the twelve years his parents dated.

Taken together, all of these patterns help Houston make his point that dating has changed from a "simple process" to one that is much more complex.

Hillary Rodham Clinton

Hillary Rodham Clinton, a graduate of Wellesley College and Yale Law School, was the First Lady of the United States (1993–2001), a U.S. Senator (2001–2009), and the sixty-seventh U.S. Secretary of State (2009–2013). In 1988 and 1991, she was on *The National Law Journal*'s list of the "One Hundred Most Powerful Lawyers in America." Clinton's publications include five books: *It Takes a Village* (1996); *Dear Socks, Dear Buddy: Kids' Letters to the First Pets* (1998); *An Invitation to the White House* (2000); *Living History* (2003); and *Hard Choices* (2014). She is widely respected as a champion for women's rights, child care, and health care reform. Clinton presented the speech that follows at the plenary session (general meeting of all participants) of the United Nations Fourth World Conference on Women in Beijing, China, on September 5, 1995.

Remarks to the United Nations Fourth World Conference on Women Plenary Session

Introductory remarks

Description of purpose of conference: to celebrate the contributions of women

Exemplification used to provide examples of the ways women contribute and the roles they play

Continuation of *description* of purpose of conference: for women to "come together" and find "common ground"

Exemplification used to provide examples of the places women "come together"

1   Thank you very much, Gertrude Mongella,[1] for your dedicated work that has brought us to this point, distinguished delegates, and guests:

2   I would like to thank the Secretary General for inviting me to be part of this important United Nations Fourth World Conference on Women. This is truly a celebration, a celebration of the contributions women make in every aspect of life: in the home, on the job, in the community, as mothers, wives, sisters, daughters, learners, workers, citizens, and leaders.

3   It is also a coming together, much the way women come together every day in every country. We come together in fields and factories, in village markets and supermarkets, in living rooms and board rooms. Whether it is while playing with our children in the park, or washing clothes in a river, or taking a break at the office water cooler, we come together and talk about our aspirations and concerns. And time and again, our talk turns to our children and our families. However different we may

---

[1]Gertrude Mongella is the former President of the Pan-African Parliament and was Secretary General of the Fourth World Conference on Women (editors' note).

Comparison-contrast of women's differences and similarities.

Effects of women finding a "common ground"

Description of purpose of conference: to focus attention on issues that are a priority for women

Exemplification used to provide examples of issues that are a priority for women

Opposing viewpoints

Exemplification used to provide examples of roles of women who have come together at the conference and in the town of Huairou

Cause-effect: beginning of causal chain

Continuation of causal chain

Narration and description: personal account of recent experiences relating to speaker's efforts to improve conditions for women and their families

Effect of discussion at the meeting of the United Nations Development Fund for Women

Cause-effect: start of causal chain resulting from women being "healthy," "educated," and " free from violence"

appear, there is far more that unites us than divides us. We share a common future, and we are here to find common ground so that we may help bring new dignity and respect to women and girls all over the world, and in so doing bring new strength and stability to families as well.

By gathering in Beijing, we are focusing world attention on issues that matter most in our lives—the lives of women and their families: access to education, health care, jobs and credit, the chance to enjoy basic legal and human rights and to participate fully in the political life of our countries. 4

There are some who question the reason for this conference. Let them listen to the voices of women in their homes, neighborhoods, and workplaces. There are some who wonder whether the lives of women and girls matter to economic and political progress around the globe. Let them look at the women gathered here and at Huairou[2]—the homemakers and nurses, the teachers and lawyers, the policymakers and women who run their own businesses. It is conferences like this that compel governments and peoples everywhere to listen, look, and face the world's most pressing problems. Wasn't it after the women's conference in Nairobi ten years ago that the world focused for the first time on the crisis of domestic violence? 5

Earlier today, I participated in a World Health Organization forum. In that forum, we talked about ways that government officials, NGOs[3], and individual citizens are working to address the health problems of women and girls. Tomorrow, I will attend a gathering of the United Nations Development Fund for Women. There, the discussion will focus on local—and highly successful — programs that give hard-working women access to credit so they can improve their own lives and the lives of their families. 6

What we are learning around the world is that if women are healthy and educated, their families will flourish. If women are free from violence, their families will flourish. If women have a chance to work and earn as full and equal 7

[2]Huairou is the small town 35 miles northeast of Beijing where the United Nations Fourth World Conference on Women was held in 1995 (editors' note).
[3]NGO is an acronym for "non-government organization" (editors' note).

Continuation of causal chain

Part of purpose/ thesis: What happens at the United Nations 4ᵗʰ Conference on Women affects everyone on the planet

Exemplification and description used to establish credentials, provide examples, and describe speaker's interactions with women

Exemplification and description used to provide examples of women with whom speaker has interacted and to describe the important work they are doing

Part of purpose/ thesis: Every woman matters. Every woman's voice should be heard.

Statistics supporting the roles women play and the conditions in which they live

Description of the undervalued work women do

Exemplification used to provide examples of those who do not value the work of women

partners in society, their families will flourish. And when families flourish, communities and nations do as well. That is why every woman, every man, every child, every family, and every nation on this planet does have a stake in the discussion that takes place here.

Over the past 25 years, I have worked persistently on 8 issues relating to women, children, and families. Over the past two and a half years, I've had the opportunity to learn more about the challenges facing women in my own country and around the world.

I have met new mothers in Indonesia, who come 9 together regularly in their village to discuss nutrition, family planning, and baby care. I have met working parents in Denmark who talk about the comfort they feel in knowing that their children can be cared for in safe, and nurturing after-school centers. I have met women in South Africa who helped lead the struggle to end apartheid and are now helping to build a new democracy. I have met with the leading women of my own hemisphere who are working every day to promote literacy and better health care for children in their countries. I have met women in India and Bangladesh who are taking out small loans to buy milk cows, or rickshaws, or thread in order to create a livelihood for themselves and their families. I have met the doctors and nurses in Belarus and Ukraine who are trying to keep children alive in the aftermath of Chernobyl.[4]

The great challenge of this conference is to give voice 10 to women everywhere whose experiences go unnoticed, whose words go unheard. Women comprise more than half the world's population, 70% of the world's poor, and two-thirds of those who are not taught to read and write. We are the primary caretakers for most of the world's children and elderly. Yet much of the work we do is not valued—not by economists, not by historians, not by popular culture, not by government leaders.

At this very moment, as we sit here, women around 11 the world are giving birth, raising children, cooking meals, washing clothes, cleaning houses, planting crops,

---

[4]Chernobyl, a city in Ukraine, was devastated by an explosion at the town's nuclear power plant on April 26, 1986. Belarus, a country across the Ukraine border and eleven miles from Chernobyl, also experienced devastating effects (editors' note).

Comparison-contrast of the positive contributions of women compared with the difficulties they endure.

Exemplification used to provide examples of the inhumane, unjust ways they are treated

Part of purpose/ thesis: Women at the conference have an ethical obligation to speak.

Exemplification used to provide examples of women in speaker's country who live in unjust conditions

Exemplification and description used to provide examples of the work women are doing and to describe the important roles they play

Classification of the types of jobs women perform

Comparison of similarities between the ways the speaker and the audience speak "for women around the world"

Exemplification used to provide examples of ways women are being denied their human rights

Articulation of the warrant

Effects of women being denied human rights

Description of conference's goals

working on assembly lines, running companies, and running countries. Women also are dying from diseases that should have been prevented or treated. They are watching their children succumb to malnutrition caused by poverty and economic deprivation. They are being denied the right to go to school by their own fathers and brothers. They are being forced into prostitution, and they are being barred from the bank lending offices and banned from the ballot box.

Those of us who have the opportunity to be here have the responsibility to speak for those who could not. As an American, I want to speak for those women in my own country, women who are raising children on the minimum wage, women who can't afford health care or child care, women whose lives are threatened by violence, including violence in their own homes.

I want to speak up for mothers who are fighting for good schools, safe neighborhoods, clean air, and clean airwaves; for older women, some of them widows, who find that, after raising their families, their skills and life experiences are not valued in the marketplace; for women who are working all night as nurses, hotel clerks, or fast food chefs so that they can be at home during the day with their children; and for women everywhere who simply don't have time to do everything they are called upon to do each and every day.

Speaking to you today, I speak for them, just as each of us speaks for women around the world who are denied the chance to go to school, or see a doctor, or own property, or have a say about the direction of their lives, simply because they are women. The truth is that most women around the world work both inside and outside the home, usually by necessity.

We need to understand there is no one formula for how women should lead our lives. That is why we must respect the choices that each woman makes for herself and her family. Every woman deserves the chance to realize her own God-given potential. But we must recognize that women will never gain full dignity until their human rights are respected and protected.

Our goals for this conference, to strengthen families and societies by empowering women to take greater control over their own destinies, cannot be fully achieved unless all

12

13

14

15

16

Effects of govern-
ments not insuring
human rights

Part of purpose/
thesis: Governments
must "protect and
promote" human
rights

Exemplification used
to provide examples
of human rights all
individuals deserve

Exemplification used
to provide examples
of mistreatment of
women and children

Effect of women
being "excluded
from the political
process"

Part of purpose/
thesis: Any discus-
sion of human rights
includes the rights
of women. The two
cannot be separated.

Effects of women
being silenced

*Exemplification and
cause-effect*: first
in a series of seven
examples of viola-
tions of women's
human rights and
their unjust causes

Second example

Purpose/thesis: We
must put an end to
"women and girls
[being] sold into the
slavery of prostitution
for human greed."

Third example

Fourth example

governments—here and around the world—accept their
responsibility to protect and promote internationally recognized human rights. The international community has
long acknowledged and recently reaffirmed at Vienna[5] that
both women and men are entitled to a range of protections
and personal freedoms, from the right of personal security
to the right to determine freely the number and spacing of
the children they bear. No one should be forced to remain
silent for fear of religious or political persecution, arrest,
abuse, or torture.

Tragically, women are most often the ones whose   17
human rights are violated. Even now, in the late 20th century, the rape of women continues to be used as an instrument of armed conflict. Women and children make up a
large majority of the world's refugees. And when women
are excluded from the political process, they become even
more vulnerable to abuse. I believe that now, on the eve of
a new millennium, it is time to break the silence. It is time
for us to say here in Beijing, and for the world to hear, that
it is no longer acceptable to discuss women's rights as separate from human rights.

These abuses have continued because, for too long, the   18
history of women has been a history of silence. Even today,
there are those who are trying to silence our words. But
the voices of this conference and of the women at Huairou
must be heard loudly and clearly:

It is a violation of human rights when babies are denied
food, or drowned, or suffocated, or their spines broken, simply because they are born girls.

It is a violation of human rights when women and
girls are sold into the slavery of prostitution for human
greed—and the kinds of reasons that are used to justify
this practice should no longer be tolerated.

It is a violation of human rights when women are
doused with gasoline, set on fire, and burned to death
because their marriage dowries are deemed too small.

It is a violation of human rights when individual
women are raped in their own communities and when

[5]Vienna, Austria, was the site of the World Conference on Human Rights where the "Vienna
Declaration and Program of Action" was adopted on June 25, 1993 (editors' note).

thousands of women are subjected to rape as a tactic or prize of war.

Fifth example ————→ It is a violation of human rights when a leading cause of death worldwide among women ages 14 to 44 is the violence they are subjected to in their own homes by their own relatives.

Sixth example ————→ It is a violation of human rights when young girls are brutalized by the painful and degrading practice of genital mutilation.

Seventh example ————→ It is a violation of human rights when women are denied the right to plan their own families, and that includes being forced to have abortions or being sterilized against their will.

Part of purpose/
thesis: All humans,
male and female,
deserve the same
rights, and "among
those rights are
the right to speak
freely and the
right to be heard."

If there is one message that echoes forth from this conference, let it be that human rights are women's rights and women's rights are human rights once and for all. Let us not forget that among those rights are the right to speak freely—and the right to be heard.   19

Cause and effect:
When women are
allowed "to participate fully in the
social and political
lives of their countries[,]...freedom
and democracy...
thrive and endure."

Women must enjoy the rights to participate fully in the social and political lives of their countries, if we want freedom and democracy to thrive and endure. It is indefensible that many women in nongovernmental organizations who wished to participate in this conference have not been able to attend—or have been prohibited from fully taking part.   20

Part of the —————
underlying warrant

Definition of —————
freedom

Part of underlying
warrant   —————

Let me be clear. Freedom means the right of people to assemble, organize, and debate openly. It means respecting the views of those who may disagree with the views of their governments. It means not taking citizens away from their loved ones and jailing them, mistreating them, or denying them their freedom or dignity because of the peaceful expression of their ideas and opinions.   21

Process involved in
the fight for suffrage
in the U.S. —————

Contrast between
types of wars —————

In my country, we recently celebrated the 75th anniversary of Women's Suffrage. It took 150 years after the signing of our Declaration of Independence for women to win the right to vote. It took 72 years of organized struggle, before that happened, on the part of many courageous women and men. It was one of America's most divisive philosophical wars. But it was a bloodless war. Suffrage was achieved without a shot being fired.   22

Part of underlying warrant	But we have also been reminded, in V-J Day[6] obser- 23 vances last weekend, of the good that comes when men
Effects of people uniting to oppose a common enemy	and women join together to combat the forces of tyranny and to build a better world. We have seen peace prevail in most places for a half century. We have avoided another
Comparison-contrast of the positive effects of World War II with impor- tant issues the war did not resolve	world war. But we have not solved older, deeply-rooted problems that continue to diminish the potential of half the world's population.
Part of purpose/ thesis: We must "take bold steps" for women.	Now it is the time to act on behalf of women every- 24 where. If we take bold steps to better the lives of women, we will be taking bold steps to better the lives of children and families too. Families rely on mothers and wives for
Start of causal chain of effects of taking a stand for women's rights	emotional support and care. Families rely on women for labor in the home. And increasingly, everywhere, families rely on women for income needed to raise healthy children and care for other relatives.
Continuation of causal chain	As long as discrimination and inequities remain so 25 commonplace everywhere in the world, as long as girls and women are valued less, fed less, fed last, overworked,
Part of purpose/ thesis: Females must be provided the same rights as males	underpaid, not schooled, subjected to violence in and out- side their homes—the potential of the human family to cre- ate a peaceful, prosperous world will not be realized.
Cause-effect: Our world will never become the "peace- ful, prosperous" place it could be if women are denied equal rights.	Let this conference be our—and the world's—call to 26 action. Let us heed that call so we can create a world in which every woman is treated with respect and dignity, every boy and girl is loved and cared for equally, and every family has the hope of a strong and stable future. That is
Full paragraph statement of thesis and call to action.	the work before you. That is the work before all of us who have a vision of the world we want to see—for our children and our grandchildren.
Conclusion: summa- rizes author's outlook and convictions and makes a call for action	The time is now. We must move beyond rhetoric. We 27 must move beyond recognition of problems to working together, to have the common efforts to build that com- mon ground we hope to see.
	God's blessing on you, your work, and all who will 28 benefit from it.
Closing comments	Godspeed and thank you very much. 29

---

[6]V-J Day (Victory over Japan Day) is the day when Japan surrendered and World War II ended (editors' note).

The following answers to the questions on page 539 will help you analyze Hillary Rodham Clinton's use of the patterns of development in the speech she presented at the United Nations Fourth World Conference on Women.

1. What are the writer's purpose and thesis?

The *purpose* of Clinton's speech at the United Nations Fourth World Conference on Women is to clarify the primary goal of the conference—to promote women's rights as human rights—and to encourage and support audience members in their efforts to press governments worldwide to address women's issues. To add force to her thesis, Clinton also articulates, in paragraph 15, the warrant that underlies her argument: "Every woman deserves the chance to realize her own God-given potential. But we must recognize that women will never gain full dignity until their human rights are respected and protected."

She states her thesis near the end of her text in paragraph 26: "Let this conference be our—and the world's—call to action. Let us heed that call so we can create a world in which every woman is treated with respect and dignity, every boy and girl is loved and cared for equally, and every family has the hope of a strong and stable future. That is the work before you. That is the work before all of us who have a vision of the world we want to see—for our children and our grandchildren." Clinton's primary message is that the value of conferences like this one is for individuals to come together and assert that women's rights are human rights and to urge governments to press ahead with addressing the priorities and concerns of women worldwide.

2. What pattern of development dominates the essay? How does this pattern help the writer support the essay's thesis and fulfill the essay's purpose?

Although Clinton uses a variety of developmental patterns in her text, she relies primarily on *exemplification*. Her purpose is to inspire her audience, and her examples are deliberately generalized and often extreme. In paragraphs 2–4, she provides examples "of the contributions women make in every aspect of life: in the home, on the job, in the community, as mothers, wives, sisters, daughters, learners, workers, citizens, and leaders" (2); examples of the places women congregate: "playing with our children in the park..., washing clothes in a river,...taking a break at the office water cooler" (3); and examples of the issues that are most important to women: "access to education, health care, jobs and credit, the chance to enjoy basic legal and human rights and to participate fully in the political life of our countries" (4).

In paragraph 5, Clinton addresses opposing viewpoints and encourages those who hold those views to "listen to the voices of women in their homes, neighborhoods, and workplaces." She provides examples of the women attending the conference and of those in Huairou, the town hosting the gathering: "the homemakers and nurses, the teachers and lawyers, the policymakers and women who run their own businesses." Clinton uses these examples to point out to those "who question the reason for [the] conference"—that women and the important work they do matters and should not be ignored.

Clinton uses paragraphs 8 and 9 to establish her credentials, and to do that, she provides examples of her interactions with women and the work they are doing.

She states that she has "worked persistently on issues relating to women, children and families" (8), and that she has met with women in Indonesia, Denmark, South Africa, North and South America, India, Bangladesh, Belarus, and Ukraine to discuss the important work they are doing (9).

In paragraphs 10 and 11, Clinton provides examples of entities and individuals who do not value the work of women (economists, historians, popular culture, government leaders) (10), along with more examples of the work women do (from "giving birth" to "working on assembly lines") and the inhumane, unjust ways women are treated (from "dying from diseases that should have been prevented or treated" to "being barred from the bank lending offices and banned from the ballot box") (11).

In paragraphs 12 and 13, the speaker stresses the ethical obligation of those attending the conference to speak for women who could not attend. She offers examples of women "who are raising children on the minimum wage, women who can't afford health care or child care, women whose lives are threatened by violence" (12). In paragraph 13, Clinton provides more examples of the work women are doing (from "fighting for good schools" to "working all night as nurses, hotel clerks, or fast food chefs so that they can be at home during the day with their children").

In her discussion of the importance of human rights for women in paragraphs 14–17, Clinton gives examples of ways women are being denied their human rights to education, health care, property ownership, and authority over their own lives (14), as well as examples of human rights all individuals deserve, "from the right of personal security to the right to determine freely the number and spacing of the children they bear" (16). In paragraph 17, Clinton points out that "the rape of women continues to be used as an instrument of armed conflict" and that "women and children make up a large majority of the world's refugees."

Clinton further uses exemplification in paragraph 18, where she lists seven examples of gross violations of women's human rights that result from unjust causes ranging from "simply because they are born girls" (18) and "human greed" (18), to women being considered "prize[s] of war" (18).

The author repeatedly uses exemplification throughout her essay to drive home her main point—that the United Nations Fourth World Conference on Women should serve as a "call to action" to "create a world in which every woman is treated with respect and dignity, every boy and girl is loved and cared for equally, and every family has the hope of a strong and stable future" (26).

3.   What other patterns appear in the essay? How do these secondary patterns help the writer support the speech's thesis and fulfill the speech's purpose?

In addition to exemplification, the author also uses *description, comparison-contrast, cause-effect, narration, classification,* and *definition* to get her points across. Clinton uses *description* in paragraphs 2, 3, and 4 when she *describes* the purpose of the conference: to celebrate the contributions of women (2), to provide a time for women to "come together" and find "common ground" (3), and to focus on issues that are important for women (4). In paragraph 6, the author *describes* her recent efforts to improve conditions for women and their families, and in paragraph 8, she *describes* the work she has done "over the past 25 years…on issues relating to women, children, and families." Then in paragraph 10, Clinton *describes* the undervalued work women do as "the primary caretakers for most of the world's children and elderly."

The author also makes extensive use of *comparison-contrast*. In paragraph 3, she *compares* and *contrasts* women's differences and similarities, and in paragraph 11, she *compares* and *contrasts* the positive contributions of women with the difficulties they endure. In paragraph 14, Clinton *compares* the similarities between the ways she and the members of her audience speak "for women around the world," and in paragraph 22, she *contrasts* wars that rely on deadly weapons with those that are won "without a shot being fired." And then in paragraph 23, she *compares* and *contrasts* the positive effects of World War II with "older, deeply rooted problems that continue to diminish the potential of half the world's population."

Another pattern that appears frequently in the text is *cause-effect*. In paragraph 3, the author points out when women come together and "share a common future," they "find common ground" that brings "new dignity and respect" to them and "new strength and stability" to their families." In paragraphs 5 and 6, she describes the *results* of gatherings such as the one at which she is speaking that draw attention to issues that are of utmost importance to women and their families. In the following paragraph, Clinton establishes a *causal chain* as she explains that when women are "healthy," "educated," and "free from violence," their families flourish: "And when families flourish, communities and nations do as well." In paragraph 15, she points out that "women will never gain full dignity until their human rights are respected and protected"—that being guaranteed human rights *results* in a sense of dignity that is otherwise impossible. Then in paragraph 16, Clinton reemphasizes the connection between "all governments… accept[ing] the responsibility to protect and promote internationally recognized human rights" and the "empowering [of] women to take greater control over their own destinies." In paragraphs 17 and 18, the author describes the *effect* of women being "excluded from the political process" and of having their voices silenced. The list of seven examples of violations of women's human rights in paragraph 18 includes references to the unjust *causes* of those violations. In paragraph 20, Clinton describes the *effects* of women being allowed "to participate fully in the social and political lives of their countries, and in paragraph 23 she points out the *effects* of people uniting to oppose a common enemy. In paragraph 24, the author establishes a causal chain of *effects* that come about when individuals take a stand for women's rights, and in paragraph 32, she points out that our world will never become the "peaceful, prosperous" place it could be if women are denied equal rights."

Four additional organizational patterns appear less frequently in the essay: *narration, classification, definition*, and *process analysis*. The author uses *narration* in paragraph 6, where she gives a personal account of recent experiences relating to her efforts to improve conditions for women and their families. She uses *classification* in paragraph 13, where she categorizes the types of jobs women perform, and she uses *definition* in paragraph 21 when she establishes what she means when she uses the word *freedom*. In paragraph 22, Clinton uses *process analysis* to relate the historical circumstances that led to women's suffrage in the United States.

Taken together, these patterns of development allow Clinton to compose a speech that is both persuasive and compelling.

Martin Luther King, Jr.

More than forty years after his assassination, Martin Luther King, Jr. (1929–1968), is still recognized as the towering figure in the struggle for civil rights in the United States. Born in Atlanta, Georgia, King earned doctorates from Boston University and Chicago Theological Seminary and served as pastor of a Baptist congregation in Montgomery, Alabama. Advocating a philosophy of nonviolent resistance to racial injustice, he led bus boycotts, marches, and sit-ins that brought about passage of the 1964 Civil Rights Act and the Voting Rights Act of 1965. Dr. King was awarded the Nobel Peace Prize in 1964. The following two selections by King are taken from *Where Do We Go from Here: Chaos or Community?* (1967).

Where Do We Go from Here: Chaos or Community?

A final problem that mankind must solve in order to survive in the world   1
house that we have inherited is finding an alternative to war and human destruction. Recent events have vividly reminded us that nations are not reducing but rather increasing their arsenals of weapons of mass destruction. The best brains in the highly developed nations of the world are devoted to military technology. The proliferation of nuclear weapons has not been halted, in spite of the limited-test-ban treaty.

In this day of man's highest technical achievement, in this day of   2
dazzling discovery, of novel opportunities, loftier dignities and fuller freedoms for all, there is no excuse for the kind of blind craving for power and resources that provoked the wars of previous generations. There is no need to fight for food and land. Science has provided us with adequate means of survival and transportation, which make it possible to enjoy the fullness of this great earth. The question now is, do we have the morality and courage required to live together as brothers and not be afraid?

One of the most persistent ambiguities we face is that everybody talks   3
about peace as a goal, but among the wielders of power peace is practically nobody's business. Many men cry "Peace! Peace!" but they refuse to do the things that make for peace.

The large power blocs talk passionately of pursuing peace while expand-   4
ing defense budgets that already bulge, enlarging already awesome armies
and devising ever more devastating weapons. Call the roll of those who sing
the glad tidings of peace and one's ears will be surprised by the responding
sounds. The heads of all the nations issue clarion calls for peace, yet they
come to the peace table accompanied by bands of brigands each bearing
unsheathed swords.

The stages of history are replete with the chants and choruses of the   5
conquerors of old who came killing in pursuit of peace. Alexander, Genghis
Khan, Julius Caesar, Charlemagne and Napoleon were akin in seeking a
peaceful world order, a world fashioned after their selfish conceptions of an
ideal existence. Each sought a world at peace which would personify his ego-
tistic dreams. Even within the life span of most of us, another megalomaniac
strode across the world stage. He sent his blitzkrieg-bent legions blazing
across Europe, bringing havoc and holocaust in his wake. There is grave irony
in the fact that Hitler could come forth, following nakedly aggressive expan-
sionist theories, and do it all in the name of peace.

So when in this day I see the leaders of nations again talking peace while   6
preparing for war, I take fearful pause. When I see our country today intervening in what is basically a civil war, mutilating hundreds of thousands of
Vietnamese children with napalm, burning villages and rice fields at random,
painting the valleys of that small Asian country red with human blood, leaving broken bodies in countless ditches and sending home half-men, mutilated
mentally and physically; when I see the unwillingness of our government to
create the atmosphere for a negotiated settlement of this awful conflict by
halting bombings in the North and agreeing unequivocally to talk with the
Vietcong—and all this in the name of pursuing the goal of peace—I tremble
for our world.[1] I do so not only from dire recall of the nightmares wreaked
in the wars of yesterday, but also from dreadful realization of today's possible
nuclear destructiveness and tomorrow's even more calamitous prospects.

Before it is too late, we must narrow the gaping chasm between our   7
proclamations of peace and our lowly deeds which precipitate and perpetuate
war. We are called upon to look up from the quagmire of military programs
and defense commitments and read the warnings on history's signposts.

One day we must come to see that peace is not merely a distant goal that   8
we seek but a means by which we arrive at that goal. We must pursue peaceful ends through peaceful means. How much longer must we play at deadly
war games before we heed the plaintive pleas of the unnumbered dead and
maimed of past wars?

---

[1]Only after more than 58,000 Americans had been killed did the United States withdraw from
Vietnam. The war then continued until the North Vietnamese, aided by the Vietcong, took
over all of Vietnam (editors' note).

President John F. Kennedy said on one occasion, "Mankind must put 9
an end to war or war will put an end to mankind." Wisdom born of experience should tell us that war is obsolete. There may have been a time when
war served as a negative good by preventing the spread and growth of an
evil force, but the destructive power of modern weapons eliminates even the
possibility that war may serve any good at all. If we assume that life is worth
living and that man has a right to survive, then we must find an alternative to
war. In a day when vehicles hurtle through outer space and guided ballistic
missiles carve highways of death through the stratosphere, no nation can
claim victory in war. A so-called limited war will leave little more than a
calamitous legacy of human suffering, political turmoil and spiritual disil-
lusionment. A world war will leave only smoldering ashes as mute testimony
of a human race whose folly led inexorably to ultimate death. If modern
man continues to flirt unhesitatingly with war, he will transform his earthly
habitat into an inferno such as even the mind of Dante[2] could not imagine.

Therefore I suggest that the philosophy and strategy of nonviolence 10
become immediately a subject for study and for serious experimentation in
every field of human conflict, by no means excluding the relations between
nations. It is, after all, nation-states which make war, which have produced
the weapons that threaten the survival of mankind and which are both geno-
cidal and suicidal in character.

We have ancient habits to deal with, vast structures of power, indescribably 11
complicated problems to solve. But unless we abdicate our humanity altogether and succumb to fear and impotence in the presence of the weapons we
have ourselves created, it is as possible and as urgent to put an end to war and
violence between nations as it is to put an end to poverty and racial injustice.

The United Nations is a gesture in the direction of nonviolence on a 12
world scale. There, at least, states that oppose one another have sought to
do so with words instead of with weapons. But true nonviolence is more
than the absence of violence. It is the persistent and determined applica-
tion of peaceable power to offenses against the community—in this case the
world community. As the United Nations moves ahead with the giant tasks
confronting it, I would hope that it would earnestly examine the uses of
nonviolent direct action.

I do not minimize the complexity of the problems that need to be faced 13
in achieving disarmament and peace. But I am convinced that we shall not
have the will, the courage and the insight to deal with such matters unless in
this field we are prepared to undergo a mental and spiritual re-evaluation, a
change of focus which will enable us to see that the things that seem most
real and powerful are indeed now unreal and have come under sentence of

---

[2]In The *Divine Comedy* (1321), Italian poet Dante depicts the burning torments of hell
endured by a lost soul before it can attain salvation (editors' note).

death. We need to make a supreme effort to generate the readiness, indeed the eagerness, to enter into the new world which is now possible, "the city which hath foundation, whose Building and Maker is God."

It is not enough to say, "We must not wage war." It is necessary to love   14 peace and sacrifice for it. We must concentrate not merely on the eradication of war but on the affirmation of peace. A fascinating story about Ulysses and the Sirens[3] is preserved for us in Greek literature. The Sirens had the ability to sing so sweetly that sailors could not resist steering toward their island. Many ships were lured upon the rocks, and men forgot home, duty and honor as they flung themselves into the sea to be embraced by arms that drew them down to death. Ulysses, determined not to succumb to the Sirens, first decided to tie himself tightly to the mast of his boat and his crew stuffed their ears with wax. But finally he and his crew learned a better way to save themselves: They took on board the beautiful singer Orpheus, whose melodies were sweeter than the music of the Sirens. When Orpheus sang, who would bother to listen to the Sirens?

So we must see that peace represents a sweeter music, a cosmic melody   15 that is far superior to the discords of war. Somehow we must transform the dynamics of the world power struggle from the nuclear arms race, which no one can win, to a creative contest to harness man's genius for the purpose of making peace and prosperity a reality for all the nations of the world. In short, we must shift the arms race into a "peace race." If we have the will and determination to mount such a peace offensive, we will unlock hitherto tightly sealed doors of hope and bring new light into the dark chambers of pessimism.

---

[3]Ulysses and the Sirens, as well as Orpheus (mentioned later in the paragraph), are all figures in Greek mythology (editors' note).

Joan Didion

Known for her taut prose style and sharp social commentary, Joan Didion (1934–) graduated from the University of California at Berkeley. Her essays have appeared in *The Saturday Evening Post, The American Scholar,* and the *National Review,* as well as in three collections: *Slouching Towards Bethlehem* (1969), *The White Album* (1979), and *After Henry* (1992). *Salvador* (1983) is a book-length essay about a 1982 visit to Central America. The coauthor of several screenplays (including *A Star Is Born* in 1976 and *Up Close and Personal* in 1996), Didion has also written novels, including *Run River* (1963), *A Book of Common Prayer* (1977), *Democracy* (1984), *The Last Thing He Wanted* (1996), and *Where I Was From* (2003), as well as *Fixed Ideas: America Since 9.11* (2003), a book of political commentary. In 2005, Didion published *The Year of Magical Thinking,* a memoir, "and in 2011, she published a second memoir, *Blue Nights.*" "Marrying Absurd" is from *Slouching Towards Bethlehem.*

Marrying Absurd

To be married in Las Vegas, Clark County, Nevada, a bride must swear 1
that she is eighteen or has parental permission and a bridegroom that he is
twenty-one or has parental permission. Someone must put up five dollars
for the license. (On Sundays and holidays, fifteen dollars. The Clark County
Courthouse issues marriage licenses at any time of the day or night except
between noon and one in the afternoon, between eight and nine in the
evening, and between four and five in the morning.) Nothing else is required.
The State of Nevada, alone among these United States, demands neither
a premarital blood test nor a waiting period before or after the issuance of
a marriage license. Driving in across the Mojave from Los Angeles, one sees
the signs way out on the desert, looming up from that moonscape of rattle-
snakes and mesquite, even before the Las Vegas lights appear like a mirage
on the horizon: "GETTING MARRIED? Free License Information First Strip
Exit." Perhaps the Las Vegas wedding industry achieved its peak operational
efficiency between 9:00 P.M. and midnight of August 26, 1965, an otherwise
unremarkable Thursday which happened to be, by Presidential order,[1] the last
day on which anyone could improve his draft status merely by getting married.
One hundred and seventy-one couples were pronounced man and wife in the
name of Clark County and the State of Nevada that night, sixty-seven of them
by a single justice of the peace, Mr. James A. Brennan. Mr. Brennan did one
wedding at the Dunes and the other sixty-six in his office, and charged each
couple eight dollars. One bride lent her veil to six others. "I got it down from
five to three minutes," Mr. Brennan said later of his feat. "I could've married
them *en masse*, but they're people, not cattle. People expect more when they
get married."

What people who get married in Las Vegas actually do expect—what, 2
in the largest sense, their "expectations" are—strikes one as a curious
and self-contradictory business. Las Vegas is the most extreme and alle-
gorical of American settlements, bizarre and beautiful in its venality and
in its devotion to immediate gratification, a place the tone of which is set
by mobsters and call girls and ladies' room attendants with amyl nitrite
poppers[2] in their uniform pockets. Almost everyone notes that there is
no "time" in Las Vegas, no night and no day and no past and no future
(no Las Vegas casino, however, has taken the obliteration of the ordinary

[1]Refers to a declaration made by President Lyndon Johnson regarding the draft for the Vietnam
conflict (editors' note).
[2]An illegal liquid drug, inhaled through the nose, that originally came in small capsules that
would "pop" upon opening. Known for heightening sexual arousal, it also causes dizziness and
sometimes a blackout (editors' note).

time sense quite so far as Harold's Club in Reno, which for a while issued, at odd intervals in the day and night, mimeographed "bulletins" carrying news from the world outside); neither is there any logical sense of where one is. One is standing on a highway in the middle of a vast hostile desert looking at an eighty-foot sign which blinks "STARDUST" or "CAESAR'S PALACE." Yes, but what does that explain? This geographical implausibility reinforces the sense that what happens there has no connection with "real" life; Nevada cities like Reno and Carson City are ranch towns, Western towns, places behind which there is some historical imperative. But Las Vegas seems to exist only in the eye of the beholder. All of which makes it an extraordinarily stimulating and interesting place, but an odd one in which to want to wear a candlelight satin Priscilla of Boston wedding dress with Chantilly lace insets, tapered sleeves and a detachable modified train.

And yet the Las Vegas wedding business seems to appeal to precisely   3 that impulse. "Sincere and Dignified Since 1954," one wedding chapel advertises. There are nineteen such wedding chapels in Las Vegas, intensely competitive, each offering better, faster, and, by implication, more sincere services than the next: Our Photos Best Anywhere, Your Wedding on A Phonograph Record, Candlelight with Your Ceremony, Honeymoon Accommodations, Free Transportation from Your Motel to Courthouse to Chapel and Return to Motel, Religious or Civil Ceremonies, Dressing Rooms, Flowers, Rings, Announcements, Witnesses Available, and Ample Parking. All of these services, like most others in Las Vegas (sauna baths, payroll-check cashing, chinchilla coats for sale or rent) are offered twenty-four hours a day, seven days a week, presumably on the premise that marriage, like craps, is a game to be played when the table seems hot.

But what strikes one most about the Strip chapels, with their wish-   4 ing wells and stained-glass paper windows and their artificial bouvardia, is that so much of their business is by no means a matter of simple convenience, of late-night liaisons between show girls and baby Crosbys. Of course there is some of that. (One night about eleven o'clock in Las Vegas I watched a bride in an orange minidress and masses of flame-colored hair stumble from a Strip chapel on the arm of her bridegroom, who looked the part of the expendable nephew in the movies like *Miami Syndicate*.[3] "I gotta get the kids," the bride whimpered. "I gotta pick up the sitter, I gotta get to the midnight show." "What you gotta get," the bridegroom said, opening the door of a Cadillac Coupe de Ville and watching her crumple on the seat, "is sober.") But Las Vegas seems to offer something

---

[3]The actual title is *The Miami Story,* a 1954 film about a group of citizens destroying a crime syndicate with the help of a reformed criminal (editors' note).

other than "convenience"; it is merchandising "niceness," the facsimile of proper ritual, to children who do not know how else to find it, how to make the arrangements, how to do it "right." All day and evening long on the Strip, one sees actual wedding parties, waiting under the harsh lights at a crosswalk, standing uneasily in the parking lot of the Frontier while the photographer hired by The Little Church of the West ("Wedding Place of the Stars") certifies the occasion, takes the picture: the bride in a veil and white satin pumps, the bridegroom usually in a white dinner jacket, and even an attendant or two, a sister or a best friend in hot-pink *peau de soie,* a flirtation veil, a carnation nosegay. "When I Fall in Love It Will Be Forever," the organist plays, and then a few bars of *Lohengrin.* The mother cries; the stepfather, awkward in his role, invites the chapel hostess to join them for a drink at the Sands. The hostess declines with a professional smile; she has already transferred her interest to the group waiting outside. One bride out, another in, and again the sign goes up on the chapel door: "One moment please—Wedding."

I sat next to one such wedding party in a Strip restaurant the last   5
time I was in Las Vegas. The marriage had just taken place; the bride still wore her dress, the mother her corsage. A bored waiter poured out a few swallows of pink champagne ("on the house") for everyone but the bride, who was too young to be served. "You'll need something with more kick than that," the bride's father said with heavy jocularity to his new son-in-law; the ritual jokes about the wedding night had a certain Panglossian character, since the bride was clearly several months pregnant. Another round of pink champagne, this time not on the house, and the bride began to cry. "It was just as nice," she sobbed, "as I hoped and dreamed it would be."

Jonathan Swift

The Irish author and journalist Jonathan Swift (1667–1745) graduated from Trinity College in Dublin and became a priest in the Church of Ireland, the Irish branch of the Anglican Church. He served as dean of St. Patrick's Cathedral in Dublin from 1713 to 1742. Swift is best known for his satirical writings about the injustices imposed on the people of Ireland by the English. Most of his writings were published anonymously. His two most famous works are *Gulliver's Travels* (1726), a social satire about human nature and the politics of Ireland and Britain, and "A Modest Proposal" (1729), a disturbing, unforgettable satire meant to bring attention to the extreme poverty and starvation suffered by the Irish people.

A Modest Proposal

For Preventing the Children of Poor People in Ireland from Being a Burden to Their Parents or Country, and for Making Them Beneficial to the Public

It is a melancholy object to those who walk through this great town[1] or travel in the country, when they see the streets, the roads, and cabin doors, crowded with beggars of the female sex, followed by three, four, or six children, all in rags and importuning every passenger for an alms. These mothers, instead of being able to work for their honest livelihood, are forced to employ all their time in strolling to beg sustenance for their helpless infants: who as they grow up either turn thieves for want of work, or leave their dear native country to fight for the Pretender[2] in Spain, or sell themselves to the Barbadoes.[3]

I think it is agreed by all parties that this prodigious number of children in the arms, or on the backs, or at the heels of their mothers, and frequently of their fathers, is in the present deplorable state of the kingdom a very great additional grievance; and, therefore, whoever could find out a fair, cheap, and easy method of making these children sound, useful members of the commonwealth, would deserve so well of the public as to have his statue set up for a preserver of the nation.

But my intention is very far from being confined to provide only for the children of professed beggars; it is of a much greater extent, and shall take in the whole number of infants at a certain age who are born of parents in effect as little able to support them as those who demand our charity in the streets.

As to my own part, having turned my thoughts for many years upon this important subject, and maturely weighed the several schemes of other projectors,[4] I have always found them grossly mistaken in the computation. It is true, a child just dropped from its dam may be supported by her milk for a solar year, with little other nourishment; at most not above the value of 2s.,[5] which the mother may certainly get, or the value in scraps, by her

---

[1] The "great town" is Dublin, and the country is Ireland (editors' note).
[2] James Francis Edward Stuart, the Catholic son of King James II, was an unsuccessful claimant to the English throne, and many in Ireland, a Catholic country, were loyal to him (editors' note).
[3] Because of the poverty in Ireland, many Irish emigrated to the West Indies as indentured servants (editors' note).
[4] *Projector* is an archaic term for a person who plans and schemes (editors' note).
[5] The abbreviation means "2 shillings" (48 pennies); there are 20 shillings (240 pennies) in a British pound (editors' note).

lawful occupation of begging; and it is exactly at one year old that I propose to provide for them in such a manner as instead of being a charge upon their parents or the parish, or wanting food and raiment for the rest of their lives, they shall on the contrary contribute to the feeding, and partly to the clothing, of many thousands.

There is likewise another great advantage in my scheme, that it will prevent those voluntary abortions, and that horrid practice of women murdering their bastard children, alas! too frequent among us! sacrificing the poor innocent babes I doubt more to avoid the expense than the shame, which would move tears and pity in the most savage and inhuman breast. 5

The number of souls in this kingdom[6] being usually reckoned one million and a half, of these I calculate there may be about two hundred thousand couple whose wives are breeders; from which number I subtract thirty thousand couples who are able to maintain their own children, although I apprehend there cannot be so many, under the present distresses of the kingdom; but this being granted, there will remain an hundred and seventy thousand breeders. I again subtract fifty thousand for those women who miscarry, or whose children die by accident or disease within the year. There only remains one hundred and twenty thousand children of poor parents annually born. The question therefore is, how this number shall be reared and provided for, which, as I have already said, under the present situation of affairs, is utterly impossible by all the methods hitherto proposed. For we can neither employ them in handicraft or agriculture; we neither build houses (I mean in the country) nor cultivate land: they can very seldom pick up a livelihood by stealing, till they arrive at six years old, except where they are of towardly[7] parts, although I confess they learn the rudiments much earlier, during which time, they can however be properly looked upon only as probationers, as I have been informed by a principal gentleman in the county of Cavan,[8] who protested to me that he never knew above one or two instances under the age of six, even in a part of the kingdom so renowned for the quickest proficiency in that art. 6

I am assured by our merchants, that a boy or a girl before twelve years old is no salable commodity; and even when they come to this age they will not yield above three pounds, or three pounds and half-a-crown[9] at most on the exchange; which cannot turn to account either to the parents or kingdom, the charge of nutriment and rags having been at least four times that value. 7

I shall now therefore humbly propose my own thoughts, which I hope will not be liable to the least objection. 8

[6]By "kingdom" Swift means Ireland (editors' note).
[7]*Towardly* is an archaic word meaning "compliant" (editors' note).
[8]Cavan is a county in Ireland (editors' note).
[9]Half a crown equals 2.5 shillings, or 30 pennies (editors' note).

I have been assured by a very knowing American of my acquaintance 9 in London, that a young healthy child well nursed is at a year old a most delicious, nourishing, and wholesome food, whether stewed, roasted, baked, or boiled; and I make no doubt that it will equally serve in a fricassee or a ragout.

I do therefore humbly offer it to public consideration that of the hun- 10 dred and twenty thousand children already computed, twenty thousand may be reserved for breed, whereof only one-fourth part to be males; which is more than we allow to sheep, black cattle or swine; and my reason is, that these children are seldom the fruits of marriage, a circumstance not much regarded by our savages, therefore one male will be sufficient to serve four females. That the remaining hundred thousand may, at a year old, be offered in the sale to the persons of quality and fortune through the kingdom; always advising the mother to let them suck plentifully in the last month, so as to render them plump and fat for a good table. A child will make two dishes at an entertainment for friends; and when the family dines alone, the fore or hind quarter will make a reasonable dish, and seasoned with a little pepper or salt will be very good boiled on the fourth day, especially in winter.

I have reckoned upon a medium that a child just born will weigh 11 12 pounds, and in a solar year, if tolerably nursed, increaseth to 28 pounds.

I grant this food will be somewhat dear, and therefore very proper for 12 landlords, who, as they have already devoured most of the parents, seem to have the best title to the children.

Infant's flesh will be in season throughout the year, but more plentiful 13 in March, and a little before and after; for we are told by a grave author, an eminent French physician,[10] that fish being a prolific diet, there are more children born in Roman Catholic countries about nine months after Lent than at any other season; therefore, reckoning a year after Lent, the markets will be more glutted than usual, because the number of popish infants is at least three to one in this kingdom: and therefore it will have one other collateral advantage, by lessening the number of papists among us.

I have already computed the charge of nursing a beggar's child (in 14 which list I reckon all cottagers, laborers, and four-fifths of the farmers) to be about two shillings per annum, rags included; and I believe no gentleman would repine to give ten shillings for the carcass of a good fat child, which, as I have said, will make four dishes of excellent nutritive meat, when he hath only some particular friend or his own family to dine with him. Thus the squire will learn to be a good landlord, and grow popular among his tenants; the mother will have eight shillings net profit, and be fit for work till she produces another child.

---

[10]Swift is referring to François Rabelais, a writer of the French Renaissance who was known for his bawdy and satirical works (editors' note).

Those who are more thrifty (as I must confess the times require) may   15
flay the carcass; the skin of which artificially dressed will make admirable
gloves for ladies, and summer boots for fine gentlemen.

As to our city of Dublin, shambles[11] may be appointed for this purpose   16
in the most convenient parts of it, and butchers we may be assured will not
be wanting; although I rather recommend buying the children alive, and
dressing them hot from the knife, as we do roasting pigs.

A very worthy person, a true lover of his country, and whose virtues   17
I highly esteem, was lately pleased in discoursing on this matter to offer a
refinement upon my scheme. He said that many gentlemen of this kingdom,
having of late destroyed their deer, he conceived that the want of venison
might be well supplied by the bodies of young lads and maidens, not exceed-
ing fourteen years of age nor under twelve; so great a number of both sexes
in every country being now ready to starve for want of work and service; and
these to be disposed of by their parents, if alive, or otherwise by their nearest
relations. But with due deference to so excellent a friend and so deserving
a patriot, I cannot be altogether in his sentiments; for as to the males, my
American acquaintance assured me, from frequent experience, that their
flesh was generally tough and lean, like that of our schoolboys by continual
exercise, and their taste disagreeable; and to fatten them would not answer
the charge. Then as to the females, it would, I think, with humble submis-
sion be a loss to the public, because they soon would become breeders
themselves; and besides, it is not improbable that some scrupulous people
might be apt to censure such a practice (although indeed very unjustly), as a
little bordering upon cruelty; which, I confess, hath always been with me the
strongest objection against any project, however so well intended.

But in order to justify my friend, he confessed that this expedient   18
was put into his head by the famous Psalmanazar,[12] a native of the island
Formosa, who came from thence to London above twenty years ago, and
in conversation told my friend, that in his country when any young person
happened to be put to death, the executioner sold the carcass to persons of
quality as a prime dainty; and that in his time the body of a plump girl of
fifteen, who was crucified for an attempt to poison the emperor, was sold to
his imperial majesty's prime minister of state, and other great mandarins of
the court, in joints from the gibbet, at four hundred crowns. Neither indeed
can I deny, that if the same use were made of several plump young girls in
this town, who without one single groat to their fortunes cannot stir abroad
without a chair, and appear at playhouse and assemblies in foreign fineries
which they never will pay for, the kingdom would not be the worse.

[11]*Shambles* is an archaic word meaning "slaughterhouse" (editors' note).
[12]The Frenchman George Psalmanazar impersonated a native Formosan among the British
(editors' note).

Some persons of a desponding spirit are in great concern about that 19
vast number of poor people, who are aged, diseased, or maimed, and I have
been desired to employ my thoughts what course may be taken to ease the
nation of so grievous an encumbrance. But I am not in the least pain upon
that matter, because it is very well known that they are every day dying and
rotting by cold and famine, and filth and vermin, as fast as can be reasonably expected. And as to the young laborers, they are now in as hopeful a
condition; they cannot get work, and consequently pine away for want of
nourishment, to a degree that if at any time they are accidentally hired to
common labor, they have not strength to perform it; and thus the country
and themselves are happily delivered from the evils to come.

I have too long digressed, and therefore shall return to my subject. I think 20
the advantages by the proposal which I have made are obvious and many,
as well as of the highest importance. For first, as I have already observed,
it would greatly lessen the number of papists, with whom we are yearly
overrun, being the principal breeders of the nation as well as our most dangerous
enemies; and who stay at home on purpose with a design to deliver the
kingdom to the Pretender, hoping to take their advantage by the absence of
so many good protestants, who have chosen rather to leave their country than
stay at home and pay tithes against their conscience to an episcopal curate.

Secondly, The poorer tenants will have something valuable of their 21
own, which by law may be made liable to distress[13] and help to pay their
landlord's rent, their corn and cattle being already seized, and money a thing
unknown.

Thirdly, Whereas the maintenance of an hundred thousand children, 22
from two years old and upward, cannot be computed at less than ten shillings a-piece per annum, the nation's stock will be thereby increased fifty
thousand pounds per annum, beside the profit of a new dish introduced to
the tables of all gentlemen of fortune in the kingdom who have any refinement in taste. And the money will circulate among ourselves, the goods
being entirely of our own growth and manufacture.

Fourthly, The constant breeders, beside the gain of eight shillings 23
sterling per annum by the sale of their children, will be rid of the charge of
maintaining them after the first year.

Fifthly, This food would likewise bring great custom to taverns; where 24
the vintners will certainly be so prudent as to procure the best receipts for
dressing it to perfection, and consequently have their houses frequented by
all the fine gentlemen, who justly value themselves upon their knowledge in
good eating: and a skilful cook, who understands how to oblige his guests,
will contrive to make it as expensive as they please.

---

[13]"Distress," now regulated by statutes, is the right of a landlord to seize property in payment
of a debt (editors' note).

Sixthly, This would be a great inducement to marriage, which all   25
wise nations have either encouraged by rewards or enforced by laws and
penalties. It would increase the care and tenderness of mothers toward
their children, when they were sure of a settlement for life to the poor
babes, provided in some sort by the public, to their annual profit instead
of expense. We should see an honest emulation among the married
women, which of them could bring the fattest child to the market. Men
would become as fond of their wives during the time of their pregnancy
as they are now of their mares in foal, their cows in calf, their sows when
they are ready to farrow; nor offer to beat or kick them (as is too frequent
a practice) for fear of a miscarriage.

Many other advantages might be enumerated. For instance, the addition   26
of some thousand carcasses in our exportation of barreled beef, the propa-
gation of swine's flesh, and improvement in the art of making good bacon,
so much wanted among us by the great destruction of pigs, too frequent at
our tables; which are no way comparable in taste or magnificence to a well-
grown, fat, yearling child, which roasted whole will make a considerable
figure at a lord mayor's feast or any other public entertainment. But this and
many others I omit, being studious of brevity.

Supposing that one thousand families in this city, would be constant   27
customers for Infant's Flesh, besides others who might have it at merry
meetings, particularly at weddings and christenings, I compute that Dublin
would take off annually about twenty thousand carcasses, and the rest of the
Kingdom (where probably they will be sold somewhat cheaper) the remaining eighty thousand.

I can think of no one objection, that will possibly be raised against   28
this proposal, unless it should be urged, that the number of people will
be thereby much lessened in the Kingdom. This I freely own, and 'twas
indeed one principal design in offering it to the world. I desire the reader
will observe, that I calculate my remedy for this one individual kingdom
of Ireland, and for no other that ever was, is, or I think, ever can be upon
Earth. Therefore let no man talk to me of other expedients:[14] of taxing our
absentees at five shillings a pound: of using neither clothes, nor household
furniture, except what is of our own growth and manufacture: of utterly
rejecting the materials and instruments that promote foreign luxury: of cur-
ing the expensiveness of pride, vanity, idleness, and gaming in our women:
of introducing a vein of parsimony, prudence and temperance: of learning to
love our country, wherein we differ even from Laplanders, and the inhabitants of Topinamboo:[15] of quitting our animosities, and factions, nor act any

---

[14]The "expedients" Swift now enumerates are ideas he himself had formerly proposed (editors'
note).
[15]*Topinamboo* refers to the indigenous peoples of Brazil (editors' note).

longer like the Jews, who were murdering one another at the very moment their city[16] was taken: of being a little cautious not to sell our country and consciences for nothing: of teaching our landlords to have at least one degree of mercy towards their tenants. Lastly, of putting a spirit of honesty, industry, and skill into our shop-keepers, who, if a resolution could now be taken to buy only our native goods, would immediately unite to cheat and exact upon us in the price, the measure and the goodness, nor could ever yet be brought to make one fair proposal of just dealing, though often and earnestly invited to it.

Therefore I repeat, let no man talk to me of these and the like expedients, till he hath at least some glimpse of hope, that there will ever be some hearty and sincere attempt to put them into practice.   29

But as to myself, having been wearied out for many years with offering vain, idle, visionary thoughts, and at length despairing of success, I fortunately fell upon this proposal, which as it is wholly new, so it hath something solid and real, of no expense and little trouble, full in our own power, and whereby we can incur no danger in disobliging England. For this kind of commodity will not bear exportation, the flesh being of too tender a consistence, to admit a long continuance in salt, although perhaps I could name a country,[17] which would be glad to eat up our whole nation without it.   30

After all, I am not so violently bent upon my own opinion as to reject any offer proposed by wise men, which shall be found equally innocent, cheap, easy, and effectual. But before something of that kind shall be advanced in contradiction to my scheme, and offering a better, I desire the author or authors will be pleased maturely to consider two points. First, as things now stand, how they will be able to find food and raiment for an hundred thousand useless mouths and backs. And secondly, there being a round million of creatures in human figure throughout this kingdom, whose whole subsistence put into a common stock would leave them in debt two millions of pounds sterling, adding those who are beggars by profession to the bulk of farmers, cottagers, and laborers, with their wives and children who are beggars in effect: I desire those politicians who dislike my overture, and may perhaps be so bold as to attempt an answer, that they will first ask the parents of these mortals, whether they would not at this day think it a great happiness to have been sold for food, at a year old in the manner I prescribe, and thereby have avoided such a perpetual scene of misfortunes as they have since gone through by the oppression of landlords, the impossibility of paying rent without money or trade, the want of common sustenance,   31

---

[16]Jerusalem was captured and King Solomon's Temple destroyed by the Roman Emperor Titus in 70 C.E. (editors' note).
[17]The country Swift alludes to is England (editors' note).

with neither house nor clothes to cover them from the inclemencies of the weather, and the most inevitable prospect of entailing the like or greater miseries upon their breed for ever.

I profess, in the sincerity of my heart, that I have not the least personal interest in endeavoring to promote this necessary work, having no other motive than the public good of my country, by advancing our trade, providing for infants, relieving the poor, and giving some pleasure to the rich. I have no children by which I can propose to get a single penny; the youngest being nine years old, and my wife past child-bearing.   32

MyWritingLab Visit Chapter 12, "Combining the Patterns," in MyWritingLab to test your understanding of the chapter objectives.

A GUIDE TO USING SOURCES

Many assignments in *The Longman Reader* suggest that you might want to do some research in the library or on the Internet. Such research enlarges your perspective and enables you to move beyond off-the-top-of-your-head opinions to those that are firmly supported. This appendix will be useful if you do decide to draw on outside sources when preparing an essay. The appendix explains how to (1) evaluate articles, books, and Web sources; (2) analyze and synthesize sources you find; (3) use quotation, summary, and paraphrase correctly to avoid plagiarism; (4) integrate source material into your writing; and (5) document print, Internet, and other sources.

EVALUATING SOURCE MATERIALS

The success of your essay will depend in large part on the evidence you provide. (See Chapter 2 on the characteristics of evidence.) Evidence from sources, whether print or electronic, needs to be evaluated for its relevance, timeliness, seriousness of approach, and objectivity.

Relevance

Titles can be misleading. To determine if a source is relevant for your essay, review it carefully. For a book, read the preface or introduction, skim the table of contents, and check the index to see whether the book is likely to contain information that's important to your topic. If the source is an influential text in the field, you may want to read the entire book for background and specific ideas. Or if a text devotes just a few pages to your topic, you might read those pages, taking notes on important information. For an article, read the abstract of the article, if there is one. If not, read the first few paragraphs and skim the rest to determine if it might be useful. For a website or other nonprint source, skim the site to see if it includes pertinent, reliable information that might help you write a stronger essay. When considering using information from a website, you must make certain that the site is reputable and that the information it includes has been recently updated. As you read a source, make use of the reading checklists in Chapter 1 to get the most from the material. If a source turns out to be irrelevant, just make a note to yourself that you consulted the source and found it didn't relate to your topic.

Timeliness

To some extent, the topic and the kind of research you're doing will determine whether a work is outdated. If you're researching a historical topic such as the internment of Japanese Americans during World War II, you would most likely consult sources published in the 1940s and 1950s, as well as more up-to-date sources. In contrast, if you're investigating a recent scientific development—cloning, for example—it would make sense to restrict your search to current material. For most college research, a source older than ten years is considered outdated unless it was the first to present key concepts in a field.

Seriousness of Approach

As you review a source, ask yourself if it is suitable for your purpose and your instructor's requirements. Articles from general periodicals (newspapers and widely read magazines such as *The New Yorker* and *The Atlantic*) and serious publications (such as *National Geographic* and *Scientific American*) may be sufficient to provide support in a personal essay. But an in-depth research paper in your major field of study will require material from scholarly journals and texts (for example, *American Journal of Public Health* and *Film Quarterly*).

Objectivity

As you examine your sources for possible bias, keep in mind that a strong conclusion or opinion is not in itself a sign of bias. As long as a writer doesn't ignore opposing positions or distort evidence, a source can't be considered biased. A biased source presents only those facts that fit the writer's predetermined conclusions. Such a source is often marked by emotionally charged language. Publications and websites sponsored by special-interest groups—a particular industry, religious association, advocacy group, or political party—are usually biased. Reading such sources does familiarize you with a specific point of view, but remember that contrary evidence has probably been ignored or skewed. The following checklist provides some questions to ask yourself as you evaluate print sources.

✓ EVALUATING ARTICLES AND BOOKS: A CHECKLIST

❑ If the work is scholarly, is the author well-known in his or her field? Is the author affiliated with an accredited college or university? A nonscholarly author, such as a journalist, should have a reputation for objectivity and thoroughness.

❑ Is the publication reputable? If a scholarly publication is *peer-reviewed*, experts in the field have a chance to comment on the author's work before it is published. Nonscholarly publications such as newspapers and magazines should be well-established and widely respected.

❑ Is the source recently published and up to date? Alternatively, is it a classic in its field? In the sciences and social sciences, recent publication is particularly critical.

❑ Is the material at an appropriate level—neither too scholarly nor too general—for your purpose and audience? Make sure you can understand and digest the material for your readers.

❑ Does the information appear to be accurate, objectively presented, and complete? Statistics and other evidence should not be distorted or manipulated to make a point.

Special care must be taken to evaluate the worth of material found on the Web. Electronic documents often seem to appear out of nowhere and can disappear without a trace. And anyone—from scholar to con artist—can create a Web page. How, then, do you know if an Internet source is credible? The following checklist provides some questions to ask when you work with online material.

✓ EVALUATING INTERNET MATERIALS: A CHECKLIST

❑ Who is the author of the material? Does the author offer his or her credentials in a résumé or biographical note? Do these credentials qualify the author to provide reliable information on the topic? Does the author provide an e-mail address or a "Contact Us" link so you can request more information? The less you know about an author, the more suspicious you should be about using the data.

❏ Can you verify the accuracy of the information presented? Does the author refer to studies or to other authors you can investigate? If the author doesn't cite other works or other points of view, that may suggest the document is opinionated and one-sided. In such a case, it's important to track down material addressing alternative points of view.

❏ Who's sponsoring the website? Check for an "About Us" link on the home page, which may tell you the site's sponsorship and goals. Many sites are established by organizations—businesses, agencies, lobby groups—as well as by individuals. If a sponsor pushes a single point of view, you should use the material with great caution. Once again, make an extra effort to locate material addressing other sides of the issue.

❏ What does the Internet address (URL) of the site tell you? A URL ending with .com indicates a commercial website, which will probably be interested in selling a product or service. The URL extension .edu indicates an educational institution. Though educational institutions can be trustworthy, remember that often students at a university can post documents using their institution's Web address; such materials are not necessarily reliable. A URL that includes .gov identifies a government site. These sites can be valuable for statistical information and background material, but they may not include all points of view. Finally, .org in a URL points to a nonprofit organization. Nonprofits may support worthy causes, but they usually advocate a specific position and don't always provide counterarguments.

❏ Is the cited information up to date? Being on the Internet doesn't guarantee that information is current. To assess the timeliness of Internet materials, check at the top or bottom of the document for copyright date, publication date, or revision date. Those dates will help you determine whether the material is recent enough for your purposes.

❏ Is the information original or taken from another source? Is quoted material accurate? Some Web pages may reproduce material from other sources without identifying them. Watch out for possible plagiarism. Nonoriginal material should be accurately quoted and acknowledged on the site.

ANALYZING AND SYNTHESIZING SOURCE MATERIAL

As you read your sources and begin taking notes, you may not be able to judge immediately how helpful a source will be. At that time, you probably should take fairly detailed notes. After a while, you'll become more selective.

You'll find that you are thinking more critically about the material you read, isolating information and ideas that are important to your thesis, and formulating questions about your topic.

Analyzing Source Material

To begin with, you should spend some time analyzing each source for its central ideas, main supporting points, and key details. (See Chapter 1 for tips on effective reading techniques.) As you read, keep asking yourself how the source's content meshes with your working thesis and with what you know about your subject. Does the source repeat what you already know, or does it supply new information? If a source provides detailed support for important ideas or suggests a new angle on your subject, read carefully and take full notes. If the source refers to other sources, you might decide to consult those.

Make sure you have all necessary citation information for *every* source you consult. (See "How to Document: MLA List of Works Cited" in this appendix for information you will need for documenting citations.) Then, as you read relevant sources, make sure to take plenty of notes. Articles you have printed out can be highlighted and annotated with your comments. (See "Second Reading: A Checklist" in Chapter 1 for annotation techniques.) In addition, you may wish to photocopy selected book pages to annotate or copy and paste material from online sources into a word processing document. However, you will also have to take handwritten or typewritten notes on some material. When you do so, make sure to put quotation marks around direct quotes. Annotating and note-taking will help you think through and respond to the source's ideas. (For help with analyzing images in your sources—for example, graphs and illustrations—see Chapter 1.)

Your notes might include any of the following: facts, statistics, anecdotal accounts, expert opinion, case studies, surveys, reports, results of experiments. When you are recording data, check that you have copied the figures accurately. Also note how and by whom the statistics were gathered, as well as where and when they were first reported.

Take down your source's interpretation of the statistics, but be sure to scrutinize the interpretation for any "spin" that distorts them. For example, if 80 percent of Americans think violent crime is our number-one national problem, that doesn't mean that violent crime actually *is* our main problem; it simply means that 80 percent of the people *polled* think it is. And if a "majority" of people think that homelessness should be among our top national priorities, it may be that a mere 51 percent—a bare majority—feel that way. In short, make sure the statistics mean what your sources say they mean. If you have any reason to suspect distortion, it's a good idea to corroborate such figures elsewhere; tracking down the original source of a statistic is the best way to ensure that numbers are being reported fairly.

Synthesizing Source Materials

As you go along, you may come across material that challenges your working thesis and forces you to think differently about your subject. Indeed, the more you learn, the more difficult it may be to state anything conclusively. This is a sign that you're synthesizing and weighing all the evidence. In time, the confusion will lessen, and you'll emerge with a clearer understanding of your subject.

Suppose you find sources that take positions contrary to the one that you had previously considered credible. When you come across such conflicting material, you can be sure you've identified a pivotal issue within your topic. To decide which position is more valid, you need to take good notes or carefully annotate your photocopies, electronic materials, and printed documents. Then evaluate the sources for bias. On this basis alone, you might discover serious flaws in one or several sources. Also compare the key points and supporting evidence in the sources. Where do they agree? Where do they disagree? Does one source argue against another's position, perhaps even discrediting some of the opposing view's evidence? The answers to these questions may very well cause you to question the quality, completeness, or fairness of one or more sources.

To resolve such a conflict, you can also research your subject more fully. For example, if your conflicting sources are at the general or serious level, you should probably turn to more scholarly sources. By referring to more authoritative material, you may be able to determine which of the conflicting sources is more valid.

When you attempt to resolve discrepancies among sources, be sure not to let your own bias come into play. Try not to favor one position over the other simply because it supports your working thesis. Remember, your goal is to arrive at the most well-founded position you can. In fact, researching a topic may lead you to change your original viewpoint. In this case, you shouldn't hesitate to revise your working thesis to accord with the evidence you gather.

☑ ANALYZING AND SYNTHESIZING SOURCE MATERIAL: A CHECKLIST

❏ As you read sources, note central ideas, main supporting points, and key details.

❏ Make sure to record all bibliographic information carefully, identify any quotations, and copy statistical data accurately.

❏ Annotate or take full notes on sources that deal with ideas that are important to your topic or suggest a new angle on your subject.

❏ Examine statistics and other facts for any distortions.

❏ Carefully read material that causes you to take a different view of your subject. Keep an open mind and do additional research to confirm or change your thesis.

USING QUOTATION, SUMMARY, AND PARAPHRASE WITHOUT PLAGIARIZING

Your essay should contain your own ideas stated in your own words. To support your ideas, you can introduce evidence from sources in three ways—with direct quotations, summaries, and paraphrases. Knowing how and when to use each type is an important part of the research process.

Quotation

A *quotation* reproduces, word for word, that which is stated in a source. Although quoting can demonstrate the thoroughness with which you reviewed relevant sources, don't simply use one quotation after another without any intervening commentary or analysis. To do so would mean you hadn't evaluated and synthesized your sources sufficiently. Aim for one to three quotations from each major source; more than that can create a problem in your essay. Consider using quotations in the following situations:

- If a source's ideas are unusual or controversial, include a representative quotation in your essay to show you have accurately conveyed the source's viewpoint.
- Record a quotation if a source's wording is so eloquent or convincing that it would lose its power if you restated the material in your own words.
- Use a quotation if a source's ideas reinforce your own conclusions. If the source is a respected authority, such a quotation will lend authority to your own ideas.
- In an analysis of a literary work, use quotation from the work to support your interpretations.

Remember to clearly identify quotes in your notes so that you don't confuse the quotation with your own comments when you begin drafting your paper. Record the author's statement exactly as it appears in the original work, right down to the punctuation. In addition, make sure to properly document the quotation. See "How to Document: MLA In-Text References" and "How to Document: MLA List of Works Cited" on pages 592–604.

Original Passage 1

In this excerpt from *The Canon: A Whirligig Tour of the Beautiful Basics of Science*, by Natalie Angier, page 22, the author is discussing the subject of scientific reasoning.

> Much of the reason for its success is founded on another fundamental of the scientific bent. Scientists accept, quite staunchly, that there is a reality capable of being understood, and understood in a way that can be shared with and agreed upon by others. We can call this "objective" reality if we like, as opposed to subjective reality, or opinion, or "whimsical set of predilections." The concept is deceptive, however, because it implies that the two are discrete entities with remarkably little in common.

Original Passage 2

The following is the entire text of Amendment I of the Constitution of the United States.

> Congress shall make no law respecting an establishment of religion, or prohibiting the free exercise thereof; or abridging the freedom of speech, or of the press; or the right of the people peaceably to assemble, and to petition the Government for a redress of grievances.

Acceptable Uses of Quotation   For a paper on perceptions of freedom, a student writer used this quotation (highlighted) in its entirety:

The First Amendment of the Constitution of the United States delineates what were thought to be society's most cherished freedoms: "Congress shall make no law respecting an establishment of religion, or prohibiting the free exercise thereof; or abridging the freedom of speech, or of the press; or the right of people peaceably to assemble, and to petition the Government for a redress of grievance."

In an essay on science education in schools, one student writer used this quotation:

In explaining scientific reasoning, Angier says, "Scientists accept, quite staunchly, that there is a reality capable of being understood, and understood in a way that can be shared with and agreed upon by others" (22).

Notice that both quotations are reproduced exactly as they appear in the source and are enclosed in quotation marks. The parenthetical reference to the page number in the second example is a necessary part of documenting the quotation. (See pages 592–595 for more on in-text references.) The first example requires no page number because quotations from well-known sources such as the Constitution and the Bible are sufficiently identified by their own numbering systems, in this case, the text's use of "First Amendment of the Constitution."

Incorrect Use of Quotation   Another student writer, attempting to provide some background on the scientific method, used the source material incorrectly.

To understand the scientific method, it is important to understand that scientists believe there is a reality capable of being understood (Angier 22).

The phrase "a reality capable of being understood," which gives the source's exact words, should have quotations around it. Even though the source is identified correctly in the parenthetical reference, the lack of quotation marks actually constitutes plagiarism, which is the use of someone's words or ideas without proper acknowledgement. (See pages 583–584 to see the discussion in this appendix.)

Summary

A *summary* is a condensation of a larger work. You extract the essence of someone's ideas and restate it in your own words. The length of a summary depends on your topic and purpose, but generally a summary is much shorter than the item you are summarizing. For example, you may summarize the plot of a novel in a few short paragraphs, or you might summarize a reading from this book in a few sentences. You might choose to use a summary for the following reasons:

- To give a capsule presentation of the main ideas of a book or an article, use a summary.
- If the relevant information is too long to be quoted in full, use a summary.
- Use a summary to give abbreviated information about such elements such as plot, background, or history.
- To present an idea from a source without including all the supporting details, use a summary.

To summarize a source, read the material; jot down or underline the main idea, main supporting points, and key details; and then restate the information in shortened form in your own words. Your summary should follow the order of information in the original. Also, be sure to treat any original wording as quotations in your summary. A caution: When summarizing, don't use the ellipsis to signal that you have omitted some ideas. The ellipsis is used only when quoting.

Original Passage 3

This three-paragraph excerpt is from Michael Marlow and Sherzod Abdukadirov's "Government Intervention Will Not Solve Our Obesity Problem," published as a blog post in *U.S. News and World Report*, on June 5, 2012.

> It is clear the United States is facing a rising obesity problem. But the challenge remains: We have yet to determine a successful way to tackle it. According to the National Center for Health Statistics, the prevalence of obesity among adults more than doubled from 13.4 percent in 1960 to 34.3 percent in 2008 (Ogden and Carroll). A new report released this month by the *American Journal of Preventive Medicine* predicts that by 2030, 42 percent of Americans will be obese and 11 percent will be severely obese, or 100 pounds overweight (Finkelstein, Khavjou et al. 563).
>
> Despite the myriad of studies showing American obesity is increasing, research does not clearly support that government can solve this complex problem. And yet, government solutions that provide information the public already knows—weight gain occurs when we eat too much and exercise too little—have been the focus to eliminate this epidemic.
>
> Not only is this method not solving the problem, we may actually be increasing the social stigma associated with weight gain. Rather than pursuing a one-size-fits-all solution, we need to push back against government intervention, and allow people to find the solution that best meets their needs.

Acceptable Use of Summary   The following summary was written by a student working on a paper related to obesity in the United States.

In their blog post "Government Intervention Will Not Solve Our Obesity Problem," Marlow and Abdukadirov assert that while there is no doubt that obesity is a growing problem in the United States, government should not attempt to find a blanket solution that will supposedly work for everyone. Solutions to the problem of obesity must be determined by individuals and must be based on what works best for them.

The writer gives the gist of Marlow and Abdukadirov's argument in his own words. There is no parenthetical reference at the end because the reader has already referenced the authors, as well as the title of the selection, and there is no page number for the Web source. (See pages 592–595 for more on in-text references.)

Incorrect Use of Summary   The student who wrote the following has incorrectly summarized ideas from the Marlow and Abdukadirov passage.

Who are the obese? According to Marlow and Abdukadirov, they are the people who do not control the amount of food they consume and do not exercise regularly. Because they fail to understand what makes them obese, they do not know what to do about the problem.

The writer was so determined to put things her way that she added her own ideas and ended up distorting Marlowe and Abdukadirov's meaning. For instance, note the way she emphasizes that obese individuals don't understand what causes them to gain weight. Marlowe and Abdukadirov do just the opposite and highlight that although people understand the causes of weight gain, that understanding alone is not enough to help them control obesity.

Paraphrase

Unlike a summary, which condenses the original, a *paraphrase* recasts material by using roughly the same number of words and retaining the same level of detail as the original. The challenge with paraphrasing is to capture the information without using the original language of the material. Paraphrasing is useful in these situations:

- If you want to include specific details from a source but you want to avoid using a long quotation or string of quotations, paraphrase the material.
- To interpret or explain material as you include it, try using a paraphrase.
- Paraphrase to avoid injecting another person's style into your own writing.

One way to compose a paraphrase is to read the original passage and then set it aside while you draft your restatement. As you write, make sure to use appropriate synonyms and to vary the sentence structure from that of the original. Then compare the passages to make sure you have not used any of the original language, unless you have enclosed it in quotation marks.

Acceptable Use of Paraphrase   In the following example, the student writer paraphrases the third paragraph of Marlowe and Abdukadirov's original, fitting the restatement into her argument.

Can we find a solution to our nation's obesity problem? Two leading researchers urge us to reject the idea that government should take charge of finding "a one-size-fits-all solution." They stress that this approach only makes the problem worse. Obesity is a complex issue that cannot be solved with a simple answer. Solutions to obesity must be determined on an individual basis (Marlowe and Abdukadirov).

Note that the paraphrase is roughly the same length as the original. Apart from the single instance of original language, enclosed in quotation marks, the writer has not used phrases or even sentence structures from the original. Notice also that it is easy to see where the paraphrase starts and ends: The phrase "Two leading researchers" begins the paraphrase, and the parenthetical reference ends it. Because the text does not identify the source by name, the source's authors are included in the parenthetical reference.

Incorrect Use of Paraphrase   When preparing the following paraphrase, the student stayed too close to the source and borrowed much of Marlowe and Abdukadirov's language word for word (highlighted). Because the student did not enclose the original phrases in quotation marks, this paraphrase constitutes plagiarism, even though this student acknowledged the authors in the essay. The lack of quotation marks implies that the language is the student's when, in fact, it is Marlowe and Abdukadirov's.

Most Americas clearly understand that the United States is facing a rising obesity problem. Even so, we have yet to figure out how to tackle it. Many individuals are depending on our government to intervene and take charge of the issue, but research does not clearly support that government can solve this complex problem. We need to realize that it is time for us to push back against government intervention, and allow people to find the solution that works best for them.

As the following example shows, another student believed, erroneously, that if he changed a word here and there and jumped from one part of the original text to another, he'd be preparing an effective paraphrase. Note that the language is all Marlow and Abdukadirov's except for the words not highlighted, which are the student's.

It is clear the United States is facing a rising obesity problem, but research does not clearly support that our government can solve this difficult problem. Rather than pursuing a one-size-fits-all solution, we need to resist government intervention, and allow individuals to find the solution that best meets their needs (Marlow and Abdukadirov).

The near-quotes in the two preceding examples are deceptive; the lack of quotation marks suggests that the language is the student's when actually it's substantially (but not exactly) Marlow and Abdukadirov's. Such near-quotes are considered plagiarism, even if, when writing the essay, the student supplies a parenthetical reference citing the source.

☑ USING QUOTATION, SUMMARY, AND PARAPHRASE: A CHECKLIST

❏ For a quotation, give the statement exactly as it was originally written.

❏ Always accompany quotations with your own commentary or analysis.

❏ Don't string quotations together one after the other without intervening text.

❏ Avoid using too many quotations. One to three quotations from any major source is sufficient.

❏ For a summary, restate ideas from the source in your own words.

❏ Keep summaries much shorter than the original material.

❏ Make sure your summary does not distort the meaning or tone of the original.

❏ For a paraphrase, recast ideas with the same level of detail as the original.

❏ Make sure to use your own language in a paraphrase—finding appropriate synonyms and varying sentence structure from that of the original.

❏ Check that any original source language used in a summary or paraphrase is enclosed in quotation marks.

AVOIDING PLAGIARISM

Plagiarism occurs when a writer borrows someone else's ideas, facts, or language but doesn't properly credit that source. Copyright law and the ethics of research require that you give credit to those whose words and ideas you borrow; that is, you must represent the source's words and ideas accurately and provide full documentation (see pages 591–604).

Sometimes, plagiarism is *intentional*. A writer understands that what she is doing is wrong. However, plagiarism can also be *unintentional*.

- Forgetting to use quotation marks around direct quotations is plagiarism.
- Inadvertently omitting a parenthetical reference or a works-cited entry is plagiarism.
- Mistakenly including a source's language in your paraphrase or summary without giving credit is plagiarism.

The consequence—missing or faulty documentation—can undermine your credibility. For one thing, readers may suspect that you're hiding something if you fail to identify your sources clearly. Further, readers planning follow-up research of their own will be perturbed if they have trouble locating your sources. Finally, weak documentation makes it difficult for readers to distinguish your ideas from those of your sources.

You can avoid unintentional plagiarism by taking careful notes on sources you use and making sure you can identify, at every stage in the writing process, which words and ideas are your own and which come from another source.

Some writers may fall into the trap of using "patchwork writing"—that is, stringing together words from one or more sources—which can easily lead to plagiarism. In the first place, if you pile up quotations without adding your own ideas in your own language (or adding only a few words of your own here and there), readers will feel you haven't thought deeply about your subject and don't really have much to say. In addition, patchwork writing can lead to confusion: it's easy to omit quotation marks and forget where your writing ends and someone else's begins, and it's also easy to omit or confuse parenthetical references and works-cited entries. Plagiarism can be the result.

In a college-level course, ignorance is no excuse for plagiarism. As a college student, you must understand how to avoid plagiarism because, whether it is intentional or unintentional, plagiarism can lead to failing a course or even suspension.

To avoid plagiarizing, you must provide proper documentation in the following situations:

- When you include a word-for-word quotation from a source.
- When you paraphrase or summarize ideas or information from a source, unless that material is commonly known and accepted (whether or not you yourself were previously aware of it), or is a matter of historical or scientific record.
- When you combine a summary or paraphrase with a quotation.

One exception to formal documentation occurs in writing for the general public. You may have noticed that although the authors of this book's essays, as well as newspaper and magazine writers, identify sources they have used, some writers don't use full documentation. Academic writers, though, must provide full documentation for all borrowed information.

INTEGRATING SOURCES INTO YOUR WRITING

On the whole, your essay should be written in your own words. As you draft your essay, indicate places where you might want to add evidence from sources to support your ideas. Depending on the source and the support you need, you may choose to use quotations, paraphrases, or summaries to present this evidence, as discussed in the preceding section.

Take care to blend the evidence seamlessly into your own writing through the use of introductions, transitions, and conclusions. At a minimum, each paragraph should have a topic sentence, and it may also be useful to introduce evidence with an attribution, a phrase that identifies the source and forms part of the documentation you will need to use (see pages 585–587).

A quotation, by itself, won't always make your case for you. In addition, you will need to interpret quotations, showing why they are significant and explaining how they support your central points. Indeed, such commentary is often precisely what's needed to blend source material gracefully into your discussion. Also, use quotations sparingly; draw on them only when they dramatically illustrate key points you want to make or when they lend authority to your own conclusions. A string of quotations signals that you haven't sufficiently evaluated and distilled your sources.

Awkward Use of a Quotation   In the following example, note how the quotation is dropped awkwardly into the text, without any transition or commentary. (For an explanation of the parenthetical reference at the end of the quotation, see pages 592–593.)

Recent studies of parenting styles are designed to control researcher bias. "Recent studies screen out researchers whose strongly held attitudes make objectivity difficult" (Layden 10).

Effective Use of Quotation   Adding brief interpretive remarks in this example provides a transition that smoothly merges the quotation with the surrounding material:

Recent studies of parenting styles are designed to control researcher bias. The psychologist Marsha Layden, a harsh critic of earlier studies, acknowledges that nowadays most investigations "screen out researchers whose strongly held beliefs make objectivity difficult" (10).

Introducing a Source

Try to avoid such awkward constructions as these: *According to Michael Marlow and Sherzod Abdukadirov, they say that...*, and *In the blog post by Michael Marlow and Sherzod Abdukadirov, they argue that....* Instead, follow these hints for writing smooth, graceful attributions.

Identifying the Source   An introduction to a source may specify the author's name, it may inform readers of an author's expertise, or it may refer to a source more generally. To call attention to an author who is prominent in the field, important to your argument, or referred to many times in your essay, you may give the author's full name and identifier at the first mention in the text. Then in subsequent mentions, you may give only the last name. Don't use personal titles such as *Mr.* or *Ms.* In the following two examples, language that identifies or explains the source is highlighted.

Natalie Angier, a Pulitzer Prize–winning journalist who writes about science, says that.... Angier goes on to explain....

The leading researchers Michael Marlow and Sherzod Abdukadirov argue that.... As Marlow and Abdukadirov explain....

For other sources, use a more general attribution (highlighted) and include the source's name, along with any page numbers, in the parenthetical citation.

One writer points out...(Angier 22).

According to statistics, 42 percent... (Marlow and Abdukadirov).

As part of an introduction, you may mention the title of the book, article, or other source.

In "Government Intervention Will Not Solve Our Obesity Problem," Marlow and Abdukadirov maintain that...

According to the National Aeronautics and Space Administration (NASA),...

When the author's name is provided in the text, don't repeat the name in the parenthetical reference. (See pages 592–595 for more details on parenthetical references.)

One psychologist who is a harsh critic of earlier studies acknowledges that nowadays most investigations "screen out researchers whose strongly held beliefs make objectivity difficult" (Layden 10).

The psychologist Marsha Layden acknowledges that...(10).

Using Variety in Attributions   Don't always place attributions at the beginning of the sentence; experiment by placing them in the middle or at the end:

To begin to solve our nation's obesity problem, Marlow and Abdukadirov explain, we must "allow people to find the solution that best meets their needs."

Close to half of Americans will be obese by 2030, according to statistics (Marlow and Abdukadirov).

Try not to use a predictable subject-verb sequence (*Marlow and Abdukadirov argue that, Marlow and Abdukadirov explain that*) in all your attributions. Aim for variations such as the following:

The information compiled by Marlow and Abdukadirov shows....

In Marlow and Abdukadirov's opinion,...

Marlow and Abdukadirov's study reveals that....

Rather than repeatedly using the verbs *says* or *writes* in your introductions, seek out more vigorous verbs, making sure the verbs you select are appropriate to the tone and content of the piece you're quoting. The list that follows offers a number of options.

acknowledges	demonstrates	reports
adds	endorses	responds
admits	grants	reveals
argues	implies	says
asserts	insists	shows
believes	maintains	speculates
compares	notes	states
confirms	points out	suggests
contends	questions	wonders
declares	reasons	writes

Shortening or Clarifying Quotations

To make the best use of quotations, you will often need to shorten or excerpt them. It's acceptable to omit parts of quotations as long as you do not change the wording or distort the meaning of the original.

Quoting a Single Word, a Phrase, or Part of a Sentence   Put double quotation marks around a quoted element you are integrating into your own sentence. In the following examples, the quotations are highlighted.

Angier says that to speak of "objective" and "subjective" realities is to imply that these are "discrete entities" (22).

As we try to find a way to curb the rate of obesity in our country, we must keep in mind that "research does not clearly support that government can solve this complex problem," according to Marlow and Abdukadirov.

Omitting Material in the Middle of the Original Sentence   Insert three spaced periods, called an *ellipsis* (. . .), in place of the deleted words. Leave a space before each period and a space after the third period before continuing with the quoted matter.

"Rather than pursuing a one-size fits all solution, we need to . . . allow people to find the solution that best meets their needs" (Marlow and Abdukadirov).

Omitting Material at the End of the Original Sentence   If no parenthetical reference is needed, insert a period before the first ellipsis point and provide the closing quotation mark, as in the first example that follows. If a parenthetical reference is needed, use only the ellipsis and add the period after the parentheses.

The First Amendment of the Constitution of the United States lays the foundation for the doctrine of free speech: "Congress shall make no law respecting an establishment of religion, or prohibiting the free exercise thereof; or abridging the freedom of speech, or of the press...."

In discussing scientific reasoning, Angier states, "We can call this 'objective' reality if we like, as opposed to subjective reality..." (22).

Omitting Material at the Start of a Quotation   No ellipses are required. Simply place the quotation marks where you begin quoting directly. Capitalize the first word if the resulting quotation forms a complete sentence.

"The United States is facing a rising obesity problem," a reality confirmed by leading researchers Michael Marlow and Sherzod Abdukadirov.

Adding Material to a Quotation   If, for the sake of clarity or grammar, you need to add a word or short phrase to a quotation (for example, by changing a verb tense or replacing a vague pronoun with a noun), enclose your insertion in brackets:

Moreover, Angier discredits the concept that "the two [objective reality and subjective reality] are discrete entities with remarkably little in common" (22).

Capitalizing and Punctuating Short Quotations

The way a short quotation is used in a sentence determines whether it begins or doesn't begin with a capital letter and whether it is or isn't preceded by a comma. For the formatting and punctuation of a long (block) quotation, see pages 594–595.

Introducing a Quotation That Can Stand Alone as a Sentence If a quotation can stand alone as a grammatical sentence, capitalize the quotation's first word. Also, precede the quotation with a comma:

Marlow and Abdukadirov observe, "Despite the myriad of studies showing American obesity is increasing, research does not clearly support that government can solve this complex problem."

According to Marlow and Abdukadirov, "Not only is this method not solving the problem, we may actually be increasing the social stigma associated with weight gain."

Using *That*, *Which*, or *Who* (Stated or Implied) If you use *that*, *which*, or *who* to blend a quotation into the structure of your own sentence, don't capitalize the quotation's first word and don't precede it with a comma.

Marlow and Abdukadirov maintain that "research does not clearly support" government intervention.

Angier describes scientists as firmly believing there is "a reality capable of being understood" (22).

Even if the material being quoted originally started with a capital letter, you still use lowercase when incorporating the quotation into your own sentence. Note that in the second example, the word *that* is implied (before the word *there*).

Interrupting a Full-Sentence Quotation with an Attribution Place commas on both sides of the attribution, and resume the quotation with a lowercase letter.

"Rather than pursuing a one-size-fits-all solution," Marlow and Abdukadirov comment, "we need to push back against government intervention, and allow people to find the solution that best meets their needs."

Using a Quotation with a Quoted Word or Phrase When a source you're quoting contains a quoted word or phrase, place single quotation marks around the quoted words. (See page 594 for how to treat a source that is quoting another source.)

"We can call this 'objective' reality if we like, as opposed to subjective reality, or opinion, or 'whimsical set of predilections,'" Angier posits (22).

Punctuating with a Question Mark or Exclamation Point If the question mark or exclamation point is part of the quotation, place it inside the quotation marks. If the mark is part of the structure of the framing sentence, as in the second example that follows, place it outside the quotation marks and after any parenthetical reference.

Discussing a child's epileptic attack, the psychoanalyst Erik Erikson asks, in *Childhood and Society*, "What was the psychic stimulus?" (26).

On the other hand, in what ways can society "allow people to find the solution that best meets their needs" (Marlow and Abdukadirov)?

Presenting Statistics

Citing statistics can be a successful strategy for supporting your ideas. Be careful, though, not to misinterpret the data or twist their significance, and remember to provide an attribution indicating the source. Also, be sure not to overwhelm readers with too many statistics; include only those that support your central points in compelling ways. Keep in mind, too, that statistics won't speak for themselves. You need to interpret them for readers, showing how the figures cited reinforce your key ideas.

Ineffective Use of Statistics   In an essay on the issue of obesity in the United States, one student writer presented the following statistics from Marlowe and Abdukadirov:

The authors report that 13.4 percent of adults were obese in 1960 and that 34.3 percent were obese in 2008, an increase of little more than 20 percentage points. They go on to state that reports indicate that "by 2030, 42 percent of Americans will be obese," an increase of less than 10 percentage points over a 22-year period.

Although the statistics that the student cited were those reported by Marlow and Abdukadirov, they were incomplete, and the omission of the additional statistics distorted the meaning intended by the authors. The student's comment led readers to believe that obesity rates would not continue to rise at the drastic rate at which they had risen between 1960 and 2008. However, the student failed to point out that the statistics also stated that "by 2030...11 percent [would] be severely obese, or 100 pounds overweight."

Effective Use of Statistics   Instead of distorting the statistics, the writer could have clearly presented them and could have clearly explained their significance.

The authors cite figures from the National Center of Health Statistics that report that 13.4 percent of adults were obese in 1960, and that 34.3 percent were obese in 2008, an increase of little more than 20 percentage points. Marlow and Abdukadirov go on to cite the predictions of a report published by the *American Journal of Preventive Medicine* which states that reports indicate that "by 2030, 42 percent of Americans will be obese and 11 percent will be severely obese, or

100 pounds overweight." These figures clearly indicate that we can no longer simply tell people that they need to eat less and exercise more. We must understand the necessity of taking steps to help individuals figure out how to best deal with this serious issue.

☑ INTEGRATING SOURCES INTO YOUR WRITING: A CHECKLIST

❑ Introduce an important or oft-used source by giving the author's full name and credentials at the first mention. Thereafter, refer to author by last name only. Don't use personal titles such as *Mr.* or *Ms.*

❑ Use general introductions (*One researcher says...*) for less important sources.

❑ Vary the style of attributions by sometimes positioning them at the middle or end, using different verbs, or blending quotations into your own sentences.

❑ Words may be deleted from a quotation as long as the author's original meaning isn't changed. Insert an ellipsis (...) in place of the deleted words. An ellipsis is not needed when material is omitted from the start of a quotation. Use a period plus an ellipsis when the end of a sentence is deleted.

❑ Use brackets to add clarifying information to quotations.

❑ If a quotation can stand alone as a grammatical sentence, capitalize its first word and precede it with a comma. If a quotation is blended into the structure of your own sentence, don't capitalize the quotation's first word and don't precede it with a comma. If an attribution interrupts a quotation, place commas before and after the attribution and resume the quotation with a lowercase letter.

❑ For a quotation within a quotation, use single quotation marks.

❑ Place question marks and exclamation points inside quotation marks only if they belong to the quotation.

❑ Limit statistics and explain them fully to convey essential information.

DOCUMENTING SOURCES: MLA STYLE

In Chapter 11, you learned the importance of documentation—giving credit to all the various sources whose words and ideas you borrow in an essay. The following pages will show you how to use the documentation system of the Modern Language Association (MLA) when citing sources in your essays. MLA documentation is appropriate in essays written for humanities courses, such as your composition class. If you're writing a composition for a course in the social sciences (for example, psychology, economics, or sociology), your professor will probably expect you to use the citation format developed by the American Psychological Association (APA).

To avoid plagiarism, you must provide documentation when you quote from, summarize, or paraphrase a source. However, if the information is commonly known or is a matter of historical or scientific record (the date of the Gettysburg Address, for example), you need not document it.

This discussion covers key features of the MLA system. For more detailed coverage, consult the latest edition of the *MLA Handbook* or the online MLA resource (style.MLA.org). For a sample essay with MLA documentation, see the student essay on pages 470–475.

HOW TO DOCUMENT: MLA IN-TEXT REFERENCES

The MLA documentation system uses the *parenthetical reference*, a brief note in parentheses inserted into the text after borrowed material. The parenthetical reference presents enough information so that readers can turn to the Works-Cited list at the end of the paper for a complete citation.

In the parenthetical reference, you must identify the source (usually an author) and, if possible, specify the page(s) in the source on which the material appears. The author's name may be given either in an introduction (or *attribution*) or in the parenthetical reference. The page number always appears in parentheses that are usually placed at the end of the sentence just before the period. The examples that follow illustrate the MLA documentation style. You may also consult pages 585–590 for additional examples.

Source Identified by Author in the Works-Cited List

The following parenthetical references are to a Works-Cited entry with a single author. No comma should appear after the author's name.

One writer says that to speak of "objective" and "subjective" realities is to imply that these are discrete entities" (Angier 22).

Angier says that to speak of "objective" and "subjective" realities is to imply that these are discrete entities" (22).

The example below refers to a work by two authors. Since the source was found online, there are no page numbers to cite.

Government intervention is not enough to solve the obesity issue in our country. Obesity is a complex issue and individuals must find the solution that is most effective for them (Marlow and Abdukadirov).

If a source has three or more authors, the in-text reference uses only the first author followed by *et al.* (Latin for "and others").

Some researchers found that the Seattle law did not affect consumers' purchases of high-calorie foods (Elbel et al. 1110).

Source Identified by Title in the Works-Cited List

If a source is alphabetized by title in your Works-Cited list, use a shortened version of the title—usually the first noun or noun phrase minus any articles—in the parenthetical reference. In the following example, the full title of the source is "Supreme Court of the United States."

The U.S. Supreme Court is fundamentally an appeals court, responsible for "cases arising under the Constitution, laws, or treaties of the United States" among others ("Supreme Court").

More Than One Source by the Same Author

When your paper includes references to more than one work by the same author, you must specify—either in the parenthetical reference or in the attribution—the particular work being cited. You do this by providing the title, as well as the author's name and the page(s). Here are examples from an essay in which two works by the psychologist Jean Piaget were used.

In *The Language and Thought of the Child*, Jean Piaget states that "discussion forms the basis for a logical point of view" (240).

Piaget considers dialogue essential to the development of logical thinking (*Language* 240).

The Child's Conception of the World shows that young children think that the name of something can never change (Piaget 81).

Young children assume that everything has only one name and that no others are possible (Piaget, *Child's Conception* 81).

Notice that when a work is named in the attribution, the full title appears; when a title is given in the parenthetic citation, though, only the first few significant words appear.

Source Within a Source

If you quote or summarize a *secondary source* (a source whose ideas come to you only through another source), you need to make this clear. The parenthetical documentation should indicate "as quoted in" with the abbreviation *qtd. in*:

Sherman explains that recycling can be surprisingly costly (qtd. in Pratt 3).

If the material you're quoting includes a quotation, place single quotation marks around the secondary quotation:

Pratt believes that "recycling efforts will be successful if, as Sherman argues, 'communities launch effective public-education campaigns'" (3).

Note: Your Works-Cited list should include the source you actually read (Pratt), rather than the source you refer to secondhand (Sherman).

Long (Block) Quotations

A quotation longer than four lines starts on a new line and is indented, throughout, one-half inch from the left margin. Because this block format indicates a quotation, quotation marks are unnecessary. Double-space the block quotation, as you do the rest of your paper. Don't leave extra space above or below the quotation. Long quotations, always used sparingly, require a lead-in. A lead-in that isn't a full sentence is followed by a comma; a lead-in that is a full sentence (see below) is followed by a colon:

Marlow and Abdukadirov argue that government efforts to control the increase in obesity are ineffectual:

> Despite the myriad of studies showing American obesity is increasing, research does not clearly support that government can solve this complex problem. And yet, government solutions that provide information the public already knows—weight gain occurs when we eat too much and exercise too little—have been the focus to eliminate this epidemic.

If there had been a page number for the extended quote, it would have appeared *after* the period at the end of the extended quote, not before as it would with a short quotation:

> ... eliminate this epidemic. (2)

Key Points to Remember

Take a moment to look again at the preceding examples and note the points presented in the following checklist.

☑ USING MLA PARENTHETICAL REFERENCES: A CHECKLIST

❏ The parenthetical reference is usually placed immediately after the borrowed material.

❏ The parenthetical reference is placed before any internal punctuation (a comma or semicolon) as well as before any terminal punctuation (a period or question mark), except in a block quotation, where the reference appears after the period.

❏ The first time the author is referred to in an attribution, give the author's full name; afterward, give only the last name. To inform readers of an author's area of expertise, identify the author by profession, title, or affiliation.

❏ When an author's name is provided in the attribution, the name is not repeated in the parentheses. When the author's name is provided in the parentheses, only the last name is given.

❏ If a source is cited by title rather than author, use a shortened form of the title in the parenthetical reference.

❏ The page number comes directly after the author's name with no intervening punctuation, and there is no *p.* or *page* preceding the page number. (If the source is only one page long or has no page numbers, only the author's name is needed.)

HOW TO DOCUMENT: MLA LIST OF WORKS CITED

A documented essay ends with a Works-Cited list, which includes only the sources you cite in your paper. It provides full bibliographic information about the sources cited in the parenthetical references (see pages 585–590).

- The list starts on a new page.
- The list is organized alphabetically by authors' last names or by the first word in each title other than *A, An,* or *The.*
- For entries longer than one line, each additional line is indented half an inch.
- Entries are double-spaced with no extra space between entries.

Given here are the MLA guidelines for creating Works-Cited entries. In addition, sample Works-Cited entries for the most commonly used kinds of sources are listed. (See also the Works-Cited list at the end of the student essay on pages 474–475.) Refer to these samples when you prepare your own Works-Cited list, taking special care with punctuation and spacing.

General Guidelines for MLA Works-Cited Entries

The goal of a Works-Cited entry is to give, clearly and concisely, all the information readers need to find the original source. That means you need to list the core elements of a source, including where you found it. Carefully examining a source can usually yield the necessary information:

- **Books.** Consult (1) the title page and (2) the copyright notice (on the back of the title page in print books). You will also need to know the specific page numbers of any material you are citing.
- **Periodicals.** Consult (1) the page with the journal title and copyright information and (2) all the pages (in print periodicals) on which the article appears.
- **Websites, including blogs and social media sites.** Consult (1) the homepage, (2) the source's page, and (3) any "About us" pages. Look for copyright notices at the bottom of a site's homepage.
- **Other sources including films, television shows, works of art, and the like.** Consult any (1) lists of credits, (2) exhibit or program catalogs, (3) official websites, and (4) packaging or labels.

Core Elements of an Entry

Suppose you are writing a research essay on Alexander Hamilton. An online search at your college library offers a wide range of sources, including books, journal articles, videos, and even reviews of a popular Broadway musical. You may notice that some of these sources are available in several different formats. For example, Ron Chernow's book *Alexander Hamilton* comes in hardcover, paperback, e-book, and audiobook editions.

These different delivery systems—print, electronic, and audio—can be seen as "containers" for the book. A complete citation would specify all the containers involved in the version consulted. If you read the *Alexander Hamilton* e-book on Google Books, your citation would include the information for the print book (if available) plus the information about Google Books.

Take another example. As part of your search, you find Clement Fatovic's article "Reason and Experience in Alexander Hamilton's Science of Politics." The article was originally printed in an academic journal, *American Political Thought*, but in your library you can access the journal only through *JSTOR*, an online academic database. Your citation would cite the original container (print journal) and the secondary container (*JSTOR*).

To create a Works-Cited entry, you need to provide the basic information common to all versions of a source (author's name and source title) as well as information for each container. Note that specific punctuation follows each element. The author's name and source title are each followed by a period. The last item in the container information ends with a period, and commas separate the other items within the list. Here's how to organize information for Clement Fatovic's article.

Common Information

Author.	Fatovic, Clement.
Title of source.	"Reason and Experience in Alexander Hamilton's Science of Politics."

Container 1 Information

Title of container,	*American Political Thought,*
Other contributors,	
Version,	
Number,	vol. 2, no. 1,
Publisher,	
Publication date,	Spring 2013,
Location.	pp. 1-30.

Container 2 Information

Title of container,	*JSTOR,*
Other contributors,	
Version,	
Number,	
Publisher,	
Publication date,	
Location.	doi: 10.1086/666658.

And here's the completed citation entry for the Fatovic article:

Fatovic, Clement. "Reason and Experience in Alexander Hamilton's Science of Politics." *American Political Thought,* vol. 2, no. 1, Spring 2013, pp. 1-30. *JSTOR,* doi: 10.1086/666658.

It's important to realize that one container may be nested within another. In the Fatovic citation, the journal (*American Political Thought*) is the container of the article, and the academic database (*JSTOR*) is the container of the journal.

Formatting Entry Elements

A citation always specifies a source title and usually specifies an author, but not all citations specify every element of information described here. If you cannot locate a specific element, you can omit it from the Works-Cited entry. Try to keep from repeating information unnecessarily.

- **Author.** List the author's last name followed by a comma, the first name, and a period. For use of a pseudonym, see the examples. Do not use *Anonymous* in place of an author's name; if no author is cited, start the entry with the source title.
- **Title of source.** Put the title of a complete work, such as a book, in italics. If the source is part of a larger work—for example, an article in a journal—put the source's title in quotation marks. Capitalize the first and last words in the title and all major words. However, do not capitalize articles, coordinating conjunctions, and *to* in infinitives (*to* walk, *to* begin).
- **Title of container.** Containers are named when a source is part of a larger work or has been consulted in a format different from that of the original. For example, a book of collected essays is the container for an individual essay, and a newspaper is the container for an article. Container names are given in full and are italicized.
- **Other contributors.** Contributors should be introduced by a term such as *edited by, translated by, directed by,* or *illustrated by.* Some sources require a phrase such as *introduction by, performance by,* or *general editor.* Both the source and its containers can have contributors.
- **Version.** Indicate any particular version of the source (*revised, updated, expanded*) that is consulted. Numbered editions (*2nd, 3rd, 10th*) are also considered unique versions.
- **Number.** For scholarly journals, give the abbreviation *vol.* and the volume number, then a comma, and then the abbreviation *no.* and the issue number (if available). Use arabic, not roman, numerals.
- **Publisher.** The publisher is the entity responsible for producing, not simply containing, the source. Unless confusion is likely, do not include a book's city of publication. Also, do not italicize the publisher's name. Provide each publisher's full name; however, omit terms like *Co., Corp., Inc., Ltd.,* and shorten *University Press* to *UP.* Two or more publishers that are equally responsible for a work are separated by a forward slash (/) with a space on either side. Remember that the title of a journal, magazine, or newspaper is given as a container, not a publisher.
- **Publication date.** For scholarly publications, include the month (if available) and year after the issue number. Abbreviate the names of months having more than four letters (*Jan., Feb., Mar., Apr., Aug., Sept., Oct., Nov., Dec.*). Capitalize the names of seasons (*Spring 2016*). For newspapers and weekly magazines, include the day, month, and year—in that order. For books, supply the most recent year of copyright.

- **Location.** Use the abbreviation *p.* or *pp.* before page numbers. If the pages in an article are continuous, give the page range (for example, 67–72, 321–25, or 497–502). If the pages in an article are not printed on consecutive pages, write the first page number and a plus sign (67+). For a source accessed online, include the URL (minus *http://* or *https://*). If an online source has a permanent Internet address—such as a digital object identifier (DOI) or a Permalink—include that in place of the URL (precede a DOI with *doi:*). In formatting the list, break long URLs *before* a mark of punctuation.
- **Optional elements.** For some sources, it may be useful to add the date of original publication right after the source title. For pre-1900 sources, it is customary to give original city and date of publication in place of a publisher's name. Additional optional elements are more appropriately placed at the end of the citation: the total number of volumes or discs (*6 vols.*), the unexpected nature of the material (*Transcript*), or the date the source was accessed for online material that is likely to be updated or hard to locate (*Accessed 3 June 2016*).

What follows are examples of Works-Cited entries. However, no list can cover all types of sources. If you encounter a source not listed here, consult the *MLA Handbook*, 8th ed. (2016) and its online resource (style.mla.org/) for more examples. If you still do not find an exact example, choose a close model and modify it. Be guided by the most important requirement of a Works-Cited entry: it should enable readers to find the cited source on their own. Remember also that a citation can often be formatted in more than one way.

Book with One Author

Note the formatting of *Jr.* in the second entry, which also gives the book series title (*King Legacy*) as optional information. A book accessed in electronic format (such as Kindle) is treated in the same way as a print book.

King, Martin Luther, Jr. *Where Do We Go from Here: Chaos or Community?* Beacon Press, 2010. King Legacy.

Book with Two Authors

Provide all the authors' names in the order in which they appear on the title page of the book, but reverse only the first author's name.

Lewis, Robin, and Michael Dart. *The New Rules of Retail: Competing in the World's Toughest Marketplace.* 2nd ed., St. Martin's Press, 2014.

Book with Three or More Authors

For a work by three or more authors, give only the first author's name followed by a comma and *et al.* (Latin for "and others"). Do not italicize "et al."

Yancey, Kathleen Blake, et al. *Writing across Contexts: Transfer, Composition, and Sites of Writing*. Utah State UP, 2014.

Two or More Works by the Same Author

List each source separately. Give the author's name in the first entry only; begin the other entries for that author with three hyphens followed by a period. Arrange the works alphabetically by title.

McChesney, Robert W. *Communication Revolution: Critical Junctures and the Future of Media*. New Press, 2007.

---. *The Political Economy of Media: Enduring Issues, Emerging Dilemmas*. Monthly Review, 2008.

Works by Different Author Teams Led by Same Author

For different author teams with the same lead author, give the first two author names, followed by a comma, and then *et al.* If the first two names are the same, give the first three, and so on. Alphabetize the entries by the last name of the final author cited in the entry.

West, Margaret Mary, Cecelia Borden, et al. "Enhancing the Clinical Adjunct Role to Benefit Students." *The Journal of Continuing Education in Nursing*, vol. 40, no. 7, 2009, pp. 305-10, doi: 10.3928/00220124-20090623-05.

West, Margaret Mary, Susan M. Hallick, et al. "A Rural Academic-Service Partnership." *JONA: The Journal of Nursing Administration*, vol. 36, no. 2, 2006, pp. 63-66.

Editor, Translator, or Other Contributors

Ferrante, Elena. *My Brilliant Friend*. Translated by Ann Goldstein, Europa Editions, 2012.

See the "Jackson" entry under "Specific Edition or Version" for an example of contributors to a film.

Anthology or Compilation of Works by Different Authors

Zake, Ieva, and Michael DeCesare, editors. *New Directions in Sociology: Essays on Theory and Methodology in the 21st Century*. McFarland, 2011.

Section of an Anthology or Compilation

Note that the example gives the page numbers on which the source selection appears.

DeCesare, Michael. "'Shut Up in Measureless Content': Confronting the Measurement Problem in Sociology." *New Directions in Sociology: Essays on*

Theory and Methodology in the 21st Century, edited by Ieva Zake and Michael DeCesare, McFarland, 2011, pp. 145-59.

Section or Chapter in a Book by One Author

Mayor, Joseph B. "Chapter VI: Metrical Metamorphosis." *Chapters on English Metre,* London, 1886, pp. 81-98.

Introduction, Preface, or Foreword

King, Coretta Scott. Foreword. *Where Do We Go from Here: Chaos or Community?,* by Martin Luther King, Jr., Beacon Press, 2010, pp. xxiii-xxiv. King Legacy.

Work by a Corporate Author

If an organization or institution is both author and publisher, give its name in the publisher position only. Do not include any article (*A, An, The*) that precedes the name.

Human Development, Health, and Education: Dialogues at the Economic and Social Council. Department of Economic and Social Affairs, United Nations, 2004.

New York City 2015 Drinking Water Supply and Quality Report. Department of Environmental Protection, New York City, 2015, www.nyc.gov/html/dep/pdf/wsstate15.pdf.

Article in a Scholarly Journal

Njeng, Eric Sipyinyu. "Achebe, Conrad, and the Postcolonial Strain." *CLCWeb: Comparative Literature and Culture,* vol. 10, no. 1, 2008, doi: 10.7771/1481-4374.1328.

Qin, Desiree Baolian. "The Role of Gender in Immigrant Children's Educational Adaptation." *Current Issues in Comparative Education,* vol. 9, no. 1, 7 Dec. 2006, pp. 8-19. *ERIC: Institute of Education Sciences,* ERIC ID: EJ847390.

Article in a Magazine

AN at the end of the entry stands for "Accession number" and is the permanent number for the source on this database.

Leo, John. "Campus Censors in Retreat." *U.S. News & World Report,* 16 Feb. 2004, pp. 64–65.

Leo, John. "Campus Censors in Retreat." *U.S. News & World Report,* vol. 136, no. 616, 16 Feb. 2004, pp. 64-65. *EBSCOhost Connection,* AN 12180673.

Wheeler, Jacob. "Outsourcing the Public Good." *Utne,* Sept.-Oct. 2004, www.utne.com/community/outsourcingthepublicgood.aspx?PageId=1.

Article in a Daily Newspaper

In the second example, a series name is given as optional information at the end of the entry. For a locally published newspaper, give the place in square brackets, if it is not already part of the newspaper name.

Meier, Barry. "Energy Drinks Promise Edge, but Experts Say Proof Is Scant." *The New York Times*, 2 Jan. 2013, pp. A1+.

Phillips, Dave. "Left Behind: No Break for the Wounded." *The Gazette* [Colorado Springs], 20 May 2013, cdn.csgazette.biz/soldiers/day2.html. Other Than Honorable.

Specific Edition or Version

Weiss, Thomas G., et al. *The United Nations and Changing World Politics*. 6th ed., Westview, 2011.

Jackson, Peter, director. *The Lord of the Rings: The Motion Picture Trilogy*. Performances by Elijah Wood, Ian McKellen, Viggo Mortensen, Sean Astin, and Sean Bean, special extended edition, New Line Home Video, 14 Dec. 2004. 12 discs.

Reference Work

For reference works arranged alphabetically, omit page numbers. Give the latest update or copyright date.

"Ethic." *Merriam-Webster's Collegiate Dictionary*, 2015, www.merriam-webster. com/dictionary/ethic. Accessed 11 Feb. 2016.

McGhee, Karen, and George McKay. "Insects." *Encyclopedia of Animals*, National Geographic Society, 2007.

The Oxford English Dictionary. 2nd CD-ROM ed., edited by John Simpson, version 4.0, Oxford UP, 21 May 2009.

Editorial, Letter to the Editor, or Reader's Comment

You may indicate the type of piece as optional information at the end. For comments, give the time of posting if it's available.

"Earthquake in Pakistan." *The New York Times*, 13 Oct. 2005, p. A26. Editorial.

Sisyphus. Comment on "Work in the Only Industrialized Country without Paid Maternity Leave," by Jessica Shortall. *The Atlantic*, 11 Apr. 2016, 9:39 a.m., www.theatlantic.com/business/archive/2016/04/no-family-leave /476577/#article-comments.

Review

Mellow, Beth. Review of *Hell Is a Very Small Place: Voices from Solitary Confinement*, edited by Jean Casella et al. *Bookslut*, Mar. 2016, www.bookslut.com/nonfiction/2016_03_021390.php.

Review of *The Firebrand and the First Lady*, by Patricia Bell-Scott. *The New Yorker*, 4 Apr. 2016, p. 84.

Personal, Professional, Business, or Organizational Website

An entry can cite an entire website or an individual page on a website. Indicate the date of access if the site is updated frequently, or if there is no publication date on the item you are citing.

King, Stephen. *StephenKing.com*. 2000-2016. Accessed 7 Mar. 2016.

Web Project

Note that *Uncle Tom's Cabin* is *not* italicized. It's a title that would ordinarily be italicized, but because the rest of the archive title is italicized, the book title is set off in regular type.

Railton, Stephen, director. Uncle Tom's Cabin & *American Culture: A Multi-Media Archive*. Electronic Text Center, Institute for Advanced Technology in the Humanities, Special Collections Alderman Library, U of Virginia / Harriet Beecher Stowe Center at Hartford, 2009, utc.iath.virginia.edu/. Accessed 8 Apr. 2016.

Blog

The first example shows a posting to a blog (*Respectful Insolence*) found on a site that has many blogs (*ScienceBlogs*). A newspaper or magazine blog can be treated like an article.

Orac. "Better Late Than Never: Orac Comments on the Hijacking of Evidence-Based Medicine." *Respectful Insolence*, 4 Apr. 2016. *ScienceBlogs*, scienceblogs.com/insolence/2016/04/04/better-late-than-never-orac-comments-on-the-hijacking-of-evidence-based-medicine/.

Podcast

Filreis, Al, host and producer. "Amplitude and Awe: A Discussion of Emily Dickinson's 'Wild Nights – Wild Nights!' and 'She rose to His Requirement.'" *PoemTalk 87*, Kelly Writers House / Penn Sound / Poetry Foundation, 21 Apr. 2015, www.poetryfoundation.org/features/audioitem/4948.

Television or Radio Program, Film, Sound Recording, or Similar Source

Pelley, Scott, correspondent. "The Health Wagon." *60 Minutes*, CBS News, 27 Mar. 2016, www.cbsnews.com/videos/the-health-wagon/.

Monk, Thelonious. "I Mean You." *Thelonious Monk: The Complete Blue Note Recordings*, Capitol Records, 1994, disc 4.

"1963 World Series Part 1." *YouTube*, uploaded by Kevin Kunkel, 11 Oct. 2009, www.youtube.com/watch?v=fjmkVNG1_-M.

Interview, Lecture, or Address

Specify "Personal interview" or "Telephone interview" for an interview you conducted.

Blacksmith, James. "Urban Design in the New Millennium." Cityscapes Lecture Series. Urban Studies Institute, 18 Apr. 2005, Metropolitan College, Washington, DC.

Crittenden, Alicia. Personal interview. 20 Jan. 2015.

E-mail Message

Start with the sender's name. Then give the title (from the subject line) in quotation marks. Add *Received by* and the recipient's name. End with the date received.

Lunsford, Ronald. "New Developments in Mixed Media Compositions." Received by Jane Smith, 30 Jan. 2015.

Posting on *Twitter*

For a tweet, repeat the entire text of the tweet, in quotation marks, in place of a title. When alphabetizing, ignore the @ or any other special character.

@POETSorg. "Congrats to Marilyn Nelson on winning the LA Times Book Prize for Young Adult Literature for 'My Seneca Village.'" *Twitter*, 10 Apr. 2016, 10:00 a.m., twitter.com/POETSorg/status /719178281405157377?lang=en.

Works of Art and Other Objects

The first citation below is to the sculpture on display at an outdoor location; the second citation is to a painting in a museum.

Bergmann, Meredith. *Phillis Wheatley*. 2003, Boston Women's Memorial, Commonwealth Ave. and Fairfield St., Boston.

Rousseau, Henri. *The Sleeping Gypsy*. 1897, Museum of Modern Art, New York.

AVOIDING TEN COMMON
WRITING ERRORS

Many students consider grammar a nuisance. Taking the easy way out, they cross their fingers and hope they haven't made too many mistakes. They assume that their meaning will come across, even if their writing contains some errors—perhaps a misplaced comma here or a dangling modifier there. Not so. Surface errors annoy readers and may confuse them. Such errors also weaken a writer's credibility because they defy language conventions, customs that readers expect writers to honor. By mastering grammar, punctuation, and spelling conventions, students can increase their power and versatility as writers.

This concise appendix, "Avoiding Ten Common Writing Errors," will help you brush up on the most useful rules and conventions of writing. It's organized according to the broad skill areas that give writers the most trouble. Throughout this appendix, grammatical terminology is kept to a minimum. Although we assume that you know the major parts of speech (noun, verb, pronoun, and so on), we do, when appropriate, provide on-the-spot definitions of more technical grammatical terms.

Here are the ten common writing errors covered:

1. Fragments
2. Comma Splices and Run-ons
3. Faulty Subject–Verb Agreement
4. Faulty Pronoun Agreement

Appendix

B

605

5. Misplaced and Dangling Modifiers
6. Faulty Parallelism
7. Comma Misuse
8. Apostrophe Misuse
9. Confusing Homonyms
10. Misuse of Italics and Underlining

1 FRAGMENTS

A full *sentence* satisfies two conditions: (1) it has a subject and a verb, and (2) it can stand alone as a complete thought. Although a *fragment* is punctuated like a full sentence, it doesn't satisfy these two requirements.

NO   Meteorologists predict a drought this summer. *In spite of heavy spring rains.*

NO   *A victim of her own hypocrisy.* The senator lost the next election.

Some Easy Ways to Correct Fragments

A. Attach the fragment to the beginning or end of the preceding (or following) sentence, changing punctuation and capitalization as needed.

YES   In spite of heavy spring rains, meteorologists predict a drought this summer.
or
Meteorologists predict a drought this summer, in spite of heavy spring rains.

B. Attach the fragment to a newly created sentence.

YES   Meteorologists predict a drought this summer. *They do so* in spite of heavy spring rains.

C. Insert the fragment into the preceding (or following) sentence, adding commas as needed.

YES   The senator, *a victim of her own hypocrisy,* lost the next election.

D. Supply the missing subject and/or verb, changing other words as necessary.

YES   *The senator became* a victim of her own hypocrisy. *She* lost the next election.

2 COMMA SPLICES AND RUN-ONS

Consider the following faulty sentences:

NO   The First Amendment cannot be taken for granted, it is the bedrock of our democracy.

NO   The First Amendment cannot be taken for granted it is the bedrock of our democracy.

The first example is a *comma splice:* a comma used to join, or splice together, two complete thoughts, even though the comma alone is not strong enough to connect the two independent ideas. The second example is a *run-on,* or fused, sentence: two sentences run together without any punctuation indicating where the first sentence ends and the second begins.

Some Easy Ways to Correct Comma Splices and Run-ons

A. Place a period, question mark, or exclamation point at the end of the first sentence, and capitalize the first letter of the second sentence.

YES   The First Amendment cannot be taken for *granted. It* is the bedrock of our democracy.

B. Use a semicolon to mark where the first sentence ends and the second begins.

YES   The First Amendment cannot be taken for *granted; it* is the bedrock of our democracy.

C. Turn one of the sentences into a dependent phrase.

YES   *Because* it is the bedrock of our democracy, the First Amendment cannot be taken for granted.

D. Keep or add a comma at the end of the first sentence, but follow the comma with a coordinating conjunction (*and, but, for, nor, or, so, yet*).

YES   The First Amendment cannot be taken for granted, *for* it is the bedrock of our democracy.

3 FAULTY SUBJECT–VERB AGREEMENT

A verb should match its subject in number. If the subject is singular (one person, place, or thing), the verb should have a singular form. If the subject is plural (two or more persons, places, or things), the verb should have a plural form. Always determine the verb's subject and make sure that the verb agrees with it, rather than with some other word in the sentence.

> NO   The *documents* from the court case *was* unsealed for the first time in three decades.
>
> YES The *documents* from the court case *were* unsealed for the first time in three decades.

Some Easy Ways to Correct Faulty Subject-Verb Agreement

A. When there are two or more singular subjects (joined by *and*) in a sentence, use a plural verb. (However, when the word *or* joins the subjects, use a *singular* verb.)

> YES A sprawling maple *and* a lush rose bush *flank* [not *flanks*] my childhood home.

B. When the subject and verb are separated by a prepositional phrase, be sure to match the verb to its subject—not to a word in the prepositional phrase that comes between them.

> YES The *quality* of student papers *has* [not *have*] been declining over the past semester.

C. When the words *either ... or* or *neither ... nor* connect two subjects, use the verb form (singular or plural) that agrees with the subject *closer* to the verb.

> YES *Neither* the employees *nor* the store *owner was* [not *were*] aware of the theft.
>
> YES *Neither* the store owner *nor* her *employees were* [not *was*] aware of the theft.

D. When using the indefinite pronouns *anybody, anyone, anything, each, either, everybody, everyone, everything, neither, nobody, none, no one, nothing, one, somebody, someone,* or *something,* use a *singular* verb.

> YES *Neither* of the candidates *is* [not *are*] willing to address the issue.

When you use the indefinite pronouns *all, any, most, none,* or *some,* use a **singular** or a **plural** verb, depending on whether the pronoun refers to one thing or to a number of things.

> YES The spokesperson announced that only *some* of the *report has* been confirmed.

In the preceding sentence, *some* refers to a single report and therefore takes a *singular* verb. In the following sentence, *some* refers to *multiple* reports and therefore takes a *plural* verb.

> YES   The spokesperson announced that only *some* of the *reports have* been confirmed.

E. When the subject of a sentence refers to a group acting as a unit, use a *singular* verb.

> YES   The local baseball *team is* [not *are*] boycotting the new sports stadium.

F. When words such as *here, there, how, what, when, where, which, who,* and *why* invert normal sentence order—so that the verb comes before the subject—look ahead for the subject and make sure that it and the verb agree.

> YES   There *is* [not *are*] a *series* of things to consider before deciding on a college major.
> YES   What *are* [not *is*] the *arguments* against energy conservation?

4 FAULTY PRONOUN AGREEMENT

A *pronoun* must agree in number with its *antecedent*—the noun or pronoun it replaces or refers to. If the antecedent is singular, the pronoun must be singular. If the antecedent is plural, the pronoun must be plural.

Some Easy Ways to Correct Faulty Pronoun Agreement

A. A compound subject (two or more nouns joined by *and*) requires plural pronouns.

> YES   Both the car *manufacturers* and the tire *company* had trouble restoring *their* reputations after losing the class-action lawsuit.

However, when the nouns are joined by *or* or *nor*, the pronoun form (singular or plural) should agree with the noun that is *closer* to the verb.

> YES   Neither the car manufacturers *nor* the tire *company* restored *its* reputation after losing the class-action lawsuit.
> YES   Neither the tire company *nor* the car *manufacturers* restored *their* reputations after losing the class-action lawsuit.

B. A subject that is a *collective noun* (referring to a group that acts as a unit) takes a singular pronoun.

> **YES**   The *orchestra* showed *its* appreciation by playing a lengthy encore.

Or, if a singular pronoun sounds awkward, simply make the antecedent plural.

> **YES**   The orchestra *members* showed *their* appreciation by playing a lengthy encore.

C. The indefinite pronouns *anybody, anyone, anything, each, either, everybody, everyone, everything, neither, nobody, no one, nothing, one, somebody, someone,* and *something* are singular and therefore take singular pronouns.

> **YES**   *Each* of the buildings had *its* [not *their*] roof replaced.
> **YES**   *Neither* of the executives resigned *his* [not *their*] position after the revelations.

Using the singular form with indefinite pronouns can be awkward or sexist when the pronoun encompasses both male and female. To avoid these problems, you can make the antecedent plural and use a plural pronoun.

> **AWK**   *Anyone* who exhibits symptoms should see her or his doctor immediately.
> **YES**   *Individuals* who exhibit symptoms should see *their* doctor immediately.

D. Within a sentence, pronouns should be in the same *person* (point of view) as their antecedents.

> **NO**   To register to vote, *citizens* [third person] can visit the state government's website, where *you* [second person] can download the appropriate forms.
> **YES**   To register to vote, *citizens* [third person] can visit the state government's website, where *they* [third person] can download the appropriate forms.

5 MISPLACED AND DANGLING MODIFIERS

A *modifier* is a word or group of words that describes something else. Sometimes sentences are written in such a way that modifiers are misplaced. Here is an example of a *misplaced modifier:*

> **NO**   Television stations carried the story of the disastrous tornado *throughout the nation.* [The tornado was throughout the nation?]

YES   Television stations *throughout the nation* carried the story of the disastrous tornado.

Modifiers are commonly misused in another way. An introductory modifier must modify the subject of the sentence. If it doesn't, it may be a *dangling modifier*. Here's an example:

NO   *Faded and brittle with age,* archaeologists unearthed a painted clay pot near the riverbank. [The archaeologists were faded and brittle with age?]

YES   Archaeologists unearthed a painted clay pot, *faded and brittle with age,* near the riverbank.
or
Faded and brittle with age, a painted clay pot was unearthed near the riverbank by archaeologists.

An Easy Way to Correct Misplaced Modifiers

A. Place the modifier next to the word(s) it describes.

NO   Passengers complained about the flight at the customer service desk, *which was turbulent and delayed.* [The customer service desk was turbulent and delayed?]

YES   Passengers complained about the flight, *which was turbulent and delayed,* at the customer service desk.

NO   She *nearly* ran the marathon in four hours. [Did she or didn't she run?]

YES   She ran the marathon in *nearly* four hours.

Some Easy Ways to Correct Dangling Modifiers

The following dangling modifier can be corrected in one of two ways.

NO   *Leaping gracefully across the stage,* spectators were in awe of the agile dancer.

A. Rewrite the sentence by adding to the modifying phrase the word that is being described.

YES   *As the agile dancer leaped* gracefully across the stage, spectators were in awe of him.

B. Rewrite the sentence so that the word being modified becomes the subject.

YES   Leaping gracefully across the stage, the agile dancer awed the spectators.

6 FAULTY PARALLELISM

Items in a pair, a series, or a list should be phrased in *parallel* (matching) grammatical structures. Otherwise, *faulty parallelism* results.

> **NO**   After hiking all day, the campers were *exhausted, hungry,* and *experienced soreness.* [Of the three items in the series, the first two are adjectives, but the last is a verb plus a noun.]
>
> **YES**   After hiking all day, the campers were *exhausted, hungry,* and *sore.*

Words that follow *correlative conjunctions—either...or, neither...nor, both...and, not only...but also*—should also be parallel.

> **NO**   Every road to the airport is **either** *jammed* **or** *is closed* for repairs. [The word *either* is followed by an adjective (*jammed*), but *or* is followed by a verb and adjective (*is closed*).]
>
> **YES**   Every road to the airport is **either** *jammed* **or** *closed* for repairs.

An Easy Way to Correct Faulty Parallelism

A. Use the *same grammatical structure* for each item in a pair or series.

> **NO**   The finalists for the sales job possess *charismatic personalities, excellent references,* and *they are extensively experienced.*
>
> **YES**   The finalists for the sales job possess *charismatic personalities, excellent references,* and *extensive experience.*
>
> **NO**   We observed *that the leaves were changing color, the sun was setting earlier,* and *that the air was becoming chillier.* [The word *that* precedes the first and last clauses, but not the second. It must be inserted before the second clause or, preferably, deleted from before the last clause.]
>
> **YES**   We observed *that the leaves were changing color, the sun was setting earlier,* and *the air was becoming chillier.*
>
> **NO**   Students go to college with many goals:
>
> 1. To become more educated.
> 2. Preparing for future careers.
> 3. They also want to meet new people.
>
> **YES**   Students go to college with many goals:
>
> 1. To become more educated.
> 2. To prepare for future careers.
> 3. To meet new people.
>
> **NO**   The romantic comedy that premiered last night was neither *romantic* nor *was it funny.*
>
> **YES**   The romantic comedy that premiered last night was neither *romantic* nor *funny.*

7 COMMA MISUSE

The *comma* is so frequent in writing that mastering its use is essential. By dividing a sentence into its parts, commas clarify meaning.

Most Common Uses of the Comma

A. When two complete sentences are joined with a coordinating conjunction (*and, but, for, nor, or, so, yet*), a comma is placed *before* the conjunction.

> YES   Many attended the political rally, *but* few demonstrated enthusiasm for the cause.

B. Introductory material, which precedes a sentence's main subject and verb, usually is followed by a comma.

> YES   *Like most kids,* the children in the study were powerfully influenced by TV advertisements.

Similarly, material attached to the end of a sentence may be preceded by a comma.

> YES   The children in the study were powerfully influenced by TV advertisements, *which peddled expensive toys and unhealthy snacks.*

C. When a word or phrase describes a noun but isn't crucial for identifying that noun, it is set off from the rest of the sentence with a comma.

> YES   First-year film students are required to analyze *Metropolis*, a late-1920s film that exhibited important artistic innovations.

D. When words or phrases inserted into the body of a sentence can be removed without significant loss of meaning, such elements are considered *interrupters*. Interrupters should be preceded and followed by commas when they occur midsentence.

> YES   Dr. Gene Nome, *a leading genetic researcher*, testified before Congress on the need for increased funding.

E. In a list of *three or more* items in a series, the items should be separated by commas.

> YES   The writing process usually entails *prewriting, drafting,* and *revising.*

F. A comma should be inserted between a short quotation and a phrase that indicates the quotation's source.

> **YES**   One voter commented, "This is the first candidate I've voted for enthusiastically."
> *or*
> "This is the first candidate I've voted for enthusiastically," one voter commented.
> *or*
> "This is the first candidate," one voter commented, "I've voted for enthusiastically."

G. Commas are placed between the numbers in a date and between the elements of the address with the exception that no comma precedes a zip code.

> **YES**   On November 17, 2014, the fourth graders mailed "Dear President" letters to The White House, 1600 Pennsylvania Avenue, Washington, DC 20500.

8 APOSTROPHE MISUSE

Like the comma, the *apostrophe* is a commonly used—and misused—punctuation mark.

Most Common Uses of the Apostrophe

A. In standard contractions, an apostrophe replaces any omitted letters.

> **YES**   can't, don't, I'm, she's, we've

B. The possessive form of most singular nouns requires adding *'s*.

> **YES**   Senator Ross's position is that health care is every person's right.

For ***plural nouns*** ending in *s,* an apostrophe only is added to show possession.

> **YES**   The twelve senators' position on Native Americans' rights is clear.

Plural nouns that do not end in *s* need *'s* to show possession.

> **YES**   Improvement in the children's test scores enabled the school to rise in rank.

However, an apostrophe is *not* used to form the simple plural of a noun.

NO   The central role of *radio's* in American homes has declined in recent decades.

YES   The central role of *radios* in American homes has declined in recent decades.

C. Beware of confusing possessive pronouns with contractions. The possessive forms of personal pronouns do *not* include an apostrophe. Here are the correct forms:

YES   mine, yours, his, hers, its, ours, theirs

Note that *its* (*without* an apostrophe) is the possessive form of *it*, whereas *it's* (*with* an apostrophe) means "it is" or "it has."

YES   The factory closed *its* [not *it's*] doors last week.

YES   The company president determined that *it's* [for "it is"] time to close down the factory.

Similarly, *whose* (*without* an apostrophe) is the possessive form of *who*, whereas *who's* (*with* an apostrophe) means "who is" or "who has."

YES   The sculptor *whose* [not *who's*] work is being exhibited just arrived at the gallery.

YES   The sculptor *who's* [for *who is*] exhibiting his work just arrived at the gallery.

9 CONFUSING HOMONYMS

Homonyms are words that sound alike but have different spellings and meanings. Here are some of the most troublesome.

Accept means "receive" or "agree to." **Except** means "but" or "excluding."

YES   *Except* for your position on mandatory school uniforms, I *accept* your ideas about changing the education system.

Affect means "influence" (verb). **Effect** means "result" (noun) or "bring about" (verb).

YES   It's amazing how much a hurricane's *effects* can *affect* a region's economy.

Its means "belonging to it." **It's** means "it is" or "it has."

YES   *It's* been years since the factory produced *its* last car.

Principal means either "main" (adjective) or "the person in charge of a school (noun)." **Principle** (noun) means "a law or concept."

> YES   The *principal* topic you should study for your midterm is the *principle* of gravity.

Than is a word used in comparisons. **Then** means "at that time."

> YES   The insurance agent assessed the house and *then* wrote a report stating that the damage was worse *than* expected.

Their means "belonging to them." **There** refers to a place other than "here." **They're** means "they are."

> YES   *They're* planning to drop off *their* donations for the food drive in the bin over *there*.

To can be part of a verb (as in *to smile* or *came to*) or a preposition meaning "toward." **Too** means "overly" (as in *too hot*) or "also." **Two** refers to the number 2.

> YES   *Two* of my coworkers go outside *to* eat lunch every day; today they invited me, *too*.

Whose means "belonging to someone or something." **Who's** means "who is" or "who has."

> YES   We're trying to determine *who's* going to call my aunt, *whose* son was injured in an accident.

Your means "belonging to you." **You're** means "you are."

> YES   When *your* mother calls you by *your* first, middle, and last name, you know *you're* in trouble.

10 MISUSE OF ITALICS AND UNDERLINING

Computers and other printing innovations have allowed italics (*slanted type*) to replace underlining (underlined type) in printed text. The following are the most common uses of italics (or of underlining, if you're writing by hand or if your instructor prefers underlining).

A. The titles of works that are published (or, in the case of visual works, displayed) individually should be italicized. Such works, which are often lengthy, include books, magazines, journals, newspapers, websites, online databases, movies (including DVDs), TV and radio programs, musical recordings (albums, CDs, audiocassettes), plays, paintings, and sculptures.

Note: The titles of shorter works—such as poems, short stories, articles, essays, songs, and TV episodes—published as part of a magazine, anthology, or other collection are not italicized; use quotation marks for such titles.

YES   After reading Anne Sexton's poem "The Starry Night" from the collection *All My Pretty Ones*, the students went online to look at Van Gogh's painting *The Starry Night*.

YES   The Discovery Channel program *The Beatles: The Later Years* focused primarily on the band's albums *Sgt. Pepper's Lonely Hearts Club Band* and *Abbey Road*.

B. Foreign words not fully incorporated into mainstream English should be italicized or underlined.

YES   The labor union leaders sought a *tête-à-tête* with the company's executives to resolve a work strike.

C. Words that you wish to emphasize should be italicized or underlined. However, this should be done sparingly at the risk of actually *weakening* emphasis.

YES   Users of the new computer program report that they don't like it. They *love* it.

D. When a word is being referred to *as a word* or as a *defined term*, it should be italicized or underlined. Definitions of italicized terms are often put in quotation marks.

YES   When writing, avoid using a word like *conflagration* when *fire* will do.
YES   The word *conflagration* actually means "fire."

GLOSSARY

Abstract and concrete language refers to two different qualities of words. Abstract words and phrases convey concepts, qualities, emotions, and ideas that we can think and talk about but not actually see or experience directly, such as *conservatism, courage, avarice, joy,* and *hatred.* Words or phrases whose meanings are directly seen or experienced by the senses are concrete terms, such as *split-level house, waddling penguin,* and *short pink waitress uniform.*

Adequate—see *Evidence.*

Ad hominem **argument**—see *Logical fallacies.*

Analogy refers to an imaginative comparison between two subjects that seem to have little in common. Often a writer can make a complex idea or topic understandable by comparing it to a more familiar subject. For example, to explain how the economic difficulties of farmers weaken an entire nation, a writer might create an analogy between failing farms and a cancer that slowly destroys a person's life.

Argumentation-persuasion tries to encourage readers to accept a writer's point of view on some controversial issue. In *argumentation,* a writer uses objective reasoning, facts, and hard evidence to demonstrate the soundness of a position. In *persuasion,* the writer uses appeals to the emotions and value systems, often in the hope of encouraging readers to take a specific action. Argumentation and persuasion are frequently used together in an essay. For example, a writer might argue for the construction of a highway through town by pointing out that the road would bring new business, create new jobs, and lighten traffic. The writer also might try to persuade readers to vote for a highway appropriations bill by appealing to their emotions, claiming that the highway would allow people to get home faster, thus giving them more time for family life and leisure activities.

Assertion refers to the *thesis* of an *argumentation-persuasion* essay. The assertion, or *proposition,* is a point of view or opinion on a controversial issue or topic. The assertion cannot be merely a statement of a fact. Such statements as "Women still experience discrimination in the job market," "General Rabb would make an ideal mayor for our town," and "This university should devote more funds to raising the quality of the food services" are examples of assertions.

Attribution is a phrase or sentence that identifies a source and helps incorporate source material into an essay.

Audience refers to a writer's intended readers. In planning the content and tone of an essay, you should identify your audience and consider its needs. How similar are the members of your audience to you in knowledge and point of view? What will they need to know for you to achieve your *purpose?* What *tone* will make them open to receiving your message? For example, if you wrote an essay for an economics professor about the high cost of clothing, you would choose a serious, analytic tone and supply statistical evidence for your points. If you wrote about the same topic for the college newspaper, you might use a tone tinged with humor and provide helpful hints on finding bargain clothing.

Begging the question—see *Logical fallacies.*

Brainstorming is a technique used in the *prewriting* stage. It helps you discover the limited subject you can successfully write about and also generates raw material—ideas and details—to develop that subject. In brainstorming, you

618

allow your mind to play freely with the subject. You try to capture fleeting thoughts about it, no matter how random, minor, or tangential, and jot them down rapidly before they disappear from your mind.

Causal analysis—see *Cause-effect.*

Causal chain refers to a series of causes and effects, in which the result or effect of a cause becomes itself the cause of a further effect, and so on. For example, a person's alarm clock failing to buzz might begin a causal chain by causing the person to oversleep. Oversleeping then causes the person to miss the bus, and missing the bus causes the person to arrive late to work. Arriving late causes the person to miss an important phone call, which causes the person to lose a chance at a lucrative contract.

Cause-effect, sometimes called *causal analysis,* involves analyzing the reasons for or results of an event, action, decision, or phenomenon. Writers develop an essay through an analysis of causes whenever they attempt to answer such questions as "Why has this happened?" or "Why does this exist?" When writers explore such questions as "What happens or would happen if a certain change occurs?" or "What will happen if a condition continues?" their essays involve a discussion of effects. Some cause-effect essays concentrate on the causes of a situation, some focus on the effects, and others present both causes and effects.

Characteristics—see *Formal definition.*

Chronological sequence—see *Narrative sequence* and *Organization.*

Circularity is an error in *formal definition* resulting from using variations of the to-be-defined word in the definition. For example, "A scientific hypothesis is a hypothesis made by a scientist about the results of an experiment" is circular because the unknown term is used to explain itself.

Class—see *Formal definition.*

Coherence refers to the clear connection among the various parts of an essay. As a writer, you can draw on two key strategies to make writing coherent. You can use a clear *organizational format* (for example, a chronological, spatial, emphatic, or simple-to-complex sequence). You can also provide *appropriate signaling* or *connecting devices* (transitions, bridging sentences, repeated words, synonyms, and pronouns).

Comparison-contrast means explaining the similarities and/or differences between events, objects, people, ideas, and so on. The comparison-contrast format can be used to meet a purely factual purpose ("This is how A and B are alike or different"). But usually writers use comparison-contrast to make a judgment about the relative merits of the subjects under discussion. Sometimes a writer will concentrate solely on similarities *or* differences. For instance, when writing about married versus single life, you would probably devote most of your time to discussing the differences between these lifestyles. Other times, comparison and contrast are found together. In an essay analyzing two approaches to U.S. foreign policy, you would probably discuss the similarities *and* the differences in the goals and methods characteristic of each approach.

Conclusion refers to the one or more paragraphs that bring an essay to an end. Effective conclusions give the reader a sense of completeness and finality. Writers often use the conclusion as a place to reaffirm the *thesis* and to express a final thought about the subject. Methods of conclusion include summarizing main points, using a quotation, predicting an outcome, and recommending an action.

Conflict creates tension in the readers of a *narration*. It is produced by the opposition of characters or other forces in a story. Conflict can occur between individuals, between a person and society or nature, or within a person. Readers wonder how a conflict will be resolved and read on to find out.

Connotative and denotative language refers to the ability of language to emphasize one or another aspect of a word's range of meaning. *Denotative language* stresses the dictionary meaning of words. *Connotative language* emphasizes the echoes of feeling that cluster around some words. For example, the terms *weep, bawl, break down,* and *sob* all denote the same thing: to cry. But they have different associations and call up different images.

Controlling idea—see *Thesis.*

Deductive reasoning is a form of logical thinking in which general statements believed to be true are applied to specific situations or cases. The result of deduction is a conclusion or prediction about the specific situation. Deduction is often expressed in a three-step pattern called a *syllogism.* The first part of the syllogism is a general statement about a large class of items or situations, the *major premise.* The second part is the *minor premise,* a more limited statement about a specific item or case. The third part is the *conclusion,* drawn from the major premise, about that specific case or item.

Definition explains the meaning of a word or concept. The brief formal definitions found in the dictionary can be useful if you need to clarify or restrict the meaning of a term used in an essay. In such cases, the definition is short and to the point. But you may also use an *extended definition* in an essay, taking several paragraphs, even the entire piece, to develop the meaning of a term. You may use extended definition to convey a personal slant on a well-known term, to refute a commonly held interpretation of a word, or to dissect a complex or controversial issue.

Definition by negation is a method of defining a term by first explaining what the term is *not,* and then going on to explain what it is. For example, you might begin a critical essay about television with a definition by negation: "Television, far from being a medium that dispenses only light, insubstantial fare, actually disseminates a dangerously distorted view of family life." Definition by negation can provide a stimulating introduction to an essay.

Denotative language—see *Connotative and denotative language.*

Description involves the use of vivid word pictures to express what the five senses have experienced. The subject of a descriptive essay can be a person, a place, an object, or an event. In an *objective description,* a writer provides details about a subject without conveying the emotions the subject arouses. For example, if you were involved in a traffic accident, your insurance agent might ask you to write an objective description of the events leading up to and during the crash. But in a *subjective description,* the writer's goal is to evoke in the reader the emotions felt during the experience. For example, in a cautionary letter to a friend who has a habit of driving dangerously, you might write a subjective description of your horrifyingly close call with death during a car accident.

Development—see *Evidence.*

Dialogue is the writer's way of directly presenting the exact words spoken by characters in a *narration.* By using dialogue, writers can convey people's individuality and also add drama and immediacy to an essay.

Directional process analysis—see *Process analysis.*

Division-classification refers to a logical method for analyzing a single subject or several related subjects. Though often used together in an essay, division and classification are separate processes. *Division* involves breaking a subject or idea into its component parts. For instance, the concept "an ideal vacation" could be divided according to its destination, accommodations, or cost. *Classification* involves organizing a number of related items into categories. For example, in an essay about the number of communications in our everyday lives, you might classify the typical kinds most people receive: personal e-mails, work e-mails, text messages, and post office mail.

Dominant impression refers to the purpose of a descriptive essay. Although some descriptive essays have a thesis, others do not; instead, they convey a dominant impression or main point. For example, one person writing a descriptive essay about New York City might use its architectural diversity as a focal point. Another person writing a description of Manhattan might concentrate on the overpowering sense of hustle and speed about everyone and everything in the city. Both writers would select only those details that supported their dominant impressions.

Dramatic license refers to the writer's privilege, when writing a narrative, to alter facts or details to strengthen the support of the *thesis* or *narrative point.* For example, a writer is free to flesh out the description of an event whose specific details may be partially forgotten or to modify or omit details of a narrative that do not contribute to the meaning the writer wishes to convey.

Either-or fallacy—see *Logical fallacies.*

Emphatic sequence—see *Organization.*

Ethos refers to a writer's reliability or credibility. Such an image of trustworthiness is particularly important to readers of an *argumentation-persuasion* essay or piece. Writers establish their *ethos* by using reason and logic, by being moderate in their appeals to emotions, by avoiding a hostile tone, and by demonstrating overall knowledgeability of the subject. The most effective argumentation-persuasion involves an interplay of *ethos, logos,* and *pathos.*

Etymology refers to the history of a word or term. All English words have their origins in other, often ancient, languages. Giving a brief etymology of a word can help a writer establish the context for developing an *extended definition* of the word. For example, the word *criminal* is derived from a Latin word meaning "accusation" or "accused." Today, our word *criminal* goes beyond the concept of "accused" to mean "guilty."

Evidence lends substance, or support, to a writer's main ideas and thus helps the reader to accept the writer's viewpoint. Evidence should meet several criteria. First of all, it should be *unified,* in the sense that all supporting ideas and details should relate directly to the key point the writer is making. Second, evidence should be *adequate*; there should be enough evidence to convince the reader to agree with the thesis. Third, evidence should be *specific*; that is, vivid and detailed rather than vague and general. Fourth, evidence must be *accurate* and not overstate or understate information. Fifth, evidence should be *representative,* relying on the typical rather than the atypical to make a point. The bulk of an essay is devoted to supplying evidence.

Exemplification, at the heart of all effective writing, involves using concrete specifics to support generalizations. In exemplification, writers provide examples or instances that support or clarify broader statements. You might support the thesis statement "I have a close-knit family" by using such examples as the following: "We have a regular Sunday dinner at my grandmother's house with at least ten family members present"; "My sisters and brothers visit my parents every week"; "I spend so much time on the phone talking with my sisters that sometimes I have trouble finding time for my new college friends."

Extended definition—see *Definition.*

Fallacies—see *Logical fallacies.*

False analogy—see *Logical fallacies.*

Figures of speech are imaginative comparisons between two things usually thought of as dissimilar. Some major figures of speech are *simile, metaphor,* and *personification.* *Similes* are comparisons that use the signal words *like* or *as:* "Superman was as powerful as a locomotive." *Metaphors,* which do not use signal words, directly equate unlike things: "The boss is a tiger when it comes to landing a contract"; "The high-powered pistons of the boxer's arms pummeled his opponent." *Personification* attributes human characteristics to inanimate things or nonhuman beings: "The angry clouds unleashed their fury on the town"; "The turtle shyly poked his head out of his shell."

First draft refers to the writer's first try at producing a basic, unpolished version of the whole essay. It is often referred to as the "rough" draft, and nothing about it is final or unchangeable. The process of writing the first draft often brings up new ideas or details. Writers sometimes break off writing the draft to *brainstorm* or *freewrite* as new ideas occur to them and then return to the draft with new inspiration. You shouldn't worry about spelling, grammar, or style in the first-draft stage; instead, you should keep focused on casting your ideas into sentence and paragraph form.

Flashback—see *Narrative sequence.*

Flashforward—see *Narrative sequence.*

Formal definition involves stating a definition in a three-part pattern of about one sentence in length. In presenting a formal definition, a writer puts the *term* in a *class* and then lists the *characteristics* that separate the term from other members of its class. For example, a formal definition of a word processor might be "A word processor (term) is an electronic machine (class) that is used to write, edit, store, and produce typewritten documents (characteristics)." Writers often use a formal definition to prepare a reader for an extended definition that follows.

Freewriting is most often used during the *prewriting* stage to help writers generate ideas about a limited topic. To use this method, write nonstop for five or ten minutes about everything your topic brings to mind. Disregard grammar, spelling, and organization as you keep writing. Freewriting is similar to *brainstorming,* except that the result is a rambling, detail-filled paragraph rather than a list. Freewriting can also be used to generate ideas during later stages of the writing process.

Gender-biased language gives the impression that one sex is more important, powerful, or valuable than the other. When writing, you should work to replace such sexist language with *gender-neutral* or *nonsexist* terms that convey no sexual prejudice. First of all, try to avoid *sexist vocabulary* that demeans or excludes one of the sexes: *stud, jock, chick, fox,* and so on. Also, just as adult males should be called *men,* adult females should be referred to as *women,* not *girls.* And men shouldn't be empowered with professional and honorary titles (*President* Barack Obama), whereas professional women—such as congressional representatives—are assigned only personal titles (*Ms.* Gwen Moore). Third, recognize that indefinite pronouns like *anyone, each,* and *everybody* may also pave the way to sexist pronoun use.

Hasty generalization—see *Logical fallacies.*

Inductive reasoning is a form of logical thinking in which specific cases and facts are examined to draw a wider-ranging conclusion. The result of inductive reasoning is a generalization that is applied to situations or cases similar to the ones examined. Induction is typical of scientific investigation and of everyday thinking. For example, on the basis of specific experiences, you may have concluded that when you feel chilly in a room where everyone else is comfortable, you are likely to develop a cold and fever in the next day or two. In an *argumentation-persuasion* essay, the conclusion reached by induction would be your *assertion* or *thesis.*

Inference is the term for a conclusion based on *inductive reasoning.* Because the reasoning behind specific cases may not be simple, there is usually an element of uncertainty in an inductive conclusion. Choosing the correct explanation for specific cases is a matter of carefully weighing and selecting alternative conclusions.

Informational process analysis—see *Process analysis.*

Introduction refers to the first paragraph or several paragraphs of an essay. The introduction serves three purposes. It informs readers of the general subject of the essay, it catches their attention, and it presents the controlling idea or thesis. The methods of introducing an essay include the use of an anecdote, a quotation or surprising statistic or fact, and questions.

Irony occurs when a writer or speaker implies (rather than states directly) a discrepancy or incongruity of some kind. *Verbal irony,* which is often tongue-in-cheek, involves a discrepancy between the literal words and what's actually meant ("I know you must be unhappy about receiving the highest grade in the course"). If the ironic comment is designed to be hurtful or insulting, it qualifies as *sarcasm* ("Congratulations! You failed the final exam"). In *situational irony,* the circumstances are themselves incongruous. For example, although their constitutional rights were violated when the federal government detained them in internment camps, Japanese-Americans nevertheless played American football, sang American songs, and saluted the American flag during their imprisonment.

Journal writing is a form of prewriting in which writers make frequent entries in a private journal, much as they would in a diary. Whether they focus on one topic or wander freely, journal writers jot down striking incidents, images, and ideas. Such journal material can produce ideas for future essays.

Logical fallacies are easily committed mistakes in reasoning that writers must avoid, especially when writing *argumentation-persuasion* essays. There are many kinds of logical fallacies. Here are several:

Ad hominem argument occurs when someone attacks another person's point of view by criticizing that person, not the issue. Often called "mudslinging," *ad hominem* arguments try to invalidate a person's ideas by revealing unrelated, past or present, personal or ethical flaws. For example, to claim that a person cannot govern the country well because it can be proven he or she has little sense of humor is to use an *ad hominem* argument.

Begging the question is a fallacy in which the writer assumes the truth of something that needs to be proven. Imagine a writer argues the following: "A law should be passed requiring dangerous pets like German shepherds and Doberman pinschers to be restrained by fences, leashes, and muzzles." Such an argument begs the question because it assumes readers will automatically accept the view that such dogs are indeed dangerous.

Either-or fallacies occur when it's argued that a complex situation can be resolved in only one of two possible ways. Here's an example: "If the administration doesn't grant striking professors more money, the college will never be able to attract outstanding teachers in years ahead." Such an argument oversimplifies matters. Excellent teachers might be attracted to a college for a variety of reasons, not just because of good salaries.

False analogy erroneously suggests that because two things are alike in some regards, they are similar in all ways. In the process, significant differences between the two are disregarded. If you argue that a woman prosecuting a rapist is subjected to a second rape in court, you're guilty of a false analogy. As embarrassing, painful, and hurtful as the court proceedings may be, the woman is not physically assaulted, as she was when she was raped. Also, as difficult as her decision to seek justice might be, she's in court by choice and not against her will.

Hasty generalizations are unsound *inductive inferences* based on too few instances of a behavior, situation, or process. For example, it would be a hasty generalization to conclude that you're allergic to an unfamiliar food because you once ate it and became ill. There are several other possible explanations for your illness, and only repetitions of this experience or a lab test could prove conclusively that you're allergic to this food.

Non sequiturs are faulty conclusions about cause and effect. Here's an example: "Throughout this country's history, most scientists have been male. Women apparently have little interest in becoming scientists." The faulty conclusion accords one factor—the possible vocational preferences of women—the status of sole cause. The conclusion fails to consider pressures on women to avoid an occupation sexually stereotyped as "masculine."

Post hoc thinking results when it's presumed that one event caused another just because it occurred first. For instance, if your car broke down the day after you lent it to your brother, you would be committing the *post hoc* fallacy if you blamed him, unless you knew he did something to your car's engine.

Questionable authority, revealed by such phrases as "studies show" and "experts claim," undercuts a writer's credibility. Readers become suspicious of such vague and unsubstantial appeals to authority. Writers should demonstrate the reliability of their sources by citing them specifically.

Red herring arguments are deliberate attempts to focus attention on a peripheral matter rather than examine the merits of the issue under discussion. Imagine that a local environmental group advocates stricter controls for employees at a nearby chemical plant. The group points out that plant employees are repeatedly exposed to high levels of toxic chemicals. If you respond, "Many of the employees are illegal immigrants and shouldn't be allowed to take jobs from native-born townspeople," you're throwing in a red herring. By bringing in immigration policies, you sidetrack attention from the matter at hand.

Logos is a major factor in creating an effective argument. It refers to the soundness of *argumentation,* as created by the use of facts, statistics, information, and commentary by authoritative sources. The most effective arguments involve an interplay among *logos, pathos,* and *ethos.*

Major premise—see *Deductive reasoning.*

Minor premise—see *Deductive reasoning.*

MLA documentation is the system developed by the Modern Language Association for citing sources in an essay. When you quote or summarize source material, you must do two things within your essay's text: (1) identify the author and (2) specify the pages on which the material appears. You may provide the author's name in a lead-in sentence or within parentheses following the borrowed material; the page number always appears in parentheses, inserted in the text after the borrowed material. The material in the parentheses is called a *parenthetical reference.* A paper using MLA documentation ends with a *Works Cited* list, which includes only those sources actually acknowledged in the essay. Entries are organized alphabetically by authors' last names. Entries without an author are alphabetized by the first major word in the title.

Narration means recounting an event or a series of related events to make a point. Narration can be an essay's principal pattern of development, or it can be used to supplement a composition organized primarily around another pattern. For instance, to persuade readers to avoid drug use, a writer might use the narrative pattern by recounting the story of an abuser's addiction and recovery.

Narrative point refers to the meaning the writer intends to convey to a reader by telling a certain story. This narrative point might be a specific message, or it might be a feeling about the situation, people, or place of the story. This underlying meaning is achieved by presenting details that support it and eliminating any that are nonessential. For example, in an essay about friendship, a writer's point might be that friendships change when one of the friends acquires a significant romantic partner. The writer would focus on the details of how her close female friend had less time for her, changed their usual times of getting together, and confided in her less. The writer would omit judgments of the friend's choice of partner and her friend's declining grades because these details would distract the reader from the essay's narrative point.

Narrative sequence refers to the order in which a writer recounts events. When you follow the order of the events as they happened, you're using *chronological sequence.* This sequence, in which you begin at the beginning and end with the last event, is the most basic and commonly used narrative sequence. If you interrupt this flow to present an event that happened before the beginning of the narrative sequence, you're employing a *flashback*. If you skip ahead to an event later than the one that comes next in your narrative, you're using the *flashforward* technique.

Non sequiturs—see *Logical fallacies.*

Objective description—see *Description.*

One-side-at-a-time method refers to one of the two techniques for organizing a *comparison-contrast* essay. In using this method, a writer discusses all the points about one of the compared and contrasted subjects before going on to the other. For example, in an essay titled "Single or Married?" a writer might first discuss single life in terms of amount of independence, freedom of career choice, and companionship. Then the writer would, within reason, discuss married life in terms of these same three subtopics. The issues the writer discusses in each half of the essay would be identical and presented in the same order. See also *Point-by-point method.*

Organization refers to the process of arranging evidence to support a thesis in the most effective way. When organizing, a writer decides what ideas come first, next, and last. In *chronological* sequence, details are arranged according to occurrence in time. In *spatial* sequence, details appear in the order in which they occur in space. In *emphatic* order, ideas are sequenced according to importance, with the most significant, outstanding, or convincing evidence being reserved for last. In *simple-to-complex* order, easy-to-grasp material is presented before more-difficult-to-comprehend information.

Outlining involves making a formal plan before writing a *first draft.* Writing an outline helps you determine whether your supporting evidence is logical and adequate. As you write, you can use the outline to keep yourself on track. Many writers use the indentation system of Roman numerals, letters, and Arabic numbers to outline; sometimes writers use a less formal system.

Paradox refers to a statement that seems impossible, contrary to common sense, or self-contradictory, yet that can—after consideration—be seen to be plausible or true. For example, Oscar Wilde produced a paradox when he wrote "When the gods wish to punish us, they answer our prayers." The statement doesn't contradict itself because often, Wilde believes, that which we wish for turns out to be the very thing that will bring us the most pain.

Parenthetical reference—see *MLA documentation.*

Pathos refers to the emotional power of an *argumentation-persuasion* essay. By appealing to the needs, values, and attitudes of readers and by using *connotative language,* writers can increase the chances that readers will come to agree with the ideas in an essay. Although *pathos* is an important element of persuasion, such emotional appeals should reinforce rather than replace reason. The most effective argumentation-persuasion involves an interplay among *pathos, logos,* and *ethos.*

Peer review is the critical reading of another person's writing with the intention of suggesting changes. To be effective, peer review calls for readers who are objective, skilled, and tactful enough to provide useful feedback. Begin by giving your readers a clear sense of what you expect from the review. To promote specific responses, ask the reviewers targeted (preferably written) questions. Following the review, rank the problems and solutions that the reviewers identified. Then enter your own notes for revising in the margins of your draft so that you'll know exactly what changes need to be made in your draft as you rework it.

Plan of development refers to a technique whereby the writer supplies the reader with a brief map of the main points to be covered in an essay. If used, the plan of development occurs as part of the *thesis* or in a sentence following the thesis. In it, the main ideas are mentioned in the order in which they'll appear in the supporting paragraphs. Longer essays and term papers usually need a plan of development to maintain unity, but shorter papers may do without one.

Point-by-point method refers to one of the two techniques for organizing a *comparison-contrast* essay. A writer using this method moves from one aspect of one subject to the same aspect of another subject before going on to the second aspect of each subject. For example, in an essay titled "Single or Married?" a writer might first discuss the amount of independence a person has when single and when married. Then, the writer might go on to discuss how much freedom of career choice a person has when single and when married. Finally, the writer might discuss, in turn, the amount of companionship available in each of the two lifestyles. See also *One-side-at-a-time method.*

Point of view refers to the perspective a writer chooses when writing about a subject. If you narrate events as you experience them, you're using the *first-person* point of view. You might say, for example, "*I* noticed jam on the child's collar and holes in her shirt." If you relate the events from a distance—as if you observed them but did not experience them personally—you're using the *third-person* point of view; for instance, "Jam splotched the child's collar, and her shirt had several holes in it." The point of view should be consistent throughout an essay.

Post hoc **thinking**—see *Logical fallacies.*

Prewriting is the first stage of the writing process. During prewriting, you jot down rough ideas about your subject without yet moving to writing a draft of your essay. Your goals at this stage are to (1) understand the boundaries of the assignment, (2) discover the limited subject you could write about, (3) generate raw material about the limited subject, and (4) organize the raw material into a very rough *scratch outline.* If you keep in mind that prewriting is "unofficial," it can be a low-pressure, even enjoyable activity.

Process analysis refers to writing that explains the steps involved in doing something or the sequence of stages in an event or behavior. There are two types of process analysis. In *directional process analysis,* readers are shown how to do something step by step. Cookbook recipes, tax form instructions, and how-to books are some typical uses of directional process analysis. In *informational process analysis,* the writer explains how something is done or occurs, without expecting the reader to attempt the process. "A Senator's Road to Political Power," "How Bees Make Honey," and "How a Convict Gets Paroled" would be titles of essays developed through informational process analysis.

Proofreading involves rereading a final draft carefully to catch any errors in spelling, grammar, punctuation, or typing that have slipped by. While such errors are minor, a significant number of them can seriously weaken the effectiveness of an essay.

Proposition—see *Assertion.*

Purpose is the reason a writer has for preparing a particular essay. Usually, writers frame their purposes in terms of the effect they wish to have on their *audience.* They may wish to explore the personal meaning of a subject or experience, explain an idea or process, provide information, influence opinion, or entertain. Many essays combine purposes, with one purpose predominating and providing the essay's focus.

Red herring argument—see *Logical fallacies.*

Refutation is an important strategy in *argumentation-persuasion.* In refutation, writers acknowledge that there are opposing views on the subject under discussion and then go on to do one of two things. Sometimes they may admit that the opposing views are somewhat valid but assert that their own position has more merit and devote their essay to demonstrating that merit. For example, a writer might assert, "Business majors often find interesting and lucrative jobs. However, in the long run, liberal arts graduates have many more advantages in the job market because the breadth of their background helps them think better, learn faster, and communicate more effectively." This writer would concentrate on proving the advantages that liberal arts graduates have. At other times, writers may choose to argue actively against an opposing position by dismantling that view point by point. Such refutation of opposing views can strengthen the writer's own arguments.

Repeated words, synonyms, and pronouns —see *Signaling devices.*

Revision means, literally, "reseeing" an earlier draft with a fresh eye, as if the writer had not actually prepared the draft. When revising, you move from more global issues (like clarifying meaning and organization) to more specific matters (like fine-tuning sentences and word choice). While revising, you make whatever changes are necessary to increase the essay's effectiveness. You might strengthen your thesis, resequence paragraph order, or add more transitions. Such changes often make the difference between mediocre and superior writing.

Satire is a humorous form of social criticism usually aimed at society's institutions or human behavior. Often irreverent as well as witty, satire is serious in purpose: to point out evil, injustice, and absurdity and bring about change through an increase in awareness. Satire ranges widely in tone: it may be gentle or biting; it may sarcastically describe a real situation or use fictional characters and events to spoof reality. Satire often makes use of *irony.*

Scratch outline refers to your first informal plan for an essay, devised at the end of the *prewriting* stage. In making a scratch outline, you select ideas and details from your raw material for inclusion in your essay and discard the rest. You also arrange these ideas in an order that makes sense and that will help you achieve your *purpose.* A scratch outline is tentative and flexible, and can be reshaped as needed.

Sensory description vividly evokes the sights, smells, tastes, sounds, and physical feelings of a scene or event. For example, if a writer carefully chooses words and images, readers can see the vibrant reds and oranges of falling leaves, taste the sourness of an underripe grapefruit, hear the growling of motorcycles as a gang sweeps through a town, smell the spicy aroma of a grandmother's homemade tomato soup, and feel the pulsing pain of a jaw after Novocain wears off. Sensory description is particularly important in writing *description* or *narration.*

Sentence variety adds interest to the style of an essay or paragraph. In creating sentence variety, writers mix different kinds of sentences and sentence patterns. For example, you might vary the way your sentences open or intersperse short sentences with long ones, simple sentences with complex ones. Repetitive sentence patterns tend to make readers lose interest.

Signaling devices indicate the relationships among ideas in an essay. They help the reader follow the train of thought from sentence to sentence and from paragraph to paragraph. There are three types of connectives. *Transitions* are words that clarify flow of meaning. They can signal an additional or contrasting point, an enumeration of ideas, the use of an example, or other movement of ideas. *Linking sentences* summarize a point just made and then introduce a follow-up point. *Repeated words, synonyms,* and *pronouns* create a sense of flow by keeping important concepts in the mind of the reader.

Spatial sequence—see *Organization.*

Specific—see *Evidence.*

Stipulative definition is a way of restricting a term for the purposes of discussion. Many words have multiple meanings that can get in the way of clarity when a writer is creating an *extended definition.* For example, you might stipulate the following definition of *foreign car:* "While many American automobiles use parts or even whole engines made by foreign car manufacturers, for the purposes of discussion, 'foreign car' refers only to those automobiles designed and manufactured wholly by a company based in another country. By this definition, a European vehicle made in Pennsylvania is *not* a foreign car."

Subjective description—see *Description.*

Support—see *Evidence.*

Syllogism—see *Deductive reasoning.*

Term—see *Formal definition.*

Thesis is the central idea in any essay, usually expressed in a one- or two-sentence *thesis statement.* Writers accomplish two things by providing a thesis statement in an essay: They indicate the essay's limited subject and express an attitude about that subject. Also called the *controlling idea,* the thesis statement consists of a particular slant, angle, or point of view about the limited subject.

Tone conveys your attitude toward yourself, your purpose, your topic, and your readers. As in speaking, tone in writing may be serious, playful, sarcastic, and so on. Generally, readers detect tone more by how you say something (that is, through your sentence structure and word choice) than by what you say.

Topic sentence is the term for the sentence(s) that convey the main idea of a paragraph. Such sentences are often, but not always, found at the start of a paragraph. They provide a statement of the subject to be discussed and an indication of the writer's attitude toward that subject. Writers usually concern themselves with topic sentences during the writing of the first draft.

Transitions—see *Signaling devices.*

Unified—see *Evidence.*

Works Cited—see *MLA documentation.*

ACKNOWLEDGMENTS

Adams, Charlene. "Professors Open Up About the Benefits of a College Degree." First appeared in *The Penn*, the student newspaper of the Indiana University of Pennsylvania, on February 19, 2013.

Ahmed, Leila. "Reinventing the Veil." Originally published in *The Financial Times*, May 20, 2011. Copyright © 2011. Used by permission of the author.

Appleton, Josie. "The Body-Piercing Project." Originally appeared in *SPIKED ONLINE*, July 9, 2003. Copyright © 2003. Used by permission.

Barber, Houston. "Dating Then and Now: A Convoluted Mess."

Barry, Dave, "Beauty and the Beast." *The Miami Herald*, February 1, 1998. Used by permission of Dave Barry.

Barry, Lynda. "The Sanctuary of School." Originally published by *The New York Times*, January 5, 1992. Copyright © 1992. All Rights reserved. Used with permission.

Baum, L. Frank. "The Wizard of Oz." Puffin Classics, May 10, 2012.

Berry, Wendell. "Another Turn of the Crank." Reprinted by permission of *Counterpoint*.

Bittman, Mark. "What Causes Weight Gain?" From *The New York Times*, June 11 © 2014, *The New York Times*. All rights reserved. Used by permission and protected by the Copyright Laws of the United States. The printing, copying, redistribution, or retransmission of this Content without express written permission is prohibited.

Bosker, Bianca. "How Teens Are Really Using Facebook: It's a 'Social Burden,' Pew Study Finds." From *The Huffington Post*, May 21 © 2013 AOL Inc. All rights reserved. Used by permission and protected by the Copyright Laws of the United States. The printing, copying, redistribution, or retransmission of this Content without express written permission is prohibited.

Brooks, David, "Psst! 'Human Capital.'" From *The New York Times*, November 13, 2005. Copyright © 2005 *The New York Times*. All rights reserved. Used by permission and protected by the Copyright Laws of the United States. The printing, copying, redistribution, or retransmission of this Content without express written permission is prohibited.

Chapman, Stephen. "The Prisoner's Dilemma." From *The New Republic*, March 8, 1980. Copyright © 1980. Used with permission.

Cofer, Judith Ortiz. "A Partial Remembrance of a Puerto Rican Childhood." "Casa" reprinted with permission from the publisher of *Silent Dancing: A Partial Remembrance of a Puerto Rican Childhood* by Judith Ortiz Cofer. Copyright © 1990. Arte Publico Press—University of Houston.

Comas-Díaz, L. "Hispanics, Latinos, or Americanos: The Evolution of identity." *Cultural Diversity and Ethnic Minority Psychology*, 7(2), 115–120. doi:10.1037/1099-9809.7.2.115. Copyright © 2001 by the American Psychological Association. Reproduced with permission.

D'Amboise, Jaques. "Showing What Is Possible." Used with permission.

Darley, John M., and Bibb Latané. "When Will People Help in a Crisis?" Reprinted with permission from *Psychology Today Magazine*, (Copyright © 1969 Sussex Publishers, LLC).

Didion, Joan. "Marrying Absurd." From *Slouching Towards Bethlehem* by Joan Didion. Copyright © 1966, 1968, renewed 1996 by Joan Didion. Reprinted by permission of Farrar, Straus and Giroux, LLC. Reprinted by permission of the author throughout the United Kingdom.

Divakaruni, Chitra. "Common Scents: The Smell of Childhood Never Fades." Copyright © 1997. First appeared on *Salon.com*. Reprinted by permission of the author and the Sandra Dijkstra Literary Agency.

Dunn, Laura Rose. "Letters from Dad."

Ehrenreich, Barbara. "Serving in Florida" from the book *Nickel and Dimed: On (Not) Getting By in America* by Barbara Ehrenreich. Copyright © 2001 by Barbara Ehrenreich. Used by permission of Henry Holt and Company, LLC. All rights reserved.

Ericsson, Stephanie. "The Ways We Lie." Originally published by *The Utne Reader*. Copyright © 1992 by Stephanie Ericsson. Reprinted by the permission of Dunham Literary as agents for the author.

Fish, Stanley. "Free Speech Follies." From *The Chronicle*. June 13, 2003. Copyright © 2003. Used with permission.

Fletcher, Olivia. "'Tweet, Tweedle-lee-dee' (118 Characters Left)."

Francis, Caylah. "Aggression, Addiction, Isolation, and More: The Dark Side of Video Game Play." Pearson Essay Contest, Perason Education, Inc.

Fraser, Laura. "The Inner Corset." Originally published in "The Inner Corset" from *Losing It: American's Obsession with Weight and The Industry That Feeds It*. Used by permission.

Garibaldi, Gerry. "How the Schools Shortchange Boys." From *City Journal*, 2006. Copyright © 2006. Used with permission.

Gispert, Catherine. "The Benchers, the Nappers, the Jellyfish, and the Musicians."

Goodman, Ellen. "Family Counterculture." From *The Boston Globe*, August 16, 1991. Copyright © 1991 by The Boston Globe. All rights reserved. Used by permission and protected by the Copyright Laws of the United States. The printing, copying, redistribution, or retransmission of this Content without express written permission is prohibited.

Grandin, Temple. "Seeing in Beautiful, Precise Pictures." Copyright © 2006. From the book *This I Believe: The Personal Philosophies of Remarkable Men and Women*, edited by Jay Allison and Dan Gediman. Copyright © 2006 by This I Believe, Inc. Reprinted by permission of Henry Holt and Company, LLC. All rights reserved.

Gumm, Lydia. "It's About Time, Augusta!"

Gundersheimer, Werner. "A Mother's Secret." Reprinted from *The American Scholar*, Volume 78, No. 3, Summer 2009. Copyright © 2009 by the author.

Helvarg, David. "The Storm This Time." *Multinational Monitor*, September/October 2005. Copyright © 2005. Used with permission.

Horton, Alex. "On Getting By." From *Army of Dude Blog*. January 13, 2010. Used with permission. http://armyofdude.blogspot.com/2010/01/on-getting-by.html.

Hughes, Langston. "Salvation." From *The Big Sea*. Copyright © 1940 by Langston Hughes. Copyright renewed 1968 by Arna Bontemps and George Houston Bass. Reprinted by permission of Hill and Wang, a division of Farrar, Straus and Giroux, LLC and reprinted by permission of Harold Ober Associates.

Hulbert, Ann. "Beyond the Pleasure Principle." Originally published in *The New Yorker*. Copyright © 2007 by Ann Hulbert. Used with permission of The Wylie Agency LLC.

Hymowitz, Kay S. "Tweens: Ten Going On Sixteen." Manhattan Institute, *City Journal*, Autumn 1998. Used with permission.

Johnson, Beth. "Bombs Bursting in Air." Used with permission.

Johnson, Keith. "Who's a Pirate? In Court, A Duel over Definitions." Reprinted by permission of The Wall Street Journal. Copyright © August 20, 2010.

Khan, Amir. "America Tops List of 10 Most Obese Countries." US News: Health and Wellness, May 28, 2014. Based on figures from the CDC. Copyrighted 2014. U.S. News & World Report. 113229:1114BC. Used with permission.

Kimmel, Michael. "A War Against Boys?" © 2009 by Michael Kimmel. Reprinted by permission. All rights reserved.

King, Martin Luther, Jr. "Where Do We Go from Here: Chaos or Community?" Reprinted by arrangement with The Heirs to the Estate of Martin Luther King Jr., c/o Writers House as agent for the proprietor, New York, NY. Copyright © 1967 Dr. Martin Luther King Jr; Copyright renewed 1995 Coretta Scott King.

Lorde, Audre. "The Fourth of July" from *Zami: A New Spelling of My Name*. Published by Crossing Press. Copyright © 1982, 2006. Used herewith by permission of the Charlotte Sheedy Literary Agency.

Madden, Mary. "Where teens have social media accounts." From "Teens, Social Media, and Privacy" by Mary Madden. May 21, 2013. Copyright © 2013. Used by permission of Pew Research Center. http://www.pewinternet.org/2013/05/21/teens-social-media-and-privacy-2/

Madden, Mary, et al. "Teens, Social Media, and Privacy." May 21, 2013. Copyright © 2013. Used by permission of Pew Research Center. http://www.pewinternet.org/2013/05/21/teens-social-media-and-privacy-2/

Marlow, Michael, and Sherzod Abdukadirov. "Government Intervention Will Not Solve Our Obesity Problem." *USNews.com*, June 5 2012. Copyrighted 2014. U.S. News & World Report. 113228:1114BC. Used with permission.

McDonald, Cherokee Paul. "A View from the Bridge," by Cherokee Paul McDonald. First published in the *Florida Sun Sentinel*, February 12, 1989. Reprinted by permission of the Author. All rights reserved.

Mosely, Jared. "Don't Write Poetry–Be a Poet."

Norman, Blake. "Buying a Cross-Country Mountain Bike."

Postrel, Virginia. "Need Transplant Donors? Pay Them." Copyright © June 10, 2006 in *Los Angeles Times*.

Quindlen, Anna. "Driving to the Funeral." Copyright © 2007 by Anna Quindlen. Used by Permission. All rights reserved.

Raspberry, William. "The Handicap of Definition." From *The Washington Post*, January 6, 1982. Copyright © 1982. Washington Post Company. All rights reserved. Used by permission and protected by the Copyright Laws of the United States. The printing, copying, redistribution, or retransmission of the Material without express written permission is prohibited.

Rego, Caroline. "The Fine Art of Complaining." Used by permission of the author.

Riverbend, "Bloggers without Borders..." (October 22, 2007) from *Baghdad Burning* blog, http://riverbendblog.blogspot.com. Reprinted by permission of The Permissions Company, Inc., on behalf of The Feminist Press at the City University of New York, www.feministpress.org. All rights reserved.

Roberts, Paul, "How to Say Nothing in 500 Words." From *Understanding English* by Paul Roberts. Copyright © 1958 by Paul Roberts. Reprinted by permission of Pearson Education, Inc. Upper Saddle River, New Jersey.

Shaw, George Bernard. "The Quintessence of Ibsenism." 1981.

Shaw, Jane S. "Nature in the Suburbs." From the Heritage Foundation, February 18, 2004. Copyright © 2004. Used with permission.

Sherry, Mary. "In Praise of the F Word." Used with permission of Mary Sherry.

Staples, Brent. "Black Men and Public Space." Originally published as "Just Walk on By: A Black Man Ponders His Power to Alter Public Space." Literary Cavalcade: Sep 98, Vol. 50 Issue 5, p. 38. Used with permission.

Stoufer, Leanna. "Enduring with Dignity: *Akua's Surviving Children*." Pearson Essay Contest 2013.

Suárez, Mario. "El Hoyo." From *Chicano Sketches: Short Stories by Mario Suárez*. Copyright © 2004. The Arizona Board of Regents. Reprinted by permission of the University of Arizona Press.

Sutherland, Amy, "What Shamu Taught Me About a Happy Marriage." Originally appeared in *The New York Times*, June 25, 2006. Copyright © 2006. Reprinted by permission of the author.

Tabarrok, Alexander T. "A Moral Solution to the Organ Shortage." Reprint commentary. © Copyright February 19, 2001, *The Independent Institute* (www.independent.org).

Tan, Amy. "Mother Tongue." Copyright © 1989. First appeared in *The Threepenny Review*. Reprinted by permission of the author and the Sandra Dijkstra Literary Agency.

Twain, Mark. "The Damned Human Race." (pp. 221–42) from *Letters from the Earth* by Mark Twain. Copyright © 1938, 1944, 1946, 1959, 1962 by The Mark Twain Company. Copyright © 1942 by The President and Fellows of Harvard College. Reprinted by permission of HarperCollins Publishers.

Wasserstrom, Jeffrey N. "A Mickey Mouse Approach to Globalization." Reprinted with permission of YaleGlobal Online. Copyright © 2003. Yale Center for the Study of Globalization.

Weiner, Eric. "Euromail and Amerimail." Originally published in *Slate Magazine*, March 25, 2005. Copyright © 2005. Used by permission of Eric Weiner.

Williams, Juan. "The Ruling That Changed America." Reprinted with permission from *American School Board Journal*, April 2004. Copyright © 2004 National School Boards Association. All rights reserved.

Zinsser, William. "College Pressures." Originally appeared in *Blair & Ketchum's Country Journal*, Vol. VI, No. 4, April 1979. Copyright © 1979 by William K. Zinsser. Reprinted by permission of the author.

Zwieg, Erica. "Party with a Purpose."

pp. 1, 15, 537, 571, 605: Alexander Chaikin/Shutterstock

p. 6: Ricardo Arduengo/AP Images

p. 7: From data reported in the *World Malaria Report*, 2012. World Health Organization.

p. 78: Eco Images/UIG/AGE Fotostock

p. 86: Collection of the artist and October Gallery, London. Photo: Andy Keate. Courtesy the artist and Jack Shainman Gallery, New York. © El Anatsui.

p. 99, 100: David Helvarg

p. 165: Dove Campaign for Real Beauty, Advertising Archives.

p. 175: Pew Economic Mobility Project. "How Much Protection Does a College Degree Afford? The Impact of the Recession on Recent College Graduates." The Pew Charitiable Trusts, 10. Jan. 2013. Web 7. Feb. 2013. http://www.pewtrusts.org/en/research-and-analysis/reports/0001/01/01/ how-much-protection-does-a-college-degree-afford/2013/Pew_college_grads_recession_report.pdf

p. 205: Dann Tardif/LWA/Corbis

p. 256: Jack Hollingsworth/Photodisc/Getty Images

p. 302: "Family Portrait" by Werner Gundersheimer. Used by permission of Werner Gundersheimer.

p. 352: Coco Robicheaux/Alamy

p. 401: Donald Miralle/Getty Images

p. 421: The Piracy Reporting Centre (PRC), ICC International Maritime Bureau

p. 427: Brand X Pictures/Getty Images

p. 507: CDC/NCHS, National Health and Nutrition Examination Survey III 1968–1994 and 2007–2008.

p. 309: The Advertising Archive/ZUMA Press

INDEX

☑ Peer Review/Revision Checklist

1. *Revise Overall Meaning and Structure*
☐ Considering the essay's purpose, audience, and tone (pages 20–23), in what ways does or doesn't the paper accomplish what was intended?
☐ What is the essay's thesis (pages 31–34)? Is it explicit or implied? Does it focus on a limited subject and express the writer's attitude toward that subject (pages 31–34)? If not, what changes need to be made?
☐ What are the main points supporting the thesis (pages 35–36)? List the points. If any stray from or contradict the thesis (pages 37–49), what changes need to be made?
☐ What overall format is used to sequence the essay's main points: chronological, spatial, emphatic, or simple-to-complex (pages 44–46)? Does this format reinforce the thesis? Why or why not?
☐ Which patterns of development (page 44) are used in the essay? How do these patterns reinforce the thesis?

2. *Revise Paragraph Development*
☐ Where in each paragraph does support seem irrelevant, vague, insufficient, inaccurate, or nonrepresentative (pages 37–41)? How could these problems be fixed?
☐ What format is used to sequence the ideas in each paragraph? Does this format reinforce the paragraph's main point? Why or why not?
☐ What signal devices (pages 53–56) are used to connect ideas within and between paragraphs? Where are there too few signals or too many?
☐ What strategies are used to open (pages 56–58) and close (pages 58–59) the essay? How could the introduction and conclusion be made more effective?

3. *Revise Sentences and Words*
☐ Which sentences seem inconsistent with the essay's intended tone (pages 21–22)? How could the problem be fixed?
☐ Where does sentence structure become monotonous and predictable (pages 83–85 and 127–128)? Where could a different sentence pattern add variety?
☐ Which words seem vague and overly general (pages 83–85 and 126–127)? How could they be made more vigorous and concrete?
☐ Where does gender-biased language (page 623) appear? How could the problem be fixed?

4. *Proofread for Grammar, Punctuation, and Typing Errors*
☐ Before handing in the final draft of your essay, proofread it closely, keeping a dictionary and English handbook nearby. When proofing, people tend to see what they think is on the page rather than what really is there. Reading the essay out loud and backwards, starting with the last word first, can highlight errors that otherwise might slip by.

Note: Each pattern-of-development chapter contains a *Peer Review/Revision Checklist* that fits the demands of that particular pattern.